SIXTH EDITION

A Reader for College Writers

SANTI V. BUSCEMI

Praise for *A Reader for College Writers*

"This book reads to me like a generous behind-the-scenes exposé on the secrets of writing/thinking. I like how this text walks the reader through every step of the process but somehow avoids talking down to the readers; it also avoids making writing sound like something one only does in school. The examples are well-grounded in the real world that our budding intellectuals are going to be living (and writing) in."
    Wayne Berninger, Long Island University—Brooklyn Campus

"A Reader for College Writers is a strong collection of readings with a wonderful guiding focus through the process of developing an essay."
    J. Elizabeth Clark, LaGuardia Community College—CUNY

"For students to become real writers, they need to become real readers. This text does an excellent job of showing the connection between reading and writing. The pre-reading activities successfully prepare students to read, and the pre-writing activities effectively prepare the students to write."
                    Timothy R. Cramer, Santa Monica College

"This text is altogether unique. It's rigorous but compassionate."
    Wayne Berninger, Long Island University—Brooklyn Campus

"The reading selections are impressive, to say the least. [. . .] This is a thorough textbook, one designed to challenge the student to read, think, and write better."

Sandra Barnhill, South Plains College

"The range of topics, voices, and views is excellent. The student essays are wonderful. [. . .] A Reader for College Writers is a very fine and useful textbook."

Michael R. Scott, D. S. Lancaster Community College

"I particularly like the visual treatment of selected essays; the annotations are apt and the graphic nature of those pages would work with many basic writers who are struggling to understand the architecture of an essay."

Bobbie Robinson, Abraham Baldwin College

"A Reader for College Writers is a high-interest reader with excellent writing prompts. It offers a wide variety of examples of specific writing techniques and has, I think, one of the best chapters on writing introductions and conclusions I've seen."

Laura L. Apfelbeck, University of Wisconsin—Manitowoc

"Questions, pre-writing strategies, vocabulary, critical reading apparatus, etc. are excellent. [Buscemi] gives lots of help but does not talk down to students."

Vivian Thomlinson, Cameron University

"A Reader for College Writers might eliminate the need for a writing handbook and a critical-thinking workbook. This book does an excellent job in teaching pre-writing strategies and editing/revision techniques."

Tracy E. Miller, Towson University

"The group activities are very distinctive in this reader. I've seen no other reader that plans out the group work so carefully."

Kristine Dassinger, Genesee Community College

SIXTH EDITION

A Reader for College Writers

Santi V. Buscemi

Middlesex County College

Boston   Burr Ridge, IL   Dubuque, IA   Madison, WI   New York
San Francisco   St. Louis   Bangkok   Bogotá   Caracas   Kuala Lumpur
Lisbon   London   Madrid   Mexico City   Milan   Montreal   New Delhi
Santiago   Seoul   Singapore   Sydney   Taipei   Toronto

Higher Education

A Division of The McGraw-Hill Companies

A READER FOR COLLEGE WRITERS

Published by McGraw-Hill, a business unit of The McGraw-Hill Companies, Inc., 1221 Avenue of the Americas, New York, NY, 10020. Copyright © 2005, 2002, 1999, 1996, 1993, 1990, by The McGraw-Hill Companies, Inc. All rights reserved. No part of this publication may be reproduced or distributed in any form or by any means, or stored in a database or retrieval system, without the prior written consent of The McGraw-Hill Companies, Inc., including, but not limited to, in any network or other electronic storage or transmission, or broadcast for distance learning.

Some ancillaries, including electronic and print components, may not be available to customers outside the United States.

This book is printed on acid-free paper.

1 2 3 4 5 6 7 8 9 0 DOC/DOC 0 9 8 7 6 5 4

ISBN 0 07 288554 8

President of McGraw-Hill Humanities/Social Sciences: *Steve Debow*
Senior sponsoring editor: *Alexis Walker*
Executive marketing manager: *David S. Patterson*
Senior media producer: *Todd Vaccaro*
Project manager: *Ruth Smith*
Senior production supervisor: *Carol A. Bielski*
Senior designer: *Gino Cieslik*
Associate supplement producer: *Meghan Durko*
Associate photo research coordinator: *Natalie C. Peschiera*
Permissions editor: *Marty Granahan*
Cover design: *Gino Cieslik*
Cover photo: *Toledo, Spain. Courtesy of Santi V. Buscemi*
Typeface: *10/12 Berkely Book*
Compositor: *Carlisle Communications, Ltd.*
Printer: *R. R. Donnelley and Sons, Inc.*

Library of Congress Cataloging-in-Publication Data

Buscemi, Santi V.
    A reader for college writers / Santi V. Buscemi.--6th ed.
      p. cm.
    Rev. ed. of: A reader for developing writers. 5th ed. c2002.
    Includes index.
    ISBN 0-07-288554-8 (alk. paper)
    1. College readers. 2. English language—Rhetoric—Problems, exercises, etc. 3. Report writing—Problems, exercises, ec. I. Buscemi, Santi V. Reader for dveloping writers. II. Title.
PE1417.B853 2005
808'.0427--dc22

                                                  2003068631

www.mhhe.com

*For **Joseph** and
Theresa Buscemi and
for all the other Sicilian
heroes who came to this
country to make a
better life for their
children*

About the Author

*Santi V. Buscemi teaches reading and writing at Middlesex County College
in Edison, NJ. He is the author of* AllWrite! 2.0 with Online Handbook,
McGraw-Hill's interactive electronic writing program, and co-author of
The Basics *and* 75 Readings Plus. *He has lectured on developmental
education at national conferences in the United States and South Africa.*

To the Instructor

Known as *A Reader for Developing Writers* through its first five editions, *A Reader for College Writers* is a complete rhetoric and reader for students in writing courses that emphasize the close relationship between reading and writing. In addition to reflecting what many instructors have told us—that the text works well across a range of levels of proficiency—the title change reflects the fact that students are, after all, already writers when they arrive at college: *A Reader for College Writers* is designed to help them develop and refine the writing, reading, and thinking skills that they already possess.

Though enriched and expanded, the text retains its original purpose: to help students read carefully, respond thoughtfully, and use those responses as creative springboards for writing. More than ever, research continues to affirm the close relationship between analytical reading and effective writing. *A Reader for College Writers* insists on this connection.

This is not to say that the reading selections have been chosen to serve as blueprints or models for the students' own writing. However, they do illustrate important principles and techniques clearly, and they inspire students to use writing as a way to explore their own values, ideas, concerns, and opinions. The connection between reading and writing is first discussed in depth in "Getting Started." This emphasis is maintained throughout the text via the instructional apparatus. Section and chapter introductions discuss fundamental principles of rhetoric and composition that are illustrated in the reading selections, and questions and writing suggestions encourage students to use what they read in order to write, and to think, more powerfully.

About the Sixth Edition

THE READING SELECTIONS
Thirty percent of the readings in the sixth edition are new. As in previous editions, I have actively sought out reading selections that allow students to use their own experiences and perceptions as sources of information and insight for writing projects that explore questions suggested by—if not drawn directly from—the reading. More than ever, the paragraphs, essays, and poems I have included reflect a **diversity of cultural and academic interests,** and many of them speak about phenomena, cultures, and lifestyles with which some students may be unfamiliar.

For example, in addition to an essay about the suffering a student writer endured under the Pol Pot regime in Cambodia, Chapter One contains an essay on the scourge of AIDS in Africa, by UN Secretary General Kofi Annan. In Chapter Two, students read a short essay about the agony of Afghani people, who have had to endure drought, earthquakes, and the Taliban. An essay in Chapter Ten discusses the heroism of hundreds of women who, disguised as men, fought in the American Civil War next to their male

vii

counterparts. In addition, two new essays provide **first-hand accounts of the events of September 11, 2001.** Another addition, "Macho Girls and Vanishing Females," talks about a new sexual revolution that threatens to make men obsolete.

In earlier editions, I included a number of poignant and eloquent pieces that explore the nature of what it means to be human. Among them is a letter by Elie Wiesel, which addresses the Master of the Universe about the question of evil in the context of the Holocaust. Another is a moving essay by a medical doctor who must deal with the knowledge that her sister has breast cancer and, in the process, come to grips with her own mortality. Both have been very successful with students, and they have been retained in the sixth edition. At the suggestion of the reviewers, however, I also added several pieces that portray the lighter side of life, including **essays by Dave Barry and satirist P. J. O'Rourke.**

As in previous editions, the selections demonstrate variety in length, subject matter, difficulty, and purpose. Included in most chapters is at least one short, readily accessible piece designed to promote confidence and prepare students for the longer, more challenging selections that follow.

The table of contents continues to address a variety of academic disciplines and a wide range of social, political, economic, and scientific concerns. While most selections are non-fiction prose, **poetry** continues to play a significant role. As in the past, each is appropriate to the reading abilities of students in college writing courses, but I have also included several that promote healthy intellectual stretching.

The sixth edition also contains a **thematic table of contents** so that students and teachers can more easily make their own connections between themes, questions, and issues. In addition, the title of each selection in the table of contents is now accompanied by a short description intended to pique student interest.

STUDENT ESSAYS

Because students need realistic models, and, perhaps more importantly, because they need to know that their writing matters, *A Reader for College Writers* offers **at least one student piece in every chapter.** The Appendix on research paper-writing contains "Victims of Violent Crime," a paper by Angela Brandli that was so well researched and so convincing that it prompted the New Jersey State legislature to pass measures increasing compensation to victims of violent crime. The other student essays in the text represent a range of similarly compelling issues. A student essay new to the sixth edition contrasts the sources and types of anxiety faced by today's young people with those their parents and grandparents endured. Another essay explores the relationship between part-time work and full-time college study. A third argues for the humane treatment of the mentally ill, and yet another explains the horror a student and her family endured in communist Romania.

In this sixth edition, I have once again made it a point to show that the student essays are products of careful, sustained effort. Thus, **each chapter introduction contains samples of rough and corrected drafts of student essays** appearing in that chapter. Comments in the margins relevant to techniques and skills covered in the chapter demonstrate the riches revising can yield.

REVISED AND ENHANCED INSTRUCTION ON WRITING AND READING

The sixth edition continues to emphasize the notion that writing is a process of discovery to be approached with care, commitment, and energy. In order to explain the process more fully, the **"Getting Started"** section, which opens the book, **traces the evolution of an essay from prewriting through the final draft,** with each stage fully explained and illustrated via samples taken from the work of a college student.

In addition, materials to help students learn to gather information for and plan their writing have been added, as has been **complete coverage of purpose, audience, and style** as they relate to academic writing. **Techniques for writing outlines**—both formal and informal—are also included, as are new templates that students can use to organize essays for special purposes, including comparison/contrast and argumentation.

However, the most important change to "Getting Started" has to do with the expansion of the critical reading section, now called **"Becoming an Active College Reader."** This new section **traces the process of critical reading from surveying and reading the text initially, through re-reading for better comprehension and a more accurate appraisal, through summarizing, critiquing, and synthesizing texts.** Special attention is paid to taking notes in the margins and conversing with the text through active dialogue and questioning. Outlining skills are also explained in the light of textual analysis, and several student examples that respond to professional essays (one of them to multiple essays) are included.

EXPANDED COVERAGE OF ARGUMENT AND PERSUASION

Another major new feature of the sixth edition is the revision and expansion of the two-chapter section entitled Argumentation and Persuasion. It now contains a total of **thirteen student and professional selections and additional coverage of relevant techniques and approaches** students can use when they pursue such writing. Among these are a reliance on claims and warrants (the **Toulmin method**) as the basis of argument as well as the application of **Rogerian strategies,** such as establishing common ground, which are especially useful to writers of persuasion. The introduction to this section also includes expanded discussion of ways to evaluate and approach potential audiences of argumentative and persuasive essays. Coverage of **logical fallacies,** which appears in this introduction, has been doubled. Several **new visual pieces** – political cartoons, an ad, and a public service announcement – encourage students to explore the persuasive power of words and images used together. Finally, both the argument and persuasion chapters contain several **paired pieces**, which offer opposing views on important contemporary issues from bilingual education to American foreign policy to the question of paying reparations for slavery.

APPARATUS ACCOMPANYING THE SELECTIONS

Because many—if not the vast majority of college students—have taken naturally to the idea of seeking information on the Internet, the sixth edition of *A Reader for College Writers* offers a new category of apparatus accompanying the selections: **"Read More on the Web,"** providing students who want to know more about an author or a topic with references to relevant websites – all of which have been thoroughly researched for accuracy and appropriateness to college study.

As in earlier editions, each reading selection in the sixth edition is accompanied by **well-integrated apparatus** that helps students practice techniques explained in chapter introductions and illustrated in the reading selections. **Introductions** to the selections provide a context for the piece, including information on the author, and they illustrate important principles and techniques. Questions and comments under **Preparing to Read** and the definitions under **Vocabulary** help students preview the content and structure of each selection.

At the same time, this "pre-reading" material prepares students for the **Questions for Discussion** and the **Thinking Critically** questions that follow each reading. Questions for Discussion direct students' attention to important features of the text and prompt them to respond to ideas and techniques presented there. Thinking Critically prompts offer students challenging topics for discussion and writing that will help them practice a variety of important critical skills. For example, some items ask students to practice techniques learned in the reading and note-taking sections of "Getting Started." Others ask them to extend or respond to the discussion of ideas or opinions found in what they have just read. Still others require them to make comparisons between two or more selections in the text.

Suggestions for Journal Entries encourage students to record insights and ideas that are inspired by the reading and that can serve as springboards for longer writing projects outlined in **Suggestions for Sustained Writing,** which appear near the end of each chapter of readings. As in previous editions, the clear connection between the Suggestions for Journal Entries and the Suggestions for Sustained Writing has been maintained. Each and every Suggestion for Sustained Writing reminds students that composing is more than simply gathering information and arranging it on a page. Indeed, woven into the fabric of each item is a reminder that successful writing demands careful planning, the creation of multiple drafts, frequent reorganization and revision, and painstaking editing.

Also retained in the sixth edition are the end-of-chapter **"Writing to Learn" group activities.** These assignments take student groups through a step-by-step process of discussion, research, writing, and revision that culminates in a major collaborative project. Students are encouraged to research and discuss trends, problems, events, and figures from a variety of disciplines by interviewing professors, using the college library, and searching the Internet.

SUPPLEMENTS

The following supplements are designed to help instructors and students derive the full benefit from the sixth edition of *A Reader for College Writers:*

- An **Instructor's Resource CD-ROM** (0-07-297669-1) contains a guide to *A Reader for College Writers* written by Santi Buscemi, with strategies for teaching individual essays, suggested answers to questions, tips for using the text in class, and more.
- A **companion website** (www.mhhe.com/rcw) includes links to information on authors, topics, and essays included in the print text.
- **Teaching Composition faculty listserv** (www.mhhe.com/tcomp), moderated by Chris Anson of North Carolina State University, and **Teaching Basic Writing faculty listserv** (www.mhhe.com/tbw), moderated by Laura Gray Rosendale of Northern Arizona University, are offered by McGraw-Hill as a service to the academic community. These listservs bring senior members of composition programs together with newer members—junior faculty, adjuncts, and graduate teaching assistants—in an online newsletter and discussion group that addresses issues of pedagogy, in theory and in practice.

Used in many colleges across the United States and in other parts of the world, *Reader for College Writers* has been far more successful than I could have hoped when I completed the first edition in 1990. No matter what the future brings, I will always be grateful for the support that so many teachers and students have given me in the thirteen years since the text was first published.

No textbook is the product of one person, even a book that carries a single byline. I am indebted to several good friends and fellow teachers whose counsel, direction, and encouragement helped this book evolve into what it is. I would like to thank several of my teaching colleagues from across the country for carefully reviewing the sixth edition and making excellent suggestions for improving it:

Laura L. Apfelbeck, University of Wisconsin—Manitowoc
Sandra Barnhill, South Plains College
Wayne Berninger, Long Island University, Brooklyn Campus
J. Elizabeth Clark, LaGuardia Community College—CUNY
Timothy R. Cramer, Santa Monica College
Kristine Dassinger, Genesee Community College
Tracy E. Miller, Towson University

Bobbie Robinson, Abraham Baldwin College
Michael R. Scott, Lancaster Community College
Vivian Thomlinson, Cameron University

Among my friends and colleagues at Middlesex County College, I want to thank Lucille Alfieri, Betty Altruda, the late Jamie Daley, Sallie Del Vecchio, Barry Glazer, James Keller, Jack Moskowitz, Georgianna Planko, Renee Price, Yvonne Sisko, and Mathew Spano for their support and loyalty. I also want to express my thanks to my editors, Alexis Walker, Laura Barthule, and Lisa Moore, at McGraw-Hill. Finally, I want to thank my wife, Elaine, my daughter Pamela, and my grandson Matthew for putting up with my "imperfections" and for granting me their patience and support during the writing of this and of earlier editions.

Santi V. Buscemi

CHAPTER 3

Development   121

CHAPTER 4

Introductions and Conclusions   155

S E C T I O N   T W O   1 9 9

Word Choice and Sentence Patterns   199

C H A P T E R   5

Word Choice: Using Concrete, Specific, and Vivid Language   201

CHAPTER 6

Word Choice: Using Figurative Language   229

CHAPTER 9

Narration   347

CHAPTER 12

Process Analysis   471

CHAPTER 14

Persuasion   561

THEMATIC TABLE OF CONTENTS

Getting Started

A Reader for College Writers is a collection of short readings by professional and student authors. Each paragraph, essay, and poem is accompanied by discussion questions, suggestions for short and sustained writing, and other instructional aids. The reading selections use techniques you will want to learn as you develop your reading and writing skills. Many will serve as models for the writing you do in college.

The reading selections act as springboards to your own writing. Some supply facts and ideas you can include and make reference to in your own work. Others inspire you to write paragraphs, letters, or essays about similar subjects by drawing details from what you know best—your own experiences, observations, and readings. In short, this book helps you make connections between your reading and your writing, and it shows you ways to improve both. The rest of this introduction, Getting Started, discusses:

1. How to Use This Book
2. Using the Writing Process: A Tool for Discovery
3. The Making of a Student Essay: From Prewriting to Proofreading
4. Becoming an Active College Reader.

Part 1: How to Use This Book

Each of the paragraphs, essays, and poems that you will read is accompanied by instructional aids including (1) a note that profiles the author and/or explains text's origins, (2) comments that help you prepare to read, (3) a vocabulary list, (4) Questions for Discussion, and (5) Suggestions for Journal Entries (short writing). In addition, each chapter contains several Suggestions for Sustained Writing, as well as one group assignment that you might work on with your classmates. These materials will help you make the most of your reading and get started on your own writing projects. Here's one way to use *A Reader for College Writers* (your teacher may suggest others):

1. The book is divided into five sections, each containing at least two chapters. Begin by reading the section introduction. Section introductions are not long, but they contain information important to reading the selections in the chapters that follow. The introduction to Section One begins on page 53.
2. Next, read the chapter introduction. It explains principles and strategies illustrated by the reading selections in that chapter. The introduction to Chapter 1 begins on page 55.

3. When you get to the reading selections in a chapter, you will see that each is preceded by the author's biography, a section called Preparing to Read, and a vocabulary list. Read these instructional aids before you begin the selection itself. They provide information important to previewing the selection. The first selection begins on page 66.

4. Read each selection carefully, making notes in the margins, underlining important ideas, and marking unfamiliar words and phrases that you need to look up in a dictionary or encyclopedia.

5. After you read and re-read the selection, read and answer the Questions for Discussion that follow it. It is a good idea to put your answers in writing, in a computer file, in a notebook dedicated to this class, or at least in the margins of your book.

6. Next, read and complete the items under Thinking Critically, which follow the Questions for Discussion. Again, it is wise to put your responses to these items in writing. Incidentally, responding to the Thinking Critically items also provides ideas you might use in longer and more formal writing projects.

7. Now, respond to the Suggestions for Journal Entries, which follow Thinking Critically. Write your responses in a journal (notebook)—paper or electronic—kept only for this purpose. Making regular journal entries is critical to developing your writing abilities. First, like any skill, writing is mastered only through constant practice, and keeping a journal provides this practice. Second, your journal contains responses to the readings, so it helps you make what you have read your own. Finally, responding to Suggestions for Journal Entries is an easy way to gather information for longer projects. Almost all of the Suggestions for Sustained Writing (found at the end of each chapter) refer to journal entries, so keeping a journal means you will have already taken the first step in completing major writing assignments.

8. Respond to one of the Suggestions for Sustained Writing at the chapter's end. Read each suggestion carefully; then, choose one that interests you. Almost all Suggestions for Sustained Writing refer to earlier journal suggestions. If you haven't made a journal entry like the one referred to in the Suggestions for Sustained Writing, go back and do so.

9. If your teacher asks you to use library or Internet research when writing a paper, you may find it helpful to refer to the Appendix on writing research papers using Modern Language Association (MLA) style. It is found near the end of this book. In addition, important terms are defined in the glossary, which follows the Appendix. Refer to the glossary if you have questions about a term used to define a writing technique, rule, or principle.

10. Depending upon your instructor's preferences, you might be asked to complete one or more of the collaborative assignments called Writing to Learn: A Group Activity. They are found at the end of each chapter.

Part 2: Using the Writing Process: A Tool for Discovery

This section of Getting Started (GS) helps you follow steps in the process of writing an essay, letter, or any other document. It covers the following:

GS 2.1 The Writing Process: An Overview

GS 2.2 Prewriting:
>   Determining Purpose, Audience, and Style
>   Gathering Information for Writing

GS 2.3 Outlining

GS 2.4 Drafting and Revising

GS 2.5 Editing and Proofreading

GS 2.1 THE WRITING PROCESS: AN OVERVIEW

Both writing and reading are processes (Becoming an Active College *Reader* is discussed later in Getting Started.) One way to explain the writing process is to divide it into four major steps: prewriting, outlining, drafting/revising, and editing/proofreading.

Prewriting, also called invention, consists of two major steps:

• Determining your intended audience (your readers) and purpose and style.

• Gathering information.

Here's what Gilbert Muller and Harvey Wiener, two veteran professors and writers, have to say about prewriting:

> Few writers begin without some warm-up activity. Generally called prewriting, the steps they take before producing a draft almost always start with thinking about their topic. They talk to friends and colleagues; they browse in libraries . . . ; they read newspaper and magazine articles. Sometimes they jot down notes and lists in order to put on paper some of their thoughts in very rough form. Some writers use free-association; they record as thoroughly as possible their random, unedited ideas. . . . Using the raw, often disorganized materials produced in this preliminary stage, many writers try to group related thoughts with a scratch outline. ("On Writing")

Don't skip this important stage. In addition to helping you decide on the nature of your writing project and its focus, prewriting provides insights about how your writing might be arranged and leads you to the second step in the process: outlining.

Outlining provides a blueprint or organizational framework through which to present information and ideas in a manner that readers will have no trouble following. As you will see later in this section of Getting Started, there are two major types of outlines you might use: formal and informal.

Drafting and revising are the heart of the composing process. Begin drafting after having decided on important questions such as purpose and audience, having gathered information, and having made at least an informal outline. Remember, first drafts are also called "rough" drafts. Spend time revising—that is, completely rewriting and restructuring—your first, second, and third drafts until your paper says what it needs to clearly, completely, and logically.

Editing and proofreading may come last, but they are as important as all of the other steps. Neglect them and you risk embarrassing yourself or, even worse, confusing and frustrating your reader.

Note: These steps are neatly defined, but they are not always distinct from each other. For example, while editing, you might realize that you have to add more information or correct a serious organizational problem. If this happens, don't worry. Go back and make the needed changes. It's the way the process is supposed to work.

GS 2.2 PREWRITING

This section covers two types of prewriting activities: 1) determining purpose, audience, and style and 2) gathering information.

GS 2.2a Determining Purpose, Audience, and Style

Determine Your Purpose. Writing is a practical activity. It always serves a purpose, whether the writer is producing a technical report that explains an electronic process, an argumentative essay on a current social issue, a thank-you letter to a business client, a review of a film or book, a pamphlet that describes a beautiful vacation resort, or simply an entry in a diary. The purpose of the writing determines the major approach or method that the writer uses and the form that the document will take. For example, in order to explain the workings of a cellular phone system, you might use a technique called *process analysis* to list steps required for the transmission of voice and fax messages over a wireless system. If you are trying to convince the state legislature to increase assistance to victims of violent crime, you would probably use techniques associated with *argumentation* and *persuasion*. If you are simply recording the day's events in a diary, narration (recalling events in time order) might be the best tool.

However, pieces of writing rarely rely on only one method or approach. For instance, a *process analysis* explaining how cellular phones transmit messages might also use *definition* to explain what a cellular phone or a transmission tower is. It might even *contrast* a cellular phone to the more traditional, wired models. An argument attempting to convince legislators to increase aid to crime victims might also include paragraphs of pure *narration* to tell the history of recent crime legislation or recall the experience of a particular crime victim. A simple diary entry that relies heavily on narration might also include a *description* of what the writer heard or saw during the day.

In short, even though a piece of writing relies on one major approach, it may also use other approaches to achieve its purpose. The choice of approaches depends, of course, on the writer's purpose.

For students enrolled in first-year college writing classes, the assignment an instructor makes might indicate a specific purpose and even require a definite approach. However, this is not always the case. With some assignments, instructors ask students to determine their own purposes and then decide for themselves how best to achieve them. This is part of a process intended to help developing writers grow and gain experience. Although we sometimes think of effective writing as a matter of sticking to the rules of grammar and mastering the techniques of rhetoric, mature and effective writing also demands an ability to make judgments. For example, writers must decide on a topic's particular focus, gather information appropriate to that focus, define their purpose, and determine ways to fulfill that purpose. No textbook can do these things for them.

A writer develops judgment only by experience. As with any other craft, this is a process of trial and error. So, don't get discouraged if you suddenly discover that you have chosen the wrong approach or that you haven't defined your purpose clearly. Most new writers—and many experienced writers—often have the same problems. Simply go back and rethink your purpose and your approach; then, start again. Of course, this might require doing more information-gathering by using some of the prewriting tools explained in the next few pages. It might also require you to get rid of information you gathered earlier simply because it is no longer relevant to your new purpose. However, all of this is normal—writing is a process of discovery and revision.

The best time to think about your purpose for an academic essay is *before* you begin gathering facts, ideas, and insights about your topic through *listing, clustering,* or some other method explained below. After carefully considering the assignment you have been given, write a statement of purpose (a sentence or two should do) on an index card. However, keep in mind that you might revise this statement of purpose later in the process, after you have gathered information, after you have made an outline, or even after you have written a first draft of the essay. You will learn more about purpose in Chapter 1.

Consider the Audience. The audience for any piece of writing is its reader or readers. It is certainly important to consider the readers before you begin writing a first draft, but you should also do so even before you begin gathering information. Let's say your purpose is to convince your classmates to use the library's online periodical database to find recent information on their majors. You might first have to define "professional journals" and distinguish such publications from "weekly news magazines." You might also have to define "periodical," "database," and even "online." Finally, you might want to explain ways students can find relevant articles so as to convince them of the ease with which this tool can be used.

On the other hand, what if you are writing to the members of the library staff to convince them that your college should subscribe to a particular database? You would not have to explain such basic things to get your point across. Indeed, taking time to do so would probably bore these readers.

The primary audience for academic essays is usually the professor. Often, however, your classmates will also be asked to read your work, especially if you discuss papers in small writing groups. In such cases, you must consider your whole audience—both instructor and students—and you might need to include explanatory information and definitions of specialized terms in addition to what you would have included had you been writing for your instructor alone.

Even if you are writing for the instructor alone, evaluating the needs of your reader can get tricky. Many instructors of first-year composition classes have advanced degrees in English or related disciplines. Therefore, you can assume that they are well trained in their field. But does that mean that they are acquainted with other specialized fields of knowledge? Would they know the process by which atoms are split, the most effective methods for tracking economic growth, or the latest theories on criminology and prison reform? If you were writing on recent developments in American music, would your instructor be able to distinguish "hip-hop" from "rap" music? Would he or she be familiar with the "boy-band sound"? If not, you would have to define these specialized terms.

As in determining your purpose, considering your audience requires the use of your judgment as a writer. Evaluate your audience's needs before you begin to gather information, but again, remember that you may later revise your understanding of your readers' needs at any time in the writing process. You will learn more about evaluating an audience in Section Five.

Use Formal Style in Academic Writing. Style refers to the level of language you use. Essentially there are three levels of language you can use in writing, but *formal* style—the third of these—is preferable in academic writing.

Informal Style You use this style when writing to a very limited audience—yourself, a close friend, a classmate—in email, short notes, or personal letters. Such writing may contain *colloquialisms,* or conversational expressions used only in certain locales or by a familiar group. Informal style also allows *slang,* or language that has a special meaning within a limited group and that changes rapidly. Such style sometimes makes reference to people, events, or things that have special meaning only to the reader and writer. Consider the terms "tanking" and "Geek Patrol," for example, in this passage from a student's email to a former high school classmate:

> Most guys in my fraternity are pretty brainy, and
> they hit the books hard. But they aren't that stuck
> up, not like the Geek Patrol we knew at Jefferson
> High. In fact, they're all right! They even tutor kids
> whose grades are tanking.

Familiar Style You might use a familiar style in a short business memo, in a letter to the editor of your college newspaper, or in a letter or e-mail to a relative or acquaintance. Here is a sample from a student's letter about his first year in college, which he sent to the boss he worked for during the summer:

> You would like the students in my fraternity. They
> are fairly smart, and they really put their noses to
> the grindstone when they want to ace a big exam.
> However, they're not snobs. In fact, they often tutor
> other kids who are having trouble with school work.

This version is somewhat more formal than the last, and it resembles every-day conversation among intelligent people. It does not include slang or private language, but it does use colloquialisms such as "ace a big exam." For the sake of easy communication, it also includes a cliché (a phrase that lacks original-ity): "put their noses to the grindstone." In the familiar style, it addresses the reader directly by using the word "you."

Formal Style This is the kind of language that belongs in academic papers, in answers to essay questions, in business letters, and in business, technical, and government reports. Notice that the writer now replaces all colloquialisms, slang, and clichés and that he no longer addresses the reader directly by using "you." The vocabulary he uses is more sophisticated than the more relaxed choice of words he used in the two versions above.

> Students in my fraternity are quite likable. They are
> intelligent, and they are also diligent, studying hard
> especially when it comes to major examinations.
> However, they are not snobs. In fact, they often tutor
> other students who are having difficulty with their
> studies.

It is best to use a formal style from the moment you begin drafting your paper. However, you can always check for and eliminate clichés, slang, collo-quialisms, and other less-than-formal elements when you edit your work.

GS 2.2b Gathering Information for Writing

Another important aspect of prewriting is gathering information. You can use the following seven techniques to gather facts, ideas, and opinions for any assignment, especially for journal en-tries. A good way to start a journal entry is to read the notes you made on a read-ing selection (You can learn more about taking notes in Part IV of Getting Started: Becoming an Active College Reader, which begins on p. 31). This should get you mentally set for writing. Then, follow the Suggestions for Journal Entries, which often recommend using the information-gathering techniques that follow.

Listing. You can use your journal to make a list of details by recording what you think is most important, most startling, or most obvious about your topic.

Sometimes, in fact, you can compile a useful list of details simply by putting down whatever comes to mind about your topic. Here's a list that student Aggie Canino made when asked to describe a recent storm and its effects:

Cloged rain sewers overflowing

Giant tree limbs across the road

Flooding

Strong winds

Birch trees bent duble in the wind

Cracked utility poles

Downed power lines

Loss of electric

Lasted only one hour

Dog hidding under bed

Flooded basements

Thunder/lightening

Loss of power

Frightening sounds—howling of the wind, crash of thunder

Complete darkness in the middle of the day

Oak on corner struck by lightening-bark ripped

This list is repetitious and has spelling errors, but don't worry about such problems at first; you can correct them later. Just concentrate on your topic, and record the details as fast as they pop into your head.

Make sure to read your list after—but only *after*—you run out of things to say. Doing so will allow you to eliminate repetition and correct obvious errors. More important, it will help you make various items more specific and even come up with a few new details. For instance, Aggie expanded her mention of "cracked utility poles" by describing the "white sparks that flew from downed power lines" and by detailing the terror she felt as she heard the "splintering of a utility pole struck by lightning."

Focused Freewriting. Freewriting is a very common technique to help overcome *writer's block,* a problem that results in staring at a blank piece of paper while trying unsuccessfully to come up with something to say. Freewriting involves writing nonstop for 5 or 10 minutes and simply recording ideas that come into your mind at random. Focused freewriting is similar, but it involves concentrating on a predetermined topic.

Let's say that you want to do some focused freewriting on a storm. The results might look like this:

> The clogged rain sewers were overflowing, and there was a lot of flooding with strong winds knocking down power lines. Thunder crashed, and lightning flashed. Giant tree limbs fell across the road and a birch was bent double, and there were lots of flooded basements. Even so, the storm lasted only one hour. Several downed power lines threw threatening sparks and flashes across the road. My street was blocked; a large oak had fallen across it. We lost our electricity. The crash of thunder shook me to my bones. My dog hid under the bed. We were terrified.

Again, don't worry about grammar and other errors at this point in the process. Simply focus on your topic and record your ideas quickly and completely.

As always, read your journal entry immediately after you've recorded your ideas. Doing so helps you cut out repetition, rework parts that require clarification, and add more details that come to mind in the process.

Clustering. Clustering is a good way to turn a broad subject into a limited and more manageable topic for a short essay. Also called *mapping* and *webbing,* it is another effective way to gather information for an essay.

Like focused freewriting, clustering uses free association. To cluster ideas, begin with a blank sheet of paper. In the center, write and circle the word or phrase that expresses the broad subject you want to write about. Let's say it is dancing. Think of ideas and details related to this subject. Write down whatever pops into your mind. For example, you might think of subheadings such as ballet, ballroom dancing, dancing as exercise, modern dance, dancing in the movies, and folk/ethnic dancing. If you arrange these subheadings in circles around your general subject, you might create a diagram that looks like this:

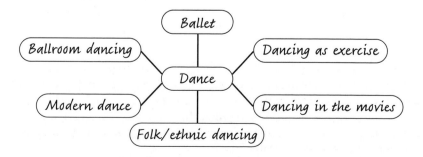

Now write down ideas and details related to these subheadings, and continue in this way until you have run out of ideas. Circle each word or phrase, and draw lines between each of your subheadings and the ideas and details that relate to them. Here's what your paper might look like when you are finished:

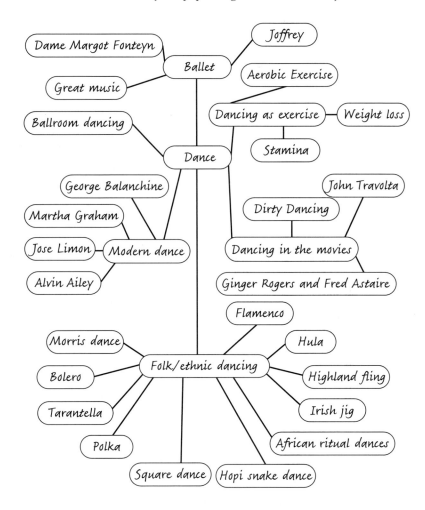

Notice that some subheadings have been given more attention than others. That just means that you may know more or have more to say about folk/ethnic dancing than about ballroom dancing. In fact, then, clustering has helped you focus on the topic that you know most about or that you are most interested in.

Of course, you can stop at this stage, review your notes, and begin planning a preliminary thesis statement (and even an outline) for a paper on ethnic dancing. On the other hand, you might focus your topic even further by getting more specific. Let's say you know a lot about African ritual dancing or are interested in learning more about it through library research. You can extend your clustering by focusing in on that subtopic. Here's what yet another cluster might look like:

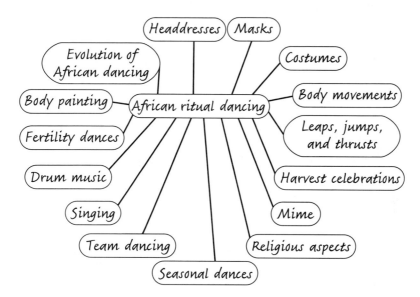

Drawing a Subject Tree. Still another way to settle on a manageable topic and to gather information is to draw a subject tree. As with clustering, start with a broad subject. Then, divide it into two or three subheadings, or branches. Next, subdivide each of these branches, and so on, until you feel comfortable that your topic is limited enough and that you have enough information to begin writing an outline or a rough draft of your paper. On the next page is an example that begins with "uses of computers" as a general subject.

As you create a subject tree, you will almost naturally put down more details and ideas under subheadings with which you are most familiar or in which you have the greatest interest. For example, the writer who created the subject tree for "uses of computers" would probably feel most comfortable writing about ways in which computers help both students and teachers.

Brainstorming. Unlike most other ways to gather information, brainstorming usually results in a collection of words and phrases scribbled across a page randomly. Another difference is that brainstorming is done with friends or classmates. Using this method, a small group can come up with many more interesting questions and answers about a topic than someone working alone.

You can begin brainstorming in a variety of ways. One of the most effective is to ask journalists' questions. Reporters ask these when they plan their stories: *What happened? When did it happen? Where did it happen? Who was involved? Why did it happen?* and *How did it happen?* (An easy way to remember the six questions journalists use is to think of them as the 5Ws and the H.)

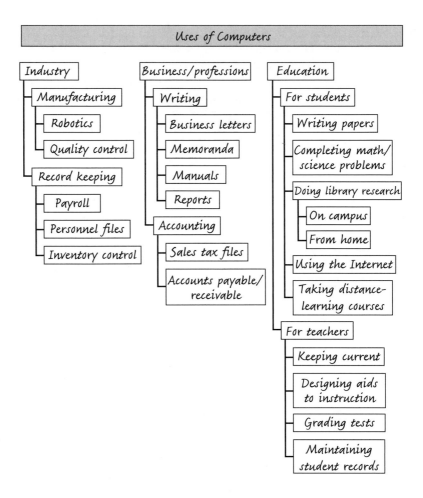

Journalist questions work best if you want to tell a story or explain how or why something happens or should happen. However, you will probably have to think of different questions if you have other purposes in mind. Say you want to describe your Uncle Charlie. You might ask: What does he look like? How old is he? Who are his friends? Where does he live? What kind of job does he have? In any case, remember that prewriting is also called *invention,* so be creative and invent as many kinds of questions as you like.

Not all the questions you ask will yield useful information. However, the answers to only one or two might suggest ideas and details to other members of your brainstorming group. In a little while, a mental chain reaction will occur, and you will find yourself discussing ideas, facts, and opinions that seem to pop up naturally. Working together, then, you will inspire each other to produce information for a fine journal entry and even for a longer piece of writing based on that entry.

EXERCISE 1: *Practice what you have learned*   Pick a topic related to your academic major or to an interest you have held for a long time. If you are majoring in nursing, you might focus on pediatric nursing, emergency-room nursing, or nursing in an extended-care facility. If you are a psychology major, you might consider the causes and treatment of an emotional disorder such as kleptomania, claustrophobia, anorexia nervosa, or obsessive–compulsive syndrome. Then again, you might think about your interest in model trains, in camping, or in cooking. Begin to gather what you already know about this topic through the listing method. Then, using the same topic, try clustering or drawing a subject tree.

Interviewing. Asking appropriate questions of people who know about your topic is an excellent way to gather detail. Like brainstorming, interviewing gives you other perspectives from which to view your topic, and it often yields information that you might otherwise never have learned.

The kinds of questions you ask should be determined by your purpose. If you are trying to learn why something happened, what someone did, or how something works, for example, you might begin your interview with a group of questions like those journalists rely on and that you read about under Brainstorming.

Just make sure that the person you interview is knowledgeable about your subject and willing to spend enough time with you to make your interview worthwhile. People who can give you only a few minutes might not be good sources of information. When you make the appointment to meet with the person you want to interview, tell him or her a little about your topic, your purpose, and the kinds of questions you will ask. This will give your subject a chance to think about the interview in advance and prepare thoughtful responses to your questions.

Finally, come to the interview prepared. Think carefully about the questions you need answered ahead of time. Write them down—at least those you feel are most important—in your journal or on a piece of notebook paper. Bring them to the interview, and use them to get your subject talking. If your questions are clear and interesting, you should gather more information than you bargained for. On the other hand, don't get upset if the interview doesn't go exactly as you planned. Your subject might not answer any of your questions but simply discuss ideas as they come to mind. Such interviews sometimes provide a lot of useful information. Just take good notes.

Summarizing. This prewriting method involves condensing another writer's ideas and putting them into your own words. It is especially effective if you want to combine information found in your reading with details you have gathered from your own experiences or from other sources. Just be sure to use your own language throughout the summary. In addition, if you plan to use any of this information in an essay, make certain to tell your readers that it comes from the work of another writer by mentioning the writer's name. For instance, if you decide to summarize Bertrand Russell's "Three Passions I Have Lived For" (a selection in Chapter 1), you might begin: "As Russell explained in his autobiography . . . ."

EXERCISE 2: Practice what you have learned   Read Bertrand Russell's "Three Passions I Have Lived For" or Siu Chan's "Suffering," essays found in Chapter 1. Then, summarize this essay paragraph by paragraph. Try to capture the content of each paragraph in one sentence.

GS 2.3 OUTLINING

After gathering information and deciding on a working central idea, many writers construct an outline for the essay. An outline can often make the writing of a working draft of your paper easier. Think of an outline as a sort of a blueprint, which will guide you through the beginning of the drafting process.

For most short essays, an informal or scratch outline is sufficient. However, if you are writing a lengthy essay, such as a library research paper, you might want to use a formal outline, which can also serve as a table of contents. Ask your instructor if you should submit an outline as part of the assignment and, if so, which type is required. In any event, your essay will be more successful if you spend a few minutes constructing a working thesis statement, the central idea of your essay, and then jotting down a scratch outline of the main points you want to make in the body of your essay. (You will learn more about writing thesis statements and developing ideas in the body of your essay in Chapters 1 and 3.)

GS 2.3a Writing an Informal (Scratch) Outline   Let's say you have just reviewed the notes you took when you completed a clustering exercise about African ritual dancing (page 11). Realizing that the most important aspect of what you know about such dancing is that it is dramatic, colorful, and exciting, you decide to write an essay showing this. Your thesis might be: "African ritual dances are the most dramatic, colorful, and exciting folk dances I have ever witnessed."

As you review your notes a second time, you realize that several of the ideas you have put down in your clusters do not relate to your working thesis. For example, the fact that some African dances are seasonal does not relate to—develop or support—your working thesis. So you decide to leave it out and focus on aspects of the dances that are dramatic, colorful, and exciting. Here's what your scratch outline might look like:

Working Thesis: African ritual dances, which I observed on my visit to Zimbabwe, are the most dramatic, colorful, and exciting folk dances I have ever seen.

1. Colorful masks.

2. Frightening costumes.

3. Bodies painted in bright colors, eye-catching patterns.

4. Joyful music.

5. Vivid body movements.

As you can see, this scratch outline is no more than a brief list of details—most of them just words and phrases—pulled from the clustering exercise completed earlier. However, it is enough to provide a pattern that the writer can follow to construct a successful first, or working draft.

GS 2.3b Writing a Formal Outline   A formal outline differs from a scratch outline in that it is more complete and more consistent in structure. A formal outline for an essay on African ritual dancing might look like this:

I.   Introduction.

    A.   Folk dances differ in form and purpose from culture to culture.

    B.   Many European and American folk dances reveal much about the cultures in which they originated.

    C.   Thesis: African ritual dances, which I observed on my visit to Zimbabwe, are the most dramatic, colorful, and exciting folk dances I have ever seen.

II.   Many dancers wear bizarre masks intended to startle and even frighten the audience.

    A.   Patterns painted on these masks are varied and vivid.

    B.   They take odd shapes and are often very large.

        1.   Many are triangular or pointed; others resemble shields used in warfare.

        2.   Some triple the size of the wearer's face so as to make him appear monstrous.

        3.   Some look like the faces of animals; others suggest that the dancer has come from another planet.

III.   The costumes are rich, complex, and colorful.

    A.   Some are made of animal skins; others are woven from native vegetable fibers.

    B.   All are extremely colorful.

    C.   The costumes make great use of fascinating geometric patterns.

    D.   Huge headdresses are worn, some resembling the heads of animals.

IV.   Drum music gets the heart pounding; the air is sometimes filled with song.

    A.   The musicians keep the pace energetic, often adding to the dramatic effect.

    B.   A chorus of women singing sweetly often accompanies the dancers.

V.   The real spectacle comes in the dancers' acrobatics.

    A.   Each dancer conveys a message or vivid story through movement.

    B.   Performers run, stomp, and leap high into the air.

    C.   Some prance around on huge stilts, standing 15 feet tall.

    D.   They even approach members of the audience, pretending to threaten them with lunges and howls.

Though not very long, this formal outline is still quite different from the scratch outline that might be used for this essay:

1. It contains major sections, each of which is subdivided into more specific subheadings. Therefore, it contains more detail than the scratch outline.

2. Each heading is expressed as a complete sentence. As a result, the writer might be able to use each of these sentences as the topic sentence of the major paragraphs of the essay. A topic sentence expresses a paragraph's main or central idea. (You will learn more about it in Chapters 1 and 2.)

3. Sections of the formal outline are identified by number or letter. The major headings have Roman numerals (I, II, III, IV). These are subdivided into items with capital letters (A, B, C, D), and these are followed by Arabic numerals (1, 2, 3).

4. It is not necessary to divide each major heading into as many subheadings as you divide another. For example, IV is divided into two subheadings, but V is subdivided into four. Sometimes you might divide

a subheading as in IIB, but you need not do so all the time. Actually, the pattern to follow in a formal outline is straightforward:

I. (Roman numeral)
    A. (Capital letter)
        1. (Arabic numeral)
            a. (Lowercase letter)

5. Each unit in the outline is divided into at least two subunits. If you can't divide a heading into two or more subheadings, leave it alone.

Not	But	Or
I.	I.	I.
A.	A.	II.
II.	B.	
	II.	

Whether you make a scratch or a formal outline, remember that outlines are intended only to guide you through the task of drafting your essay. No outline is written in stone. As you begin your first draft, stick to your outline as closely as you can. However, don't be afraid to add new information, make changes in organization, replace or delete parts of the outline, or revise your working thesis. Of course, if you are writing a long paper and want your outline to serve as a table of contents, you will have to revise it to reflect changes you have made. But this can be done after the essay itself has been completed. Just remember that writing is a process of discovery; the deeper you get into it, the better you will understand what you have to say.

GS 2.3c. Writing Other Types of Outlines for Special Purposes

Here are some other kinds of outlines you might use, depending upon the purpose of the paper you are writing.

I. AN ESSAY THAT MAKES MORE THAN ONE POINT IN ITS THESIS

If your thesis makes more than one point, you might expand upon each of those points in a separate body paragraph or group of paragraphs. Here's a blueprint based upon student Siu Chan's essay, "Suffering," which appears in Chapter 1.

(Paragraph 1): Introduces Essay and States Following Thesis:

[Living] in Cambodia from 1975 to 1979 was the worst time in

(continued)

Point A	Point B

my life: I was allowed little personal freedom, I witnessed the

Point C

death of my family, and I nearly died of starvation.

(Paragraph 2): Develops Point A: . . . when the communists took over, the government destroyed nearly all my personal freedom.

(Paragraph 3): Develops Point B: During those years, I lost six members of my family.

(Paragraph 4): Develops Point C: I can still remember a three-month period during which I nearly starved to death.

(Paragraph 5): States Essay's Conclusion: Having gone through [that suffering], I can appreciate the life I have now.

II. AN ESSAY THAT COMPARES OR CONTRASTS

As you will see in Chapter 13, there are two methods to outline an essay that compares subjects (i.e., explains their similarities) or contrasts them (i.e., explains their differences). These are the point-by-point method and the subject-by-subject method.

Point-by-Point: This method compares or contrasts various aspects of the two subjects you are discussing, one-by-one, in a separate paragraph or group of paragraphs. Let's say you want to point out differences between (contrast) attending a small college and going to a large university.

(Paragraph 1): Introduces Essay and States Following Thesis: The advantages of attending a small college, as opposed to a university, outweigh the disadvantages.

(Paragraph 2): First Point—Class Size: In small colleges, class sizes tend to be smaller than at large universities, making it easier to ask questions and to enter into discussion with faculty and other students.

(Paragraph 3): Second Point—Access to Faculty: Some students attending small colleges say they have easy access to their teachers, who are often available for tutoring. Friends attending large universities have greater access to a professor's teaching assistants than to the professor.

(Paragraph 4): Third Point—Campus Life: Most large universities offer a fuller and more diverse exposure to the arts, lectures, and other cultural activities than smaller colleges do. On the other hand, small campuses are more intimate and more welcoming to new students.

(Paragraph 5): Fourth Point: Life After Graduation: Thanks to name recognition, graduating from a large and prestigious university may increase one's career opportunities. On the other hand, students who learn better in intimate settings will probably exit a small college with a higher GPA, which will make them better candidates for jobs or professional training.

(Paragraph 6): States Conclusion: Although large universities offer students a great deal, attending a small college is a smarter choice for many. Students who learn better in more intimate environments should choose a smaller school.

(continued)

Subject-by-Subject: This method compares or contrasts two subjects one at a time, in separate sections of the paper. It is best used for shorter papers.

(Paragraph 1): Introduces Essay and States Following Thesis: The advantages of attending a small college, as opposed to a university, outweigh the disadvantages.

(Paragraph 2): Attending a Large University

· Class Size

· Access to Faculty

· Campus Life

· Life after Graduation

(Paragraph 3): Attending a Small College

· Class Size

· Access to Faculty

· Campus Life

· Life after Graduation

(Paragraph 4): Conclusion

III. AN ESSAY THAT SUPPORTS AN OPINION

As you will see in Chapter 13, one of the best ways to argue an opinion is through the conclusion-and-support method. Start by stating a general idea (your thesis, also known as a "conclusion" in argumentation). Then, in the essay's body paragraphs, discuss in detail ideas that support the thesis. In other words, explain the reasons you hold this opinion. Of course, some supporting ideas may need more than one paragraph to be developed adequately. (Note that authors of argument papers often find it effective to anticipate and answer the opposition's arguments, in addition to supporting their own. In the sample outline following, the writer does this in paragraph 5.)

(Paragraph 1): Introduces Essay and States Following Thesis: Term limits should be established for all elected officials, local, state, and national.

(Paragraph 2): Develops Supporting Idea A: Limiting the time politicians can serve prevents them from becoming too powerful.

(Paragraph 3): Develops Supporting Idea B: Term limits create an opportunity for a greater number of people to serve, thereby making government more representative.

(Paragraph 4): Develops Supporting Idea C: Term limits would remove the incumbents' advantage over lesser-known opponents at election time. This would make it easier to infuse government with the new ideas new people will bring.

(Paragraph 5): Anticipates and Answers Opposing Argument: Opponents of term limits argue that politicians with seniority can do more for the people back home than newcomers. However, this just supports the notion that long-time office holders have too much power.

(Paragraph 6): Concludes the Essay by Summing up and Restating Thesis

GS 2.4 DRAFTING AND REVISING

Write your first draft several days before it is due. Doing so will give you time to revise, edit, and proofread it without rushing. Begin **drafting** by reviewing the decisions you made about audience, purpose, and style. With these in the back of your mind, carefully re-read the notes you made when gathering information for your paper through focused freewriting, researching, or another method discussed in earlier in Getting Started (pages 7–14). Also, review your formal or informal outline, and make last-minute changes to it if necessary. (For example, when re-reading your notes, you might discover that you left out an important point when you wrote your outline.)

Next, write down a working thesis statement. This is a sentence that expresses the main point you want to make about your subject. (You will learn more about thesis statements in Chapter 1: The Central Idea.) Keep your working thesis statement and your outline in front of you as you begin to draft.

Don't worry about spelling or grammar problems at this stage; you can correct those when you edit. For now, concentrate on putting down important ideas and concrete details that support the paper's thesis. Include as much information as you can. If you repeat yourself or put down more than you need, no matter. You can remove words, sentences, and even whole paragraphs later.

If you get tired before completing this draft, take a 10- or 20-minute break. However, try not to leave it unfinished before going on to another project. Once you have completed the rough draft, put it aside for 24 hours, if possible. When you go back to it, you will approach it with a fresher mind and clearer eye.

Start **revising** by reading over your rough draft two or three times. Refine your working thesis if you believe that what you wrote in your paper no longer matches exactly what your thesis claims. As you will see at the end of Getting Started and in Chapter 1, writing the final draft will often reveal exactly what you meant to say in the first place. (This is only one reason that writing is called a "process of discovery.") So don't be afraid to rewrite your working thesis or your outline once you have completed a rough draft.

You might also decide to add facts and ideas that will make your paper clearer and stronger. If so, return to prewriting and find this information. (You can do so during or after you have written your second draft.) Add this material by combining it with an existing paragraph or by giving it a paragraph of its own.

Now, read your second draft. Do you need still more information? If so, find and add it. Next, divide paragraphs that are too long or that contain unrelated information. Combine those that relate to the same point. Change the positions of paragraphs if doing so will make your paper easier to follow or more logical. Do the same things with sentences: add to, combine, separate, and reposition them in ways that make better sense. (Chapters 3 and 7 discuss paragraph organization and sentence structure in great detail.)

Don't be afraid to cut out information you don't need. Perhaps you have repeated information. There is no sin in that; eliminate one version. Perhaps you have presented three examples when two will do. If so, remove the last one. Throughout the process, keep repeating the old adage, "All writing is rewriting."

EXERCISE 3: Practice what you have learned   Review the notes you collected through listing, clustering, or drawing a subject tree as explained in an earlier information-gathering exercise (see Exercise 1, page 13). Then, write an informal or outline for an essay that might use this information.

GS 2.5 EDITING AND PROOFREADING

Editing means reading the best of your drafts to correct errors in grammar, punctuation, sentence structure, and mechanics. Editing also involves cutting out wordiness and redundancies and correcting word choice and usage. Proofreading involves the final check for spelling and typographical errors.

There are many ways to edit and proofread. Some writers read their papers backwards, sentence by sentence. Others read their work aloud to friends to make sure they haven't left out words and that their sentences make sense. Some writers, in fact, break up the editing process by reading their final drafts several times and concentrating on one major editing problem or area during each pass. For example, they read the paper once to correct sentence-structure errors such as fragments and comma splices. During a second reading, they focus on punctuation, and so on. Whatever method you use, take your time. Editing carefully can often save you from producing a paper that, while well developed and organized, contains annoying errors and prevents readers from taking your writing seriously.

After you have edited the paper, proofread for spelling and typographical errors. You can use your computer's spell checker, but don't *rely* on it. Electronic spell checkers are simply limited data banks of words. They can't distinguish between homonyms such as "you're" and "your," and they won't tell you if the name Leif Ericsson, the explorer, is spelled correctly. Use electronic grammar checkers with caution, too. The best way to edit and proofread is to rely on yourself, your grammar handbook, dictionary, and thesaurus.

For more on editing and proofreading, try these websites: http://owl.english.purdue.edu/handouts/general/gl_edit.html (Purdue University Online Writing Center) and http://leo.stcloudstate.edu/acadwrite/genproofed.html (St. Cloud University's Site on editing and proofreading).

EXERCISE 4: *Practice what you have learned* In Exercise 1 (page 13), you were asked to gather information on a particular topic. In Exercise 3 (page 22), you were asked to write an outline using this information. Following the outline you have created, draft a short essay that uses the information you have collected. Revise this essay at least once. Then edit and proofread it.

Part 3: The Making of a Student Essay: From Prewriting to Proofreading

This part of Getting Started traces the writing of a full-length essay by Deborah Diglio, who was a first-year nursing student when she wrote it. Her essay shows clearly that she sees writing as a process of important steps:

GS 3.1 Prewriting to gather information

GS 3.2 Making a scratch outline

GS 3.1 Prewriting to Gather Information

The process began when Diglio was inspired by Carl Sandburg's "Child of the Romans," a poem in Chapter 9 about the difficult life of an immigrant laborer. In a computer file she kept for this purpose, Diglio responded to one of the Suggestions for Journal Entries that recommended using focused freewriting to gather details about a job she once held. Here's what she wrote in her journal about waitressing:

> People ordering food. The night was going by fast. Nervous. First nights can be scary. Keep a pleasant attitude. I could do the job easily. Training period over, I was on my own. I needed this job. We needed the money. I felt confident, too confident. I can now laugh at it. Not then. Society may not place waitressing high on the social ladder, but you have got to be surefooted, organized, you have to have a sense of humor, and a pleasant personality. You have to be able to learn from your mistakes. Eventually, I did learn but then I thought I would die. This old woman left her walker in the corner. How did I know it wasn't a tray stand? Still I should have! Why didn't I just look more closely. Why didn't my brain take over. And the old folks didn't mind. We should look back at ourselves and laugh sometimes.

As you can see, there is no particular order to Diglio's notes, and like most freewriting, it uses quick phrases as much as full sentences. Nonetheless, an event that might make interesting reading is coming through. So is the idea that Diglio learned something from the experience and can now look back at it with a smile.

GS 3.2 MAKING A SCRATCH OUTLINE

After discussing her journal entry with her teacher, Diglio decided to tell her story in a full-length essay. She reviewed what she had written in her journal and thought more about the central idea, the point she wanted her essay to make. After adding notes to her original journal entry, she made a scratch outline to organize and began drafting her essay. Here is her scratch outline for that working draft:

> Working thesis: Sometimes, we need to look back at ourselves and laugh.
>
> 1. Describe the restaurant, set the stage.
>
> 2. State the thesis.
>
> 3. Describe the job.
>
> 4. Tell what happened that first night:
>
>   How well it went first—thought I was a "born natural."
>
>   The old couple and their walker.
>
>   I wanted to crawl into a hole.
>
> 5. What I learned from my mistake.

GS 3.3 WRITING A WORKING DRAFT

Diglio used her scratch outline as a blueprint for her first draft. As you will see, each of the paragraphs in that draft corresponds roughly to the five major headings in her scratch outline. However, the act of writing inspired her. As she wrote, more and more details and ideas came to mind, and she included them wherever she could.

All of this goes to prove an important point: an outline—especially a quick, scratch outline—can be used only to get started. You need not be a slave to your outline, and if the act of writing adds brand new details or takes you in a new direction, so be it. Remember, writing is a process of discovery, and good writers can and often do change their minds at many points along the way.

When Diglio stopped writing, she read her draft, a process that helped her recall even more details, which she squeezed in between paragraphs and sentences and in the margins of her paper. The result was messy, so she retyped the working draft as shown below. This is the first version of her paper. It contains more detail and is better written than her journal entry or her outline, but it is only a working draft. (Note: This first draft contains numerous, unacceptable errors. No one would suggest that these are right at any stage, merely that first drafts like this one may have them.)

Waitressing

It was a typical Saturday night. I was standing there,
paying no attention to the usual racket of the dinner
crowd. The restaurant was crowded. I was waiting for
my next table. I try to listen to the sounds around
me. I hear the stereo.

In come my eight oclock reservation, fifteen
minutes late. There is an elderly woman with them.
She reminded me of something that happened when I
started working there many years before. Recalling
that story taught me to look back and laugh at myself.

When my second child was born. It became clear
that I needed to find a part-time job to help make
ends meet. A friend said I should waitress at the
restaurant where she worked. I thought about it for a
few days. I decided to give it a try. I bluffed my way
thru the interview. A new chapter in my life began.
Since then, I have learned from many mistakes like
the one I am going to describe. My friends told me
that, someday, I would look back and laugh at that
night. I guess after fifteen years that day has come!

I followed another waitress for a few days and
then I was released on my own. All went well that
first week. When Saturday night came, I had
butterflies in my stomache. I was given four tables
not far from the kitchen. It was an easy station. Oh,
God, was I happy, however I still felt awkward
carrying those heavy trays. Before I new it, the

restaurant was packed resembling mid-day on wall street. I moved slowly organising every move. I remember the tray stand in my station. It looked a little different than the one I was trained on. It had nice grips for handles of which made it easier to move around. I was amazed at how well things were going. I was too confident. I remember thinking that I was a born natural. Than, this jovial looking old man came over, and taped me on the shoulder, and said "Excuse me, dear, my wife and I loved watching you work. It seems your tray stand has been very handy for you, but we are getting ready to leave now, and my wife needs her walker back." I wanted to crawl into a hole and hide. What a fool I had made of myself. I was so glad when that night ended.

Since then, I have learned from many mistakes such as the one I just described.

GS 3.4 REVISING THE WORKING DRAFT

The essay above makes for entertaining reading. But Diglio knew it could be improved, so she revised it *several times* to get to the last draft (but not final version) of her paper, which appears below. Although this draft is not perfect, it is more complete, effective, and polished than the one you just read. Note, again, the unacceptable errors that *must* be corrected in the editing stage.

Lessons Learned

It was a typical Saturday night at Carpaccio's Restaurant. I was standing there, paying no attention to the usual merrymaking of the dinner crowd. Just two of the restaurant's twenty-five tables were vacant. As I waited for my next table, I absorbed a few of the sounds around me: clanging trays, the ringing of the cash register. I could even hear Dean Martin belting out a familiar Italian song in the background.

Finally, in come my eight o'clock party. As they were seated, my attention was drawn to an elderly woman with a walker slowly shuffling behind the others. She brought back a memory I had locked away for fifteen years.

After the birth of my second child, I needed a part-time job to help make ends meet. A friend suggested I apply for a waitressing job at a new restaurant where she worked. I decided to give it a shot. I bluffed my way through the interview and was hired. A new chapter in my life began the next evening.

After trailing an experience waitress for a few days, I was allowed to wait tables on my own. All went well that first week. When Saturday night came, the butterflies in my stomach were set free. I was given the apprentice station that night, four tables not far from the kitchen. Oh, God, was I relieved, however I still felt awkward carrying the heavy trays.

Before I new it, the restaurant was packed; it resembled mid-day on wall street. I moved slowly, organising every step. I remember how impressed I was with the tray stand in my station, it looked different than the one I was trained on. It had nice grip-like handles, of which made it easier to manuver. I was amazed at how well things were going. I began to believe I was a natural at this job.

Then, a jovial, old man approached, tapped me on the shoulder, and said, "Excuse me, dear, my wife and I loved watching you work. It seems your tray stand has been very handy for you, but we are getting ready to leave now, and my wife needs her walker back."

At first his message did not register. "What was he talking about!" Then, it sank in. I had set my trays on his wife's orthopedic walker. I stood there frozen as ice, but my face was on fire. I wanted to crawl into a hole; I wanted to hibernate.

Since then; I have learned from many mistakes such as the one I just described. I have learned to be more observant and more careful. I have learned to guard against overconfidence, for no matter how well things are going, something will come along eventually to gum up the works. Most of all, I have learned that the best way to get over honest embarrassment is to look back and laugh at yourself.

As this last draft shows, Diglio made several important changes to improve her essay:

1. She changed the title to make her purpose clearer; "Waitressing" didn't say much about the point of her story.
2. She moved the central idea—the point she wants it to make—to the end. This allows her to tell her story first and then to explain its importance in a way that is both clear and interesting. It also makes her conclusion more effective and memorable.

3. She added details to make her writing exact and vivid. Just compare the beginning of each draft. In the later version, Diglio names the restaurant, and she explains that just two of its "twenty-five tables were vacant," not simply that it was "crowded." She even mentions that "Dean Martin [was] belting out a familiar Italian song."

4. She reorganized paragraph 4 into several new paragraphs. Each of these focuses on a different idea, makes a new point, or tells us another part of the story. Thus, the essay becomes easier to read.

5. She removed unnecessary words to eliminate repetition and make her writing more direct.

6. She replaced some words with more exact and interesting substitutes. In paragraph 1, the dinner crowd's "racket" is changed to "merrymaking"; in paragraph 4, "I was happy" becomes "I was relieved."

7. She combined short, choppy sentences into longer, smoother ones to add variety and interest.

8. She corrected some—but not all—problems with spelling, verb tense, punctuation, sentence structure, and mechanics.

GS 3.5 EDITING AND PROOFREADING

Although Diglio's last version is much better than the draft with which she began, she owed it to her readers to review her paper once more. She wanted to remove annoying errors that could interfere with their appreciation of her work. Using a pencil, a dictionary, and a handbook of college writing skills recommended by her instructor, she corrected problems in grammar, spelling, punctuation, capitalization, and style in her final draft. Here's what just two paragraphs from that draft looked like after she edited them. (If you want to practice you own editing skills, you can go back and correct the rest of Diglio's paper after you review her changes in what follows.)

> After trailing an experience$_\wedge^d$ waitress for a few days, I was allowed to wait tables on my own. All went well that first week. When Saturday night came, the butterflies in my stomach were set free. I was given the apprentice station that night, four tables not far from the kitchen. Oh, God, was I relieved/$_\wedge^{\cdot}$ however, I still felt awkward carrying the heavy trays.
>
> Before I $_\wedge^k$new it, the restaurant was packed; it resembled mid-day on $\not{W}^W$all $\not{S}^S$treet. I moved slowly, organi$\not{z}^z$ing every step. I remember how impressed I

was with the tray stand in my station,/^ it looked

different *than*, the one I was trained on. It had nice

grip-like handles, of which made it easier to maneuver.

I was amazed at how well things were going. I began

to believe I was a natural at this job.

Of course, an entire paper full of such corrections is too sloppy to submit in a college composition class. Therefore, after correcting her final draft in pencil, Diglio prepared one last, clean copy of her paper. It was this copy that she gave her instructor.

Each person is unique in the way he or she writes. The methods you use to put together a paper may be different from those Deborah Diglio used. They also may be different from the ways your friends or classmates choose to write. And no one says any step outlined above has to be done separately from the others. In fact, some folks revise while they edit. Some continue to gather information as they write their second, third, and even fourth drafts. Nevertheless, writing is serious business. Completing just one or two drafts of an essay will never allow you to produce the quality of work you are capable of. You owe it to your readers and to yourself to respect the process of writing and to work hard at every step in that process, regardless of the way or the order in which you choose to do so. (If you want to learn more about the process of writing, read Richard Marius's "Writing and Its Rewards" in Chapter 2.)

Part IV: Becoming an Active College Reader

This section of Getting Started discusses:

GS 4.1 Preparing to read: Survey

GS 4.2 Reading and taking notes: Engage the text

GS 4.3 Writing an informal outline: Strengthen your grasp of the text

GS 4.4 Conversing with the text: Read it again

GS 4.5 Summarizing: Make what you have read your own

GS 4.6 Responding and critiquing: Evaluate what you have read

GS 4.7 Synthesizing: Bring ideas together in a new statement

The more you read, the better you will write. Like writing, reading is an *active* process. Effective readers don't just sit back and absorb words. They *digest, interpret,* and *evaluate* what they read. They interact with the text by considering both *stated* and *unstated* (*implied*) messages. They question *facts* and *assumptions,* evaluate *evidence,* ask *questions,* and apply their own *insights* and *experiences* to what is read.

In college you will read textbooks; essays in newspapers, magazines, journals, and anthologies; monographs, which discuss one issue or question; scientific and technical materials; poetry, fiction, and other literature; and academic, professional, and government websites. Many of us read such materials without fully understanding them the first time. If this happens to you, read them a second or third time. Discuss them with friends and classmates, or put them aside for a few days to let ideas develop. Doing these things is similar to writing multiple drafts of an essay, getting feedback from others, and putting the paper aside for a while before rewriting it.

SPECIAL TIPS ON READING SELECTIONS IN THIS BOOK

1. Prepare for a selection by first reading the author's biography, the vocabulary words, and the Preparing to Read section, which come before it.

2. Take notes while you read. You can do this in many ways, such as listing or outlining ideas on your computer or on a notepad. Two especially good methods are to make notes in the margins of the text and to keep a double-entry notebook. Both are explained below.

3. Answer the Questions for Discussion that appear after each selection in this textbook. Then, complete at least one of the Suggestions for Journal Entries and the Thinking Critically exercise.

GS 4.1 PREPARING TO READ: SURVEY

Surveying, also called *previewing,* is an essential first step in reading: it reveals much that will help you read more easily, effectively, and enjoyably.

- Begin by looking for clues in the *title,* especially in essays or scholarly articles. Writers of such texts provide hints about content, purpose, and thesis in their titles.

- If a *biographical or introductory note* precedes the essay or article—as with the selections in this book—read this first. It should help you understand the cultural, historical, or political context in which the text was written, and it might provide clues to the author's *main idea (thesis).* If the note indicates the publication date or the title of the publication in which the text first appeared, you might be able to conclude something about the author's purpose and intended audience.

- Sometimes, essay writers state their theses (main ideas) in their *introductions or conclusions,* so read the first and last paragraphs carefully. The introductory paragraph(s) can also provide clues about the organization, purpose, and supporting ideas of the essay.

- Read *subheadings or subtitles.* They provide additional insight into the essay's organization. Then *skim* every paragraph for ideas that support the thesis. Often supporting ideas are expressed as conclusions—statements drawn from evidence. Look for words and phrases such as "therefore," "thus," and "as a result," which often introduce such statements.

EXERCISE 5: Practice what you have learned Survey a chapter in a textbook, an editorial in a newspaper or magazine such as *Time, US News & World Report,* or *The National Geographic,* or an article assigned by your instructor. (Each of the magazines mentioned above offers access to some of their articles online: find them at www.time.com, www.usnews.com, and www. nationalgeographic.com.)

GS 4.2 READING AND TAKING NOTES: ENGAGE THE TEXT

Some texts can be understood on the *literal level.* They mean exactly what they say, with little need for interpretation. Others require you to draw *inferences* (*conclusions*). In such cases, different readers might come up with different but equally valid interpretations of a statement or even of an entire essay. The more sophisticated a text—the richer its fabric of words and ideas—the more subject it is to interpretation.

As you read something for the first time, keep the following in mind:

• Your aim this time around is to comprehend the literal meaning.

• *Reading with a pencil in hand* will enable you to underline words and phrases, make notes in the margins, and highlight sentences. (When you read the text a second time, you might want to change, delete, or clarify your notes by erasing old material and adding new. That's why using a pencil is better than using a highlighter or pen.)

• If you come upon unfamiliar words or historical/cultural references, don't be alarmed. Reading, like writing, involves discovery and growth. However, don't break your focus and look up these items immediately. Instead, underline or circle them and look them up in a dictionary or encyclopedia later.

• Mark the thesis and important ideas that support the thesis.

• In the margins, write short questions about points that you don't fully understand, you find interesting, or you question.

Study the notes and comments a student made when she first read a *USA Today* editorial entitled "Overreaction to Cloning Claim Poses Other Risks." This editorial, published on January 3, 2003, was a statement of *USA Today's* position on possible action by Congress to ban all cloning, including the cloning of human embryos, which is used to gather stem cells for medical research. An opposing view, by Kansas Senator Sam Brownback, also appeared in that issue of *USA Today.* It appears later in this chapter.

Overreaction to Cloning Claim Poses Other Risks

A *USA Today* Editorial

Much of the world is now holding its breath, wondering whether Eve, the supposed first-ever human
clone, born Dec. 26 [2002] is real or a <u>twisted publicity</u>
stunt. Her existence certainly sounds like something out
of science fiction: announced by the Raelians, a bizarre
sect that believes the human race was cloned from aliens
25,000 years ago.

Interesting phrase.
Meaning?

1

The Raelians Clonaid organization promises to provide scientific proof of Eve's authenticity through genetics
experts, though it <u>refuses to produce Eve or her 31-year-
old American mother</u>. It also claims that four more clones
are due to be born by February [2003]—a statistic that
stretches credulity given that the cloning of mammals
since <u>Dolly the sheep in 1997</u> has usually taken hundreds
of tries and produced Frankenstein-leaning deformities.

Meaning?
Yea, right! probably a hoax!
Meaning?
Check out on Internet.

2

Whether or not Eve proves to be genuine, any clone
would <u>catch Americans spectacularly unprepared</u>. That's
because conservative Republicans and the Bush administration have insisted on pursuing a ban on all cloning.
Their overreach overlooks <u>a more sensible alternative</u>:
outlawing the morally reprehensible cloning of humans
but permitting cellular cloning that could cure ailments
from Alzheimer's to spinal injuries.

Why?
Meaning?
Meaning?

3

True to form, within day's of Eve's birth announcement, conservatives promised a push for Senate legislation to ban all human cloning. . . . Yet such a <u>knee-jerk
reaction ignores critical differences between cloning of the
human and</u> therapeutic variety:

Which ones?
Thesis?
Meaning?

4

- **Human cloning aims to replicate humans.** It
  requires implanting a cloned embryo into a
  woman's uterus. The Raelians' claims aside, the
  practice holds moral, technical and practical risks.
  Attempts to clone humans are certain to follow the

path of animal cloning. That means hundreds of failures and the death within days of most clones that do not reach birth. Survivors, even if they seem healthy, could be time bombs with unknown genetic abnormalities. Besides such vexing moral questions as who has the right to clone another person, family relationships and rights would become a minefield of ambiguity. Eve's mother, for example, would really be her twin.

Meaning?

- **Therapeutic cloning aims to develop medical therapies.** Cloned embryos are grown only up to 14 days, long enough to harvest their stem cells, which may eventually prove useful in treating diseases including Parkinson's, leukemia and diabetes. Embryos aren't implanted in a woman's uterus, the step required to clone a human.

Strong argument!

Supporters of a total ban would shut off this promising avenue of U.S. research. Yet investigations would continue overseas.

Is this point really valid? So what?

5

A far more sensible approach was proposed last year when the National Academy of Sciences called for a five-year renewable ban on the cloning of human beings while allowing research on therapeutic cloning.

Appeal to experts! Seems reasonable.

6

Regardless whether Eve is a clone, her announced arrival delivers a call for responsible action. Like it or not, we already are in a brave new world of medical advances.

Why brave?

7

GS 4.3 WRITING AN INFORMAL OUTLINE: STRENGTHEN YOUR GRASP OF THE TEXT

After your first reading, look over the words, phrases, and sentences you have underlined or marked. Then, read the notes you made in the margins. If you've marked the text effectively, this review alone can provide enough information for you to create an informal outline. (This outline resembles the informal outlines you make before writing an essay, as explained earlier, on pp. 14–15 in Getting Started). Creating this kind of outline will strengthen your understanding of what you have read.

1. Start by stating the essay's thesis.
2. List each of the major ideas the author uses to support that thesis.
3. Under each of these major ideas, list or summarize important details that illustrate, develop, or otherwise support each of these supporting ideas.

You can find several examples of such outlines in Getting Started: Part 2 (pages 14–21) and in Getting Started: Part 3 (page 25).

EXERCISE 6: Practice what you have learned   Use a pencil to take notes on an editorial in a newspaper or other periodical. (Current and some back issues of many newspapers and magazines are available online. See, for example, the *New York Times* at www.nyt.com.) Underline the thesis and supporting ideas, and ask questions or make comments by writing brief notes in the margins.

An Alternative: Keep a Double-Entry (Summary/Response) Notebook

If you don't care to annotate the text, you might try keeping a double-entry notebook as a way to summarize and respond to a text. In the long run, it will help you become a more efficient and effective reader. In the short run, keeping a double-entry notebook will help you respond to the Suggestions for Journal Entries, which appear after each of the reading selections in this textbook. Here's an easy way to do it:

1. Before reading, draw a line from top to bottom down the middle of notebook page. (This can also be done as a table in a computer file.)
2. Label the left column *Summary,* the right column *Response.*
3. As you read the essay, poem, or other kind of text, *summarize* the major ideas in each paragraph or section under the left column. (As you have learned, a summary condenses—puts in a briefer form—what you have read and expresses it in your own words.)
4. Next, in the right column, write brief responses to the summary statements you made. Your responses can take any form, but they will probably be similar to notes you might have written in the margins. For example, you might 1) ask a question, 2) agree or disagree with an opinion, 3) identify the central idea (thesis) and other important ideas, 4) mark a word or phrase you especially like 5) note a word or reference you will need to look up later (6) explain how the reading relates to you.

As an example, here is Alfred Lord Tennyson's "The Eagle," followed by a student's notebook entry summarizing and responding to this poem.

The Eagle

He clasps the crag with crooked hands;
Close to the sun in lonely lands,
Ring'd with the azure world, he stands.

The wrinkled sea beneath him crawls;
He watches from his mountain walls,
And like a thunderbolt he falls.

Summary	**Response**
Stanza 1—Grasping a large rock, an eagle stands on high and lonely cliff.	The eagle is "close to the sun." He's higher than we are, but also alone. Why are his feet called "hands"?
Stanza 2—The eagle looks down at the sea from on top of a high mountain. He drops down quickly, furiously.	Why is the sea "wrinkled"? Because he's so high up? When he falls, what is he going after? Food? An enemy? "Thunderbolt" is a great word. He's an incredibly majestic, powerful animal—and dangerous, maybe?

GS 4.4 CONVERSING WITH THE TEXT: READ IT AGAIN

As you approach the text again, pretend you are having a conversation with the author. The text represents his or her part of the conversation. Your part involves making marginal notes that do the following:

- Add information that helps you understand a point, state agreement or disagreement, or express another point of view.
- Draw conclusions from the material presented, and add insights, facts, opinion taken from your own experiences, observations, or reading.

- Challenge facts, opinions, statistics, "expert" testimony, or other evidence.
- Challenge illogical conclusions. For example, if a writer claimed that because your new college president has a doctorate in English she will not support programs in the technologies, you would challenge that statement as illogical.
- Question the author's reference to undocumented sources. If you read that "A recent study proves that listening to rap music makes children more aggressive," you might ask: "Which study?" "Who conducted it?" "Where can I find a copy of the study?" and other questions.
- Comment on the author's tone and language.
  1. Is the language the author uses fair and objective or is it "loaded"— that is, do the words call up emotions that might interfere with a reader's logical and reasoned response to the material?
  2. Does the author express a legitimate concern, complaint, or purpose, or is the author's position compromised by self-interest, personal feelings, or even ignorance?
  3. If the essay's purpose is to persuade, does the writer remain fair while appealing to the reader's emotions or self-interest, or is his/her approach biased—that is, does the author tell the reader everything, or does he or she withhold critical information or present it in a misleading way
- Make changes as appropriate to the marginal and other notes you made during your first reading.
- During this stage in the process, look at everything with a healthy dose of skepticism—that is, don't believe everything you read. After all, even the worst villains and liars can sometimes have their works published. Questioning, challenging, and demanding proof are the signs of an enlightened reader.

Here are notes and comments a student made on her second reading of "Overreaction to Cloning Claim Poses Other Risks."

Interesting language draws reader into editorial

Much of the world is now holding its breath, wondering whether Eve, the supposed first-ever human clone, born Dec. 26 [2002] is real or a twisted publicity stunt. Her existence certainly sounds like something out of science fiction: announced by the Raelians, a bizarre sect that believes the human race was cloned from aliens 25,000 years ago.

interesting phrase.

meaning? = strange odd.

1

The Raelians Clonaid organization promises to provide . . . scientific proof of Eve's authenticity through

2

meaning?
= science
of heredity.

meaning? =
believability.

good image!

Why? We've
known about
Dolly since
1997.

Thesis!

meaning? =
embryonic

Tone sarcastic
why?

Which ones?

good detail!

meaning? =
lack of clarity

(genetics) experts, though it refuses to produce Eve or her 31-year-old American mother. It also claims that four more clones are due to be born by February[2003]—a statistic that stretches (credulity) given that the cloning of mammals since Dolly the sheep in 1997 has usually taken hundreds of tries and produced Frankenstein-leaning deformities.

Whether or not Eve proves to be genuine, any clone would catch Americans spectacularly unprepared. That's because conservative Republicans and the Bush administration have insisted on pursuing a ban on all cloning. Their overreach overlooks a more sensible alternative: outlawing the morally (reprehensible) cloning of humans but permitting (cellular) cloning that could cure ailments from Alzheimer's to spinal injuries.

True to form, within day's of Eve's birth announcement, conservatives promised a push for Senate legislation to ban all human cloning. . . . Yet such a knee-jerk reaction ignores critical differences between cloning of the human and (therapeutic) variety:

- **Human cloning aims to replicate humans.** It requires implanting a cloned embryo into a woman's uterus. The Raelians' claims aside, the practice holds moral, technical and practical risks. Attempts to clone humans are certain to follow the path of animal cloning. That means hundreds of failures and the death within days of most clones that do not reach birth. Survivors, even if they seem healthy, could be time bombs with unknown genetic abnormalities. Besides such vexing moral questions as who has the right to clone another person, family relationships and rights would become a minefield of (ambiguity) Eve's mother, for example, would really be her twin.

- **Therapeutic cloning aims to develop medical therapies.** Cloned embryos are grown only up to 14 days, long enough to harvest their stem cells,

Yea, right!
Probably a
hoax!

Check out on
Internet British
scientists
produced first
cloned mammal.   3

Why conservatives?
Generalization.

meaning? = evil

4

Thesis? - No

meaning? =
relating to
medical
treatment

supporting idea

good example!

supporting idea

strong argument

which may eventually prove useful in treating   5
diseases including Parkinson's, leukemia and
diabetes. Embryos aren't implanted in a woman's
uterus, the step required to clone a human.

Should we
do this
because
others will?

Supporters of a total ban would shut off this   Is this point   6
promising avenue of U.S. research. Yet   really valid?
investigations would continue overseas.   So what?

A far more sensible approach was proposed last Appeals to experts!
year when the National Academy of Sciences called Seems
for a five-year renewable ban on the cloning of   reasonable.
human beings while allowing research on   A reasonable
therapeutic cloning.   compromise!

Why brave? =
Reference to
Huxley's Brave
New World,
a novel about
cloning.

Regardless whether Eve is a clone, her   7
announced arrival delivers a call for responsible
action. Like it or not, we already are in a brave new
world of medical advances.

EXERCISE 7: Practice what you have learned   Re-read the editorial
from a newspaper or other periodical that you read earlier. Converse with the author: underline words and sentences and make additional marginal notes. You
might also revise or remove notes you made during your first reading. Then, review
and, if appropriate, revise the informal outline you made after your first reading.

GS 4.5 SUMMARIZING: MAKE WHAT YOU HAVE READ YOUR OWN

Summarizing re-states the text's main and supporting ideas in your own words.
It requires you to wrestle with someone else's language as you transform it into
your own. Thus, it forces you to put into concrete form ideas and insights that
otherwise would have remained abstract and vague. Summarizing always en-
hances comprehension. If you can summarize accurately, you can be sure that
you've understood a selection.

Be Original: Avoid Plagiarism

You can find out more about summarizing, paraphrasing, and quoting in
the Appendix of this text: Writing a Research Paper Using Modern Language Association Style. For now, make sure your summary is your original restatement of the text and that it contains no traces of *plagiarism*—
that is, passing off the words or ideas of another person as your own.

The two items below summarize the first paragraph of the *USA Today* editorial you read earlier. The first contains inadvertent (unintentional) plagiarism; the second does not.

Inadvertent plagiarism: Many people are now wondering whether the claim that a cloned baby girl has actually been born is real or whether the whole thing is just a stunt to get publicity. The claim was made at the end of December 2002 by the Raelians, a cult that believes that humans were cloned from aliens 25,000 years ago.

More original summary. In late December 2002, a group called the Raelians claimed that the world's first cloned human had been born. The Raelians also claim that visitors from outer space cloned the human race into existence thousands of years ago. However, some people believe that the Raelians' news may be a hoax to get media attention.

Note that the underlined words in the first example come directly from the editorial. This version also follows the organization of editorial too closely. However, the second example is a completely new version, both in terms of its language and its organization. It's clear from the second that the student has truly understood the content of the editorial.

USING THE SPLIT-SCREEN FUNCTION TO CHECK FOR PLAGIARISM

Most word processors offer a split-screen function, which aids in checking for plagiarism and in summarizing material. The split-screen function allows you to scan the original version of a text on the top half of the screen. (This works best, of course, for original material in electronic form. Otherwise you will have to type it up yourself.) You can then independently summarize that text on the bottom half of the screen. Each half of the screen can be scrolled separately, allowing you to compare sentences and paragraphs carefully so as to make your summary more accurate and to eliminate inadvertent plagiarism.

Unlike a paraphrase, which only restates the original in new words, a summary also *condenses* the original. Depending on length and complexity, a chapter in a textbook or an article in journal might be summarized in a few paragraphs. A summary of an essay of 1500–2000 words might span no more than 150 words. Read the following tips on writing summaries. Then, read the summary of the *USA Today* editorial, which follows these tips:

- After rereading the text again, review marginal notes and ideas you have marked.
- As a general rule, begin your summary by stating the essay's thesis, whether explicit or implied. Also, consider stating the author's purpose and intended audience.
- Next, state each of the supporting ideas used to develop the thesis.
- Depending upon the thoroughness required, include one or two examples of the details used to develop each supporting idea.
- If you need to use some of the author's own words, introduce them appropriately and place quotation marks around them (see Appendix to this book)
- Don't summarize each of the essay's paragraphs into a sentence, one by one. Authors often develop supporting ideas with details spread over more than one paragraph, so summarizing every paragraph is often unnecessary. (Again, a summary is a condensation, not the restating of every detail.) Including too much detail can be misleading, because it gives emphasis to minor aspects of the essay. Finally, it shows that the reader's grasp of the text's purpose and main idea is weak.

Here is an example of a student's summary of the *USA Today* editorial:

Student Summary of <u>USA Today</u> Editorial

A <u>USA Today</u> editorial of January 3, 2003 argues that, while US lawmakers should prohibit human cloning, they should encourage cellular cloning, which will help medical researchers find cures to many illnesses. The editorial appeared shortly after the announcement by a group called the Raelians that "the supposed first-ever human clone" was born late last year. According to <u>USA Today</u>, legislation proposed by conservatives in Congress that would prevent human cloning will go too far by also

banning research into cellular or "therapeutic"

cloning, which produces human embryos from which

stem cells can be gotten. Such stem cells can be used

in the fight against diseases "including Parkinson's,

leukemia and diabetes." Therapeutic cloning poses

none of the scientific or ethical problems of cloning

human beings. Unlike attempts to clone another

individual, it does not involve the placement of a

cloned embryo in a host mother, a practice that, in

the case of experimentation with animals, has often

resulted in the death of the embryo before birth.

Even if therapeutic cloning is banned in the United

States, it is sure to continue in other parts of the

world.

EXERCISE 8: Practice what you have learned   Write a summary of a newspaper or periodical article. Try to make use of your word processor's split-screen function to do this.

GS 4.6 RESPONDING AND CRITIQUING: EVALUATE WHAT YOU HAVE READ

You can respond to the ideas and opinions in a text, you can critique (evaluate) a text's message and presentation, or you can do both.

In a response paper, you comment on the author's ideas by agreeing, disagreeing, drawing comparisons, adding evidence of your own, presenting another point of view, raising questions, applying these ideas to other things you have read or observed, or doing all of the above. You are trying to engage the text just as you do when making notes in the margins or underlining important points. Now, however, your part of the conversation is more formal and organized. You are creating your own text, which might serve as a complement to, an addition to, or a rejection of the original text. In fact it might serve as all of these things.

A critique *evaluates* a text's message and its presentation. Although the words "critique" and "criticism," are related, a critique is not just "critical": it can and should mention both strengths and weaknesses.

A critique can be a full-length essay. Begin by reviewing your marginal notes and your summary. If necessary, go back to the text itself and reread it. Revise the notes you have already made in light of criteria (measuring sticks) you are using to evaluate what you have read.

Criteria used to evaluate a text can differ from reader to reader. Below are only a few questions you might ask as you critique a text. Perhaps they will help you create some of your own criteria. After you have read all of these questions, read the student critique of the *USA Today* editorial, which follows them.

SUGGESTED CRITERIA FOR EVALUATION

- What are the author's credentials? Is the source in which the essay was first published a reputable periodical, book, or other publication?
- Are the essay's thesis and purpose clear and reasonable?
- Are supporting ideas clear, credible, and logical? Are they well developed?
- Does the author make unsubstantiated claims?
- Does the author use evidence from studies, experts, or other authorities to support his or her thesis without identifying these authorities by name?
- Is the author impartial, or does he or she use language intended to appeal to the reader's emotions and self-interest? If the latter, is this language simply strong and moving, or is it unfair, biased, or inappropriate in any way?
- Does the author use information that is incomplete or incorrect? If so, how much does this problem affect the essay's credibility?
- Does the essay lack important information that you know might contradict one of its supporting ideas or even its thesis?
- Does the author raise important questions and answer them adequately? Does he or she include opposing arguments and address them fairly and completely?
- Is the language of the essay appropriate to the intended audience? Does it contain jargon and other language that is unnecessarily complicated?

Note: Again, when critiquing and responding, feel free to include some of the author's own words if you believe it is important, but remember to *use quotation marks*.

Matthew Roberts

Professor Spano

ENG 101-33

19 November, 2004

Critique of **USA Today** Editorial:

"Overreaction to Cloning Claim Poses Other Risks"   1
In arguing for the continuation of research into cellular or
therapeutic cloning, USA Today's editorial "Overreaction to Cloning
Claim Poses Other Risks" (January 3, 2003) takes a reasonable
approach to an issue that, in the last several months, has been
hotly debated in a less-than-productive manner. Citing a
recommendation from the National Academy of Sciences, the
editors argue that, while the cloning of people may be morally
wrong, the cloning of embryos to gather stem cells, which are
important to medical research, should be encouraged. The editorial
makes a clear distinction between the dangers of human cloning
and the benefits of cellular or "therapeutic" cloning. Especially
important are the technical and moral arguments against cloning
that "aims to replicate humans."

At first glance, then, the editorial's argument against the Bush   2
administration's proposed ban on all human cloning, including
that of embryos, is convincing. Its recommendation to continue
cloning "to harvest stem cells" for medical research seems like a
middle path we should follow. Still, one has to ask why the editorial
gives so much coverage to the bizarre claim by the Raelians that a

human child has been successfully cloned? Shouldn't this claim have been given no more than passing notice in so serious an article? It is interesting that mention of the Raelians is used to introduce a proposal by "conservative Republicans" to ban cloning of any sort, a proposal that the editorial describes with loaded words such as "overreaction," "knee-jerk reaction," and "overreach." Aren't there people other than conservative Republicans who are against all cloning?

In addition, the claim the "any clone would catch Americans spectacularly unprepared" seems hard to believe. The media has covered cloning and stem-cell research extensively in the recent past. Most Americans know that sheep can be cloned ever since hearing about Dolly in 1997.

3

In fact, Americans may have "vexing moral questions" about both kinds of cloning, questions that the article never addresses. For example, the article skirts the issue that many Americans believe that human embryos—whether grown in a test tube or implanted in a uterus—are human beings. What about the fact that destroying embryos to harvest stem cells devalues human life, even if it is important to research that may save lives? And if we say therapeutic cloning is unethical, should we allow it simply because others countries will do it?

4

There are compelling arguments on both sides of the issue of therapeutic cloning, but such questions must be addressed if we are to understand this issue and make informed choices. Nonetheless, the editorial is correct: the announcement of a cloned human—true or false—"is a call for responsible action." We are in fact "in a brave new world of medical advances."

5

EXERCISE 9: *Practice what you have learned*   Write a critique of an essay, article, or textbook chapter you have been reading. Begin by reviewing the suggested criteria for evaluation on p. 44.

GS 4.7 SYNTHESIZING: BRINGING IDEAS TOGETHER IN A NEW STATEMENT

Learning to synthesize or to bring ideas together from different sources is a logical step in the development of critical reading skills. Synthesizing requires the *restating, combining, and reconciling* of ideas, opinions, and information from disparate sources logically and coherently.

Courses you take in college will ask you to evaluate one writer's position against another's, compare/contrast ideas on the same issue, and even create an entirely new perspective after reading several different discussions on a related issue. However, this new product should be more than a collection of borrowed elements. It should also reflect your own thinking, perspectives, and experiences. Just as important, it should be developed and organized in a way you think suits your purpose.

An effective synthesis, then, is a well-crafted and purposeful piece that uses the writer's ideas as well as those of others to create a new statement or a new focus on the issue at hand.

Read "All Human Cloning is Wrong" by US Senator Sam Brownback. This guest editorial appeared in *USA Today* as an opposing view to "Overreaction to Cloning Claim Poses Other Risks." Then, read Matthew Roberts' "Adult Stem-Cell Research: An Alternative to Cloning," a student essay that synthesizes materials from both editorials as well as from a third source.

All Human Cloning Is Wrong

Senator Sam Brownback

The announcement of the possible first live-born human clone came as a shock to many. And it should.   1

However, what the Raelians claim to have done is at its most basic level no different from what numerous biotech companies in this country and elsewhere are attempting to do. As observers of this issue know, there are several biotech companies and university research labs engaged—or soon will be—in the mass production of human embryos for research purposes. The human embryos will be harvested for their material, then destroyed.   2

This grisly prospect—creating human life merely to conduct research on it—must be outlawed.   3

Some proponents of human cloning would have society believe that there are two different types of cloning: so-called reproductive and so-called therapeutic. Science, however, tells us that there are not two types of cloning—there is only one, and it always results in the creation of a new human embryo.   4

The essential point: cloning is cloning is cloning, and all cloning is the   5
same.

Whether the embryo created through the process of somatic-cell transfer   6
(the technical name for cloning) is destined for implantation or for destructive
research that ultimately kills him or her—it is the same, and it should be
banned.

Some Congress members who favor cloning in certain circumstances are   7
offering a bill that bans the implantation of clonal human embryos while at the
same time authorizing biotech companies to create thousands of human
embryos.

Let us be clear: this proposal is not in any way a ban on human cloning. It   8
is an endorsement of human cloning that attempts to restrict some of the ways
the human clones may be used.

If we do not ban the cloning of human embryos now, we will quickly find   9
ourselves unable to put the genie back in the bottle.

The only solution to the problem now facing humanity is to act quickly 10
and to ban all human cloning now.

Along with Sen. Mary Landrieu, D–La., I have authored a bipartisan bill 11
that bans all human cloning. The House has passed such a bill, and the president had indicated his strong support for this measure. Congress and the country can afford to wait no longer.

Student Synthesis

Matthew Roberts

Professor Spano

ENG 101–33

November 29, 2003

Adult Stem-Cell Research: An Alternative to Cloning   1

The controversy over human cloning, which began in earnest in

1997, after British scientists announced the cloning of a sheep, is

coming to a head. The Bush administration supports legislation to

prohibit all human cloning. However, many medical researchers,

such as those in the National Academy of Sciences, oppose the ban

because it would outlaw therapeutic cloning, which creates

embryos from which stem cells used in medical research can be taken ("Overreaction . . ." A8). In short, what the Bush administration considers unethical, many researchers believe is important to the advancement of medicine and ultimately to the saving of lives. However, there is an alternative that accommodates both of these positions: the use of adult stem cells.

The Bush administration's opposition to all human cloning "ignores critical differences between cloning of the human and the therapeutic variety," claim the editors of USA Today. ("Overreaction . . ." A8). The editors forthrightly condemn the implanting of a cloned embryo into a uterus, the process by which a human being might be duplicated. However, they support therapeutic cloning, which provides stem cells used in research to combat leukemia, diabetes and other terrible diseases. It is difficult, then, to argue with the "end" to which the cloning of human embryos is aimed. But what about the "means"?

2

It can be argued that cloning human embryos in order to grow stem cells—therapeutic cloning—is as morally offensive as cloning human beings. (Brownback A8). Senator Sam Brownback (R-Kansas), who, with Senator Mary Landrieu (D-Louisiana), is co-sponsoring a ban on all cloning, objects to therapeutic cloning because it destroys human life. It is a "grisly prospect," says Brownback, "creating human life merely to conduct research on it." Researchers clone human embryos only to harvest stem-cells, and then they dispose of them. "If we do not ban the cloning of human embryos now," says Brownback, "we will quickly find ourselves unable to put the genie back in the bottle" (Brownback A8). For Senators Brownback and Landrieu, the end does not justify the means.

3

However, there is a middle ground that should be explored to   4
meet the needs of medical researchers and to address the
objections of those opposed to embryonic cloning. It is the
harvesting of a patient's own stem cells for use in treating his or
her disease. "Adult stem cells are now beginning to ameliorate
suffering in human beings," claims Wesley J. Smith, a senior fellow
at the Discovery Institute (2).

After culturing stem cells taken from a Parkinson's sufferer,   5
Smith reports, doctors were able to inject the cells into the patient's
brain, resulting in a 37% increase in his motor skills. "One year
after the procedure, the patient's overall Unified Parkinson's Disease
Rating Scale had improved by 83 percent—this at a time when he
was not taking any other Parkinson's medications!" (Smith 2).

Adult stem cells have also been used to treat patients with   6
multiple sclerosis at Seattle's Washington Medical Center. Twenty-
six patients were involved; of these, twenty showed marked
improvement after receiving treatment using their own stem cells.
As reported in the Globe and Mail, Canadian researchers have
treated four other MS patients using therapies involving adult
stem cells (Smith 3).

Stem-cell research offers far too many promises for advances   7
in medical research not to be pursued vigorously. Fortunately,
there is some evidence that we can avoid the ethical problem of
cloning embryos to harvest the stem cells we need to save lives.
But more needs to be done. Medical researchers must be willing to
consider new avenues and to pursue the use of adult stem cells as
a realistic alternative to cloning. And government must be willing

not simply to ban all cloning, but to provide the money that researchers will need to continue and accelerate adult stem-cell research.

Works Cited

Brownback, Sam. "All Human Cloning is Wrong. Opposing Opinion." USA Today 3 Jan. 2003: A8.

"Overreaction to Cloning Claim Poses Other Risks." Editorial, USA Today 3 Jan. 2003: A8.

Smith, Wesley. "Spinning Stem Cells." National Review Online 23 Apr. 2002. 5pp. 30 Dec. 2002 <http://www.nationalreview.com/comment/ comment-smith042302.asp>.

CREDITING YOUR SOURCES

When you use other authors' materials in a synthesis, you must provide parenthetical citations, thereby informing your reader that the material is not your own. *You must do this whether you paraphrase, summarize, or quote directly.* Follow standard guidelines such as those published by the Modern Language Association (see the Appendix to this book), the American Psychological Association, or some other professional group, as required by your instructor.

EXERCISE 10: *Practice what you have learned* Find another essay or editorial that relates directly to the topic or issue addressed in an essay or editorial you have read recently. Synthesize ideas from what you have read with your own ideas.

Organization and Development

In "Getting Started" you learned several ways to gather facts, ideas, and opinions about the subjects you choose to write about. Collecting sufficient information about your subject—making sure that you know as much about it as you need to—is an important first step in the writing process.

Next, you will need to determine what it is about your subject that you wish to communicate and how to use your information to get your point across clearly and effectively. Learning how to make such decisions is what the four chapters of Section One are all about.

In Chapter 1 you will learn that two of the most crucial steps early in the writing process are *focusing and limiting* the information you've collected so that you can begin to decide upon a *central idea.* Sometimes referred to as the *main* or *controlling* idea, the central idea of a paragraph or essay expresses the main point its writer wishes to develop.

The process of deciding on a central idea begins with a review of information you collected in your journal through focused freewriting, brainstorming, and the other prewriting techniques explained in "Getting Started." You can then evaluate these details to determine what they say about your subject and to decide exactly what you want to tell your readers about it. Always keep your journal handy. The more information you collect about a subject, the easier it is to find an interesting central idea. Once you have found it, the central idea will help you choose the kinds and amounts of detail needed to develop your writing effectively.

Chapter 2 introduces you to *unity* and *coherence,* two key principles to observe in organizing information. The section on unity explains how to choose details that best accomplish your purpose and relate most directly to your central idea. The section on coherence shows you how to create connections in and between paragraphs to maintain your reader's interest and to make your writing easy to follow.

Chapter 3, "Development," shows you how to determine the amount of detail a paragraph or essay should contain. It also explains ways to arrange these details and develop ideas. Chapter 4, "Introductions and Conclusions," suggests techniques to create effective openings and closings in essays.

The reading selections in Section One contain examples of the important principles of organization and development explained in the chapter introductions. They are also a rich source of interesting topics to develop in your own writing. However, like the other selections in *A Reader for College Writers,* each has a value all its own. Whether written by professionals or by college students like you, these paragraphs and essays discuss people, places, or ideas you are sure to find interesting, informative, humorous, and even touching. Here's hoping they will inspire you to continue reading and writing about a variety of subjects, especially those you care about most!

CHAPTER 1

The Central Idea

An important concern for any writer is the ability to organize information in a form that is easy to follow. The best way to do this is to arrange, or focus, the details you've collected around a central idea.

Identifying the Central Idea

The central idea is often called the *main idea* because it conveys the writer's main point. It is also called the *controlling idea,* for it controls (or determines) the kinds and amounts of detail that a paragraph or essay contains.

The central idea is the focal point to which all the other ideas in an essay or paragraph point. Just as you focus a camera by aiming at a fixed point, you focus your writing by making all the details it contains relate directly to the central idea. Everything you include should help prove, illustrate, or support the central idea. You might also think of a central idea as an umbrella. It is the broadest or most general statement in an essay or paragraph; all other information fits under it. The diagrams on page 56 illustrate these two concepts.

Read these next two paragraphs; their central ideas (in italics) act as focal points to which everything else points. Notice that the central ideas are broader than the details that support them.

> *Talk about bad days: today is a classic.* First, I woke up to hear my parents screaming in my ear about a bill I have to pay. Then I went to school to find out I had failed my art project. After that, I called home to learn that I might have my license revoked, and the accident wasn't even my fault. Finally, while walking out of the cafeteria, I tripped over somebody's book bag and made myself look like an ass. And it's only two in the afternoon! (Donna Amiano, "Bad Days")

> *My life is full of risks.* As a stair builder who works with heavy machinery, I risk cutting off a finger or a limb every day. Each Monday and Thursday, I risk four or five dollars on the state lottery. Every time I take my beat-up, 1981 Chevy Caprice Classic for a drive, I risk breaking down. However, the biggest risk I've ever taken was my decision to attend DeVry Institute this year. (Kenneth Dwyer, "Risks")

In most cases the central idea of a paragraph is expressed in a *topic sentence,* and the central idea of an essay is expressed in a *thesis statement.* In some pieces of writing, however, the central idea is so obvious that the author does not

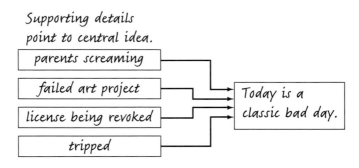

Central idea = focal point

Supporting details
point to central idea.

parents screaming

failed art project

license being revoked

tripped

Today is a
classic bad day.

Central Idea = umbrella under which supporting details fit

My life is full of risks.

risk at work
risk driving old car

risk playing lottery
risk attending DeVry

need to state it in a formal topic sentence or thesis statement. In such cases, the central idea is said to be implied. This is often true of narration and description, the kinds of writing you will read in Section Three. However, it can apply to all types of writing. In this chapter, for example, a paragraph in which the central idea is only implied appears on page 67; it is entitled "The Way We Were."

Nonetheless, as a college writer, you should always state the central idea outright—as a topic sentence when you write a paragraph or as a thesis statement when you tie several paragraphs together in an essay. Doing so will help you focus on specific ideas and organize information.

Often, authors state the central idea early, placing the topic sentence or thesis at the very beginning of a paragraph or essay. However, this is not always the best place for it. For example, you first might have to give readers explanatory details or background materials. In such cases, you can place your topic sentence or thesis somewhere in the middle or even at the end of a paragraph or essay. Delaying the central idea can also create suspense. Finally, it is a good way to avoid offending readers who at first may be opposed to an opinion you are presenting.

Writing a Preliminary Topic Sentence or Thesis Statement

As a developing writer, make sure you have a good grasp of the central ideas that will control the paragraphs and essays you write. You can do this early in the writing process by jotting down a working version of your central idea on a piece of scratch paper or in your journal. This will be your *preliminary* topic sentence or thesis statement. It is called *preliminary* because you can and often should make significant changes in this version of your topic sentence or thesis statement after you've begun to write your paragraph or essay.

Of course, before you draft a preliminary topic sentence or thesis, you must choose a subject to write about. Keep in mind that by its very nature a subject represents a kind of thinking that is abstract, general, and incomplete. A central idea, on the other hand, is a concrete, specific, and complete expression of thought. For example, notice how much more meaningful the subject "waterskiing" becomes when you turn it into a central idea: "Waterskiing can be *dangerous.*"

To turn any subject into a central idea, whether it winds up as the topic sentence of a paragraph or the thesis of an essay, you will have to *focus* and *limit* your discussion of a subject by saying something concrete and specific about it. Focusing and limiting are important thinking processes that will help you begin to organize the information you've collected about your subject. Here's how they work.

FOCUS YOUR DISCUSSION

A good time to think about focusing on a central idea and drafting a working thesis or topic sentence is immediately after you have reviewed your journal for facts, ideas, and opinions that you gathered through prewriting as explained in "Getting Started." While these important details are still fresh in your mind, ask yourself three questions:

1. *Purpose:* What do I want this piece of writing to accomplish?
2. *Main point:* What is the main point I wish to communicate about my subject?
3. *Details:* What details can I use to develop this main point?

Purpose   As well as you can at this stage in the writing process, determine your purpose—what you want your essay or paragraph to do. For instance, it may be to entertain the reader with a humorous story, to explain a natural process, to compare two types of music, to warn readers of a health hazard, or to convince them to adopt your position on a social issue. You can read more about purpose in "Getting Started."

Once you have determined your purpose, you will be able to decide on your main point more easily, for you will already have begun determining which of the details you have gathered will be useful and which will not.

Let's say your purpose is to describe a forest you hiked through last fall. You review your notes and decide to include details about the colors—brilliant reds, burnt oranges, bright yellows—against which you saw a small herd of white-tailed deer. You also consider describing other things you saw, such as the old truck tire dumped on the side of the trail or the two hunters dressed in green and orange camouflage gear. On the other hand, you decide not to tell readers that you traveled three hours in an old pickup to get there, that you bumped into a high school friend as you were leaving, or that you met a forest ranger who had dated Aunt Bertha. None of these facts describe the forest.

Main Point   The next step is to determine exactly what you want to say about your walk through the woods. Ask yourself what for *you* is the most interesting or important aspect of the subject. This will be your *main point,* the point that will help you tie all the details together logically.

In short, you can turn a subject into a central idea by making a main point about the subject. If you decide that the most interesting or important aspect of your walk in the forest is that it was *inspiring,* your central idea might read: "The forest I hiked through this autumn was inspiring."

As you learned earlier, focusing lets the writer turn an abstract, general, incomplete subject into the central idea for a paragraph or essay. Notice how much clearer, more specific, and more complete the central ideas on the right are than the abstract subjects on the left:

Subject	**Central Idea**
My fall walk in the forest	My fall walk in the forest was inspiring.
Rock music	Rock music can damage your hearing.
Electric cars	Electric cars can replace gasoline models.
The Battle of Gettysburg	The Battle of Gettysburg was the turning point of the Civil War.

Homeless children	The government should guarantee homeless children proper nutrition, education, and health care.
The Brooklyn Bridge	The Brooklyn Bridge is an engineering marvel.
The Spanish influenza epidemic of 1917	The Spanish influenza epidemic of 1917 killed more people than did World War I.

As you can see, focusing on a main point helps change an abstract idea into something specific and concrete—into a central idea.

Details   Focusing also provides a starting point for a first draft of an essay because it helps you choose between the details to include and those to discard. If you decide to focus on the inspirational aspects of the forest, for example, you ought to include a description of the changing leaves and of the deer, but should you also mention the old tire and the hunters? They are certainly part of the experience, but do they relate to the notion that your hike was inspirational? Probably not.

LIMIT YOUR DISCUSSION TO A MANAGEABLE LENGTH

Typically, students are asked to write short essays, usually ranging between 250 and 750 words, with paragraphs seldom longer than 75 words. That's why one of the most important things to remember when writing a thesis statement or topic sentence is to limit your central idea as much as you can. Otherwise, you won't be able to develop it in as much detail as will be necessary to make your point clearly, effectively, and completely.

Let's say you are about to buy a car and want to compare two popular makes. In a short essay it would be foolish to compare these automobiles in more than two or three different ways. Therefore, you might limit yourself to cost, appearance, and comfort rather than discuss their performance, handling, and sound systems as well. You might even limit your central idea to only one of these aspects—cost, for instance. You can then divide cost into more specific subsections, which will be easier to organize when it comes time to write your first draft. The thesis for such an essay might read: "I chose the 2001 Mountain Marauder over the 2001 Cross-Country Schooner because it costs less to buy, to operate, and to repair."

SOME TIPS ON WRITING TOPIC SENTENCES AND THESIS STATEMENTS

1. Make sure your topic sentence or thesis is a complete sentence. A complete sentence contains a subject and a verb, and it expresses a complete thought.

   Not: Computers and being a successful college student.

   Or: Using computers to succeed in college.

   Or: How computers can help students succeed in college.

   But: Computers can help students succeed in college.

2. State your main point directly; don't announce it.

   Not: I am going to write about how computers can help students succeed in college.

   Or: This paper will discuss the fact that computers can help students succeed in college.

   But: Computers can help students succeed in college.

3. In most cases, readers will naturally assume that what you are writing about is your own opinion or is what you believe. There is no need to explain that.

   Not: I believe that computers can help students succeed in college.

   Or: It is my opinion that computers can help students succeed in college.

   But: Computers can help students succeed in college.

4. Make sure your topic sentence or thesis clearly states the point you want to make about your subject.

   Not: Computers affect student performance in college.

   But: Computers can help students succeed in college.

Controlling Unity and Development

At the beginning of this chapter, you read that the central idea can be called the *controlling idea* because it helps the writer determine the kind and amount of information a paragraph or essay contains. This is explained further in Chapters 2 and 3.

For now, remember that the kinds of details a piece of writing contains determine whether it is unified. A paragraph is unified if its sentences relate directly to its central idea, whether or not that idea is expressed formally in a topic sentence. An essay is unified if its paragraphs relate directly to its central idea, whether or not that idea is expressed in a thesis statement.

The amount of detail a piece of writing contains determines whether it is well developed. A paragraph or essay is well developed if it contains all the detail it needs to prove, illustrate, or otherwise support its central idea.

Revising the Central Idea

One last and very important bit of advice: Always revise the working, or preliminary, versions of your thesis statements and topic sentences during the writing process. Like taking notes or writing a first draft of a paper, writing a preliminary version of a thesis statement or topic sentence is intended only to give you a starting point and a sense of direction. Don't be afraid to reword, edit, or completely rewrite your central idea at any point. Like all processes, writing involves a series of steps or tasks to be completed. However, there is no rule that prevents you from stopping at any point along the way, looking back at what you've done, and changing it as thoroughly and as often as you like. What's more, the process of writing always includes discovery. The more you discover about your subject, the more likely you are to understand it better and to revise what you *thought* you had wanted to say about it.

As an example, study three drafts of the introductory paragraphs from Maria Cirilli's essay "Echoes." Each time she revised her work, Cirilli came to a clearer understanding of her subject and of what she wanted to say about it. This can be seen best in the last sentence, which is Cirilli's thesis statement. A complete version of "Echoes" appears at the end of this chapter.

Cirilli—Draft 1

I hardly remember my grandmother except for the fact that she used to bounce me on her knees by the old-fashioned brick fireplace and sing old songs. I was only four years old when she died. Her face is a faded image in the back of my mind.

In contrast, I remember my grandfather very well. He was 6'4" tall. He possessed a deep voice, which distinguished him from others whether he was in the streets of our small picture-perfect town in southern Italy or in the graciously sculptured seventeenth-century church. He appeared to be strong and powerful. In fact he used to scare all my girlfriends away when they came to play or do homework. Yet, I knew that there was nothing to be afraid of.

Is this thesis clear? Does it tell what the essay will say about Cirilli 's grandfather?

Cirilli—Draft 2

I hardly remember my grandmother except for the fact that she used to bounce me on her knees by the old-fashioned brick fireplace and sing old songs. I was only four years old when she died.

The last sentence of draft 1 has been removed.

In contrast, I remember my grandfather very well. He was 6'4" tall, a towering man with broad shoulders and a pair of mustaches that I watched turn from black to grey over the years. He possessed a deep voice, which distinguished him from others whether he was in the streets of our small picture-perfect town in southern Italy or in the graciously sculptured seventeenth-century church. He appeared to be strong and powerful. In fact, he used to scare all my girlfriends away when they came to play or do homework, yet he was the most gentle man I have ever known.

Detail added to describe him better.

The thesis is clearer. But, will essay also discuss fear?

Cirilli—Draft 3

I hardly remember my grandmother except for
the fact that she used to bounce me on her
knees by the old-fashioned brick fireplace
and sing old songs. I was only four years
old when she died. <u>Her face is a faded image</u>   *Cirilli reuses*
<u>in the back of my mind.</u>   *this sentence*
from draft 1.

    In contrast, I remember my grandfather
very well. He was 6'4" tall, a towering man
with broad shoulders and a mustache that I
watched turn from black to grey. His voice
was deep, distinguishing him from others in
our small picture-perfect town in southern
Italy. To some, my grandfather appeared very
powerful, and he used to scare my
girlfriends away when they came to play or
do homework. <u>In fact, he was strong, but he</u>
<u>was the gentlest and most understanding man</u>
<u>I have ever known.</u>

Detail about
church removed;
not needed.

Thesis is expanded;
now includes
"most understanding."

Thesis stands alone in its
own sentence; much clearer.

Practicing Writing Central Ideas

To turn a subject into a central idea, you must express a main point about the
subject. In the left column are subjects you might discuss in a paragraph or essay. Turn them into central ideas by writing your main point in the spaces provided. To think of an effective main point, ask yourself what is most interesting
or most important about the subject. When you join your subject and main
point, be sure to create a complete sentence. A complete sentence has a subject
and a verb. The first item is done for you as an example.

┌──────── **Central Idea** ────────┐

Subject   **Main Point**

1. A successful diet   *requires much will power.*

2. College textbooks   _____
                                               _____

3. Computers   _____
                                               _____

4. My family   _____
                                               _____

5. Noise pollution   _____
                                               _____

6. Listening to music   _____
                                               _____

7. Professional athletes   _____
                                               _____

8. AIDS (or another disease)   _____
                                               _____

9. Learning to drive (swim, play tennis,   _____
   use a computer, cook, fix cars, etc.)   _____

10. Studying mathematics (science,   _____
    accounting, a foreign language, etc.)   _____

The reading selections that follow illustrate the organizational principles just discussed. Read them carefully, take notes, and respond to the Questions for Discussion and the Suggestions for Journal Entries that accompany them. Doing so will give you an even better understanding of the central idea and its importance to organization.

Four Paragraphs for Analysis

The four paragraphs that follow show the importance of focusing on a central idea. Written by various authors, they discuss four different ideas, but each focuses clearly on a main point developed through detail.

Barbara Dafoe Whitehead is a noted social historian and author. Her writing has appeared in several American magazines and professional journals. Gen X is an abbreviation for Generation X, a term that, roughly speaking, includes people in their late teens to late twenties. "The Girls of Gen X" first appeared in The American Enterprise *magazine (1998).*

Stephen Fox is the author of "The Education of Branch Rickey," one of many essays published in 1995 to mark the fiftieth anniversary of Jackie Robinson's breaking of professional baseball's color barrier. Branch Rickey was the owner of the Brooklyn Dodgers at the time. The paragraph included here is from that essay.

Ernest Albrecht is a professor of English, a drama critic, and the author of two books on the circus.

Lewis Lord writes for U.S. News & World Report. *The paragraph he wrote appeared as part of a history of the year 1000 AD, published in that magazine in the summer of 1999.*

Preparing to Read

1. As the following four paragraphs show, a writer who wants to express a central idea in a topic sentence need not start with that sentence. Depending on the paragraph's purpose, he or she might provide a few sentences of background or explanation first. To create emphasis, a writer might even wait until the end of a paragraph before stating the central idea. In fact, as you will see in Lewis Lord's paragraph from "The Way We Were," sometimes writers choose not to express central ideas in a topic sentence at all. Instead, they allow readers to draw their own conclusions. In such cases the central idea is said to be "implied."

2. As you read the first sentence of paragraph 1, try to identify Whitehead's main point. Keep this in mind as you read the details in the rest of the paragraph, which relate to that point.

3. Paragraphs 2, 3, and 4 contain several personal and place names, such as Branch Rickey, Brooklyn Dodgers, Jackie Robinson, Madison Square Garden, and Roman Empire. Be on the lookout for them. If you are unsure about what they contribute to the meaning of the paragraph, look them up in an encyclopedia or on the Internet. In fact, if you have never heard of these people or places, look them up now.

Vocabulary

adolescence (noun)	The stage of growth between childhood and maturity, roughly from 10 to 18 years.
binge (adjective)	Excessive, uncontrolled.
controversial (adjective)	Causing disagreement; disputable, arguable.
debris (noun)	Waste, litter.
depression (noun)	A psychological disorder in which the patient feels sad, hopeless.
dialects (noun)	Various forms of the same language.
enigmatic (adjective)	Puzzling, mysterious.
harbinger (noun)	Sign of things to come, forerunner.
hippodrome (noun)	Arena for horses.
innovate (verb)	Invent, create something new.
lathe (noun)	Machine for shaping wood.
millennium (noun)	One thousand years, ten centuries.
novel (adjective)	New.
ordeals (noun)	Trials.
relics (noun)	What's left of, remnants.
roustabouts (noun)	Workers, laborers.
venereal (adjective)	Relating to sexual indulgence, most commonly as in a disease resulting from sexual contact.
replete with (adjective)	Full of.
wary (adjective)	Careful, cautious.

The Girls of Gen X

Barbara Dafoe Whitehead

ALL IS NOT well with the women of Generation X. Consider the evidence: Close to 40 percent of college women are frequent binge drinkers, a behavior related to date rapes and venereal disease. Young women suffer higher levels of depression, suicidal thoughts and attempts than young men from early adolescence on. Between 1980 and '92, the rate of completed suicides more than tripled among white girls and doubled among black girls. For white women between 15 and 24, suicide is the third leading cause of death.

The Example of Jackie Robinson*

Stephen Fox

FIFTY YEARS ago this fall, Branch Rickey announced that Jackie Robinson had signed a contract to play with the Brooklyn Dodgers organization, thus breaking the "color line" that had kept African-Americans out of white organized baseball in the 20th century. With that single stroke, the crafty, enigmatic 63-year-old white man and the wary, explosive 26-year-old black man helped spark a social revolution. Intensely controversial at the time, the signing of Robinson now seems a harbinger of the postwar civil-rights movement: three years before the integration of the armed forces, nine years before the Supreme Court's *Brown* decision, ten years before the Montgomery, Alabama, bus boycott.

Sawdust

Ernest Albrecht

AS A TEN year old, I watched as miniature mountains of the magical debris took shape around my father's lathe or his table saw, and with hardly any effort at all I imagined three rings and a hippodrome track sprinkled with the stuff in various colors. Having once conjured that, it didn't take much more effort to envision the ropes and cables that the circus roustabouts spun into a fantastic web transforming the old Madison Square Garden on Eighth Avenue and 49th Street (New York) into an exotic world of wonder and fantasy. That is why, of all the changes that progress has wrought upon the circus, I lament the loss of the sawdust the most. Rubber mats may be practical, but they have no magic.

The Way We Were

Lewis Lord

ONE MILLENNIUM AGO, the best roads in Europe were several centuries old, the neglected relics of the Roman Empire. Most routes were so bad that the well-to-do chose to travel by horseback. Only the poor and sick bumped along in wagons. Perhaps 19 of every 20 people lived in villages, typically surrounded by forests replete with wolves, bears, and outlaws. The outside

---

*Editor's title.

world was everything beyond the village fence, and local dialects often could not be understood by people residing only a few miles away. Generations of villagers lived their 30 or 40 years unaware of important events elsewhere: floods, wars, and deaths of popes, kings, and emperor. Few ever saw a single thing that was both significant and novel. With learning scorned, hardly anyone knew how to innovate. What existed was deemed God's way, and those who dared change it risked suspicion and possible ordeals by fire and water to prove their innocence.

Read More on the Web*

St. Cloud State University's Literacy Education Online: http://leo.stcloudstate.edu/acadwrite/thesistatement.html

University of North Carolina Writing Center: http://www.unc.edu/depts/wcweb/handouts/thesis.html

Generation X Sources on the Web: http://membres.lycos.fr/coupland/coupgx.html

Site of the Jackie Robinson Foundation: http://www.jackierobinson.org/

Site of the Jackie Robinson Society: http://www.utexas.edu/students/jackie/

Site of the Circus World Museum: http://www.circusworldmuseum.com/

English History's Site on the Year 1000: http://englishhistory.info/year1000/

Questions for Discussion

1. What are the topic sentences in the first three paragraphs?

2. What in your own words is the central idea of Lord's paragraph from "The Way We Were"?

3. Would "The Girls of Gen X" have been as effective and easy to read had the topic sentence appeared in the middle of the paragraph? At the end of the paragraph?

4. What important information does Fox provide before the topic sentence in "The Example of Jackie Robinson"?

5. What is the main point of "Sawdust?" Why does Albrecht wait until the end of the paragraph to reveal it"?

---

*Note that URLs change frequently. If a site in which you're interested doesn't appear at the URL listed, try typing the *name* of the site into a search engine such as Google. If the site still exists, you're likely to find it.

Thinking Critically

Remember that a central idea acts as an umbrella under which all the details and other, more limited, ideas in a paragraph or essay fit. The central idea for the following paragraph is unstated. Read the paragraph; then, in your journal, write your own central idea for it in a complete topic sentence. Remember, the idea in a topic sentence is broader than any other idea in a paragraph.

> The planet Mars takes its name from the Roman god of war. Mercury is the Roman god of commerce; and Venus, the goddess of love. Pluto is named for the Greek god of the underworld, Neptune rules the sea, and Jupiter reigns as king of the gods. Even the planets Saturn and Uranus borrow their names from ancient deities.

Suggestion for a Journal Entry

This journal entry is in three parts:

First, pick a limited subject you know a lot about. Here are some examples: waiting on tables, last year's Fourth of July picnic, your bedroom at home, feeding a baby, your car, studying math, your Uncle Mort, going to a concert, watching baseball on television.

Second, decide what are the most interesting or important points you can make about that subject. Choose *one* of these as the main point of a central idea. Write that central idea down in the form of a topic sentence for a paragraph you might want to write later.

Third, do the same with three or four other limited subjects you know about. Here's what your journal entry might look like when you're done:

1. **Limited subject:** Feeding a baby
    Main points: Sometimes messy, always fun
    Topic sentence: Feeding a baby can be messy.

2. **Limited subject:** Uncle Mort
    Main points: Old, handsome, outgoing, considerate
    Topic sentence: My Uncle Mort was one of the most considerate people in my family.

3. **Limited subject:** Last year's Fourth of July picnic
    Main points: Much food, many people, lots of rain
    Topic sentence: Last year's Fourth of July picnic was a washout.

Suffering

Siu Chan

Siu Chan was born in Cambodia of Chinese parents. Her father owned a small business in Phnom Penh, the capital, where Siu lived with her parents and her five brothers and sisters. In 1975 her life changed drastically. That was the year that the Khmer Rouge, the movement headed by communist leader Pol Pot, took control of the country. The atrocities committed by this group resulted in the extermination of millions of native Cambodians and other people with millions more displaced from their homes and sent to live in work camps. In fact, the communists nearly evacuated the city of Phnom Penh and redistributed the people in rural areas.

This essay tells of Siu Chan's experience during the four years she lived under the tyranny of the Khmer Rouge. In 1979, she and three younger brothers and sisters escaped from Cambodia into Vietnam traveling by bus, boat, bicycle, and on foot. They spent five years in Vietnam before immigrating to the United States, where an uncle who sponsored them was waiting. Today, Siu works two jobs to help support her family and attends college part-time, majoring in accounting. As she explained to her writing instructor, she works seven days a week and has not had a day off in over three years.

Preparing to Read

1. Chan states a thesis in her first paragraph. It contains three main points. Make sure you understand each before going on to the rest of the essay.

2. This is a five-paragraph essay. Paragraph 1 is the introduction, with the essay's thesis statement. Each of the three main points in Chan's thesis is the basis for the topic sentence you will find in each body paragraph—2, 3, and 4. Paragraph 5 is the essay's conclusion.

3. Think about the significance of Chan's title. Doing so makes reading her essay easier.

4. The horrors that the Khmer Rouge created in Cambodia are documented in *The Killing Fields,* a film that you can find on videotape.

Vocabulary

authorities (noun)	People in charge.
craved (verb)	Desired.
malnutrition (noun)	Lack of proper food, inadequate diet.
nourishment (noun)	Proper food, sustenance.
tyranny (noun)	Oppression, dictatorship.

Suffering

Siu Chan

WHENEVER I THINK about the word "suffering," the first thought that comes 1 to mind is the time I lived under the dictatorship of the Khmer Rouge from 1975 though 1979 in my homeland of Cambodia. It was the worst time in my life: I was allowed very little personal freedom, I witnessed the death of my family, and I nearly died of starvation. *Thesis*

Starting in 1975, when the communists under Pol Pot took over, the gov- 2 ernment destroyed nearly all personal freedom. Families were split apart, with each member being forced to live separately. Even my two-year-old brother was taken away to live with a group of children the same age. We were never able to visit each other, and when my parents passed away I wasn't even able to see them for a final goodbye. In addition, the communists forced me into slave labor. I got up at 3:00 AM every day, sometimes to work on a road-building project for which I carried water and earth and sometimes to dig a hole for an artificial pond. Our work day sometimes ended at 11:00 PM. More-over, I was allowed to speak only one language: Cambodian. At home, we had spoken Chinese. The authorities would not allow any criticism of the govern-ment, and I had to be very careful about what I said and did. Otherwise, they would kill me.

During those four years, I lost six members of my family. First my grand- 3 parents passed away about two months apart. They were old and ill. Because my country had experienced war and tyranny for many years, they could not get the medicines they needed. Approximately four months later, my uncle died; he was overworked and did not have enough food to eat, so he became ill. There was no medicine to help him either. One year later, my little brother died after suffering from a fever for one full week. Again, no medication was available. After another six months, my parents also died one month apart. They starved to death.

I had to eat food that the communist government gave me whether it was 4 good or not. Usually it was just plain white rice, sometimes with a few wild veg-etables mixed in, but it was never enough to fill me up. I can still remember a three-month period during which I nearly starved to death. The rice crop had failed because of flooding, so I had to go into the woods to search for tree roots and other wild foods. But they satisfied me only temporarily, and they did not have enough nourishment to keep me healthy. I began to suffer from malnutri-tion, and my body became swollen. In fact, I was so hungry for real food that I sometimes burst into tears. I craved food all the time. I even dreamt about it. I would have been very satisfied with only a bowl of plain rice or a slice of bread.

Throughout those four years, I suffered a great deal. I cannot find the ap- 5 propriate words to describe that horror. However, having gone through it, I can appreciate the life I have now. My spirit and my mind get stronger each day. I learned not to waste anything—especially food—when I was in Cambodia, and

I am doing well in the United States. I work hard and I have even started going to college. What's more I feel confident about the future. My suffering has prepared me to face any obstacle.

Read More on the Web

The Cambodian Genocide Project Website: http://www.yale.edu/cgp/

Questions for Discussion

1. What is Chan's thesis? What are the three main points found in that thesis?
2. Identify each of the topic sentences Chan uses in paragraphs 2, 3, and 4.
3. Explain how the details in paragraphs 2, 3, and 4 relate to their topic sentences.

Thinking Critically

1. Why do you think the authorities allowed people to speak only Cambodian?
2. What questions might you ask Chan if you had the opportunity? Write those questions in the margins.
3. Compare the structure of this essay with the structure of Russell's "Three Passions I Have Lived For," which follows.

Suggestions for Journal Entries

1. Recall a personal experience in which your freedom was limited and/or your well-being was threatened because of the power someone had over you. Use clustering, a subject tree, or listing to record details.
2. Recall a battle with serious illness from which you or someone you know well suffered. What caused it? What were its symptoms? What kind of suffering did it cause? Was the illness ever overcome? How?

Three Passions I Have Lived For

Bertrand Russell

One of the most widely read philosophers and mathematicians of the twentieth century, Bertrand Russell (1872–1970) is even better remembered as a social and political activist. For many years, he was considered an extremely unorthodox thinker because of his liberal opinions on sex, marriage, and homosexuality. Politically, Russell was a socialist and pacifist. In the 1950s and 1960s he became one of the leaders of the ban-the-bomb movement in Europe, and later he helped organize opposition to U.S. involvement in Vietnam.

Among his most famous works are Principles of Mathematics, A History of Western Philosophy, *and a three-volume autobiography in which the selection that follows first appeared. Russell won the Nobel Prize in literature in 1950.*

Preparing to Read

1.   The first paragraph contains Russell's thesis. Read it carefully; it will give you clues about the topic sentences on which he develops three of the paragraphs that follow.

2.   The word *passions* should be understood as deep, personal concerns that Russell developed over the course of his life and that had a significant influence on the way he lived.

Vocabulary

abyss (noun)	Deep hole.
alleviate (verb)	Lessen, soften, make less harsh or painful.
anguish (noun)	Grief, sorrow, pain.
consciousness (noun)	Mind, intelligence.
mockery (noun)	Ridicule, scorn.
prefiguring (adjective)	Predicting, forecasting.
reverberate (verb)	Resound, repeatedly echo.
unfathomable (adjective)	Unmeasurable.
verge (noun)	Edge.

Three Passions I Have Lived For

Bertrand Russell

THREE PASSIONS, simple but overwhelmingly strong, have governed my life: 1
the longing for love, the search for knowledge, and unbearable pity for the
suffering of mankind. These passions, like great winds, have blown me hither
and thither, in a wayward course over a deep ocean of anguish, reaching to the
very verge of despair.

I have sought love, first, because it brings ecstasy—ecstasy so great that I 2
would often have sacrificed all the rest of my life for a few hours of this joy. I
have sought it, next, because it relieves loneliness—that terrible loneliness in
which one shivering consciousness looks over the rim of the world into the cold
unfathomable lifeless abyss. I have sought it, finally, because in the union of
love I have seen, in a mystic miniature, the prefiguring vision of the heaven that
saints and poets have imagined. This is what I sought, and though it might
seem too good for human life, this is what—at last—I have found.

With equal passion I have sought knowledge. I have wished to understand 3
the hearts of men. I have wished to know why the stars shine. . . . A little of
this, but not much, I have achieved.

Love and knowledge, so far as they were possible, led upward toward the 4
heavens. But always pity brought me back to earth. Echoes of cries of pain re-
verberate in my heart. Children in famine, victims tortured by oppressors,
helpless old people a hated burden to their sons, and the whole world of loneliness, poverty, and pain make a mockery of what human life should be. I long
to alleviate the evil, but I cannot, and I too suffer.

This has been my life. I have found it worth living, and would gladly live 5
it again if the chance were offered me.

Read More on the Web

The Bertrand Russell Society Website: http://users.drew.edu/~jlenz/
brs.html

The Bertrand Russell Archives at McMaster University: http://www.
mcmaster.ca/russdocs/russell1.htm

Questions for Discussion

1. The title gives us a clue about why Russell wrote this selection. What
was his purpose?

2. Russell expresses the central idea—the thesis—in paragraph 1. What is his thesis?

3. In your own words, explain each of the central ideas—topic sentences—in paragraphs 2, 3, and 4. In other words, what three passions did Russell live for?

4. How do these three passions relate to the thesis?

5. What details does Russell use to develop the topic sentence in paragraph 2? In paragraph 3? In paragraph 4? Explain how these details relate to their topic sentences in each case.

6. You've learned in this chapter how to limit your discussion to a manageable length. In what ways did Russell make sure to limit his essay's length?

Thinking Critically

Russell lists reasons for seeking love and knowledge. What *other* reasons might someone have for seeking them? In your journal, write a paragraph of between 50 and 100 words explaining why you are seeking love or knowledge, or are pursuing some other personal passion. Focus on only one of these. Start your paragraph with a topic sentence modeled after the ones Russell uses.

Suggestions for Journal Entries

1. In your own words, summarize the three reasons Russell has "sought love."

2. In Preparing to Read you read that Russell used the word *passions* to describe the deep, personal concerns that determined the way he lived. Using Russell's essay as a model, write a series of topic sentences for paragraphs that describe the passions—at least three of them—that *you* live for. The kinds of passions you mention should be personal and real. Remember to limit each topic sentence to one and only one passion. If you're embarrassed to write about yourself, write about someone else's passions. Here are some examples:

   One of the most important concerns in my life is getting a good education.

   My religion is the cornerstone of my existence.

   My brother lives to eat.

   My grandmother's most important concern was her children.

   Mother Teresa's sole purpose in life was to serve the poor.

In Africa, AIDS Has a Woman's Face

Kofi A. Annan

Kofi Annan has been the Secretary-General of the United Nations since 1997. Annan was born in Kuamsi, Ghana, in 1938. He graduated with a bachelor's degree in economics from Macalester College in St. Paul, Minnesota in 1961 and completed a master's in management at the Massachusetts Institute of Technology in 1972. Before becoming Secretary-General, he served in several United Nations' positions, including Assistant Secretary-General for Human Resources Management. In 2002, Kofi Annan proposed the New Partnership for African Development, a program to fight the effects of drought, famine, and especially AIDS, a disease that has attacked Africa even more viciously than it has other parts of the world.

Preparing to Read

1. Although the title of this essay tells us it will focus on AIDS and African women, Annan also discusses the effects of drought and famine. These long-time enemies have become even stronger because of the effects of the AIDS epidemic.
2. Annan's thesis appears in the first paragraph, but he repeats it later on. Try to find it as you read subsequent paragraphs.
3. The Horn of Africa, mentioned in paragraph 3, is the northeastern part of the continent. It includes the countries of Somalia, Ethiopia, and Eritrea.

Vocabulary

capacity (noun)	Ability.
depleted (adjective)	Weakened, reduced.
disproportionately (adverb)	Out of keeping with their numbers.
epidemics (noun)	Widespread diseases.
exponentially (adverb)	At a tremendous rate.
innovative (adjective)	New, creative.
nurture (verb)	Support.
replicate (verb)	Duplicate, copy.
resilient (adjective)	Hardy, strong.
stigma (noun)	Sign of shame, blemish.
sustain (verb)	Support, keep alive.

In Africa, AIDS Has a Woman's Face

Kofi A. Annan

A COMBINATION OF famine and AIDS is threatening the backbone of Africa— 1
the women who keep African societies going and whose work makes up
the economic foundation of rural communities. For decades, we have known
that the best way for Africa to thrive is to ensure that its women have the freedom, power and knowledge to make decisions affecting their own lives and
those of their families and communities. At the United Nations, we have always
understood that our work for development depends on building a successful
partnership with the African farmer and her husband.

Study after study has shown that there is no effective development strat- 2
egy in which women do not play a central role. When women are fully involved, the benefits can be seen immediately: families are healthier; they are
better fed; their income, savings and reinvestment go up. And what is true of
families is true of communities and, eventually, of whole countries.

But today, millions of African women are threatened by two simultaneous 3
catastrophes: famine and AIDS. More than 30 million people are now at risk of
starvation in southern Africa and the Horn of Africa. All of these predominantly
agricultural societies are also battling serious AIDS epidemics. This is no coin-
cidence: AIDS and famine are directly linked.

Because of AIDS, farming skills are being lost, agricultural development ef- 4
forts are declining, rural livelihoods are disintegrating, productive capacity to
work the land is dropping and household earnings are shrinking—all while the
cost of caring for the ill is rising exponentially. At the same time, H.I.V. infection and AIDS are spreading dramatically and disproportionately among
women. A United Nations report released last month shows that women now
make up 50 percent of those infected with H.I.V. worldwide—and in Africa that
figure is now 58 percent. Today, AIDS has a woman's face.

AIDS has already caused immense suffering by killing almost 2.5 million 5
Africans this year alone. It has left 11 million African, children orphaned since
the epidemic began. Now it is attacking the capacity of these countries to resist
famine by eroding those mechanisms that enable populations to fight back—
the coping abilities provided by women.

In famines before the AIDS crisis women proved more resilient than men. 6
Their survival rate was higher, and their coping skills were stronger. Women
were the ones who found alternative foods that could sustain their children in
times of drought. Because droughts happened once a decade or so, women who
had experienced previous droughts were able to pass on survival techniques to
younger women. Women are the ones who nurture social networks that can
help spread the burden in times of famine.

But today, as AIDS is eroding the health of Africa's women, it is eroding the 7
skills, experience and networks that keep their families and communities

going. Even before falling ill, a woman will often have to care for a sick husband, thereby reducing the time she can devote to planting, harvesting and marketing crops. When her husband dies, she is often deprived of credit, distribution networks or land rights. When she dies, the household will risk collapsing completely, leaving children to fend for themselves. The older ones, especially girls, will be taken out of school to work in the home or the farm. These girls, deprived of education and opportunities, will be even less able to protect themselves against AIDS.

Because this crisis is different from past famines, we must look beyond re- 8 lief measures of the past. Merely shipping in food is not enough. Our effort will have to combine food assistance and new approaches to farming with treatment and prevention of H.I.V. and AIDS. It will require creating early-warning and analysis systems that monitor both H.I.V. infection rates and famine indicators. It will require new agricultural techniques, appropriate to a depleted work force. It will require a renewed effort to wipe out H.I.V.-related stigma and silence.

It will require innovative, large-scale ways to care for orphans, with spe- 9 cific measures that enable children in AIDS-affected communities to stay in school. Education and prevention are still the most powerful weapons against the spread of H.I.V. Above all, this new international effort must put women at the center of our strategy to fight AIDS.

Experience suggests that there is reason to hope. The recent United Na- 10 tions report shows that H.I.V. infection rates in Uganda continue to decline. In South Africa, infection rates for women under 20 have started to decrease. In Zambia, H.I.V. rates show signs of dropping among women in urban areas and younger women in rural areas. In Ethiopia, infection levels have fallen among young women in the center of Addis Ababa.

We can and must build on those successes and replicate them elsewhere. 11 For that, we need leadership, partnership and imagination from the international community and African governments. If we want to save Africa from two catastrophes, we would do well to focus on saving Africa's women.

Read More on the Web

CNN.com site, *AIDS, Africa in Peril:* http://www.cnn.com/SPECIALS/
2000/aids/

Washington Post site with several links and current reports: http://www.
washingtonpost.com/wp-dyn/world/issues/aidsinafrica/

Questions for Discussion

1. What is the essay's thesis?
2. Where does Annan repeat the thesis?
3. What are the topic sentences or central ideas in paragraphs 2 through 10? How do they relate to the thesis?
4. Why does AIDS among women worsen the effects of drought and famine?
5. How does Annan propose to fight the spread of AIDS in Africa?

Thinking Critically

1. What is Annan suggesting about the AIDS epidemic in Africa when, in paragraph 8, he calls for a "renewed effort to wipe out H.I.V-related stigma and silence"?
2. To American ears, the statement that the UN needs to build a "successful partnership with the African farmer and her husband" (paragraph 1) might sound strange. Explain why.
3. Paragraph 7 explains the importance of women in African society. Discuss the long-term effects that the death of a mother might have on her family. In what ways are these effects similar to what we might expect upon the death of an American mother?

Suggestions for Journal Entries

1. Complete the following statements by filling in the blanks:

    In America, _____ has a woman's face.

    In America, _____ has a man's face.

    In America, _____ has a child's face.

2. In many ways, this is an essay in praise of women who are heads of families. Do you know such a woman? If so, use listing to record what you believe are her major strengths or virtues. List at least three.

    Then add examples or facts to this list that might help you discuss or describe each of these strengths or virtues. For example, you might begin by saying that your grandmother is 1) hardworking,

2) patient, and 3) courageous. You could then list details like the following under each item:

Hardworking:

Held two jobs to support three children after husband died.

Worked fifteen hours a day.

Did most of the repairs on her home.

Kept a vegetable garden and raised chickens.

Made sure her children always had clothes that were clean and pressed.

Patient:

Never raises her voice at her children or grandchildren.

Puts up with her nasty sister and her busybody neighbors.

Didn't even get angry when three of my cousins and I trampled three of her prize rose bushes or when I broke a hundred-year old gravy dish.

Has spent hundreds of hours getting her hyperactive dog, Duncan, to calm down.

Courageous

Never complains about her diabetes.

Lived through the death of two children, one at birth, the other when he was twenty.

Buried her husband when he was only 40.

Once, the bank almost foreclosed on her home.

Echoes

Maria Cirilli

Born in a small town in southern Italy, Maria Cirilli immigrated to the United States in 1971. She earned her associate's degree in nursing from a community college and is now an assistant head nurse at the Robert Wood Johnson University Hospital in New Brunswick, New Jersey. Cirilli has completed her bachelor's in nursing from the University of Medicine and Dentistry of New Jersey. Since writing "Echoes" for a college composition class, she has revised it several times to add detail and make it more powerful.

Preparing to Read

1. Cirilli chose not to reveal the central idea of this essay—her thesis statement—in paragraph 1. However, the first paragraph is important because it contains information that we can contrast with what we read in paragraph 2.

2. The two main points in the thesis (paragraph 2) are important because they give us clues about the topic sentences in the body paragraphs, which follow.

Vocabulary

distinguishing (adjective)	Making different from.
exuberance (noun)	Joy, enthusiasm.
manicured (adjective)	Neat, well cared for.
mediator (noun)	Referee, someone who helps settle disputes.
negotiating (adjective)	Bargaining, dealing.
placate (verb)	Pacify, make calm.
siblings (noun)	Sisters and brothers.
solemnly (adverb)	Seriously.
tribulation (noun)	Trouble, distress.
vulnerable (adjective)	Open, without defenses.
with a vengeance (adverb)	Skillfully, earnestly.

Echoes

Maria Cirilli

I HARDLY REMEMBER my grandmother except for the fact that she used to bounce 1
me on her knees by the old-fashioned brick fireplace and sing old songs. I
was only four when she died. Her face is a faded image in the back of my mind.

In contrast, I remember my grandfather very well. He was 6'4" tall, a tow- 2
ering man with broad shoulders and a mustache that I watched turn from black
to grey. His voice was deep, distinguishing him from others in our small
picture-perfect town in southern Italy. To some, my grandfather appeared very
powerful, and he used to scare my girlfriends away when they came to play or
do homework. In fact, he was strong, but he was the gentlest and most understanding man I have ever known.

I still see him weeping softly as he read a romantic novel in which his fa- 3
vorite character died after many trials and much tribulation. And I will never
forget how carefully he set the tiny leg of our pet bird, Iario, who had become
entangled in a fight with frisky Maurizio, our cat. Once, my brother and I accompanied him to our grandmother's grave at a nearby cemetery that was small
but manicured. As we approached the cemetery, my tall grandfather bent down
from time to time to pick wild flowers along the road. By the end of the journey, he had a dandy little bouquet, which he placed solemnly at my grandmother's grave while bountiful tears streamed down his husky, vulnerable face.

My grandfather was always available to people. Mostly, he helped senior 4
citizens apply for disability or pension benefits or file medical-insurance
claims. Several times, however, he was asked to placate siblings who had quar-
reled over a family inheritance. Many angry faces stormed into our home dissatisfied with what they had received, but they usually left smiling, convinced
by my grandfather that their parents had, after all, distributed their possessions fairly.

At times, he could even play Cupid by resolving disputes between couples 5
engaged to be married. Whether the problem concerned which family would
pay for the wedding or who would buy the furniture, he would find a solution.
As a result, our family attended many weddings in which my proud grandfather sat at the table of honor.

On Sundays, there was always a tray of fresh, homemade cookies and a pot 6
of coffee on our oversized kitchen table for visitors who stopped by after Mass.
Seeking advice about purchasing land or a house, they asked my grandfather if
he thought the price was fair, the property valuable, the land productive. After
a time, he took on the role of mediator, negotiating with a vengeance to obtain
the fairest deal for both buyer and seller.

I remember most vividly the hours we children spent listening to our 7
grandfather's stories. He sat by the fireplace in his wooden rocking chair and
told us about the time he had spent in America. Each one of us kids would aim

for the chair closest to him. We didn't want to miss anything he said. He told us about a huge tunnel, the Lincoln Tunnel, that was built under water. He also described the legendary Statue of Liberty. We were fascinated by his stories of that big, industrialized land called America.

As I grew up and became a teenager, I dreamt of immigrating to America   8
and seeing all the places that my grandfather had talked about. His exuberance about this land had a strong influence on my decision to come here.

A few months before I arrived in America my grandfather died. I still miss   9
him very much, but each time I visit a place that he knew I feel his presence close to me. The sound of his voice echoes in my mind.

Read More on the Web

University of Wisconsin site on parenting and grandparenting:
   http://www1.uwex.edu/topics/Parenting_and_grandparenting.cfm
Extensive annotated bibliography on the relationship between
   grandchildren and grandparents: http://www.nnfr.org/igen/
   stressc.html

Questions for Discussion

1. What important information does Cirilli give us in paragraph 1?
2. What is her thesis? Why does she wait until paragraph 2 to reveal it?
3. Pick out the topic sentences in paragraphs 3 through 7, and explain what each tells us about Cirilli's grandfather.
4. What evidence does the author give to show that her grandfather was "gentle?" How does she prove he was "understanding?"
5. What about the fact that Cirilli's grandfather scared her girlfriends? Why does the author give us this information?
6. Why is "Echoes" a good title for this essay?

Thinking Critically

1. Reread the three drafts of Cirilli's introduction, which appear earlier in this chapter (pages 61–63). Then, in your journal, write a paragraph that explains the major differences you see among the versions. Use the notes in the margins as guides, but write the paragraph in your own words. If you read carefully, you will find even more differences than those described in the margins.
2. Cirilli tells us that her grandmother's "face is a faded image in the back of [her] mind." Why did she put this line back into the third version after taking it out of the second (page 62)? Explain in two or three sentences why keeping this line is important to Cirilli's essay.

Suggestions for Journal Entries

1. Use focused freewriting to gather information that shows that someone you know practices a particular virtue. Like Cirilli's grandfather, your subject might be gentle or understanding. Then again, he or she might be charitable, hardworking, generous, or considerate of others. Reread paragraph 3 or 4 in "Echoes" to get an idea of the kind of details you might put in your journal. After completing your entry, read it carefully and add details if you can. Finally, write a sentence that expresses the main point you have made and that might serve as a topic sentence to a paragraph using this information.

2. Think of someone special in your life, and write down a wealth of details about this person. Use brainstorming, interviewing, or any other information-gathering techniques discussed in "Getting Started." Then, discuss this special person in three or four well-written sentences. Like the topic sentences in "Echoes," each of yours should focus on only one main point you want to make about your subject or about your relationship with this person.

Suggestions for Sustained Writing

1. Recall what you have read about writing central ideas at the beginning of this chapter: a central idea contains a subject and makes a point about that subject, a point that is focused and specific. Think about a subject you know a great deal about. Then write four or five sentences that express different points about that subject. Let's say your subject is Thanksgiving dinner. You might write the following central ideas:

Subject	Main Point
Thanksgiving dinner at my house	is always very noisy.
In my family, Thanksgiving dinner	means eating a lot and watching football.
Our Thanksgiving dinners	are not very traditional.
A typical Thanksgiving dinner	can kill a diet.
Preparing a Thanksgiving dinner	takes a lot of work.

    Next, use each of these sentences as the topic sentence for a different paragraph. When you write each paragraph, remember to include details that support or explain the paragraph's central idea as expressed in its topic sentence. Here's what one of the paragraphs you are going to write might look like:

Preparing a Thanksgiving dinner takes a lot of work.

First you'll have to prepare the stuffing. This means peeling and cutting up the apples, chopping up and soaking the bread, mixing in the raisins and the spices. After you're done, you'll have to stuff the turkey with this gooey mixture. While you're waiting for the bird to roast, you should peel, boil, and mash the potatoes, and cook any other vegetables you will serve. You'll also have to bake the biscuits, set the table, pour the cider, and put the finishing touches on the pumpkin and apple pies you spent three hours preparing the night before.

As you learned in "Getting Started," don't be satisfied with the first draft of your work; rewrite it several times. Then, correct spelling, grammar, punctuation, and other distracting problems.

2. If you haven't done so already, complete the Suggestion for a Journal Entry after "Four Paragraphs for Analysis." Use *each* of the topic sentences you were asked to write as the beginning of a paragraph in which you explain the main point you are making in that topic sentence. You should wind up with the rough drafts of four or five paragraphs, each of which is several sentences long.

   Rewrite these rough drafts until you are satisfied that your topic sentences are clear and that you have included enough information to help your readers understand the main point in each paragraph easily. Complete the writing process by editing your work just as student writer Deborah Diglio did with her paper in "Getting Started."

3. Have you ever lived under the tyranny of a government, organization, or person? If so, explain how this experience affected you in two or three ways. Like Siu Chan ("Suffering," page 70), begin your essay with an introductory paragraph that contains a thesis statement. Make sure that the two or three main points in this thesis statement express the effects that living under this oppression caused you. Then, make these main points the basis of the topic sentences you use in your essay's body paragraphs. Again, use Chan's essay as your model.

Begin by reviewing the notes you made in your journal after reading Chan's essay. They might provide you with materials with which you can get started. Then, do some more prewriting to gather even more information. Next, write a preliminary thesis statement, which might appear in your introductory paragraph. Also write a preliminary or working topic sentence for each of your essay's body paragraphs. Again, base each topic sentence on one of the main points stated in your thesis. Next, make a rough outline of your essay.

Write a rough draft and several revisions of your essay. Don't be afraid to revise your working thesis and topic sentences if you need to. End your essay with a conclusion, such as the one Chan used. Finally, edit and proofread the whole paper carefully.

4. In "Three Passions I Have Lived For," Bertrand Russell explains three deep, personal concerns that have "governed" his life. If you responded to item 2 in the Suggestions for Journal Entries following this essay, you have probably written a few topic sentences about the passions you or someone you know well lives for.

Use each of your topic sentences as the basis or beginning of a fully developed paragraph about each of these passions. Next, take the main points expressed in your topic sentences and combine them into a sentence that might serve as the thesis statement to an essay made up of the paragraphs you have just written.

Refer to Russell's essay as a model. Remember that his thesis statement mentions three passions: "the longing for love, the search for knowledge, and unbearable pity for the suffering of mankind." These three passions are used individually as the main points in each of the topic sentences of the paragraphs that follow and develop his thesis.

You should end up with the draft of an essay that contains a thesis statement followed by a few paragraphs, each of which develops one of the points mentioned in that thesis. Don't forget to revise and edit this draft.

5. If you answered the second of the journal-entry suggestions after Kofi Annan's "In Africa, AIDS Has a Woman's Face," you have probably listed information that describes the strengths or virtues of a woman who is or was the head of a household. Read over your notes, and add information to expand upon what you have already written. To gather more detail, you might even interview another person who also knows this woman well.

Next, turn your notes into a full length essay. Come up with a thesis that you can support with information from your notes. State this thesis in your first paragraph. Then, discuss each one of your subject's strengths or virtues— which you listed in your journal—in at least one paragraph of your essay.

When it comes time to write a concluding paragraph, consider restating your central idea in different words or summarizing what we can all learn—both men and women—from the person you have written about.

Write several drafts of your paper, adding detail and improving paragraph structure as you go along. As you revise, make sure that each body paragraph has a clear topic sentence that relates directly to your thesis. Finally, edit and proofread your work.

6. Write a short essay in which you explain three reasons that you are doing something important in your life. Include these three reasons in a central idea that you will use as your thesis statement. Let's say that you decide to explain three of your reasons for going to college. You might write: "I decided to attend Metropolitan College to prepare for a rewarding career, to meet interesting people, and to learn more about music and literature." Put this thesis somewhere in your introductory paragraph.

Next, use *each* of the reasons in your thesis as the main point in the topic sentences of the three paragraphs that follow. In keeping with the example on the previous page, you might use the following as topic sentences for paragraphs 2, 3, and 4. The main point in each topic sentence is in italics:

Paragraph 2: The most important reason I decided to attend Metropolitan College was *to prepare myself for a rewarding career.*

Paragraph 3: *The opportunity to meet interesting people* was another reason I thought that going to college would be a good idea.

Paragraph 4: My decision to continue my schooling also had a lot to do with my desire to *learn more about literature and music.*

Try to develop each of these in a paragraph of three or four sentences that will help you explain the main point of your topic sentence completely and effectively. Finally, as with other assignments in this chapter, revise and edit your work thoroughly.

7. In item 2 of the Suggestions for Journal Entries after Maria Cirilli's "Echoes," you were asked to write three or four sentences, each of which was to focus on a single aspect or characteristic of someone special in your life. Make each of these the topic sentence of a paragraph that describes or explains that aspect or characteristic. If necessary, reread "Echoes." Many of the paragraphs in the body of this essay will serve as models for your writing.

Next, write an appropriate thesis statement for an essay containing the three or four paragraphs you've just written. Make sure that your thesis statement somehow reflects the main points found in the topic sentences of the three or four paragraphs in your essay. Make this thesis part of your essay's first or introductory paragraph.

Again, approach this writing assignment as a process. Complete several drafts of your paper, and don't submit your final product until you are satisfied that you have dealt with problems in grammar, spelling, punctuation, and the like.

Writing to Learn: A Group Activity

THE FIRST MEETING

Meeting in a group of three or four classmates, reread Stephen Fox's paragraph, "The Example of Jackie Robinson" on page 67. Ask each member of the group to research a person, place, event, or thing that played an important role in the struggle to secure civil rights for African-Americans. Here are some examples.

Martin Luther King, Jr.'s "I Have a Dream" Speech

Rosa Parks

Medgar Evers

Malcolm X

Jesse Jackson

The Montgomery, Alabama, bus boycott

The U.S. Supreme Court's Brown v. the Board of Education decision

The 1965 Civil Rights Law

The Ku Klux Klan

RESEARCH

You can learn about the subject you choose by looking it up in a current encyclopedia or on the World Wide Web or by interviewing someone, such as a history, political science, law, or other professor, who knows a great deal about the civil rights movement.

Find out why your subject is important to the struggle for civil rights for African-Americans. After completing your research, summarize what you have learned in a paragraph of about 100 of your own words. A good way to start is with a topic sentence that explains your subject's importance to the civil rights movement. Then, fill your paragraph with details that prove, support, or explain that idea. Finally, in another, shorter paragraph, explain the steps you took to gather information.

THE SECOND MEETING

When you meet with your group again, give each member a copy of your paragraph. As you discuss each other's work, make suggestions that will help each student revise and edit his or her writing.

CHAPTER 2

Unity and Coherence

Chapter 1 explained the importance of focusing on a central idea. The central idea is also called the controlling idea. It controls, or determines, the kind of information a writer uses in an essay or paragraph.

Deciding how much information to include in a piece of writing has to do with development, a principle discussed in the next chapter. Deciding what kinds of information to include and making sure such information fits together logically relates to two principles of organization discussed in this chapter: unity and coherence.

Creating Unity

A piece of writing is unified if it contains only those details that help develop—explain or support—the central idea. You probably remember from Chapter 1 that a central idea contains both a subject and a main point the writer wishes to make about that subject. The following paragraph by Dorian Friedman describes the much discussed weather-maker El Niño. To maintain unity, the author has included only those details that support or explain the central idea, which he has put into the first sentence, the paragraph's topic sentence. Its subject is "the child"; its main point is "appears unusually cranky."

> It was South American fishermen who first dubbed [named] the December arrival of warm coastal currents "El Niño"—for the baby Christ—and this year, *the child appears unusually cranky.* Scientists tracking a mass of warm water building along the equatorial Pacific say it may signal the most pronounced El Niño of the century. The cyclical phenomenon—El Niño visits every two to seven years—occurs when trade winds and ocean currents change course for reasons still not understood. Already this year's system is scrambling climatic conditions worldwide, causing droughts in Asia and Brazil and torrential rains in Peru. Meanwhile, Californians are bracing [preparing] for rains and flooding this winter [1997–1998] that could match the 1982–83 El Niño.

Sometimes, beginning writers lose focus on the main point of a paragraph or essay, and they include irrelevant information—information that does not help explain or support the writer's central idea. Including such information sidetracks readers by drawing their attention to ideas that don't serve the writer's purpose. Make sure to check for unity when you revise your rough drafts.

Writing that lacks unity makes it difficult for readers to determine exactly what you are trying to say.

The following paragraph is based on one written by Geoffery Ward from a *National Geographic* article that commemorates the fiftieth anniversary of India's independence. However, it has been rewritten so that it now contains details unrelated to its central idea. The material was added to show that irrelevant details destroy the focus of a piece of writing.

> [1] Indian civilization has an astonishingly long history, and Delhi has witnessed a good deal of it. [2] There have been at least eight cities here in the past 3,000 years, beginning with Indraprastha, the capital mentioned in the Hindu epic [heroic poem], the *Mahabharata*. [3] Some scholars believe that if all the smaller settlements and fortifications and military outposts whose remnants are scattered across the landscape were taken into account, the actual number would be closer to 15. [4] Today, remnants of several old civilizations can also be found in Rome, Italy. [5] Monuments, ruins, and relics of the rich past are everywhere. [6] The high-rise office buildings that have gone up near Connaught Place in recent years cast their reflections into the green waters of a 14th-century steppe well. [7] In fact, as one of the world's fastest growing countries, India is experiencing a great deal of urban construction. [8] Traffic on one of New Delhi's busiest thoroughfares has to swerve around the masonry slab that marks a Muslim saint's grave. [9] Under the Independence Act of 1947 the Muslim state of Pakistan emerged as a separate country. [10] Even on the fairways on the New Delhi Golf Club . . . royal tombs offer unique hazards.

Ward establishes his focus in the first sentence. His subject is "Delhi"; his main point is that this city "has witnessed a good deal" of Indian civilization's "long history." This is what he sets out to prove. Therefore, each sentence and each detail that he includes should relate directly to that point. With the added information, however, that is not the case.

Sentence 1 the topic sentence, expresses the central idea.

Sentence 2 tells us about cities that existed on this site as far back as 3,000 years ago, so it helps explain the "long history" mentioned in the topic sentence.

Sentence 3 continues the idea begun in sentence 2, so it too is relevant to the topic sentence.

Sentence 4 makes an interesting comparison between Rome and Delhi. However, it does not help convince the reader that Delhi has witnessed a great deal of Indian history. It should be removed.

Sentence 5 mentions the city's "rich past." Therefore, it belongs in the paragraph.

Sentence 6 tells us about a 600-year-old well, another sign of Delhi's "long history." It too belongs.

Sentence 7 makes no reference to the past; it is entirely about the present. It is irrelevant and should be removed.

Sentence 8 is relevant; it explains that a modern highway has been designed in such a way as to preserve a historical site, in this case the grave of a Muslim saint.

Sentence 9 is irrelevant. It has nothing to do with Delhi, the paragraph's subject, or about the long history that the city has witnessed. It doesn't belong.

Sentence 10 is relevant to the topic sentence. The royal tombs are more evidence that Delhi has seen much of the country's history.

This analysis shows that details added to Ward's original paragraph are irrelevant. Compare the disunited version above with the correct version below.

Indian civilization has an astonishingly long history, and Delhi has witnessed a good deal of it. There have been at least eight cities here in the past 3,000 years; beginning with Indraprastha, the capital mentioned in the Hindu epic [heroic poem], the *Mahabharata*. Some scholars believe that if all the smaller settlements and fortifications and military outposts whose remnants are scattered across the landscape were taken into account, the actual number would be closer to 15. Monuments, ruins, and relics of the past are everywhere. The high-rise office buildings that have gone up near Connaught Place in recent years cast their reflections into the green waters of a 14th-century steppe well. Traffic on one of New Delhi's busiest thoroughfares has to swerve around the masonry slab that marks a Muslim saint's grave. Even on the fairways on the New Delhi Golf Club . . . royal tombs offer unique hazards.

Maintaining Coherence

The second principle important to organization is coherence. A paragraph is coherent if the sentences it contains are connected clearly and logically in a sequence (or order) that is easy to follow. An essay is coherent if the writer has made sure to create logical connections between paragraphs. The thought expressed in one sentence or paragraph should lead directly—without a break—to the thought in the following sentence or paragraph.

Logical connections between sentences and between paragraphs can be created in two ways: (1) by using transitional devices and (2) by making reference to words, ideas, and other details the writer has mentioned earlier.

USE TRANSITIONAL DEVICES

Transitional devices, also called *transitions* or *connectives,* are words, phrases, and even whole sentences that establish or show definite relationships in and between sentences and paragraphs. As seen in the following, transitional devices can be used for many different purposes.

To Indicate Time   You would be describing the passage of time if you wrote: "Henry left home just before dawn. *After a short while,* sunlight burst over the green hills." Other connectives that relate to time include:

After a few minutes	In the meantime
Afterward	Meanwhile
All the while	Now
Already	Prior to
As soon as	Right away
At that time	Soon
Back then	Still
Before	Subsequently
Before long	Suddenly
Before that time	Then
During	Thereafter
Immediately	Until
In a few minutes (hours, days, etc.)	When
In a while	While

To Indicate Similarities or Differences   You can also use transitions to show that things are similar or different: "Philip seems to be following in his sister's footsteps. *Like* her, he has decided to major in engineering. *Unlike* her, he doesn't do very well in math." Other transitions that indicate similarities and differences include:

Similarities	Differences
And	Although
As	But
As if	Even though
As though	However
In addition	In contrast
In the same way	Nevertheless
Like	Nonetheless
Likewise	On the other hand
Similarly	Still
	Though
	Unless
	Yet

To Introduce Examples, Repeat Information, or Emphasize a Point   You would be using a transition to introduce an example if you wrote: "Mozart displayed his genius early. *For example,* he composed his first symphony when he was only a boy."

You would be using a transition to repeat information if you wrote: "At the age of 21, Mozart was appointed court composer for the emperor of Austria. This event was *another* indication of how quickly the young man rose to fame."

You would be using a transition to emphasize a point if you wrote: "The end of Mozart's career was hardly as spectacular as its beginnings. *In fact,* he died in poverty at age 35."

Other transitional devices useful for these purposes include:

Introducing Examples	Repeating Information	Emphasizing a Point
As an example	Again	As a matter of fact
For instance	Once again	Indeed
Specifically	Once more	More important
Such as		To be sure

To Add Information   If you wanted to add information by using a transition, you might write: "When Ulysses S. Grant and Robert E. Lee met at Appomattox Courthouse in 1865, they brought the Civil War to an end. *What's more,* they opened a whole new chapter in U.S. political history." Here are some other connectives you will find useful when adding information:

Also	Furthermore
And	In addition
As well	Likewise
Besides	Moreover
Further	Too

To Show Cause and Effect   If you wanted to explain that an action or idea led to or was the cause of another, you could indicate this relationship by using a transitional device like *consequently,* the word that draws a connection between the two thoughts in these sentences: "During the early days of the Revolution, General George Washington was unable to defend New York City. *Consequently,* he was forced to retreat to Pennsylvania." Other transitional devices that show cause-effect relationships are:

As a result	So that
Because	Then
Hence	Therefore
Since	Thus

To Show Condition   If you need to explain that one action, idea, or fact depends on another, you might create a relationship based on condition by using words like *if,* as in these sentences: "Professor Jones should arrive in a few minutes. *If* she doesn't, we will have to go on without her." Some other transitions that show condition include:

As long as	In order to
As soon as	Provided that
Even if	Unless
In case	When

Make Reference to Material That Has Come Before

Two other effective ways to connect details and ideas in a sentence or paragraph with what you have discussed in earlier sentences or paragraphs are (1) to use pronouns to link details and ideas and (2) to restate important details and ideas.

Using Pronouns to Link Details and Ideas   A good way to make reference to material that has come before is to use *linking pronouns,* pronouns that point clearly and directly to specific names, ideas, or details you've mentioned earlier. Such pronouns direct the reader's attention to nouns in earlier sentences or paragraphs; these nouns are called *antecedents.* Relying on pronouns to maintain coherence also helps you avoid mentioning the same noun over and over, a habit that might make your writing repetitious.

The most important thing to remember about using linking pronouns is to make sure they refer directly and unmistakably to the nouns you want them to. In other words, all pronouns of reference should have antecedents that the reader will be able to identify easily and without question.

Read this paragraph, from the writings of Mother Teresa, the Roman Catholic nun who dedicated her life to the poor of Calcutta. Pronouns used to maintain coherence appear in italics:

> Here in Calcutta, we have a number of non-Christians and Christians *who* work together in the house of the dying and other places. There are also *some who* offer *their* care to the lepers. One day an Australian man came and made a substantial donation. But as *he* did *this he* said, "*This* is something external. Now I want to give something of *myself.*" *He* now comes regularly to the house of the dying to shave the sick men and to converse with *them. This* man gives not only *his* money but also *his* time. *He* could have spent it on *himself,* but what *he* wants is to give *himself.*

The paragraph above includes only a few of the pronouns you might want to use to make your writing more coherent. Here are others:

Personal Pronouns. These are pronouns that refer to people and things:

I (me, my, mine)	We (us, our, ours)
He, she, it (him, his; her, hers; its)	You (your, yours)
	They (them, their, theirs)

Relative Pronouns. These are pronouns that help describe nouns by connecting them with clauses (groups of words that contain nouns and verbs):

Who (whose, whom)	Whatever
That	Which
What	Whichever

Demonstrative Pronouns. These are pronouns that precede and stand for the nouns they refer to. Sentences like "*Those* are the best seats in the house" or "*That* is my book" make use of demonstrative pronouns. The most common demonstrative pronouns are:

This	These
That	Those

Indefinite Pronouns. These are pronouns used for general rather than specific reference. You can make good use of these pronouns as long as you are sure the reader can identify their antecedents easily. For instance: "Both Sylvia and Andrew were released from the hospital. *Neither* was seriously injured." In this case, the antecedents of *neither* are Sylvia and Andrew. Here are other indefinite pronouns:

All	Either	Nobody	Several
Another	Everybody	None	Some
Both	Everyone	No one	Someone
Each	Neither	Others	

Restating Important Details and Ideas   The second way to make reference to material that has come before is to restate important details and ideas by repeating words and phrases or by using easily recognizable *synonyms,* terms that have the same (or nearly the same) meaning as those words or phrases.

The following paragraph is from a pamphlet by Shen C. Y. Fu, who was curator of Chinese Art for the Freer Gallery of the Smithsonian Institute in Washington, DC. Fu uses the word *calligraphy* four times, but for the sake of variety he also uses recognizable synonyms (italics added):

> *Calligraphy* is generally defined as beautiful *writing*. In the West the *term* applies to *decorative writing* or may simply mean *good penmanship*. In China, however, *calligraphy* is regarded as the ultimate artistic expression, requiring years of training, discipline, and dedication before mastery can be achieved. Like music and dance, *calligraphy* is an art of performance. But unlike music and dance, each performance of *calligraphy* results in a tangible [material] creation that both captures the artist's technical skills at the time and provides concrete evidence of his or her immediate mood and innate [inborn] personality.

Visualizing Unity and Coherence

The following paragraph is from Rudy Chelminsky's "The Curse of Dracula," an essay published in *Smithsonian* magazine in 2003. Notes in the margins explain how the paragraph is unified. Shaded words and phrases show how the writer maintained coherence.

Sheds light on central idea and introduces it.

Over the past year and a half, a furious controversy surrounding a proposal [to build a Dracula theme park] has focused attention on an area so obscure that many people today still assume it's fictitious:

States central idea in a topic sentence.

Transylvania. But located high within the curling grip of the rugged Carpathian Mountains in central Romania, Transylvania is as real as real can be—rich in mineral resources, blessed with fertile soil and filled with picturesque scenery.

Definition adds information relating to topic sentence.

Adds information to show this place "is as real as real can be."

Although its name means "land beyond the forest," this historical province of more than seven million souls was not known as a particularly spooky place until 1897, when the Irish writer and critic Bram Stoker published his sensational gothic novel *Dracula*.

Explains why the "real" Transylvania became known as "spooky"

"Backdrop" (setting) connects with description of Transylvania in topic sentence.

Casting about for a suitable backdrop for his eerie yarn about a nobleman who happened to be a bloodsucking vampire, Stoker hit upon Transylvania, which he described as "one of the wildest and least known portions of Europe."

Another reference to natural environment of Transylvania, as mentioned in topic sentence.

Revising to Improve Unity and Coherence

Read the following sets of paragraphs, which are taken from the rough draft and the final draft of "Oma," an essay written by student Maria Scamacca. The final draft appears in its entirety later in this chapter. Pay particular attention to the notes in the margins. They explain how the essay was revised to improve unity and coherence.

Maria Scamacca—Rough Draft

Paragraphs 1–3

Use a transitional expression to explain when this meeting occurred?

Oma looked about eighty-years old, a bit over-weight, and slightly hunched over. She wore a flowered house dress, a starched white apron, and old, scuffed leather loafers. Oma was deaf in one ear from a neglected childhood ear infection. Symptoms of Bell's palsy were present. She shuffled her feet and held on to the

Add transition and combine sentences for smoothness?

furniture with swollen, scarred hands as she walked. She lived alone. The house looked neat, but there were small crumbs and stains on the tables, and

Add transition to bridge paragraphs

particles of old food were stuck to some of the dishes.

    She led me to a back door to a garden that she boasted of planting and maintaining alone. It was like no garden I had ever seen, an acre of food and beauty. I sensed immediately that this paradise was the creation of a unique energy, courage and beauty I

OK, but include information to prove this idea?

Paragraph unified? This information belongs elsewhere, for it does not relate to garden.

came to see in Oma. She had married a widower with a young daughter; the couple eventually had three other children. They lived on a farm near the Rumanian border on which they grew and raised all their food, even the grapes from which they made their own wine.

Combine with material about the garden in preceding paragraph?

    Ready to be picked in the garden were neat and orderly rows of potatoes, carrots, asparagus, onion, peppers, lettuce, lima beans, and string beans as well

Add a transition?

as many other vegetables I had never heard of.　*Vagne? Remove?*

There were fruits and flowers were everywhere.　*Provide examples of fruits and flowers?*

Paragraphs 7–10

Add transition for smoothness?

Farm life was hard. Oma took it well. She cooked and kept house. The horses and other farm animals had to be looked after. She baked bread, made sausage, and salted the meats the family would eat year round.

Combine with preceding paragraph?

Oma is fond of telling me how she force-fed geese by stuffing balls of bread down their long necks with her fingers. Her geese got so fat they couldn't fly, but they brought the best prices at the market, she often reminds me.

Add transitions and combine sentence for smoothness?

Her family raised their own pigs. Her husband, Opa, asked his neighbor to slaughter the animals. Opa slaughtered the neighbor's pigs. "He felt bad, you know, killing his own pig," Oma said. Oma and Opa hired outside help, whom they paid with bread and salted meat. They did most of the work themselves, and they prospered.

Seems contradictary. Use transition make clearer?

Add transition to bridge paragraphs? Strengthen coherence between sentences?

The war came. The horses were stolen by Russian soldiers. The family was removed from their farm, and Oma found herself in a Russian concentration camp. The stories are confusing. I have heard bits and pieces repeatedly over the past six years, and I have had to reconstruct them myself. Once in a while I ask Oma to clarify the order of

Which stories? When did they take place?

events, but she doesn't get very far until she starts an entirely new story.

Maria Scamacca—Final Draft

Paragraphs 1–2

Adds transition to explain when this meeting occurred.

When I first met Oma six years ago, she looked about eighty-years old, was a few pounds over-weight for her medium frame, and was slightly hunched over. She wore a flowered house dress, a starched white apron, and old, scuffed leather loafers. She was deaf in one ear from a neglected childhood ear infection, and half of her face drooped from Bell's palsy. She shuffled her feet and held on to the furniture with swollen, scarred hands as she walked. Despite Oma's

Adds transition and combines sentences for smoothness.

disability and the fact that she lived alone, her house looked neat, but there were small crumbs and stains on the tables, and particles of old food were stuck to some of the dishes, unnoticed by eyes weakened with age.

Adds transition to bridge paragraphs.

That's why I was shocked when she led me to a back door to a garden that she boasted of planting and maintaining alone. It was like no garden I had ever seen, an acre of food and beauty. Ready to be picked in the garden were neat and orderly rows of potatoes, carrots, asparagus, onion, peppers, lettuce, lima beans, and string beans. Her garden also boasted strawberries, blueberries, gooseberries, currant, peaches, watermelons and many other

Rewrites entire paragraph to ensure unity.

Adds information needed to support last sentence in paragraph.

Adds a transition.

fruits. And there were flowers everywhere: zinnias, day lilies, marigolds, irises, and petunias. I sensed immediately that this paradise was the creation of a unique energy, courage and beauty I came to see in Oma.

Paragraphs 7–9

Adds transitions for smoothness.

Farm life was hard. However, Oma took it well. In addition to cooking and housekeeping, she had to tend the horses and other farm animals, bake bread, make sausage, and salt the meats the family would

Combines two paragraphs into one.

eat year round. Oma is fond of telling me how she force-fed geese by stuffing balls of bread down their long necks with her fingers. Her geese got so fat they couldn't fly, but they brought the best prices at the market, she often reminds me.

Adds transitions and information for smoothness.

Her family also raised their own pigs. But when it came time to slaughter the animals, her husband, Opa, asked his neighbor to do it. In return, Opa slaughtered the neighbor's pigs. "He felt bad, you know, killing his own pig," Oma said. At times, Oma and Opa hired outside help, whom they paid with bread and salted meat. However, they did most of the work themselves, and they prospered.

Adds transitions to clarify ideas.

Adds transitions to bridge paragraphs and to strengthen coherence between sentences

Then he war came. First the horses were stolen by Russian soldiers. Then the family was removed from their farm, and Oma found herself in a Russian concentration camp. The stories from this period of her life are confusing. I have heard bits and

Adds detail; explains when these stories took place.

pieces repeatedly over the past six years, and I have

had to reconstruct them myself. Once in a while I ask

Oma to clarify the order of events, but she doesn't get

very far until she starts an entirely new story.

Practicing Unity and Coherence

Read this paragraph—written by Stacy Zolnowski for a first-year writing class—to learn more about paragraph unity. Then, using complete sentences, answer the questions that follow in the spaces provided:

> [1] Throughout history, left-handedness has been deemed a nasty habit, a social infraction, a symptom of neurosis, or even a sign of mental retardation. [2] More recently, however, its social, educational, and psychological implications have acquired a more enlightened appreciation. [3] Nonetheless, left-handers continue to be discriminated against in an environment that conforms to the needs and prejudices of a right-handed society. ("The Left-Handed Minority")

1. Assume that the paragraph's topic sentence is the third sentence. What, in your own words, is the paragraph's central idea?

   _____

   _____

   _____

   _____

2. How do sentences 1 and 2 relate to the central idea?

   _____

   _____

   _____

3. What transitional devices does the writer use to maintain coherence?

   _____

   _____

   _____

4. In what other ways does the writer maintain coherence?

_____

_____

_____

This chapter has introduced you to two important principles of organization: unity and coherence. A paragraph or essay is *unified* if all its ideas and details relate to and contribute to the central idea. A paragraph or essay is *coherent* if the reader can move from sentence to sentence and paragraph to paragraph easily because the writer has connected the ideas logically.

Look for signs of unity and coherence as you read the following selections. More important, apply these principles in your own writing as you respond to the Suggestions for Journal Entries and the Suggestions for Sustained Writing.

I Don't Know What God Wants. . . .

Bay Fang

Bay Fang is a correspondent for US News and World Report, *where this essay appeared in April 2002. It tells of the devastation suffered by the people of Afghanistan because of civil war, drought, and earthquake.*

Preparing to Read

1. Judging from the title, what might be the central idea in this short essay?
2. Pay special attention to the way in which the author opens and closes this essay.
3. The Taliban, a group of extremist Islamic militants, controlled Afghanistan for about 10 years until the Northern Alliance, aided by US forces, toppled their repressive regime.

Vocabulary

parched (verb)   Dried, dehydrated
refrain (noun)   Verse of a poem or song that is repeated.

I Don't Know What God Wants. . . .

Bay Fang

NAHRIN, AFGHANISTAN—Shaima rocks on her heels amid mounds of mud- 1 brick rubble and wails a low, mournful refrain. "Oh, my children. Oh, my children." She will not leave this particular pile of earth because this, at least, is hers. And after an earthquake hit her village Monday night, killed four of her children, and flattened her home, this is all she has left. "I don't know what God wants anymore," she says.

For the residents of Nahrin, their God must seem very far away right now. 2 This town in northern Afghanistan, once a front line of fighting between the Northern Alliance and the Taliban, has weathered more than its share of hardships. For the past five years, the men of the village lived mostly in the mountains to fight or flee the Taliban. For the past three years, the land has been parched by drought. And now an earthquake, which killed an estimated 800 people and left about 100,000 homeless in dozens of area villages.

It is night, and by the light of a full moon an aid worker reads out names, 3 one by one. Villagers wait patiently for their names to be called and then load up their donkeys to take their goods back home, wherever home is. And still Shaima sits. "Oh, my children," she cries. "If they gave me Afghanistan I would not want it now, for I have lost my sons. I have lost everything."

More on the Web

Bay Fang's wartime diary of her time with the Northern Alliance troops as they fought against the Taliban: http://www.usnews.com/usnews/news/terror/articles/frontline011114.htm.

Library of Congress Country Studies on Afghanistan: http://lcweb2.loc.gov/frd/cs/aftoc.html

Times Educational Supplement on Afghanistan: http://www.tes.co.uk/afghanistan/appeal_news_afghanistan.asp?id=12550

Questions for Discussion

1. In your own words, explain the essay's central idea? Is it stated or implied?
2. What use of repetition does the author make to maintain coherence?
3. Identify the transition that connects paragraphs 1 and 2.
4. Find the transitional devices used to maintain coherence within paragraphs.
5. What is the topic sentence in paragraph 3? How does this paragraph help develop the essay's thesis?

Thinking Critically

1. What similarities do you find between the first and third paragraphs? Why did the author include these similarities?
2. Over 800 people died in the earthquake, while thousands more were made homeless. Why does the author choose to focus on only one? Why does she not list the losses that many of the others experienced?

Suggestions for Journal Entries

1. Review what you learned about summarizing in Getting Started: Becoming an Active College Reader (pages 40–43). Then, summarize "I Don't Know What God Wants . . ." into one paragraph.
2. Jump ahead to Chapter 4 and read Elie Wiesel's "A Prayer for the Days of Awe." (page 179). Make notes in the margins of the text as you learned how to do in Getting Started: Becoming an Active Reader" (pages 33–36). Then use these notes as you write a one-paragraph summary of that essay.

Writing and Its Rewards

Richard Marius

Richard Marius directed the expository writing program at Harvard University. He began his career as a historian and has authored biographies of Thomas More and Martin Luther. He also wrote four novels and several books on writing, including The McGraw-Hill College Handbook, *which he co-authored with Harvey Wiener. "Writing and Its Rewards" is from* A Writer's Companion, *Marius's splendid guide for both experienced and developing writers. Richard Marius died in 1999.*

Preparing to Read

1. Writing is a process of drafting and revising, Marius tells us. As you probably learned in "Getting Started," *drafting* means putting down facts and ideas in rough form, no matter how disorganized your paragraph or essay might seem at first. *Revising* involves rewriting, reorganizing, adding to, deleting from, and correcting earlier drafts to make them more effective and easier to read.

2. In paragraph 5, Marius mentions three writers whose work you may want to read: Geoffrey Chaucer, Leo Tolstoy, and W.H. Auden. To learn more about them, look up their names in an encyclopedia or reference book recommended by your college librarian.

Vocabulary

eighteenth century (adjective and noun)	The 1700s.
embodied (adjective)	Contained.
enduring (adjective)	Lasting.
lexicographer (noun)	Writer of a dictionary.
parable (noun)	Story with a lesson or moral.
profound (adjective)	Deep, extreme.
weighing (adjective)	Carefully considering.

Writing and Its Rewards

Richard Marius

WRITING IS hard work, and although it may become easier with practice it 1 is seldom easy. Most of us have to write and rewrite to write anything well. We try to write well so people will read our work. Readers nowadays will seldom struggle to understand difficult writing unless someone—a teacher perhaps—forces them to do so. Samuel Johnson, the great eighteenth-century

English writer, conversationalist, and lexicographer, said, "What is written without effort is in general read without pleasure." Today what is written without effort is seldom read at all.

Writing takes time—lots of time. Good writers do not dash off a piece in an hour and get on to other things. They do not wait until the night before a deadline to begin to write. Instead they plan. They write a first draft. They revise it. They may then think through that second draft and write it once again. Even small writing tasks may require enormous investments of time. If you want to become a writer, you must be serious about the job, willing to spend hours dedicated to your work.

Most writers require some kind of solitude. That does not mean the extreme of the cork-lined room where the great French writer Marcel Proust composed his huge works in profound silence. It does mean mental isolation—shutting yourself off from the distractions around you even if you happen to be pounding a computer keyboard in a noisy newspaper office. You choose to write rather than do other things, and you must concentrate on what you are doing.

In a busy world like ours, we take a risk when we isolate ourselves and give up other pursuits to write. We don't know how our writing will come out. All writers fail sometimes. Successful writers pick themselves up after failure and try again. As you write, you must read your work again and again, thinking of your purpose, weighing your words, testing your organization, examining your evidence, checking for clarity. You must pay attention to the thousands and thousands of details embodied in words and experience. You must trust your intuitions; if something does not sound right, do it again. And again. And again.

Finally you present your work to readers as the best you can do. After you submit a final draft, it is too late to make excuses, and you should not do so. Not everybody will like your final version. You may feel insecure about it even when you have done your best. You may like your work at first and hate it later. Writers wobble back and forth in their judgments. Chaucer, Tolstoy and Auden are all on record for rejecting some of their works others have found enduring and grand. Writing is a parable of life itself.

Read More on the Web

University of British Columbia's Writer's Workshop: http://www.cstudies.ubc.ca/wc/workshop/tools/unity.htm

Troy State University Writing Center: http://www.troyst.edu/writingcenter/handouts/unity_support_and_coherence.html

Wheaton College Writing Center: http://www.wheaton.edu/learnres/writectr/Resources/coherence.htm

Questions for Discussion

1. Reread Marius's introduction. What is his thesis? What is the main point in this thesis?

2. This essay is unified because each paragraph clearly develops the essay's central idea (thesis). Explain how each topic sentence in paragraphs 2, 3, and 4 relates to Marius's thesis.

3. Reread paragraphs 2 and 3. Which techniques does Marius use to maintain coherence?

4. Reread paragraph 4. Which words and phrases are used to repeat ideas and, thus, to maintain coherence?

5. What does Marius mean by writing "is a parable of life itself" (paragraph 5)? Why is this conclusion effective?

Thinking Critically

One assumption Marius makes is that all educated people need to be competent writers. Is that true of you? Will you need strong writing skills for the job you take after college? Contact someone practicing in that field or profession. Ask her or him about the need for good writing skills. Then write a short report of your interview.

Suggestions for Journal Entries

1. Marius says "Most writers require some kind of solitude." Do you? Use your journal to describe the place in which you write or study most often. Is it comfortable? Can you concentrate there? Should you find another place to work?

2. "Writing and Its Rewards" contains advice to make us better writers. Use your journal to list three or more specific pieces of advice to help you or a classmate become better at an important activity you know a lot about. Here are examples of such an activity: studying or doing homework; dressing for school or work; driving in heavy traffic or bad weather; communicating with parents, children, teachers, or classmates; maintaining a car; losing weight; sticking to a nutritious diet; or treating members of a different race, age group, religion, or sex with respect.

    Express each piece of advice in a complete sentence, the kind that can serve as the topic sentence to a paragraph you might write later on to explain that piece of advice more fully.

Study Calculus!

William J. Bennett

Secretary of Education and Chairman of the National Endowment for the Humanities in the Reagan administration, William J. Bennett holds a doctorate in political philosophy from the University of Texas and a law degree from Harvard University. Under the first President Bush, Bennett directed the war on drugs as head of the Office of National Drug Control Policy. This essay, which reveals much about Bennett's thinking when he was secretary of education, is taken from The De-Valuing of America: The Fight for Our Children. *Bennett is also the author of the best-selling* Book of Virtues: A Treasury of Great Moral Stories *as well as several other books.*

Preparing to Read

1. Bennett maintains coherence in and between paragraphs well. Look for linking pronouns and other connective words and phrases as you read his essay.

2. In paragraph 2, Bennett reports that some of Escalante's colleagues claimed "his plan to teach calculus was a quixotic fantasy." The word *quixotic* is taken from the name of the title character of Miguel de Cervantes's seventeenth-century Spanish novel *Don Quixote.* Although admirable in many respects, Cervantes's hero was a dreamer who often got himself into trouble by attempting the impossible. Therefore, the term *quixotic* has come to mean "foolish," "silly," or "totally impractical."

3. The essay ends with several one-sentence paragraphs. Although not often found in formal writing, such paragraphs are useful here because they convey dialogue, conversation between two or more people.

4. The title of this essay provides a strong hint about its thesis. Why was "Calculus" and not "math" or "arithmatic" used?

Vocabulary

calculus (noun)	A branch of mathematics important to science, engineering, and other disciplines.
canard (noun)	False belief, principle, rule, or story.
ethic (noun)	Principle, belief in.
pedagogy (noun)	Education, schooling, teaching.
skepticism (noun)	Doubt, distrust, disbelief.

Study Calculus!

William J. Bennett

PRINCIPAL HENRY Gradillas at Garfield High School in East Los Angeles let   1
Jaime Escalante teach. And did the students ever learn. Escalante, a Bolivian
immigrant, arrived at the school in 1974 to teach math. Now perhaps America's most famous teacher, he wanted to return something to the country that
had taken him in and given him opportunity.

His plan to teach calculus to disadvantaged Hispanic youngsters was   2
greeted with skepticism and laughter by his colleagues, and he encountered resistance from his students. But he told me that the greatest resistance came not
from the students but from others in the profession, other teachers and counselors who urged him not to push so hard. They told him that his plan to teach
calculus was a quixotic fantasy. "If you try," some told him, "the students will
fail. They can't do it. They will be embarrassed, and their self-esteem will suffer. What you want to do—teach calculus—will be dangerous."

Escalante told me what he told his critics: "If you are fifteen or sixteen years   3
old, in the barrio of East Los Angeles, there are a lot of things that are dangerous. But calculus isn't one of them." His principal, Henry Gradillas, encouraged
him to proceed.

Escalante persisted, and in 1982 eighteen of his students took the Ad-   4
vanced Placement (AP) calculus test. By 1991, 160 students from Garfield took
the test. According to Jay Mathews, author of *Escalante: The Best Teacher in
America,* Escalante has given Garfield the most successful inner-city mathematics program in the United States. In recent years only four or five secondary
schools in the country have prepared more students for the AP calculus examination (tests so difficult that fewer than 2 percent of American students even
attempt them). Because of Escalante's efforts, about a fourth of all the Mexican-
American students in the country who pass AP calculus come from Garfield.

Escalante's methods and approach (celebrated in the movie *Stand and De-*   5
liver) are in marked contrast to the theory and practice of pedagogy as taught
in most American schools of education. He consistently violates the canard that
a teacher shouldn't "impose his values on students." Indeed, he seeks every opportunity to impose his ethic of achievement, success, and hard work on them.
His reason, as expressed to me, is simple: "My values are better than theirs." His
way of doing this is direct, manly, no nonsense. In the early days of his career
at Garfield, he asked a student whether he wanted to study calculus. "No," said
the student, "I want to see my girlfriend."

"Well, then," responded Escalante, "go over to woodworking class on your   6
way out."

"Why," the student asked.   7

"So you can learn how to make shoeshine boxes so you can have a career   8
shining the shoes for Anglos as they pass through Los Angeles International Airport on their business trips."

"I don't want to shine Anglos' shoes," protested the student.   9

"Then study calculus," was Escalante's reply.   10

Read More on the Web

Website of the Bolivia Hall of Fame containing more information on
  Escalante: http://www.boliviaweb.com/hallfame/escalante.htm

The Math Forum at Drexel University: http://mathforum.org/library/
  drmath/drmath.college.html

Questions for Discussion

1. What is the essay's thesis?
2. What is the topic sentence in paragraph 4? Explain how each of the
   sentences it contains relates to or develops that topic sentence.
3. What does the dialogue in paragraphs 6–10 contribute to the essay?
4. Why didn't Bennett combine paragraphs 6–10 into one paragraph?
5. Explain how Bennett uses linking pronouns to maintain coherence in
   paragraph 2.
6. Find two transitional words or phrases in paragraph 1. Find at least
   three more in the rest of the essay.
7. What use does Bennett make of repetition to maintain coherence
   within paragraphs?

Thinking Critically

1. Do you agree with the way in which Escalante challenged his
   students? Think of another way that you might motivate students to
   study a difficult subject if you were a teacher. Explain this in a
   paragraph or two.
2. What kind of values is Escalante talking about in paragraph 5?
   Should teachers be allowed to impose other values—social, political,
   or moral, for example—on students? On a separate sheet of paper list
   the advantages and disadvantages of allowing them to do so.
3. Why do you think some teachers had a low opinion of the abilities of
   students whom Escalante helped? What connection, if any, is there
   between a teacher's attitude and student success?

Suggestions for Journal Entries

1. Use clustering or listing to come up with several characteristics or qualities of a good teacher. You might begin by thinking about the best teacher or teachers you have had. Consider those qualities that caused you to admire them or that made them effective instructors. For example you might write that:

    Ms. Jones challenged students.

    Mr. Mendoza graded homework and tests carefully.

    Dr. Patel inspired confidence in you.

    Ms. Fernandez made geometry interesting and easy to understand.

    By the way, you don't need to limit yourself to teachers you have had in school. Family members, employers, neighbors, coaches, and members of the clergy often teach us a lot as well.

2. Freewrite for about 10 minutes to gather information about the teacher who has influenced you most. Again, don't limit yourself to teachers you have had in school.

Oma: Portrait of a Heroine

Maria Scamacca

Maria Scamacca graduated from college with a degree in nursing and is now a critical-care registered nurse at a large hospital. "Oma: Portrait of a Heroine" was written in a freshman composition class in response to an assignment that asked students to describe people they found inspiring. After reading Scamacca's essay, it is easy to understand why she chose to write about Oma.

Preparing to Read

1. *Oma* means grandmother in German, *Opa* means grandfather.
2. Scamacca's essay provides several examples of tools useful for maintaining coherence. Look for transitions between paragraphs and within sentences in this essay and try to use such devices in your own writing.
3. Scamacca mentions events from twentieth-century history. During World War II (1939–1945), the Germans conquered much of eastern Europe but were pushed back by the Soviets. At the war's end, Hungary, Romania, East Germany, and other eastern nations became Soviet satellites. In the Korean War (1950–1953), American troops formed the bulk of a United Nations force that defended South Korea from communist North Korea and China.

Vocabulary

black market (noun)	Underground commercial system in which banned or stolen goods are sold or traded.
compensation (noun)	Payment.
displaced (adjective)	Forced to move.
equivalent (noun)	The equal of.
humane (adjective)	Kind, charitable, benevolent.
implores (verb)	Begs.
palsy (noun)	Paralysis.
provisions (noun)	Necessities, supplies.

Oma: Portrait of a Heroine

Maria Scamacca

WHEN I FIRST met Oma six years ago, she looked about eighty years old, was 1
a few pounds over-weight for her medium frame, and was slightly
hunched over. She wore a flowered house dress, a starched white apron, and
old, scuffed leather loafers. Oma was deaf in one ear from a neglected childhood ear infection, and half of her face drooped from Bell's palsy. She shuffled
her feet and held on to the furniture with swollen, scarred hands as she walked.
Despite Oma's disability and the fact that she lived alone, her house looked
neat, but there were small crumbs and stains on the tables, and particles of food
were stuck to some of the dishes, unnoticed by eyes weakened with age.

That's why I was shocked when she led me through the back door to a gar- 2
den that she boasted of planting and maintaining alone. It was like no garden
I had ever seen, an acre of food and beauty. Ready to be picked and eaten were
neat and orderly rows of potatoes, carrots, asparagus, onions, peppers, lettuce,
lima beans, and string beans. Her garden also boasted strawberries, blueberries,
gooseberries, currant, peaches, watermelons, and many other fruits. And there
were flowers everywhere: zinnias, day lilies, marigolds, irises, and petunias. I
sensed immediately that this paradise was the creation of a unique energy,
courage, and beauty I came to see in Oma.

Each year the impossible garden yields bushels of fruits and berries for the 3
jams and jellies that Oma cooks and jars herself. She also cans fruit and vegetables, and she uses the fruit in the fillings of luscious pastries that, as I was to
learn, have made her famous among friends, family, and neighbors. She still
does all of her own cooking and had been known, until only recently, to throw
holiday dinners for more than twenty people.

From the day I met Oma, I grew to admire her and have looked forward 4
to visiting. Almost every Sunday after church, my husband's family and I gather
around her dining room table for fresh coffee, homemade Prinz Regent Torte (a
seven-layer cake), Schwarzwälder Kirschtorte (Black Forest cherry cake), warm
cookies, and good talk.

Oma dominates the conversation, filling us with stories of her childhood 5
and of World War II; she hardly stops to take a breath unless one of us asks a
question or implores her to translate the frequent German or Hungarian
phrases that pop out of her mouth. At such times, we play guessing games as
Oma tries to explain in broken English a word or expression for which she
knows no English equivalent.

Oma was born in Hungary. She was an only child—rare in the early days 6
of this century—the only surviving baby of four pregnancies. Her mother died
when Oma was in her teens, and she was left alone to keep house for her father. At eighteen, she married a widower with a young daughter; the couple

eventually had three other children. They lived on a farm near the Romanian border on which they grew and raised all their food, even the grapes from which they made their own wine.

Farm life was hard. However, Oma took to it well. In addition to cooking   7
and housekeeping, she had to tend to the horses and other farm animals, bake bread, make sausage, and salt the meats the family would eat year round. Oma is fond of telling me how she force-fed geese by stuffing balls of bread down their long necks with her fingers. Her geese got so fat they couldn't fly, but they brought the best prices at the market, she often reminds me.

Her family also raised their own pigs. But when it came time to slaughter   8
the animals, her husband, Opa, asked his neighbor to do it. In return, Opa slaughtered the neighbor's pigs. "He felt bad, you know, killing his own pig," Oma said. At times, Oma and Opa hired outside help, whom they paid with bread and salted meat. However, they did most of the work themselves, and they prospered.

Then the war came. First her horses were stolen by Russian soldiers. Then   9
the family was removed from their farm, and Oma found herself in a Russian concentration camp. The stories from this period of her life are confusing. I have heard bits and pieces of them repeatedly over the past six years, and I have had to reconstruct them myself. Once in a while I ask Oma to clarify the order of events, but she doesn't get very far until she starts an entirely new story.

After the war, the borders of countries were redrawn, and Oma's family   10
was displaced with only a few hours' notice. Allowed to take only the clothes on their backs and whatever they could carry, they were put into a cattle car on a long freight train. The new government provided no compensation for their land and told them to leave all of their possessions behind. The only explanation was that their family had originally come from Germany and that they were required to leave Hungary and return to the land of their ancestors. This was not punishment, the authorities explained; it was "humane displacement."

Before they boarded the train, the family had to collect enough grain and   11
other provisions to feed themselves during the long trip. But they saw little of their food; Oma thinks it was stolen and sold on the black market. "There were no bathrooms on the train," Oma explained. "If someone had to defecate or urinate, they were held by others out of the open doors over the side of the moving train. And they call that humane!"

When they arrived in Germany, Oma and her family were placed in a room   12
in a run-down building that had holes in the walls and was full of rats. Her husband developed pneumonia. Sick for months, he almost lost the will to live and just lay in bed. When he finally recovered, they moved to America, but they had to leave their daughter behind because she had tuberculosis. Oma still weeps openly whenever she recalls being forced to abandon her child. Luckily, however, things turned out well for "Tante Vicki," who still lives in Germany and now has a family of her own.

In time, the family settled in Millstone, New Jersey, and began to build a 13 new life in what was then a small rural community. In the early 1950s, however, Oma and Opa lost their oldest son in the Korean War, so when the other two boys married and moved out of the house, the two old people were on their own.

Several years ago, Opa died of lung cancer contracted from many years of 14 working in an asbestos factory. Oma continues to receive a good pension and health benefits from his employer. They come in handy, for over the past few years she has been hospitalized several times. Last summer she got so sick she couldn't even plant her garden, so all of her grandchildren got together to plant it for her. That is the only request she has ever made of them.

It is hard to see a woman who was once so strong grow old and weak. At 15 times, Oma feels quite useless, but she can still tell wonderful stories, and we listen avidly. I wonder if there will be a garden this year.

Read More on the Web

Holocaust Learning Center site with links to other information:
http://www.ushmm.org/wlc/article.jsp?ModuleId=10005186
Library of Congress country study site on Hungary:
http://memory.loc.gov/frd/cs/hutoc.html

Questions for Discussion

1. Where in this essay does Scammaca state her central idea? In other words, what is her thesis?
2. Where does the topic sentence in paragraph 2 appear? Identify the topic sentence in at least one other paragraph.
3. The central idea in paragraph 6 is implied. State it in your own words.
4. Is this essay well unified? If so, explain how paragraphs 4 and 5 support Scammaca's thesis.
5. Pick out devices that create coherence between paragraphs 1 and 2; 2 and 3; 3 and 4; 7 and 8; 8 and 9; 9 and 10; 10 and 11; 11 and 12; 12 and 13; and 13 and 14.
6. Reread paragraphs 9 through 12. Circle transitions and other elements the author uses to maintain coherence.

Thinking Critically

1. If you were able to meet Oma, what would you ask her about her life? As you reread this essay, write questions to her in the margins of the text when they occur to you. Then do some creative guessing. On

the basis of what you know about Oma, answer your questions in a paragraph or two.

2. Reread Maria Cirilli's "Echoes" in Chapter 1. In what ways is this essay similar to Scamacca's? In what ways are these essays different?

3. Pretend that the government has decided to take almost everything you own and send you to another country. Would you resist? If so, how? If not, how would you prepare for this drastic change? Put your answer in two or three paragraphs that are unified and coherent. Make sure to include transitions between paragraphs as well.

Suggestions for Journal Entries

1. Do you have an older relative, friend, or neighbor whose attitude toward life you consider heroic? Choose your own definition of the word *heroic*. Freewrite for about five minutes about an event from this person's life that might show his or her heroism.

2. Interview the person mentioned above. Try to find out more about his or her attitude toward life. A good way to do this is to ask your subject to tell you about a difficult or depressing time and to explain how he or she dealt with it.

3. Brainstorm with one or two others who know the person mentioned above. Try to gather facts, direct quotations, and opinions that you could use in a paper that describes your subject as heroic.

Suggestions for Sustained Writing

1. Review the journal entries you made after reading "I Don't Know What God Wants. . . ." If you haven't responded to both of the Suggestions for Journal Entries after this essay, do so now.

   Now, write a 75 to 100-word paragraph in which you point out the similarities between Fang's "I Don't Know What God Wants . . ." and Wiesel's "Prayer for the Days of Awe." Focus on the situations they are describing and on the questions they ask about the nature of God. Do both give an answer to these questions?

   Next, write a paragraph in which you discuss an incident that tested your own faith in God. How did this incident turn out? Did your faith become weaker or stronger? Did your idea of God change? Did you stop believing in God altogether? In the case of both paragraphs, make sure that the details they contain relate directly to their topic sentences. Also, check for coherence between and within paragraphs. Add transitional devices or use pronouns or repetition as needed. If you feel ambitious, write a short essay that uses information from both of the paragraphs you wrote. The thesis of our essay night address this question: "Why does God allow suffering?"

2. If you responded to item 2 in the Suggestions for Journal Entries after Marius's "Writing and Its Rewards," you have probably listed three or four sentences that give advice on a particular activity you know a lot about. Use *each* of these sentences as the topic sentence of a paragraph that explains the advice you are giving in detail. For example, if you are trying to help a friend lose weight, one thing you might suggest is that he or she get a lot of exercise. That would make a good topic sentence of a paragraph that goes like this:

    > *Get a lot of exercise.* Wake up early and jog two or three miles. Use the weight room in the college gymnasium several times a week or ride one of the stationary bicycles you will find there. If all else fails, walk the three miles to school every day, do sit-ups in your room, or jump rope in your backyard.

    After you have written three or four such paragraphs, decide on a thesis statement that might express the central idea of the essay in which these paragraphs will appear. Make your thesis broad enough to include the main points you made in all three or four of your topic sentences. Use the thesis statement as the basis of a paragraph that comes before and introduces the three or four body paragraphs you have just completed.

    Now, rewrite your paper several times. Make sure it is clear and well organized. Check to see that you have included enough transitional devices to maintain coherence as explained in this chapter.

3. Review the notes you made for the first journal entry following Bennett's "Study Calculus!" If you have not responded to that journal prompt yet, do so now. Use this information to write the thesis statement for an essay that might be entitled "The Ideal Teacher." In that thesis, mention at least three qualities that make for excellent teaching. Here's how such a thesis might read:

    > The best teachers challenge their students, inspire confidence in them, and work harder than anyone else in class.

    Place this thesis statement in your first paragraph, your introduction. Now use each of the three or four characteristics of good teaching in your thesis as the basis for the topic sentences of your essay's body paragraphs. Here's how each of the topic sentences for paragraphs 2, 3, and 4 or your essay might read:

    Paragraph 2: The best teachers challenge their students.

Paragraph 3: Inspiring confidence in students is another sign of good teaching.

Paragraph 4: Good teachers work harder than their students.

Develop each of these body paragraphs with examples relating to a teacher or teachers you have known. You need not discuss the same teacher in each paragraph. If you completed the second journal suggestion after Bennett's essay, you might have already gathered some information you can use.

After writing several drafts of your paper, check that you have maintained coherence in and between paragraphs by using techniques explained in this chapter. Finally, remember that the best essays are those that are reviewed and edited carefully.

4. Review the journal entry or entries you made after reading Maria Scamacca's "Oma: Portrait of a Heroine." Then, write a short essay in which you use this information to explain why you think a person you know is heroic. Provide at least three reasons to support your view. Here's one way you might organize your essay:

Paragraph 1: Captures your readers' interest and states your thesis. For example, your **thesis statement** might resemble this: *My neighbor, Mrs. Rozowski faces life with a smile even though she has experienced much suffering and heartache.* In the rest of your introduction you might also explain that *Mrs. Rozowski suffers constant pain from arthritis, lives on a very small pension, and recently lost her husband of 50 years after a long illness.*

Paragraph 2: Mentions Mrs. Rozowski's illness and its symptoms. It also discusses the many things she does to keep active—like gardening, sewing, and cooking at a local soup kitchen—despite her pain.

Paragraph 3: Explains that, living on a small pension, Mrs. Rozowski, has learned several ways to save money such as growing much of her own food, making her own clothes, and even doing simple house repairs.

Paragraph 4: Discusses her devotion to her husband, her willingness to care for him during his long battle with Alzheimer's disease, and her refusal to become dependent on her children after he died.

Paragraph 5: Restates your admiration for Mrs. Rozowski, summarizes the major reasons you think she is heroic, and expresses a wish that someday you might be able to follow her example.

Writing to Learn: A Group Activity

THE FIRST MEETING

Pretend you and several others have been asked to contribute to a brochure that will help students choose an academic major. (For inspiration, reread Bennett's "Study Calculus!") Meet in a group of three or four students and ask each to research one (only one) major, perhaps from the list below or from a list that the group makes for itself:

Accounting	Dental hygiene	Nursing
Anthropology	Economics	Pharmacy
Architecture	History	Physical education
Biology	Journalism	Political science
Business	Literature	Psychology
administration	Mathematics	Rehabilitation science
Chemistry	Mechanical	Sociology
Computer science	engineering	Speech therapy
Civil engineering	Modern languages	Theater
Criminal justice		

RESEARCH

Make sure each member covers a different major. Search the Internet, do some research in your college's career placement center, or interview professors who teach courses in the assigned areas of study. Find out:

• What courses are required of students who major in this area.

• What careers are open to students who graduate with this major.

• What rewards (monetary and other) do these careers offer.

• What are some of the negative aspects of these careers.

WRITING

Then, write an essay that discusses most or all of these points for the major each of you chose. In your second group meeting, share early drafts (not first drafts) of each other's papers and suggest revisions. Be especially concerned with changes that will help the writer improve unity and coherence as explained in this chapter. In your third group meeting, distribute final versions of your papers. Finally, ask everyone to write a paragraph that explains whether the reading of these essays has influenced his or her choice of a major.

CHAPTER 3

Development

By now you know from practice that you use the central idea to focus your writing on a main point and to keep it unified. You do so by making sure that all the information in your paragraphs and essays relates clearly to the central idea. This chapter explains how the central idea also controls *development*—how much information a piece of writing contains and how this information is organized.

A paragraph or essay is well developed if it contains all the details it needs to prove, support, or illustrate its central idea. You should provide enough details to make your point clearly and convincingly. You should also arrange these details in a way that fits your purpose and allows readers to follow your train of thought easily.

Determining How Much a Paragraph or Essay Should Contain

There is no simple rule to tell how long a piece of writing should be. Depending on your thesis, you might be able to develop an essay in only a few paragraphs. But in some cases, your central idea will require that you write several more paragraphs of explanation and support.

Something similar is true for paragraphs. In some, you will have to supply many concrete details, illustrations, and other information important to your topic sentence. In others, you will be able to make your point clearly with only one or two supportive details. In a *few,* you might find that one sentence is all you need to achieve your purpose. (Keep in mind, however, that using too many one-sentence paragraphs can make your writing seem choppy.)

It is a good idea to rely on your central idea as a guide for development. After all, the central idea contains the main point you want to make. Therefore, it can give you a good clue about the kinds and amount of detail you should use to develop that point effectively.

Let's say you want to explain that there are *several* career opportunities for people majoring in biology. You might start by discussing teaching and medicine. But you will also have to include other fields (such as laboratory research, environmental management, and forestry) if you want your reader to understand all of what you meant when, in your topic sentence or thesis, you wrote, "Majoring in biology can provide a good foundation for *several* careers."

The subject in the sentence above is "Majoring in biology." The main point you want to make about this subject is that it can lead to "*several* careers." To write a paragraph or essay that develops this point fully, therefore, you will have to discuss *several*—at least three—careers.

In short, you can think of the central idea as a promise you make to your readers at the beginning of a paragraph or essay—a promise to discuss your main point in as much detail as is appropriate. If you start off by writing that "Three types of birds visit your backyard regularly during the winter," make sure to discuss all *three* birds. If you set out to explain that "There are many ways to decrease cholesterol in the bloodstream," discuss *many* ways, not just one or two. If you want to prove that your brother is not neat, don't be content to describe his closet and leave it at that. Talk about the mess of papers and books he often leaves scattered across the floor, and mention the jumble of sporting equipment and dirty clothes on the back seat of his car.

Deciding how many details are enough to develop a paragraph or essay fully is not always easy. However, the more experienced you become, the easier it will be to determine how much to include. For now, remember that providing too much detail is better than not providing enough. Too much information might bore your readers, but too little might leave them unconvinced or even confused. The first of these sins is forgivable; the second is not.

Just how much detail to include is what physician Lewis Thomas had to decide when he wrote this paragraph:

> Everyone must have had at least one personal experience with a computer error by this time. Bank balances are suddenly reported to have jumped from $379 into the millions, appeals for charitable contributions are mailed over and over to people with crazy-sounding names at your address, department stores send the wrong bills, utility companies write that they're turning everything off, that sort of thing. If you manage to get in touch with someone and complain, you then get instantaneously typed, guilty letters from the same computer, saying, "Our computer was in error, and an adjustment is being made in your account." ("To Err Is Human")

Obviously, Thomas could not include an example of every computer error he had ever heard of. So, he limited himself to those that would make his point most effectively and that his readers would recognize. His decision to include a specific number of examples—four in this case—is not important. We know without counting that Thomas has provided enough information to get his point across.

Choosing the Best Method of Development

You can develop an idea in many ways. The method you choose depends on your purpose—the point you wish to make and the effect you want your writing to have on your readers. Your purpose can be descriptive, narrative, explanatory, persuasive, or any combination of these.

DESCRIPTION

If your purpose is to introduce your reader to a person, place, or thing, you might *describe* your subject in concrete detail. The easiest way to gather detail for this kind of paragraph or essay is to use your five physical senses. Sight, smell, hearing, taste, and touch provide details that make writing vivid and effective. Description is also discussed in Chapter 8.

NARRATION

If you want to tell a story—to explain what happened—you will likely *narrate* a series of events as they occurred in time, explaining each event or part of an event in the order it took place. Narration is also discussed in Chapter 9.

EXPLANATION AND ARGUMENT

If your purpose is to *explain* an idea (expository writing) or to *argue* that an opinion or belief is correct (argumentative writing), you can choose from several methods to develop your ideas. Among these, of course, are narration and description, as well as the simple method called *conclusion and support,* which allows you to defend an opinion or explain an idea by using concrete and specific details that relate to it directly. However, you may want *to explain* or *to argue* by choosing from seven other methods:

- Illustration: Develop an idea with examples.
- Definition: Explain a term or concept.
- Classification: Distinguish between types or classes.
- Comparison and contrast: Point out similarities and differences.
- Analogy: Compare an abstract or difficult idea to something that is concrete and that the reader knows; usually, the subjects being compared seem unrelated at first.
- Cause and effect: Explain why something happens.
- Process analysis: Explain how something happens or how to do something.

Deciding which method of development is best for your purpose depends on the idea you are explaining or the point you are making. Let's say you want to persuade your readers that the best way to clean up the rivers in your town is to fine polluters. The cause-and-effect method might work well. If you decide to explain that the daily routine you followed in high school is quite different from the one you follow in college, you might choose contrast. If you want to prove how serious a student you are, you can support your opinion with specific details that show how often you visit the library, how infrequently you miss class, or how seldom you go to parties on nights before important tests.

Various methods of development appear in the sample paragraphs and essays that follow in this chapter. You will learn even more about exposition in Section Four of this book. There you will find separate chapters on three very common and useful methods of development: illustration, comparison and contrast, and process analysis. Section Five contains two chapters on techniques useful in argument and persuasion. For now, just remember that any method of development can be used by itself or in combination with others to develop paragraphs and essays that explain, that persuade, or that do both.

Deciding How to Arrange the Ideas and Details in a Paragraph

FOR NARRATIVE AND DESCRIPTIVE WRITING

Often, the best way to organize narration or description is simply to recall details naturally—just as you saw or experienced them. When *narrating,* you can arrange events in the order they happened, from beginning to end; this is called *chronological order,* or order of time. In the following narrative paragraph, John Steinbeck tells of a young man who is being chased by the police in the wilderness. Words that relate to time or that show action are in italics:

> Pepé *stumbled* down the hill. His throat was almost closed with thirst. *At first* he *tried to run,* but immediately he *fell* and *rolled. After that* he *went* more carefully. The moon *was just disappearing* behind the mountains *when* he *came* to the bottom. He *crawled* into the heavy brush *feeling* with his fingers for water. There was no water in the bed of the stream, only damp earth. Pepé *laid* his gun *down* and *scooped up* a handful of mud and put it in his mouth, and *then* he *spluttered* and *scraped* the earth from his tongue with his finger, for the mud *drew* at his mouth like a poultice [plaster dressing]. He *dug* a hole in the stream bed with his fingers, *dug* a little basin to catch water; but *before* it was very deep his head *fell forward* on the damp ground and he *slept.* ("Flight")

When *describing,* you can put concrete details into a *spatial* pattern, according to any arrangement you think best. For example, you might describe a place from east to west or from left to right; an object from top to bottom or from inside to outside; and a person from head to toe. In the following paragraph, John Steinbeck introduces a character from his short story "The Chrysanthemums" by telling us about both her facial and physical characteristics and then by describing what she wore:

> Elisa watched [the men] for a moment and then went back to her work. She was thirty-five. Her face was lean and strong and her eyes were as clear as water. Her figure looked blocked and heavy in her gardening costume, a man's black hat pulled low down over her eyes, clodhopper shoes, a figured print dress almost completely covered by a big corduroy apron with four big pockets to hold the snips, the trowel and scratcher, the seeds and the knife she worked with. She wore heavy leather gloves to protect her hands while she worked.

FOR EXPOSITORY AND ARGUMENTATIVE WRITING

Again, several choices are available when trying your hand at exposition—writing that explains—and at argument—writing that proves a point or defends an opinion. Here are a few patterns of arrangement you can use.

From General to Specific   Starting with a general statement and supporting it with specific details or ideas is a common way to organize a paragraph. Each of the following paragraphs has a different purpose and uses a different method of development. However, all begin with a general statement (the topic sentence) that is followed and developed by specific information.

Conclusion and Support: Use Details That Explain or Prove

Columbine. For years, it was simply the name of a big high school in Littleton, Colo. But last April, it became a code word for a kind of killing disease that has been sweeping America's schools. When students Eric Harris and Dylan Klebold massacred a teacher and 12 classmates (as well as themselves), they set a new standard for the bloody horror that may confront teenagers showing up for class each day. Columbine capped a long season of school killings in Pearl, Miss.; Paducah, Ky.; and Springfield, Ore.; and left the nation in a state of confusion and grief. Despite a national outbreak of finger pointing at everyone from gun manufacturers to Hollywood to uninvolved parents, the rampages have continued. Just last month, a 13-year-old boy opened fire and wounded five classmates in Fort Gibson, Okla., with a semiautomatic handgun. (Editors of *US News & World Report*)

Comparison and Contrast: Point Out Similarities and Differences

Grant and Lee were in complete contrast, representing two diametrically opposed elements in American life. Grant was the modern man emerging: behind him, ready to come on the stage, was the great age of steel and machinery, of crowded cities and a restless, burgeoning [blossoming] vitality. Lee might have ridden down from the old age of chivalry, lance in hand, silken banner fluttering over his head. Each man was the perfect champion of his cause, drawing both his strengths and his weaknesses from the people he led. (Bruce Catton, "Grant and Lee: A Study in Contrasts")

Classification: Distinguish between Types or Classes

Many religions have definite beliefs regarding hell. Some Christians see it as a fiery pit—much like what Dante described in the *Inferno*—where sinners suffer eternal damnation. Islamic texts describe it as a lake of fire spanned by a bridge over which souls must travel to get to heaven. Evil doers, who fall off the bridge, are cast into the lake, there to spend eternity. Buddhism and Hinduism describe many hells through which a soul must pass in order to be cleansed of any evil so as to be reincarnated and eventually to reach a state of perfection. For the ancient Greeks and Romans, Hades, or the underworld, was populated by the shades or shadows of people who had once walked the earth. Few ever escaped this miserable place. In Judaic theology, hell was once a real place, but for most modern Jews, hell is merely an idea discussed in the scriptures so as to help people un-derstand evil. (Karen Staples, "Deep Down Under")

Analogy: Compare an Abstract Idea to Something that Is Concrete and that the Reader Knows

The American political system is like a gigantic Mexican Christmas fiesta. Each political party is a huge piñata—a papier-maché donkey, for example. The donkey is filled with full employment, low interest rates, affordable housing, comprehensive medical benefits, a bal-anced budget and other goodies. The American voter is blindfolded and given a stick. The voter then swings the stick wildly in every di-rection, trying to hit a political candidate on the head and knock some sense into the silly bastard. (P. J. O'Rourke, *Parliament of Whores*)

From Specific to General   Beginning with specific details and moving to-ward a general conclusion (the topic sentence) that relates to these details is an-other way to arrange information. Although the following paragraphs use different methods of development, all move from specific to general.

Illustration: Develop Ideas with Examples

The ancient Chinese thought they were celestial brooms wielded [operated] by the gods to sweep the heavens free of evil. In the West they were believed to presage [foretell] the fall of Jerusalem, the death of monarchs and such anomalies as two-headed calves. The Norman Conquest of England was attributed to the 1066 flyby of Halley's, history's most famous comet, which has been linked to everything from Julius Caesar's assassination to the defeat of Attila the Hun. Told that Earth would pass through Halley's tail during its 1910 visit, many Americans pan-icked and bought gas masks and "comet pills." Alan Hale calls these waves of fear and mysticism "comet madness," and as co-discoverer of Comet Hale-Bopp, he's seen more than his share. (Leon Jaroff, "Crazy about Comets")

Comparison and Contrast: Point Out Similarities and Differences

In *The Expression of the Emotions in Man and Animals,* Darwin made a systematic study of how animals look when they are afraid. In both humans and animals, he found, some or all of the following may occur: the eyes and mouth open, the eyes roll, the heart beats rapidly, hairs stand on end, muscles tremble, teeth chatter, and the sphincter loosens. The frightened creature may freeze in its place or cower. These rules hold true across a remarkable array of species. Somehow it is surprising to learn that when dolphins are terrified, their teeth chatter and the whites of their eyes show, or that a frightened gorilla's legs shake. Such familiar behavior in a wild animal is a reminder of our ultimate kinship. Melvin Konner has written, "We are—not metaphorically, but precisely, biologically—like the doe nibbling moist grass in the predawn misty light; chewing, nuzzling a dewy fawn, breathing the foggy air, feeling so much at peace; and suddenly, for no reason, looking about wildly." (Jeffrey M. Masson and Susan McCarthy, *When Elephants Weep*)

You learned earlier that various methods of development can be used together. The paragraph above uses both comparison and description.

From Question to Answer   A good way to begin a paragraph is with an interesting question. You can then devote the rest of your paragraph to details that develop an effective answer to that question.

Definition: Explain a Term or Concept

What does it mean to be poor in America? We can offer no single description of American poverty. But for many, perhaps most, it means homes with peeling paint, inadequate heating, uncertain plumbing. It means that only the very lucky among the children receive a decent education. It often means a home where some go to bed hungry and malnutrition is a frequent visitor. It means that the most elementary components of the good life in America—a vacation with kids, an evening out, a comfortable home—are but distant and unreachable dreams, more likely to be seen on the television screen than in the neighborhood. And for almost all the poor it means that life is a constant struggle to obtain the merest necessities of existence, those things most of us take for granted. We can do better. (U.S. Senator Paul Wellstone, "If Poverty Is the Question . . .")

Analogy: Compare an Abstract or Difficult Idea to Something that Is Concrete or that the Reader Knows

How can a telescope provide information about the beginning of the Universe? The answer is that when we look out into space, we look into the past. If a galaxy is five billion light-years away, it takes five billion years for the light from this galaxy to reach the earth. Consequently, our telescopes show the galaxy not as it is today, but as it was five billion years ago, when the light we are receiving now had just left that galaxy on its way to the earth. A telescope is a time machine; it carries us back to the past. (Robert Jastrow, *Journey to the Stars*)

The paragraph above is another that uses more than one method of development. Here, analogy combines with process analysis.

From Problem to Solution   Organizing a paragraph by stating a problem and explaining how to solve it in the sentences that follow is much like asking a question and answering it. It is especially effective when you are explaining a process or analyzing causes and effects. But it can be used with other methods of development as well.

Process Analysis: Explain How to Do Something

For most people, being overweight is not simply a matter of vanity. Excess weight is a threat to health and longevity. You should start losing weight by getting a thorough physical examination, then begin following a regular exercise program prescribed by your doctor. Next, start counting calories; read labels or look up the caloric content of your favorite foods in diet guides available at most supermarkets and drugstores. Finally, stay away from high-fat animal products and rich desserts. Fill up on fruits, vegetables, natural grains and other high-fiber foods. (Diana Dempsey, "Tightening Our Belts")

By Order of Importance   Writers of fiction often place the most important bit of information last. This makes their work suspenseful and creates a more effective climax. If arranged in this pattern, an expository or argumentative paragraph can help you create emphasis by guiding your readers to the details and ideas you believe are most important.

Cause and Effect: Explain Why Something Happens

The greatest moral imperative [obligation] we face is replacing the welfare state with an opportunity society. For every day that we allow the current conditions to continue, we are condemning the poor—and particularly poor children—to being deprived of their basic rights as Americans. The welfare state reduces the poor from citizens to clients. It breaks up families, minimizes work incentives, blocks people from saving and acquiring property, and overshadows dreams of a promised future with a present despair born of poverty, violence, and hopelessness. (former Speaker of the U.S. House of Representatives Newt Gingrich, *To Renew America*)

Around a Pivot   The pivoting pattern begins with one idea, then changes direction—pivots—by presenting a different or contrasting idea. The topic sentence normally appears in the middle of the paragraph and announces the shift. Often, but not always, the topic sentence is introduced by a transition such as *but, however,* and *nonetheless.*

Definition: Explain a Term or Concept

The government is huge, stupid, greedy and makes nosy, officious [pompous] and dangerous intrusions into the smallest corners of life—this much we can stand. But the real problem is that government is boring. We could cure or mitigate [lessen] the other ills Washington visits on us if we could only bring ourselves to pay attention to Washingtonton itself. But we cannot. (P. J. O'Rourke, *Parliament of Whores*)

Illustration: Develop an Idea with Examples

I sometimes hear people who should know better saying that we would be healthier if we depended solely on herbal remedies and refused to take the synthetic drugs purveyed [supplied] by modern scientific medicine. Browse through a pharmacopoeia [list of medicines] and see how many of the medicines prescribed by doctors and sold by druggists are prepared from plants. Quinine for malaria, ephedrine for asthma, cascara for constipation, digitalis for heart conditions, atropine for eye examinations and a great host of other valuable medicines in constant use came directly from folk herbal medicines, and are still prepared from wild plants or those recently brought under cultivation. (Euell Gibbons, *Stalking the Wild Asparagus*)

Visualizing Paragraph Development

The following paragraphs are from "Which Side of the Fence?" freshman Dan Roland's essay that recalls a honeymoon trip to Jamaica. The first uses the conclusion-and-support method of development and a general-to-specific pattern of organization. The second, which is arranged in the specific-to-general pattern, illustrates three methods of development: description, cause/effect, and contrast.

Topic sentence expresses a conclusion.

Arriving at the resort is like stepping into another world. This ultra-modern hotel is

Paragraph moves from general to specific.

surrounded by a golf course; tennis courts; a huge swimming pool; outdoor lounges complete with palm trees, calypso bands, and elegant bamboo cages that hold parrots and other exotic birds; and a beach that features water skiers, wind surfers, yachts, and hundreds of tourists wearing the latest summer fashions and sipping numerous fruit and rum drinks with little umbrellas in them.

Specific details support conclusion.

Paragraph moves from specific to general.

　　All of the luxury in this hotel is surrounded by a barbed-wire fence, with only one entrance on each side patrolled by armed security guards. This protects the tourist from a constant bombardment of sales pitches

Description

from native Jamaicans, who can feed their families for weeks by selling just a few of their homemade souvenirs. Hotel guests are

Cause/effect

allowed to go out through the gate, but natives may not come in. Many of them live in small shacks right next to the fence, so as never to miss a selling opportunity. The symbolism is staggering: on one side are wealth and luxury, on the other poverty and hunger. The fence is a barrier to the good life.

Contrast

Topic sentence

Revising to Improve Development

Read these two versions of paragraphs from "Exile and Return," an essay appearing later in this chapter, which discusses the author's return to his high school after many years. Compare the second version with the first to learn how James Keller added to, corrected, and clarified his rough draft to improve the effectiveness of his essay.

Keller—Rough Draft

Eventually my eyes come to rest on the

chalkboards. I remember staring at them

Why faces? bored at what I was listening to. Faces turn

and face me from seats in front and to my

side. They are only shadows from the past,

only memories. They're looking for me. And

through me. They've left. Some gone to

Check meaning? school, some gone to the world. Others gone

quite literally to hell, not soon to return.

Vague. What "places" are these? Out of the building, I walk on grassy

playing fields that were greener

then. . . . Places where many of us found

brief, insignificant glory. I no longer

remember who won and who lost. Only that

somehow we all walked away winners and

losers to the same heart. It is more than I

can bear.

I leave now, maybe forever, if I ever

existed at all.

Why was he "bored"?

Choppy, vague, and weak. Needs detail.

Explain this term?

Keller—Final Draft

Eventually my eyes come to rest on the chalkboards. Old habits die hard. I remember staring at them through teachers whose words "had forked no lightning." My <u>teachers</u> and <u>classmates</u> are gone, but many faces remain. From seats in front and to my side, they turn and stare. They are shadows of the past, bloodless visions, returned from long exile to mock my exile and return. They're looking for me and through me. But they're only memories. They've left, you know—some gone to school, some gone to the world, others gone to their own private hells. Faces that laughed, young and innocent, now cry, worn and haggard. Their expressions hide lives that were true and alive but now are neither.

Out of the building, I walk on grassy playing fields where so many of us found brief insignificant glory. They were greener in another spring. The <u>empty stands</u> play sentinel to the <u>lonely track</u> and <u>football field</u>, and a thousand ghosts <u>applaud a hundred athletes</u> only I can see. I no longer remember who won and lost, only that somehow we all walked away winners and losers to the same heart, veterans of so much happiness and so much pain. It is more than I can bear.

Margin annotations:

Identifies "faces."

Adds narrative and descriptive details.

Adds quotation to explain why he was "bored."

Has removed "literally."

Smoother and developed more fully. Adds information about classmates.

Identifies "places" with specific information.

Adds information to explain "insignificant glory."

A stronger
conclusion:
adds detail
to convey
his emotional
reaction.

> I leave now, maybe forever. I wonder if I ever existed and was ever here at all. To say good-bye is to die a little. And so I do.

Practicing Methods of Development

Complete the paragraphs begun below. Include information based on your own observations and experiences. Use whatever method of development you think the topic sentence, which begins each paragraph, calls for.

1. My family provides me with a great deal of emotional support. For example,

    _____

    _____

    _____

    _____

    _____

    _____

    _____

    _____

2. There are three types of students at my college. The first _____

    _____

    _____

    _____

    _____

    _____

3. If you want to flunk a test, do the following:

    _____

    _____

    _____

    _____

4. Most people gain weight because _____

_____

_____

_____

_____

_____

5. My sister (brother, best friend) is a _____ type of person. I, on
   the other hand, am

_____

_____

_____

_____

_____

_____

_____

As you read the following selections, remember what you've just learned about (1) the methods that writers use to develop their ideas and (2) the patterns they use to organize their paragraphs. Approach each selection carefully, and devote as much effort to determining *how* the author has organized and developed the material as you do to understanding what the essay means. Doing so will help you develop your own writing more effectively.

The Last Safe Haven

Joannie M. Schrof

"The Last Safe Haven" appeared in the December 26, 1994, issue of U.S. News and World Report, *a weekly news magazine. It analyzes the spread of violence to the small town, once considered a refuge from the kinds of crime found in the city.*

Preparing to Read

1. This essay was printed in an end-of-year column called "Farewells: Faces We Knew, Ways We Were: Now They Are Gone." This information is important to understanding the author's purpose.

2. Schrof makes good use of transitions and other devices to maintain coherence. Read her essay twice. The second time, circle words and phrases that make it coherent.

3. What does the first sentence of the essay tell us about what is to come?

Vocabulary

hamlet (noun)	Small town, village.
maelstrom (noun)	Storm.
mayhem (noun)	Violence.
palpable (adjective)	Obvious, plain, evident.
recital (noun)	Speech, reading, presentation.
refuge (noun)	Safe place, shelter.
relentless (adjective)	Without end, unceasing.
sanctuary (noun)	Holy place, haven, refuge.
seared (verb)	Burned.

The Last Safe Haven

Joannie M. Schrof

NINETEEN NINETY-FOUR SEARED a series of disturbing images into the American memory: a mother drowning her sons, children shooting each other, a 5-year-old boy thrown from a high-rise window. The relentless recital of mayhem added to the fear, to the feeling—however illusory—that there was once true refuge, and that it has disappeared.

Nowhere is this sense more palpable than in the nation's small towns. 2 While cities have always battled crime, the small town has been celebrated as a sanctuary, where doors are left unlocked and children roam freely. But even the smallest towns are growing more dangerous, often at the hands of the very children they are famous for protecting.

Geneseo, Ill. (population 5,990), is one such place. A decade ago its quiet 3 streets won the state's "Hometown Award." This year, after a series of violent incidents, the police department created a gang investigation unit. Every other week now, it seems, a teenager is badly beaten in gang-related violence: Recently, a local boy was clubbed to death in a nearby town. Stolen cars, burglarized homes and vandalism are on the rise. And nightfall brings the sound of doors locking all around town.

City dwellers have long imagined that if things got too bad, they could 4 pack up and move to a place like Geneseo, a cozy, self-enclosed hamlet far from the maelstrom. It was probably always a fantasy. Now that we know it, the only alternative left is to stand and fight back.

Read More on the Web

Associated Press News Story on crimes migrating to small towns:
    http://www.eagletribune.com/news/stories/19990417/FP_003.htm
Reality Check Online Site explaining serious crime problems in small communities: http://www.health.org/reality/articles/2002/smalltown.asp
National Center for Policy Analysis presents another view:
    http://www.ncpa.org/pi/crime/pd050900b.html

Questions for Discussion

1. Identify the essay's thesis.
2. In Preparing to Read, you read that the title of the column in which this essay appeared, "Faces We Knew, Ways We Were: Now They Are Gone," tells us something about the author's purpose. Explain.
3. What is the chief method of development used in paragraphs 1 and 4?
4. What is the chief method of development used in paragraphs 2 and 3?
5. What pattern of organization does Schrof use in paragraphs 2 and 4? In paragraph 3?
6. Explain the function of paragraph 2's first sentence in terms of maintaining coherence.
7. Find places in which Schrof uses transitions to maintain coherence.

Thinking Critically

1. In paragraph 2, Schrof writes: "even the smallest towns are growing more dangerous, often at the hands of the very children they are famous for protecting." Are children getting more and more violent? If so, what do you think is causing this?
2. Schrof concludes by saying that "the only alternative left is to stand and fight back." What are some ways we can combat the growing trend toward violence?
3. Explain in what way the tragedy at Columbine High School (1999) supports Schrof's thesis.

Suggestions for Journal Entries

1. Whether you come from a city or small town, do you think your community is a safe haven? Ask yourself whether or not you feel safe walking the streets at night, leaving the front door unlocked, carrying around a lot of cash, parking your car on the street, and so on. Try asking and answering a variety of questions that will help you determine how safe your community is.
2. Many of us have "safe havens," places where we can feel safe and at ease. There we seek advice, safety, sympathy, or encouragement, or just a peaceful atmosphere where we can relax and rejuvenate ourselves ("recharge our batteries"). Where is your safe haven? Freewrite for about 10 minutes to describe this place.

Exile and Return

James Keller

As managing editor for his college newspaper, James Keller wrote many news and feature stories that attracted the attention of professors and fellow students. Today he is a college English professor. "Exile and Return" recalls his visit to his suburban high school several years after graduation. This before-and-after portrait reveals as much about the author as it does about his school.

Preparing to Read

1. Keller's thesis statement appears at the end of his first paragraph. Identify the main point he makes in this essay as you read this sentence.
2. "Had forked no lightning" (paragraph 5) is from "Do Not Go Gentle into That Good Night," a poem by Dylan Thomas.
3. You know what the subject of this essay is. Can you guess Keller's purpose in writing this essay? Who might his primary readers be?

Vocabulary

arcane (adjective)	Secret, known only by a few.
asbestos (noun)	Insulating material now considered a health hazard.
banality (noun)	Boring quality.
predicting (adjective)	Giving signs of, foretelling.
stifling (adjective)	Suffocating.

Exile and Return

James Keller

IT'S ALL DIFFERENT, quiet and grey now, like the sun reflecting on the previous 1 night's darkness or predicting the afternoon's storm. On this stifling summer morning, I scarcely recognize the school I had attended for four years. The life and laughter have died. It is another world.

I walk down the vacant halls, and what light there is shines a path on the 2 mirrored beige floors, leading me past imposing grey lockers that stand erect in columns. At one time, they woke the dead in closing but now remain closed in silence. I remember the faces of people who stood and sometimes slumped before them at day's end. They were friendly faces that looked up and nodded or said "Hello" as I galloped past. Now there are other faces, faces of people I never got to know.

The lockers soon give way to the classrooms, cement cells we once lived 3
in, learned in, and often slept in. Steel I-beams I had once hardly noticed now hang like doom over cracked and peeling walls. The architect left them exposed, for want of talent, I assume. From the color scheme of putrid green to the neutral asbestos ceiling and steel rafters, the banality of the classrooms overwhelms me.

The rooms are empty now save the ancient desks. They are yellow clay 4
and steel and much smaller than I remember. I can still read arcane graffiti, its meaning forgotten, on their dull surfaces. The handwriting is my own. I recognize the doodles drawn as every minute ran past like a turtle climbing up a glass wall. Back then, they killed the time. They didn't do much for the furniture either.

Eventually my eyes come to rest on the chalkboards. Old habits die hard. 5
I remember staring at them through teachers whose words "had forked no lightning." My teachers and classmates are gone, but many faces remain. From seats in front and to my side, they turn and stare. They are shadows of the past, bloodless visions, returned from long exile to mock my exile and return. They're looking for me and through me. But they're only memories. They've left, you know—some gone to school, some gone to the world, others gone to their own private hells. Faces that laughed, young and innocent, now cry, worn and haggard. Their expressions hide lives that were true and alive but now are neither.

Out of the building, I walk on grassy playing fields where so many of us 6
found brief insignificant glory. They were greener in another spring. The empty stands play sentinel to the lonely track and football field, and a thousand ghosts applaud a hundred athletes only I can see. I no longer remember who won and lost, only that somehow we all walked away winners and losers to the same heart, veterans of so much happiness and so much pain. It is more than I can bear.

I leave now, maybe forever. I wonder if I ever existed and was ever here at 7
all. To say good-bye is to die a little. And so I do.

Read More on the Web

University of Ottawa site on paragraph development:
> http://www.uottawa.ca/academic/arts/writcent/hypergrammar/
> rvpardev.html
Orangeburg-Calhoun Technical College site on paragraph development:
> http://www.kent.k12.wa.us/KSD/KR/WRITE/GEN/para-develop.html

Questions for Discussion

1. What is Keller's thesis statement? What words in that thesis express his main point? In short, what is he telling us about his high school?

2. In which paragraphs does the topic sentence not appear at the very beginning? Can you find a paragraph in which the central idea is only implied?

3. The author's purpose is to contrast his memories of a place with its present reality. However, he uses other methods of development as well. In which paragraph or paragraphs does he use cause and effect?

4. Where in this essay can you find examples of narration and description?

5. Find an instance in which Keller uses analogy.

6. Which pattern of organization discussed earlier in this chapter does Keller use in paragraph 2?

7. Which pattern of organization does he use in paragraphs 6 and 7?

Thinking Critically

The biographical note on Keller, which appears before the essay, claims that this selection reveals as much about the author as about the place he is discussing. What have you learned about Keller's personality from this essay?

Suggestions for Journal Entries

1. Take a mental stroll through the hallways, classrooms, or athletic fields of your high school. What do you remember most about it and about your classmates, your teachers, and yourself? Use focused freewriting or listing to record these memories in your journal.

   Next, read your journal entry. What main impression about your high school experience can you draw from these details? Did you enjoy it? Were you happy and secure around the teachers and students you met each day? Is the opposite true? Or do you have mixed feelings? Put your main impression into a preliminary thesis statement that might get you started on a longer assignment described in the Suggestions for Sustained Writing at the end of this chapter.

2. "To say good-bye is to die a little," Keller writes. Recall an incident in which you had to say good-bye to someone, something, or some place. Use focused freewriting to write a brief story about the event. Try to reveal why saying good-bye was so hard.

Burger Queen

Erin Sharp

Erin Sharp was a sophomore at Cornell University when she wrote this essay. It first appeared in The American Enterprise Magazine.

Preparing to Read

1. The information in this essay comes from Sharp's employment at a McDonald's restaurant. Before you begin reading, think about the layout and appearance of such a restaurant, the people who might work there, and people who might eat there.

2. If you were writing an essay about your place of employment, what subjects would you discuss to give your readers a good understanding of this place?

3. What do you think Sharp is hinting at in the title?

4. As you read, you might find unfamiliar words not listed in the vocabulary below. If so, try to get at their meanings by using context clues within the essay. For example, in paragraph 4, the author says that some customers have "bickered" with her "for five minutes over a measly ten-cent increase in the price of an Egg McMuffin." What might "bickered" and "measly" mean in this sentence?

Vocabulary

coveted (adjective)	Desired.
forfeited (verb)	Gave up.
freelance (adjective)	Self-employed, temporary, hired for a one-time job.
hoard (verb)	Save, hide away.
quipped (verb)	Answered in a joking or sarcastic way.
pathologist (noun)	Doctor who diagnoses physical changes caused by disease.
perspective (noun)	Point of view.
reimbursement (noun)	Refund.
scam (verb)	To cheat.
stereotypes (noun)	Labels, types.
tackiness (noun)	Bad taste.
tempered (adjective)	Moderated, lessened, toned down.

Burger Queue

Erin Sharp

WHEN I ANNOUNCED the change of my major from biology with pre-med as- 1
pirations to English, my advisor simply raised an eyebrow and asked if I
planned to work at McDonald's for the rest of my life. "Actually," I quipped,
"I've been working at McDonald's for two and a half years, and it's sort of fun."
His surprise was evident, a typical reaction to my shocking side occupation. I
spoke the truth, though; I have held a dozen jobs ranging from camp counselor
to pathologist's assistant (now including, I suppose, freelance journalism), yet
none have been as entertaining as my stints at the Golden Arches.

My double life as Erin Sharp, Ivy League McDonald's Worker, has revealed 2
twin stereotypes to me. People told I go to Cornell view me as bright and ambitious. Put me behind the counter at McDonald's, however, and I am usually
assumed to be a high school dropout with fifteen unseen piercings.

When I was six years old, McDonald's was my favorite place to eat, and 3
kids have not changed much in the last dozen years. I am often asked whether
I have actually met "The Ronald" McDonald, and have been given letters to pass
along to him, like one of Santa Claus's elves. Among kids, McDonald's workers
rank right up there with policemen and firefighters.

Yet this perspective rarely survives adolescence. Respect for the workers of 4
the fast food industry is lost among most adults, with absurd results. Many
adults seem to assume that McWorkers are stupid, attempting to scam us out
of free food and coupons. The depths of tackiness to which some human beings will stoop in order to save a few pennies at a drive-thru window are worthy of "Candid Camera." Grown men driving Lincoln Town Cars have bickered
with me for five minutes over a measly ten-cent increase in the price of an Egg
McMuffin. Perhaps they imagine that I overcharge each patron and hoard mis-
begotten dimes in a piggy bank behind the shake machine?

Once, my store even received a phone call at noon from a furious woman 5
demanding reimbursement for the breakfast she had bought that morning via
drive-thru; apparently, it was cold when she arrived at work over an hour later.
Our most famous TIC (Truculent, Irate Customer) lost her temper when we
could not (in her eyes, would not) provide the grilled chicken sandwich she
craved in the middle of breakfast rush hour. An entirely new traffic pattern was
created in drive-thru for the 25 minutes spent in fruitless argument and ac-
commodation attempts by our managers as the grill team thawed frozen meat,
heated a grill to cook on and produced the coveted sandwich for her. When
at last presented with it, she lofted the bag triumphantly and accused us of
withholding it from her for the entire time, then zoomed off with the last
words: "I'm never coming back here again!" The effectiveness of this condemnation was tempered by her license plate, which proclaimed her to be from
Delaware—over an hour away.

A small portion of our patrons are so confused that there is really nothing   6
to do but wait for them to leave. My most prominent example of this sort of
"guest" is the infamous Snack Attack Lady, who ordered hotcakes and sausage
during our 90-second-guaranteed-service hour and then ate her breakfast right
outside the drive-thru window. Heedless of the frenzied honking behind her,
she carefully opened the platter, poured a puddle of syrup, rolled the sausage
in a hotcake and dipped both daintily into the syrup. My co-workers and I
watched in speechless amazement. When asked what she was doing, she rolled
her eyes and snapped, "What does it look like I'm doing? I'm eating my breakfast!" That woman has permanently forfeited all rights to complain about slow
drive-thru service.

And yet, there are some great customers out there, like the Morning Crew: 7
the seven retired men and one active police officer who wait for our doors to
open every day so that they can enjoy their dawn coffee and conversation. If I
missed a day of work, I would return to inquiries about my health and concern
that all was well. The greatest customers ever to grace our store were two de-
liverymen who drove up to the window one spring afternoon two years ago
with armfuls of roses for my co-worker and me. They were moving their business out of state, they explained, and wanted to thank us for making their afternoons brighter.

Well, boys, if you are reading this article, thank you again for that fabulous   8
surprise. I still have the ribbon which bound them.

Read More on the Web

HRZone.com article on image of fast-food restaurant workers:
> http://www.hrzone.com/articles/applicant_attract2.html

US Department of Labor Occupational Outlook Handbook:
> http://www.bls.gov/oco/ocos024.htm

Questions for Discussion

1. In which paragraphs does Sharp make use of illustration?
2. Which paragraph uses the cause-and-effect method? Which uses contrast?
3. What method of development can be seen in paragraph 1?
4. Identify the pattern of organization used in paragraphs 1 through 7.
5. What is Sharp's central idea?
6. Why does Sharp tell us that her advisor was surprised when she told him she had worked at McDonald's? How does doing so help introduce her central idea?

Thinking Critically

1. In Preparing to Read, you were asked to use context clues to determine the meaning of some of Sharp's vocabulary. What does she mean by "pre-med," "aspirations," and "stints" in paragraph 1; "truculent," "irate," "fruitless," and "lofted" in paragraph 5; "heedless" and "frenzied" in paragraph 6?

2. What are the Ivy League, "Candid Camera," and McWorkers? You might find more about the first two terms on the Internet or in your college library, but you will have to figure out the third term on your own.

3. What is the pun (play on words) Sharp uses in the title?

Suggestions for Journal Entries

1. Use focused freewriting, listing, or clustering to gather information that describes customers or employees or both at a place at which you work or have worked. Focus on people with the most interesting or distinctive personalities.

2. Sharp's essay is more than a listing of complaints about annoying customers. It is a statement—and a positive one at that—about her role and image as a worker in a fast-food restaurant. Use clustering or any other prewriting method to explain your feelings—be they positive, negative, or mixed—about a job you hold or once held.

A Brother's Dreams

Paul Aronowitz

Paul Aronowitz was a medical student at Case Western Reserve University when he wrote this very sensitive essay comparing his dreams, hopes, and ambitions with those of his schizophrenic brother. Schizophrenia is a mental illness characterized by withdrawal from reality.

Aronowitz's love, compassion, and understanding come across clearly as he unfolds the story of how he learned to deal with the fact that his brother's strange, sometimes violent behavior was the symptom of an illness and not a defect in character. This essay is also Aronowitz's admission and unselfish affirmation that, however "elusive" and "trivial," his brother's dreams might be even more meaningful than his own.

"A Brother's Dreams" first appeared in "About Men," a weekly column in the New York Times Magazine.

Preparing to Read

1. Aronowitz's central idea concerns how he came to understand his brother's illness and to accept the fact that his brother's dreams were meaningful and important. However, the author does not begin to reveal this central idea until near the end of this essay, and he never puts the idea into a formal thesis statement.

2. Many of the paragraphs in this selection are developed through narration and description, but Aronowitz also makes good use of cause and effect, comparison and contrast, illustration, and conclusion and support.

3. Josef Mengele, whom Aronowitz mentions in paragraph 5, was a Nazi medical researcher who conducted unspeakable experiments in which he tortured and maimed or killed thousands of human beings.

Vocabulary

acrid (adjective)	Bitter, harsh, sharp.
aimlessly (adverb)	Without purpose.
alienate (verb)	Make enemies of, isolate oneself from.
delusions (noun)	Misconceptions, fantasies.
depravity (noun)	Immorality, corruption.
elusive (adjective)	Hard to grasp, intangible.
paranoid (adjective)	Showing unreasonable or unwarranted suspicion.

prognosis (noun)   Prediction about the course or outcome of an
                        illness.
resilient (adjective)   Able to bounce back.
siblings (noun)   Sisters and brothers.

A Brother's Dreams

Paul Aronowitz

EACH TIME I go home to see my parents at their house near Poughkeepsie,   1
N.Y., my brother, a schizophrenic for almost nine years now, comes to visit
from the halfway house where he lives nearby. He owns a car that my parents
help him to maintain, and his food and washing are taken care of by the halfway
house. Somewhere, somehow along the way, with the support of a good physician, a social worker and my ever-resilient parents, he has managed to carve a
niche for himself, to bite off some independence and, with it, elusive dreams
that, to any healthy person, might seem trivial.

My brother sits in a chair across from me, chain-smoking cigarettes, trying   2
to take the edge off the medications he'll be on for the rest of his life. Sometimes
his tongue hangs loosely from his mouth when he's listening or pops out of his
mouth as he speaks—a sign of tardive dyskinesia, an often-irreversible side effect of his medication.

He draws deeply on his cigarette and tells me he can feel his mind healing—   3
cells being replaced, tissue being restored, thought processes returning. He
knows this is happening because he dreams of snakes, and hot, acrid places in
which he suffocates if he moves too fast. When he wakes, the birds are singing
in the trees outside his bedroom window. They imitate people in his halfway
house, mocking them and calling their names. The birds are so smart, he tells
me, so much smarter than we are.

His face, still handsome despite its puffiness (another side effect of the   4
medications that allow him to function outside the hospital), and warm brown
eyes are serious. When I look into his eyes I imagine I can see some of the suffering he has been through. I think of crossed wires, of receptors and neuro-
transmitters, deficits and surpluses, progress and relapse, and I wonder, once
again, what has happened to my brother.

My compassion for him is recent. For many years, holidays, once happy   5
occasions for our family of seven to gather together, were emotional torture sessions. My brother would pace back and forth in the dining room, lecturing us,
his voice loud, dominating, crushing all sound but his own, about the end of
the world, the depravity of our existences. His speeches were salted with para-
noid delusions: our house was bugged by the F.B.I.; my father was Josef Mengele; my mother was selling government secrets to the Russians.

His life was decaying before my eyes, and I couldn't stand to listen to 6
him. My resentment of him grew as his behavior became more disruptive
and aggressive. I saw him as being ultimately responsible for his behavior.
As my anger increased, I withdrew from him, avoiding him when I came
home to visit from college, refusing to discuss the bizarre ideas he brought
up over the dinner table. When I talked with my sister or other two brothers about him, our voices always shadowed in whispers, I talked of him as
of a young man who had chosen to spend six months of every year in a pleasant, private hospital on the banks of the Hudson River, chosen to alienate his
family with threats, chosen to withdraw from the stresses of the world. I
hated what he had become. In all those years, I never asked what his diag-
nosis was.

Around the fifth year of his illness, things finally changed. One hot sum- 7
mer night, he attacked my father. When I came to my father's aid, my brother
broke three of my ribs and nearly strangled me. The State Police came and took
him away. My father's insurance coverage had run out on my brother, so this
time he was taken to a locked ward at the state hospital where heavily sedated
patients wandered aimlessly in stockinged feet up and down long hallways.
Like awakening from a bad dream, we gradually began talking about his illness.
Slowly and painfully, I realized that he wasn't responsible for his disease any
more than a cancer patient is for his pain.

As much as I've learned to confront my brother's illness, it frightens me to 8
think that one day, my parents gone from the scene, my siblings and I will be
responsible for portions of my brother's emotional and financial support. This
element of the future is one we still avoid discussing, much the way we avoided
thinking about the nature of his disease and his prognosis. I'm still not capable
of thinking about it.

Now I come home and listen to him, trying not to react, trying not to show 9
disapproval. His delusions are harmless and he is, at the very least, communicating. When he asks me about medical school, I answer with a sentence or
two—no elaboration, no revelations about the dreams I cradle in my heart.

He talks of his own dreams. He hopes to finish his associate's degree—the 10
same one he has been working on between hospitalizations for almost eight
years now—at the local community college. Next spring, with luck, he'll get a
job. His boss will be understanding, he tells me, cutting him a little slack when
he has his "bad days," letting him have a day off here or there when things aren't
going well. He puts out his cigarette and lights another one.

Time stands still. This could be last year, or the year before, or the year be- 11
fore that. I'm within range of becoming a physician, of realizing something I've
been working toward for almost five years, while my brother still dreams of
having a small job, living in his own apartment and of being well. As the smoke
flows from his nose and mouth, I recall an evening some time ago when I drove
upstate from Manhattan to tell my parents and my brother that I was getting

married (an engagement later severed). My brother's eyes lit up at the news, and then a darkness fell over them.

"What's wrong?" I asked him.   12

"It's funny," he answered matter-of-factly. "You're getting married, and I've 13 never even had a girlfriend." My mother's eyes filled with tears, and she turned away. She was trying her best to be happy for me, for the dreams I had—for the dreams so many of us take for granted.

"You still have us," I stammered, reaching toward him and touching his 14 arm. All of a sudden my dreams meant nothing; I didn't deserve them and they weren't worth talking about. My brother shrugged his shoulders, smiled and shook my hand, his large, tobacco-stained fingers wrapping around my hand, dwarfing my hand.

Read More on the Web

Schizophrenia Home Page: http://www.schizophrenia.com/

National Institute of Mental Health Page on Schizophrenia:
    http://www.nimh.nih.gov/publicat/schizoph.cfm

Questions for Discussion

1. If you wanted to write a formal thesis statement for this essay, what would it be?

2. "A Brother's Dreams" contains at least two paragraphs that are developed through description. Identify one of them. What important idea does this paragraph communicate?

3. The purpose of paragraph 6 is to explain a cause and an effect. What is the paragraph's topic sentence (cause)? What details (effect) does Aronowitz provide to develop the paragraph fully?

4. Which paragraphs use narration?

5. Aronowitz gets specific about his brother's dreams in paragraph 10, which he develops by stating a conclusion and then supporting this conclusion with details. Identify these details.

6. Paragraph 11 contrasts some of Aronowitz's dreams to some of his brother's. In what other paragraph do we see their dreams contrasted?

7. Most paragraphs in this essay are organized in the general-to-specific pattern. However, paragraphs 11 and 13 are organized according to order of importance. What is the most important idea in each of these paragraphs?

8. This is a powerful essay. Which paragraph affects you most strongly? What do the details in this paragraph tell you about the author or his brother or both?

Thinking Critically

Explaining how he came to terms with his brother's illness, Aronowitz says his compassion for his brother is only "recent." Pretend you are interviewing Aronowitz. What would he say is the reason for not feeling compassion earlier? What caused his change in attitude?

Suggestions for Journal Entries

1. Aronowitz writes about a person whose lifestyle and dreams are very different from those of most other people. Do you know someone like this? If so, write a paragraph showing how this person's lifestyle or dreams differ from those of most others. Use one major method of development; for instance, you might *describe* what this individual looks like (much in the way Aronowitz describes his brother in paragraphs 2 and 4), or you might use *narration* to tell a story about the kind of behavior you have come to expect from the person (as Aronowitz does in paragraphs 3, 5, and 7). You might even want to try your hand at the cause-and-effect method by telling your reader how you normally react to or deal with this person and then explaining what causes you to react in this way.

2. Aronowitz's essay contrasts his brother's dreams to his own. Write a paragraph in which you show how different you are from your brother, sister, or other close relative by contrasting a major goal in your life to one of his or hers.

   Clearly identify the two different goals in your topic sentence, and fill the rest of your paragraph with details showing how different they are; that is, develop the paragraph by contrast. Your topic sentence might go something like this: "My sister Janet intends to move to the city and find a high-paying job, even if she hates every minute of it; I'll be happy earning the modest income that comes with managing our family farm."

Suggestions for Sustained Writing

1. Write a paragraph that uses the cause-and-effect method to explain why you do something habitually. For instance, explain why you are late for work every day, why you take the same road home, why you frequent a particular restaurant or bar, or why you study in the same place every night.

Arrange the paragraph in a general-to-specific or specific-to-general pattern, provide enough details to develop your central idea clearly and convincingly, and check for unity and coherence. You will find examples of effective cause-and-effect paragraphs in "Exile and Return" and "A Brother's Dreams."

As with other assignments, revise your work as necessary; never be satisfied with an early draft. Add or remove detail as appropriate, and insert transitions that will make your ideas easy to follow. Then edit carefully for mechanical errors that might reduce your writing's effectiveness.

2. If you responded to the first of the Suggestions for Journal Entries after "The Last Safe Haven," you have begun to gather information on whether or not you believe your community is safe. If you think it isn't, use what you have written thus far as the basis of a longer essay that supports your opinion. Here's a sample outline for the first draft of such an essay:

Paragraph 1: Thesis: *An increase in serious crime is making my hometown unsafe.* (You might include general information about kinds of crime you have seen, read about, or heard about.)

Paragraph 2: Discusses specific examples of criminal acts you know about. A good way to organize this paragraph is the general-to-specific pattern.

Paragraph 3: Uses cause and effect to explain the increase in crime. A good way to organize this paragraph is the question-to-answer pattern.

Paragraph 4: Uses process analysis to explain what your community should do to combat crime. A good way to organize this paragraph is the order-of-importance pattern.

Paragraph 5: Concludes the essay by referring to the thesis and expressing hope that things will get better.

Make sure to revise your rough draft several times. As you do, practice the techniques for maintaining coherence and unity discussed in Chapter 2. Whenever possible, add detail to make your ideas more convincing. Finally, edit and proofread the final version carefully.

3. After you read Keller's "Exile and Return," you might have used your journal to take a mental stroll through your high school and to write a preliminary thesis statement for an essay explaining your main impression or opinion of the time you spent there. If so, you might also have begun collecting memories that explain that impression.

Read your journal notes carefully. Add information if you can. Then, use your preliminary thesis as the beginning of an essay on your high school experience. Express your main impression or opinion of the experience through the thesis statement's main point.

Next, write three or four paragraphs that explain or support your thesis. Give each paragraph a topic sentence about one aspect of your experience. Make sure the topic sentence expresses a main point, and focus the information in your paragraph on that point.

Here's what an outline for such an essay might look like:

Paragraph 1

Thesis: *The thing I appreciate most about Valley High is that it helped me gain confidence as a student.* (This paragraph might also include information about the kind of high school you attended, your overall impression of the place, and things you most remember about it.)

Paragraph 2

Topic sentence: *My classmates were supportive.*
Method of development: Illustration
Pattern: General to specific

Paragraph 3

Topic sentence: *My teachers taught me to study for tests.*
Method of development: Process analysis or contrast
Pattern: Order of importance

Paragraph 4

Topic sentence: *With the help of math tutors, I finally overcame my fear of algebra.*
Method of development: Cause and effect or contrast
Pattern: Pivot

Paragraph 5:

Conclusion: This paragraph makes reference to the thesis. It also explains that the confidence you developed in high school will help you in college.

Read your rough draft carefully. Add details as needed to make your essay complete and convincing. After completing several drafts, edit and proofread the best of them.

4. Read any journal notes you made after reading Sharp's "Burger Queen." Use as much of this material as you can to write an essay that gives your general impression or opinion of a job you have held or a place at which you have worked. Your opinion might be positive, negative, or mixed, but make sure to state it clearly in your thesis statement, which should appear in your first paragraph.

To practice writing various kinds of paragraphs, try to include at least one of the following:

- A paragraph that defines the kind of business conducted or work performed at this job or place.
- A paragraph that provides examples of your usual duties or tasks.
- A paragraph that describes the physical environment in which you work or have worked—the factory, office building, restaurant, etc. If your job is or was outdoors, describe the kind of locations in which you most often work or worked.
- A paragraph that contrasts this job with another you have held.
- A paragraph that narrates incidents with customers and/or employees to explain the social environment or atmosphere in which you work or worked.

In addition, vary the patterns by which you organize your paragraphs. Try to include at least one that is arranged from general to specific; one that is arranged from specific to general; and one that uses the pivot pattern.

You might want to begin writing by making a formal outline of your paper based on what has been said above. Then, after carefully drafting and revising each paragraph and the paper as a whole, edit and proofread slowly and methodically.

5. After completing Paul Aronowitz's "A Brother's Dreams," you might have written a paragraph in your journal explaining how different your goal in life is from that of your brother, sister, or other close relative. If so, the method by which you developed this paragraph was contrast.

Reread this paragraph. What does it tell you about your subject's character? What kind of person is he or she? Turn your answer into the central idea (thesis statement) of an essay in which you continue to discuss this relative. In fact, make the paragraph you've already written the introduction to your essay.

As you plan this essay, consider writing a paragraph or two in which you describe this individual—the way he walks, the way she dresses, and so on. You might also want to include a narrative paragraph, one in which you tell a story that helps support what you say about him or her in your thesis. Finally, think about using additional methods of development—illustration, and conclusion and support, for example—in other paragraphs to develop your thesis further.

Once again, remember that writing is a process. You owe it to yourself and your readers to produce the most effective paper you can through painstaking rewriting and editing.

Writing to Learn: A Group Activity

THE FIRST MEETING

For inspiration, read Joannie M. Schrof's "The Last Safe Haven" aloud. Then, ask each group member to gather information about methods communities (both police and ordinary citizens) are using to prevent crime. Ideally, each member should gather the equivalent of two or three typewritten pages of information.

RESEARCH

Start with what you already know about crime prevention. However, interviewing a sociology or criminal justice professor, the head of the campus security force, or even a local police officer might be very worthwhile.

Another way to gather information is library research. Find informative magazine articles by checking recent editions of the *Readers' Guide to Periodical Literature* under headings such as crime, crime prevention, gang violence, vandalism, violent crime, rape, theft, burglary, automobile theft, and homicide. Also, search the Internet or any of your college library's electronic databases (CD-ROM or online). Ask your librarian for assistance.

Make enough photocopies of your interview notes or articles for each member of the group.

THE SECOND MEETING

Begin by exchanging interview notes or articles. Then, take turns reporting and discussing what each of you has found. Next, have each student choose the method of crime prevention he or she wants to make the topic of a paragraph of about 75–125 words. Each of you should write on a different method of crime prevention. Ideally, you should each write your paragraphs using a different pattern of paragraph organization as explained in this chapter: general-to-specific; specific-to-general; question-to-answer; problem-to-solution; order of importance; and around a pivot.

Make enough photocopies of your paragraphs for each member of your group.

THE FINAL MEETING

Share your paragraphs with each other and offer suggestions for revision and editing. Keep these questions in mind as you do so:

• Does the paragraph have a clear topic sentence?

• Is it developed in enough detail?

• Does the paragraph follow a pattern resembling one explained in this chapter?

• Is the paragraph unified and coherent? (Remember what you learned in Chapter 2.)

• Does the writer need to correct errors in grammar, sentence structure, punctuation, and spelling?

CHAPTER 4

Introductions and Conclusions

In the previous chapters you learned important principles to help you focus on the central idea of a paragraph or essay and to express this central idea in a topic sentence or thesis statement. You also learned how to develop paragraphs adequately and to make sure that each paragraph in an essay clearly develops the essay's thesis.

Most effective essays begin with an interesting and informative introduction—a paragraph or a series of paragraphs that reveals the essay's thesis and captures the reader's attention. Similarly, most successful essays end with a paragraph or a series of paragraphs that bring the writer's discussion of the subject to a timely and logical conclusion. Effective conclusions always leave the reader satisfied that everything the writer set out to discuss from the very beginning has been discussed.

Clearly, then, introductions and conclusions have special uses and are important to the success of an essay. That's why this chapter explains how to write them.

Writing Introductions

Before deciding exactly what to include in an introduction, how to organize it, or even how to begin it, ask yourself whether the essay you're writing actually calls for a formal introduction. If you're writing a narrative, for instance, you might simply want to start with the very first event in your story. Of course, you can always begin with colorful details, exciting vocabulary, or intriguing ideas that will spark your readers' interest. But you need not provide a thesis statement, background information, explanatory details, or other introductory material before getting into the story proper. If you feel the need to express your central idea in a formal thesis statement, you can do so later, at a convenient point in the body of your essay or even in its conclusion.

On the other hand, you might decide that your essay needs a formal introduction. If so, remember that the *most important* function of an introduction is to capture the attention of the readers and make them read on. However, you can also use an introduction to:

- Reveal the essay's central idea as expressed in the thesis.
- Guide readers to important ideas in the body of the essay.
- Provide background or explanatory information to help readers understand the essay's purpose and thesis.

Consider these four objectives when you plan your introduction. But if you are unable to decide how to begin, simply write out a preliminary thesis statement and go directly to the body of your essay. You can always get back to your introduction later in the writing process. It certainly does not have to be the very first part of the essay you write.

However you choose to get started, remember that an exciting part of writing is deciding *exactly* what you want to say about your subject. You usually won't make this discovery until after you have completed at least one draft—and often more than one draft—of the middle or body paragraphs of your essay. Once you have done that, your chances of going back and drafting a clearer, more substantial thesis will have improved. So will your chances of writing an interesting and effective introduction.

The simplest and sometimes best way to write an introductory paragraph or series of introductory paragraphs is to state your thesis at the very beginning and follow it with explanatory details that prepare readers for what they will find in the body of the essay. This is the method used by Shimon Peres, former prime minister of Israel, in an essay that appeared in *Civilization* magazine. Peres's thesis appears in italics.

> *[A nation's] strength and wealth today are products of science and technology.* No matter what the size of your land, no matter what the wealth of your natural resources, no matter what the number of your people, what really counts is the level of your scientific effort, your investment in education, your ability to encourage the human mind to flow freely and stimulate new ideas. ("The Bull in the Garden")

However, depending on your purpose, your thesis, and your audience, this may not always be the best way to begin. In Chapter 3, you learned several ways to develop the essay's body paragraphs. Here are several ways to write introductions:

1. Use a startling remark or statistic.
2. Ask a question or present a problem.
3. Challenge a widely held assumption or opinion.
4. Use a comparison, a contrast, or an analogy.
5. Tell an anecdote or describe a scene.
6. Use a quotation.
7. Define an important term or concept.
8. Address your readers directly.
9. Open with a paradox (an apparent contradiction).

Often, beginning writers limit their introductions to one paragraph. Doing so will help you get to the point quickly. On the other hand, you can—and sometimes must—spread your opening remarks over two or three short paragraphs. This may help you increase your readers' interest because it allows you to use a variety of methods to write your introduction. Each method is described below and illustrated by one or more sample paragraphs. In some samples, the central idea is expressed in a formal thesis statement (shown in italics); in others, the central idea is only implied, and no formal thesis statement can be identified.

USE A STARTLING REMARK OR STATISTIC

Some pieces of writing begin with statements or statistics (numbers) that, while true to the author's intent, have an effective shock value—one sure to make readers want to continue. Take this example of a lead paragraph from an essay on the state of the American family:

> Divorce and out-of-wedlock childbirth are transforming the lives of American children. In the postwar generation more than 80 percent of children grew up in a family with two biological parents who were married to each other. By 1980 only 50 percent could expect to spend their entire childhood in an intact family. If current trends continue, less than half of all children born today will live continuously with their own mother and father throughout childhood. *Most American children will spend several years in a single-mother family.* (Barbara Dafoe Whitehead, "Dan Quayle Was Right")

You might find this technique particularly effective if you have to take an unpopular stand on a well-known subject, as did former Philadelphia Phillies pitcher Robin Roberts in the opening of "Strike Out Little League":

> In 1939, Little League baseball was organized by Bert and George Bebble and Carl Stotz of Williamsport, Pa. What they had in mind in organizing this kids' baseball program, I'll never know. But *I'm sure they never visualized the monster it would grow into.*

A startling statement is often followed by details—some of them statistics—that explain the writer's point. In *Victims of Vanity,* a book criticizing laboratory tests on animals, Lynda Dickinson decided that spreading startling remarks and statistics over three short paragraphs would be a better way to capture the readers' attention and prepare them for her thesis than using one long unit:

> Lipstick, face cream, anti-perspirant, laundry detergent . . . these products and hundreds of other personal care and household items have one common ingredient: the suffering and death of millions of animals.
>
> An average of 25 million animals die every year in North America for the testing of everything from new cosmetics to new methods of warfare. Five hundred thousand to one million of these animals are sacrificed each year to test new cosmetics alone.

> *Of all the pain and suffering caused by animal research, cosmetic and household product testing is among the least justifiable, as it cannot even be argued that tests are done to improve the quality of human life.*

ASK A QUESTION OR PRESENT A PROBLEM

If you begin by asking a question or presenting a problem, you can devote the rest of your essay to discussing that question or problem and, perhaps, to providing answers or solutions. In "Old, Ailing, and Abandoned," an editorial on care of the elderly, which appeared in the *Philadelphia Inquirer,* the writer begins with three thought-provoking questions:

> How would you punish the people responsible for letting 18 hours pass before getting emergency medical help to an epileptic with second- and third-degree burns, while large sections of her skin were peeling off? What justice is there for a man whose amputated foot is allowed to become infested with maggots while he's paying for care in a specialized rooming house? And what's the proper penalty for someone who leaves a mentally ill woman alone for three days with little food and no medication?

In the first paragraph of "The Ambivalence of Abortion," Linda Bird Francke introduces the problem she and her husband faced over an unplanned pregnancy, thus preparing us for her discussion of abortion later in the essay:

> We were sitting in a bar on Lexington Avenue when I told my husband I was pregnant. It is not a memory I like to dwell on. Instead of the champagne and hope which had heralded [announced] the impending [coming] births of the first, second and third child, the news of this one was greeted with shocked silence and Scotch. "Jesus," my husband kept saying to himself, stirring the ice cubes around and around, "Oh Jesus."

CHALLENGE A WIDELY HELD ASSUMPTION OR OPINION

In "Gen X Is OK," Professor Edward E. Ericson, Jr., writes an introduction that both challenges an opinion and surprises his readers:

> Today's young adults read little. They're poorly prepared for college. They're suckers for the instant gratification of booze and drugs. They're enormously confused about sex and scared to death of marriage. They're all for a woman's right to choose an abortion, especially the men. They force metal rings through the most unwelcoming of facial orifices [openings]. They're so light on civic duty that few vote and fewer still can imagine why one would die for one's country. *And I like them.*

The last line of this paragraph—the author's thesis—captures our attention. We want to learn why in the world Ericson likes people whom he has just described so negatively. So, we read on!

Sometimes you can challenge an opinion or assumption by using a rhetorical question, as does Jeffrey Winters, author of "That Ozone Hole? Never Mind":

> Remember that hole in the ozone layer over Antarctica, the one thought to be caused by chlorofluorocarbons? It may be on the mend, say Japanese researchers. They say the hole could be on its way to recovery more quickly than anticipated.

USE A COMPARISON, A CONTRAST, OR AN ANALOGY

Comparison points out similarities; contrast points out differences. Both methods can help you provide important information about your subject, clarify or emphasize a point, and catch the reader's attention.

Donald M. Murray offers students good advice by contrasting the way they sometimes complete writing assignments with the more thorough and careful process used by professionals:

> When students complete a first draft, they consider the job of writing done—and their teachers too often agree. *When professional writers complete a first draft, they usually feel that they are at the start of the writing process.* When a draft is completed, the job of writing can begin. ("The Maker's Eye")

In the following paragraph, student Dan Roland uses both comparison and contrast. He begins by likening Kingston, Jamaica, to any city the reader might recognize, only to follow with a stark contrast between the extremes of wealth and poverty found there. The effect is startling and convincing. Roland has prepared his readers well for the thesis at the end of the paragraph.

> From my seat on an American Airlines 727, Kingston, Jamaica, looks like any other large urban center to me: tall buildings dominate the skyline, traffic weaves its way through roadways laid out like long arteries from the heart of the city. But Kingston is not like other cities, for it is here that some of the most extreme poverty in the world exists. The island of Jamaica was founded as a slave colony to help satisfy Europe's great demand for sugar cane, and its inhabitants are the descendants of slaves. Despair and poverty are part of everyday life and have been for centuries. The leading industry is tourism; every year thousands of well-to-do vacationers, mostly Americans and Canadians, come to stay in the multitudes of luxurious hotels and resorts. *Jamaica is one of the most beautiful places on Earth; it is also one of the most destitute [poorest].* ("Which Side of the Fence?")

Analogy serves the same purposes as comparison or contrast; the most important of these is, once again, to keep the reader's attention. But analogy also helps explain ideas that are hard to grasp by allowing you to compare them with things readers can understand more easily. Analogy points out similarities between subjects that are unrelated. This is what happens in "The Tapestry" when student Steven Grundy compares his family to a fine wall hanging:

> *My family is an ancient tapestry*, worn in places, faded by the passage of time, its colors softened by accumulated dust. It has hung there for so long that we rarely stop to appreciate its value. Yet beneath the dusty coating lies a precious masterpiece, a subtle composition of woven thread.

TELL AN ANECDOTE OR DESCRIBE A SCENE

Anecdotes are brief, interesting stories that illustrate or support a point. An anecdote can help you prepare readers for the issues or problems you will be discussing without having to state the thesis directly. For example, this anecdote, which begins a *Wall Street Journal* editorial, makes the essay's central idea clear even though it does not express it in a thesis statement:

> We don't know if Janice Camarena had ever heard of *Brown v. Board of Education* when she enrolled in San Bernadino Valley College in California, but she knows all about it now. Mrs. Camarena was thrown out of a class at her public community college because of the color of her skin. When she sat down at her desk on the first day of the semester in January 1994, the instructor asked her to leave. That section of English 101 was reserved for black students only, she was told; Mrs. Camarena is white. ("Affirmative Reaction")

Another way to prepare readers for what follows is to describe a scene in a way that lets them know your feelings about a subject. Take the introduction to "A Hanging," an essay in which George Orwell reveals his view on capital punishment. Orwell does not express his opinions in a thesis statement; the essay's gloomy setting—its time and place—does that for him:

> It was Burma, a sodden [soggy] morning of the rains. A sickly light, like yellow tinfoil, was slanting over the high walls into the jail yard. We were waiting outside the condemned cells, a row of sheds fronted with double bars, like small animal cages. Each cell measured about ten feet by ten and was quite bare within except for a plank bed and a pot for drinking water. In some of them brown silent men were squatting at the inner bars, with their blankets draped around them. These were the condemned men, due to be hanged within the next week or two.

USE A QUOTATION

Quoting an expert or simply using an interesting, informative statement from another writer, from someone you've interviewed formally, or even from someone with whom you've only been chatting can lend interest and authority to your introduction. If you use this method, however, remember to quote your source accurately. Also be sure that the quotation relates to the other ideas in your paragraph clearly and logically.

Philip Shabecoff uses a quotation from world-famous scientist and writer Rachel Carson to lead us to his thesis in the introduction to his essay on pesticides:

> "The most alarming of all man's assaults upon the environment is the contamination of air, earth, rivers, and sea with dangerous and even lethal materials," Rachel Carson wrote a quarter of a century ago in her celebrated book *Silent Spring*. Today there is little disagreement with her warnings in regard to such broad-spectrum pesticides as DDT, then widely used, now banned. *But there is still hot debate over how to apply modern pesticides—which are designed to kill specific types of weeds or insects—in ways that do not harm people and their environment.* ("Congress Again Confronts Hazards of Killer Chemicals")

DEFINE AN IMPORTANT TERM OR CONCEPT

Defining a term can explain aspects of your subject that will make it easier for readers to understand your central idea. But don't use dictionary definitions. Because they are often limited and rigid, they will make the beginning of an essay uninteresting. Instead, rely on your own ingenuity to create definitions that are interesting and appropriate to your purpose. This is what student Elena Santayana has done in the introduction to a paper about alcohol addiction:

> Alcoholism is a disease whose horrible consequences go beyond the patient. Families of alcoholics often become dysfunctional; spouses and children are abandoned or endure physical and emotional abuse. Co-workers suffer too. Alcoholics have high rates of absenteeism, and their work is often unreliable, thereby decreasing office or factory productivity. Indeed, alcoholics endanger the whole community. One in every two automobile fatalities is alcohol-related, and alcoholism is a major cause of violent crime. ("Everybody's Problem")

ADDRESS YOUR READERS DIRECTLY

Speaking to your readers directly is an excellent way to get their attention. Notice how effectively Claudia Wallis does this at the very beginning of an article from *Time* magazine:

> To grasp what it means to be 120 years old, consider this: a woman in the U.S. now has a life expectancy of 79 years. Jeanne Calment of Arles, France, reached that advanced age back in 1954, when Eisenhower was in the White House and Stalin had just passed from the scene. Twenty-two years later, at age 100, Calment was still riding

her bicycle around town, having outlived both her only child and grandchild. And 20 years after that, she was charming the photographers and reporters who arrived in droves last week, . . . to mark her 120th birthday. ("How to Live to Be 120")

In "What Is Poverty?" Jo Goodwin Parker has also chosen to address her readers directly, but she begins with a question. Her introduction is both urgent and emphatic:

You ask me what is poverty? Listen to me. Here I am, dirty, smelly, and with no "proper" underwear on and with the stench of my rotting teeth near you. I will tell you. Listen to me. Listen without pity. I cannot use your pity. Listen with understanding. Put yourself in my dirty, worn out, ill-fitting shoes, and hear me.

OPEN WITH A PARADOX

A paradox is a statement that, while true, seems to contradict itself. Because such statements are interesting in themselves, they make effective beginnings. For example, take this opening paragraph to Angie Cannon's "Crime Stories of the Century," which appeared in a December 1999 issue of *U.S. News & World Report*. Cannon's thesis, which contains a paradox, appears in italics.

We are at once disgusted and fascinated by crime. First we avert [turn away] our eyes. Then we reach for the newspapers with their grisly headlines and stare for hours at our televisions as the accused villains go on trial. *Every decade, it seems, produces a "crime of the century."* As E. L. Doctorow noted in *Ragtime*, headline writers way back in 1906 had already anointed [labeled] the murder of renowned architect Stanford White the "Crime of the Century," even though there were still 94 more years to go.

Writing Conclusions

Sometimes, it is on the basis of your conclusion alone that your readers respond to your essay and remember the point it tries to make. The conclusion's length depends on the essay's length and purpose. For a very short essay, you can simply end the last paragraph with a concluding sentence, which might itself contain details important to developing your thesis. Such is the case in Kenneth Jon Rose's "2001 Space Shuttle." Rose's last paragraph, a description of the shuttle's landing on its return to Earth, also contains his conclusion (shown in italics):

[T]he sky turns lighter and layers of clouds pass you like cars on a highway. Minutes later, still sitting upright, you will see the gray runway in the distance. Then the shuttle slows to 300 mph and drops its landing gear. Finally, with its nose slightly up like the Concorde SST and at a speed of about 225 mph, the shuttle will land on the asphalt runway and slowly come to a halt. *The trip into space will be over.*

Although one-sentence conclusions are fine for short essays, you will often need close with at least one full paragraph. Either way, a conclusion should bring your discussion of the thesis to a timely and logical end. Try not to conclude abruptly; always give a signal that you are about to wrap things up. And never use your conclusion to introduce new ideas—ideas for which you did not prepare your readers earlier in the essay.

There are many ways to write conclusions. Here are eight:

1. Rephrase or make reference to your thesis.
2. Summarize or rephrase your main points.
3. Offer advice; make a call to action.
4. Look to the future.
5. Explain how a problem was resolved.
6. Ask a rhetorical question.
7. Close with a statement or quotation readers will remember.
8. Respond to a question in your introduction.

REPHRASE OR MAKE REFERENCE TO YOUR THESIS

In Chapter 1 you learned that it can be appropriate to place the thesis statement not in the introduction, but in a later paragraph or even in the conclusion. As a beginning writer, however, you might want to use the more traditional pattern which is to place your thesis at the beginning of the essay. Of course, this doesn't mean you shouldn't rephrase or refer to the thesis in your conclusion. Doing so can emphasize your central idea.

Take this three-part conclusion from Professor Edward E. Ericson, Jr.'s "Gen X Is OK," the introduction to which appears on page 158.

> I didn't plan to develop a special fondness for today's young. My students made me do it. Of course I haven't stopped worrying. This generation does not seem headed for greatness. They have suffered too much cultural despoliation [loss], too much distortion of personhood, for that. It would take a global cataclysm [catastrophe] for them to have any chance of rising to the heights of human valor.
>
> But will they be basically sensible, productive adults? Were I a betting man, I'd put my money on them. And the more intergeneration friendships they form, the better their odds will be.
>
> All in all, I think Gen X is OK.

Ericson rephrases his thesis when he says, "Gen X Is OK." But he also restates four important points he made in the body of his essay:

1. His students caused him "to develop a special fondness for today's young."
2. Members of Gen X don't seem "headed for greatness."
3. They will become "sensible, productive adults."
4. Friendships between members of different generations will help improve their chances for success.

SUMMARIZE OR REPHRASE YOUR MAIN POINTS

For long essays, restating your thesis can be combined with summarizing or rephrasing each of the main points you have made in the body paragraphs. Doing so will help you write an effective summary of the entire essay and emphasize important ideas. This is exactly what Robin Roberts has done in his two concluding paragraphs of "Strike Out Little League" (see his introduction on page 157):

> I still don't know what those three gentlemen in Williamsport had in mind when they organized Little League baseball. I'm sure they didn't want parents arguing with their children about kids' games. I'm sure they didn't want young athletes hurting their arms pitching under pressure. . . . I'm sure they didn't want young boys . . . made to feel that something is wrong with them because they can't play baseball. I'm sure they didn't want a group of coaches drafting the players each year for different teams. I'm sure they didn't want unqualified men working with the young players. I'm sure they didn't realize how normal it is for an 8-year-old boy to be scared of a thrown or batted baseball.
>
> For the life of me, I can't figure out what they had in mind.

OFFER ADVICE; MAKE A CALL TO ACTION

An example of a conclusion that offers advice appears in Elena Santayana's "Everybody's Problem," the introduction to which appears on page 161.

> If you have alcoholic friends, relatives, or co-workers, the worst thing you can do is to look the other way. This disease and its effects are simply not theirs to deal with alone. Try persuading them to seek counseling. Describe the extent to which their illness is hurting their families, co-workers, and neighbors. Explain that their alcoholism endangers the entire community. Above all, don't pretend not to notice! Alcoholism is everybody's problem.

LOOK TO THE FUTURE

If you believe the future can bring significant changes or new developments in regard to a topic you have discussed in your essay, you might end by discussing those changes. This is what Barbara Dafoe Whitehead does in "Dan Quayle Was Right." (You will find her introduction on page 157.)

> People learn; societies can change; particularly when it becomes apparent that certain behaviors damage the social ecology, threaten the public order, and impose new burdens on core institutions. Whether Americans will act to overcome the legacy of family disruption is a crucial but as yet unanswered question.

In "Crime Stories of the Century" (its introduction appears on page 162), Angie Cannon concludes with a much darker vision of the future. Given her subject matter and the points she makes in her essay, however, it seems appropriate to her purpose:

> And in the new millennium? "Oklahoma City, I'm afraid, is the future," says [historian Roger] Lane." At the end of this American century and the beginning of the next, all the world's grievances center on Uncle Sam." Sadly, there will be many more "crimes of the century."

Note that Cannon's conclusion uses more than one method. In addition to looking to the future, she inserts a direct quotation that readers will remember. All of this is perfectly appropriate. So, when it comes time to writing your own essays—especially those of the longer variety—don't be afraid to combine methods or to spread your conclusion over two or three paragraphs.

EXPLAIN HOW A PROBLEM WAS RESOLVED

In "The Ambivalence of Abortion" (see page 158 for the introduction to this essay), Linda Bird Francke writes about the difficulty she and her husband had in deciding whether to have or abort their fourth child. Francke's conclusion tells us how they resolved the question:

> My husband and I are back to planning our summer vacation and his career switch. And it certainly does make sense not to be having a baby right now—we say to each other all the time. But I have this ghost now. A very little ghost that only appears when I'm seeing something beautiful, like the full moon on the ocean last weekend. And the baby waves to me. And I wave at the baby. "Of course, we have room," I cry to the ghost. "Of course, we do."

ASK A RHETORICAL QUESTION

A rhetorical question (a question whose answer is obvious) asks your readers to participate in your essay's conclusion by answering the question. If you believe the essay has made the answer so obvious that all readers will respond to the question as you want them to, ending with a rhetorical question can be a fine way to make your essay memorable. As a reader, it's hard to forget an essay when you've answered its question in your own words.

Jo Goodwin Parker uses this device in "What Is Poverty?" (See her introduction on page 162):

> I have come out of my despair to tell you this. Remember I did not come from another place to another time. Others like me are all around you. Look at us with an angry heart, anger that will help you help me. Anger that will let you tell of me. The poor are always silent. Can you be silent too?

CLOSE WITH A STATEMENT OR QUOTATION READERS WILL REMEMBER

Deciding whether a statement or quotation will stick in readers' memories isn't easy. Trust your instincts. If a particular remark has made a strong impression on you, it may work for others. As always, however, make your conclusion relate directly to your essay's content. In "How to Live to Be 120," Claudia Wallis closes her discussion with a direct quotation from her fascinating subject, whom you read about in the introduction to Wallis's essay on page 161.

> As for Jeanne Calment, she seems to embody the calm resilience associated with long life. "I took pleasure when I could," she said. . . . "I acted clearly and morally and without regret. I'm very lucky."

RESPOND TO A QUESTION IN YOUR INTRODUCTION

After asking a question in your introduction, you can fill your essay with information that discusses the question or prepares the reader for an answer in your conclusion, or both. In the introduction to "Old, Ailing, Abandoned," the writer raises serious questions about caring for the elderly (see page 158). Here is the conclusion to that essay:

> Communities, stretched though they may be, need to remember these forgotten elderly living in our midst. What if every church in the region agreed to regularly visit residents at just one [nursing] home? How about local government, or advocate agencies, linking the owners of small facilities more closely with existing services, such as rehab grants that could improve conditions?
>
> One simple question need guide us: How would we want *our* parents treated?

Interestingly, the writer phrases much of this conclusion in questions; but these are rhetorical questions, for which the answers are obvious.

Visualizing Ways to Write Introductions and Conclusions

Read the introduction and conclusion to Michael Ryan's "They Track the Deadliest Viruses," which appear below. Comments in the margins identify effective techniques you might use in your own introductions and conclusions.

Ryan—Introduction

Makes a startling statement and challenges an assumption.

"A disease that's in a faraway place today may be in our own backyard tomorrow," said Dr. James Hughes [of] the Centers for Disease Control and Prevention (CDC) in Atlanta. "We're certainly not immune."

Creates a contrast.

A few years ago, this statement would have surprised many Americans. The advent [coming] of "miracle drugs and vaccines that conquered such plagues as polio, smallpox and even measles led many of us—including some scientists—to believe that the age of killer diseases was coming to an end.

The AIDS epidemic changed that . . . *States essay's thesis*

Ryan—Conclusion

On my visit to Atlanta I . . . met with the associate director of the CDC, Dr. James Curran. He has been involved in the fight against AIDS since 1981. "The first five years, through 1985, was the age of discovery. . . . We discovered the global extent of the epidemic, the virus, antibody tests, AZT.

Refers to thesis.

It was an exciting time, but when it ended, half a million people in the U.S. already were infected.

Looks to the future.

Today, Dr. Curran said, the Centers for Disease Control and Prevention's response to the AIDS epidemic has changed. "We're trying

Uses a quotation readers will remember.

to help the country evaluate the blood supply, develop test kits and work on prevention and counseling strategies. . . .

Information alone isn't sufficient. We have to find ways to change behavior—especially in young people, who sometimes think they're invulnerable."

Makes a call to action.

Revising Introductions and Conclusions

Later in this chapter, you will read Anita DiPasquale's "The Transformation of Maria Fernandez." DiPasquale knew that the first version of her essay was not the best she could do, so she rewrote her paper several times. Compare the rough and final drafts of the paragraphs she used in her essay's introduction and conclusion.

DiPasquale's Introduction—Rough Draft

Maria's story is a very shocking testimony

A good first try; add stronger details?

to a brutal war. Her country is Nicaragua. This impoverished yet beautiful land is the site in which the Reagan Administration became involved in a series of actions known as the Iran-Contra fiasco. The only good

Is this essay's thesis?

that has come from our country's involvement in this dreadful war is that the apathetic American, hopefully, has finally realized that Kansas does not mean Central America, Contra does not mean freedom fighter, and Sandinista   does not mean repressive regime.

<u>We</u> meet Maria on a trip through hell. The month was June; the year was 1988. Maria is seventeen, no longer a child, no longer a woman. She is a soldier in the FSLN.

Is author with someone or does "we" include her readers?

Maria is a thin girl with shoulder-length raven hair, which she keeps in a braid and tucks away under her camouflage hat. Her nose is long, her chin is proud. She is olive in color, and her cheekbones are high like those of a *Vogue* model.

Will this move the reader?

DiPasquale's Introduction—Final Draft

Maria's story is testimony to the horror of war. Her country is Nicaragua, one of America's greatest embarrassments and yet another battleground in what the superpowers called the "cold" war. In this impoverished, <u>merciless</u>, yet beautiful land, the Reagan Administration became <u>mired</u> in a series of <u>covert</u> operations known as the Iran-Contra fiasco. <u>Ironically,</u> our shame over this dreadful incident may be the only good thing to come from our presence in Nicaragua. Perhaps Americans who were once parochial and apathetic will realize that Kansas is not Central America, that *Sandinista* and

Final draft combines sentences for smoothness.

Adds detail; improves word choice.

Focuses her essay on a revised, more specific thesis.

"repressive" are not synonymous, that *Contra* may not mean "freedom fighter," and that all wars, no matter who the adversaries, are barbarous!

My friend Michael and I meet Maria on a trip through hell in Nicaragua's capital, Managua. The month is June, the year 1988.

Adds information to clarify a point.

Explains important historical information and abbreviation.

Maria is seventeen, no longer a child, no longer a woman. She is a soldier in the FSLN (*Frente Sandinista de Liberacion Nacional*), the national liberation front named for Augusto Sandino, a guerrilla fighter martyred in an earlier war of liberation.

Maria is thin, with shoulder-length raven hair, which she braids and tucks away under her camouflage hat. Her nose is long and straight, her chin prominent and proud. A silky olive complexion and cheekbones straight out of *Vogue* magazine reveal a face

Adds a question that startles reader and sets essay's tone.

that is truly delicate. How, then, has it come to harbor the deadest eyes I have ever seen?

DiPasquale's Conclusion—Rough Draft

My stomach grew heavy and sank to a depth I did not know was possible. A truck pulled into the street. It was filled with dead Contra bodies on the way to burial. Another truck pulled up behind, and this one was filled with Sandinista soldiers. My heart sank in desperation. These soldiers were children: eight, ten, fifteen. All toting rifles, passing cigarettes among the crowd. When I looked in the other truck, I grew ill with fear. This truck was also filled with children, men, and women, but all were dead.

Needs to describe in more detail.

Sentences are choppy.

It is practically impossible to tell the Contras and Sandinistas apart. Their youth, their camaraderie, and dead have a lot in common.

Needs expansion, stronger detail.

DiPasquale's Conclusion—Final Draft

As Maria finishes her story, my stomach grows heavy and sinks to a depth I did not think was possible. Suddenly, a truck pulls onto the street. It is filled with dead Contras on the way to burial. Another truck pulls up behind; this one is filled with Sandinista soldiers, none of whom look over twenty. Most are between ten and fifteen. Some might be eight. They are all toting rifles, passing cigarettes out among the crowd. When I look into the first truck, I become desperate with fear. Piled one on top of another are men, women, and children. They are all dead.

Uses present tense to create excitement.

Combines sentences to correct and smooth out sentence structure.

Uses stronger vocabulary and adds stark details.

Adds a new paragraph that refers to someone mentioned earlier in the essay.

Back at the ledge, I slump against Michael. Maria emerges from the daze of her horrid memory and kisses Michael on the cheek. She points to the trucks. "If he [Maria's younger brother] were here, his world would be all too real."

Adds quotation readers will remember.

Expands this paragraph with stronger, smoother wording.

Sometimes it is nearly impossible to tell Contra soldiers and Sandinistas apart. They have a lot in common: their youth, their camaraderie, their mortality. When Salvadoran Archbishop Rivera y Damas spoke of the role of the superpowers in his country's civil war, he could have been describing the tragedy of Nicaragua: "They supply the weapons, and we supply the dead."

Practicing Writing Introductions

Write a one-paragraph introduction for an essay you might compose on one of the following topics. Try using one of the methods for writing introductions suggested with each topic.

1. **Topic:** A terrifying, tragic, or emotionally charged experience.

   Method: Use a startling remark or statistic.

   _____

   _____

   _____

   _____

   _____

2. **Topic:** Dealing with an allergy or other common health problem.

   Method: Ask a question or present a problem.

   _____

   _____

   _____

   _____

   _____

3. **Topic:** The benefits (or dangers) of physical exercise.

   Method: Tell an anecdote or use contrast.

   _____

   _____

   _____

   _____

   _____

4. **Topic:** Ways to overcome pain other than using drugs.

   Method: Challenge a widely held opinion, use contrast, or present a problem.

   _____

   _____

   _____

   _____

   _____

5. **Topic:** What your clothes (car, home, or room) say about you.

   Method: Describe a scene, use a quotation, or address your readers directly.

   _____

   _____

   _____

   _____

   _____

6. **Topic:** The role of a father or mother in a young family.

   Method: Ask a question or challenge a widely held opinion.

   _____

   _____

   _____

   _____

7. **Topic:** Overcoming a fear of math (heights, closed-in places, water, etc.).

   Method: Address your readers directly, ask a question, or define a term.

   _____

   _____

   _____

   _____

8. **Topic:** Practicing safe sex.

   Method: Present a problem, define a term, or address your readers directly.

   _____

   _____

   _____

   _____

Read the introductions and conclusions to the following four essays carefully, and take some time to respond to the Questions for Discussion and the Suggestions for Journal Entries that follow each selection. As always, you will also want to try your hand at the Suggestions for Sustained Writing at the end of the chapter. Doing so will help you develop the skills needed to write good introductions and conclusions of your own—the kind that will capture your readers' attention and make them look forward to more of your writing.

I Was Just Wondering

Robert Fulghum

Robert Fulghum wrote All I Really Need to Know I Learned in Kindergarten, *the best-selling collection of essays from which this one is taken. The contents of this funny book are summed up by its subtitle:* Uncommon Thoughts
on Common Things. *Fulghum has worked as a cowboy, IBM sales representative, bartender, teacher, artist, and minister. Judging from this selection, he has a
curiosity and love for life that make it easy to understand why his writing is so
popular.*

Preparing to Read

1. As you read this essay, ask yourself why Fulghum's introduction and
    conclusion are effective. Identify methods for writing beginnings and
    endings you learned earlier in this chapter.
2. In paragraphs 1, 5, and 8, Fulghum intentionally uses incomplete
    sentences, known as fragments, to create emphasis and establish a
    conversational tone. They are part of a carefully considered style that
    this experienced writer chose for his essay. As a rule, however,
    developing writers should avoid fragments.

Vocabulary

curry (verb)	Groom.
epidemic (noun)	Widespread occurrence.
meditate (verb)	Think, ponder, contemplate.
oracle (noun)	Advisor, prophet. (Here, *oracle* is used figuratively; Fulghum describes the habit some folks have of questioning themselves as they look in the mirror.)
Ph.D. (noun)	Advanced academic degree, also known as a doctorate.
potions (noun)	Liquid medicines, remedies.
preen (verb)	Make ready, prepare.
unguents (noun)	Salves, ointments.
spelunking (noun)	Cave exploring.

I Was Just Wondering

Robert Fulghum

I WAS JUST wondering. Did you ever go to somebody's house for dinner or a 1
party or something and then use the bathroom? And while you were in there,
did you ever take a look around in the medicine cabinet? Just to kind of compare notes, you know? Didn't you ever—just look around a little?

I have a friend who does it all the time. He's doing research for a Ph.D. in 2
sociology. He says lots of other people do it, too. And they aren't working on a
Ph.D. in sociology, either. It's not something people talk about much—because
you think you might be the only one who is doing it, and you don't want people to think you're strange, right?

My friend says if you want to know the truth about people, it's the place to 3
go. All you have to do is look in the drawers and shelves and cabinets in the
bathroom. And take a look at the robes and pajamas and nightgowns hanging
on the hook behind the door. You'll get the picture. He says all their habits and
hopes and dreams and sorrows, illnesses and hangups, and even their sex life—
all stand revealed in that one small room.

He says most people are secret slobs. He says the deepest mysteries of the 4
race are tucked into the nooks and crannies of the bathroom, where we go to
be alone, to confront ourselves in the mirror, to comb and curry and scrape and
preen our hides, to coax our aging and ailing bodies into one more day, to clean
ourselves and relieve ourselves, to paint and deodorize our surfaces, to medi-
tate and consult our oracle and attempt to improve our lot.

He says it's all there. In cans and bottles and tubes and boxes and vials. Po- 5
tions and oils and unguents and sprays and tools and lotions and perfumes and
appliances and soaps and pastes and pills and creams and pads and powders
and medicines and devices beyond description—some electric and some not.
The wonders of the ages.

He says he finds most bathrooms are about the same, and it gives him a 6
sense of the wondrous unity of the human race.

I don't intend to start an epidemic of spelunking in people's bathrooms. 7
But I did just go in and take a look in my own. I get the picture. I don't know
whether to laugh or cry.

Take a look. In your own. And from now on, please go to the bathroom be- 8
fore you visit me. Mine is closed to the public.

Read More on the Web

Fulghum's short essay "That Kindergarten Thing," which he expanded
into *All I Really Need to Know I Learned in Kindergarten:*
http://darriendesign.com/serendipity/wisdom.htm

Short biography of Fulghum: http://www.taemag.com/taeja95u.htm
January Magazine online interview with Fulghum:
    http://www.januarymagazine.com/fulghum.html

Questions for Discussion

1. What two ways of writing introductions discussed in this chapter did
    you find in paragraph 1?
2. Which of the methods for concluding discussed earlier best describes
    Fulghum's approach in paragraph 8?
3. What method of development that you learned about in the previous
    chapter does Fulghum use in paragraph 3?
4. What techniques does Fulghum use to maintain coherence in and
    between paragraphs?

Thinking Critically

1. Pretend you caught someone snooping around in your bathroom,
    bedroom, closet, or other private part of your home. Write this
    person a letter explaining your reaction.
2. What does Fulghum mean when he says that bathrooms are places
    where we go "to meditate and consult our oracle and attempt to
    improve our lot"?

Suggestions for Journal Entries

1. Are most people "secret slobs"? What about you? Think of a
    particular place you call your own. Does the way you keep it show
    how neat or sloppy you are? If so, use focused freewriting to describe
    what it looks like. A place to write about might be your bedroom,
    bathroom, car, closet, area in which you study, or location where you
    spend most of your time at work.
2. Like Fulghum, do some wondering. Focus on someone you know
    very well. Can you describe or at least imagine what the inside of his
    or her room, closet, apartment, house, refrigerator, garage, basement,
    or bathroom looks like? What might you see in such places that
    would describe this individual's personality?

A Prayer for the Days of Awe

Elie Wiesel

Elie Wiesel was born in Romania in 1928. In 1944, he was imprisoned in Auschwitz and Buchenwald, two of the many infamous Nazi death camps where six million Jews and millions of other people were murdered. This horror is now called the Holocaust, a word derived from the fact that the bodies of many victims of this mass murder were burned in ovens after having been gassed or killed in other ways. Wiesel's autobiographical novel Night *recalls his experience in the camps, and his many other novels, plays, and stories are aimed at making sure the Holocaust is never forgotten. Wiesel was awarded the Nobel Peace Prize in 1986. He now teaches at Boston University.*

Preparing to Read

1. This essay appeared in the *New York Times* shortly before Rosh Hashanah, the Jewish New Year Holiday, which is observed in prayer and begins the Ten Days of Penitence, ending with Yom Kippur, the Day of Atonement. These Days of Awe conclude with the faithful's praying for forgiveness for the previous year's sins.

2. As Wiesel's title indicates, this is not just an essay; it is a prayer. Keep this in mind as you read this selection, for Wiesel is addressing two—and perhaps three—different audiences.

3. How might Wiesel be using the word "awe"? Look this word up in a dictionary.

Vocabulary

annihilate (verb)	Destroy completely, exterminate.
culpability (noun)	Guilt, responsibility.
fervor (noun)	Enthusiasm, eagerness, passion.
Sabbath (noun)	Day of worship.
testimony (noun)	Written or spoken statement that something is true.
theological (adjective)	Having to do with the study of God.
Treblinka (noun)	Another Nazi concentration camp.
tribunal (noun)	Council, court.
Zionism (noun)	A movement that attempted to reestablish the Jewish state in Palestine.

A Prayer for the Days of Awe

Elie Wiesel

MASTER OF THE Universe, let us make up. It is time. How long can we go on   1
being angry?

More than 50 years have passed since the nightmare was lifted. Many   2
things, good and less good, have since happened to those who survived it. They
learned to build on ruins. Family life was recreated. Children were born,
friendships struck. They learned to have faith in their surroundings, even in
their fellow men and women. Gratitude has replaced bitterness in their hearts.
No one is as capable of thankfulness as they are. Thankful to anyone willing to
hear their tales and become their ally in the battle against apathy and forget-
fulness. For them every moment is grace.

Oh, they do not forgive the killers and their accomplices, nor should they.   3
Nor should you, Master of the Universe. But they no longer look at every
passer-by with suspicion. Nor do they see a dagger in every hand.

Does this mean that the wounds in their soul have healed? They will never   4
heal. As long as a spark of the flames of Auschwitz and Treblinka glows in their
memory, so long will my joy be incomplete.

What about my faith in you, Master of the Universe?   5

I now realize I never lost it, not even over there, during the darkest hours   6
of my life. I don't know why I kept on whispering my daily prayers, and those
one reserves for the Sabbath, and for the holidays, but I did recite them, often
with my father and, on Rosh Hashanah eve, with hundreds of inmates at
Auschwitz. Was it because the prayers remained a link to the vanished world
of my childhood?

But my faith was no longer pure. How could it be? It was filled with an-   7
guish rather than fervor, with perplexity more than piety. In the kingdom of
eternal night, on the Days of Awe, which are the Days of Judgment, my traditional prayers were directed to you as well as against you, Master of the Universe. What hurt me more: your absence or your silence?

In my testimony I have written harsh words, burning words about your   8
role in our tragedy. I would not repeat them today. But I felt them then. I felt
them in every cell of my being. Why did you allow if not enable the killer day
after day, night after night to torment, kill and annihilate tens of thousands of
Jewish children? Why were they abandoned by your Creation? These thoughts
were in no way destined to diminish the guilt of the guilty. Their established
culpability is irrelevant to my "problem" with you, Master of the Universe. In
my childhood I did not expect much from human beings. But I expected everything from you.

Where were you, God of kindness, in Auschwitz? What was going on in   9
heaven, at the celestial tribunal, while your children were marked for humiliation, isolation and death only because they were Jewish?

These questions have been haunting me for more than five decades. You 10 have vocal defenders, you know. Many theological answers were given me, such as "God is God. He alone knows what He is doing. One has no right to question Him or His ways." Or: "Auschwitz was a punishment for European Jewry's sins of assimilation and/or Zionism." And: "Isn't Israel the solution? Without Auschwitz, there would have been no Israel."

I reject all these answers. Auschwitz must and will forever remain a ques- 11 tion mark only: it can be conceived neither with God nor without God. At one point, I began wondering whether I was not unfair with you. After all, Auschwitz was not something that came down ready-made from heaven. It was conceived by men, implemented by men, staffed by men. And their aim was to destroy not only us but you as well. Ought we not to think of your pain, too? Watching your children suffer at the hands of your other children, haven't you also suffered?

As we Jews now enter the High Holidays again, preparing ourselves to pray 12 for a year of peace and happiness for our people and all people, let us make up, Master of the Universe. In spite of everything that happened? Yes, in spite. Let us make up: for the child in me, it is unbearable to be divorced from you so long.

Read More on the Web

Biography of Elie Wiesel with links to bibliography of his works and to
    Report to the President on the President's Commission on the
    Holocaust: http://xroads.virginia.edu/~CAP/HOLO/ELIEBIO.HTM
Home page of the United States Holocaust Memorial Museum:
    http://www.ushmm.org/
Noble Prize Internet Archive on Elie Wiesel: http://almaz.com/nobel/
    peace/1986a.html

Questions for Discussion

1. What method or methods for writing introductions does Wiesel use?
2. What method does he use to close the essay?
3. Why does the author refer to God as "Master of the Universe" rather than use a more personal form of address?
4. This selection is addressed to at least two audiences: God and the readers of the *New York Times*. Why did Wiesel choose to address both? Why didn't he write it solely for human readers?
5. Is Wiesel also writing to himself? Explain.

6. In paragraph 10, Wiesel tells us that many questions have been "haunting [him] for more than five decades." What are those questions?

7. Reread paragraphs 11 and 12. What do they reveal about the reason or reasons Wiesel wants to make peace with God?

Thinking Critically

1. In a 1998 interview with George Plimpton, Wiesel said: "I rarely speak about God. To God, yes. I protest against Him. I shout at Him. But to open a discourse [discussion] about the qualities of God, about the problems that God imposes . . ., no. And yet He is there, in silence." What light does this quotation shed on "A Prayer for the Days of Awe"? What is Wiesel's purpose in writing this prayer? Has his attitude toward God changed from what it was when he spoke with Plimpton?

2. Do you have a favorite prayer, poem, or hymn? Read it carefully; then, summarize it in your journal. In the process explain why this particular piece is meaningful to you.

Suggestions for Journal Entries

1. Sometimes life seems illogical, and tragedies strike for no apparent reason and with no warning. If such an incident has occurred in your life or in the life of someone you know, write down everything you know about this event.

2. Have you ever been angry with God or with the universe for allowing some difficulty or horror to visit you or others? Record the particulars of this situation. Make sure to explain why you are or were angry.

Code of Denial

Tena Moyer

Like many of the authors whose work appears in this text, Tena Moyer's primary occupation is not writing. However, she is an articulate professional who is passionate enough about a subject to communicate it brilliantly to others. Moyer is a physician practicing in a small town in the mountains of southern California, where she runs a breast-cancer screening clinic. Once having worked for a large health maintenance organization (HMO) in Los Angeles, Moyer moved to a rural community to practice the kind of medicine that allowed her to develop a more personal understanding of her patients and their needs.

First published in Discover magazine, this selection is taken from a longer essay that describes Moyer's reaction to her sister's getting and dying from breast cancer. But this is no straightforward medical report; Moyer reveals a great deal of herself, not simply as a doctor and sister, but in a variety of roles.

Preparing to Read

1. Search the Internet to find out all you can about breast-cancer examinations. What are they like? How often should women get them? Why are they so important? Do men get breast cancer? What are the treatments for such an illness?

2. Above you read that the author reveals herself through a variety of roles. Besides recalling this experience through the eyes of a doctor and of a sister, what other ways might she be looking at it? Think about such perspectives as you read this essay.

3. What concerns, fears, plans might run through an author's mind as he or she writes an essay on losing a sister to cancer? Begin thinking about this question by considering the title of this essay.

4. In the conclusion, the author distinguishes medicine as science from medicine as art. Look for clues to this distinction earlier in the essay.

Vocabulary

alien (adjective)	Foreign, strange.
bat mitzvahs (noun)	Ceremonies that celebrate a daughter's coming of age in Judaism.
bereft (adjective)	Deprived of.
biopsy (noun)	Laboratory test on tissue to determine presence of disease.

cataclysm (noun)	Catastrophe.
chemotherapeutic (adjective)	Pertaining to chemotherapy, a treatment for cancer.
desolate (adjective)	Barren.
fitfully (adverb)	Erratically, irregularly.
indelible (adjective)	Nonerasable, permanent.
obfuscate (verb)	Confuse, complicate, bewilder.
palette (noun)	Hand-held board on which a painter places blobs of paint.
pathology (noun)	Study of diseases.
prognosis (noun)	Prediction of the effects or outcome of an illness.
protoplasm (noun)	Basic matter that makes up the cells of living things.
sadistic (adjective)	Taking pleasure from inflicting pain.
sentient (adjective)	Alive and conscious, aware.

Code of Denial

Tena Moyer

CANCER IS LIKE a nuclear bomb that detonates in the middle of your family. 1
Before the phone call, the explosion, you go about your life unaware and unconcerned that a cataclysm of such proportion could possibly disrupt your life. Sure, there are the warning signs that scream like air raid sirens—the lump, the unhealed sore, the bloody stool, the shortness of breath. But we have learned to live with denial. After all, we are the generation that learned to duck and cover during the Cold War. And so when the physician, with drawn and serious face, says we need to run a few tests, we hear the siren and shudder at the thought, but we dismiss it just as quickly saying, praying, "It could never happen to me or my family." Duck and cover.

But the phone rings and the bomb falls and in a heartbeat the once famil- 2
iar landscape of your life becomes desolate and devastated, alien and treacherous. All the landmarks, the road signs, you have used to orient and guide yourself are blown away, and suddenly you don't know what to do or where to turn or whom to call or how to feel. You will never forget that moment; it will replay itself over and over again in your thoughts, like a slow-motion scene from some disaster movie.

I remember that instant more clearly and completely than any other mo- 3
ment of my life. My husband, Jim, and I had gone to the Midwest to visit his family, to take a long-overdue vacation from the stress of life and work and moving. I had left for that vacation knowing that my sister's biopsy report was

pending. I heard the sirens but was unconcerned. I had seen enough negative biopsy reports to know that this couldn't possibly happen to my family, to my sister, to someone I loved so much. But as we turned into the driveway of my in-laws' home, the bomb exploded. I remember the color of the light—pale yellow and sky blue—on that late May afternoon: the fall of the shadows, the hot sun on my face, the moist air in my nostrils, the smell of hay and freshly turned Iowa farmland. I remember the lines and angles of my nephew Eric's face, drawn tense and tight, when we drove up the driveway and he approached the car. He didn't know how to tell me that my sister had called, that she had cancer. "I'm sorry," he said. "I'm sorry."

That moment is frozen in my memory like a held breath, tattooed into 4 my sensory system in indelible and undeniable ink. Even after I have recovered from the initial shock, the fear and doubt and pain and anger linger night after night, month after month, like radiation slowly and silently consuming my soul.

Once I return to California and see my mother, Geraldine, for the first time 5 since the news, she turns to me. I have fulfilled the dreams and fantasies of her own youth: I have become a physician. She has paid almost $100,000 for this, and now she turns to me with her pleading eyes and her beseeching face, asking for a return on her investment. "What does this all mean? Explain it to me." She wants a prognosis, a script for the future, a prescription for a cure. She wants me to save my sister. I cannot look her in the eye; I cannot give her the reassurance she so desperately wants and needs and wishes for. I cannot look myself in the eye, plumb the depths of my own heart, give myself what I desperately need—reassurance—and what I desperately want—ignorance. I have read too many pathology reports, memorized too many statistics.

I don't know how to tell my mother that her daughter has cancer, serious 6 cancer. I don't know how to tell myself, and so I retreat to my professional vocabulary and obfuscate, muttering things about chemotherapeutic agents and tissue receptors and treatment outcomes. "Speak English!" she says. The language that she once beamed with pride and pleasure to hear me speak has now become a barrier between us, a barrier between my brain and my heart, my intellect and my emotions.

My poor mother. I cannot imagine what it must feel like to know your 7 child has an illness that you cannot defend against. No matter how religious you have been about vaccinations, about nutrition, about safety, you cannot protect your child from this. You cannot protect yourself from this. It is a parent's worst nightmare. Children are supposed to outlive their parents. Children are supposed to weather their parents' illnesses and mourn their passing. Not vice versa.

And my sister. Mother of two young children, wife of a physician, painter 8 of magnificent and fantastic landscapes. Andrea tells me that she stands in front of her unfinished canvases without the knowledge of how to complete them, indecisive, not knowing what palette to choose or which brush stroke to use.

At night she sits in the doorways of her children's bedrooms and watches them as they sleep, fitfully and restlessly, breathing softly, sometimes crying out in their dreams. As she watches them she cries over the lives she may not see to adulthood, the dance recitals unapplauded, the bat mitzvahs uncelebrated, the graduations unrewarded, the weddings unplanned, the grandchildren unheld. My sister stands in front of the unfinished canvas of her life and wishes for the time to complete it.

My sister's husband, Russell—the doctor—and I look at each other with- 9 out speaking, yet a silent dialogue passes between us—words we don't want to say and things we don't want to hear. Andrea and Russell's daughters, Sophie, just under 7, and Allie, not quite 4, named for their great-grandmothers, too young to understand and too old to be unaffected, have taken to fighting more during the day and sleeping together at night. "Mommy, are you going to die?" asks Sophie. The younger child angrily hits my sister in the breast.

My poor sister. She cannot protect her children from this, the most horri- 10 ble of children's nightmares. I turn to my husband and say, "I wish it was me instead of her. At least I don't have children."

"Don't say that!" Jim recoils from the thought, afraid someone might hear 11 me, afraid this could happen to his wife, almost as if he's crossing himself or reciting a prayer or fending off the evil eye. Duck and cover.

I am determined that no tumor will escape detection during my breast 12 screening clinic today. So I pinch and press and probe deep into these breasts, searching for the lump or the lymph node or the nipple discharge. I do this be-cause I am a committed and caring physician, but I also do this because I am an angry and frightened and hurting sister. In my mind the tumor is sentient and is purposefully devouring my sister's life with a voracious appetite and sadistic pleasure. I am so angry.

I am angry at the cancer for invading my sister's body. I am angry at her im- 13 mune system for failing to overwhelm and destroy the disease. I am angry with my sister for getting cancer and causing me so much pain. I am angry with my mother because she is bereft and desperate and I have no words to comfort her. I am angry with the nurse who, when my sister called requesting an appoint-ment because of a lump she felt, told her to wait until after her period was over. Three precious weeks lost. I am angry with the physicians because they don't seem to recognize that my sister is not a pathology report but a living, breath-ing person with two beautiful young children and plans for the future and a family who loves her absolutely and without reservation.

I am angry with everybody, acquaintance and stranger alike, because they 14 are going about their lives unaware and unconcerned, as if nothing has changed, when my own life has been transformed so terribly and irretrievably. I am angry at the world because nothing in the world can undo the damage or turn back time. I am angry with myself because it is my sister who got cancer and not me, and for the briefest moment I breathed a sigh of relief and said, "Bad luck, bad protoplasm." But today, mostly, I am angry at breasts because they become cancerous, and despite all my education and training there is nothing I can do about it; I cannot make it go away. So I press and probe and pinch maybe a little too hard and a little too aggressively because I hate breasts for what they have done to my family and me.

By the end of the day my hands and fingers are aching and cramped. It has been an exhausting day. The science of medicine may be doing a thorough breast exam, but the art of medicine is talking with your patients, listening to their stories and learning about their lives. Today I have gotten to know 30 women who will become my patients and friends. But there is still one task left, I take a sheet of paper and make circles and scribbles and comments on it. "History of fibrocystic disease," it says. "Status post biopsy times two, family history of breast cancer." I walk down the hall and hand it to the mammographer as I unbutton my blouse.

Read More on the Web

Links to information about breast cancer and breast-cancer support
groups: http://www.cancernews.com/bcs.htm

Cancer Information Network Home Page with links to further reading:
http://www.cancerlinksusa.com/top10.htm

Questions for Discussion

1. What method or methods discussed earlier in this chapter does Tena Moyer use to introduce this essay?

2. Is Moyer's introduction limited to one paragraph? What function does paragraph 2 play?

3. What methods does she use in her concluding paragraph?

4. What is the "task" that Moyer mentions in paragraph 15?

5. Preparing to Read, you were asked to consider the various roles Moyer plays in this essay. What role is she playing in paragraph 15?

6. Why does the author mention the names of her nieces, her mother, and other family members?

7. In most of this essay, the author writes in the present tense, even when she is recalling the past. What is the effect of her doing so? Why does she use the past tense in paragraph 3?

8. Comment on Moyer's title.

Thinking Critically

1. The author tells us that medicine is both an art and a science. Write notes in the margins of this selection to identify places in which Moyer discusses medicine as an art, as a science, or as both. Then, write two or three paragraphs that explain her vision of medicine and her role as a doctor.

2. In Chapter 3, you might have read "A Brother's Dreams," in which medical student Paul Aronowitz describes his brother's mental illness. What does this essay have in common with "Code of Denial"?

Suggestions for Journal Entries

1. Many of us play two or more roles in life. We are students, employees, family members, church- or temple-goers, and so on. Does your personality seem to change or do you see things differently when you are asked to play different roles? Use listing or draw a subject tree to gather details that explain differences in your personality, your approach to life, your self-image, or the image you portray to others as you take on different roles.

2. Moyer expresses frustration that she cannot reassure her mother about her sister's prognosis. This frustration is increased when she realizes that no mother can really protect her daughter from this illness. Think about an illnesss or condition that we can attempt to prevent or to lessen the effects of. For example, we can avoid the ill effects of obesity by eating carefully and exercising regularly. We can decrease our chances of contracting lung cancer by not smoking. Use focused freewriting, clustering, or brainstorming with a friend to gather information that you could use if you wanted to advise someone on how to prevent an illness.

The Transformation of Maria Fernandez

Anita DiPasquale

Anita DiPasquale had the rare opportunity to visit Nicaragua near the end of the civil war that devastated that Central American country in the 1980s. She went there with a friend to bring news to relatives of a Nicaraguan child who had been adopted by a family in California. When a college writing instructor asked Di-Pasquale to narrate an unforgettable experience, she had no trouble deciding what to write about.

The Iran-Contra affair, which is mentioned in paragraph 1, involved the sale of arms to Iran as part of an illegal plan to provide American military aid to the Contras of Nicaragua. The Contras were a group trying to overthrow Nicaragua's communist government led by a group called the Sandinistas. The "superpowers," mentioned twice in this essay, are the United States and the former Soviet Union.

Preparing to Read

1. Think about what the word "transformation" in the title prepares us for in the essay. What is a "transformation"?

2. DiPasquale's introduction is longer than one paragraph, and it uses more than one of the methods for writing introductions explained earlier in this chapter. Read her introduction carefully; make sure you understand what she is saying and how she is saying it.

3. Although her story takes place in the past, DiPasquale writes in the present tense. In paragraph 2, for example, she tells us that Michael and she "meet," not "met" Maria. Using the present tense often adds excitement to a narrative essay and makes it more convincing.

4. The author kept an informal journal of her conversations with Maria by recording what she remembered of their talks from time to time. What we read may not be exactly what she and Maria said, word for word, but it is a fair re-creation of their conversations.

Vocabulary

adversaries (noun)	Opponents, enemies.
apathetic (adjective)	Unconcerned, uninterested.
communal (adjective)	Having to do with a community.
covert (adjective)	Secret, hidden.
defiled (adjective)	Dirtied, violated.
diverse (adjective)	Various, assorted.
eking out (verb)	Struggling to make or get.

eradicate (verb)	Destroy, annihilate.
ironically (adverb)	Contrary to what is expected.
meager (adjective)	Poor, little.
mired (adjective)	Stuck.
parochial (adjective)	Isolated, provincial.
raven (adjective)	Black.
repressive (adjective)	Tyrannical, dictatorial.
synonymous (adjective)	Similar in meaning.

The Transformation of Maria Fernandez

Anita DiPasquale

MARIA'S STORY IS testimony to the horror of war. Her country is Nicaragua, 1 one of America's greatest embarrassments and yet another battleground in what the superpowers called the "cold" war. In this impoverished, merciless, yet beautiful land, the Reagan Administration became mired in a series of covert operations known as the Iran-Contra fiasco. Ironically, our shame over this dreadful incident may be the only good thing to come from our presence in Nicaragua. Perhaps Americans who were once parochial and apathetic will realize that Kansas is not Central America, that *Sandinista* and "repressive" are not synonymous, that *Contra* may not mean "freedom fighter," and that all wars, no matter who the adversaries, are barbarous!

My friend Michael and I meet Maria on a trip through hell in Nicaragua's 2 capital, Managua. The month is June, the year 1988. Maria is seventeen, no longer a child, no longer a woman. She is a soldier in the FSLN (*Frente Sandinista de Liberacion Nacional*), the national liberation front named for Augusto Sandino, a guerrilla fighter martyred in an earlier war of liberation.

Maria is thin, with shoulder-length raven hair, which she braids and tucks 3 away under her camouflage hat. Her nose is long and straight, her chin prominent and proud. A silky olive complexion and cheekbones straight out of *Vogue* magazine reveal a face that is truly delicate. How, then, has it come to harbor the deadest eyes I have ever seen?

Maria, Michael and I make our way along the gray and blue cobblestone 4 street and sit on a curb so large it would be considered a ledge in the United States. The masonry buildings around us are old, bruised, and defiled. Bullet holes and political graffiti have stained the faces of these tired shelters. Some still lie battered and tormented by the earthquake that devastated Nicaragua on December 23, 1972.

A young woman bathes in rain water that has collected in an old metal 5 drum across the street. No one notices; people walk by as if she were invisible. Maria catches me staring: "It's a way of life here; so many people are without water, without homes."

She is safer here on the street than at the river, I am told. "Listen, haven't   6
you heard the gunfire or seen the blood?" asks Maria.

"Have my eyes and ears deceived me?" I wonder. I have seen no blood and   7
heard no shooting. I know there is a war, but not until many days later will I
fully realize what she means.

Michael pulls a photograph from his shirt pocket and hands it to Maria. It   8
is a picture of her brother Alberto; he is seated on a bright red Big Wheel. Alberto is seven and lives in Los Angeles with Michael's uncle. The child is smiling; he knows his world is make-believe, like that of most children in countries
free of war.

"I remember," she proclaims, as she stares at the photo. "I remember when   9
I was a child; we lived in the north, in Matagalpa." Matagalpa is known for its
mountains and its hard living. Aside from the small towns every five miles or
so, nothing but small shacks dot the landscape. The people of Matagalpa work
alone on small plots of land, eking out a meager existence. There are no real
communities here as there are in the Pacific culture, which is known for its
communal involvement with the land.

Maria lights a cigarette and sighs. "We were very poor and lived close to   10
the earth. I can still smell Mama's tortillas cooking in the oven. Our house had
two rooms, and the roof was made of corrugated tin. The floor was dirt except
for a small area which Papa dug out and covered with wood in order to hide us
when the soldiers came through."

Her face grows solemn for a moment. But she lifts her strong chin and   11
continues proudly. "As a small girl, I would wear pretty dresses that Mama
made from spare pieces of cloth. They always had flowers on them, pink and
yellow. I never had a pair of shoes; there was no need for them. My job on the
land was to spread the fertilizer." Maria's nose crinkles as if she can still smell
the manure.

"Once we went on a trip to Puerto Cabezas; Alberto was so small he had   12
just learned to walk. There the Miskito Indians were catching giant sea tortoises
on the shore. The tortoises were larger than Alberto," she chuckles. "A Miskito
woman gave us a ride on her boat. It was made from a hollowed out tree. That
was the last family outing I remember."

"How did Alberto come to live in America?" I ask. Michael has never told   13
me, and I know by the look on his face that I should not have asked the question. The story Maria tells is more horrifying than any horror film. It makes the
ravages of war real to me. I no longer look on them as someone else's problems.
It also explains how a happy little girl in flowered dresses could have become
a soldier, a killer, how her eyes can be so dead.

"I must go back a few years to help you understand what led to Alberto's   14
departure," began Maria. "In August of 1978, when I was a very small child, before Alberto was born, our world changed forever. The FSLN had seized the National Palace, taking 1,500 hostages. When the attackers and 59 newly freed
prisoners drove to the airport to get a flight to Panama, thousands of people

lined the streets and cheered their victory. After the Palace assault, there were many attacks on the National Guard throughout Nicaragua—in Matagalpa, Leon, Masaya, Esteli, and Chinandega. The people lifted up arms against President Anastasio Somoza Debayle. So, to stop the rebels, the Guard destroyed our cities from the air. It took about two weeks and left over 4,000 dead. As the Sandinistas withdrew, they took thousands of newly recruited soldiers. My father was one.

"Later, in 1979, Somoza was driven into exile, to America's Miami. We 15 thought there was hope for our country. Your President Carter worked with us, but then Reagan came. He reorganized Somoza's National Guard, which became the Contras. They were given haven in Honduras. The 75,000 Sandinistas had few weapons and little money, so they could not eradicate the 10,000 Contras, who were well equipped with U.S. weapons and money.

"Back to Alberto. The last day I saw my brother started like any other. I was 16 fourteen or so, Alberto about four. We were home alone with my mother. Papa was off fighting in the jungle. It was September, and a wonderful rain had fallen the night before, leaving the air fragrant with a lush tropical scent. However, smoke hovered over the village, casting shadows on houses and streets and plunging the land into a deep, damp calm.

"Suddenly, I heard our neighbor Guillermo run into our house. He was 17 covered with blood. 'Contras,' he screamed before darting into the mist. Mama moved the heavy trunk that covered the hiding place my father had made. She was eight months pregnant, so I helped. First we placed Alberto into the hole, and I climbed on top of him. Mama placed the wood back on top and threw a rug over the floor.

"Just then the soldiers must have arrived. They were yelling and laughing. 18 I covered Alberto's ears and tried to muffle his crying. I heard my mother's screams; I still hear her screams. They were finally silenced by gunfire.

"The soldiers must have stayed about an hour; it felt like an eternity. The 19 house grew quiet. 'I dare not move,' I thought, so we lay there for several hours. Before I climbed out of the hole, I tied a piece of my dress around Alberto's eyes and around his hands so he wouldn't remove the blindfold. When I entered the daylight I was instantly sick. Mama was dead; they had cut my baby sister from her stomach; they lay there in a pool of blood. Both bodies were riddled with bullets.

"The soldiers had stayed there with their dead bodies long enough to eat 20 our breakfast. There was blood everywhere. I don't know how long I stood motionless when a shadow crossed the doorway. It was Chris, a U.S. reporter who often came by to feed his stories and his belly. He buried Mama and the baby, Isabel. That would have been her name.

"Chris told me my father had died the week earlier in a battle in Jinotega. 21 He said he could get Alberto out of Nicaragua, away from the Contras. He knew someone who was smuggling small, light-skinned children into California. He promised he would personally get him a good home as repayment for the help my family had given him. He was crying when he said I was too big to go. I had forgotten how to cry. Right then, at that moment, I was reborn into this world all alone. You do what you have to do in order to survive. I now know the meaning in the smoke. You do what you have to do to survive."

As Maria finishes her story, my stomach grows heavy and sinks to a depth 22 I did not think was possible. Suddenly, a truck pulls onto the street. It is filled with dead Contras on the way to burial. Another truck pulls up behind; this one is filled with Sandinista soldiers, none of whom look over twenty. Most are between ten and fifteen. Some might be eight. They are all toting rifles, passing cigarettes out among the crowd. When I look into the first truck, I become desperate with fear. Piled one on top of another are men, women, and children. They are all dead.

Back at the ledge, I slump against Michael. Maria emerges from the daze of 23 her horrid memory and kisses Michael on the cheek. She points to the trucks. "If he were here, his world would be all too real."

Sometimes it is nearly impossible to tell Contra soldiers and Sandinistas 24 apart. They have a lot in common: their youth, their camaraderie, their mortality. When Salvadoran Archbishop Rivera y Damas spoke of the role of the superpowers in his country's civil war, he could have been describing the tragedy of Nicaragua: "They supply the weapons, and we supply the dead."

Read More on the Web

Library of Congress Country Study site on Nicaragua: http://memory.loc. gov/frd/cs/nitoc.html

Information Please site on Nicaragua: http://www.infoplease.com/ipa/ A0107839.html

Questions for Discussion

1. A transformation is a very significant change. What significant change has Maria experienced? Has the author experienced a change as a result of meeting Maria?

2. What is DiPasquale's thesis? What events in the story support or develop that thesis best?

3. The introduction to the essay includes several startling remarks. Identify two or three.

4. Where in the introduction does DiPasquale challenge widely held assumptions or opinions?

5. How does the question at the end of paragraph 3 help us understand her thesis?

6. This essay closes with quotations and statements that might stick in your mind long after you have read them. Which of these do you think is most memorable?

7. In what way does the scene described in paragraph 22 support the essay's thesis?

8. In paragraph 24, DiPasquale mentions the "superpowers," which we recall from paragraph 1. What is she trying to accomplish by repeating this word at the end of the essay?

Thinking Critically

1. Do a little reading on Nicaragua in a recently published encyclopedia or other reference work. Your college librarian can help you find such resources. Then, write a short explanation of DiPasquale's first paragraph. Make sure to identify the *Sandinistas* and the *Contras* and to explain the significance of her hope that Americans will no longer confuse Central America with Kansas.

2. Read "Growing Up in Romania," another student essay, which appears in Chapter 10. What does it have in common with DiPasquale's work?

Suggestions for Journal Entries

1. Recall a horrifying or dangerous event that showed you the sad or dark side of life. Ask the journalists' questions (you can find these in "Getting Started," under Brainstorming) to collect as many details about it as you can. Examples of such an incident include military combat; a bad automobile or industrial accident; a building fire; a tornado; a bout with a serious illness; a violent crime; a fall from a ledge or down a stairs; a mishap at sea, in a lake, river, or other body of water; or a fight in which someone was seriously hurt. Whatever event you write about, make sure to show why it was horrifying or dangerous.

2. Do you know someone who experienced a tragic or horrifying event like those mentioned above? If so, interview him or her using the techniques described in "Getting Started." Gather as much information as you can about the incident, and determine how it affected the person you interview.

3. Do you have a friend or relative who went through a drastic and sudden personality change as a result of an important event or development in his or her life? Write about this person by making three lists: one that contains details describing your subject before the change; one that describes him or her after the change; and one that explains what caused the change.

Suggestions for Sustained Writing

1. Reread one of the papers you've written this semester. Try to pick the one you or your instructor liked best, but don't limit your choice to papers you've completed for English class. Then, rewrite the beginning and ending to that essay by using techniques for writing introductions and conclusions discussed in this chapter.

2. Do you agree with Robert Fulghum that people's bathrooms tell a lot about them? How about their cars, bedrooms, closets, or refrigerators? Write an essay in which you introduce your readers to a close friend or relative by describing his or her room, home, apartment, car, work area, or the like. Include details that focus on one and only one aspect of your subject's personality. For example, to show that this person has expensive tastes, mention the brand names and estimate the costs of clothes you saw in his or her closet. Then talk about the luxurious furniture and expensive stereo equipment in his or her living room, and so on. If you responded to the second suggestion for journal writing after "I Was Just Wondering," you have already gathered useful details for this assignment.

   When you write your introduction, you might use a startling statement or, like Fulghum, ask a question that helps reveal your thesis. Here's an example of such a question: "How do I know Andy has expensive tastes?"

   You can conclude by summarizing your main points, offering advice, or looking to the future. For example:

   > Andy spends money faster than he can make it. Unless he gets a better-paying job, cuts back on expensive purchases, or inherits money from a rich relative, the finance company will repossess his furniture.

3. If you responded to either of the suggestions for journal writing after Wiesel's "A Prayer for the Days of Awe," read the notes you made in preparation for the writing of a letter to God or to the Master of the Universe (in other words, a prayer). You might write about your concerns and frustrations over an incident in which someone has been harmed, or you might express your anger to the Creator for allowing evil, sorrow, and injustice to exist either in general or in a particular situation you have observed. Or you might simply discuss some questions that have been bothering you about yourself, about your relationship with God, or about life in general.

   Whichever path you choose, remember that your letter/prayer will be read by a human audience, so provide enough details to ensure that your readers will understand the situations, concepts, and emotions you are discussing. In addition, use one or more of the methods for writing introductions and conclusions that you have learned in this chapter. Whether human or divine, your audience deserves interesting and effective openings and closings.

Finally, write several drafts of your paper. Revise and edit it carefully. God may forgive sloppy writing, but other readers won't.

4. Look back at the notes you made in response to either of the journal suggestions following Moyer's "Code of Denial." Use your notes as a springboard for the completion of a piece of writing that contains an interesting and focused introduction and an effective conclusion. Try using more than one technique explained in this chapter to open and close your work.

If you responded to the first of the Suggestions for Journal Entries after Moyer's essay, explain the changes that your personality or self-image undergoes when you take on different roles during a typical day or week. If you responded to the second journal suggestion, write a letter to a relative or friend offering advice on how to prevent contracting an illness or how to detect signs of that illness. In the Preparing to Read section that precedes Moyer's essay, you were advised to learn more about breast-cancer examinations via the Internet. Try using this information if you decide to write about breast cancer. Return to the Internet to find information if you decide to write about another disease.

Again, pay particular attention to your introduction (include an effective thesis statement) and to your conclusion. You may wish to write both your introductory and concluding paragraphs after you have completed a rough draft of the body paragraphs. In any case, remember that writing is a process. So, write and revise several drafts, edit them carefully, and proofread your final copy.

Note: If you take information from the Internet, you must cite (give credit to) your source(s), whether you use a direct quotation or put the information into your own words. The Appendix which appears at the end of this textbook explains how to cite sources using Modern Language Association (MLA) style.

5. "The Transformation of Maria Fernandez" tells of tragic events that Anita DiPasquale witnessed or that she learned about from someone else. If you responded to either of the first two suggestions for journal writing after this essay, you have collected information about a terrifying incident you experienced directly, witnessed, or heard about from another person. Turn these notes into a full-length essay that tells your story in detail. Like the author of "The Transformation of Maria Fernandez," you might quote yourself or others in your story.

DiPasquale opens by making startling statements, challenging popular assumptions, and asking a rhetorical question. Any of these methods is a good way to introduce your essay, but you can also describe a scene, use a quotation, or explain a problem. When concluding, try a memorable quotation from someone in the story, make a call to action, or look to the future.

You can tell from the final product that DiPasquale wrote several drafts of her essay and edited it quite well. Do the same with yours.

6. Have you ever known anyone who, because of a single experience, went through a drastic and sudden change in personality, lifestyle, or attitude like the one you read about in "The Transformation of Maria Fernandez"? Write the story of this transformation by telling your readers about the experience and by explaining how it changed the person you are writing about. First, however, review the notes you made after reading Di-Pasquale's essay. If you responded to the third journal suggestion, you may have gathered details you can use in this assignment.

A startling statement, an interesting question or analogy, or the vivid description of a place might make an interesting introduction to your story. Quoting your subject, looking to the future, or asking a rhetorical question might make an effective conclusion.

Once again, remember that writing is a process, so draft, revise, and edit!

Writing to Learn: A Group Activity

The First Meeting

For inspiration, reread and discuss Elie Wiesel's "A Prayer for the Days of Awe" as well as the following short prayer from the Koran, the Islamic holy book:

In the Name of God, the Compassionate, the Merciful

Praise be to God, Lord of the worlds!
The compassionate, the merciful!
King on the Day of reckoning!
Thee *only* do we worship, and to Thee do we cry for help.
Guide Thou us on the straight path,
The path of those to whom Thou has been gracious;—with
whom Thou art not angry, and who go not astray. (Sura I)

Now pretend that you have been asked to write a group letter to the Master of the Universe. Brainstorm for at least 20 minutes to come up with three or four questions that you might ask about the nature of life, of the universe, of the afterlife, of God Himself, or of any other relevant issues important to you. Write out each question in a clear and complete sentence. Assign each student of the group—except one—to discuss this question in a fully developed paragraph that he or she will complete for homework. Assign the remaining student the task of writing the introduction and conclusion for an essay that will include the three or four paragraphs written by the other group members. Everyone should bring several copies of his or her work to the next meeting.

THE SECOND MEETING

Distribute the materials everyone has brought. Now decide which paragraphs need to be expanded or revised in any way. Make suggestions as needed. Then decide on the order in which each paragraph should appear in the paper. Rewrite your paragraphs for homework, making enough copies to distribute at the next meeting.

THE THIRD MEETING

Distribute the materials everyone has brought. Arrange all the paragraphs in the order they are to appear in the essay's final version. Collectively, make sure that there are transitions in and between paragraphs, that the paper begins and ends in interesting and logical ways, and that it makes sense over all. Next, edit the paper for grammar, spelling, sentence structure, and other errors. Finally, assign one person the job of typing the paper as a whole and of making enough copies for each member of the group and for the instructor.

Word Choice and Sentence Patterns

In Section One you learned how to approach a subject, to focus on a purpose and central idea, and to organize and develop the information you collected. The three chapters in Section Two explain how to use language and sentence structure to make your writing clearer, more interesting, and more emphatic.

What you will learn in Section Two is just as important as what you learned earlier. In most cases, however, the techniques discussed in this section—refining word choice, creating figures of speech, and reworking sentence structure for emphasis and variety—are things you will turn your attention to after having written at least one version of a paper, not while you are focusing on a central idea, organizing details, or writing your first rough draft.

Keep this in mind as you read the next three chapters. Chapter 5 explains how to choose vocabulary that is concrete, specific, and vivid. You will learn even more about using words effectively in Chapter 6, which explains three types of figurative language: metaphor, simile, and personification. Finally, Chapter 7 will increase your ability to create variety and emphasis through sentence structure.

Enjoy the selections that follow. Reading them carefully and completing the Questions for Discussion, the Suggestions for Journal Entries, and the Suggestions for Sustained Writing will not only help you learn more about the writing process but should also inspire you to continue developing as a writer.

CHAPTER 5

Word Choice: Using Concrete, Specific, and Vivid Language

A writer has three ways to communicate a message: by (1) implying it, (2) telling it, or (3) showing it. Of course, all three types of writing serve specific and important purposes. Usually, however, writing that is the clearest and has the greatest impact uses language that shows what you wish to communicate. Words that show are more concrete, specific, and usually more interesting than those that simply tell the reader what you want to say, and they are always more direct than language that only implies or suggests what you mean.

Although the following two paragraphs discuss the same subject, they contain very different kinds of language. Which of the two will have the greater impact on the reader?

Writing That Tells

Smith's old car is the joke of the neighborhood. He should have gotten rid of it years ago, but he insists on keeping this "antique" despite protests from his family and friends. The car is noisy and unsafe. What's more, it pollutes the environment, causes a real disturbance whenever he drives by, and is a real eyesore.

Writing That Shows

Whenever Smith drives his 1957 Dodge down our street, dogs howl, children scream, and old people head inside and shut their windows. Originally, the car was painted emerald green, but the exterior is so covered with scrapes, dents, and patches of rust that it is hard to tell what it looked like when new. His wife, children, and close friends have begged him to junk this corroded patchwork of steel, rubber, and chicken wire, but Smith insists that he can restore his "antique" to its former glory. It does no good to point out that its cracked windshield and bald tires qualify it as a road hazard. Nor does it help to complain about the roar and rattle of its cracked muffler, the screech of its well-worn brakes, and the stench of the thick, black smoke that billows from its rusty tail pipe.

As you will learn in the chapters on narration and description, language that shows makes for effective and interesting writing, especially when your purpose is to describe a person or place or to tell a story. But such language is important to many kinds of writing, and learning how to use it is essential to your development as a writer.

There are three important things to remember about language that shows: It is concrete, it is specific, and it is vivid.

Making Your Writing Concrete

Concrete language points to or identifies something that the reader can experience or has experienced in some way. Things that are concrete are usually material; they can be seen, heard, smelled, felt, or tasted. The opposite of *concrete* is *abstract*, a term that refers to ideas, emotions, or other intangibles that, while very real, exist in our minds and hearts. That's why readers find it harder to grasp the abstract than the concrete.

Compare the nouns in the following list. The ones on the left represent abstract ideas. The ones on the right stand for concrete embodiments of those ideas; that is, they are physical representations, showing us what such ideas as *affection* and *hatred* really are.

Abstract	Concrete
Affection	Kiss, embrace
Hatred	Sneer, curse
Violence	Punch, shove
Anger	Shout
Fear	Scream, gasp
Joy	Laugh, smile

Here are three ways to make your writing concrete.

USE YOUR FIVE SENSES TO RECALL AN EXPERIENCE

Giving your readers a straightforward, realistic account of how things look, smell, sound, taste, or feel is one of the most effective ways to make your writing concrete. There are examples of how authors appeal to the five senses in the later chapter on description. For now, read the following passage from "Once More to the Lake," in which E. B. White recalls concrete, sensory details about arriving at the camp in Maine where he spent his summer vacations as a boy. The only sense that White does not refer to is taste; see if you can identify details in this paragraph that appeal to the other four:

> The arriving . . . had been so big a business in itself, at the railway station the farm wagon drawn up, the first smell of the pine-laden

air, the first glimpse of the smiling farmer . . . and the feel of the wagon under you for the long ten-mile haul, and at the top of the last long hill catching the first view of the lake after eleven months of not seeing this cherished body of water. The shouts and cries of the other campers when they saw you, and the trunks to be unpacked, to give up their rich burden.

CREATE A CONCRETE IMAGE

An image is a mental picture that expresses an abstract concept in concrete terms. Therefore, it helps readers understand more easily. You can create images by packing your writing with details, usually in the form of nouns and adjectives. The word *image* is related to the word *imagine*. Therefore, a good time to create an image is when you write about something that your readers have never experienced or that they can only imagine from the information you provide. This is what happens in the following paragraph from "Searching for El Dorado," an essay that likens modern-day gold mining in South America to the search for the mythical golden land of El Dorado. Here, author Marc Herman uses an image to explain "a natural paradise."

> The Guiana Shield region of South America is a natural paradise. The moisture from its waterfalls sifts over lush forests, producing daily rainbows that span hundreds of miles at their base and widen into double spectra across cliff faces. Tourists come here to see Angel Falls, the world's highest, or Canaima National Park, a plateau with Wyoming's sky, Yosemite's waterfalls, and New Mexico's mesas. The tallest of these mesas, Mount Roraima, creates its own weather, as clouds slip off the top and twist beside the cliffs like dropped scarves, catching the sunlight and staining the brush below a dense, woven brown the color of a monk's robe. The landscape is studded with Pemon Indian houses shaped like rockets—wood and mud cylinders with conical roofs made of dried leaves.

USE EXAMPLES

Using easily recognizable examples is a very effective way to help your readers grasp abstract ideas, which might otherwise seem vague or unclear. For instance, if you want to explain that your Uncle Wendell is eccentric, you can write that "he has several quirks," that "he is odd," or that "he is strange." But such synonyms are as abstract and as hard to grasp as *eccentric*. Instead, why not provide examples that your readers are sure to understand? In other words, show them what *eccentric* means by explaining that Uncle Wendell never wears the same color socks, that he often cuts his own hair, that he refuses to speak for days at a time, and that he sometimes eats chocolate-covered seaweed for dessert.

In "The Human Cost of an Illiterate Society," Jonathan Kozol uses easily recognizable, well-developed examples to portray the frustration, loss, and risks faced by people who cannot read and write:

Illiterates cannot read the menu in a restaurant.

They cannot read the cost of items on the menu in the window of the restaurant before they enter.

Illiterates cannot read the letters that their children bring home from their teachers. They cannot study school department circulars that tell them of the courses that their children must be taking if they hope to pass the SAT exams. They cannot help with homework. They cannot write a letter to the teacher. They are afraid to visit the classroom. They do not want to humiliate their child or themselves.

Illiterates cannot read instructions on a bottle of prescription medicine. They cannot find out when a medicine is past the date of safe consumption; nor can they read of allergenic risks, warnings to diabetics, or the potential sedative effects of certain kinds of non-prescription pills. They cannot observe preventive health care admonitions. They cannot read about "the seven warning signs of cancer" or the indications of blood-sugar fluctuations or the risks of eating certain foods that aggravate the likelihood of cardiac arrest.

Making Your Writing Specific

As you've learned, writing that shows uses details that are both specific and concrete. Writing that lacks specificity often contains language that is general, which makes it difficult for the writer to communicate clearly and completely. One of the best ways to make your language more specific is to use carefully chosen nouns and adjectives. As you probably know, nouns name persons, places, and things; adjectives modify (or help describe) nouns, thereby making them more exact and distinct. In the following list, compare the words and phrases in each column; notice how much more meaningful the items become as you move from left to right:

General	More Specific	Most Specific
automobile	sports car	Corvette
residence	house	three-bedroom ranch
fruit	melon	juicy cantaloupe
school	college	University of Kentucky
baked goods	pastries	chocolate-filled cream puffs
beverage	soft drink	caffeine-free diet cola

| television show | situation comedy | Seinfeld |
| public transportation | train | Orient Express |

You probably noticed that several of the "Most Specific" items contain capitalized words. These are proper nouns, which name specific persons, places, and things. Use proper nouns that your readers will recognize whenever you can. Doing so will show how much you know about your subject and will increase the readers' confidence in you. More important, it will help make your ideas more familiar and easier to grasp.

At first, you might have to train yourself to use specifics. After a while, though, you will become skilled at eliminating flat, empty generalizations from your writing and at filling it with details that clarify and focus your ideas.

Notice the differences between the following two paragraphs. The first uses vague, general language; the second uses specific details—nouns and adjectives—that make its meaning sharper and clearer and that hold the reader's interest better.

General

The island prison is covered with flowers now. A large sign that is visible from a long way off warns visitors away. But since the early 1960s, when they took the last prisoners to other institutions, the sign has really served no purpose, for the prison has been abandoned. The place is not unpleasant; in fact, one might enjoy the romance and solitude out there.

Specific

Alcatraz Island is covered with flowers now: orange and yellow nasturtiums, geraniums, sweet grass, blue iris, black-eyed Susans. Candytuft springs up through the cracked concrete in the exercise yard. Ice plant carpets the rusting catwalks. "WARNING! KEEP OFF! U.S. PROPERTY," the sign still reads, big and yellow and visible for perhaps a quarter of a mile, but since March 21, 1963, the day they took the last thirty or so men off the island . . . the warning has been only *pro forma* [serving no real purpose]. It is not an unpleasant place to be, out there on Alcatraz with only the flowers and the wind and the bell buoy moaning and the tide surging through the Golden Gate. (Joan Didion, "Rock of Ages")

The differences between these two paragraphs can be summed up as follows:

• The first calls the place an "island prison." The second gives it a name, "Alcatraz."

• The first claims that the prison is covered with flowers. The second shows us that this is true by naming them: "nasturtiums, geraniums," and so on. It also explains exactly where they grow: "through the cracked concrete" and on "rusting catwalks."

- The first tells us about a sign that can be seen "from a long way off." The second explains that the sign is "visible for perhaps a quarter of a mile" and shows us exactly what it says.
- The first mentions that the last prisoners were removed from Alcatraz in the 1960s. The second explains that they numbered "thirty or so" and that the exact date of their departure was March 21, 1963.
- The first tells us that we might find "romance and solitude" on Alcatraz Island. The second describes the romance and solitude by calling our attention to "the flowers and the wind and the bell buoy moaning and the tide surging through the Golden Gate."

Making Your Writing Vivid

Besides using figurative language (the subject of the next chapter), you can make your writing vivid by choosing verbs, adjectives, and adverbs carefully.

1. Verbs express action, condition, or state of being. If you wrote that "Jan *leaped* over the hurdles," you would be using an action verb. If you explained that "Roberta *did not feel* well" or that "Mario *was* delirious," you would be describing a condition or a state of being.

2. Adjectives describe nouns. You would be using adjectives if you wrote that "the *large, two-story white* house that the *young Canadian* couple bought was *old* and *weather-beaten.*"

3. Adverbs modify (tell the reader something about) verbs, adjectives, or other adverbs. You would be using adverbs if you wrote: "The *easily* frightened child sobbed *softly* and hugged his mother *very tightly* as she *gently* wiped away his tears and *tenderly* explained that the knee he had *just* scraped would stop hurting *soon.*"

Choosing effective verbs, adjectives, and adverbs can turn dull writing into writing that keeps the reader's interest and communicates ideas with greater emphasis and clarity. Notice how much more effective the rewritten version of each of the following sentences becomes when the right verbs, adjectives, and adverbs are used:

1. The old church needed repair.

   The pre–Civil War Baptist church cried out for repairs to its tottering steeple, its crumbling stone foundation, and its cracked stained-glass windows.

2. The kitchen table was a mess. It was covered with the remains of peanut butter and jelly sandwiches.

   The kitchen table was littered with the half-eaten remains of very stale peanut-butter sandwiches and thickly smeared with the crusty residue of strawberry jelly.

3. A pathetic old homeless person was in an alley among some garbage.

   The body of a homeless man, his face wrinkled and blistered, lay in a pile of oil-covered rags and filthy cardboard boxes piled in the corner of a long alley devoid of life and light.

Visualizing Concrete, Specific, and Vivid Details

In the following paragraphs from "Where the World Began," Margaret Laurence describes her small hometown on the Canadian prairie. Comments in the margins of the first paragraph point to examples of the kinds of language you just learned about. After studying the first paragraph, find and circle similar examples of effective language in the second.

Adjectives appeal to senses. Summers were scorching, and when no rain came and the wheat became bleached and dried

Startling image. before it headed, the faces of farmers and townsfolk would not smile much, and you took for granted, because it never seemed to have been any different, the frequent knocking at the back door and the young men standing there, mumbling or thrusting defiantly their *Vivid adjectives.* requests for a drink of water and a sandwich *Vivid adverb.* if you could spare it. They were riding the

Specific type of train. freights, and you never knew where they had come from, or where they might end up, if anywhere. The Drought and Depression were *Proper nouns.* like evil deities which had been there always. You understood and did not understand.

Yet the outside world had its continuing marvels. The poplar bluffs and the small river were filled and surrounded with a

zillion different grasses, stones, and weed
flowers. The meadowlarks sang undaunted
[courageously] from the twanging telephone
wires along the gravel highway. Once we
found an old flat-bottomed scow [small
boat] and launched her, poling along the
shallow brown waters, mending her with
wodges [chunks] of hastily chewed Spearmint,
grounding her among the tangles of yellow
marsh marigolds that grew succulently along
the banks of the shrunken river, while the
sun made our skins smell dusty-warm.

Revising to Include Concrete, Specific, and Vivid Language

Read these two versions of a paragraph from Nancy J. Mundie's ironic (tongue-in-cheek) essay that proposes to use the mentally ill in scientific experimentation. It is clear that, by revising her work, Mundie was able to make her language more concrete, specific, and vivid. You will find a complete version of Mundie's essay—"The Mentally Ill and Human Experimentation: Perfect Together"—later in this chapter.

Mundie—Rough Draft, Paragraph 2

This proposal would have an immediate impact
on the condition of our cities. For the
homeless a dirty, litter-strewn corner would
be replaced by a clean living environment.
Tourism would become more attractive to out-
of-towners, for the mentally ill would be
off the streets. Public transportation would

flourish as bus, train, and subway stations would be devoid of ranting vagabonds. Houses of worship would see an increase in membership, for the "street-corner preacher" would be unavailable. Crime would decrease, for police could concentrate on serious offenders as opposed to acting as street sweepers of the homeless.

Mundie—Final Draft, Paragraphs 2 and 3

This proposal would have an immediate impact on the homeless, many of whom are afflicted with mental disorders. For them, a filthy, *Adds concrete details, vivid language.* litter-strewn street corner would be replaced by a sterile environment in a research hospital, sheltered from rains, sleet, and snow, from the heat of summer and the biting winds of winter. Of course, their absence would improve our cities' landscapes as well. Tourism would increase *Adds detail that appeals to senses; creates an* dramatically, for the mentally ill, many of whom walk around encrusted with filth and reeking of their own excrement, would be off the streets. Public transportation would flourish as bus, train, and subway stations would be devoid of ranting vagabonds.

Houses of worship would see an increase in membership, for "street-corner preachers" would be hauled off to hospitals where, *Added detail causes author to create two paragraphs from one.*

Adds specifics and a quotation.
> while undergoing extensive neurological observation, they could shout that the "world is coming to an end" to their heart's content.

Crime would decrease, for police would concentrate on serious offenders as

Expands original to create a startling image.
> opposed to acting as street sweepers of the homeless, of beggars, and of vagrants shouting obscenities to passersby or mumbling incoherently to themselves as they lie in dark and dirty doorways.

Practicing Using Concrete, Specific, and Vivid Language

In the spaces provided, rewrite the following sentences to improve word choice. Use techniques you have just read about to turn language that *tells* into language that *shows*. The first item has been completed for you as an example.

1. When the proud, old woman graduated, her classmates showed their approval.

    When the eighty-year-old chemistry major strutted across the stage to get

    her diploma, her classmates stood up and cheered.

2. A construction worker hung from a beam above the street.

    _____

    _____

    _____

3. The woman was overjoyed to be reunited with her lost son.

    _____

    _____

    _____

4. The exterior of the house needed painting.

    _____

    _____

    _____

Tenelya

5. His desk was cluttered.

_____

_____

_____

6. The garden contained a variety of beautiful flowers and trees.

_____

_____

Danira

7. The children became frightened when the dog came into the room.

_____

_____

Charmigne

8. The bus was crowded.

_____

_____

Charmigne

9. The supermarket was doing a brisk business.

_____

_____

_____

Juan

10. The Greasy Spoon Restaurant was a breeding ground for bacteria.

_____

_____

_____

Word choice is extremely important to anyone who wants to become an effective writer. Using the right kind of language marks the difference between writing that is flat, vague, and uninteresting and writing that makes a real impact on its readers. The following selections present the work of authors who have written clear and effective explanations of very abstract ideas, ideas they would have been unable to explain without language that is concrete, specific, and vivid.

Those Winter Sundays

Robert Hayden

Robert Hayden (1913–1980) taught English at Fisk University and at the University of Michigan. For years, the work of this talented African-American writer received far less recognition than it deserved. Recently, however, his reputation has grown, especially since the publication of his complete poems in 1985.

"Those Winter Sundays" uses the author's vivid memories of his father to show us the depth and quality of love that the man had for his family. Unlike much of Hayden's other work, this poem does not deal with the black experience as such, but it demonstrates the same care and skill in choosing effective language that Hayden used in all his poetry.

If you want to read more by Hayden, look for these poetry collections in your college library: A Ballad of Remembrance, Words in Mourning Time, Angle of Ascent, *and* American Journal.

Preparing to Read

1. Hayden's primary purpose is to explain his father's love for his family. Look for details that are physical signs of that love.
2. The author says his father "made/banked fires blaze." Wood and coal fires were "banked" by covering them with ashes to make them burn slowly through the night and continue giving off heat.
3. The word *offices* isn't used in its usual sense in this poem. Here, it means important services or ceremonies.

Vocabulary

austere (adjective)	Severe, harsh, difficult, without comfort.
chronic (adjective)	Persistent, unending, constant.
indifferently (adverb)	Insensitively, without care or concern.

Those Winter Sundays

Robert Hayden

Sundays too my father got up early
and put his clothes on in the blueblack cold,
then with cracked hands that ached
from labor in the weekday weather made
banked fires blaze. No one ever thanked him.

I'd wake and hear the cold splintering, breaking.
When the rooms were warm, he'd call,

5

and slowly I would rise and dress,
fearing the chronic angers of that house,

Speaking indifferently to him,   10
who had driven out the cold
and polished my good shoes as well.
What did I know, what did I know
of love's austere and lonely offices?

Read More on the Web

Academy of American Poets site on Hayden: http://www.poets.org/poets/
poets.cfm?prmID=200

Modern American Poetry site on Hayden: http://www.english.uiuc.edu/
maps/poets/g_l/hayden/life.htm

Questions for Discussion

1. What details in this poem appeal to our senses?
2. In line 2, Hayden uses "blueblack" to describe the cold in his house
    on Sunday mornings. What other effective adjectives do you find in
    this poem?
3. Hayden shows us his father in action. What were some of the things
    this good man did to show his love for his family?
4. What was Hayden's reaction to his father's "austere and lonely offices"
    when he was a boy? How did he feel about his father when he wrote
    this poem?

Thinking Critically

Hayden mentions that he feared "the chronic angers of that house." What
might he mean by that? Do you associate any "chronic angers" with your
home?

Suggestions for Journal Entries

1. In Preparing to Read, you learned that Hayden describes his father's
    love by using language that is concrete, specific, and vivid. In your own
    words, discuss the kind of love that Hayden's father showed his family.
2. Do you know someone who demonstrates love for other people day
    in and day out, as Hayden's father did? In your journal, list the offices
    (services, tasks, or activities) that he or she performs to show this
    love. Include as many concrete and specific terms as you can. Then
    expand each item in your list to a few short sentences, showing that
    these activities are clearly signs of love.

Jeffrey Dahmer, Cannibal

Angie Cannon

Angie Cannon is a writer for US News & World Report, *a weekly news magazine. In December 1999, the magazine ran a multipart feature entitled "Crimes of the Century." This essay was one of the many that made up that feature.*

Preparing to Read

1. Consider Cannon's title. Is the author trying to shock us, or is she warning sensitive readers about the gory nature of her subject? What other purposes might this title serve?
2. Given the length of the essay, its introduction is fairly long, but it clearly states the central idea. The thesis is repeated later in the essay. Look for it in both places.

Vocabulary

barbell (noun)	Used in body building, a metal bar with weights at both ends that can be added or removed.
biceps (noun)	Muscle that has two points of origin.
depraved (adjective)	Degenerate, mentally and spiritually twisted.
fetish (noun)	Mania, compulsion, obsession.
forensic (adjective)	Having to do with legal proceedings including criminal investigations and trials.
putrid (adjective)	Disgusting, rotten, rank.
repulsive (adjective)	Horrible, disgusting.
revolting (adjective)	Offensive, disgusting, nauseating.
torso (noun)	Trunk of the body.
zombies (noun)	In folklore, dead bodies that have been taken over by a spirit or outside power.

Jeffrey Dahmer, Cannibal

Angie Cannon

HE WAS A former chocolate factory worker with a fetish for flesh. In his pu-   1
trid, one-bedroom apartment in Milwaukee, he saved painted skulls and severed heads, including one stashed in the fridge next to a box of baking soda. He had a kettle and a freezer of body parts. He stored torsos in a vat of acid. He drilled holes in his victims' heads and had sex with dead bodies. He chewed on

body parts, once using Crisco and meat tenderizer on a biceps. Over 13 years, mostly through the excessive 1980s, Jeffrey Dahmer, alone in his poisoned world, was monstrous, repulsive, depraved. But the most frightening thing about Dahmer is what he was not: insane. He was objectively judged to be sane. He did what he did with his wits intact. "He was a man who made a decision that he would satisfy himself," says E. Michael McCann, the Milwaukee district attorney who put Dahmer away in 1992. "He liked sex with dead bodies. It was the ultimate in self-indulgence."

In an interview with NBC's *Dateline* in March 1994, Dahmer said lust drove 2 him to lure his victims, most of them black and gay, from bars, bus stops, and shopping malls, to his apartment, where he drugged, strangled, and dismembered them. "Once it happened the first time, it just seemed like it had control of my life from there on in," he said. "The killing was just a means to an end. That was the least satisfactory part. I didn't enjoy doing that. That's why I tried to create living zombies with . . . acid and the drill."

His killing spree started in 1978 with an 18-year-old hitchhiker whom 3 Dahmer met and brought home for a few beers. Dahmer, who had just graduated from high school, battered him with a barbell, cut up the body, and scattered the crushed bones behind his parents' house. By the time he was arrested on July 22, 1991, after a man he had handcuffed escaped from his apartment and flagged down a police car, Dahmer had killed 17 men and boys. He confessed, saying simply, "I carried it too far, that's for sure."

The only issue at his 1992 trial was whether to accept his plea that he was 4 criminally insane—and therefore not responsible for his revolting actions. Dr. Park Dietz, a respected California forensic psychiatrist, determined that he was not insane. "Dahmer was quiet, introverted, and performed his job pretty well until he finally fell asleep and couldn't do his work because he couldn't keep up with his nighttime dastardly deeds," says prosecutor McCann.

Dahmer was serving 16 consecutive life terms when inmates beat him to 5 death in a prison bathroom in November 1994. Two years later, a businessman offered more than $400,000 to buy his implements—the refrigerator, the vats, the drills, the saws—to prevent a public auction. They were secretly buried.

Read More on the Web

Case study of Dahmer: http://www.extentia.net/thrillers/case_study.htm

Links to sites about mass murderers and serial killing: http://crime.about. com/cs/massmurderers/

Questions for Discussion

1. Reread paragraph 1, and identify verbs and adjectives that are particularly vivid. Where else in this essay does Cannon use vivid details?

2. What examples of concrete language appear in paragraph 1? What about paragraph 3?

3. Why didn't Cannon say that Dahmer put vegetable shortening on a body part rather than that he used "Crisco on a biceps"?

4. The journalist who wrote this essay was careful about researching specific facts and statistics. What evidence do you find of such research?

5. Why does Cannon include direct quotations in this essay? Who are the sources for such quotations?

6. What method or methods explained in Chapter 4 does the author use to introduce her essay? To conclude it?

Thinking Critically

1. "The most frightening thing about Dahmer," claims the author, "is what he was not: insane." Consider this statement. Then explain why it was necessary for Cannon to include so many gruesome details in paragraph 1.

2. What does Cannon's concluding paragraph say about our society?

Suggestions for Journal Entries

1. This essay is the portrait of a serial killer, but concrete, specific, and vivid language can be used to discuss anyone's life—unknown or famous, good or evil. Think about an individual you admire or dislike. Your subject can be someone you know personally or someone you have only read or heard about such as an entertainer, a politician, or even an historical figure. Make a list of as many concrete, specific, and vivid details as you can to describe this individual's personality or character.

2. Cannon quotes Dahmer directly so as to help us understand his motives and his character. Freewrite for at least 10 minutes about having done something or having made a decision that you now deeply regret. Explain what it was, why you did it, and why you regret it.

The Haunting Final Words: "It Doesn't Look Good, Babe"

James Glanz

This short essay appeared in the New York Times *one year after the terrorist attacks of September 11, 2001, on New York's World Trade Center and on the Pentagon. Through the use of concrete and vivid language, it captures, as the author tells us, "what is was like" to be in the WTC towers when the jets hit and "as death neared." In this piece, James Glanz has given us something invaluable as we continue to try to come to grips with the tragedy of 9/11.*

Glanz writes on astronomy and astrophysics. His articles have appeared in Science *magazine and the* New York Times. *He also co-authored a series of articles explaining the physics behind the collapse of the Twin Towers.*

Preparing to Read

1. Glanz makes excellent use of direct quotations from victims and family members. Ask yourself why he chose these particular quotations since, as he tells us "at least 353 people trapped inside the towers . . . managed to communicate with the outside world."

2. Glanz compares telephone conversations of the victims and their loved ones to the appearance of Ceyx to his lover Halcyon in a dream. Ceyx and Halcyon are characters in ancient mythology, whom the poet Ovid wrote about in *Metamorphoses.* Make sure you understand the basis of that comparison.

3. At the end of this essay, Glanz contrasts the story of Ceyx and Halcyon with what happened to the WTC victims. Make sure you understand why he creates that contrast.

Vocabulary

bequeath (verb)	Grant, give.
bereaved (adjective)	Grieving over a death.
colloquial (adjective)	Conversational, familiar, everyday as it relates to language.
commodities broker	Person who buys/sells sugar, grains, metals and other basic goods.
indelible (adjective)	Permanent, unable to be erased.
intimately (adverb)	Personally, closely.
juxtaposed (adjective)	Placed side by side for comparison.
panoramic (adjective)	Wide angle.
solace (noun)	Comfort, relief.
uncanny (adjective)	Strange, mysterious.

The Haunting Final Words:
"It Doesn't Look Good, Babe"

James Glanz

PERHAPS ONLY mythology can convey the strangeness of this story: that peo- 1
ple trapped high in the World Trade Center spoke to their loved ones even
as the flames rose and the towers fell. The channels of communication—cell
phones and BlackBerry communicators and a few surviving land lines—were
the by-now familiar miracles of modern technology.

But the experience of those outside the buildings who received the final 2
messages was as timeless and uncanny as the story of Halcyon and Ceyx in
Ovid's "Metamorphoses." Ceyx died in a tempest at sea, but was allowed by the
gods to return to his lover, Halcyon, in a dream and reveal his death.

At least 353 people trapped inside the towers on Sept. 11 managed to com- 3
municate with the outside world before they died. In a way, all of us reporting
about their fates, and those who read about it, became the dreaming Halcyon.
We learned, intimately, what it was like up there as death neared, and are now
left to make sense of it on our own.

The final transmissions reveal as nothing else the full scale of the events of 4
Sept. 11—something that carries beyond the panoramic camera shots of the
burning towers and delves at least some distance into the measureless depths
of the heart. The power of those calls from the towers emerges in part from the
way in which instant communication almost seemed to slow down the tragedy
so that it could be explained, as it happened, to people who meant the world
to the doomed.

"They, died alone," said Sophie Pelletier, whose husband, Mike, a com- 5
modities broker, phoned her from the 105th floor of the north tower. "No one
was there to help them. They did everything they could to get out, and they
fought with their heart and soul and there was just no way out, and that was
torture."

The colloquial directness and easy intimacy of those communications from 6
the sky, juxtaposed against the sheer scale of the disaster they describe, made
them all the more haunting.

"It doesn't look good, babe," said Jeff Shaw, an electrician who was on the 7
105th floor of the north tower when it was hit by a plane 10 floors below, in a
cell phone conversation with his wife, Debra.

Some of those conversations have been burned into the minds of those 8
who survived in ways that are as indelible as they are painful. Patricia and Louis
Massari had just learned that morning that she was pregnant with their first
child. They were talking on the phone when the first plane hit, very near her
office. Mrs. Massari said, "Oh my God," and the connection was cut forever.

"She had seen something, she felt something," Mr. Massari said, "I kept say- 9
ing, 'Not now, not my wife, not just when we heard this news about the baby.'"

Of Mrs. Massari's last communication with the outside world, Mr. Massari   10
said, "I hear it every day in my mind."

Technology in the end, is not god-like; it cannot bequeath to men and   11
women the solace the gods sometimes give in myth.

Zeus turned Ceyx and Halcyon into graceful birds after her dream, while   12
ordinary life goes on for the bereaved families. But the stories of their loved
ones have been written into history.

Read More on the Web

Links to personal stories about the terrorist attacks:
   http://www.christianitytoday.com/ctmag/special/personalstories.html

Academic Information resources on 9/11/01: http://www.academicinfo.
   net/usa911.html

Questions for Discussion

1. What examples of specific language do you find in this essay?

2. Why does Glanz mention that Sophie Pelletier's husband was a
    "commodities broker," who "phoned her from the 105 floor of the
    north tower"?

3. Re-read paragraphs 2 and 3. What words in those paragraphs do you
    find vivid or especially effective in communicating Glanz's message?
    Where else in the essay does such language appear?

4. Explain how the quotations in this essay help give it a concreteness it
    would have lacked had they been left out.

5. Where in this essay does Glanz draw verbal images?

6. In what way does Glanz's comparing the Ovid story to the WTC
    stories add emphasis to this essay?

7. What is so haunting about the quotation from Jeff Shaw? What about
    the conversation between Patricia and Louis Massari?

8. Summarize paragraph 4. What is Glanz's thesis?

Thinking Critically

1. Explain the comparison that Glanz makes between the victims of the
    WTC attack and Ceyx and Halcyon. What contrasts does he draw
    between them?

2. In what way are the readers of this article similar to the "dreaming
    Halcyon"?

Suggestions for Journal Entries

1. Jump ahead and read "The Buried Sounds of Children Crying," an essay in Chapter 7, which discusses the terrorist attack in Oklahoma City in 1995. In what way is this essay similar to and different from "The Haunting Final Words"? Make sure you have made marginal and textual notes on both essays before you begin your comparison. Then, use listing or freewriting to record what is similar and different in these essays.

2. Pretend that you just learned that your life is in danger. Perhaps you are in a building that is about to fall, are in a ship that is about to sink, or are about to enter a fierce military battle. Now pretend that you have only a few minutes to write what might be your last letter to a loved one. Use freewriting to record the thoughts you might put into such a letter.

3. Most of us remember exactly where we were when we heard about the events of September 11. But do we really understand how those events have affected our lives? Working on your own or in a small group, brainstorm about ways in which your life and/or life in America has changed since 9/11/01. For example, is traveling more difficult? Are we as secure about national defense as we used to be? Do we need to have a greater awareness of world events and of other cultures?

The Mentally Ill and Human Experimentation: Perfect Together

Nancy J. Mundie

Mundie wrote this essay in a composition class after reading Jonathan Swift's "A Modest Proposal," an eighteenth-century essay that uses irony to expose the abuse of the Irish poor by the rich. Irony is a technique writers use to state the opposite of what they really mean. Often, it adds sting to social criticism. For example, Swift suggested ironically that poor children be bred like cattle and sold for food to the rich. His point was that the poor were being "eaten alive" by the economic practices of the powerful and wealthy.

Mundie uses irony to condemn society's treatment of the mentally ill. Thus, although she seems to suggest we use the mentally ill for experimentation, she is arguing just the opposite. As she makes clear at the essay's end, she is a strong advocate for the mentally ill. In fact, Mundie is majoring in psychological/social rehabilitation.

Preparing to Read

Mundie refers to Willowbrook and Salem in paragraph 1. Willowbrook is a psychiatric hospital on Staten Island, New York, which was criticized for its treatment of patients in an investigation by Geraldo Rivera in the 1970s. Salem, Massachusetts, is often remembered for its seventeenth-century trials, as a result of which several people accused of being witches were burned at the stake.

Vocabulary

advocates (noun)	Supporters.
afflicted (adjective)	Adversely affected by, hurt by.
consistent (adjective)	Compatible with, conforming to.
diverse (adjective)	Varied.
incompetent (adjective)	Unfit, incapable.
paramount (adjective)	Most important.
pesky (adjective)	Annoying, troublesome.
psychotropic (adjective)	Affecting one's behavior, changing one's psychological state or mood.
squalor (noun)	Misery, poverty, filth.
suffice (verb)	Be enough.

The Mentally Ill and Human Experimentation: Perfect Together

Nancy J. Mundie

THE HUMAN RACE has always failed at attempting to solve the problem of the   1
mentally ill. In previous generations, this segment of society had been handled in ways consistent with the thinking of the times. However, whether burned at the stake in Salem, Massachusetts, or condemned to live in squalor at Willowbrook, the mentally ill have never fulfilled a constructive purpose. Therefore, I propose that we begin using the mentally incompetent as test subjects for scientific and social research.

This proposal would have an immediate impact on the homeless, many of   2
whom are afflicted with mental disorders. For them, a filthy, litter-strewn street corner would be replaced by a sterile environment in a research hospital, sheltered from rains, sleet, and snow, from the heat of summer and the biting winds of winter. Of course, their absence would improve our cities' landscapes as well. Tourism would increase dramatically, for the mentally ill, many of whom walk around encrusted with filth and reeking of their own excrement, would be off the streets. Public transportation would flourish as bus, train, and subway stations would be devoid of ranting vagabonds.

Houses of worship would see an increase in membership, for "street-   3
corner preachers" would be hauled off to hospitals where, while undergoing extensive neurological observation, they could shout that the "world is coming to an end" to their heart's content. Crime would decrease, for police would concentrate on serious offenders as opposed to acting as street sweepers of the homeless, of beggars, and of vagrants shouting obscenities to passersby or mumbling incoherently to themselves as they lie in dark and dirty doorways.

Those classified as mentally ill (except women with children, for their be-   4
havior mimics that of the unstable) would be housed in a common area close to the hospital or research center. Public homeless shelters—notorious for filth, crime, and vermin—would suffice, for the patients' stay would not be long. This would keep housing costs down.

Moreover, only short-term, unskilled care would be required, for research   5
on patients would be unmonitored and as such would probably result in high fatality rates. Since the patients' stay would be brief, the use of psychotropic drugs would be unnecessary; hence, another cost savings. At the same time, the housing industry would be stimulated by the need to build more low-quality public shelters, the medical professions given yet another opportunity to grow and profit as a result of the need for more research.

The advantages of this proposal to the scientific community are numerous.   6
Human experimentation is usually preferred over experimenting with animals to determine a procedure's or product's effectiveness. However, in much research as we know it, animal experimentation must precede work on human

beings. Using the mentally ill as guinea pigs, so to speak, would eliminate this requirement, thereby saving much time, effort, and money. In addition, a diverse test pool is paramount to reliable and accurate scientific research. Using the mentally ill will enable us to create a large and varied pool, for mental illness knows no social, economic, ethnic, or gender boundaries. Finally, researchers will not be forced to contend with pesky animal-rights activists such as members of the ASPCA. Moreover, there is no need to worry about civil-rights advocates, for the American Civil Liberties Union's attorneys and the like will make up a large portion of the "research pool."

This proposal is of course preposterous and inhumane at best. The mentally ill have a right to decent living conditions and proper care. Because their illness is largely "unseen" in the physical realm and misunderstood in the intellectual sense, they are often undiagnosed, misclassified, or ignored. But the mentally ill are our beloved family members and friends: the aging grandfather with Alzheimer's disease, the teenager battling depression, the daughter suffering from bulimia, the uncle addicted to alcohol, the neighbor victimized by schizophrenia. Mental illness is so widespread, so close to us, that we would do well always to remember the saying "there but for the grace of God go I." 7

Read More on the Web

Article from *The Guardian* (UK) on mental patients with dangerous personality disorders with links to other information on treating mental patients: http://society.guardian.co.uk/mentalhealth/story/ 0,8150,744126,00.html

Google's Web Directory for Patients' Rights: http://directory.google.com/ Top/Health/Mental_Health/Policy_and_Advocacy/ Patients'_Rights/81

Questions for Discussion

1. Mundie begins by saying that we have "failed at attempting to solve the problem of the mentally ill." Why didn't she write "failed at attempting to solve the problem of mental illness"? Would this have meant the same thing?

2. What is Mundie's thesis (or supposed thesis)?

3. Where in this essay do you find proper nouns?

4. Find and explain at least one image Mundie creates.

5. Discuss the language in paragraph 4. Which words contribute most to the effect of this paragraph?

6. What is Mundie suggesting at the end of paragraph 6?

7. What type of conclusion does Mundie use? (Recall various types of conclusions you read about in Chapter 4.)

Thinking Critically

1. This proposal is "preposterous," Mundie admits. However, many of the social problems she describes are all too real. Focus on one such problem—say the one mentioned at the end of paragraph 3—and offer a solution you think is both practical and humane. Put your "proposal" in a paragraph of between 75 and 100 words.
2. Reread Paul Aronowitz's "A Brother's Dreams" in Chapter 3. Explain how that selection helps us understand Mundie's essay, especially her conclusion.

Suggestions for Journal Entries

1. Are you concerned about the way victims of poverty, disease, or a social problem are treated by others? If so, use your journal to list your complaints about the way society treats members of any one of these groups.
2. Reread Mundie's last paragraph. Do any of the people she mentions remind you of people you know? If so, use freewriting to describe the effects of their illnesses on themselves or on their families.

Suggestions for Sustained Writing

1. Hayden's "Those Winter Sundays" praises a man who demonstrates his love for others. If you responded to the second journal suggestion after this poem, you have probably made a list of the offices (activities, tasks, or services) that someone you know performs to show his or her love.

    Focus on at least three offices that mean the most to you, and expand your discussion into an essay in which you show how much this individual does for others. Begin with a preliminary thesis that expresses your feelings about your subject, but remember once again that you will probably want to revise this statement after you write your first draft.

    Limit each of the body paragraphs to only one of the offices in your list. Try developing these paragraphs by using methods described in Chapter 3; narration, description, conclusion and support, illustration, and process analysis might work well in such an assignment. Whatever you decide, follow Hayden's lead and use language that is concrete and specific.

    Express your revised thesis in an effective introduction that uses one or more of the techniques for effective openings explained in Chapter 4. Close with a conclusion like one you read about in that chapter. As usual, write several drafts of your paper and edit it carefully.

2. Read the notes you made in response to either of the Suggestions for Journal Entries after Angie Cannon's "Jeffrey Dahmer, Cannibal." Do more listing or freewriting to add concrete and specific nouns and vivid verbs, adjectives, and adverbs to this information. Then use this prewriting to develop an essay that either describes a person's character (Suggestion 1) or that explains the motivations behind your once doing something or making a decision that you now regret (Suggestion 2). After writing the first draft, try gathering direct quotations from others. If you are describing someone's character or personality, interview people who know your subject. (If your subject is well-known, read what others have said about him or her in newspapers or other sources.) If you are writing about yourself, interview people who witnessed or heard about the action or decision you now regret. Put such quotations into your second draft; they will make your writing more believable, realistic, and convincing. Revise this draft by adding details, refining your thesis statement, and sharpening your introduction and conclusion. Finally, edit the work carefully and systematically, and proofread it before you hand it in.

3. Read the journal notes you made if you responded to the item #2 under Suggestions for Journal Entries after James Glanz's "The Haunting Final Words: 'It Doesn't Look Good, Babe.' " Expand your journal entry into a full-length letter to someone you love. (Remember, you are pretending to be in a life-threatening situation.) Begin by reading your notes, and identify those ideas and points that you want your reader to know about you and about your relationship with him or her. As you write your essay, organize it in order of importance. In other words, move from the least important to the most important idea.

   If this assignment doesn't interest you, read over the notes you made in response to item #3 of the Suggestions for Journal Entries after Glanz's essay. Explain what you think are the most important changes in your life or in the life of this country as a result of the events of 9/11/01. Again, organize your essay beginning with the least important idea and ending with the most important.

   In either case, make sure to state your thesis clearly. If you are writing a letter to a loved one, you might define the way that individual has changed or enriched your life. If you are writing about changes caused by the events of 9/11, you might briefly state two or three of these changes in your thesis, then develop each of them in separate paragraphs or sections of your essay.

4. In the second suggestion for journal entries after Nancy Mundie's "The Mentally Ill and Human Experimentation: Perfect Together," you were asked to describe the effects of an illness on someone you know or on his or her family. Turn this journal entry into a full-length essay by explaining the causes or symptoms of the illness. Then, in language that is concrete,

specific, and vivid, show to what degree it has changed the lives of the people it touches. If appropriate, conclude your essay by looking to the future. Try to predict what will become of the people you are writing about.

As you revise the first draft of your paper, include language that will show your readers what you mean by using the techniques discussed in this chapter. In other words, try to create forceful images, use concrete and specific nouns, and fill your writing with lively verbs, adjectives, and adverbs.

After you are satisfied with the result, edit and proofread your work. A great paper deserves a final polishing.

Writing to Learn: A Group Activity

In "The Mentally Ill and Human Experimentation," Nancy J. Mundie argues for humane treatment for people suffering from mental or psychological disorders. To this end, we first need to understand the diseases from which they are suffering and become aware of treatments currently available.

THE FIRST MEETING

Decide on a group of related psychological disorders to research. For example, you might want to study addictions to alcohol, drugs, gambling, shopping, or even work. Or your group could research eating problems such as anorexia nervosa, bulimia, and binge eating. Another possibility is to research disorders that affect children such as oppositional defiant disorder, conduct disorder, attention deficit hyperactive disorder, and separation anxiety disorder. You might even focus your search on various types of learning disabilities or depressions.

RESEARCH

Assign each student the task of researching one of the psychological problems in the classification of mental disorders your group has decided to study. Ask each to gather information on causes, symptoms, and treatments. Internet and library print sources will probably provide ample information, but members of your group might also interview psychology, nursing, or other faculty who teach in health-related disciplines.

THE SECOND MEETING

Make sure everyone has gathered sufficient information to describe the illness he or she has been assigned. If not, ask him or her to continue searching. Once you are satisfied that your group has collected sufficient information, ask each student to write a short (200–400-word) summary that discusses causes, symptoms, and treatment options. Remind the group members that, whenever possible, they should describe the disorder realistically by employing language that is concrete, specific, and vivid. Also remind them that information taken from researched sources must be cited. Check with your instructor on the required format. (An explanation of the Modern Language Association format appears in the appendix to this textbook).

The Third Meeting

Collect each student's work. Then, assign one member of your group to combine all of this information into a sustained research project that defines the class of disorder your group has been researching. Assign another person to write an introduction and conclusion to this paper. Ask still another to compile a bibliography for this paper using information on the sources that each student has used and cited in his or her report.

The Fourth Meeting

Read over and rewrite/edit the paper. Whenever possible, revise to include language that is more concrete, specific, and vivid. Also, eliminate grammatical and mechanical errors, and correct problems in sentence structure and wordiness. Finally, assign a student to type and proofread the final version before submitting it to the instructor.

CHAPTER 6

Word Choice: Using Figurative Language

In Chapter 5 you learned that you can bring to life and clarify abstract ideas by using concrete language. You can engage your reader by filling your writing with specific details and creating verbal images (pictures in words) that appeal to the reader's senses. You also learned that using effective verbs, adjectives, and adverbs can help make your writing vivid. All of these techniques help you *show*—and not simply tell—your readers what you mean.

Another way to make your writing clearer and more vivid is to use figurative language. Such language is called *figurative* because it does not explain or represent a subject directly. A figure of speech works by creating a comparison or other relationship between the abstract idea you want to explain and something concrete that readers will recognize easily. In that way, it can help you explain an idea more clearly and emphatically than if you used literal language alone.

In fact, figures of speech provide a way to create images, mental pictures that allow readers to *see* what you mean. Notice how effective your description of a "clumsy" friend becomes when you compare him to a "bull in a china shop." The concrete image of a bull in a china shop—complete with shattered teacups, bowls, and plates—is sharper and more dramatic than the abstraction *clumsy* can ever be.

The most common figures of speech take the form of comparisons. The three discussed in this chapter are simile, metaphor, and personification.

Simile

A simile creates a comparison between two things by using the words *like* or *as*. For example, say that you're writing your sweetheart a letter in which you want to explain how much you need him or her. You can express your feelings literally and directly by writing "I need you very much." Then again, you can *show* how strongly you feel by writing that you need him or her "as an oak needs sunlight," "as an eagle needs the open sky," or "as the dry earth needs spring rain."

Read the following list carefully. Notice how much more concrete, exciting, and rich the ideas on the left become when they are expressed in similes:

Literal Expression	Simile
She arrived on time.	She arrived as promptly as the sunrise.
Snerdly's face was sunburned.	Snerdly's face was as red as the inside of a watermelon.

Eugene is a fancy dresser.	Eugene dresses like a peacock.
The tires made a loud noise.	The tires screeched like a wounded animal.
The dog moved slowly.	The dog moved like corn syrup on a cold day.

Finally, have a look at "Harlem" by Langston Hughes, an important twentieth-century American poet, who was one of the lights of the Harlem Renaissance, an artistic and cultural flowering of the 1920s. Hughes uses five similes in eleven lines.

What happens to a dream deferred?

Does it dry up
like a raisin in the sun?
Or fester like a sore—
And then run?
Does it stink like rotten meat?
Or crust and sugar over—
like a syrupy sweet?

Maybe it just sags
like a heavy load.

Or does it explode?

Metaphor

A metaphor also uses comparison to show the relationship between things in order to make the explanation of one of these things clearer and livelier. In fact, a metaphor works just like a simile except that it does not make use of *like* or *as*. For instance, you can turn the simile "Eugene dresses like a peacock" into a metaphor by writing "Eugene is a peacock." In neither case, of course, do you actually mean that Eugene is a bird; you're simply pointing out similarities between the way he dresses and the showiness we associate with a peacock.

Remember that, like all figures of speech, similes and metaphors turn abstract ideas (such as "Eugene is a fancy dresser") into vivid, concrete images. In other words, they communicate more emphatically and clearly than if the writer had used literal language alone. Study the following list of similes and metaphors. What effect do they have on you, especially when compared with the literal expressions on the left?

Literal Expression	Simile	Metaphor
My old car is hard to drive.	My old car drives like a tank.	My old car is a tank!

She works too hard for her family.	She works like a slave for her family.	She is a slave to her family.
During holidays, shopping malls are crowded and noisy.	During holidays, shopping malls are so crowded and noisy that they seem like madhouses.	During holidays, shopping malls are so crowded and noisy that they become madhouses.
The hayloft was hot.	The hayloft was as hot as a blast furnace.	The hayloft was a blast furnace.

Read the following excerpt from Martin Luther King's "I Have a Dream," a speech he delivered at the Lincoln Memorial during the 1963 march on Washington. Identify the metaphors and similes that Dr. King used to captivate the thousands in his audience and to make his message more concrete, vivid, and effective:

> Five score years ago, a great American, in whose symbolic shadow we stand today, signed the Emancipation Proclamation. This momentous decree came as a great beacon light of hope to millions of Negro slaves who had been seared in the flames of withering injustice. It came as a joyous daybreak to end the long night of their captivity.
>
> But one hundred years later, the Negro still is not free. One hundred years later, the life of the Negro is still sadly crippled by the manacles of segregation and the chains of discrimination.

Personification

Personification is the description of animals, plants, or inanimate objects by using terms ordinarily associated with human beings. Like metaphor and simile, personification is an effective way to turn abstract ideas into vivid and concrete realities that readers will grasp easily and quickly.

One common example of personification is Father Time, the figure of an old man trailing a white beard and carrying a scythe and hourglass. Another is the Grim Reaper, the representation of death pictured as a skeleton holding a scythe. Shakespeare often used personification to enrich the language of his poems and plays. In "Sonnet 18," for example, he described the sun as "the eye of heaven." William Least Heat Moon does something similar when, in *Blue Highways*, he describes the saguaro cactus of the southwestern United States:

> Standing on the friable slopes . . . saguaros mimic men as they salute, bow, dance, raise arms to wave, and grin with faces carved in by woodpeckers. Older plants, having survived odds against their reaching maturity of sixty million to one, have every right to smile.

Visualizing Figurative Language

You may recall reading two paragraphs from Margaret Laurence's "Where the World Began" in Chapter 5 (pages 207–208). Here are two more paragraphs from that essay. Read the first paragraph, which is accompanied by notes that identify figures of speech. Then, read the second paragraph and circle or box examples of figurative language you find.

In winter we used to hitch rides on the back
of the milk sleigh, our moccasins squeaking
and slithering on the hard rutted
snow . . . our hands in ice-bubbled mitts   *Metaphor*
hanging onto the box edge of the sleigh for
dear life. . . . Those mornings, rising, there
would be the perpetual fascination of the
Metaphor   frost feathers on windows, the ferns and *Metaphor*
flowers and eerie faces traced there during *Personification*
the night by unseen artists of the wind.
Evenings, coming back from skating, the sky
would be black but not dark, for you could
see a cold glitter of stars from one side of
the earth's rim to the other. And then the
sometime astonishment when you saw the
Northern Lights flaring across the sky, like
Simile   the scrawled signature of God.

My best friend lived in an apartment
above some stores on Main Street (its real
name was Mountain Avenue, goodness knows
why), an elegant apartment with royal-blue
velvet curtains. The back roof, scarcely
sloping at all, was corrugated tin, of a

furnace-like warmth on a July afternoon, and
we would sit there drinking lemonade and
looking across the back lane at the Fire
Hall. Sometimes our vigil would be rewarded.
Oh joy! Somebody's house was burning
down. . . . Then the wooden tower's bronze
bell would clonk and toll like a thousand
speeded funerals in a time of plague, and in
a few minutes the team of giant black horses
would cannon forth, pulling the fire wagon
like some scarlet chariot of the Goths,
while the firemen clung with one hand,
adjusting their helmets as they went.

Revising to Include Figurative Language

Read these two versions of a paragraph from Louis Gonzalez's "Music," a student essay that appears in this chapter. As you will see, the revision process has
enabled Gonzalez to make his writing stronger, livelier, and more interesting.

Gonzalez—Rough Draft

As I became a little older and entered high
school, my interests shifted toward learning
to play a musical instrument. After a little
experimentation, the bass guitar became my
love. It produced warm, confident tones.
They danced around my head. The guitar
became the implement of my creativity. It
soon became the center of my existence. I

felt naked and insecure without it. Its

weight was a lover's hand upon my shoulder.

Gonzalez—Final Draft

When I entered high school, my interests

shifted toward learning to play a musical

instrument. After a little experimentation,

I fell in love with the bass guitar. It

covered me with warm, confident tones—

blankets of pure ecstasy. They were poised

ballroom dancers waltzing elegantly around

my head. The guitar became the implement of

my creativity, the brush with which I

painted portraits of candid love and dark

emotion. I was naked and insecure without

it. Its weight was a lover's hand upon my

shoulder, and its smooth hourglass body was

a pleasure to hold. It whispered sweet

kisses in my ear.

Adds personification by comparing guitar to lover. Creates an image; personifies "tones."

Adds a metaphor; compares guitar to a painter's brush.

Adds detail to continue personifying guitar as lover.

Practicing Creating Simile, Metaphor, and Personification

In the spaces provided, put the idea you find in the literal expressions into a simile, metaphor, or personification as indicated. The first item is done for you as an example.

1. **Literal expression:** The two men fought hard through the night.
   Simile: <u>The two men fought like gladiators through the night.</u>

2. **Literal expression:** Cheryl treats her mother well.
    Simile: _____

    _____

    _____

3. **Literal expression:** He ran to the end of the street and jumped over the barricade.
    Simile: _____

    _____

    _____

4. **Literal expression:** Modern appliances have made our homes more comfortable and convenient than ever before.
    Simile: _____

    _____

    _____

5. **Literal expression:** I enjoy the sounds of robins in the morning.
    Metaphor: _____

    _____

    _____

6. **Literal expression:** The small boat was overloaded.
    Metaphor: _____

    _____

    _____

7. **Literal expression:** In the last 20 years, medical researchers have produced wondrous cures.
    Metaphor: _____

    _____

    _____

8. **Literal expression:** The wind was strong.
    Personification: _____

    _____

    _____

9. **Literal expression:** We did not feel welcome as we entered the dark house.
    Personification: _____

    _____

    _____

10. **Literal expression:** The front-page photograph contained a warning about driving drunk.

    Personification: _____

    _____

    _____

The following selections demonstrate very careful uses of language, both literal and figurative. As you read them, identify their similes, metaphors, and personifications and ask yourself if these figures of speech have made the selections clearer, more vivid, and more effective than if their authors had relied on literal language alone.

What the Gossips Saw

Leo Romero

A native of New Mexico, Leo Romero is among a growing number of contemporary Southwestern writers whose poetry and fiction are becoming popular across the country. Romero studied at the University of New Mexico, where he took a degree in English. His poems have appeared in several recent collections of poetry and prose. "What the Gossips Saw" was first published in 1981 in a collection of his poetry called Agua Negra.

Preparing to Read

1. This is the story of a community's response to a woman who had her leg amputated. What it says about the way society reacts to those who are "different" can be compared with what we learn in other selections in this book. Take, for example, Schwartz's essay "The Colossus in the Kitchen," (Chapter 9), which you might read after completing "What the Gossips Saw."

2. Romero chooses to leave out periods and other end marks. Doing so can help a poet create dramatic effects. Nonetheless, developing writers should always use such punctuation.

Vocabulary

alluring (adjective)	Appealing, tempting.
conjecture (noun)	Guessing, speculation.
hobble (verb)	Limp.
in cohorts (adjective)	In league with, cooperating with.
murmur (verb)	Mumble discontentedly.

What the Gossips Saw

Leo Romero

Everyone pitied Escolastica, her leg
had swollen like a watermelon in the summer
It had practically happened over night
She was seventeen, beautiful and soon
to be married to Guillermo who was working   5
in the mines at Terreros, eighty miles away
far up in the mountains, in the wilderness
Poor Escolastica, the old women would say
on seeing her hobble to the well with a bucket

carrying her leg as if it were the weight   10
of the devil, surely it was a curse from heaven
for some misdeed, the young women who were
jealous would murmur, yet they were grieved too
having heard that the doctor might cut
her leg, one of a pair of the most perfect legs   15
in the valley, and it was a topic of great
interest and conjecture among the villagers
whether Guillermo would still marry her
if she were crippled, a one-legged woman—
as if life weren't hard enough for a woman   20
with two legs—how could she manage
Guillermo returned and married Escolastica
even though she had but one leg, the sound
of her wooden leg pounding down the wooden aisle
stayed in everyone's memory for as long   25
as they lived, women cried at the sight
of her beauty, black hair so dark
that the night could get lost in it, a face
more alluring than a full moon

Escolastica went to the dances with her husband   30
and watched and laughed but never danced
though once she had been the best dancer
and could wear holes in a pair of shoes
in a matter of a night, and her waist had been
as light to the touch as a hummingbird's flight   35
And Escolastica bore five children, only half
what most women bore, yet they were healthy
In Escolastica's presence, no one would mention
the absence of her leg, though she walked heavily
And it was not long before the gossips   40
spread their poison, that she must be in cohorts
with the devil, had given him her leg
for the power to bewitch Guillermo's heart
and cloud his eyes so that he could not see
what was so clear to them all   45

Read More on the Web

Twelve poems online by Leo Romero: http://sfpoetry.org/romero.html
Notes on Leo Romero: sfpoetry.org/bionote2.html

Questions for Discussion

1. Find examples of simile in this poem. Remember that similes use words such as "like" and "as" to create comparisons.
2. Find examples of other figurative language in this piece.
3. Romero creates two images (pictures in words) in the second stanza (verse paragraph) of this poem. What are these images, and why does he include them?
4. Pick out examples of concrete language in this selection. Then, find examples of vivid verbs and adjectives.
5. The story takes place in a village where life is hard. Why is it important for us to know that?
6. The gossips believe Guillermo "could not see/what was so clear to them all." What does Guillermo see that they don't?
7. How do the gossips explain Guillermo's marrying Escolastica even after she loses her leg? What does this say about them?
8. What can we conclude about the gossips' opinion of men in general?

Thinking Critically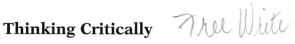

1. Many of us know people like the gossips. Do such people deserve blame or pity? Are they malicious or just ignorant? Make a list of similes or metaphors that might help describe such people.
2. Schwartz's "Colossus in the Kitchen," an essay in Chapter 9, shows that bad luck can be mistaken by small-minded people as a sign of God's punishment for sinning. Where does this theme appear in Romero's poem? Make notes in the margins to identify this theme.

Suggestions for Journal Entries

1. Think of a person or an event that was the subject of gossip in your school or community. Use listing or another method for gathering details discussed in "Getting Started" to explain how much the gossips exaggerated, twisted, or lied about the facts. Try to show how they changed the truth to make the story seem more sensational, startling, racy, or horrible than it was.
2. Not all communities react badly to people who are different. Do you agree? If so, provide evidence from personal experience, from newspapers, or from other sources to support this idea. For example, talk about how quickly people in your city responded when they heard a neighbor needed expensive medical care, or explain how well students at your school accept newcomers from other cultures.

Music

Louis Gonzalez

When asked by his professor to define a concept, idea, or activity that was important to him, Louis Gonzalez knew immediately what he would write about. The challenging part came in making this abstraction real to his readers. He did this by choosing concrete, specific, and vivid vocabulary and by filling his writing with powerful figures of speech. In other words, he showed the reader what he meant.

Gonzalez writes musical reviews for a local magazine and is considering a career as a writer. He was a first-year liberal-arts student when he wrote this essay.

Preparing to Read

1. Pay special attention to paragraph 4. You will recall that the rough draft of this paragraph appears earlier in the chapter with the author's revisions, which show how much care he puts into the process of writing.

2. Gonzalez uses all three figures of speech discussed in this chapter. He also uses hyperbole, or exaggeration. Look for an example of this technique at the end of paragraph 7.

Vocabulary

cathartic (adjective)	Cleansing, purifying.
chaotic (adjective)	Confusing, disorderly.
licks (noun)	Musical phrases created when improvising.
mesmerizing (adjective)	Absorbing, hypnotizing.
obsession (noun)	Passion, fixation.
orgasms (noun)	Sexual climaxes.
oscillating (adjective)	Moving from side to side.
poised (adjective)	Balanced.
preoccupied (adjective)	Absorbed in, wrapped up in.
reverberates (verb)	Echoes.
tangible (adjective)	Able to be touched, felt.
tenacity (noun)	Determination, persistence.
venues (noun)	Places where events take place.
yoke (noun)	Shackle, chain.

Music

Louis Gonzalez

MUSIC IS MY obsession. It reverberates across every fiber of my being. I have 1
spent endless hours of my life creating music, performing it, or even just
dreaming about it. My thoughts are filled with the angelic sigh of a bow kissing the string of a violin, or the hellish crash of batons torturing the skin of a
kettle drum. But my favorite instrument is the vociferous world around us. The
scuff of a penny loafer against a wood floor, the clinking of Crayolas across a
child's desk, or the mesmerizing hum of an oscillating fan are all part of this
chaotic symphony. It is within this sonic spectrum that I exist.

I have long been preoccupied with the audible world. When I was 2
younger, anything and everything that made a sound became a musical instrument. My mother's pots, empty soda bottles, even the railing on my front porch
became part of my private symphony orchestra. Then, for my ninth birthday, I
received a Fisher-Price record player. A single tin speaker was built into the
base, and the needle was attached to a wooden lid, which I had to shut in order to make the thing work. More often than not, the lid would fall accidentally and cut deep scratches into the record. But to my young ears, it made the
sounds of heaven.

Armed with my record player and some old jazz 45s I liberated from my 3
dad's collection, I locked myself in the garage and entered another world. Instead of remaining surrounded by tools and half-empty paint cans, I lowered
the lid of that cheap Fisher-Price and transported myself to a smokey club
somewhere in the city. As the music played, wrenches became saxophones,
boxes became a set of drums, and the workbench became a sleek black piano.
I played 'em all, man! I wore those old 45s down until there was nothing left
but pops, cracks, and the occasional high note. I spent most of my childhood
in that smelly garage listening to Miles Davis and my other patron saints, while
other kids played football and video games. Even though my parents said I
wasted my time there, the experience instilled in me a burning desire to become
a musician.

When I entered high school, my interests shifted towards learning to play 4
a musical instrument. After a little experimentation, I fell in love with the bass
guitar. It covered me with warm, confident tones—blankets of pure ecstasy.
They were poised ballroom dancers waltzing elegantly around my head. The
guitar became the implement of my creativity, the brush with which I painted
portraits of candid love and dark emotion. I was naked and insecure without
it. Its weight was a lover's hand upon my shoulder, and its smooth hourglass
body was a pleasure to hold. It whispered sweet kisses in my ear.

As my skills increased, so did my yearning to play those old jazz songs of 5
my youth. But the harder I tried, the less I succeeded. It seemed as though I was
simply incapable of playing those songs. All those wild bass licks that poured
out of that Fisher-Price record player were ripped from my dreams.

My lust for jazz was then replaced by the desire to perform in a live rock 6
band. So, I joined a local college group and began to play small venues. The
shows were like cathartic orgasms of sweaty bodies undulating as the sensation
of music overwhelmed them. While I was on stage, the power of the music
pierced through the air like a volley of arrows falling upon the flannel-clad flesh
whirling below me. But I felt as though the music was in control and I was just
letting it happen. That feeling began to consume my spirit and destroy my sense
of oneness with the music.

There was definitely something missing. Even though what I played was 7
structurally powerful, it lacked a soul. I also realized that my style of playing
lacked a human quality. So when I came upon my old jazz records, I listened
to them with new ears. I dropped all of my preconceived notions of song structure. As the records popped and scratched their way around the turntable, the
secrets of the universe were finally revealed to me.

I realized that my approach had been all wrong. All my songs were suffo- 8
cated under the weight of formality. Harnessed to the yoke of "proper" song
structure and arrangement, they were never allowed to grow fully. So, I picked
up my bass with a fresh tenacity and dropped all my inhibitions. Not, surpris-
ingly, those old jazz songs started to pour out. I played them as if I had known
them all of my life.

I look back on that day and realize that I did know how to play those songs 9
all along. It wasn't a tangible lack of something—like talent or effort—that held
me back. I just needed to *feel* the music—to feel the sweet life a musician blows
into, to feel it the way that innocent child felt in the garage all those years ago.

Read More on the Web

National Association for Music Education site: http://www.menc.org/
information/infoserv/careersinmusic.htm
University of Illinois at Urbana site on the value of teaching music in the
schools: www.ed.uiuc.edu/ups/curriculum2002/music/
phase3narr.shtml

Questions for Discussion

1. What is Gonzalez's thesis? Has he proved it?
2. How would you describe the introduction of this essay? Is it like one
    or more of the types you learned about in Chapter 4? Which one or
    ones?

3. Find examples of metaphor in paragraphs 3 and 4.
4. Where in this essay does Gonzalez use simile?
5. Find two paragraphs in which the author makes good use of personification. Explain these figures of speech.
6. Paragraphs 1, 2, and 3 show that Gonzalez uses concrete and specific nouns, like those you read about in Chapter 5. Find examples of such nouns.
7. Vivid verbs make paragraph 7 especially interesting. Identify a few of them.

Thinking Critically

1. Gonzalez uses a hyperbole, another figure of speech, in paragraph 7. Explain what he means. Is his use of exaggeration effective?
2. If you could speak to Gonzalez, what would you ask him about his experiences with music? Write these questions in the margins of the essay.

Suggestions for Journal Entries

1. What is your obsession? Use freewriting or brainstorming to record facts about your love for an activity or idea that will show how much you are committed to it.
2. Create a list of metaphors, similes, or personifications that might describe how you feel when you are doing a particular activity you really enjoy. For inspiration reread paragraphs 1, 3, 4, and 6 of "Music."

Uncommon Valor

Ken Ringle

Ken Ringle is a staff writer and film critic for the Washington Post. *This essay first appeared in the September 2002 issue of* Smithsonian Magazine, *one year after the fateful terrorist attacks on the World Trade Center in New York City and the Pentagon in Washington, D.C. on September 11, 2001. Much of Ringle's work focuses on stories of human survival, and this one is no exception. "Uncommon Valor" tells the story of two naval officers and a Pentagon employee who showed exceptional courage as well as a dedication to their fellow human beings.*

Preparing to Read

1. This is a substantial essay in which Ringle uses figurative language to convey the danger, horror, and excitement of the incident. Read this essay with a pencil in your hand and make sure to underline examples of figurative language. Then, read it again and, remembering what you learned in Chapter 5, circle examples of other words and phrases that, although being literal, are concrete, specific, and vivid.

2. Read the first two paragraphs a few times before going on to the entire essay. Ask yourself how the author has constructed his introduction and what his thesis is.

3. This is not just a story. It is a description of heroic people, and a definition of heroism itself. Keep this in mind as you read "Uncommon Valor."

4. The Pentagon is the office complex that houses the U.S. Defense Department.

Vocabulary

apocalypse (noun)	Vision of the end of the world.
cipher (adjective)	Coded.
cogs (noun)	Teeth or sprockets in a gear wheel (here used figuratively).
concentric (adjective)	Having the same center, circles within circles.
cyber (adjective)	Relating to computers, digital communication.
disparate (adjective)	Different, separate.
excruciating (adjective)	agonizing.

ganglia (noun)	Strings of nerve tissue (here used figuratively).
molten (adjective)	Liquid, melted.
rudimentary (adjective)	Simple, basic.
searing (adjective)	Burning, withering.

Uncommon Valor

Ken Ringle

THE FIRST THING TO UNDERSTAND IS THAT, UNTIL THE moment American Airlines   1
Flight 77 actually struck the Pentagon at 9:38 that morning, the three men
heard nothing. The rest of us in the Washington, D.C. area may live with the
noise of passenger jets flying in and out of Reagan National Airport every
minute, but everyone working in the great, pentagonal building, located almost
directly beneath its northern flight path, labors insulated from that roar. Some
of the same measures that secured the hum of its phones, computers and code
machines from the electronic snoopers outside also muffled the deafening rum-
ble of fuel-freighted airliners screaming by overhead. Nobody ever thought of
them as flying bombs.

The second thing to recognize is that none of the three knew one another.   2
They were three human cogs in the 24,000-strong Pentagon workforce. They
were assigned to different floors in separate rings of offices, disparate bureau-
cratic kingdoms within the concentric five sided design that gives the world's
largest office building its name. Had it not been for Osama bin Laden, the three
might never have met.

Of course, in the end none of that mattered. The three men were welded   3
together for the rest of their lives by a half-hour hellscape of searing flame and
shattered bodies and smoke so thick and suffocating they coughed up black
sludge from their lungs for days.

"It was raining molten metal and plastic," remembers Capt. David   4
M. Thomas, Jr, 44, a distant look of intensity in his eyes, "The soldered connections in the overhead wiring and the insulation were melting. I took off my
uniform blouse because it had polyester in it and I was sure it would melt. I was
wearing just my cotton T-shirt. But then the molten liquid from the ceiling
dripped on more of my body. The drops made little black holes as they burned
through my skin."

"I didn't want to go in there," says Lt. Cmdr. David Tarantino, 36, remem-   5
bering the moment he reached the crash site. "It was like an apocalypse."

Tarantino, a Navy physician who helps coordinate humanitarian relief ef-   6
forts for the Department of Defense, had rushed from his fourth-floor office in
the centermost A ring (the building, like a tree, has concentric rings, each con-
figured pentagonally) at the moment he felt a "violent shudder" of the building.

He had just returned from a meeting to find colleagues watching the burning World Trade Center on television, had seen the second plane hit and was sure that now the Pentagon, too, had come under attack. But he recalls hearing no noise when Flight 77 struck the building.

Tarantino, a 6-foot-4, 180-pound triathlete who had rowed crew for Stanford, ran down one of the corridors radiating from the Pentagon's central courtyard. The hallway was filled with smoke and with coughing, bleeding people who were sumbling around, disoriented. The heat and smoke, rising to ceiling height, had effectively hidden all exit signs. Many were uncertain, amid the wailing fire-alarm sirens, which way to go. Grabbing some wet paper towels from a nearby rest room as a rudimentary gas mask, and working his way from floor to floor, Tarantino helped direct people toward the courtyard. Then, turning against the flow of people fleeing to safety, he headed toward what appeared to be the point of greatest destruction. 7

Between B and C rings, radial corridors transect an open-air ring, a breezeway, into which Tarantino lurched to get some air. There he saw two large smoking holes in the C-ring walls and what was clearly the forward landing gear and huge tire of a jetliner. There were also body parts. "I may be a doctor," he says, "but nothing prepares you for that kind of devastation." 8

Dave Thomas worked on C ring, in a section two corridors away from the airliner's impact point. Thomas is a second-generation Naval officer with two brothers in the Navy and one in the Marines. 9

When Flight 77 hit, all Thomas could think was that his best friend worked in that section of the building. Bob Dolan had been like a brother since their days rooming together at Annapolis. He had been the best man at Thomas' wedding and was godfather to one of his kids. No one outside Thomas' immediate family was more important to him. 10

Racing down a stairway, Thomas made his way through the smoke to the breezeway and the giant tire and the gaping holes. Inside one of the holes, he heard voices behind a door. 11

Somebody handed him a metal bar and he pounded on the door. But, like many secure areas in the Pentagon, it was sealed with an electric cipher lock. The door wouldn't give. He knew he had to find another way in. Grabbing a fire extinguisher, he crawled into the smaller of the two holes. 12

"The plane had punched through an electrical closet; all these live wires were lying around and arcing in the water [from sprinklers or burst mains]. You had to crawl over the wires through the water while you were getting shocked. There was so much smoke, you could not see. But I had grabbed a flashlight from somewhere, and two people on the floor inside were able to see the beam of light and make their way out past me. I saw the head of another guy. I knew we had to get him out, but I wasn't sure I could. It was all you could do in there just to breathe." 13

Thomas had grabbed a wet T-shirt to breathe through and protect his balding scalp. Then, with his shoes literally melting on his feet, he crawled forward, into the firestorm of molten rain. 14

metaphor

The shattered room he was entering was part of the new Navy Command   15
Center, a vast war room filled with the techno-ganglia of cyber communications. One of the 50-odd staffers who worked there was Jerry Henson, a 65-
year-old former Navy commander who had returned to the Pentagon after
retirement. He liked being at the center of things.   *simile*

"It was like being hit in the head with a baseball bat," he remembers.   16
"There was no sense of gradualism, or of the plane coming through the walls
or anything like that. I heard one loud report, and all of a sudden it was dark
and hot, and the air was filled with smoke and the smell of jet fuel. I couldn't
move. And I was in excruciating pain."

A huge wall of debris—ceiling, book-cases, wallboard, desks, plumbing—   17
had slammed into him, pinning his head between his computer monitor and
his left shoulder. The rubble probably would have crushed him, but his desk
top had dislocated across the arms of his chair, imprisoning him but supporting most of the weight.

"There were two enlisted people nearby on the floor, but they couldn't get   18
to me. It was pitch dark and suffocating in the smoke. We were all coughing
and strangling and yelling for help but never heard any answer from the other
side of the wall. The room was burning and melting around us."

After about 15 minutes, he says, he was able to gradually dig enough rub-   19
ble from around his head to straighten his neck a bit. That eased the pain. But
metaphor the smoke was getting thicker; it was getting harder and harder to breathe. The
increasing rain of solder and plastic from the ceiling told him the room could-
n't last much longer. Then he saw the beam of a flashlight.

David Tarantino had worked his way with a fire extinguisher over the snarl   20
of live wires into the smaller of the two holes in the breezeway wall, throwing
aside flaming debris as he went. Somehow the physician had chosen a slightly
different route from Thomas. "When I finally saw Jerry, he was looking right at
me," Tarantino remembers. "We made eye contact. I yelled, 'Come on, man, get
out of there. You got to get out of there.' I wanted him to come to me. I didn't
want to go where he was. It was hell in there."   *metaphor*

Tarantino knew time was running out. "He crawled in through all that fire   21
and dripping metal and lay down beside me," Henson says. "He said, 'I'm a doctor and I'm here to get you out.' Then he lay on his back and leg-pressed that   *metaphor*
wall of debris enough so I could squeeze over the chair arm." Tarantino inched
Henson out, and Thomas freed him the rest of the way, Henson recalls. "Tarantino had the bruises from my fingers on his arms for a week."

One hundred twenty-five people died at the Pentagon, not counting the   22
more than 60 passengers, crew and hijackers aboard Flight 77. More than a hundred others were injured in the explosion and fire. Jerry Henson was treated at
the scene for head cuts and given an IV and oxygen and hospitalized for four
days, mostly for smoke inhalation problems. He was back at work a month later.

Thomas and Tarantino suffered burns on their hands, knees and feet as   23
well as smoke inhalation. Both were back at work the next day.

"I don't have words to describe how brave they were," Henson says of his   24
rescuers. "There's a limit to what's intelligent to do" on behalf of someone else.
"They exceeded that. Their heroism is a step beyond what any medal could
recognize."

The doctor's leg-press rescue, Thomas said, was "the bravest thing I've ever   25
seen." Tarantino downplays any heroics. "Once you've made eye contact with
someone, you can't just leave them to die." He says his desperate leg-press maneuver was more a product of adrenaline than technique—like a mother who
somehow lifts a car off a child. He sprained his knee in the effort—the next day
he could hardly walk—and doubts he could have gotten Henson out without
Thomas.

With a heavy heart, Thomas continued looking for his friend Bob Dolan,   26
all the while grieving for what he feared Dolan's wife and children would have
to face. "His cell phone kept ringing for a couple of days when we called it, so
we had hopes," Thomas says. Dolan was confirmed among the victims; some
remains were recovered. Last January 11, in the presence of Thomas and the
Dolan family, he was buried at sea.

Read More on the Web

University of Michigan site on the 9/11 attacks:
   http://www.lib.umich.edu/govdocs/usterror.html
Yale University Law School's Avalon Project site with links:
   http://www.yale.edu/lawweb/avalon/sept_11/sept_11.htm

Questions for Discussion

1. What is the essay's thesis? Explain how the introduction to this essay
   helps make the thesis statement more emphatic.

2. What metaphors are used in the thesis? What effect do they have on
   you and your understanding of what occurs in this essay? Why is the
   term "welded" in paragraph 3 appropriate?

3. Find three or four metaphors and an equal number of similes in this
   essay and explain what they mean.

4. Explain what Ringle means by the "techno-ganglia of cyber
   communications" (paragraph 15).

5. Reread and analyze at least three paragraphs. What examples of
   concrete and specific language do you find?

6. Find examples of Ringle's use of vivid verbs and adjectives.

7. In paragraph 3, "hellscape" is used to describe the scene in this essay. Find language in one or two paragraphs that helps develop that metaphor.

8. Is the conclusion fitting? In what way does it relate to the essay's thesis?

Thinking Critically

1. From what you have read in this essay, try to describe the layout of the Pentagon.

2. Tarantino and Thomas are the heroes of this story. Find and analyze places in this essay where the author provides proof of their heroism. Then, explain what you think is the source of that heroism. In what way is this story a definition of heroism?

Suggestions for Journal Entries

1. Do you know of other examples of uncommon valor that occurred on September 11, 2001 or during any other catastrophe in American history? If so, write about one of them by using the clustering or freewriting methods.

2. What this essay defines is a quality that is very rare. Think of an incident or event from your personal or family history that might define another uncommon quality. This quality can be positive or negative. For example, you might recall a story that illustrates or shows uncommon charity or uncommon kindness. Then again you might want to discuss uncommon selfishness or uncommon laziness. Begin recording notes by using listing or freewriting.

Back from the Brink

Daniel Zanoza

Daniel Zanoza wrote this essay to describe the horrors of drug addiction and to broadcast a warning. Originally published in The American Enterprise *magazine, the essay uses both literal and figurative language to get and maintain the reader's attention. Zanoza lives in Illinois.*

Preparing to Read

1. Besides using metaphors and similes to describe his life as a drug addict, Zanoza assigns human qualities to the addiction itself, thereby creating a kind of ghostly character that haunts the entire essay. He does this through personification.

2. One of Zanoza's objectives in writing this essay is to respond to those who would have us believe that the drug life can be fashionable, "chic" as he puts it. His use of figurative language helps him make his point emphatically, and it shows that such language can be used for a variety of purposes, including persuasion.

3. What does Zanoza mean by "The Brink"?

Vocabulary

accessible (adjective)	Obtainable, available.
anesthetization (noun)	Deadening of the senses.
cross a threshold (verb)	Pass through a doorway.
dastardly (adjective)	Evil, nasty, unscrupulous.
deterrents (noun)	Obstacles, barriers.
dispensary (noun)	Clinic, place where drugs are distributed.
emerging (adjective)	Arising.
euphoria (noun)	Elation, feeling of well-being.
gateway (noun)	Doorway, entrance.
illicit (adjective)	Illegal.
insidious (adjective)	Sneaky, evil.
invincibility (noun)	Indestructibility.
magnitude (noun)	Size, extent.
psychosis (noun)	Madness.
seminal (adjective)	Defining, determining.
urgency (noun)	Necessity.
veritable (adjective)	Genuine, actual.

Back from the Brink

Daniel Zanoza

I NEVER THOUGHT I'd hear the words heroin and chic mentioned in the same   1
sentence. But lately the two have been paired, in movies and other pop culture. This shakes me to my very soul, as I recall the private hell that heroin
brought to my life for over 20 years.

A single decision can determine one's life path. My seminal moment came   2
on my nineteenth birthday. A friend stopped by to help me celebrate. At the
time, I'd been experimenting with all kinds of illicit drugs. Marijuana had been
the first. Soon the world was a veritable candy store: alcohol, uppers, downers,
psychedelics—there was a pharmaceutical cocktail for every mood. Combine
this with the invincibility of youth, and life became one long party. Or so it
seemed. My true goal was self-anesthetization from the pains of life.

On my nineteenth birthday, however, I crossed a further threshold. For the first   3
time, I tried heroin, and the drug became my life partner for the next two decades.

At first, there were no meetings in dark alleys or dingy bars. Drug use was   4
easy and attractive. Heroin was just another adventure. A negative experience
might have been the best thing to happen on that nineteenth birthday, but that
wasn't the case. I felt right at home in the sedated euphoria caused by the drug.

The insidious danger of heroin is that in early use, you're in control. You   5
feel you can take it or leave it; therefore, quitting holds no urgency.

Year after year passed. I went to school and became a social worker. It was   6
all right; I just needed to use it responsibly. Can you believe that? A responsible heroin addict.

By age 30, the addiction was a way of life. The pain was great, an all-   7
consuming dull throb of hopelessness and dependence that possessed my life.
Greeting the day was a chore of the greatest magnitude. Sometimes I would
sleep until 5:00 PM because the light was too revealing. I was a creature of the
night, a vampire sucking family and friends for all they were worth.

No, I didn't commit any armed robberies or burglaries, but rarely did a gift   8
or any item of value last for long. Sold or returned for cash. After all, what was
really important? Heroin was my god. It came before parents and friends. It came
before a job. It came before food and shelter. Often, it came before life itself.

Most current and former drug addicts like me will tell you that legalization   9
of drugs is a terrible idea—and that includes marijuana. Marijuana was the first
drug used by the vast majority of us, and recent research has shown it works
on the brain in precisely the same ways "harder" drugs like cocaine and heroin
do. That's why scientists now describe marijuana as a natural "gateway" to
stronger narcotics.

Decriminalization or legalization would only create greater access to drugs.   10
With the explosion of teenage drug use during the last four years, the last thing

America should be thinking about is making drugs more accessible. One of the strongest deterrents to using drugs today is simply the fact that they are illegal.

Unlike other unhealthful "temptations," drugs actually exert a chemical power over their users. I've asked advocates of drug legalization, "What do we do with people who have been up for three days on a cocaine bender?" There is a psychosis that grips such a person, and their binge ends only when they run out of funds, or consciousness. Some dastardly crimes are committed by people under the influence of drugs. What do we do with such people if there is legalization? Give them a ticket and send them down the road to kill my family or yours? Or create a one-stop dispensary where an abuser can obtain the drug until his heart seizes?   11

In my own case, even a new faith wasn't enough to break the drug stranglehold at first. I expected a miraculous deliverance. God would do all the work; I would just sit back and wait. But that deliverance never came. It wasn't that easy: recovery takes strenuous effort. A substance abuser, I learned, must make a habit out of being sober.   12

Eventually, with the help of God and the support of others, I was ready for that commitment—after decades of misery. I've been almost five years in recovery now, living life again. The appreciation of a beautiful sunset has returned, along with my gratefulness for true love and friendship. Silly things make me laugh and sad movies make me cry. The simple pleasures of household chores are no longer unimaginable burdens but welcome responsibilities.   13

Some of my human relationships were irreparably harmed, but those who cared about me most now care again. I asked for their forgiveness, and they've welcomed back the old me that was lost and nearly forgotten. I have a wife and family who never left my side. I have an emerging new journalism career, and I'm active in public service. I'll never be a literary giant, or president, but I'm looking forward to the future. With God's help, I will be the best friend, husband, and person I can be.   14

And for me, that's quite an accomplishment.   15

Read More on the Web

National Institute on Drug Abuse home page: http://www.nida.nih.gov/

Principles of Drug Addiction Treatment: A Research Based Guide with links to many related sites: http://www.nida.nih.gov/PODAT/PODATindex.html

Questions for Discussion

1. What is Zanoza's thesis?
2. What is the author's purpose for writing this essay? Did he have more than one purpose? Reread paragraphs 9, 10, and 11 before you answer.

3. Explain the metaphors the author uses in paragraph 2.
4. In what other paragraphs does he use metaphors? Explain each example.
5. In paragraph 3, Zanoza uses personification when he refers to his addiction as his "life partner." Where else does he use personification?
6. Paragraph 11 makes good use of concrete and vivid literal language, like the kind you learned about in Chapter 5. Underline or mark such words in this paragraph.

Thinking Critically

1. Do you agree with Zanoza that drugs like heroin and marijuana should be kept illegal? If so, think of at least one reason not mentioned in his essay that supports this opinion.
2. If you disagree with Zanoza, make a list of reasons that support your view. Make sure to answer both the questions that the author asks in paragraph 11.

Suggestions for Journal Entries

1. After reading this essay, what advice might you give to a friend or relative suffering from a drug, alcohol, gambling, food, sex, shopping, or other addiction? Freewrite or use clustering to gather information. Discuss the effects of the addiction on the addict and on his or her loved ones. After you complete this entry, read what you have written. Then, revise it, creating a few figures of speech that will explain your subject more vividly. Say that you write that your cousin's life "has been ruined by alcohol." You might revise this to read that "the demon of alcohol haunts my cousin."
2. Do you know someone suffering from a serious illness? Write a paragraph in which you identify the illness and describe one of its effects on that individual and on his or her family. In the process, include figures of speech such as the ones explained in this chapter.

Suggestions for Sustained Writing

1. In "What the Gossips Saw," Romero shows that gossips can exaggerate or twist a story so badly that, in their mouths, the truth becomes unrecognizable. If you responded to the first of the journal prompts after Romero's poem, read your notes. Then, draft an essay that tells what happened when gossips spread rumors about a person or event in your school or community.

As with other assignments, you can organize your thoughts in several different ways. For example, you might start by revealing the truth of a story and then explaining—step-by-step—how the gossips distorted it. Or, you might recall how false rumors began, how they spread, and how they affected people. A good way to end this story is to tell the truth as you know it.

Whichever approach you choose, rewrite the paper several times. In your second and subsequent drafts, try hard to include figures of speech—simile, metaphor, and/or personification—to describe people, motives, places, and events and to give your writing greater variety and interest. Doing so will also make your writing more convincing.

Finally, explain what observing or experiencing the effects of gossip taught you about it and about the people who spread it. The best place to do this is in the paper's introduction or conclusion.

2. Read the journal notes you made after completing Louis Gonzalez's "Music." If you responded to either or both of the Suggestions for Journal Entries, you have a good start on an essay that will discuss an obsession of your own.

Begin with an introduction that, like Gonzalez's, explains the extent to which you are committed to a particular pursuit, idea, study, activity, hobby, art form, or sport. Then go on to explain how this obsession developed in you. End your essay by looking to the future or by using any of the other types of conclusions discussed in Chapter 4.

As always, remember that one draft is never enough. When you write your second draft, include concrete and specific nouns and adjectives. Add vivid verbs, adjectives, and adverbs as well. When you revise this draft, try to add figures of speech like those discussed in this chapter. Then, revise your third draft to improve organization, sentence structure, and grammar. The final step is, of course, to edit and proofread your work carefully.

3. Read the journal notes you made after reading "Uncommon Valor" by Ken Ringle. Turn the notes responding to either suggestion for journal entries into a full length essay. If you responded to the first prompt, you might want to do some additional research on the Internet or in the library to give your writing greater authority. However, if you use any of this material, make sure to incorporate it and cite it (give appropriate credit) correctly. You can learn how to do this using Modern Language Association style by turning to the the appendix of this textbook

If you choose to expand your notes responding to the second prompt, make sure to recall your story in detail and to include language that is concrete, specific, and vivid. To make your writing even more exciting and effective, follow Ringle's lead and add figures of speech when you write your second and third drafts. As always, edit and proofread your work carefully.

4. The first of the Suggestions for Journal Entries after Daniel Zanoza's "Back from the Brink" asks you to write down advice you might give someone suffering from an addiction. Review your entry carefully and add to it. Make a special effort to create similes and metaphors and to use personification so as to make your writing vivid. Then, put this information into a letter that tries to convince the reader to give up his or her addiction.

   After you have written your first draft, read your letter carefully. Ask yourself if you have used vocabulary that is concrete, specific, and vivid enough to convince your reader. If not, use the techniques you learned in this chapter and in Chapter 5 to make your language more effective.

   When you are satisfied that you have developed your letter well and that you have expressed your ideas in language that is powerful and convincing, edit and proofread your letter. Then send it.

5. The second journal assignment after "Back from the Brink" by Daniel Zanoza asks you to write a paragraph explaining one effect of a serious illness on someone you know and on his or her family. Review this paragraph. Then, write several more paragraphs, each of which explains another way in which the patient's life or the life of his or her loved ones has been affected. You might introduce this essay with a paragraph that explains how the patient contracted or found out about the illness. Such a paragraph might end with your thesis statement.

   As you revise your rough draft, pay special attention to your language. Add figures of speech, like those you read in Zanoza's essay. They will make your writing more effective and convincing. As always, edit and proofread the last draft of your paper.

Writing to Learn: A Group Activity

Daniel Zanoza's "Back from the Brink" describes a life nearly lost to drug abuse. Luckily for Zanoza, his wife and family helped him battle his demon. But what about people not lucky enough to have the support of loved ones—where can they seek help?

THE FIRST MEETING

Ask each group member to identify a different community, religious, volunteer, or government agency, group, or organization dedicated to helping people fight their drug habits.

RESEARCH

One of you might call your city or town government to find out what services it offers or to ask for leads about religious or other community groups that provide such services. Another might call the local hospital, board of health, or the college's counseling center, infirmary, or health office for information about health services or drug rehabilitation programs in the community or on campus. Finally, someone might research topics such as drug rehabilitation or drug addiction in the college library or on the Internet.

Ask each member of the group to find out about and take careful notes on one service, agency, or organization—whether public or private—that helps drug addicts. Everyone should photocopy his or her notes and be prepared to discuss them at the next meeting.

THE SECOND MEETING

Distribute, discuss, and critique each other's notes. Don't be afraid to recommend that a particular student find out more about the agency or service he or she has chosen to write about. Then, ask everyone to write two or three well-developed paragraphs explaining what the agency or service he or she researched does to help addicts recover. Again, ask group members to make photocopies of their work so that it can be discussed at the next meeting.

THE THIRD MEETING

Discuss the paragraphs that each member of the group has written and distributed. Make suggestions for revision and editing. Then assign one member of the group the task of incorporating this material into a letter to the editor of your local or college newspaper. The purpose of this letter would be, of course, to advise drug addicts on campus or in the community that help is available. Assign one or two other students to use this same information in a poster that could be displayed in your college's student center or in classroom buildings. Ask other members to put this information into a one- or two-page pamphlet that might be displayed and distributed at your college's counseling center.

CHAPTER 7

Sentence Structure: Creating Emphasis and Variety

In Chapters 5 and 6 you learned to express your ideas more effectively by using language that is concrete, specific, and vivid. In this chapter you will learn how to use sentence structure to give your writing emphasis and variety, making it even more interesting and effective.

Emphasis

Communicating ideas clearly often depends on the ability to emphasize, or stress, one idea over another. By arranging the words in a sentence carefully, you can emphasize certain ideas and direct your readers' attention to the heart of your message.

A good way to emphasize an idea is to express it in a short, simple sentence of its own. But you will never develop your writing skills if you stick to a steady diet of such sentences. Even the shortest writing projects require sentences containing two or more ideas. In some cases, these ideas will be equally important; in others, one idea will need to be emphasized over the other or others.

CREATE EMPHASIS THROUGH COORDINATION

Ideas that are *equal* in importance can be expressed in the same sentence by using coordination. The sentence below coordinates (makes equal) three words in a series: *found, pitched,* and *started.*

> We *found* a clearing, *pitched* the tent, and *started* a small fire.

You can also use coordination to join two or more *main clauses* to which you wish to give equal emphasis. A main clause contains a subject and verb and, even when standing by itself, expresses a complete idea. You can join main clauses with a comma and a coordinating conjunction, such as *and, but, or, nor, for,* or *so.* Here are some examples; the main clauses are shown in italics:

> *Wild ponies gallop through the surf,* and *eagles soar quietly overhead.*

> *Robert Frost is famous for poetry set in rural New England,* but *he was born in San Francisco.*

The raccoons have not been near our house in days, nor *have they been missed.*

Marlin will take the final exam, or *he will fail the course.*

The area was contaminated with a strange virus, so *the medical team wore protective gear.*

I floss my teeth daily, for *I want to avoid gum disease.*

Note that, in the above sentences, the beginning and ending clauses are given equal importance. Another way to coordinate (make equal) main clauses within a sentence is to join them with a semicolon:

Alice's car is an antique; it was built in 1927.

You can use both a semicolon and a conjunction when you want to make sure your readers see the relationship of equality between the ideas you are emphasizing. This is especially important in long sentences:

Hoping to reach Lake Soggy Bottom by noon, we left our house by 6:00 AM and took Interstate 90; but traffic was so heavy that we soon realized we would be lucky to reach the lake before dark.

CREATE EMPHASIS THROUGH SUBORDINATION

The sentences above contain complete ideas—main clauses—that are equal in importance. But what if you decide that one of your ideas is more important than the other? Sometimes, putting the less important idea into a *phrase* or *subordinate clause* helps emphasize the other. A phrase is a group of words without a subject or predicate; a subordinate clause contains a subject and predicate, but, unlike a main clause, it does not express a complete idea. Say you wrote these sentences:

Ethel turned the corner, and she noticed a large truck in her lane.

She was frightened, but she avoided the truck.

When revising, you decide that in each sentence the second idea is more important than the first. Therefore, you *subordinate* the first idea to the second:

Turning the corner, Ethel noticed a large truck in her lane.
(*The first idea has been put into a phrase.*)

Although she was frightened, she avoided the truck.
(*The first idea has been put into a subordinate clause.*)

Here are three of many ways to subordinate ideas.

Use Participles   *Participles* are adjectives formed from verbs. They describe nouns and pronouns. Each of the following sentences has been revised by turning one of its main clauses into a phrase that begins with a participle. Doing so helps put emphasis on the main clause that remains.

> **Original:** Charlotte was visiting her Uncle in Knoxville, and she decided to drive through the Great Smoky Mountains.
> (*The sentence contains two main clauses of the same importance.*)
> **Revised:** Visiting her uncle in Knoxville, Charlotte decided to drive through the Great Smoky Mountains.
> (*The first idea is expressed in a phrase that begins with the participle "Visiting." It is less important than the second idea, which remains in a main clause, "Charlotte decided" . . . .*)

> **Original:** Angel planned to visit Moscow, so he began to study Russian.
> (*The ideas are equally important.*)
> **Revised:** Planning to visit Moscow, Angel began to study Russian.
> (*The first idea is now less important than the second because it is expressed in a phrase, which begins with the participle "Planning."*)

Use Subordinating Conjunctions   You can turn a main clause into a subordinate clause with words such as *although, after, as, because, even though, if, since, unless, until,* and *while.*

> **Original:** The French military leader Joan of Arc was condemned as a witch, so she was burned at the stake.
> (*The ideas are equally important.*)
> **Revised:** Because she had been condemned as a witch, the French military leader Joan of Arc was burned at the stake.
> (*The second idea, expressed in a main clause, is emphasized. The first idea is now in a subordinate clause, which begins with "Because."*)

Use Relative Pronouns   Using pronouns such as *who, whom, whose, that,* and *which* is another way to subordinate one idea to another. Subordinate clauses beginning with relative pronouns describe nouns in the sentence's main clause.

> **Original:** My friend's parents once lived in Corsica; Corsica is the birthplace of Napoleon.
> (*The ideas are equally important.*)
> **Revised:** My friend's parents once lived in Corsica, which is the birthplace of Napoleon. (*The first idea, expressed in a main clause, is more important than the second idea, which is now in a subordinate clause introduced by "which."*)

Original: Audrey Davis has spent two years in the Marine Corps; she was sent to Saudi Arabia.
Revised: Audrey Davis, who has spent two years in the Marine Corps, was sent to Saudi Arabia.
(*The subordinate clause, introduced by "who," comes in the middle of the main clause.*)

CREATE EMPHASIS BY USING PERIODIC SENTENCES

You can create emphasis by putting the strongest or most important word or idea at the end of the sentence. Such sentences are called *periodic* because the emphasis comes just before the period. Here are three examples:

Mario forgot the tomato sauce's most important ingredient, garlic!

India, where over half a billion people have the right to vote, is the world's largest democracy.

Zora Neale Hurston is remembered not for her work in anthropology, the field in which she was trained, but for her novels.

CREATE EMPHASIS BY USING A COLON

A colon can be used in place of a semicolon in a compound sentence when the second main clause explains the first. The effect is similar to the one created by a periodic sentence.

Toni Morrison has been busy: she has written eight novels and several books of criticism over the last twenty years.

The second main clause, which follows the colon, explains what the writer means by "busy." Notice that, as with a periodic sentence, emphasis is placed on information at the end of the sentence.

CREATE EMPHASIS BY USING THE ACTIVE OR PASSIVE VOICE

Sentences that use the *active voice* contain subjects—persons, places, or things—that perform an action. Sentences that use the *passive voice* contain subjects that are acted upon. Notice how the structure of a sentence changes when it is put into the passive voice.

Active: The enthusiastic listeners applauded the young guitarist.
Passive: The young guitarist was applauded by the enthusiastic listeners.

Generally, using the active voice rather than the passive voice makes it easier to stress the subject of a sentence. For instance, if you wanted to report that the president of your college announced her decision to resign, it wouldn't make much sense to write, "Her decision to resign was announced by President Greenspan." A clearer and more emphatic version would be "President Greenspan announced her decision to resign."

However, there are times when using the passive voice can create empha-sis. In some cases, you might decide that the receiver of an action is more im-portant than the person, place, or thing who completes that action. For example,

> Ann was elected to the Monroe City Council.

is more emphatic than

> The residents of Monroe elected Ann to the City Council.

Sometimes, in fact, you might not know who or what is responsible for an action, and you will have to use the passive voice:

> Doors and windows were left open; books, furniture, and clothing were scattered across the room; and curtains, sheets, and blankets were torn to shreds.

CREATE EMPHASIS BY REPEATING KEY WORDS AND PHRASES

Repeating important words and phrases, carefully and sparingly, can help you stress important ideas over those that deserve less emphasis. This technique is used in the speeches of President John F. Kennedy and Reverend Martin Luther King, Jr.

In his inaugural address, Kennedy gave a special meaning to his plans for the nation when he said:

> All this will not be finished in the first one hundred days. Nor will it be finished in the first one thousand days, nor in the life of this ad-ministration, nor even perhaps in our lifetime on this planet. But let us begin.

Dr. King used repetition to communicate a sense of urgency about civil rights to a massive audience at the Lincoln Memorial when he delivered the speech now known as "I Have a Dream":

> Now is the time to make real the promises of democracy. Now is the time to rise from the dark and desolate valley of segregation to the sunlit path of racial justice. Now is the time to lift our nation from the quicksands of racial injustice to the solid rock of brotherhood. Now is the time to make justice a reality for all of God's children.

CREATE EMPHASIS THROUGH PARALLELISM

> We the people of the United States, in Order to *form* a more per-fect union, *establish* Justice, *insure* domestic Tranquility, *provide for* the common defence, *promote* the general Welfare, and *secure* the Blessings of Liberty to ourselves and our Posterity, do ordain and establish this Constitution for the United States of America.

The sentence you have just read begins the United States Constitution; this preamble is one of the most well-known sentences in American history. One reason it is so powerful and memorable has to do with its use of six phrases (the reasons for establishing the Constitution) that follow the same pattern. Each consists of a verb followed by a direct object. This writing technique is called *parallelism.*

Parallelism is a way to connect facts and ideas of equal importance in the same sentence and thereby give them added emphasis. Sentences that are parallel list items by expressing each of them in the same grammatical form. For instance, Adlai Stevenson's eulogy of Winston Churchill, the great British prime minister, contains several examples of parallelism:

> The voice that led nations, raised armies, inspired victories and blew fresh courage into the hearts of men is silenced. We shall hear no longer the remembered eloquence and wit, the old courage and defiance, the robust serenity of indomitable faith. Our world is thus poorer, our political dialogue is diminished, and the sources of public inspiration run more thinly in all of us. There is a lonesome place against the sky.

In the first sentence, Stevenson placed equal emphasis on Churchill's accomplishments by expressing each through a verb followed by a direct object: "led nations," "raised armies," "inspired victories," and "blew fresh courage into the hearts of men." He created parallelism in the second sentence in a series of adjectives and nouns that describe Churchill's best qualities: "the remembered eloquence and wit," "the old courage and defiance," "the robust serenity of indomitable faith." In the third sentence, he explained the effects of Churchill's death in a series of main clauses: "Our world is thus poorer," "our political dialogue is diminished," and "the sources of public inspiration run more thinly in all of us."

Consistency is the key to making sentences parallel. Express every idea in a list in the same grammatical form. Without a doubt, the eulogy you just read would have sounded awkward and been less emphatic had Stevenson written that Churchill's voice "led nations, raised armies, inspired victories, and it blew fresh courage into the hearts of men." The first three items are verbs followed by objects; the fourth is a main clause.

Here are three other examples of how parallelism creates emphasis:

> The President enjoys *reading* mystery novels, *fishing* in Maine, and *speaking* with young people.
> *(The sentence contains gerunds, nouns formed from verbs by adding "ing"; gerunds show activity.)*

> *To master* the piano, *to compose* beautiful music, and *to lead* a symphony orchestra seemed to be her destiny.
> *(The sentence contains infinitives, which are formed by placing* to *before the present tense of the verb. Infinitives act as nouns, adjectives, or adverbs.)*

They vowed to battle the invaders *on the land, on the sea,* and *in the air.*
(*The sentence contains* prepositional phrases; a preposition *is a short word—such as* at, in, *or* on—*that shows the relationship of a noun or pronoun to the rest of the sentence.*)

Variety

One sure way to make your readers lose interest in what you have to say—no matter how important—is to ignore the need for variety. Good writers try not to repeat vocabulary monotonously, and they vary the length and structure of their sentences whenever possible.

CREATE VARIETY BY CHANGING SENTENCE LENGTH

A steady diet of long, complicated sentences is sure to put your readers to sleep. On the other hand, relying solely on short, choppy sentences can make your writing seem disconnected and even childish. Therefore, one of the most important things to remember about the sentences you write is to vary their length. You can do this by combining some of them into longer, more complex units and by leaving others short and to the point.

Reread the passage from President Kennedy's Inaugural Address on page 261. One reason it holds our interest is that it contains sentences of different lengths. The last of these leaves a lasting impression, not simply because it comes at the end but because it is so much shorter than the others and carries a special punch.

You can combine two or three short sentences into a longer unit in three ways: coordination, subordination, or compounding.

Coordination This method is useful if you want to write a longer sentence in which all the main ideas receive equal emphasis. The easiest way to do this is to combine sentences with a comma and the appropriate coordinating conjunction or to use a semicolon, as explained on pages 257–258.

Subordination As you know, subordination lets you combine two or more sentences to emphasize one idea over another. It also helps you vary sentence length and make your writing more interesting. Say you've just written:

I had been waiting at the bus stop for 20 minutes. The afternoon air was hot, thick, and humid. I became uncomfortable and soon began to perspire. I wished I were home. I thought about getting under the shower, cooling off, and relaxing. My day at work had been long and hard. I looked up from the newspaper I was reading. I saw a huge truck. It sped by, and it covered me with filthy exhaust. I prayed the bus would come soon.

As you read this paragraph, you realize that you haven't emphasized your most important ideas and that your style is choppy and monotonous. Therefore, you decide to rewrite by combining sentences through subordination (you can review ways to do this by rereading pages 258–259):

> I had been waiting at the bus stop for 20 minutes. Because the afternoon air was hot, thick, and humid, I became uncomfortable and soon began to perspire. Wishing I were home, I thought about getting under the shower, cooling off, and relaxing. My day at work had been long and hard. As I looked up from the newspaper I was reading, I saw a huge truck, which sped by and covered me with exhaust. I prayed the bus would come soon.

In combining some sentences, you've made your writing smoother and more interesting because you've created sentences of different lengths. What's more, some ideas have gained emphasis.

Compounding   This method involves putting subjects, verbs, adjectives, and adverbs together in the same sentence as long as they relate to one another logically.

Sometimes, ideas that are very similar seem awkward and boring if expressed in separate sentences. For example: "Egbert has been transferred to Minneapolis. Rowena has also been transferred to that city." Notice how much more interesting these short sentences become when you combine their subjects: "Egbert and Rowena have been transferred to Minneapolis." Here are a few more examples:

> **Original:** The doctor rushed into the emergency room. She went immediately to a patient who had been bitten by wasps.
> **Compound verb:** The doctor rushed into the emergency room and went immediately to a patient who had been bitten by wasps.

> **Original:** The weather around here is sometimes unpredictable. Sometimes it becomes treacherous.
> **Compound adjective:** The weather around here is sometimes unpredictable and treacherous.

> **Original:** Grieving over the loss of her child, the woman wept openly. She wept uncontrollably.
> **Compound adverb:** Grieving over the loss of her child, the woman wept openly and uncontrollably.

CREATE VARIETY BY CHANGING SENTENCE PATTERNS

As you know, all complete sentences contain a subject, a verb, and a complete idea; many also contain modifiers (adjectives, adverbs, prepositional phrases, and the like) and other elements. However, there is no rule that all sentences must begin with a subject, that a verb must follow the subject immediately, or that everything else must be placed at the end of a sentence. Depending on their purpose, good writers create as many patterns as they need to make their writing interesting and effective. Here are a few ways you can vary the basic patterns of your sentences.

Begin with an Adverb   *Adverbs* modify verbs, adjectives, or other adverbs. They help explain *how, when, where,* or *why.* The following examples begin with adverbs or with groups of words that contain and serve as adverbs (shown in italics):

> *Soon* the rain stopped and the sun reappeared.
>
> *High above the spectators,* the hot air balloon drifted peacefully.
>
> *Slowly* and *confidently,* Maria rose to the speaker's platform.
>
> *Near the ancient Egyptian city of Thebes,* pharaohs built monuments to their wealth and power.

Begin with an Infinitive   As you learned earlier, an *infinitive* is the present tense of a verb with the word *to* in front of it. Infinitives acting as nouns often make good beginnings for sentences:

> *To study* archaeology was her childhood dream.
>
> *To defend* unpopular ideas takes courage.
>
> *To call* him a coward is unfair and inaccurate.

Begin with a Preposition or Prepositional Phrase   *Prepositions* connect or show relationships between nouns or pronouns and the rest of a sentence. *Prepositional phrases* contain prepositions, a noun or pronoun, and any words that modify that noun or pronoun.

> *Without love,* life is empty.
>
> *Between the mountains* ran a bright, clear stream.
>
> *Before the spectators* stood a Mayan priest ready to perform the harvest ritual.
>
> *To a large temple,* the worshippers carried flowers, candles, and statues.
>
> *Inside the barn,* Freda found tools that dated from the Revolution.

Begin or End with a Participle or Participial Phrase   A *participle* is a verb turned into an adjective. Many participles end in "ed" or "ing." But words like *caught, lost, found, brought,* and *drawn,* which are formed from irregular verbs, can also be participles. A *participial phrase* is a group of words containing a participle.

Screeching, the infant birds told their mother they were hungry.

Exhausted, I fell asleep as soon as my head touched the pillow.

Caught in the act, the thief gave up easily.

I stayed home that night, *having nowhere else to go.*

Suddenly, the old bicycle broke apart, *scattering spokes and bits of chain everywhere.*

Jamie wept openly, *his dream destroyed.*

Use an Appositive   An appositive is word or phrase that renames or describes a noun that comes before it.

E-mail, *an electronic marvel,* has revolutionized communications.

Insisting that her company stop selling contaminated food earned the department supervisor a severe reprimand, *her badge of honor.*

Ask a Rhetorical Question   You learned in Chapters 3 and 4 that asking a question is a good way to begin a paragraph or an essay. Rhetorical questions—those to which the writer knows the answer or to which no answer is expected—can also emphasize important points and create variety. Take this example from a speech condemning television by Federal Communications Commission head Newton Minow at a meeting of television executives in 1961:

You will see a procession of game shows, violence, audience participation shows, formula comedies about totally unbelievable families, blood and thunder mayhem, violence, sadism, murder, Western badmen, Western good men, private eyes, gangsters, more violence and cartoons. And endlessly, commercials—many screaming, cajoling, and offending. And, most of all boredom. . . .

Is there one person in this room who claims that broadcasting can't do better?

Reverse the Position of the Subject and the Verb   Say that you write, "Two small pines grew at the crest of the hill." When you read your rough draft, you realize that this is the kind of pattern you've used in many other sentences. To vary the pattern, simply reverse the position of your subject and verb: "At the crest of the hill grew two small pines."

CREATE VARIETY BY USING A COLON

Use a Colon after an Independent Clause to Introduce Information That Names or Explains Something in That Clause   Such information can be expressed in a word or phrase, a list of words, or even a sentence.

> **Word:** He was motivated by one thing and one thing only: greed. (*"Greed" names "thing."*)

> **List:** He has three loves: his dog, his car, and his stomach. (*"His dog, his car, and his stomach" name his "loves."*)

> **Sentence:** Please follow these instructions: Find the nearest exit, walk to it quickly, and help other passengers who need assistance. (*The sentence after the colon explains "instructions."*)

Use a Colon to Introduce a Quotation   Using a colon is a good way to introduce someone else's words and at the same time use a different sentence pattern. Let's say you wanted to quote from President Kennedy's Inaugural Address. You might write:

> Today we would do well to remember JFK's exhortations to his fellow Americans: "Ask not what your country can do for you—ask what you can do for your country."

CREATE VARIETY BY USING PARENTHESES

There are three major uses for parentheses when creating variety.

1. **To set off an explanatory sentence within or immediately following another sentence. Ordinarily, material within the parentheses is less important than material that is not in parentheses.**

    > My father's attempt to join the Marine Corps failed (he was only 15 at the time), so he decided to go back to school.

    > The university just opened a modern art museum. (It houses only 10 paintings, but the trustees are trying to raise money to buy more.)

2. **To enclose a brief definition**

    > The children learned to construct an anemometer (instrument for measuring wind speed) from the Franklin Institute's Web site.

3. **To set off words that clarify or specify.**

    > The leaders of Nazi Germany and the Soviet Union (Hitler and Stalin) made a pact with the devil.

CREATE VARIETY BY USING A DASH

Create a dash by typing two hyphens, but do not include a space between the dash and the words that come before and after it. A dash can be used to emphasize, expand upon, or explain information earlier in the sentence and to signal a shift in meaning or tone.

> **Emphasis:** Every employee of the company—from the president to the janitor—must now pay his or her own health insurance premiums.

> **Expansion:** Three Supreme Court justices—Scalia, O'Connor, and Kennedy—were nominated by President Reagan.

> **Explanation:** Paying your $1000 in parking fines beats the alternative—spending a week in the work house.

> **Shift:** He made his fortune in less than two years—and lost it in less than two days.

Visualizing Sentence Structure

To see how some of the principles you have just learned work in professional writing, read these paragraphs from Pete Hamill's autobiography, *A Drinking Life.* Comments in the left margin explain how Hamill created emphasis. Those on the right discuss variety. Hamill is writing about World War II.

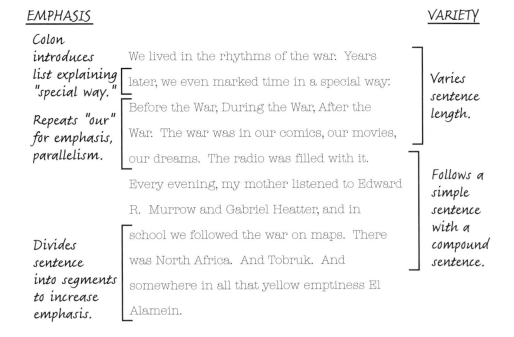

EMPHASIS

Colon introduces list explaining "special way."

Repeats "our" for emphasis, parallelism.

Divides sentence into segments to increase emphasis.

We lived in the rhythms of the war. Years later, we even marked time in a special way: Before the War, During the War, After the War. The war was in our comics, our movies, our dreams. The radio was filled with it. Every evening, my mother listened to Edward R. Murrow and Gabriel Heatter, and in school we followed the war on maps. There was North Africa. And Tobruk. And somewhere in all that yellow emptiness El Alamein.

VARIETY

Varies sentence length.

Follows a simple sentence with a compound sentence.

At Holy Name, I heard about the war from new teachers every year, each of them rolling down the maps and showing us the *Ends sentence with participial phrases.*

Subordinates one idea to another.

places that were in the newspapers and on the radio. There was so much excitement when the Allies landed in Sicily because the parents of most of the Italian kids were *Follows long sentence with short one.*

Coordinates two equally important ideas.

from that island. They wanted the Americans to win. They had brothers in our army, and some of the brothers died in those first battles. All of them said their parents *Follows simple sentence with compound sentence.*

Creates emphasis through repetition.

were worried. I got an aunt there, said Vito Pinto. My grandmother is there, said Michael Tempesta. I got an uncle over there, said George Poli. The war went on and on.

Revising to Create Variety and Emphasis

Read these two versions of paragraphs from Alice Wnorowski's "A Longing," which appears in this chapter. Although the rough draft is correct, Wnorowski knew that revising it would allow her to give important ideas the appropriate emphasis and to bring variety to her writing style.

Wnorowski—Rough Draft, Paragraphs 3 and 4

Vary length?

The morning dew chilled my naked feet. I stopped on the sandy lane. From out of the corner of my eye, I suddenly caught a movement. Something was moving in the wide, open hay field that lay before me. Five deer, three does and two fawns, were grazing

Vary structure?

in the mist-filled dips of the roller-coaster landscape. I sat down in the damp earth to watch them. I got my white nightdress all brown and wet.

What is being emphasized in this one-sentence paragraph?

The deer casually strolled through the thigh-high grass, stopping every other step to dip their heads into the growth and pop them back up again with long, tender timothy stems dangling from the sides of their mouths.

Too long?

Wnorowski—Final Draft, Paragraphs 3 and 4

Combines sentences through coordination, subordination, and compounding.

The morning dew chilled my naked feet, and I stopped on the sandy lane. From out of the corner of my eye, I suddenly caught a movement in the wide, open hay field that lay before me. In the mist-filled dips of the roller-coaster landscape grazed five deer: three does and two fawns. I sat down in the damp earth to watch them and got my white nightdress all brown and wet.

Creates variety by reversing subject and verb. Uses colon to introduce a list.

Divides paragraph into two sentences; emphasizes both ideas.

The deer casually strolled along through the thigh-high grass, stopping every other step to dip their heads into the growth and pop them back up again. Long, tender timothy stems dangled from the sides of their mouths.

Practicing Combining Sentences

The two paragraphs below lack emphasis and variety because the sentences they contain are similar in length and structure. Use techniques explained in this chapter to rewrite the paragraphs in the spaces that follow them. Combine sentences, remove words, add details, choose new vocabulary, or make any other changes you wish to create more interesting and effective paragraphs.

Ramses II

Ramses II was a pharaoh [ruler] of Egypt. He lived approximately 3,300 years ago. He took the throne when he was only 24. He ruled for 66 years. He died at about age 90. He had a huge family. He had more than 100 children. He is thought to be the pharaoh when Moses led the Hebrews from bondage in Egypt. He is also remembered for his many important building projects. He was an industrious and resourceful king. He left his mark on the Egyptian landscape. He built temples and other magnificent monuments in every major city of his kingdom. His projects included expanding the famous temples at Karnak and at Luxor. He is buried in the Valley of the Kings. This place is near Luxor. Luxor used to be called Thebes.

_____

_____

_____

_____

_____

_____

_____

_____

_____

_____

_____

_____

_____

_____

Trinity

The prefix "tri" means three. Traditional Christianity teaches that God exists in a trinity, three persons. These are the Father, the Son, and the Holy Spirit. Christianity is not the only religion that has a trinity. Hinduism also has a trinity. It is called the Trimurti. "Murti" means shape in Sanskrit. Sanskrit is the ancient language of India. Many classical religious and literary works are written in this language. The Hindu trinity has three members. They are Brahma, Vishnu, and Shiva. Brahma is the creator. Vishnu is the preserver. Shiva is the destroyer.

_____

_____

_____

_____

_____

_____

_____

_____

The following selections will help you develop the ability to create sentences that are both varied and emphatic. As you read on, try to apply the techniques you're learning in this chapter to your own writing. Don't hesitate to reread important sections in the introduction to this chapter when you need to.

Macho Girls and Vanishing Males

Suzanne Fields

Suzanne Fields is a nationally syndicated columnist whose work appears in The Washington Times *and more than 30 other American newspapers. She has a doctorate in English literature from the Catholic University of America. Having also studied social psychology and psychology in literature, she was once the mental health editor for* Vogue *magazine. Fields' columns cover a variety of contemporary social, moral, and political issues.*

Preparing to Read

1. This essay was published soon after the 2002 Congressional elections.

2. The title provides an indication of the essay's thesis. Preview this essay by reading the introductory and concluding paragraphs first.

3. "Boomer Mothers," mentioned in paragraph 6, are women who were born in the post-World War II era, during the "baby boom."

4. Charles Darwin (mentioned in paragraph 9) was the originator of the theory of evolution, which maintains that humans descended or developed from lower forms of life.

Vocabulary

cads (noun)	Rascals, rogues, scoundrels.
chromosome (noun)	Unit that carries genes.
demise (noun)	Death, passing.
genetics (noun)	Study of inherited traits in living things.
gratification (noun)	Satisfaction.
hustled (adjective)	Used, tricked, seduced.
lament (noun)	Sorrowful sound.
macho (adjective)	Aggressive, manly, virile.
morphed (verb)	Changed completely, was transformed.
narcissistic (adjective)	Self-centered.
nurture (noun)	Upbringing.
predatory (adjective)	Belligerent, rapacious, like an animal that hunts prey.
proliferating (adjective)	Growing, increasing.
pundits (noun)	Experts (here used sarcastically).
purveyors (noun)	Suppliers, sellers.
railed (verb)	Complained loudly.

Macho Girls and Vanishing Males

Suzanne Fields

POLITICS IS THE obsession of the week, with pundits and politicians busy   1
studying what's left of the tea leaves left over from Tuesday's elections, but
we shouldn't forget sex. Some of our sociologists, psychologists and biologists
think they've identified cultural changes with far greater impact on how we
govern ourselves than all the elections put together. Boys, they say, are being replaced. By girls, of all things.

Women have become the aggressors in the war between the sexes. The   2
changes that have been detected in the teenage years are so alarming that some
parents now worry over how to protect their sons from predatory females.
Gone is the young man's agonizing backache and fear of rejection. Instead he's
the "Nervous Nellie" (for Nelson) in fear of getting hustled by Hannah the
Heavy. (It's something his daddy and his granddaddy could only have dreamed
of.)

The "material girl" has morphed into the "macho girl." She's pulling his   3
chain, tightening his leash, dragging him by the hair in a role reversal of the
"Me, Tarzan/You, Jane" scenario.

"The teenage boys I see often say girls push them for sex and expect them   4
to ask them for sex and will bring it up if the boys don't ask," Tabi Upton, a
counselor at the Johnson Mental Health center in Chattanooga, Tenn., tells the
New York Times. She consults with 20 or 30 teenagers a month and identifies a
shift in the culture, where it's the girls who have all the "attitude," aggressively
approaching boys with a heightened sense of their own sexuality.

CosmoGirl, the little sister magazine to *Cosmo,* aimed at girls between 11   5
and 17, offers pullout posters of bare-chested boys reclining on bear rug or
beach. Story lines urge the macho girl to "Make him say 'I love you.' "

Trend watchers see macho girls in direct competition with the mean girls,   6
the teenagers who are aggressively nasty toward members of their own sex.
These girls are daughters of boomer mothers who told them to be all that they
can be. Unfortunately, they adopted the strategies of the cads whom their fem-
inist mothers railed against at the dawn of the sexual revolution. Now they've
become the cadettes mothers of boys warn against.

Destiny's Child captures the spirit of the macho girl in the rap song "Inde-   7
pendent Women": "(I) only ring your celly when I'm feelin' lonely/When it's all
over please get up and leave." This may be the flip side of the lament of a
Nashville guy: "My phone still ain't ringing so I guess it's still must not be you."

Explanations for all this are plentiful and you can round up the usual   8
suspects—the triumph of feminism, female "empowerment" in jobs, sports and
education as well as sitcoms such as HBO's "Sex in the City," where women
sleep around enjoying instant gratification only to complain about what rotters
men have become.

A neo-Darwinian analysis may be closer to the truth, illuminated by the   9
theories of Steve Jones, a professor of genetics at London University who's written an amusing and at the same time depressing little book called "Y: The Descent of Men" (after Darwin's "Descent of Man"). His point is that men, not
women, are the second sex, doomed by the Y chromosome, rapidly deteriorat-
ing. The final demise of the male is not exactly around the corner unless you
measure your corners in millions of years, but the distinctive male Y chromosome is in bad shape, considerably less "virile," shall we say, than the female X
chromosome, of which she has two.

The forecast of a world without men mixes the nature vs. nurture argu-   10
ments, but the professor reserves his greatest contempt for narcissistic men's
studies proliferating on American college campuses. Purveyors of this dis-
mal stuff are preoccupied with the "inner man" who they say is trying to
break out of his skin. Adding to this state of (loveless) affairs, sperm counts
are down and cloning threatens to make the male irrelevant. Professor Jones
concludes: "From sperm count to social status, and from fertilization to
death, as civilization advances those who bear Y chromosomes are in relative decline."

In an advertisement in the *New York Times,* next to the article about macho   11
girls, something called the Women's World Institute for Consciousness, Spiri-
tuality and Aging, announces a conference called "The Ways of Wise Women
Creating Fulfillment After 50-plus." One of the panelists will be Gloria Steinem,
who originally coined the phrase that "A woman needs a man like a fish needs
a bicycle."

Participants may want to treat themselves to an evolutionary update of the   12
young man who puts his fin to the pedal and pedals away, his gills purple with
fear. And you thought the congressional campaigns were dreary.

Read More on the Web

University of California at Berkeley's site on Advice to Parents of
   Teenagers: http://parents.berkeley.edu/

Site devoted to study of teenage sexual behavior: http://www.focusas.
   com/SexualBehavior.html

Links to other articles by Suzanne Fields: http://www.jewishworldreview.
   com/cols/fields.archives.asp

Questions for Discussion

1. Which techniques explained at the beginning of this chapter does
    Fields use to create variety in paragraph 2?
2. Explain how she creates variety in paragraph 10.

3. What adverbs does the author use in paragraph 6? How do they help her vary sentence structure?

4. Find an example of Fields' use of parallelism to create emphasis.

5. Identify sentences that begin or end with participial phrases.

6. Why does the author use a colon in paragraph 7? What function does the dash serve in paragraph 8?

7. How would you describe the author's tone (her attitude toward her subject) in paragraph 8?

8. What does Fields mean by "the 'material girl' has morphed into the 'macho girl' "? How is this statement related to her thesis?

Thinking Critically

1. In what way or ways does Fields believe girls are replacing boys? What evidence does she provide to support her view? Is this evidence convincing?

2. Explain the pun (play on words) in paragraph 6 and in paragraph 9.

3. Why should males be alarmed at what is written in paragraph 10?

Suggestions for Journal Entries

1. Do you agree that young women are becoming more "macho?" If so, list a few signs that shows you this change is occurring. In other words, what functions, roles, or activities once reserved for boys are now being assumed by girls?

2. Do you agree that young men are becoming "Nervous Nellies" when it comes to love? If yes, what evidence do you have to support your conclusion; should this state of affairs concern us? If no, what evidence do you have to the contrary?

A Longing

Alice Wnorowski

"A Longing" is a tender, almost dreamlike recollection of a beautiful childhood experience that continues to haunt the author. Wnorowski wrote this short essay in response to a freshman English assignment designed to help students learn to use concrete detail. However, it also illustrates several important principles about sentence structure discussed earlier in this chapter. Wnorowski began her studies at a community college. She has since earned a B.S. with honors in engineering.

Preparing to Read

1. You've learned that coordination can be used to create sentences in which two or more ideas receive equal emphasis and that subordination can be used to create sentences in which one idea is stressed over others. Look for examples of coordination and subordination in this essay.

2. The author puts variety into her writing by using techniques discussed earlier in this chapter. They include beginning sentences with an adverb and a prepositional phrase and using participles to vary sentence structure and length.

3. Remember what you learned about using details in Chapter 5, especially those that appeal to the five senses. Identify such details in "A Longing."

Vocabulary

acknowledge (verb)	Recognize.
conceived (verb)	Understood.
yearn (verb)	Desire, long for.

A Longing

Alice Wnorowski

AN EASY BREEZE pushed through the screen door, blowing into my open face 1 and filling my nostrils with the first breath of morning. The sun beamed warm rays of white light onto my lids, demanding they lift and acknowledge the day's arrival.

Perched in the nearby woods, a bobwhite proudly shrieked to the world 2 that he knew who he was. His song stirred deep feelings within me, and I was overcome by an urge to run barefoot through his woods. I jumped up so abruptly I startled the dog lying peacefully beside me. His sleepy eyes looked into mine questioningly, but I could give him no answer. I only left him bewildered, pushing through the front door and trotting down the grassy decline of the front lawn.

The morning dew chilled my naked feet, and I stopped on the sandy lane. 3 From out of the corner of my eye, I suddenly caught a movement in the wide, open hay field that lay before me. In the mist-filled dips of the roller-coaster landscape grazed five deer: three does and two fawns. I sat down in the damp earth to watch them and got my white nightdress all brown and wet.

The deer casually strolled along through the thigh-high grass, stopping 4 every other step to dip their heads into the growth and pop them back up again. Long, tender timothy stems dangled from the sides of their mouths.

The fawns were never more than two or three yards behind their mothers, 5 and I knew a buck must not be far off in the woods, keeping lookout for enemies. Suddenly, a car sped along the adjacent road, disrupting the peace of the moment. The deer jumped up in terror and darted toward the trees. They took leaps, clearing eight to ten feet in a single bound. I watched their erect, white puffs of tails bounce up and down, until the darkness of the woods swallowed them up and I could see them no more.

I don't think that at the simple age of eleven I quite conceived what a rare 6 and beautiful sight I had witnessed. Now, eight years later, I yearn to awaken to the call of a bobwhite and to run barefoot through wet grass in search of him.

Read More on the Web

Nature Writing for Readers and Writers: http://www.naturewriting.com/

Virginia Commonwealth University site on nature writing with several useful links: http://www.vcu.edu/engweb/eng385/natweb.htm

Questions for Discussion

1. Find a few examples of both coordination and subordination in this essay.

2. Identify some adverbs, prepositional phrases, and participles Wnorowski uses to create variety.

3. In which sentence are the normal positions of the subject and verb reversed?

4. In paragraph 5, the author varies the length and structure of her sentences to make her writing more interesting. What methods discussed in this chapter does she use?

5. To which of our five senses do the details in this essay appeal?
6. What is the meaning of Wnorowski's title? Why is it appropriate?
7. What techniques does the writer use to maintain coherence in and between paragraphs?

Thinking Critically

1. This selection reveals as much about the writer as about the experience she recalls. From what you have just read, what can you say about Wnorowski's personality?
2. For anyone living in or near a rural area, seeing a family of wild animals is not an unusual event. Why, then, is this event so special to the writer?

Suggestions for Journal Entries

1. Think back to an experience you would like to relive. Make a list of the things that made this experience memorable and that will explain why you have such "a longing" to relive it.
2. Use the brainstorming technique discussed in "Getting Started" to list details about a natural setting (for example, a meadow, mountain, seashore) that you experienced recently or remember vividly.

The Buried Sounds of Children Crying

Harrison Rainie

On a quiet April morning in 1995, terrorists set off a 5,000-pound bomb at a federal office building in Oklahoma City. Among the 170 people killed were many infants and small children. It is a tragedy that has been burned into the American consciousness and that will cause us pain for generations to come. Harrison Rainie writes for U.S. News & World Report, *where this essay was published shortly after the bombing.*

Preparing to Read

1. In paragraph 3, Rainie quotes lines from William Shakespeare's *King John*. In this play, Arthur, the king's nephew, is captured in battle and is killed while attempting to escape. Constance, Arthur's mother, goes mad with grief and kills herself.

2. This essay contains examples of language that shows which you learned about in Chapters 5 and 6. Look for concrete and specific nouns, vivid verbs, adjectives, and adverbs. Make a special effort to find figures of speech.

Vocabulary

distraught (adjective)	Troubled, upset, worried.
embodiment (noun)	Realization, manifestation.
gracious (adjective)	Gentle, tender, lovely.
implication (noun)	Indication, suggestion.
incessant (adjective)	Without end.
ineffable (adjective)	Indefinable, indescribable.
instinctive (adjective)	Inbred, natural.
molecular level (noun)	The most basic level, the smallest part of our being.
nourish (verb)	Feed.
nurturing (adjective)	Caring for, feeding, supporting.
pluck (noun)	Boldness, nerve, courage.
prevails (verb)	Exists, is the rule.
qualifiers (noun)	Describers.
riveting (adjective)	Captivating, engaging.
roguishness (noun)	Friskiness.
vacant (adjective)	Empty.

The Buried Sounds of Children Crying

Harrison Rainie

ALMOST TO A person, the searchers who combed the ruins at the Alfred   1
P. Murrah Federal Building said they had one thought after finishing their
work: They wanted to go home and hug their kids. The most chilling fact about
the Oklahoma City bombing was that it struck at children eating breakfast and
playing in a day-care center one floor above the street. And the only way to respond to the ache the incident created is to clasp all surviving children
tightly—even those thousands of miles from harm's way—and pour out a fear-
ful love.

While there was much talk about the meaning of this attack on "America's   2
heartland," its biggest impact was on the soul's heartland. We are fixed at the
molecular level to respond to children. Some famous experiments have shown
that their faces have been designed to draw instinctive nurturing from us; their
noises are especially riveting to adult ears. Give a mother a pile of dozens of
identical T-shirts, as one researcher did, and she can pick out the one her child
wore by its scent.

The death of such precious beings violates the order and meaning of life.   3
The only way to understand it is to describe the incessant pain of the loss, as
the distraught Constance does in Shakespeare's *King John:* "Grief fills the room
up of my absent child, / Lies in his bed, walks up and down with me, / Puts on
his pretty looks, repeats his words, / Remembers me of all his gracious parts, /
Stuffs out his vacant garments with his form." Adults nourish this grief the way
they would the child himself, psychologist Louise Kaplan says.

The tragedy of the children's deaths in Oklahoma City is compounded by   4
the loss of many adult lives and the implications of the bombing's occurrence
in a heartland city. Oklahoma holds a spot in the American imagination as the
embodiment of normality, a gritty wholesomeness, an appealing streak of rogu-
ishness and pluck, as a place where a pretty happy coexistence prevails among
American Indians, Northern Methodists whose ancestors entered through
Kansas, Southern Baptists whose kin came from Texas, and many newcomers
in the past generation.

Its capital city is a festival of Americana, home of the National Cowboy Hall   5
of Fame and Western Heritage Center, the National Softball Hall of Fame and
a nice firefighters' museum. That, though, did not prevent it from being devastated by an evil force—and an alien one, no matter what its origin is. "You don't
have terrorism in Middle America," insisted firefighter Bill Finn. Now we do.
And the city will be long haunted by the sounds described by Red Cross worker
Jennifer Harrison: "As we helped people on the street, we could hear children
crying, like blowing in the wind. You couldn't see them. You just heard their
voices."

In our language, we use parental terms in inventive ways as qualifiers: We   6
can live in fatherlands, speak in mother tongues, measure things by Father
Time and exist in Mother Nature. But our attachment to children is so ineffa-
ble, we don't use it to describe other ideas. Child love is the essence of life, and
we have all been orphaned by the slaughter of children in Oklahoma City.

Read More on the Web

CNN's site on the bombing: http://www.cnn.com/US/OKC/

PBS's site on the bombing: http://www.pbs.org/newshour/bb/law/
    mcveigh/news_4-19-95.html

Questions for Discussion

1. What function does the colon serve in the first sentence of paragraph 1?
2. Where else in this essay does the author use a colon? What function
    does it serve in those places?
3. Find examples of parallelism in this essay.
4. Explain how Rainie maintains variety in paragraph 2.
5. Paragraph 5 contains a three-word sentence. Should this sentence
    have been combined with another sentence? Why or why not?
6. Find a periodic sentence in paragraph 5.
7. Where does Rainie use images to communicate his feelings? Discuss
    two examples.
8. Where does Rainie use personification?

Thinking Critically

1. In your own words write a summary of the quotation from *King John*
    in paragraph 3.
2. Read (or reread) "The Last Safe Haven," an essay in Chapter 3 (page
    135), which also discusses violence in America. In what way is its
    message similar to that in "The Buried Sounds of Children Crying"?
3. In paragraph 3, we read: "The death of such precious beings violates
    the order and meaning of life." Explain this statement.

Suggestions for Journal Entries

1. "We are fixed at the molecular level to respond to children," Rainie says in paragraph 2. He then provides a few brief examples to explain what he means. Reread this paragraph. Then, use freewriting to recall at least one example from your own experience or observation that would support or explain this idea.

2. Use any prewriting method explained in "Getting Started" to discuss your reaction to the Oklahoma City bombing or to any other event that shocked the nation or your community, campus, or family. Don't be content to list a few words such as *stunned,* or *angry,* which will describe your immediate reaction only. Instead, explore the thoughts and feelings you have had about this event since learning about it.

Gettysburg Address

Abraham Lincoln

Perhaps the best-loved American president, Abraham Lincoln was a model of what a leader should be: decisive, principled, hard working, and compassionate. He was also among the most eloquent of public speakers. His Second Inaugural Address and Gettysburg Address are landmarks of American oratory. In November 1863, Lincoln came to Gettysburg, Pennsylvania, to dedicate a cemetery at the site of the Civil War's bloodiest battle. The turning point of the War, the Battle of Gettysburg had raged for four days and killed 50,000 Americans, both Union and Confederate, before Southern forces under General Robert E. Lee withdrew. Lincoln's Gettysburg Address is an eloquent and powerful statement of his belief that "all men are created equal"; of his grief over the death of his countrymen on both sides; and of his faith that "government of the people, by the people, for the people, shall not perish from the earth." Incidentally, Lincoln did not rely on a speech writer; he composed the Gettysburg Address himself.

Preparing to Read

1. Note that Lincoln makes excellent use of repetition. One word in particular is used seven times in this short speech. Look for and underline it each time.

2. Lincoln begins with a reference to the past, moves to the present, and ends with the future. Such references help organize the speech. Read the speech once; then, reread it to spot these references.

3. Another technique used to hold this speech together and give it greater emphasis is parallelism. Look for examples of this technique throughout the Gettysburg Address.

4. In the last sentence, Lincoln describes a "great task remaining before us." Read this important sentence several times to make sure you understand it fully.

Vocabulary

conceived (adjective)	Created.
consecrate (verb)	Bless, sanctify, make holy.
dedicate(d) (verb/adjective)	Set aside for a purpose, sometimes to honor or worship.
detract (verb)	Take away from, lessen, decrease.
hallow (verb)	Make holy or sacred, sanctify.

in vain (adjective)   For no reason or purpose.
measure (noun)   Amount.
proposition (noun)   Idea, principle.
resolve (verb)   Decide, determine.

Gettysburg Address

Abraham Lincoln

FOUR SCORE AND SEVEN years ago our fathers brought forth on this continent 1
a new nation, conceived in Liberty, and dedicated to the proposition that all
men are created equal.

Now we are engaged in a great civil war, testing whether that nation, or any 2
nation so conceived and so dedicated, can long endure. We are met on a great
battlefield of that war. We have come to dedicate a portion of that field, as a final resting place for those who here gave their lives that that nation might live.
It is altogether fitting and proper that we should do this.

But in a larger sense, we can not dedicate—we can not consecrate—we can 3
not hallow—this ground. The brave men, living and dead, who struggled here,
have consecrated it, far above our poor power to add or detract. The world will
little note, nor long remember what we say here, but it can never forget what
they did here. It is for us the living, rather, to be dedicated here to the unfinished work which they who fought here have thus far so nobly advanced. It is
rather for us to be here dedicated to the great task remaining before us—that
from these honored dead we take increased devotion to that cause for which
they gave the last full measure of devotion—that we here highly resolve that
these dead shall not have died in vain—that this nation, under God, shall have
a new birth of freedom—and that government of the people, by the people, for
the people, shall not perish from the earth.

Read More on the Web

Online biography of Lincoln: http://gi.grolier.com/presidents/ea/bios/
16plinc.html

Links to the first and second inaugural addresses and the Emancipation
Proclamation: http://libertyonline.hypermall.com/Lincoln/
Default.htm

Links to historical documents: http://www.law.ou.edu/hist/

Military History Online's history of the Battle of Gettysburg:
http://www.militaryhistoryonline.com/gettysburg/getty1.aspx

Questions for Discussion

1. What examples of repetition appear in this speech?

2. The most obvious example of parallelism in the Gettysburg Address appears at the very end: "government of the people, by the people, for the people, shall not perish from the earth." What other examples of parallelism do you find?

3. Most sentences in this speech are long, but Lincoln does vary sentence length. Where does he do this?

4. What two participial phrases does Lincoln use at the end of the first sentence? Would it have made better sense to put the information they convey into another sentence? Why or why not?

5. Where in paragraph 2 does Lincoln use a participial phrase?

6. What effect does repeating the word "dedicate" or "dedicated" have? Does the word have any religious significance?

7. Where else does Lincoln use words that have a religious significance? What is he trying to tell us by using such vocabulary?

8. What is Lincoln's central idea? What devices does he use to maintain coherence?

Thinking Critically

1. In Preparing to Read, you learned that Lincoln makes reference to the past, to the present, and to the future. Find places in which he does this. What is he trying to accomplish by setting up this pattern other than helping to organize the speech? What does he accomplish each time he references a specific time?

2. Reread the last sentence. Is there a pattern in Lincoln's resolving that "these dead shall not have died in vain," that "this nation, under God, shall have a new birth of freedom," and that democracy "shall not perish from the earth"? What is that pattern, and why would such a pattern be so effective in a speech?

Suggestions for Journal Entries

1. In what ways do you think the government should be "for the people"? What rights, and/or services should it guarantee us? Use clustering, draw a subject tree, or freewrite for about 10 minutes on this question. After you have completed your journal entry, read it to classmates or friends. Together, brainstorm for a few minutes to collect more ideas.

2. Many speeches in American history have served as sources of inspiration from decade to decade, from generation to generation.

With the help of your instructor or your college librarian, locate a speech that you'd like to read or reread. Then analyze this speech. Pick out examples of parallelism, repetition, and other techniques the writer has used to create emphasis. Here are a few speeches you might choose from:

Abraham Lincoln, Second Inaugural Address
Franklin Delano Roosevelt, First Inaugural Address
Adlai Stevenson, Eulogy for Eleanor Roosevelt
Dwight D. Eisenhower, Farewell Address
John F. Kennedy, Speech at the Berlin Wall
Martin Luther King, Jr., Speech at the Lincoln Memorial ("I Have a Dream")
Ronald Reagan, Speech at Moscow State University
George W. Bush, State of the Union Address (January 29, 2002)

3. Using as many paragraphs as you like, rewrite Lincoln's speech in your own words. Make sure that you express his central idea clearly and that you emphasize his other important ideas through parallelism, repetition, or any of the other techniques you've learned for creating emphasis.

Suggestions for Sustained Writing

1. If you haven't responded to both of the journal suggestions after Fields's "Macho Girls and Vanishing Males," do so now. Then expand what you have put into your journal into an essay that argues for or against Fields's thesis: boys are being replaced by girls. Rely on what you have read or observed in regard to the nature of romantic relationships between young men and women these days. In order to focus your essay, you might want to limit yourself to particular age group: those in high school, those 18–25, or those 26–30, for example.

    You may want to interview friends and classmates for this assignment or even see what sociology, psychology, and health professors or college counselors have to say about this question.

    Like Fields, you will have to keep your readers' interest and create emphasis. Also, use what you have learned from previous chapters about creating effective introductions and conclusions and choosing effective vocabulary (Chapter 4, 5, and 6).

2. One of the Suggestions for Journal Entries after Alice Wnorowski's "A Longing" asks you to think about an experience you would like to relive. If you responded to this suggestion, you've made a list of effective details that will help explain why you have such a longing to repeat this experience.

Add to your notes, and expand them into an essay that shows what made the experience so memorable. Develop your thesis in concrete detail, and make your writing unified and coherent by using techniques discussed in Chapter 2.

After you've written your first draft, read your essay carefully. Should you do more to emphasize important ideas or to maintain your reader's interest? If so, revise your paper by using techniques for creating emphasis and variety explained in the introduction to this chapter. As usual, edit and proofread the final draft of your paper.

3. The second item in Suggestions for Journal Entries after "A Longing" invites you to begin listing details about a natural setting—a forest, meadow, seashore, mountain, river—that you visited recently or remember vividly.

Follow the advice in item 2 of Suggestions for Sustained Writing above, and turn these notes into a short essay.

4. In the first suggestion for journal entries after Rainie's "The Buried Sounds of Children Crying," you were asked to provide an example to support the idea that "We are fixed at the molecular level to respond to children," which appears in paragraph 2. Reread that paragraph. Then, read your journal notes. Next, add at least two other examples that will help prove this point. Discuss each of these examples in a separate paragraph of an essay that uses the quotation above as its thesis.

Make sure the quotation and your explanation of it appears in your essay's introduction. You might also use a contrast, a definition, or an anecdote in the beginning of your paper. A good way to conclude is to refer to your thesis or to make a call to action. In any case, review the methods of writing introductions and conclusions in Chapter 4 before you begin to draft your essay.

5. Read the notes you made in response to the first of the Suggestions for Journal Entries following Lincoln's "Gettysburg Address." (If you haven't completed this short assignment, do so now.)

Next, focus on three or four of the rights and/or services that democratic governments should guarantee their people. Choose those you believe are essential. Define each of these items in one or two sentences; then arrange them in a list that ends with the one item you consider most important of all.

Use this list as a blueprint or outline for an essay that explains, develops, and supports each of these ideas (rights/services) in a separate paragraph or group of paragraphs. When you begin revising your rough draft, write an introductory paragraph that contains a thesis and captures the reader's attention. Also, write a concluding paragraph based upon one of the techniques explained in Chapter 4. As you rewrite this and subsequent drafts, create variety and emphasis by using the advice in this chapter. The next step, of course, is to edit and proofread your work.

Writing to Learn: A Group Activity

Abraham Lincoln's Gettysburg Address is perhaps the best pieces of oratory in world history. However, other great speeches need to be studied, not simply for their rhetorical values but also for what they tell us about the times in which they were delivered.

FIRST MEETING

Lincoln spoke at Gettysburg during a time of national emergency. Though eternal in its message, his address was aimed at the particular needs of his time. Ask each member of your group to find, read, and analyze one speech on a major issue(s) that the nation was facing during the time the speech was delivered. You might want to limit yourselves to presidential addresses such as:

• Abraham Lincoln's Second Inaugural Address
• Franklin Roosevelt's Four Freedoms Address to Congress or his First Inaugural Address
• Ronald Reagan's address at Berlin's Brandenburg Gate
• George W. Bush's speech to the UN General Assembly in November 2001

On the other hand, you might limit yourselves to speeches made by famous women, such as:

• Anna Howard Shaw's The Fundamental Principle of a Republic (1915)
• Maragret Chase Smith's Declaration of Conscience (1950)
• Mary Church Terrell's What It Means to Be Colored in the Capital of the United States (1906)
• Eleanor Roosevelt's The Struggle for Human Rights (1948)
• Barbara Bush's Commencement Address at Wellesley College (1990)
• Mary Fisher's Whisper of AIDS speech to the Republican National Convention (1992)

Or, you might also choose from the speeches of civil rights leaders such as;

• Booker T. Washington's Atlanta Compromise Speech (1895)
• WEB Dubois's Men of Niagara speech (1906)
• Dr. Martin Luther King's "I Have a Dream" speech (1963), his Nobel Prize Acceptance speech (1964), or his "I've Been to the Mountain" speech (1968)
• Malcolm X's Message to the Grass Roots (1963) or his speech at the Audubon Ball Room (1964)

Whatever speeches your group decides to research, try to select from a group of addresses that have something in common, as illustrated in the previous examples.

RESEARCH AND WRITING

You can find the speeches just mentioned as well as many more on the Internet. Make sure to locate and research at least two commentaries on the speech you are studying. Commentaries on these addresses are plentiful both on the Web and in print Then, write the first draft of a short research essay (250–500 words) that explains the purpose of the speech and the social or political environment in which it was delivered. Make sure to quote and/or paraphrase from your primary source (the speech) and from secondary sources (commentaries on the speech). Use a citation format approved by your instructor (the Modern Language Association format is explained in the appendix to this text.) Make photocopies of your work.

SECOND MEETING

Distribute and discuss copies of each student's first draft. Evaluate content, development, and the inclusion of researched material. Make suggestions for revision. In addition, evaluate the paper on the basis of sentence structure. Has the student made his or her writing varied, interesting, and emphatic? Ask students to rewrite their papers based upon the group's evaluation and to resubmit them at the third meeting.

THIRD MEETING

Distribute and review the second drafts of each student's paper. If necessary, recommend additional revision. Also, offer suggestions toward editing and /or proofreading. Once again, pay special attention to what you have learned in this chapter about improving sentence variety and emphasis.

Description
and Narration

The two chapters in this section explain how to create vivid verbal portraits of people, places, and things and to narrate stories about meaningful events. As you read Chapters 8 and 9, remember that the more details you put into any piece of writing the more believable, interesting, and effective it will be.

Knowing Your Subject

The more you know about your subject or event, the easier it is choose effective details that communicate its significance to your readers. If you need to learn more about what you are describing, you can always observe it more closely and even use your other four senses—hearing, touch, taste, and smell—to gather information. If you are narrating an event you experienced or observed, you might recall additional details about it through focused freewriting, listing, or another of the pre-writing techniques explained in Getting Started II: Using the Writing Process. You can also interview other people involved to get their recollections. In fact, interviewing is also a good way to gather information about an incident you did not observe firsthand. This is what journalists and historians often do. Finally, you might also gather narrative details through library or Internet research, but be sure to credit your sources through appropriate citations (see the Appendix to this textbook for information on the Modern Language Association citation format).

Using Language That Shows

As you learned in Chapter 5, using language that shows makes your writing more concrete, specific, and vivid than using language that simply tells. For example, it's one thing to say: "The firefighters risked their lives to save two people." It is another to say: "Their faces and protective clothing blackened from the suffocating smoke that had filled the hallways, the firefighters ran out of the tenement carrying a mother and infant whose apartment was now engulfed in flame." The first version is vague and unconvincing—a statement we soon forget. The second paints a memorable picture. It doesn't tell us that the

291

firefighters were in danger, but the details it includes make that conclusion unavoidable. It also provides information about the building, the people who were saved, and the extent of the fire.

USE CONCRETE NOUNS AND ADJECTIVES

If you are describing a friend, don't just say that "He's not a neat dresser." Include nouns and adjectives that will enable readers to come to that conclusion on their own. Talk about "the red dirt along the sides of his scuffed, torn shoes; the large rips in the knees of his faded blue jeans; and the many jelly spots on is shirt." Concrete nouns and adjectives are also important to narration. For example, in "Mid-Term Break" (Chapter 9), Seamus Heaney creates a mood appropriate to a wake when he tells us that:

> Whispers informed strangers I was the eldest
> Away at school, as my mother held my hand
>
> In hers and coughed out angry tearless sighs.
> At ten o'clock the ambulance arrived
> With the corpse stanched and bandaged by the nurses.

INCLUDE SPECIFIC DETAILS

After you have chosen important details that are concrete—that show rather than tell—make your writing more specific. For example, revise the description of your friend's attire to "The sides of his scuffed, torn loafers were caked with red clay. His knees bulged from the large rips in his faded Levis; and strawberry jam was smeared on the collar of his white Oxford shirt." Notice that "loafers" has replaced "shoes," "red clay" has replaced "red dirt," "Levis have replaced "blue jeans," and "shirt" has been revised to "white Oxford shirt."

Writers of narrative also rely on specifics. In "Child of the Romans" (Chapter 9), Carl Sandburg is not content to say that the train's dining car is filled with flowers or that the passengers are dining on expensive food. Instead, he writes:

> A train whirls by, and men and women at tables
> Alive with red roses and yellow jonquils
> Eat steaks running with brown gravy,
> Strawberries and cream, eclairs and coffee.

Sandburg then contrasts this elegant meal with the railroad worker's lunch of "dry bread and bologna," which he "washes down with a dipper from the water-boy."

CREATE FIGURES OF SPEECH

In Chapter 6, you learned that one of the best ways to make your writing clear and vivid is to use figures of speech, expressions that convey a meaning beyond their literal sense. The most common figures of speech are metaphor, simile, and personification. Writers often rely on such expressions to explain or clarify abstract, complex, or unfamiliar ideas. In "If at First You Do Not See . . ." (Chapter 8), Jesse Sullivan describes trees that seem "to bow their heads in sorrow," their branches "twisted and ill-formed, as if poisoned by the very soil in which they are rooted."

Figures of speech are also used extensively in narration. Take, for example, the metaphors Adrienne Shwartz uses in a passage from "The Colossus in the Kitchen," a story about her childhood home in South Africa (Chapter 9): "In those days . . . the adults were giants bestriding the world with surety and purpose. Tandi, the cook, reigned with the authoritarian discipline of a Caesar. She held audience in the kitchen. . . ."

RELY ON YOUR FIVE SENSES

Personal observation and experience often yield visual details. However, using your other four senses can provide even more important information, especially when you are describing. Of course, explaining what something sounds, tastes, smells, or feels like can be harder than showing what it looks like. But the extra effort is worthwhile. Whether you are describing or telling a story, the greater the variety of details you include, the more realistic and convincing your writing will be.

Next to sight, hearing is the sense writers rely on most. In "Flavio's Home" (Chapter 8), an essay that combines narration and description, Gordon Parks describes a boy holding a "bawling naked baby in his arms." He goes on to explain that the boy "whacked" the baby's bottom and that, later, two of the family's daughter's "burst into the shack, screaming and pounding on one another."

When writers describe rain-covered sidewalks as "slick," scraped elbows as "raw" or "tender" or the surfaces of bricks as "coarse" or abrasive," they appeal to the sense of touch. Another example appears in "Watching the Reapers" by Po Chu-i (Chapter 8) when he writes that the reapers' "feet are burned by the hot earth."

Tastes and smells, though sometimes difficult to re-create, can also make your writing interesting and believable. Notice how well Mary Taylor Simeti uses them to recall an Easter picnic of take-out food from a hillside restaurant in Sicily:

> . . . [Our] obliging host produces [brings out] three foil-covered plates, a bottle of mineral water, and a round kilo loaf of fragrant, crusty bread. We drive back along the road a little way to a curve that offers space to park and some rocks to sit on. Our plates turn out to hold spicy olives, some slices of *prosciutto crudo* [cold ham] and of a peppery local salami, and two kinds of pecorino [sheep's milk] cheese, one fresh and mild, the other aged and sharper. With a bag of oranges from the car, the sun warm on our backs, the mountains rolling down at our feet to the southern coast and the sea beyond, where the heat haze clouds the horizon and hides Africa from view, we have as fine an Easter dinner as I have ever eaten. (*On Persephone's Island*)

Being Objective or Subjective

Objective writing requires you to report what you see, hear, or experience accurately and thoroughly—without revealing your feelings or opinions. Subjective writing allows you to convey your personal perspective on or reactions to a subject or experience. Both types of writing have their places in description and narration.

Most journalists and historians try to remain objective by communicating facts, not opinions about those facts. In other words, they try to give us the kind of information we'll need to make up or own minds about the subject. This is what Meg Potter does when she describes a woman living on the streets of a large American city:

> This particular [woman] had no shoes on, but her feet were bound in plastic bags that were tied with filthy rags. It was hard to tell exactly what she was wearing. She had on . . . a conglomeration of tattered material that I can only say . . . were rags. I couldn't say how old she was, but I'd guess in her late fifties. The woman's hair was grey and silver, and she was beginning to go bald.
>
> As I watched for a while, I realized she was sorting out her bags. She had six of them, each stuffed and overflowing. . . . I caught a glimpse of ancient magazines, empty bottles, filthy pieces of clothing, an inside-out umbrella, and several mismatched shoes. The lady seemed to be taking the things out of one bag and putting them into another. All the time she was muttering to herself. ("The Shopping Bag Ladies")

In some cases, however, authors find it important to make their feelings known. Doing so adds interest to their work. Take this paragraph from Carl Sagan's "Frederick Douglass: The Path to Freedom," a narrative which appears in Chapter 9.

> . . . picture Frederick Bailey in 1828—a 10-year old African-American child, enslaved, with no legal rights of any kind, long since torn from his mother's arms, sold away from the tattered remnants of his extended family as if he were a calf or a pony, conveyed to an unknown household in a strange city of Baltimore, and condemned to a life of drudgery with no prospect of reprieve.

Watch for examples of objective and subjective writing throughout Section Three. At the same time, identify concrete and specific details and figures of speech to better appreciate and understand what makes for effective description and narration.

CHAPTER 8

Description

This chapter presents selections that describe people, places, and things. It also discusses some techniques discussed in the introduction to Section Three, which are important to both description and narration. For example, you might recall the importance of using concrete nouns and adjectives, including specific details, relying on your five senses, and creating figures of speech (simile, metaphor, and personification). You might also remember the need to decide whether to remain objective or to take a more subjective approach when you write. Keeping this advice in mind will help you make your subjects as interesting and vivid to your readers as they are to you. In addition, however, you should learn several techniques especially important to description whether your subject is a place, a thing, or a person.

Techniques for Describing Places and Things

USING PROPER NOUNS

In addition to filling your writing with concrete details and figures of speech, you might also want to include a number of *proper nouns*, which, as you know, are the names of particular persons, places, and things. Here are some examples: Arizona, University of Tennessee, Lake Michigan, Farmers and Merchants' Savings and Loan, First Baptist Church, Spanish, Chinese, Belmont Avenue, Singer Sewing Machine Company, Harold Smith, San Francisco Opera House, *Business Week* magazine, and Minnesota Vikings.

Including proper nouns that readers recognize easily can make what you are describing more familiar to them. At the very least, it makes your writing more believable. Notice how Alfred Kazin's recollection of his childhood home is enriched by the names of places and things (shown in italics) he uses in this passage from "My Mother in Her Kitchen":

> In the corner next to the toilet was the sink at which we washed, and the square tub in which my mother did our clothes. Above it, tacked to the shelf on which were pleasantly arranged square, blue-bordered white sugar and spice jars, hung calendars from the *Public National Bank* on *Pitkin Avenue* and the *Minsker Progressive Branch* of the *Workman's Circle;* receipts for the payment of insurance premiums and household bills on a spindle; two little boxes engraved with *Hebrew* letters. One of these was for the poor, the other to buy back the *Land of Israel.*

USING EFFECTIVE VERBS

We know how important verbs are to narration, but effective verbs can also add much to a piece of description. Writers use verbs to make descriptions more specific, accurate, and interesting. For instance, "the wind had chiseled deep grooves into the sides of the cliffs" is more specific than "the wind had made deep grooves." The verb *chiseled* also gives the reader a more accurate picture of the wind's action than *made* does.

In the introduction to Section Three, you've just read about how to enrich the description of a friend's clothing by adding specific details. Returning to that sentence, notice that lively verbs (in italics) make as much of a difference as do concrete nouns and adjectives:

> Red clay *was caked* along the sides of his scuffed, torn loafers; his knees *bulged* from the large rips in his faded Levi's; and strawberry jelly *was smeared* on the collar of his white Oxford shirt.

Something similar can be said about the verbs Robert K. Massey uses in a portrait of the Russian countryside that opens his biography of Peter the Great:

> Around Moscow, the country *rolls* gently up from the rivers *winding* in silvery loops across the pleasant landscape. Small lakes and patches of woods *are sprinkled* among the meadowlands. Here and there, a village *appears, topped* by the onion dome of its church. People *are walking* through the fields on dirt paths lined with weeds. Along the riverbanks they *are fishing, swimming* and *lying* in the sun. It is a familiar Russian scene, *rooted* in centuries. (*Peter the Great*)

INCLUDING ACTION AND PEOPLE IN THE DESCRIPTION OF A PLACE

Narration and description are closely related, and they often appear together. Storytellers describe places where their narratives take place. Writers of description often reveal the character or atmosphere of a place by narrating events that occur in it or by describing people who appear in it.

A selection in this chapter that shows how actions and the people who perform them can help reveal the character of a place is Gordon Parks's "Flavio's Home." In the following passage, Parks reveals the hopelessness and poverty that fills the da Souza home when he tells us about the fear, sadness, and anger with which the family's children conduct themselves:

> Maria's eyes flashed anger. " . . . I'll beat you, you little bitch." Liza threw a stick at Maria and fled out the door. Zacarias dropped off to sleep. Mario . . . slouched in the corner and sucked his thumb. Isabel and Albia sat on the floor, clinging to each other with a strange tenderness. Isabel held on to Albia's hair and Albia clutched at Isabel's neck. They appeared frozen in an act of quiet violence.

Techniques for Describing People

You just learned that writers often go beyond physical appearance when describing a place or thing; they reveal its character as well. This is even more true when they describe people. Writers describe human beings because they are fascinated by their personalities, values, and motivations, as well as by their looks and the sound of their voices. Writers may start by describing physical appearance—what's on the outside. But they often end up talking about their subjects' characters—what's on the inside.

DESCRIBING A SUBJECT'S APPEARANCE AND SPEECH

Describing someone's appearance—height and weight, eye color, and so on—can be an end in itself. More often, however, physical appearance is used as an indication of what a person is like inside. Describing the kinds of clothes someone wears or the sound of her voice can help you begin discussing her personality.

Indeed, writers sometimes see outward details as indications of character. For instance, how often have you heard people mention deep-set, shifty eyes, or a sinister smile when describing a villain? Aren't heavy people often described as jolly? And often, aren't the clothes people wear or the way they comb their hair seen (fairly or unfairly) as a sign of their character?

In "Two Gentlemen of the Pines," John McPhee uses physical details to introduce Bill Wasovwich, a child of nature, who has lived in the wilderness all of his life:

> . . . .near the doorway to the kitchen sat a young man with long black hair, who wore a visored red leather cap that had darkened with age. His shirt was coarse-woven and had eyelets down a V neck that was laced with a thong. His trousers were made of canvas, and he was wearing gum boots.

REVEALING WHAT YOU KNOW ABOUT YOUR SUBJECT

Earlier you learned that narrating events can help capture the character or atmosphere of a place you are describing. Similarly, you can reveal a lot about someone by discussing his or her actions or behavior. One of the best ways to do so is to tell anecdotes, brief stories that highlight or illustrate an important aspect of a subject's personality. For example, Barry Shlachter in "Charisma Fortified by 'Chutzpah' " demonstrates Mother Teresa's ability to inspire others by telling a brief story about her directing relief efforts in a town devastated by a cyclone. Anecdotes like this one help us understand how someone reacts to various people, problems, and situations. They say a lot about a person's attitude toward life.

Another way to reveal character is to tell readers important facts about your subject's life, home, or family. In "Two Gentlemen of the Pines," we learn that

Bill's parents abandoned him when he was a child and that, except for help from a few neighbors, Bill raised himself. This information helps account for his shyness. In the same selection, we get a good look at the house and yard of Fred Brown, a picture that helps us understand much about the old man's character beyond what is revealed by his appearance and speech.

REVEALING WHAT OTHERS SAY ABOUT YOUR SUBJECT

One of the quickest ways to learn about someone is to ask people who know this individual to tell you about his or her personality, lifestyle, morals, disposition, and so on. Often, authors use dialogue or quotations from other people to reveal something important about their subject's character. In "Crazy Mary," student Sharon Robertson combines physical description (concrete details) with information she learned from other people (dialogue) to create a memorable and disturbing portrait of an unfortunate woman she once knew:

> She was a middle-aged woman, short and slightly heavy, with jet-black hair and solemn blue eyes that were bloodshot and glassy. She always looked distant, as if her mind were in another place and time, and her face lonely and sad. We called her "Crazy Mary."
>
> Mary came to the diner that I worked in twice a week. She would sit at the counter with a scowl on her face and drink her coffee and smoke cigarettes. The only time she looked happy was when an old song would come on the radio. Then Mary would close her eyes, shine a big tobacco-stained smile, and sway back and forth to the music.
>
> One day an elderly couple came in for dinner. They were watching Mary over their menus and whispering. I went over to their table and asked if they knew who she was. The old man replied, "Aw, dat's just old Mary. She's loonier than a June bug, but she ain't nutten to be afraid of. A few years back, her house caught fire and her old man and her kids got kilt. She ain't been right since."
>
> After hearing this, it was easy to understand her odd behavior.

Other people can make good sources of information. We know from experience, however, that what others say about a person is often inaccurate. Sometimes, in fact, different people express very different—even contradictory—opinions about the same person. Consider how differently supporters and critics of a particular politician or entertainer view their subject. Today, President Abraham Lincoln enjoys the greatest respect among historians and the public alike. When he was alive, however, opinions about him differed; he was seen as a rustic frontiersman by some people, as a crafty tyrant by others, and as an embattled defender of human rights by still others.

Visualizing Details That Describe Places and Things

The following paragraphs from John Ciardi's "Dawn Watch," describe the sights, sounds, and smells of sunrise in his backyard.

Appeals to senses.

Uses simile.

The traffic has just started, not yet a roar and stink. One car at a time goes by, the tires humming almost like the sound of a brook a half mile down in the crease of a mountain I know—a sound that carries not because it is loud but because everything else is still.

Includes action.

The lawns shine with a dew not exactly dew. There is a rabbit bobbing about on the lawn and then freezing. If it were truly a dew, his tracks would shine black on the grass, and he leaves no visible track. Yet, there is something on the grass that makes it glow a depth of green it will not show again all day. Or is it something in the dawn air?

Relies on concrete, specific nouns.

Uses metaphor.

Uses simile.

Appeals to senses.

Our cardinals know what time it is. They drop pure tones from the hemlock tops. The black gang of grackles that makes a slum of the pin oak also knows the time but can only grate at it. They sound like a convention of broken universal joints grating up hill. The grackles creak and squeak, and the cardinals form tones that only occasionally sound through the noise. :

Reveals subjective reaction to cardinals and grackles.

Visualizing Details That Describe People

The two short selections that follow use techniques important to describing people. The first, by Dr. Richard Selzer, describes the physical appearance of an AIDS patient in Haiti. The second, by Jade Snow Wong, describes the personality of a man who works in a factory that is run by the author's family and that doubles as their home.

"Miracle" by Richard Selzer

Uses specific details: nouns, adjectives.

A twenty-seven-year-old man whose given name is Miracle enters. He is wobbly, panting, like a groggy boxer who has let down his arms and is waiting for the last punch. He is neatly dressed and wears, despite the heat, a heavy woolen cap. When he removes it, I see that his hair is thin, dull reddish and straight. It is one of the signs of AIDS in Haiti. . . .The man's skin is covered with a dry, itchy rash. Throughout the interview and examination he scratches himself slowly, absentmindedly. The rash is called prurigo. It is another symptom of AIDS in Haiti. The telltale rattling of the tuberculous moisture in his chest is audible without a stethoscope. He is like a leaky cistern [tank for liquid] that bubbles and froths.

Uses vivid adjectives

Uses simile to describe appearance.

Conveys action.

Appeals to hearing.

Uses a simile to create an image.

"Uncle Kwok" by Jade Snow Wong

Recalls a recurring action that tells us about Kwok's personality.

After Uncle Kwok was settled in his chair, he took off his black, slipperlike shoes. Then taking a piece of stout cardboard from a miscellaneous pile which he kept in a box near his sewing machine, he traced the outline of his shoes on the cardboard. Having closely examined the blades of his scissors and tested their sharpness, he would cut out a pair of cardboard soles, squinting critically through his inaccurate glasses. Next he removed from both shoes the cardboard soles he had made the day before and inserted the new pair. Satisfied with his inspection . . . he got up . . . disposed of the old soles, and returned to his machine. He had not yet said a word to anyone.

Uses vivid adjectives/adverb to create an image.

Reveals an important aspect of his personality.

Daily this process was repeated. . . .

Describes his clothing as a clue to his personality.

The next thing Uncle Kwok always did was to put on his own special apron, homemade from double thicknesses of heavy burlap and fastened at the waist by strong denim ties. This long apron covered his thin, patched trousers and protected him from dirt and draft. After a half hour had been consumed

by these chores, Uncle Kwok was ready to
wash his hands. He sauntered into the Wong   *Uses*
kitchen, stationed himself at the one sink   *vivid verbs.*
which served both family and factory, and
with characteristic meticulousness [care],
now proceeded to clean his hands and
fingernails.

It was Mama's custom to begin cooking the
evening meal at this hour . . . . but every
day she had to delay her preparations at the
sink until slow-moving Uncle Kwok's last   *Recalls an*
clean fingernail passed his fastidious   *action to*
[close] inspection. One day, however, the   *describe*
inconvenience tried her patience to its   *Kwok.*
final limit.

Trying to sound pleasantly persuasive,   *Explains what*
she said, "Uncle Kwok, please don't be so   *someone else*
slow and awkward. Why don't you wash your   *thinks of*
hands at a different time, or else wash them   *Kwok.*
faster?"

Uncle Kwok loudly protested . . . "Mama,
I am not awkward. The only awkward thing   *Allows Kwok*
about my life is that it has not yet   *to reveal*
prospered!" And he strode off, too hurt even   *himself in*
to dry his hands, finger by finger, as was   *his own*
his custom.   *words.*

Revising Descriptive Essays

Read these two versions of three paragraphs from Jessie Sullivan's "If at First You Do Not See . . .," a student essay that appears later in this chapter in its entirety. Though the rough draft is powerful, Sullivan's revision smooths out rough spots, improves wording, and provides additional detail that makes her writing even more vivid and effective.

Sullivan—Rough Draft

I live in an apartment on the outskirts of New Brunswick, New Jersey. To the right of my building is Robeson Village, a large low-income housing project with about two-hundred apartments facing each other on opposite sides of a wide, asphalt driveway that runs the length of the complex. In this driveway, drug dealers and buyers congregate   *Wordy?* daily, doing business in front of anyone who cares to watch. Sometimes, children who have witnessed these transactions look over paraphernalia the dealers and their   *What kind of paraphernalia?* customers have left in their wake.

To the left of my building is Henry Street, a street that has grown to be synonymous with illegal drugs over the years. It is truly a pathetic sight. The block consists of a half dozen vacant and   *If "vacant," how can they be "inhabited"?* condemned buildings, all of which are still inhabited by addicts and dealers who have set up store there in much the same way a

Wordy? legitimate business <u>owner decides on a</u>

<u>particular</u> location where business will be

most profitable.

. . .

Whose eye? <u>To the eye</u>, the community appears to be

in a state of depression. Even trees, which   *Make this*

traditionally symbolize life and vitality   *more vivid?*

What kinds
of "pungent reflect this. <u>Pungent odors</u> are made worse
odors"?
by the stench of rotting food, spilled from   *Make this*

overturned garbage cans onto the sidewalk   *image more*
active, lively?"
and cooking in the heat of the sun.

Sullivan—Final Draft

I live in an apartment on the outskirts of

New Brunswick, New Jersey. To the right of

my building is Robeson Village, a large low-

income housing project with about two-

hundred apartments facing each other on

opposite sides of a wide, asphalt driveway

that runs the length of the complex. <u>Here</u>,   *Substitutes one*
word for three.
drug dealers and buyers congregate daily,

doing business in front of anyone who cares

to watch. Sometimes, children who have
Adds
witnessed these transactions look over the   *specific*
detail to
<u>crack vials</u>, <u>hypodermic needles</u>, <u>syringes</u>,   *define*
"paraphernalia."
and other paraphernalia the dealers and

their customers have left in their wake.

Uses fewer words than original.

To the left of my building is Henry Street, which <u>has become</u> synonymous with illegal drugs. It is a pathetic place. The

block consists of a half dozen condemned buildings, all of which are <u>lived</u> in or <u>frequented</u> by addicts and dealers. The

Changes wording to be more accurate.

latter have set up stores there in much the

Uses fewer words than original.

same way legitimate merchants choose locations where they think business will be profitable.

. . .

Adds effective adjective.

To the eye <u>of the visitor,</u> the community appears to be in a <u>chronic</u> state of

Adds detail.

depression. Even trees, symbols of life and vitality, seem to bow their heads in sorrow. Rather than reaching up in praise, their branches are twisted and ill-formed, as if poisoned by the very soil in which they are

Uses personification to create a vivid image.

Uses specifics to explain what kinds of odors.

rooted. The pungent odors of <u>urine</u>, <u>feces</u>, and <u>dead, wet leaves</u> are made worse by the stench of rotting food, which <u>spills</u> from overturned garbage cans onto the sidewalk and <u>cooks</u> in the heat of the sun.

Uses verbs to make image active, lively.

Practicing Techniques that Describe

1. Write a paragraph that describes an eating area in your college's student center, a reading area in your college's library, or a coffee shop, a bar, a restaurant, or some other public place where people gather. Appeal to the senses, and include information about the appearance and behavior of people who frequent the place.

_____

_____

_____

_____

_____

_____

2. In a short paragraph or two, describe a specific animal (your pet frog "Meteor") or a type of animal (frogs, in general). Use simile, metaphor, or personification. Also appeal to the senses.

_____

_____

_____

_____

_____

_____

3. Describe the inside of your car, your bedroom, your family's kitchen, or any other room in which you spend a great deal of time. Appeal to the senses and use simile.

_____

_____

_____

_____

_____

_____

4. Write a paragraph that describes your physical appearance. Include details that appeal to the senses, and try to use figures of speech. Be specific about your height, weight, hair color, eye color, and so on. Write the rough draft on scratch paper. Put your final draft on the lines below.

_____

_____

_____

_____

_____

_____

_____

_____

5. Write a paragraph that describes your best or worst quality. For example, discuss your patience or impatience, your tolerance or lack of tolerance for differences in people, your ambition or laziness, or your knack for making or losing friends. Show readers what you mean by using examples and by recalling what others have said about you. Write the rough draft on scratch paper. Put your final draft on the lines below.

_____

_____

_____

_____

_____

_____

_____

_____

6. How do others see you? Write a paragraph that explains how someone you know well would describe your best or worst quality. Focus on only one aspect of your personality. Use any of the techniques for describing that you have learned so far. Write the rough draft on scratch paper. Put your final draft on the lines below.

_____

_____

_____

_____

_____

_____

_____

_____

_____

_____

Enjoy the selections that follow. Each contains examples of the practices discussed on the previous page, and each provides additional hints to help you make your writing stronger and more interesting.

Watching the Reapers*

Po Chü-i

Perhaps one of the most productive of all Chinese poets, Po Chü-i lived between 772 and 846. Many of his works, though seemingly simple in content, reveal a profound concern for others. Some of them, aimed at the consciences of the ruling class, recall the social evils of his day. Others use description as a tool for exposing guilt, heartache, or other strong emotion in the poet. "Watching the Reapers" does all of these things.

Preparing to Read

1. In the introduction to this chapter, you learned that including action is a good way to capture the character of a place or scene. "Watching the Reapers" makes good use of this technique.
2. Description can have many uses. Here it becomes a tool for self-reflection as well as social commentary.
3. The "fifth month" in line 2 refers to midsummer. In lines 19 and 20, Po mentions that the reapers have paid a tax to the state equal to the amount of grain they had raised themselves. This statement is a clear indication that one of the purposes of this poem is to expose a political and economic evil. In line 23, Po tells us that, as a government official, he is paid in "stones," which are measures of grain.

Vocabulary

glean (verb)   Gather.
grudging (adjective)   Resenting.
lingered (verb)   Remained, stayed around.

Watching the Reapers

Po Chü-i

Tillers of the earth have few idle months;
In the fifth month their toil is double-fold.
A south wind visits the field at night;
Suddenly the ridges are covered with yellow corn.
Wives and daughters shoulder baskets of rice,   5

---

*Translated by Arthur Waley.

Youths and boys carry flasks of wine,
In a long train, to feed the workers in the field—
The strong reapers toiling on the southern hill,
Whose feet are burned by the hot earth they tread,
Whose backs are scorched by the flames of the shining sky.   10
Tired they toil, caring nothing for the heat,
Grudging the shortness of the long summer day.
A poor woman with a young child at her side
Follows behind, to glean the unwanted grain.
In her right hand she holds the fallen ears,   15
On her left arm a broken basket hangs.
Listening to what they said as they worked together
I heard something that made me very sad:
They lost in grain-tax the whole of their own crop;
What they glean here is all they will have to eat.   20
And I today—in virtue of what desert
Have I never once tended field or tree?
My government pay is three hundred stones;
At the year's end I have still grain in hand.
Thinking of this, secretly I grew ashamed   25
And all day the thought lingered in my head.

Read More on the Web

Selected poems of Po Chu-I (AD 772–846) Translated by Howard
        S. Levy and Henry Wells: http://www.darsie.net/library/pochui.html
Links to Literature site including biography of the poet and several
        translated poems: http://www.linkstoliterature.com/po.htm

Questions for Discussion

1. What concrete nouns does Po use in this poem?
2. Where does he use effective verbs and adjectives?
3. Explain how Po's description of the reapers helps him describe the
   fields in which they toil.
4. One of Po's objectives is to make us aware of how hard a life the
   reapers have. How do his descriptions of the fields, the wind, and
   other natural objects help him do this?
5. Why does Po make sure to include action in this poem?
6. What emotion does Po reveal in his conclusion?

Thinking Critically

1. If Po were writing in our day, what would he say about the way our society treats its workers? As you think about this topic, focus on a particular industry, business, or trade.

2. Jump ahead to Chapter 9 and read Carl Sandburg's "Child of the Romans." In what ways are its message and content similar to those of Po's poem?

3. Reread line 12. What does Po mean by the "shortness of the long summer day?"

Suggestions for Journal Entries

1. Use listing, clustering, or freewriting to begin gathering concrete details about a place that you have worked in and that you have found interesting. You don't have to have liked this place; you need only have found it interesting. Try to remember the kind of people and activities that one would normally find there, but keep your information factual and objective. Do not include details that would reveal your feelings about the place.

2. Read over your response to Suggestion 1. Now, be subjective. Through freewriting, explain your feelings about this workplace, the people in it, and the kind of work that goes on there. Finally, answer this question: Would you recommend this job to one of your friends?

Flavio's Home

Gordon Parks

Gordon Parks (1912) is a film director/producer, author, composer, and photographer. His feature films include Shaft *(1972),* The Super Cops *(1974),* Leadbelly *(1976), and* Moments without Proper Names *(1986). He also made the television documentary* The Diary of a Harlem Family *(1968), for which he won an Emmy Award. Perhaps his most memorable film is* The Learning Tree *(1969), a fictionalized account of his childhood in Kansas.*

Parks is the founder and was the editorial director (1970–73) of Essence *magazine, and he has written many works of nonfiction—including several memoirs and many books on the art of photography—as well as a novel,* Shannon *(1981). Today, however, his fame rests chiefly on his photography and on the writings that accompany his photography collections. In* Voices in the Mirror *(1990), a memoir in which "Flavio's Home" first appeared, Parks says that he uses "photography as a weapon against poverty and racism." As a staff writer for* Life *magazine, he was once assigned to complete a photo-essay on poverty in one of the "favelas," or slums, of Rio de Janeiro, Brazil. The essay that follows is based on what he witnessed on that trip.*

Preparing to Read

1. Read Parks's first paragraph several times to determine his purpose.
2. Is the first line of this essay a warning of what is to come?
3. Look for images of and references to death starting with paragraph 2. What do you think "Catacumba," the name of the slum where Flavio lives, means in English? Look up words that begin with "cata" in the dictionary if necessary.
4. Read paragraph 3 carefully. Like other paragraphs, it uses effective language, but it also hints at something we will learn about at the essay's end.

Vocabulary

afflictions (noun)	Troubles, suffering, illnesses.
excrement (noun)	Bodily waste.
hemmed and hawed (verbs)	Hesitated before speaking.
jaundiced (adjective)	Yellowed because of illness or malnutrition.
maze (noun)	Confusing set of passageways in which one gets lost easily.
mobilize (verb)	Put into action.

plankings (noun)	Rough boards.
plush (adjective)	Rich, luxurious.
scurried (verb)	Ran around or hurried nervously.
skepticism (noun)	Lack of trust or faith.
wallowing (adjective)	Rolling around, as a pig does in the mud.

Flavio's Home

Gordon Parks

I'VE NEVER LOST my fierce grudge against poverty. It is the most savage of all   1
human afflictions, claiming victims who can't mobilize their efforts against it,
who often lack strength to digest what little food they scrounge up to survive.
It keeps growing, multiplying, spreading like a cancer. In my wanderings I attack it wherever I can—in barrios, slums and favelas.

Catacumba was the name of the favela where I found Flavio da Silva. It was   2
wickedly hot. The noon sun baked the mud-rot of the mountainside. Garbage
and human excrement clogged the open sewers snaking down the slopes. José
Gallo, a *Life* reporter, and I rested in the shade of a jacaranda tree halfway up
Rio de Janeiro's most infamous deathtrap. Below and above us were a maze of
shacks, but in the distance alongside the beach stood the gleaming white homes
of the rich.

Breathing hard, balancing a tin of water on his head, a small boy climbed   3
toward us. He was miserably thin, naked but for filthy denim shorts. His legs
resembled sticks covered with skin and screwed into his feet. Death was all over
him, in his sunken eyes, cheeks and jaundiced coloring. He stopped for breath,
coughing, his chest heaving as water slopped over his bony shoulders. Then
jerking sideways like a mechanical toy, he smiled a smile I will never forget.
Turning, he went on up the mountainside.

The detailed *Life* assignment in my back pocket was to find an impover-   4
ished father with a family, to examine his earnings, political leanings, religion,
friends, dreams and frustrations. I had been sent to do an essay on poverty. This
frail boy bent under his load said more to me about poverty than a dozen poor
fathers. I touched Gallo, and we got up and followed the boy to where he entered a shack near the top of the mountainside. It was a leaning crumpled place
of old plankings with a rusted tin roof. From inside we heard the babblings of
several children. José knocked. The door opened and the boy stood smiling
with a bawling naked baby in his arms.

Still smiling, he whacked the baby's rump, invited us in and offered us a   5
box to sit on. The only other recognizable furniture was a sagging bed and a
broken baby's crib. Flavio was twelve, and with Gallo acting as interpreter, he
introduced his younger brothers and sisters: "Mario, the bad one; Baptista, the
good one; Albia, Isabel and the baby Zacarias." Two other girls burst into the

shack, screaming and pounding on one another. Flavio jumped in and parted them. "Shut up, you two." He pointed at the older girl. "That's Maria, the nasty one." She spit in his face. He smacked her and pointed to the smaller sister. "That's Luzia. She thinks she's pretty."

Having finished the introductions, he went to build a fire under the 6 stove—a rusted, bent top of an old gas range resting on several bricks. Beneath it was a piece of tin that caught the hot coals. The shack was about six by ten feet. Its grimy walls were a patchwork of misshapen boards with large gaps between them, revealing other shacks below stilted against the slopes. The floor, rotting under layers of grease and dirt, caught shafts of light slanting down through spaces in the roof. A large hole in the far corner served as a toilet. Beneath that hole was the sloping mountainside. Pockets of poverty in New York's Harlem, on Chicago's south side, in Puerto Rico's infamous El Fungito seemed pale by comparison. None of them had prepared me for this one in the favela of Catacumba.

Flavio washed rice in a large dishpan, then washed Zacarias's feet in the 7 same water. But even that dirty water wasn't to be wasted. He tossed in a chunk of lye soap and ordered each child to wash up. When they were finished he splashed the water over the dirty floor, and, dropping to his knees, he scrubbed the planks until the black suds sank in. Just before sundown he put beans on the stove to warm, then left, saying he would be back shortly. "Don't let them burn," he cautioned Maria. "If they do and Poppa beats me, you'll get it later." Maria, happy to get at the licking spoon, switched over and began to stir the beans. Then slyly she dipped out a spoonful and swallowed them. Luzia eyed her. "I see you. I'm going to tell on you for stealing our supper."

Maria's eyes flashed anger. "You do and I'll beat you, you little bitch." Luzia 8 threw a stick at Maria and fled out the door. Zacarias dropped off to sleep. Mario, the bad one, slouched in a corner and sucked his thumb. Isabel and Albia sat on the floor clinging to each other with a strange tenderness. Isabel held onto Albia's hair and Albia clutched at Isabel's neck. They appeared frozen in an act of quiet violence.

Flavio returned with wood, dumped it beside the stove and sat down to 9 rest for a few minutes, then went down the mountain for more water. It was dark when he finally came back, his body sagging from exhaustion. No longer smiling, he suddenly had the look of an old man and by now we could see that he kept the family going. In the closed torment of that pitiful shack, he was waging a hopeless battle against starvation. The da Silva children were living in a coffin.

When at last the parents came in, Gallo and I seemed to be part of the fam- 10 ily. Flavio had already told them we were there. "Gordunn Americano!" Luzia said, pointing at me. José, the father, viewed us with skepticism. Nair, his pregnant wife, seemed tired beyond speaking. Hardly acknowledging our presence, she picked up Zacarias, placed him on her shoulder and gently patted his behind. Flavio scurried about like a frightened rat, his silence plainly expressing the fear he held of his father. Impatiently, José da Silva waited for Flavio to serve dinner. He sat in the center of the bed with his legs crossed beneath him, frowning, waiting. There were only three tin plates. Flavio filled them with black beans and rice, then placed them before his father. José da Silva tasted them, chewed for several moments, then nodded his approval for the others to start. Only he and Nair had spoons; the children ate with their fingers. Flavio ate off the top of a coffee can. Afraid to offer us food, he edged his rice and beans toward us, gesturing for us to take some. We refused. He smiled, knowing we understood.

Later, when we got down to the difficult business of obtaining permission 11 from José da Silva to photograph his family, he hemmed and hawed, wallowing in the pleasant authority of the decision maker. He finally gave in, but his manner told us that he expected something in return. As we were saying good night Flavio began to cough violently. For a few moments his lungs seemed to be tearing apart. I wanted to get away as quickly as possible. It was cowardly of me, but the bluish cast of his skin beneath the sweat, the choking and spitting were suddenly unbearable.

Gallo and I moved cautiously down through the darkness trying not to ap- 12 pear as strangers. The Catacumba was no place for strangers after sundown. Desperate criminals hid out there. To hunt them out, the police came in packs, but only in daylight. Gallo cautioned me. "If you get caught up here after dark it's best to stay at the da Silvas' until morning." As we drove toward the city the large white buildings of the rich loomed up. The world behind us seemed like a bad dream. I had already decided to get the boy Flavio to a doctor, and as quickly as possible.

The plush lobby of my hotel on the Copacabana waterfront was crammed 13 with people in formal attire. With the stink of the favela in my clothes, I hurried to the elevator hoping no passengers would be aboard. But as the door was closing a beautiful girl in a white lace gown stepped in. I moved as far away as possible. Her escort entered behind her, swept her into his arms and they indulged in a kiss that lasted until they exited on the next floor. Neither of them seemed to realize that I was there. The room I returned to seemed to be oversized; the da Silva shack would have fitted into one corner of it. The steak dinner I had would have fed the da Silvas for three days.

Read More on the Web

Biography of Gordon Parks: http://www.galegroup.com/free_resources/bhm/bio/parks_g.htm

Photo gallery and video clips including one in which Parks speaks about Flavio da Silva: http://www.pdnonline.com/legends/parks/mainframeset.shtml

UNICEF site on how poverty affects children: http://athena.tbwt.com/content/article.asp?articleid=2414

Questions for Discussion

1. In which parts of the essay does Parks remain objective? Where does he become subjective by reacting to and commenting upon what he witnesses?

2. What references to and images of death can be found in this essay?

3. What other examples of figurative language does Park use?

4. In what parts of the essay does the author appeal to the senses?

5. Analyze paragraphs 2, 3, and 6 carefully. What descriptive techniques discussed earlier in this chapter do they use?

6. Where does Parks use contrast, and to what purpose?

7. Why does the author describe Flavio in such detail? Isn't this supposed to be a description of a place?

8. What happens in a place helps reveal its character. What do the events Parks narrates tell us about Flavio's home? Start with paragraph 7.

9. Why does the author bother to include the names of all the da Silva children? What other proper nouns do you find?

10. Why does he include dialogue—what the people say—in this essay?

11. In what paragraph does Parks prepare us for Flavio's coughing, which we learn about in paragraph 11?

12. Why does the author describe his hotel room?

Thinking Critically

1. What do paragraphs 11 and 12 reveal about the author's character and his purpose for writing this essay?

2. Why does Parks bother to tell us about the lovers kissing in the elevator? How do you react to their ignoring his presence and carrying on with their love-making?

3. Compare this essay to Jesse Sullivan's "If at First You Do Not See . . .," which also appears in this chapter. In what ways are they different? Is Sullivan's purpose the same as Parks's?

Suggestions for Journal Entries

1. Parks has a talent for piling detail upon detail to paint a vivid and compact word picture of what he describes. In paragraph 6, for example, he tells us that the da Silvas' stove was the "rusted, bent top of an old gas range resting on several bricks." In fact, the entire paragraph shows Parks's ability to accumulate concrete, specific, and vivid detail.

Try your hand at doing the same by writing a one-sentence description of a common object. For example you might start with an ordinary piece of furniture—perhaps the desk or table you are working on right now—and then add details until you have a list that looks something like this:

> The desk
>
> The wooden desk
>
> The large wooden desk
>
> The large brown wooden desk
>
> The large brown wooden desk covered with junk
>
> The large brown wooden desk covered with junk, which squats in the corner of my room
>
> The large brown wooden desk covered with junk, books, and papers, which squats in the corner of my room.

Repeat this process, adding as many items as you can, until you've exhausted your mind's supply of nouns and adjectives. Then review your list. Can you make your description even more specific and concrete? For instance, the above example might be revised to read:

> The four-foot-long dark brown oak desk was covered with my math book, an old dictionary with the cover ripped off, two chemistry test papers, today's French notes, a half-eaten bologna sandwich, and a can of diet cola.

2. This essay contains both objective and subjective descriptions of "Catacumba," a symbol for poverty and human misery if there ever was one. Have you ever seen such a place in your own country? If so, begin recording details that might describe it. If this topic doesn't appeal to you, gather details about any public place such as a bus station, amusement park, sports arena or stadium, airport, shopping mall, or waterfront—just to name a few examples.

   Whatever topic you choose, approach this journal entry in two steps. Begin by gathering details that describe the place objectively. Then, record your subjective reaction. Use clustering or listing to gather information that might describe this location.

If at First You Do Not See . . .

Jessie Sullivan

When Jessie Sullivan began this essay for a college composition class, she wanted simply to tell her readers what her neighborhood looked like. As she revised and developed her work, however, she discovered that the place in which she lived had a vibrant character beyond what the eye can see. Slowly, she expanded and refined her purpose until description became a tool for exploring the sorrow and the promise of her world. Sullivan majors in liberal arts and business. She plans to study business administration in graduate school.

Preparing to Read

1. As you learned in Chapter 3, narration and description can sometimes be used to explain ideas. Sullivan uses description to explain what is wrong with her neighborhood but also to reveal her hope for the people and place she loves.

2. In creating the contrast explained above, Sullivan reveals much about herself: her courage, her vision, and her desire to make a difference.

3. You know that this essay uses both description and contrast. Look for examples as well.

Vocabulary

bewilderment (noun)	Astonishment, confusion.
condone (verb)	Make excuses for.
defaced (verb)	Made ugly, disfigured.
diversified (adjective)	Varied, different.
illicit (adjective)	Illegal, prohibited.
infamous (adjective)	Dishonorable, known for evil or wrongdoing.
obscenities (noun)	Words or drawings that are indecent and offensive.
oppressive (adjective)	Harsh, severe, hard to bear.
paraphernalia (noun)	Gear, equipment used in a particular activity.
pathetic (adjective)	Pitiful, wretched, miserable.
preconceived notions (noun)	Prejudices, opinions formed before having accurate information about something.
sober (adjective)	Reliable, serious, steady.
superficial (adjective)	Quick and careless, shallow, on the surface.

If at First You Do Not See . . .

Jessie Sullivan

A LOOK OF genuine surprise comes over some of my classmates when I mention where I live. My neighborhood has a reputation that goes before it. People who have never been there tend to hold preconceived notions about the place, most of which are negative and many of which are true. Those who actually visit my neighborhood usually notice only the filth, the deterioration of buildings and grounds, and the crime. What they fail to see isn't as apparent, but it is there also. It is hope for the future.

I live in an apartment on the outskirts of New Brunswick, New Jersey. To the right of my building is Robeson Village, a large low-income housing project with about two-hundred apartments facing each other on opposite sides of a wide, asphalt driveway that runs the length of the complex. Here, drug dealers and buyers congregate daily, doing business in front of anyone who cares to watch. Sometimes, children who have witnessed these transactions look over the crack vials, hypodermic needles, syringes, and other paraphernalia the dealers and their customers have left in their wake.

To the left of my building is Henry Street, which has become synonymous with illegal drugs. It is a pathetic place. The block consists of a half dozen condemned buildings, all of which are lived in or frequented by addicts and dealers. The latter have set up stores there in much the same way legitimate merchants choose particular locations where they think business will be profitable.

It is this area, three blocks in radius, that is infamous for illicit drugs, prostitution, and violence of every sort. Known as the "Vil," it is regarded as the city's hub of criminal activity and immorality.

With the growing popularity of crack, the appearance of the community has gotten worse and worse, as if it were on a collision course with destruction. Fences that once separated one property from another lie in tangled rusted masses on sidewalks, serving now only as eyesores. Almost all of the buildings are defaced with spray-painted obscenities and other foul messages. Every street is littered with candy wrappers, cardboard boxes, balled-up newspapers, and broken beer and soda bottles.

But Henry Street is undeniably the worst. The road is so covered with broken glass that the asphalt is barely visible. The way the glass catches the sunlight at every angle makes the street look almost magical, but there is nothing magical about it. Henry Street is a dead-end in more than the literal sense. In front of apartment buildings, the overgrown lawns, which more closely resemble hay than grass, are filled with old tires, cracked televisions, refrigerators and ovens with missing doors, rusted bikes, broken toys, and worn chairs and tables without legs. Dozens of abandoned cars, their windows shattered and their bodies stripped of anything of value, line the curbs. The entire block is so cluttered with refuse that strangers often mistake it for the junk yard, which is five blocks up.

To the eye of the visitor, the community appears to be in a chronic state of 7
depression. Even trees, symbols of life and vitality, seem to bow their heads in
sorrow. Rather than reaching up in praise, their branches are twisted and ill-
formed, as if poisoned by the very soil in which they are rooted. The pungent
odors of urine, feces, and dead, wet leaves are made worse by the stench of rotting food, which spills from overturned garbage cans onto the sidewalk and
cooks in the heat of the sun.

Most people familiar with the neighborhood are aware that the majority of 8
us residents are virtual prisoners in our homes because of the alarming crime
rate. Muggings, rapes, and gang-related shootings, many of which do not get
reported in newspapers, are commonplace. Many residents live in such fear
that they hide in their apartments behind deadbolt locks and chains, daring to
peer out of their peepholes only when a frequent gunshot rings out.

Many of my neighbors have adopted an I-mind-my-own-business attitude, 9
preferring to remain silent and blind to the goings-on around them. This is the
case for so many of them that many nonresidents believe everyone feels this
way. Unfortunately, most outsiders learn about our community from people
who have been here only once or twice and who leave with unfair and dangerous misconceptions about us. They see the filth and immorality, and that is all
they see. They take one quick look and assume none of us cares about the
neighborhood or about the way we live.

I see my neighborhood from the inside, and I face all of the terrible things 10
I have mentioned on a day-to-day basis. I also see aspects of my community
that cannot be appreciated with a superficial first glance. If you look at the place
closely, you will find small strong family units, like my own, scattered amid the
degeneration and chaos. Working together, struggling to free themselves from
oppressive conditions, these families are worth noticing! We are sober, moral
people who continue to live our lives according to the laws of society and, more
important, according to the laws of God Himself.

Look closely and you will find those of us who pick up the trash when we 11
see it scattered on our small lawns, sidewalks, and doorsteps. We discourage
our children from disrespecting the area in which they live, and we see to it that
they don't litter or deface public property. We emphasize the importance of
schooling, and we teach them about the evils of drugs and crime, making certain that they are educated at home as well.

Most important, we practice what we preach. We show the children with 12
our actions that we do not condone the immoral and illegal acts around us, and
we refuse to take part in any of them. We call the police whenever we hear gun-
shots, see drug transactions, or learn of any other unlawful activity. The children know that we care and that we are trying to create a brighter future for
them.

However, the most visible sign of hope is that young people from my 13
neighborhood—and from many neighborhoods like mine, for that matter—are
determined to put an end to the destruction of our communities. It angers us

that a minute yet very visible group of negative individuals has come to represent the whole. It saddens us that skills, talents, and aspirations, which are so abundant in our communities, should go untapped. Therefore, we have decided to take matters into our own hands; we will get the education we need and solve the problems of our neighborhoods ourselves.

Many of us attend the local county college, where we come together often 14 to share ideas for a better future for our community. We also give each other the moral support we need to achieve our educational goals. Our hope binds us together closely and is itself a sign that things will get better.

This May, I was proud to see a number of friends receive associate's degrees 15 and get admitted to four-year colleges and universities for advanced degrees. I hope to do the same soon. We are studying for different professions, but no matter how diversified our goals, we will use our knowledge for the benefit of all. This means returning to the community as doctors, lawyers, teachers, entrepreneurs. We will build programs to assist the people of our community directly: day care centers for children with working mothers; family mental and physical health clinics; job-training and placement facilities; legal service centers; youth centers; and drug/alcohol rehabilitation programs. Given the leadership of educated people like those we will become, such facilities can eventually be operated by community residents themselves. Most important, we intend to serve as visible and vocal role models for our children—for the leaders who will follow us and keep our hope alive. Eventually, we will bring about permanent change and make it impossible for a misguided few to represent a proud and productive community.

When friends visit me in my apartment for the first time, they frequently 16 ask in awe and bewilderment, "How can you live in such a bad place?" I always give the same reply: "It isn't where you live, but how you live and what you live for."

Read More on the Web

People's Weekly World site on the state of Black America:
   http://www.hartford-hwp.com/archives/45a/188.html

Urban Institute site with links to many other resources:
   http://www.urban.org/

Questions for Discussion

1. What does Sullivan mean in paragraph I when she says that her "neighborhood has a reputation that goes before it"? Does this statement help introduce what follows in the rest of the essay?

2. Where in this essay does Sullivan include proper nouns? How do they help her achieve her purpose?

3. One reason this essay is so powerful is that it uses specific details. Find examples of these in paragraphs 5 and 6. Then find more examples in any other paragraph of your choice.

4. What image does Sullivan create in paragraph 7? What figure of speech does she use to develop this image?

5. Does action play a role in this essay? What is it?

6. Sullivan mentions her neighbors. How do they help define the neighborhood?

7. What sense other than sight does Sullivan appeal to?

8. When does she make use of illustration (examples)?

Thinking Critically

1. Why do you think Sullivan bothers to tell us that many shootings never get reported in the newspapers?

2. Summarize Sullivan's central idea in your own words.

3. This is a thought-provoking essay. What questions might you ask Sullivan about herself or her neighborhood if you were able to interview her? (For example, who or what has been her greatest inspiration?) Write your questions in the right- and left-hand margins.

Suggestions for Journal Entries

1. Make a list of the qualities you admire most about the neighborhood in which you live or grew up. Then make another list of ways it might be improved.

2. Use any technique discussed in "Getting Started" to gather information about what your home, neighborhood, or town might look like to someone seeing it for the first time. Then, go beyond appearances and discuss the real character of the place. Like Sullivan, describe what's on the "inside."

3. Think of a community, a family, or any group of people struggling to grow, improve, or even survive. What makes their life a struggle? What hope do you see for this place or these people?

Josephine Baker: The Daring Diva

Samantha Levine

In January 2003, US News & World Report *published "Spy Stories: A History of Espionage," a series about famous spies from World War I's Mata Hari to Soviet agent Aldrich Ames. Also discussed are people commonly not known for spying, such as novelist Ernest Hemingway and gourmet Julia Child.*

Among this group is Josephine Baker (1906–75), an African-American cabaret singer and dancer. During her early career, Baker found it difficult to achieve success. A combination of racism and a refusal of the American public to accept her style of performance held her back. In the 1930s, Baker moved to Paris, eventually to become a French citizen. After a sexually provocative performance in La Revue Nègre, *she became an instant success. However, she also served as an Allied spy during World War II. After the war, she visited the United States several times to fight for the Civil Rights Movement.*

Preparing to Read

1. This essay focuses on only one aspect of Baker's life and personality. However, the central idea is only implied; it is not stated. Before you read the essay in its entirety, read the introduction and conclusion. They provide clues as to the essay's central idea, which has to do with something very positive in Baker's character.

2. On the Internet or in an encyclopedia, do some background reading on the Free French, the Nazi persecution of the Jews, Mussolini's invasion of Ethiopia, Charles de Gaulle, and the Croix de Guerre, all of which are mentioned in this essay.

Vocabulary

adulation (noun)	Praise, honor.
chanteuse (noun)	Female cabaret singer.
counterintelligence (noun)	Agency set up to limit enemy espionage.
diva (noun)	Star female performer.
ferry (verb)	Carry.
lavish (adjective)	Expensive, elegant.
liaisons (noun)	Sexual encounters, affairs.
renown (noun)	Fame.
sidle (verb)	Edge along.

Josephine Baker: The Daring Diva

Samantha Levine

A LAVISH FUR COAT made it impossible to tell that Josephine Baker's dress was 1
oddly lumpy as she boarded a train in France on Nov. 23, 1940. On that
day, and many others, the American chanteuse known for dancing in a belt
of bananas and little else was using the shield of her diva status to secretly
ferry information about German Army forces to French and British intelligence officers.

As Baker traveled around Europe and the Middle East to entertain troops 2
during World War II, she never failed to tote home at least some scrap of intelligence. She pinned photographs of German installations to her undergarments
and carried sheet music covered with messages in invisible ink detailing moves
of the Axis enemies. She was never stopped or questioned, her adopted son,
Jean-Claude Eaker, recalled in his biography, *Josephine; The Hungry Heart*. As
she herself once said: "Who would dare search Josephine Baker?"

Born into poverty in St. Louis, Baker rose to international renown in such 3
productions as *La Revue Nègre* and the *Folies Bergère* in Paris. She later became
a French citizen and pledged her life to her adopted homeland as World War II
became a dark reality. The country showered her with adulation as an African-
American star, in contrast to the racism she had encountered stateside. So when
the chief of counterintelligence in Paris recruited Baker to become a secret in-
former, she eagerly served.

Baker traded on her charms to sidle through military checkpoints and se- 4
cure prized transit visas for friends, including Spanish Moroccan passports for
Jews from Eastern Europe to get them safely to Latin America.

Dangerous liaisons. Her support of Italian dictator Benito Mussolini's in- 5
vasion of Ethiopia, a stance she later regretted, still gave her entree to Italian
diplomats. "She would go to the Embassy of Italy, dressed in a beautiful evening
gown for a liaison," says Jean-Claude Baker. "She would listen. . . . They would
talk openly about which countries they would be attacking."

It is hard to say whether the intelligence Baker gathered resulted in lives 6
saved or attacks averted. But her help was invaluable to the Free French, who
were up against the bulldozing Nazi regime.

Baker enthusiastically took every assignment and came up with some of 7
her own: When she was bedridden for months in Morocco, visitors never suspected they were feeding her information machine. Baker took mental notes as
they discussed German intentions toward Morocco, the Free French invasion
of Syria, and American probes into North Africa.

After the war, Gen. Charles de Gaulle gave Baker the Croix de Guerre and 8
the Medal of the Resistance. She died in 1975, buried in Monaco to the booms
of a 21-gun salute.

Read More on the Web

Women's History site on Baker with valuable links: http://womenshistory. about.com/library/bio/blbio_baker_josephine.htm

Official Josephine Baker site: http://www.cmgww.com/stars/baker/about/ biography.html

The Whole Spy Page with biographies and links to history's most famous spies: http://www.angelfire.com/dc/lspy/spies.html

Questions for Discussion

1. Write a sentence that captures the central idea of this essay. What is the author saying about Josephine Baker's character?

2. Why does the author bother to tell us about the flamboyant part of Baker's character such as the fact that she danced in "a belt of bananas" and nothing else.

3. Why does the author tell us about Baker's life before she went to Paris?

4. What do the comments by her son, Jean-Claude, add to Baker's portrait?

5. What do paragraphs 5 and 7 tell us about Baker's character?

6. Why does the author tell us that she once supported Mussolini's invasion of Ethiopia?

7. What does the last paragraph tell us about the nature and extent of Baker's espionage?

8. You have learned that description often aids narration. But the opposite is also true. What role does narration play in this essay?

Thinking Critically

1. Summarize this piece in one paragraph. What can you say about the Josephine Baker we see in this essay?

2. This chapter also contains a portrait of Barry Shlachter's Mother Teresa. You can read the portrait of still another woman in Maria Scamacca's "Oma: Portrait of a Heroin" (Chapter 2). Mother Teresa and Oma are quite different from Josephine Baker. But they have something in common. What quality in "Oma" and Mother Teresa do you also find in Josephine Baker?

Suggestions for Journal Entries

1. Do you see something positive in people that others can not? Do you know someone who frequently behaves in an unconventional, odd, or even negative way but whose character you admire? Perhaps this is a family member or fellow student. Use focused freewriting or clustering to write down details explaining how others see this person and how you see him or her.

2. Go online and find out more about Josephine Baker. Research and take notes on another aspect of her character or life: for example, the fact that she was married several times and that she received 1500 proposals for marriage; that she was an extremely talented albeit provocative cabaret singer and dancer; that she fought against racism in the United States; or that she achieved fame despite having suffered extreme poverty as a child.

Two Gentlemen of the Pines*

John McPhee

A productive writer with a wide range of interests, John McPhee has been a long-time essayist for The New Yorker. *Among his books are* Rising from the Plains *(1986) and* The Control of Nature *(1989). One of the things McPhee does best is to describe the human character. His portraits of people he meets on his travels are among the most memorable in contemporary American literature. McPhee ran into two of his most interesting subjects on a trip through New Jersey's Pine Barrens, a wilderness whose name he used as the title of a book from which this selection is taken.*

Preparing to Read

1. You know that we can learn a lot about people from what they say. This is very true of Fred, the first of McPhee's subjects, but less true of Bill. Nonetheless, the little that Bill lets slip out provides good clues to his personality.

2. McPhee describes the setting in which he meets his subjects; doing so helps enrich their portraits.

3. Think about the use of "gentlemen" in the title as you read this selection.

Vocabulary

cathode-ray tubes (noun)	Television picture tubes.
dismantled (adjective)	Taken apart.
eyelets (noun)	Holes through which laces can pass.
gaunt (adjective)	Lean, thin, angular.
mallet (noun)	Heavy hammer with a short handle.
poacher (noun)	Someone who uses another's land to hunt or fish there illegally.
thong (noun)	Strip of leather used as a lace.
turfing it out (noun)	Digging out the top layer of soil and grass.
understory (noun)	Underbrush.
undulating (adjective)	Changing, varying, fluctuating.
vestibule (noun)	Small room at the entrance to a building.
visored (adjective)	Having a long brim that shades the sun.

---

*Editor's title.

Two Gentlemen of the Pines

John McPhee

FRED BROWN'S HOUSE is on an unpaved road that curves along the edge of a   1
wide cranberry bog. What attracted me to it was the pump that stands in
his yard. It was something of a wonder that I noticed the pump, because there
were, among other things, eight automobiles in the yard, two of them on their
sides and one of them upside down, all ten years old or older. Around the cars
were old refrigerators, vacuum cleaners, partly dismantled radios, cathode-ray
tubes, a short wooden ski, a large wooden mallet, dozens of cranberry picker's
boxes, many tires, an orange crate dated 1946, a cord or so of firewood, man-
dolins, engine heads, and maybe a thousand other things. The house itself, two
stories high, was covered with tarpaper that was peeling away in some places,
revealing its original shingles, made of Atlantic white cedar from the stream
courses of the surrounding forest. I called out to ask if anyone was home, and
a voice inside called back, "Come in. Come in. Come on the hell in."

I walked through a vestibule that had a dirt floor, stepped up into a   2
kitchen, and went on into another room that had several overstuffed chairs in
it and a porcelain-topped table, where Fred Brown was seated, eating a pork
chop. He was dressed in a white sleeveless shirt, ankle-top shoes, and undershorts. He gave me a cheerful greeting and, without asking why I had come or
what I wanted, picked up a pair of khaki trousers that had been tossed onto
one of the overstuffed chairs and asked me to sit down. He set the trousers on
another chair, and he apologized for being in the middle of his breakfast, explaining that he seldom drank much but the night before he had had a few
drinks and this had caused his day to start slowly. "I don't know what's the matter with me, but there's got to be something the matter with me, because drink
don't agree with me anymore," he said. He had a raw onion in one hand, and
while he talked he shaved slices from the onion and ate them between bites of
the chop. He was a muscular and well-built man, with short, bristly white hair,
and he had bright, fast-moving eyes in a wide-open face. His legs were trim and
strong, with large muscles in the calves. I guessed that he was about sixty, and
for a man of sixty he seemed to be in remarkably good shape. He was actually
seventy-nine. "My rule is: Never eat except when you're hungry," he said, and
he ate another slice of the onion.

In a straight-backed chair near the doorway to the kitchen sat a young man   3
with long black hair, who wore a visored red leather cap that had darkened with
age. His shirt was coarse-woven and had eyelets down a V neck that was laced
with a thong. His trousers were made of canvas, and he was wearing gum boots.
His arms were folded, his legs were stretched out, he had one ankle over the
other, and as he sat there he appeared to be sighting carefully past his feet, as if
his toes were the outer frame of a gunsight and he could see some sort of target in the floor. When I had entered, I had said hello to him, and he had nod-

ded without looking up. He had a long, straight nose and high cheekbones, in a deeply tanned face that was, somehow, gaunt. I had no idea whether he was shy or hostile. Eventually, when I came to know him, I found him to be as shy a person as I have ever had a chance to know. His name is Bill Wasovwich, and he lives alone in a cabin about half a mile from Fred. First his father, then his mother left him when he was a young boy, and he grew up depending on the help of various people in the pines. One of them, a cranberry grower, employs him and has given him some acreage, in which Bill is building a small cranberry bog of his own, "turfing it out" by hand. When he is not working in the bogs, he goes roaming, as he puts it, setting out cross-country on long, looping journeys, hiking about thirty miles in a typical day, in search of what he calls "events"—surprising a buck, or a gray fox, or perhaps a poacher or a man with a still. Almost no one who is not native to the pines could do this, for the woods have an undulating sameness, and the understory—huckleberries, sheep laurel, sweet fern, high-bush blueberry—is often so dense that a wanderer can walk in a fairly tight circle and think that he is moving in a straight line. State forest rangers spend a good part of their time finding hikers and hunters, some of whom have vanished for days. In his long, pathless journeys, Bill always emerges from the woods near his cabin—and about when he plans to. In the fall, when thousands of hunters come into the pines, he sometimes works as a guide. In the evenings, or in the daytime when he is not working or roaming, he goes to Fred Brown's house and sits there for hours. The old man is a widower whose seven children are long since gone from Hog Wallow, and he is as expansively talkative and worldly as the young one is withdrawn and wild. Although there are fifty-three years between their ages, it is obviously fortunate for each of them to be the other's neighbor.

Read More on the Web

New Jersey Pinelands Commission Home Page with links to information on other wilderness sites across the country and the world: http://www.state.nj.us/pinelands/

National Parks Service home page: http://www.nps.gov/

Questions for Discussion

1. What do details about Fred's and Bill's physical appearances say about them?
2. Think about the way the older man welcomes his visitor. How do such actions reveal his character?
3. The original shingles on Fred's house are made of cedar "from the stream courses of the surrounding forest" (paragraph 1). In what way

is this and other information about the house helpful to
understanding Fred?

4. Does Fred's claiming there is "something the matter" with him explain
the way he views himself?

5. Bill says he goes into the woods in search of "events." What are these
events? Should the author have used a synonym for this word instead
of quoting Bill directly? Why or why not?

Thinking Critically

1. Why is it important for us to learn about Bills' childhood? In a short
paragraph that uses information from "Two Gentlemen of the Pines,"
explain how learning about Bill the child helps us to understand Bill
the man.

2. Pretend that you accompanied McPhee into the pines. What would
have been your reaction to Fred and Bill? Reread this selection and
make notes in the margins to explain what you might have said or
done in response to various events you read about. For example, how
would you have reacted to meeting Fred in his undershorts?

Suggestions for Journal Entries

1. As this selection shows, we can learn a lot about people from the
places they call home. Use listing to begin describing a place you
consider your own: your room, your kitchen, your garage, the inside
of your car, for example. You might even describe a place—public or
private, indoors or out of doors—that you enjoy visiting. Gather
details that show how this place reflects your personality or that
explain what draws you to it time and again.

2. Have you ever taken a trip and come upon strangers you found
interesting because they were different from most people you know?
Use focused freewriting to explain why they captured your attention.

3. McPhee accounts for Bill's shyness by explaining that his parents
abandoned him. Do you know someone who experienced an event or
set of circumstances that marked his or her personality? Interview
this person; learn what in his or her past contributed to a particular
characteristic or personality trait. Say your great uncle is thrifty.
When you interview him, you find that he was orphaned at age eight,
that he lived many years in poverty, and that he is afraid of being
poor again. Good subjects for this assignment include anyone with a
distinctive personality trait and a willingness to talk about his or her
past.

Charisma Fortified by "Chutzpah"

Barry Shlachter

Barry Shlachter is a reporter for the Star Telegram *in Forth Worth, Texas. For more than a decade, he worked as a correspondent for the Associated Press, a service that provides news stories to papers around the world, in both Asia and Africa. Shlachter met, interviewed, and has written about Mother Teresa, the subject of this piece, on several occasions. Mother Teresa was born in Macedonia but left her homeland to join an Irish order of Roman Catholic nuns and eventually dedicated her life to serving the poor, the homeless, and the defenseless. She died at the age of 87 on September 5, 1997, in Calcutta, India.*

Preparing to Read

1. Indira Ghandi, mentioned in paragraph 3, was the prime minister of India until her assassination in 1984. Eva Peron was the wife of Argentine dictator Juan Peron. Eva enjoyed a great deal of political power until her death of cancer at age 33 in 1954.

2. *Charisma* means personal warmth, charm, allure, or appeal. The word is often associated with political leaders. *Chutzpah* is a Yiddish word meaning courage and determination. It too is rarely used when speaking of religious leaders, but both terms capture Shlachter's vision of Mother Teresa and play important roles in his title and central idea.

3. "Fortified" is also an important word in the title. Consider its meaning as you read on.

Vocabulary

aimlessly (adverb)	Without purpose or plan, disorganized.
bureaucrats (noun)	Government officials.
clerics (noun)	Priests, nuns, or other members of the clergy.
cynical (adjective)	Critical, skeptical.
epiphany (noun)	Awakening, realization.
fended off (verb)	Fought off, avoided.
habit (noun)	Nun's attire, clothing.
hospice (noun)	Place where terminally ill are cared for.
indifferent (adjective)	Unconcerned, apathetic.
sari (noun)	Indian dress.
understated (adjective)	Subtle.
unfazed (adjective)	Undisturbed.
vestige (noun)	Trace.

Charisma Fortified by "Chutzpah"

Barry Shlachter

S HE WAS A tiny woman who spoke remarkably simple words. Yet Mother   1
Teresa used that unadorned speech to bend the will of indifferent bureaucrats, cynical journalists and at least one of the world's most despised tyrants.

I know: I watched her.   2

If she had gone into politics instead of missionary work, I thought after   3
first meeting her after a 1977 cyclone in India, she would have put an Indira
Ghandi or an Eva Peron to shame. That thought was reinforced upon seeing her
again two years later when she won the Nobel Peace Prize and during the 1984
Ethiopian famine.

Few could resist this woman in the home-spun sari-like habit. Born in   4
what is now Macedonia of ethnic Albanian parents, she came to India with an
Irish order, became a naturalized Indian and founder of her own Missionaries
of Charity at a time when foreign clerics were seen as an unwanted vestige of
the colonial era. Ministering to the poorest of Calcutta's poor, she won national,
then world, fame for her selfless work.

On a stretch of coastal road in south India, she once came upon a group of   5
government doctors stranded when their vehicle broke down. After she spoke
to them briefly, they unanimously volunteered to join her cyclone relief effort,
abandoning their own assignments.

"It's hard to say 'no' to a living saint," explained a relief official who knew   6
her, a Hindu like the majority of Indians. "Few are left unaffected by her
charisma," a priest told me. It was that understated charisma, fortified with
well-intentioned chutzpah, that helped bring about what she invariably called
"God's miracles."

Her caravan of trucks and cars made its way to Mandapakala, once a pros-   7
perous farming community flattened by the storm. It was piled with corpses
that day Mother Teresa arrived to supervise relief operations. Methodically, she
issued instructions on the disposal of bodies, a health hazard to the living.

"The best thing would be to build a single long trench and lay the bodies   8
in a file," she crisply told members of her order and a crowd of volunteers she
had attracted along the way. "That, we discovered, was the simplest method
when the floods took their toll in Jalpaiguri in Bengal last year."

Many of the survivors wandered aimlessly about the village or picked   9
through rubble in search of a pot to hold water or boil rice. A woman called to
Mother Teresa, pointing to her only surviving family member, a 6-year-old deaf
mute, and asked: "What will I do with him? Is he worth anything?" The boy approached the nun and played with her wooden rosary. Mother Teresa gathered
him in her arms and the child, unable to speak, gurgled with delight.

"See," she told the distraught mother. "The child is happy."   10

Turning to those accompanying her, the nun said: "Where there is tragedy, 11 there is salvation. Even when the mother cries, the child finds happiness. It is eternal."

In Ethiopia, I witnessed two small "miracles" during a visit by Mother 12 Teresa—and those were aside from all the life-saving efforts by her missionaries among the starving.

Toward the end of my second or third stint in Ethiopia, an Associated Press 13 colleague based in Zimbabwe flew up to relieve me. The late John Edlin was something of a legend in Africa press circles. A hard drinking New Zealander, he had lost count of the times his wife had thrown him out. Sent to cover Sen. Ted Kennedy's famine tour, Edlin was too pickled to dictate more than two paragraphs each night of what was a major story.

Then he met Mother Teresa. 14

It was an epiphany for Edlin. At first, he considered chucking his job to 15 handle her order's press relations in Ethiopia. (Mother Teresa did this all too well on her own.) In the end, the tough Kiwi became an overnight humanitarian who quietly set up and financed an orphanage for children who lost their parents in the famine. Then he returned to reporting.

If the 1984 drought was of biblical proportions, so was the raw cruelty of 16 the country's dictator, Col. Mengistu Haile Mariam. His Marxist regime killed an estimated 150,000 people, while Mengistu is widely believed to have personally strangled his predecessor, Emperor Haile Selassie.

It is well known that the country's Jews, known as Falasha, were perse- 17 cuted. But Mengistu was equally brutal toward a Lutheran-linked church and to practicing Roman Catholics, said my best source in Addis Ababa, the papal nuncio (the Vatican ambassador). Ordinary people were terrified of Mengistu and would not utter his name.

Unfazed, Mother Teresa requested a meeting with the dictator, telling re- 18 porters she would ask him to hand over the late emperor's palace for use as a hospice. She didn't get the palace, but to the amazement of everyone I ran across, she received a piece of land smack in the middle of the capital.

For a journalist, interviewing Mother Teresa about herself was a task. Not 19 that she fended off such encounters; she just wouldn't say much about herself. Instead, she'd speak of miracles, large and small, that materialized, thanks to God, when they were needed most.

"It's His work, not mine," she told me at the Calcutta home for the desti- 20 tute and dying after winning the 1979 Nobel Peace Prize. "God is our banker, He always provides." She recalled a day at the home when "we found we had nothing, not a single piece of bread to give our people."

"You know what happened? For some mysterious reason, all the schools 21 suddenly closed that day and their bread was sent to us," she said.

"Now who else but God could have done that?" 22

Read More on the Web

Site features a short biography and several important links to other
    Internet sites: http://almaz.com/nobel/peace/1979a.html
Site includes links to writings and speeches of Mother Teresa:
    http://home.attbi.com/~motherteresasite/mother.html

Questions for Discussion

1. Where in this essay does the author provide detail to show that
    Mother Teresa had charisma? Where does he provide evidence that
    she had chutzpah?

2. Barry Shlachter tells us little about Mother Teresa's appearance in
    paragraphs 1 and 4. Yet, what he tells us is important to begin
    understanding her character. Explain what this information reveals.

3. One of the ways to reveal character is to relate what others have said
    about your subject. Where does Shlachter do this, and how does it
    help him describe his subject?

4. What a person does often tells us more about his or her character
    than what others say about him or her. Where in this essay does
    Shlachter use anecdotes (brief stories) to tell us about his subject?

5. Where in this essay does Shlachter provide his own insights into
    Mother Teresa's character?

6. Why does the author bother to tell us about John Edlin's drinking
    problem (paragraph 13)? Why does he include so much about the
    brutal regime of Ethiopian dictator Mengistu Haile Miriam
    (paragraphs 16–18)?

7. Reread paragraphs 8 through 11. Explain why leaving those
    paragraphs out would have made the essay far less effective.

Thinking Critically

1. Recall what you know or have learned about Indira Ghandi and Eva
    Peron. If you need more information about these women, read about
    them in an encyclopedia. Then explain why Shlachter makes
    reference to them in paragraph 3.

2. Reread the essay, paying special attention to the quotations Shlachter
    takes from Mother Teresa herself. Underline or highlight phrases or
    sentences that you think are especially telling of Mother Teresa's
    character and beliefs. Summarize these ideas by making notes in the
    margins or on a separate piece of paper. Then turn your notes into a
    short paragraph.

Suggestions for Journal Entries

1. Many people believe that Mother Teresa will be sainted. Whether or not that ever comes to pass, Shlachter's essay paints the picture of a holy and charitable person who deserves to be held up as an example of human charity and unselfishness. If you know someone who you think might be an example to others, use interviewing, clustering, or freewriting to gather information that you might use to describe him or her. Focus on only one or two virtues that this person possesses.

2. In paragraph 15, we learn that journalist John Edlin experienced an epiphany when working with Mother Teresa. *Epiphany,* from the Greek word for "showing," means a revelation or an awakening. As was the case with Edlin, it usually results in a significant change. Do you know someone whose life has changed drastically because of an epiphany? Use focused freewriting or clustering to gather details that will help explain what brought on this realization and what changes it caused in his or her character or lifestyle.

Joe DiMaggio: The Silent Superstar

Paul Simon

Paul Simon (1941) is a musician and composer who has written, performed, and recorded songs that have become classics of American popular music. Simon worked with Art Garfunkel from 1967–1971 to produce award-winning albums such as The Sounds of Silence *(1966);* Parsley, Sage, Rosemary and Thyme *(1968); the soundtrack from* The Graduate *(1968); and* Bridge over Troubled Water *(1972). Simon's subsequent works include* Still Crazy After All These Years *(1975) and* Graceland *(1986), both of which won Grammy Awards.*

Joseph Paul DiMaggio (1914–1999), a native of North Beach, California, played centerfield for the New York Yankees from 1936 to 1951. One of the best fielders and hitters ever to play the game, DiMaggio was named the American League's Most Valuable Player in 1939, 1941, and 1947. He hit safely in 56 straight games in 1941, a record that remains unbroken 60 years later. Sportswriter George Vecsey called him a "staggering blend of power and self-control." He hit 361 home runs but struck out only 369 times in his 16-year career. Many people say that DiMaggio was the best that baseball had to offer. But he was more than a super-athlete. "The Yankee Clipper" was an American hero. The ultimate professional, he was a model for young people, someone to whom they could look for inspiration and example. He stood for values that seem to be rare today, not only in professional sports, but anywhere. DiMaggio had integrity, humility, and respect for others. And, in turn, he earned and kept the respect of the American people. After he retired from baseball, he became president of the Mr. Coffee Corporation, for which he appeared in television commercials. In the 1970s, he was named in a public survey the most trustworthy person on television. Joe DiMaggio was a gentle, honorable, and good man. To the aging baseball fan who is writing this, he will always be a hero.

Preparing to Read

1. Read a little about the life and career of Joe DiMaggio on the Internet or in a sports encyclopedia.
2. Simon mentioned DiMaggio in "Mrs. Robinson," a song featured in *The Graduate* (1967). The film criticizes the kinds of contemporary American values that are in complete opposition to those DiMaggio embraced. If you haven't yet seen *The Graduate,* borrow or rent a video copy
3. In paragraph 10, Simon mentions Mother Teresa and Jeffrey Dahmer. An essay on Mother Teresa appears earlier in this chapter. An essay on Jeffrey Dahmer appears in Chapter 5.

Vocabulary

alluded (verb)	Made an indirect reference.
anointed (adjective)	Divinely chosen, consecrated (here used metaphorically).
antithesis (noun)	Complete opposite.
attribution (noun)	Assignment of.
befouls (verb)	Soils, dirties.
deconstructed (adjective)	Analyzed to such an extent that it loses all meaning.
deify (verb)	Turn into a god.
distortion (noun)	Misrepresentation, falsification.
enthralled (verb)	Enchanted, held spellbound.
icon (noun)	Symbol.
iconoclastic (adjective)	Rebellious, ignoring the rules.
iconographic (adjective)	Relating to images of a hero, legend, or god.
idolatry (noun)	Worship of statues or images (here used metaphorically).
malice (noun)	Ill will, hatred.
neurotic (adjective)	Overly anxious, emotionally off-balance.
petty (adjective)	Mean-spirited, selfish.
scrutinized (adjective)	Analyzed, examined closely.
transgressions (noun)	Sins.
trepidation (noun)	Fear, nervousness.

Joe DiMaggio: The Silent Superstar

Paul Simon

MY OPINIONS REGARDING the baseball legend Joe DiMaggio would be of no 1
particular interest to the general public were it not for the fact that 30
years ago I wrote the song "Mrs. Robinson," whose lyric "Where have you gone
Joe DiMaggio, a nation turns its lonely eyes to you" alluded to and in turn probably enhanced DiMaggio's stature in the American iconographic landscape.

A few years after "Mrs. Robinson" rose to No. 1 on the pop charts, I found 2
myself dining at an Italian restaurant where DiMaggio was seated with a party
of friends. I'd heard a rumor that he was upset with the song and had considered a lawsuit, so it was with some trepidation that I walked over and introduced myself as its composer. I needn't have worried; he was perfectly cordial
and invited me to sit down, whereupon we immediately fell into conversation
about the only subject we had in common.

"What I don't understand," he said, "is why you ask where I've gone. I just   3
did a Mr. Coffee commercial, I'm a spokesman for the Bowery Savings Bank and
I haven't gone anywhere."

I said that I didn't mean the lines literally, that I thought of him as an Amer-   4
ican hero and that genuine heroes were in short supply. He accepted the explanation and thanked me. We shook hands and said good night.

Now, in the shadow of his passing, I find myself wondering about that ex-   5
planation. Yes, he was a cultural icon, a hero if you will, but not of my generation. He belonged to my father's youth: he was a World War II guy whose career
began in the days of Babe Ruth and Lou Gehrig and ended with the arrival of
the youthful Mickey Mantle (who was, in truth, my favorite ballplayer).

In the 50's and 60's, it was fashionable to refer to baseball as a metaphor   6
for America, and DiMaggio represented the values of that America: excellence
and fulfillment of duty (he often played in pain), combined with a grace that
implied a purity of spirit, an off-the-field dignity and a jealously guarded private life. It was said that he still grieved for his former wife, Marilyn Monroe,
and sent fresh flowers to her grave every week. Yet as a man who married one
of America's most famous and famously neurotic women, he never spoke of her
in public or in print. He understood the power of silence.

He was the antithesis of the iconoclastic, mind-expanding, authority-   7
defying 60's, which is why I think he suspected a hidden meaning in my lyrics.
The fact that the lines were sincere and that they've been embraced over the
years as a yearning for heroes and heroism speaks to the subconscious desires
of the culture. We need heroes, and we search for candidates to be anointed.

Why do we do this even as we know the attribution of heroic characteris-   8
tics is almost always a distortion? Deconstructed and scrutinized, the hero
turns out to be as petty and ego-driven as you and I. We know, but still we
anoint. We deify, though we know the deification often kills, as in the cases of
Elvis Presley, Princess Diana and John Lennon. Even when the recipient's life is
spared, the fame and idolatry poison and injure. There is no doubt in my mind
that DiMaggio suffered for being DiMaggio.

We inflict this damage without malice because we are enthralled by   9
myths, stories and allegories. The son of Italian immigrants, the father a fish-
erman, grows up poor in San Francisco and becomes the greatest baseball
player of his day, marries an American goddess and never in word or deed be-
fouls his legend and greatness. He is "the Yankee Clipper," as proud and masculine as a battleship.

When the hero becomes larger than life, life itself is magnified, and we read   10
with a new clarity our moral compass. The hero allows us to measure ourselves
on the goodness scale: O.K., I'm not Mother Teresa, but hey, I'm no Jeffrey Dahmer. Better keep trying in the eyes of God.

What is the larger significance of DiMaggio's death? Is he a real hero? Let   11
me quote the complete verse from "Mrs. Robinson":

Sitting on a sofa on a Sunday afternoon   12
Going to the candidates' debate
Laugh about it, shout about it
When you've got to choose
Every way you look at it you lose.
Where have you gone Joe DiMaggio
A nation turns its lonely eyes to you
What's that you say Mrs. Robinson
Joltin' Joe has left and gone away.

In these days of Presidential transgressions and apologies and prime-time   13
interviews about private sexual matters, we grieve for Joe DiMaggio and mourn
the loss of his grace and dignity, his fierce sense of privacy, his fidelity to the
memory of his wife and the power of his silence.

Read More on the Web

Baseball Hall of Fame site on Di Maggio: http://www.
   baseballhalloffame.org/hofers_and_honorees/hofer_bios/
   dimaggio_joe.htm

City of San Francisco's site: "Joe Di Maggio, the Yankee Clipper" with
   links to information about his early years: http://www.sfmuseum.
   org/hist10/dimaggio1.html

Questions for Discussion

1. Why doesn't Simon describe DiMaggio's appearance?
2. Where in the essay does the author use examples to define DiMaggio's
    character?
3. In paragraph 9, we learn that DiMaggio was "as proud and masculine
    as a battleship." Where else does Simon use figurative language?
4. What does the author mean by "moral compass" (paragraph 10)? In
    what way did DiMaggio fit that definition?
5. In paragraph 7, Simon tells us what DiMaggio was not. How does
    doing this help to define him?
6. Reread paragraph 2. What clues do you see about the kind of man
    Simon is about to describe?
7. Why does Simon bring up Elvis Presley, John Lennon, and Princess
    Diana in paragraph 8? How was DiMaggio different from these
    people?
8. In paragraph 9, we read that DiMaggio "never in word or deed
    befouls his legend and greatness." Explain why this statement might
    serve as the essay's thesis.

Thinking Critically

1. Besides DiMaggio's character and athletic ability, what caused the public to admire him so much? (Reread paragraph 7.)

2. Consider the essay's title. In what way is "silent" a synonym for "humble"? In what way did DiMaggio's silence actually announce his professionalism and integrity?

3. DiMaggio was nicknamed "Joltin' Joe" and "the Yankee Clipper." Look up the term "Yankee Clipper" in an encyclopedia or unabridged dictionary. In what ways might that metaphor apply to a baseball player? What is the double meaning of the word "clipper"?

Suggestions for Journal Writing

1. Think of a public figure you consider to be a "moral compass"— perhaps an athlete; a priest, minister, or rabbi; a public servant or politician; someone who has served in the military; an artist; a medical researcher; a scientist or doctor; the head of a charitable or public-service organization; or a philanthropist (someone who raises and gives money to charity). Gather information about this person's life, the difficult choices he or she has had to make, the hardships he or she has faced, and the goals he or she has achieved. Your purpose is to prove that the way this individual has conducted his or her life can serve as a model for others. Use library and/or Internet research to gather information about this individual, or interview a professor who is familiar with your subject.

2. If, as Simon believes, DiMaggio represented "the values of . . . America" in the 1940s and 50s, in what ways might the America of those decades be different from today's America? Use clustering, listing, or freewriting to record your responses. If possible, interview someone who lived during those decades to find out more about American culture and values as they existed then.

Suggestions for Sustained Writing

1. Read over the notes you made in response to both Suggestions for Journal Entries after Po's "Watching the Reapers." If you have not responded to both of these suggestions, do so now.

   Using description as your main method of development, write an essay in which you explain why you would or would not recommend that a good friend take a job at the place you have begun to describe in your journal. Before beginning your rough draft, try making an outline of your paper. For example, you might organize it in three sections, each of which covers a body paragraph or two. The first could describe the physical characteristics of the workplace itself. The second might focus on the kinds of activities—the work—that normally takes place there. The third might describe the people who work in or frequent the place.

As you begin to draft your paper, remember that you are trying to answer a specific question: Would you recommend this job to a friend? If the answer is no, make sure you include sufficient negative details to support this view and vice versa. One way to introduce this essay is to address the reader directly, ask a question, or make a startling remark. A good way to end it is to restate or summarize some of the points you have made in the body of your essay or offer your reader advice.

However you decide to proceed, make sure that you provide sufficient detail to make your argument convincing. Then, revise, edit, and proofread.

2. If you responded to the second Suggestion for Journal Entries after "Flavio's Home" by Gordon Parks, turn these notes into a full-length essay that describes a place about which you have already gathered information. Begin by recording even more details about your subject. If you can, brainstorm with a fellow student who is also familiar with this place.

In the first draft, include details that paint an objective picture of your subject. Talk about the general layout, shape, or dimensions of the place, the colors of walls, ceilings, and floors, the kinds of furniture and other objects it contains. If you're writing about an outdoor place, mention trees, rocks, streams, bridges, park benches, walls, lampposts, and so on. In your next draft(s), add information about what the place looks, smells, and sounds like. If possible, make use of narration to re-create the kind of activity that normally occurs in this place and to introduce your readers to people who frequent it. In the process, begin revealing your subjective reactions. Use concrete details and vivid verbs, adjectives, and adverbs as well as figures of speech to let readers know what you think about this place and of the people you find there. Like Parks, do not be afraid to express your emotions.

After completing your second or third draft, write a thesis stating your overall opinion. Put this thesis in an introductory paragraph designed to capture the reader's attention. Close your essay with a memorable statement or summary of the reasons you are or are not planning to visit this place again. Finally, edit your work by checking grammar, spelling, and sentence structure.

3. If you read "If at First You Do Not See . . .," follow Sullivan's lead: describe a place you know well by presenting two views of it. For example, one view might be negative, the other positive. Another way to proceed is to describe

what newcomers see when they visit this place as opposed to what you see in it. A good place to describe might be your neighborhood or other part of your hometown, your high school or college campus, a run-down but beautiful old building, or the home of an interesting relative or friend.

Although your paper need not be as long as Sullivan's, it should use techniques like those found in hers. For example, appeal to the senses, include action, use figures of speech to create images, or describe the people who live in or frequent the place.

Check the journal entries you made after reading Sullivan's essay. They might help you get started. Once you have finished several drafts, write an introduction that captures the reader's attention and expresses your central idea in a formal thesis statement. Put the finishing touches on your writing by correcting errors that will reduce its effectiveness or distract your readers. Be sure all your spelling is correct.

4. If you responded to the first of the journal prompts after the essay on Josephine Baker, review your notes now. What do you admire about a person whom others find unconventional, strange, unattractive, or negative? Add details to your notes. Then, draft an essay that begins by briefly explaining why others don't appreciate your subject. However, devote the bulk of your essay to explaining what you admire about this person. Like the author of the Josephine Baker essay, rely heavily on anecdotes (brief stories) to reveal what you admire about your subject's character. If possible, also include quotations from your subject or from others who know him or her well.

5. Describe someone you know by focusing on the strongest or most important feature of his or her personality. Here's an example of a preliminary thesis statement for such an essay: "When I think of Millie, what comes to mind first is her faith in people."

As you draft the body of your essay, tell of something in your subject's past that accounts for this characteristic. For example, explain that Millie has had an unshakable faith in the goodness of people ever since, as a child, she lost her parents and was raised by neighbors. Then, give examples of that faith. Use what you have learned about Millie from personal experience, from people who know her, or from Millie herself. Tell one or two anecdotes (brief, illustrative stories) to convince readers that what you say is true.

A good way to learn more about the person you are describing is to interview him or her. Take accurate notes. When it comes time to write your essay, try quoting your subject directly; use his or her own words to explain how he or she feels. Examples of how to put direct quotations into your work appear in McPhee's "Two Gentlemen of the Pines." In fact, if you responded to the journal suggestions after this selection, you may already have gotten a fine start on the assignment.

Revise your paper as often as necessary. Make sure it includes enough information and is well organized. As part of the editing process, check that you have used quoted material correctly. If you have doubts, speak with your instructor.

6. Reread the journal entries you made after reading Barry Shlachter's "Charisma Fortified by 'Chutzpah.' " Then, expand these notes into a full-length essay.

   If you responded to the first suggestion you will be describing a person you consider an example for others to follow. To gather more information, discuss our subject with mutual friends, interview your subject directly, or recall anecdotes (brief stories) containing facts to support your belief that this person should be looked up to.

   Use the notes you made in response to the second suggestion for journal writing to write an essay explaining how an epiphany (revelation) changed the life or character of someone you know. Like many good papers describing people, yours can rely on anecdotes as well as direct quotations. Begin by explaining what brought on this epiphany. In the rest of your paper, compare your subject's life or character after the epiphany to what it was before.

   Whichever topic you choose, begin by making at least a rough outline. Then, go through the writing process carefully, making sure to revise several times and to edit carefully.

7. Review the notes you made after responding to the first journal suggestion after Simon's "Joe DiMaggio: The Silent Superstar." If you have not yet responded to this, do so now. Turn your notes into an essay that explains why the subject you have chosen to describe is a "moral compass" or model for the rest of us. Focus on the hardships this individual has had to overcome, the goals he or she has attained, the things he or she has done for others, and the strengths of character that enabled him or her to accomplish all these things. Write the first draft of your paper by using the information you have already gathered. As you revise this draft, however, include any new details and ideas that come to mind as you are composing. You might also want to complete more Internet or library research or to interview people who know something about your subject.

8. Most people send friends and relatives store-bought greeting cards on their birthdays. Try something different. Write a birthday letter to a friend or relative whom you love and admire. Begin with a standard birthday greeting if you like. But follow this with four or five well-developed paragraphs that explain the reasons for your love and admiration. Use your knowledge of your reader's past—what you have learned firsthand or heard from others—to recall anecdotes that support your opinion. In other words, show what in his or her character deserves love and admiration.

Not everything you say in this letter has to be flattering. In fact, this is a good chance to do some mild kidding. So, don't hesitate to poke good-natured fun at your reader—and at yourself—as a way of bringing warmth and sincerity to your writing. Just remember that your overall purpose is positive.

This assignment is different from most others. Nonetheless, it demands the same effort and care. In fact, the more you love or admire your reader, the harder you should work at revising and editing this tribute.

Writing to Learn: A Group Activity

You have read Shlachter's essay on Mother Teresa in this chapter. Some say that Mother Teresa should be declared a saint. Whether or not this occurs, few can dispute the fact that this tiny nun was an example of unselfishness worthy of imitation.

THE FIRST MEETING

Assign each student to research another great humanitarian. Here's a list of some figures some might want to learn more about:

Clara Barton	Martin Luther King, Jr.
Carlos Costa	Florence Nightingale
Father Flanagan	Albert Schweitzer
Mohandas Gandhi	Raoul Wallenberg
Dolores Hope	

Of course, you might choose your own subjects. As a matter of fact, one of you might find information on an organization such as the Red Cross, the Red Crescent, Save the Children, or Doctors without Borders. Just make sure that each student researches a different subject.

RESEARCH

Search for information on the Internet, in your library's book catalog, or in a CD or online database for periodicals and newspapers. If you are researching a person, summarize important events in his or her life and list significant contributions he or she has made. If you are researching an organization, define the group's objective and report on the work it is doing. As always, make photocopies of your notes for distribution at your group's next meeting.

THE SECOND MEETING

After distributing copies of everyone's notes, ask each student to explain what he or she discovered. Make recommendations for further research, especially to students whose notes need greater detail. Then ask everyone to turn his or her notes into one or two well-developed, well-organized paragraphs whose purpose it is to prove that his or her subject is an example of humanitarianism. Ask group members to bring photocopies of their work to the next meeting.

THE THIRD MEETING

Distribute and read the paragraphs each group member has brought. Then, ask one person to organize these paragraphs into a coherent essay that defines the term *humanitarianism* by using the subjects your group wrote about as examples. Assign a second person to write an introduction (complete with thesis statement) and a conclusion to this essay. Assign still another to revise and edit it. Finally, ask one other person to type and proofread the final version before submitting it to your instructor.

CHAPTER 9

Narration

The selections in this chapter are examples of narration, a process by which events are related to readers in a particular order. Most often, this order is chronological, or order of time. In short, they tell stories.

The logical arrangement of events in a story is called its *plot*. Often, writers begin by telling us about the first event in this series, the event that sets the whole plot in motion. And they usually end their stories with the last bit of action that takes place.

But this is not always the case. Where a writer begins or ends depends on the kind of story he or she is telling and the reason or purpose for telling it. Some stories begin in the middle or even at the end and then recall what happened earlier. Other stories are preceded or followed by information the author thinks is important. For instance, Carl Sagan introduces a story about Frederick Douglass by explaining that children born into slavery were often separated from their parents, a fact significant to events that follow in the essay.

More than 2,300 years ago, the Greek philosopher Aristotle taught that a narrative must have a beginning, a middle, and an end. In other words, a successful story must be complete. It must contain all the information a reader will need to learn what has happened and to follow along easily. That's the most important idea to remember about writing effective narratives, but there are several others you should keep in mind.

Determining Purpose and Theme

Narration can be divided into two parts: fiction and nonfiction. Works of nonfiction recall events that actually happened. Fiction, though sometimes based on real-life experiences, is born of the author's imagination and does not recreate events as they actually happened.

Many nonfiction narratives are written to inform people about events or developments that affect or interest them. Newspaper and magazine articles are examples. Narration is also used by scientists to explain natural processes as they occur step by step over time. In fact, narration can explain complex ideas or make important points about very real situations. Adrienne Schwartz's "The Colossus in the Kitchen," for instance, tells a story that illustrates the evil and stupidity of apartheid, the political system whose effects the author witnessed when she was a child in South Africa.

Therefore, many narratives are written to dramatize or present an important (central) idea, often called a *theme*. They portray life in such a way as to reveal something important about people, human nature, society, or life itself. At

347

times, this theme is stated in a *moral,* as in Aesop's fables, the ancient Greek stories that teach lessons about living. More often than not, however, the theme or idea behind a story is unstated or implied. It is revealed only as the plot unfolds. In other words, most stories speak for themselves.

As a developing writer, one of the most important things to remember as you sit down to write a narrative is to ask yourself whether the story you're about to tell is important to you in some way. That doesn't mean you should limit yourself to narrating events from personal experience only, though personal experience can often provide just the kind of information you'll need to spin a good yarn. It does mean the more you know about the people, places, and events you're writing about and the more those people, places, and events mean to you, the better able you'll be to make your writing interesting and meaningful to your readers.

Finding the Meaning in Your Story

As explained above, you won't always have to reveal why you've written your story or what theme it is supposed to present. You can allow the events you're narrating to speak for themselves. Often, in fact, you won't know what the theme (central idea) of your story is or why you thought it important until you're well into the writing process. Sometimes, you won't know that until after you've finished.

But that's just fine, for writing is a voyage of discovery. It helps you learn things about your subject (and yourself) that you would not have known had you not started the process in the first place. *Just write about something you find interesting and believe is important.* This is the first step in telling a successful story. You can always figure out why your story is important or what theme you want it to demonstrate later in the process, when you write your second or third draft.

Deciding What to Include

In most cases, you won't have much trouble deciding what details to include. You'll be able to put down events as they happened or at least as you remember them. However, in some cases—especially when you are trying to present a particular theme or idea—you'll have to decide which events, people, and so on should be emphasized or talked about in great detail, which should be mentioned only briefly, and which should be excluded from the story altogether.

Showing the Passage of Time

Of course, the most important thing in a story is the plot, a series of events occurring in time. Writers must make sure that their plots make sense, that they are easy to follow, and that each event or incident flows into the next logically.

A good way to indicate the passage of time is to use transitions or connectives, the kinds of words and expressions used to create coherence within and between paragraphs. In his popular essay about future trips to outer space, Kenneth Jon Rose uses a number of such transitional devices (in italics) as he explains what it might be like to leave the earth on a tourist shuttle to the stars. Notice how they keep the story moving and make it easy to follow:

> [While] *looking out your window,* you'll see the earth rapidly falling away, and the light blue sky progressively turning blue-black. You'll *now* be about 30 miles up, traveling at about 3000 mph. *Within minutes,* the sky will appear jet black, and only the fuzzy curve of the earth will be visible. *Then,* at perhaps 130 miles above the surface of the earth and traveling at 17,000 mph, engines will shut down and . . . you'll become weightless. ("2001: Space Shuttle")

If you want to refresh your memory about other effective transitional devices to use in your writing, turn back to Chapter 2.

Describing Setting and Developing Characters

Establishing the setting of your story involves describing the time and place in which it occurs. You've probably done some of that in response to the assignments in Chapter 8, "Describing Places and Things." Developing characters involves many of the skills you practiced in Chapter 8, "Description."

In general, the more you say about the people in your narrative and about the time and place in which it is set, the more realistic and convincing it will seem to your readers. And the more they will appreciate what it has to say. Remember that your purpose in writing a narrative is to tell a story. But the kind of characters who inhabit that story and the kind of world in which it takes place can be as interesting and as important to your readers as the events themselves.

As you probably know, an important narrative element is dialogue, the words a writer allows people in the story to speak. You can use dialogue to help reveal important aspects of someone's personality, to describe setting, and even to relate events that move the plot along. In fact, several authors whose selections follow allow their characters to explain what happened or to comment on the story's action in their own words. Usually, such comments are quoted *exactly*—complete with grammatical errors and slang expressions. So, try letting your characters speak for themselves. They may be able to tell your readers a lot about themselves, about other characters, and about the narratives in which they appear.

In "The Day I Was Fat" for example, Lois Diaz-Talty's purpose is to explain how an insult she suffered actually improved her life. The event occurred while she was driving her children to a pool. Of course, the author could have included many different facts about the trip, but she chose to include only those related directly to the insult and its effect on her life.

Making Your Stories Lively, Interesting, and Believable

Once again, good stories dramatize ideas or themes. They do this through actions and characters that seem vivid and interesting, as if they were alive or real.

One of the best ways to keep your readers' interest and to make your writing vivid is to use verbs effectively. More than any other part of speech, verbs convey action. They tell *what happened*. It's important to be accurate when reporting an incident you've experienced or witnessed. You ought to recapture it exactly as you remember and without exaggeration. However, good writing can be both accurate and interesting, both truthful and colorful. You can achieve this balance by choosing verbs carefully.

In "Mid-Term Break", for example, the speaker says that his mother "*coughed* out angry tearless sighs." Of course, he could have said that she was so angry she couldn't cry, but that would not have shown us the emotional torture she experienced.

Using adverbs—words that describe verbs, adjectives, and other adverbs—can also make your writing more emphatic, specific, and interesting. Consider these two lines from Pickering's "Faith of the Father": ". . . Miss Ida was shy. She read poetry and raised guinea fowl and at parties sat *silently* in a corner. Only on Easter was she outgoing: then like a day lily she bloomed *triumphantly*. . . ."

You can also make your writing more interesting and believable by including proper nouns—names of persons, places, and things—which will help readers feel they are experiencing the story as they read it. For example in "Faith of the Father," Pickering mentions "Campbell's" grocery store, "the train to Richmond," and St. Paul's Church, "as well as the names of two parishioners, Miss Ida and Miss Emma. He goes on to include the titles of hymns and, later, to mention the names of several colorful characters such as "Beagon Hackett," "Doodlebug Healey," and "Clara Jakeways," not to mention places like "Seven Knobs," "Booger Hill," and "Caney Fork."

Writing About Ourselves and About Others: Point of View

The essays and poems in this chapter may be divided into two categories. The first, including Heaney's "Mid-Term Break" and student Diaz-Talty's "The Day I Was Fat," are autobiographical. They look inward to explain something important about the narrator (storyteller). They are told from the first-person point of view, using the pronouns *I* or *we*. In these selections, the narrator is involved in the action. Also included in this group is Schwartz's "Colossus in the Kitchen," a student essay in which the young narrator is not the major character. Nonetheless, her voice is heard clearly as she comments upon institutional racism and tells us about one of its most innocent victims.

The second category includes Sandburg's "Child of the Romans," and Sagan's "Frederick Douglass: The Path to Freedom." These selections look outward and report on events involving others. They are told from the third-person point of view, using pronouns such as *he, she, it* and *they*. One essay that looks both inward and outward is Pickering's "Faith of the Father." It begins with a personal narrative about the way a church he attended celebrated holidays when he was a boy. It ends with a third-person narrative that reports on the life of Began Hackett, a colorful Baptist minister. Often mixing humor with personal reflection that is serious, heartfelt, and moving, Pickering explains from several vantage points his idea of the role that religion should play in our lives.

Whichever point of view the essays in this chapter use, they provide a sometimes touching, sometimes terrifying, and always interesting account of the authors' reactions to the world around them. As you learned earlier, narration can serve a variety of purposes. The selections that follow prove that reporting events—whether or not the narrator is involved in those events—is one way to make a point about the nature of human beings and the world in which they live. Indeed if you have ever taken a course in psychology or sociology, you know how important narration can be to explaining human and social behavior.

Though not always expressed in a formal thesis statement, the main point in each of these selections comes across clearly and forcefully because of the writer's powerful command of language and of techniques important to telling a story. Use these poems and essays as sources of inspiration for your own work. Reporting events you have heard about, witnessed or taken part in is an excellent way to continue growing as a writer. It can also help you gain a clearer and more perceptive vision of the world, at least the world you are writing about.

Visualizing Narrative Elements

The paragraphs that follow are from "Padre Blaisdell and the Refugee Children," René Cutforth's true story of a Catholic priest's efforts to save abandoned children during the Korean War. The place is Seoul; the time, December 1950.

Describes setting and introduces the main character.

At dawn Padre Blaisdell dressed himself in the little icy room at the top of the orphanage at Seoul. He put on his parka and an extra sweater, for the Siberian wind was fluting in the corners of the big grey barrack of the school. . . . The water in his basin was solid ice. . . .

His boots clicked along the stone flags in the freezing passages which led to the main door. The truck was waiting on the snow-covered gravel in the yellow-grey light of sunrise. The two Korean nurses stood as usual, ready for duty——pig-tailed adolescents, their moon faces as passive and kindly as cows.

Describes other characters.

By the time he reached Riverside Road the padre had passed through the normal first stage of reaction to the wind . . .; he was content now in his open vehicle to lie back and admire the effortless skill of the wind's razor as it slashed him to the bone.

Uses a transition to show passage of time.

Uses a metaphor, action verb.

There's a dingy alley off Riverside Street, narrow, and strewn with trodden straw and refuse which would stink if the cold allowed it life enough. This alley leads to the arches of the railway bridge across the Han River. The truck's wheels crackled over the frozen . . . alley, passed from it down a sandy track and halted at the second arch of the bridge [in front of which] lay a pile of filthy rice sacks, clotted with dirt and stiff as boards. It was a child, practically naked and covered with filth. It lay in a pile of its own excrement in a sort of nest it had scratched

Uses vivid adjectives and proper nouns to describe setting.

Uses vivid verbs and adjectives.

out among the rice sacks. Hardly able to
raise itself on an elbow, it still had
enough energy to draw back cracked lips from
bleeding gums and snarl and spit at the
padre like an angry kitten. Its neck was not
much thicker than a broom handle and it had
the enormous pot-belly of starvation.

Uses a simile.

    At eleven o'clock in the morning, when
the padre returned to the orphanage, his
truck was full. "They are the real victims
of the war," the padre said in his
careful . . . colorless voice. "Nine-tenths
of them were lost or abandoned. . . . No one
will take them in unless they are relations,
and we have 800 of these children at the
orphanage. Usually they recover in quite a
short time, but the bad cases tend to become
very silent. . . . I have a little boy who
has said nothing for three months now but
Yes and *No*."

Uses a transition to show passage of time.

Uses dialogue to provide information and explain story's purpose.

TRACKING THE PASSAGE OF TIME "PADRE BLAISDALE AND THE REFUGEE CHILDREN"

We can divide the story roughly into three major sections, each of which is introduced by transitions that relate to time.

"At dawn . . ."
Padre Blaisdale and the nurses leave the
orphanage in search of orphans.

"By the time he reached Riverside Road . . ."
They find the child in the alley.

"At eleven o'clock in the morning . . ."
They return with a truckload of children.

Revising Narrative Essays

The fourth selection in this chapter, "The Colossus in the Kitchen," was written by Adrienne Schwartz, a student who recalls the racial prejudice aimed at Tandi, a black woman who worked for her family in her native South Africa. Realizing narrative essays require as much care as any others, Schwartz made important changes to her rough draft and turned an already fine essay into a moving and memorable experience for her readers. Compare these excerpts from her drafts.

Schwartz—Rough Draft

Our neighbors, in conformity with

established thinking, had long called my

mother, and therefore all of us, deviants,

agitators, and no less than second cousins

to Satan himself. The cause of this

Use a
quotation
to show
this?
dishonorable labeling was the fact that we

had been taught to believe in the equality

and dignity of humankind.

That was why I could not understand the apoplectic reaction of the neighbors to my excited news that Tandi was going to have a baby. After all, this was not politics; this was new life. Tandi's common-law husband lived illegally with her in the quarters

Connect these ideas better?

assigned to them; complying with the law on this and many other petty issues was not considered appropriate in our household. It was the Group Areas Act that had been responsible for the breakup of Tandi's marriage. Her lawful husband, who was not born in the same area as she, had been refused a permit to work in the Transvaal, a

Make smoother?

province in northeastern South Africa, where we lived. In the way of many others, he had   *Needed?*

been placed in such a burdensome situation and found the degradation of being taken

More vivid?

from his wife's bed in the middle of the night and joblessness more often than he

Clarify?

could tolerate. He simply went away, never to be seen or heard from again.

Find a better place for this idea?

The paradox of South Africa is complex in the extreme. It is like a rare and precious stone set amid barren wastes, and yet it feeds off its own flesh.

The days passed, and Tandi's waist got

Slow down?
Show passage
of time?

bigger and pride could be seen in her eyes.

The child died after only one day.

Schwartz—Final Draft

Our neighbors, in conformity with
established thinking, had long called my
mother, and therefore all of us, deviants,
agitators, and no less than second cousins
to Satan himself. The cause of this

Uses a
direct
quotation
to prove
an idea.

dishonorable labeling was the fact that we
had been taught to believe in the equality
and dignity of humankind.

"Never take a person's dignity away from
him," my mother had said, "no matter how
angry or hurt you might be because in the
end you only diminish your own worth."

That was why I could not understand the
apoplectic reaction of the neighbors to my
excited news that Tandi was going to have a

Moves this
information
to a more
logical
place.

baby. After all, this was not politics; this
was new life. But the paradox of South
Africa is complex in the extreme. The
country is like a rare and precious stone

Adds vivid
details in
a metaphor.

set amid barren wastes, and yet close up it
is a gangrenous growth that feeds off its
own flesh.

Tandi's common-law husband lived illegally with her in the quarters assigned to them; complying with the law on this and many other petty issues was not considered appropriate in our household. It was the Group Areas Act that had been responsible for the breakup of Tandi's marriage in the first place. Her lawful husband, who was not born in the same area as she, had been refused a permit to work in the Transvaal, and like others placed in such a burdensome situation, suffered the continuous degradation of being dragged from his wife's bed in the middle of the night and of being denied work more often than he could tolerate. Eventually he simply melted away, never to be seen or heard from again, making legal divorce impossible.

As the days passed, Tandi's waist swelled, and pride glowed in her dauntless eyes.

And then the child was born, and he lived for a day, and then he died.

Adds transition to connect ideas.

Removes unnecessary information.

Adds vivid verbs; makes sentences smoother.

Uses vivid vocabulary.

Adds transitions to show time passing.

Expands this sentence for dramatic effect.

Practicing Narrative Skills

What follows is an eyewitness account of the last moments of the Titanic, which sank in 1912 after striking an iceberg. The writer views the scene from a lifeboat about two hours after having abandoned ship. Practice your skills by following the instructions for each section of this exercise.

1. Underline words and phrases that make this an effective narrative. Look especially for vivid verbs, adjectives, and adverbs. Also underline transitions.

> In a couple of hours . . . [the ship] began to go down . . . rapidly. Then the fearful sight began. The people in the ship were just beginning to realize how great their danger was. When the forward part of the ship dropped suddenly at a faster rate . . . there was a sudden rush of passengers on all the decks towards the stern. It was like a wave. We could see the great black mass of people in the steerage sweeping to the rear part of the boat and breaking through to the upper decks. At a distance of about a mile we could distinguish everything through the night, which was perfectly clear. We could make out the increasing excitement on board the boat as the people, rushing to and fro, caused the deck lights to disappear and reappear as they passed in front of them. [Mrs. D. H. Bishop]

2. Important words have been removed from the following paragraphs. Replace them with words of your own. Use only the kinds of words indicated. Avoid *is, are, was, were, have been, had been,* and other forms of the verb *to be.*

> This panic went on, it seemed, for an hour. _____ the ship
> TRANSITION
>
> seemed to _____ out of the water and stand there perpen-
> VERB
>
> dicularly. It seemed to us that it stood _____ in the water for
> ADVERB
>
> four full minutes._____ it began to _____ gently down-
> TRANSITION   VERB
>
> wards. Its speed increased as it went down head first, so that the
>
> stern _____ down with a rush.
> VERB
>
> The lights continued to burn till it sank. We could see the
>
> people _____ _____ in the stern till it was gone. . . .
> VERB   ADVERB

_____ the ship sank we _____ the screaming a mile
ADVERB OF TIME   VERB

away. Gradually it became fainter and fainter and died away. Some

of the lifeboats that had room for more might have _____ to
VERB

their rescue, but it would have meant that those who were in the

water would have _____ aboard and sunk them.
VERB

    The six selections in this chapter are very different in style, content, and purpose. But they all make their points in interesting and meaningful ways. More important, they illustrate effective techniques important to narrative and other types of writing that you will use in both your college and professional life.

Mid-Term Break

Seamus Heaney

Seamus Heaney (1939–   ) was born in County Derry in Northern Ireland. The son of a farmer, Heaney took a B.A. at Queen's University in Belfast and then began teaching in secondary school. He is now professor of poetry at Oxford University in England and has been a visiting lecturer at Harvard University and at the University of California. Called the greatest living Irish poet, Heaney has won many awards including the Nobel Prize for literature (1995), the most prestigious honor a writer can receive. His poems focus on the land, people, and history of Northern Ireland. Some of his works also discuss the political and religious turmoil that have plagued his country. Collections of Heaney's poetry include Field Work *(1979),* Station Island *(1984), and* The Hero Lantern *(1987).*

Preparing to Read

1. What does the title tell us about the speaker of this poem?
2. As you read the first stanza (verse paragraph), ask yourself why the speaker tells us about spending "all morning in the college sick bay [infirmary]."
3. At the beginning of the poem, the speaker mentions bells ringing. For what might this prepare us?

Vocabulary

gaudy (adjective)	Conspicuous, ugly, in bad taste.
knelling (adjective)	Ringing.
poppy (adjective)	Red or deep orange.
pram (noun)	Baby carriage.
snowdrops (noun)	White flowers that bloom in early spring.
stanched (adjective)	Wrapped so as to stop the flow of blood.

Mid-Term Break

Seamus Heaney

I sat all morning in the college sick bay
Counting bells knelling classes to a close.
At two o'clock our neighbours drove me home.

In the porch I met my father crying—
He had always taken funerals in his stride—   5
And Big Jim Evans saying it was a hard blow.

The baby cooed and laughed and rocked the pram
When I came in, and I was embarrassed
By old men standing up to shake my hand

And tell me they were "sorry for my trouble."   10
Whispers informed strangers I was the eldest,
Away at school, as my mother held my hand

In hers and coughed out angry tearless sighs.
At ten o'clock the ambulance arrived
With the corpse, stanched and bandaged by the nurses.   15

Next morning I went up into the room. Snowdrops
And candles soothed the bedside; I saw him
For the first time in six weeks. Paler now,

Wearing a poppy bruise on his left temple,
He lay in the four foot box as in his cot.   20
No gaudy scars, the bumper knocked him clear.

A four foot box, a foot for every year.

Read More on the Web

Biography of Heaney with links to recordings of his readings:
    http://www.ibiblio.org/ipa/heaney/
Biography of Heaney with a bibliography of and about his works:
    http://www.nobel.se/literature/laureates/1995/heaney-bio.html

Questions for Discussion

1. What transitional words does Heaney use to move this brief story
    along.
2. Does this story contain dialogue?
3. Consider the different (and perhaps unexpected) ways in which
    Heaney's mother and father react to the death. What do their
    reactions tell us about their characters?
4. Comment upon Heaney's choice of verbs in stanzas 5, 6, and 7. What
    use of adjectives, especially participles, does he make in this poem?
5. How does Heaney establish setting? Does the setting change?
6. Find examples of figurative language in this poem.

Thinking Critically

1. We are shocked to learn of the death of a child at the end of this poem, but Heaney has prepared us all along. Make notes in the margins where you find clues about the poem's ending.

2. What contrasts does Heaney draw in this poem?

3. Heaney attended St. Columb's College before entering Queens University. What might the word "college" mean as used in "Mid-Term Break"?

Suggestions for Journal Entries

1. In the Questions for Discussion, you were asked to consider the different ways in which Heaney's mother and father reacted to the loss of their child. Some people react differently to death than others. Use freewriting, clustering, or listing to gather details that might help explain how you or someone you know reacted to the death of a loved one. Try to use vivid language and be as detailed as you can as you gather this information.

2. In stanza 6, Heaney writes: "Snowdrops/And candles soothed the bedside." Find out more about "snowdrops" in an unabridged dictionary or concise encyclopedia. Then, using freewriting, compose a detailed picture of what you imagine this scene to be. Base your description on Heaney's words, but go beyond them by adding detail from your own imagination.

The Day I Was Fat

Lois Diaz-Talty

When she isn't waitressing part-time or taking care of her family of four, Lois Diaz-Talty studies nursing and writes interesting essays such as the one below. She credits her husband and children for encouraging her academic efforts. Nonetheless, as the essay shows, she is an energetic, determined, and intelligent woman, who is sure to succeed. When asked to write about a pivotal event or turning point in her life, Diaz-Talty recalled an incident that is burned into her memory and that has helped shape her life.

Preparing to Read

1. The significance of the event narrated in this essay is explained in its thesis, which appears near the end.
2. Diaz-Talty's style is conversational, familiar, and often humorous, but her essay is always clear, correct, and focused. Pay particular attention to her use of dialogue, which helps capture the flavor of the moment.
3. Her title is unusual. What does it signal about what is to come?

Vocabulary

condiments (noun)	Seasonings, flavorings.
committed (adjective)	Determined.
ironically (adverb)	Having an effect opposite the one expected.
limber (adjective)	Able to bend easily, flexible.
notorious (adjective)	Shameful, bad.

The Day I Was Fat

Lois Diaz-Talty

I WAS NEVER in great shape. As a child, I was always called "plump," and my 1
friend "Skinny Sherri" was always, well, skinny. I could never sit Indian-style the way other kids did, and when I made the cheerleading squad in eighth grade it was because I had a big mouth and a great smile, not because I could execute limber splits or elegant cartwheels. Although I maintained a respectable weight throughout high school (after all, my "entire life" depended upon my looks and popularity), there was always a fat person inside of me just waiting to burst onto the scene.

Adulthood, marriage, and settling down had notorious effects on my   2
weight: I blew up! The fat lady had finally arrived, saw the welcome mat, and
moved right in. No one in my family could tell me I was fat. They knew that I
had gained weight, I knew that I had gained weight, and I knew that they knew
that I had gained weight. But to discuss the topic was out of the question. Once,
my mother said, "You're too pretty to be so heavy"; that was the closest anyone
had ever come to calling me fat. Later, my husband teased me because we
couldn't lie on the couch together anymore, and I just cried and cried. He never
dared to mention it again, but I didn't stop eating.

I had just given birth to my first child and was at least fifty pounds over-   3
weight. Nonetheless, I remember feeling that that was the greatest time in my
life. I had a beautiful new baby, new furniture, a great husband, a lovely house.
What more could anyone want? Well, I knew what else I wanted: I wanted to
be thin and healthy. I just didn't care enough about myself to stop my frequent
binging. I tried to lose weight every day, but I couldn't get started. Diets didn't
last through lunch, and I got bigger by the day.

One summer afternoon in 1988, as I was headed to the pool with my sister-   4
in-law Mary Gene and our children, I got into an argument with a teenager who
was driving fast and tail-gaiting our car. When he nearly ran us off the road, I
turned around and glared at him to show my disapproval and my concern for
our safety. Suddenly, we began yelling at each other. He was about 18, with an
ugly, red, swollen face. The few teeth he had were yellow and rotten. He followed us to the pool and, as he pulled into the parking lot behind us, our argument became heated.

"What's your problem, bitch?" he screamed.   5

"You drive like an idiot! That's my problem, okay?"   6

When I got out of the car and walked around to get the baby, he laughed   7
to his friend, "Ah, look at 'er. She's fat! Go to hell, fat bitch." And then they
drove away.

Once inside the gates to the pool, my sister-in-law advised me to forget the   8
whole incident.

"Come on," she said. "Don't worry about that jerk! Did you see his teeth?   9
He was gross."

But I couldn't get his words out of my mind. They stung like a whip. "I'm   10
fat," I thought to myself. "I haven't just put on a few pounds. I'm not bloated.
I don't have baby weight to lose. I'm just plain fat." Nobody had ever called me
fat before, and it hurt terribly. But it was true.

On that very day, as I sat at the pool praying that nobody would see me in   11
my bathing suit, I promised myself that no one would ever call me fat again.
That hideous, 18-year-old idiot had spoken the words that none of my loved
ones had had the heart to say even though they were true. Yes, I was fat.

From then on, I was committed to shedding the weight and getting into   12
shape. I started a rigorous program of running and dieting the very next day.
Within months, I joined a gym and managed to make some friends who are

still my workout buddies. However, in the past seven years, I've done more than lose weight: I've reshaped my attitude, my lifestyle, and my self-image. Now, I read everything I can about nutrition and health. I'm even considering becoming an aerobics instructor. I cook low-fat foods—chicken, fish, lean meats, vegetables—and I serve my family healthy, protein-rich meals prepared with dietetic ingredients. The children and I often walk to school, ride bikes, rollerblade, and run. Health and fitness have become essential to our household and our lives. But what's really wonderful is that, some time between that pivotal day in 1988 and today, my self-image stopped being about how I look and began being about how I feel. I feel energetic, healthy, confident, strong, and pretty. Ironically, the abuse I endured in the parking lot has helped me regain my self-esteem, not just my figure. My body looks good, but my mind feels great!

I hope that the kid from the pool has had his teeth fixed because I'm sure 13 they were one source of his misery. If I ever see him again, I won't tell him that he changed my life in such a special way. I won't let him know that he gave me the greatest gift he could ever give me just by being honest. I won't give him the satisfaction of knowing that the day he called me fat was one of the best days of my life.

Read More on the Web

American Obesity Association site: http://www.obesity.org/

Surgeon General's site on being overweight and obese:
   http://www.surgeongeneral.gov/topics/obesity/default.htm

Questions for Discussion

1. Where does Diaz-Talty express the essay's central idea? In other words, which sentence is her thesis?
2. What purpose does the author's quoting herself serve in this essay? Why does she quote her mother?
3. Why did the author quote the exact words of the 18-year-old who harassed her? Would simply telling us what happened have been enough?
4. Why does Diaz-Talty bother to describe this person? Why does she make sure to reveal her attitude toward him?
5. Reread three or four paragraphs, and circle the transitions used to show the passage of time and to create coherence.
6. Find places in which the author uses particularly good verbs, adjectives, and adverbs.

Thinking Critically

1. Make notes in the margins next to details that reveal important aspects of the author's personality.

2. Were you in the author's place, how would you have reacted to the insult? Now think about an aspect of your personality or lifestyle that needs improvement. Write a paragraph that explains how you might improve it.

Suggestions for Journal Entries

1. Recall a painful experience that changed your life for the better. Answer the journalists' questions to collect details about this event and to explain how it helped you. For example, here is the journal entry Lois Diaz-Talty made in preparation for "The Day I Was Fat":

   When? In 1988, shortly after I gave birth to Tommy.

   What? An argument with a teenager who had been driving behind us. He called me fat.

   Who? I and a rude, 18-year-old stranger, who looked gross.

   Where? On the way to the pool.

   Why important? Because I *was* fat.

   How? His insult shamed me. Made me work harder to lose weight and helped restore self-esteem.

2. Use focused freewriting to gather details about how you reacted to an incident in which someone hurt, insulted, or cheated you, or did something else unpleasant to you. In the process, analyze your reaction to this event. What did it reveal about your character?

Child of the Romans

Carl Sandburg

Carl Sandburg (1878–1967) is one of America's best-loved poets and biographers. He is remembered chiefly for his six-volume biography of Abraham Lincoln and his collections of poetry, such as The Chicago Poems, Cornhuskers, *and* The People, Yes, *which reveal a love for the common people. His support for labor is evident in "Child of the Romans," a sketch of an Italian immigrant railroad worker. For Sandburg, this "dago shovelman" was typical of the people who built America's factories, railroads, and cities.*

Preparing to Read

1. *Dago* is an insulting term for an Italian. The poem's title refers to the fact that 2,000 years ago Italy was the center of the powerful Roman Empire.
2. Sandburg contrasts the life of the shovelman with those of the people on the train. It is this comparison that serves as the theme of the poem.
3. Verbs and adjectives create a sense of reality in this poem and keep it interesting. Look for them as you read "Child of the Romans."

Vocabulary

eclairs (noun)   Rich, custard-filled pastries topped with chocolate.
jonquils (noun) Garden plants of the narcissus family with lovely
                 yellow or white flowers.

Child of the Romans

Carl Sandburg

The dago shovelman sits by the railroad track
Eating a noon meal of bread and bologna.
A train whirls by, and men and women at tables
Alive with red roses and yellow jonquils,
Eat steaks running with brown gravy,   5
Strawberries and cream, eclairs and coffee.
The dago shovelman finishes the dry bread and bologna,
Washes it down with a dipper from the water-boy,

And goes back to the second half of a ten-hour day's work
Keeping the road-bed so the roses and jonquils   10
Shake hardly at all in the cut glass vases
Standing slender on the tables in the dining cars.

Read More on the Web

University of Illinois at Urbana-Champagne site on Sandburg:
   http://alexia.lis.uiuc.edu/~rmrober/sandburg/home.htm
American Academy of Poets site on Sandburg:
   http://www.poets.org/poets/poets.cfm?45442B7C000C040C

Questions for Discussion

1. The poem's plot is very simple. What events take place during the shovelman's lunch?
2. Sandburg gets very detailed in listing the various items that the railroad passengers are dining on. How do these contrast with what the shovelman is eating?
3. Why does Sandburg make sure to tell us that the train "whirls" by as the man eats his lunch? How does his description of the movement of the train contrast with what you read in the last three lines of this poem?
4. How long is the shovelman's day? In what way does his work, "keeping the road-bed," affect the passengers?
5. The poem has two very different settings. What are they, and how does the contrast between the two help Sandburg get his point across?

Thinking Critically

1. Earlier you read that Sandburg was a friend to labor and the common people. Underline words or phrases in his poem that support this idea. Does the poem tell us anything about Sandburg's attitude toward the wealthy? If so, what is it?
2. "Child of the Romans" was written in 1916. Would the setting be different if Sandburg were writing this poem today? What else might change?
3. Read a little about the Romans in an encyclopedia. Besides being Italian, in what way is the shovelman a "child of the Romans"?

Suggestions for Journal Entries

1. If you know a hardworking immigrant who has come here in search of a better life, write a story about this person's typical workday.
2. If you have ever had a job in which you provided a service for other people (perhaps as a housepainter, waitress, or salesclerk), narrate one or two events from a typical workday.
3. After reading Sandburg's story of the shovelman's difficult life, many readers are inclined to count their blessings. List some things in your life that make it easier and more hopeful than that of the shovelman.

The Colossus in the Kitchen

Adrienne Schwartz

Adrienne Schwartz was born in Johannesburg in the Republic of South Africa, where she now lives. "The Colossus in the Kitchen" is about the tragedy of apartheid, a political system that kept power and wealth in the hands of whites by denying civil and economic rights to nonwhites and by enforcing a policy of racial segregation. Tandi, the woman who is at the center of this story, was Schwartz's nursemaid for several years.

Schwartz wrote this essay in 1988. Since that time, South Africa has abolished apartheid and extended civil rights to all citizens. Nelson Mandela, a black political leader who had been imprisoned by the white minority government during the apartheid era, became South Africa's first freely elected president.

Preparing to Read

1. The Group Areas Act, which Schwartz refers to in paragraph 7, required blacks to seek work *only* in those areas of the country for which the government had granted them a permit. Unfortunately, Tandi's legal husband was not allowed to work in the same region as she.

2. The Colossus was the giant bronze statue of a male figure straddling the inlet to the ancient Greek city of Rhodes. It was known as one of the seven wonders of the ancient world. More generally, this term refers to anything that is very large, impressive, and powerful. As yo 1 read this essay, ask yourself what made Tandi a colossus in the eyes of young Schwartz.

Vocabulary

apoplectic (adjective)	Characterized by a sudden loss of muscle control or ability to move.
ashen (adjective)	Gray.
bestriding (adjective)	Straddling, standing with legs spread widely.
cavernous (adjective)	Like a cave or cavern.
confections (noun)	Sweets.
cowered (adjective)	Lowered in defeat.
dauntless (adjective)	Fearless.
deviants (noun)	Moral degenerates.
disenfranchised (adjective)	Without rights or power.

entailed (adjective)	Involved.
flaying (noun)	Whipping.
gangrenous (adjective)	Characterized by decay of the flesh.
nebulous (adjective)	Without a definite shape or form.
prerogative (noun)	Privilege.
sage (adjective)	Wise.

The Colossus in the Kitchen

Adrienne Schwartz

1 I REMEMBER WHEN I first discovered the extraordinary harshness of daily life for black South Africans. It was in the carefree, tumbling days of childhood that I first sensed apartheid was not merely the impoverishing of the landless and all that that entailed, but a flaying of the innermost spirit.

2 The house seemed so huge in those days, and the adults were giants bestriding the world with surety and purpose. Tandi, the cook, reigned with the authoritarian discipline of a Caesar. She held audience in the kitchen, an enormous room filled with half-lights and well-scrubbed tiles, cool stone floors and a cavernous black stove. Its ceilings were high, and during the heat of midday I would often drowse in the corner, listening to Tandi sing, in a lilting voice, of the hardships of black women as aliens in their own country. From half-closed eyes I would watch her broad hands coax, from a nebulous lump of dough, a bounty of confections, filled with yellow cream and new-picked apricots.

3 She was a peasant woman and almost illiterate, yet she spoke five languages quite competently; moreover, she was always there, sturdy, domineering and quick to laugh.

4 Our neighbors, in conformity with established thinking, had long called my mother, and therefore all of us, deviants, agitators, and no less than second cousins to Satan himself. The cause of this dishonorable labeling was the fact that we had been taught to believe in the equality and dignity of humankind.

5 "Never take a person's dignity away from him," my mother had said, "no matter how angry or hurt you might be because in the end you only diminish your own worth."

6 That was why I could not understand the apoplectic reaction of the neighbors to my excited news that Tandi was going to have a baby. After all, this was not politics; this was new life. But the paradox of South Africa is complex in the extreme. The country is like a rare and precious stone set amid barren wastes, and yet close up it is a gangrenous growth that feeds off its own flesh.

7 Tandi's common-law husband lived illegally with her in the quarters assigned to them; complying with the law on this and many other petty issues was not considered appropriate in our household. It was the Group Areas Act that had been responsible for the breakup of Tandi's marriage in the first place.

Her lawful husband, who was not born in the same area as she, had been refused a permit to work in the Transvaal, and like others placed in such a burdensome situation, suffered the continuous degradation of being dragged from
his wife's bed in the middle of the night and of being denied work more often
than he could tolerate. Eventually he simply melted away, never to be seen or
heard from again, making legal divorce impossible.

As the days passed, Tandi's waist swelled, and pride glowed in her daunt-   8
less eyes.

And then the child was born, and he lived for a day, and then he died.   9

I could not look at Tandi. I did not know that the young could die. I   10
thought death was the prerogative of the elderly. I could not bear to see her
cowered shoulders or ashen face.

I fled to the farthest corner of the yard. One of the neighbors was out pick-   11
ing off dead buds from the rose bushes. She looked over the hedge in concern.

"Why! You look terrible . . . are you ill, dear?" she said.   12

"It's Tandi, Mrs. Green. She lost her baby last night," I replied.   13

Mrs. Green sighed thoughtfully and pulled off her gardening gloves. "It's   14
really not surprising," she said, not unkindly, but as if she were imparting as
sage a piece of advice as she could. "These people (a term reserved for the dis-
enfranchised) have to learn that the punishment always fits the crime."

Read More on the Web

A history of apartheid in South Africa: http://www-cs-students.
    stanford.edu/~cale/cs201/apartheid.hist.html

South Africa's Apartheid Era and the Transition to Multiracial
    Democracy: http://www.facts.com/cd/o94317.htm

Questions for Discussion

1. Why does Schwartz spend so much time describing the kitchen in
   paragraph 2? Does this help us understand Tandi?
2. What details do we learn about Tandi, and what do they tell us about
   her character? Why does the author call her a "colossus?"
3. Besides Tandi, who are the characters in this narrative and what do
   we know about them?
4. Why does Schwartz recall events from Tandi's past (paragraph 7)?
5. The author makes especially good use of verbs in the last half of this
   essay. Find some examples.
6. Schwartz's use of dialogue allows her to explain important ideas.
   Where in this essay does she use dialogue, and what does it reveal?

Thinking Critically

1. Apartheid was not "merely the impoverishing of the landless" but also "a flaying of the innermost spirit," says Schwartz. What does she mean by this? If necessary, use the encyclopedia to do a little research on apartheid.

2. Is Schwartz's message or central idea similar to Romero's in "What the Gossips Saw" (Chapter 6)? Write a paragraph in which you compare (point out similarities between) the central ideas of these selections.

Suggestions for Journal Entries

1. Have you or anyone you know well ever witnessed or been involved in a case of intolerance based on race, color, creed, or sex? List the important events that made up this incident and, if appropriate, use focused freewriting to write short descriptions of the characters involved.

2. Schwartz's essay is a startling account of her learning some new and very painful things about life. Using any of the prewriting methods discussed in "Getting Started," make notes about an incident from your childhood that opened your eyes to some new and perhaps unpleasant reality.

3. Were you ever as close to an older person as Schwartz was to Tandi? Examine your relationship with the individual by briefly narrating one or two experiences you shared with him or her.

Frederick Douglass: The Path to Freedom

Carl Sagan

Carl Sagan was a professor of astronomy at Cornell University and the author of many books on science. He worked on several NASA projects and researched the possibilities of life on other planets. As host of the popular television program "Cosmos," Sagan did a great deal to increase public interest in science and mathematics and to increase support for education in these subjects. Among Sagan's most widely read books are The Dragons of Eden, *for which he won the Pulitzer Prize in 1977,* Broca's Brain, Cosmos, *and* The Demon-Haunted World, *from which this selection is taken. Sagan died in 1997.*

Preparing to Read

1. Sagan uses dialogue effectively. Read his direct quotations carefully.
2. The essay begins with remarks that explain the kind of thinking that led to and supported the institution of slavery (paragraphs 1–4). Although not part of the narrative per se, this information sheds important light on the events that led to Douglass's achieving his freedom.
3. What might be "the path to freedom" discussed in this essay?

Vocabulary

antebellum (adjective)	Before the Civil War.
condoned (verb)	Tolerated, excused.
drudgery (noun)	Hard, tedious work.
eluded (verb)	Escaped.
fiendish (adjective)	Devilish.
heart-rending (adjective)	Heartbreaking.
hereditary (adjective)	By birth, genetic.
manifesting (adjective)	Showing.
nil (noun)	Nothing, zero.
prohibitions (noun)	Bans, laws against.
reprieve (noun)	Relief, pardon.
reticent (adjective)	Restrained, quiet.
subversive (adjective)	Rebellious, defiant, revolutionary.
surreptitiously (adverb)	Secretly.

Frederick Douglass: The Path to Freedom

Carl Sagan

FREDERICK BAILEY was a slave. As a boy in Maryland in the 1820s, he had no   1
mother or father to look after him. ("It is a common custom," he later wrote,
"to part children from their mothers . . . before the child has reached its twelfth
month.") He was one of countless millions of slave children whose realistic
prospects for a hopeful life were nil.

What Bailey witnessed and experienced in his growing up marked him for-   2
ever. "I have often been awakened at the dawn of day by the most heart-rending
shrieks of an aunt of mine, whom [the overseer] used to tie up to a joist, and
whip upon her naked back till she was literally covered with blood . . . From
the rising till the going down of the sun he was cursing, raving, cutting, and
slashing among the slaves of the field . . . He seemed to take pleasure in mani-
festing his fiendish barbarity."

The slaves had drummed into them, from plantation and pulpit alike, from   3
courthouse and statehouse, the notion that they were hereditary inferiors, that
God *intended* them for their misery. The Holy Bible, as countless passages confirmed, condoned slavery. In these ways the "peculiar institution" maintained
itself despite its monstrous nature—something even its practitioners must have
glimpsed.

There was a most revealing rule: Slaves were to remain illiterate. In the an-   4
tebellum South, whites who taught a slave to read were severely punished.
"[To] make a contented slave," Bailey later wrote, "it is necessary to make a
thoughtless one. It is necessary to darken his moral and mental vision, and, as
far as possible, to annihilate the power of reason." This is why the slaveholders
must control what slaves hear and see and think. This is why reading and critical thinking are dangerous, indeed subversive, in an unjust society.

So now picture Frederick Bailey in 1828—a 10-year-old African-American   5
child, enslaved, with no legal rights of any kind, long since torn from his
mother's arms, sold away from the tattered remnants of his extended family as
if he were a calf or a pony, conveyed to an unknown household in a strange city
of Baltimore, and condemned to a life of drudgery with no prospect of reprieve.

Bailey was sent to work for Capt. Hugh Auld and his wife, Sophia, moving   6
from plantation to urban bustle, from field work to housework. In this new environment, he came every day upon letters, books, and people who could read.
He discovered what he called "this mystery" of reading: There was a connection between the letters on the page and the movement of the reader's lips, a
nearly one-to-one correlation between the black squiggles and the sounds ut-
tered. Surreptitiously, he studied from young Tommy Auld's *Webster's Spelling
Book*. He memorized the letters of the alphabet. He tried to understand the
sounds they stood for. Eventually, he asked Sophia Auld to help him learn.

Impressed with the intelligence and dedication of the boy, and perhaps ignorant of the prohibitions, she complied.

By the time Frederick was spelling words of three and four letters, Captain   7
Auld discovered what was going on. Furious, he ordered Sophia to stop. In Frederick's presence he explained:

> A nigger should know nothing but to obey his master—to do as he
> is told to do. Learning would *spoil* the best nigger in the world.
> Now, if you teach that nigger how to read, there would be no keep-
> ing him. It would forever unfit him to be a slave.

Auld chastised Sophia in this way as if Frederick Bailey were not there in the room with them, or as if he were a block of wood.

But Auld had revealed to Bailey the great secret: "I now understood . . . the   8
white man's power to enslave the black man. From that moment, I understood the pathway from slavery to freedom."

Without further help from the now reticent and intimidated Sophia Auld,   9
Frederick found ways to continue learning how to read, including buttonholing white schoolchildren on the streets. Then he began teaching his fellow slaves: "Their minds had been starved . . . They had been shut up in mental darkness. I taught them, because it was the delight of my soul."

With his knowledge of reading playing a key role in his escape, Bailey fled   10
to New England, where slavery was illegal and black people were free. He changed his name to Frederick Douglass (after a character in Walter Scott's *The Lady of the Lake*), eluded the bounty hunters who tracked down escaped slaves, and became one of the greatest orators, writers, and political leaders in American history. All his life, he understood that literacy had been the way out.

Read More on the Web

The Frederick Douglass Museum and Cultural Center Website:
    http://www.ggw.org/freenet/f/fdm/

National Parks Service Web site on Frederick Douglass National Historic
    Site in Washington DC: http://www.nps.gov/frdo/

Questions for Discussion

1. This essay shows clearly that narration can be used to make a point.
    Where does Sagan place his thesis?
2. What method for writing conclusions discussed in Chapter 4 does
    Sagan use?

3. The author keeps the story moving by using transitional words and expressions in important places. Find a few of them.
4. How does Sagan's quoting Frederick Douglass directly help him tell the story?
5. Where in this essay does Sagan establish setting?
6. This is a short selection. What is the author able to reveal about his characters?

Thinking Critically

1. Why does Sagan quote Captain Auld directly in paragraph 7? What is it that Auld unknowingly reveals to Frederick?
2. In *The Demon-Haunted World,* the book from which this essay was taken, Sagan quotes Epictetus, a Roman philosopher who had once been a slave: "We must not believe the many, who say that only free people ought to be educated, but we should rather believe the philosophers who say that only the educated are free." What light does this statement shed on Sagan's essay on Frederick Douglass?
3. In Chapter 2, reread William Bennett's essay "Study Calculus!" about mathematics teacher Jaime Escalante. Explain why Escalante might hold up Frederick Douglass as an example to his students.

Suggestions for Journal Entries

1. Think of a person you know who has had to overcome obstacles to achieve an important goal in life. If you can, interview this person to learn more about his or her struggle.
2. Frederick Douglass taught himself to read without the benefit of formal education. Indeed, his owner did everything he could to keep him from learning. Do you know someone who has been discouraged from educating him- or herself? Do you know someone who had to learn an important skill on his or her own? Use clustering or freewriting to gather information about this individual. You might even brainstorm with older people who are acquainted with your subject.

Faith of the Father

Sam Pickering

Sam Pickering teaches nature writing and children's literature at the University of Connecticut. He has written many scholarly books and articles and has published in the National Review, Kenyon Review, *and* Sewanee Review, *as well as in other prestigious journals. His essay collections include* The Right Distance, A Continuing Education, *and* May Days. *Pickering was the inspiration for the character played by Robin Williams in the movie* Dead Poet's Society.

The humorous tone of "Faith of the Father" makes it different from other selections in this chapter. However, its message is just as serious as theirs. Indeed, Pickering is a master at making important ideas come alive through interesting, sometimes hilarious, characters and events. "Faith of the Father" first appeared in the Southwest Review.

Preparing to Read

Pickering makes references to the Bible and to the Christian faith throughout this essay. Lazarus (paragraph 2) is a figure from the New Testament, whom Christ brought back from the dead. Solomon (paragraph 6) is a king of Israel; in describing the lilies of the field, St. Matthew says that "Solomon in all his glory was not arrayed [dressed] like one of these." The Resurrection (paragraph 11) is the rising of Christ from the dead.

Vocabulary

analysis (noun)	Study, investigation.
articled (adjective)	Formal, made up of regulations and procedures.
ascension (noun)	Rising.
buoying (adjective)	Lifting.
carousing (noun)	Partying.
chalice (noun)	Cup for sacred bread and wine at Christian service.
deity (noun)	God.
dispassionate (adjective)	Unemotional, without feeling.
emblem (noun)	Sign.
erratically (adverb)	Unevenly, not in any pattern.
irascible (adjective)	Ill tempered, cranky.
itinerant (adjective)	Travelling.
mourning cloak (noun)	Butterfly with purplish-brown wings.
pretension (noun)	Arrogance, excessive pride.

speculated (verb)   Guessed, wondered.
sustenance (noun)   Support, nourishment.
temperate (adjective)   Calm, dignified
tempered (verb)   Moderated.

Faith of the Father

Sam Pickering

O N WEEKDAYS Campbell's store was the center of life in the little Virginia town 1
in which I spent summers and Christmas vacations. The post office was in
a corner of the store, and the train station was across the road. In the morning
men gathered on Campbell's porch and drank coffee while they waited for the
train to Richmond. Late in the afternoon, families appeared. While waiting for
their husbands, women bought groceries, mailed letters, and visited with one
another. Children ate cups of ice cream and played in the woods behind the
store. Sometimes a work train was on the siding, and the engineer filled his cab
with children and took them for short trips down the track. On weekends life
shifted from the store to St. Paul's Church. Built in a grove of pine trees in the
nineteenth century, St. Paul's was a small, white clapboard building. A Sunday
School wing added to the church in the 1920s jutted out into the graveyard.
Beyond the graveyard was a field in which picnics were held and, on the Fourth
of July, the yearly Donkey Softball Game was played.

St. Paul's was familial and comfortable. Only a hundred people attended 2
regularly, and everyone knew everyone else and his business. What was private
became public after the service as people gathered outside and talked for half
an hour before going home to lunch. Behind the altar inside the church was a
stained glass window showing Christ's ascension to heaven. A red carpet ran
down the middle aisle, and worn, gold cushions covered the pews. On the walls
were plaques in memory of parishioners killed in foreign wars or who had
made large donations to the building fund. In summer the minister put fans out
on the pews. Donated by a local undertaker, the fans were shaped like spades.
On them, besides the undertaker's name and telephone number, were pictures
of Christ performing miracles: walking on water, healing the lame, and raising
Lazarus from the dead.

Holidays and funerals were special at St. Paul's. Funerals were occasions 3
for reminiscing and telling stories. When an irascible old lady died and her
daughter had "Gone to Jesus" inscribed on her tombstone, her son-in-law was
heard to say "poor Jesus"—or so the tale went at the funeral. Christmas Eve was
always cold and snow usually fell. Inside the church at midnight, though, all
was cheery and warm as the congregation sang the great Christmas hymns: "O
Come, All Ye Faithful," "The First Noel," "O Little Town of Bethlehem," and
"Hark! The Herald Angels Sing." The last hymn was "Silent Night." The service

did not follow the prayer book; inspired by Christmas and eggnog, the congregation came to sing, not to pray. Bourbon was in the air, and when the altar boy lit the candles, it seemed a miracle that the first spark didn't send us all to heaven in a blue flame.

Easter was almost more joyous than Christmas. Men stuck greenery into their lapels and women blossomed in bright bonnets, some ordering hats not simply from Richmond but from Baltimore and Philadelphia. On a farm outside town lived Miss Emma and Miss Ida Catlin. Miss Emma was the practical sister, running the farm and bringing order wherever she went. Unlike Miss Emma, Miss Ida was shy. She read poetry and raised guinea fowl and at parties sat silently in a corner. Only on Easter was she outgoing; then like a day lily she bloomed triumphantly. No one else's Easter bonnet ever matched hers, and the congregation eagerly awaited her entrance, which she always made just before the first hymn.   4

One year Miss Ida found a catalogue from a New York store which advertised hats and their accessories. For ten to twenty-five cents ladies could buy artificial flowers to stick into their bonnets. Miss Ida bought a counter full, and that Easter her head resembled a summer garden in bloom. Daffodils, zinnias, and black-eyed Susans hung yellow and red around the brim of her hat while in the middle stood a magnificent pink peony.   5

In all his glory Solomon could not have matched Miss Ida's bonnet. The congregation could not take its eyes off it; even the minister had trouble concentrating on his sermon. After the last hymn, everyone hurried out of the church, eager to get a better look at Miss Ida's hat. As she came out, the altar boy began ringing the bell. Alas, the noise frightened pigeons who had recently begun to nest and they shot out of the steeple. The congregation scattered, but the flowers on Miss Ida's hat hung over her eyes, and she did not see the pigeons until it was too late and the peony had been ruined.   6

Miss Ida acted like nothing had happened. She greeted everyone and asked their healths and the healths of absent members of families. People tried not to look at her hat but were not very successful. For two Sundays Miss Ida's "accident" was the main subject of after-church conversation; then it was forgotten for almost a year. But, as Easter approached again, people remembered the hat. They wondered what Miss Ida would wear to church. Some people speculated that since she was a shy, poetic person, she wouldn't come. Even the minister had doubts. To reassure Miss Ida, he and his sons borrowed ladders two weeks before Easter, and climbing to the top of the steeple, chased the pigeons away and sealed off their nesting place with chicken wire.   7

Easter Sunday seemed to confirm the fears of those who doubted Miss Ida would appear. The choir assembled in the rear of the church without her. Halfheartedly the congregation sang the processional hymn, "Hail Thee, Festival Day." Miss Ida's absence had taken something bright from our lives, and as we sat down after singing, Easter seemed sadly ordinary.   8

We were people of little faith. Just as the minister reached the altar and   9
turned to face us, there was a stir at the back of the church. Silently the minister raised his right hand and pointed toward the door. Miss Ida had arrived. She
was wearing the same hat she wore the year before; only the peony was missing. In its place was a wonderful sunflower; from one side hung a black and
yellow garden spider building a web while fluttering above was a mourning
cloak, black wings, dotted with blue and a yellow border running around the
edges. Our hearts leaped up, and at the end of the service people in Richmond
must have heard us singing "Christ the Lord Is Risen Today."

St. Paul's was the church of my childhood, that storied time when I thought   10
little about religion but knew that Jesus loved me, yes, because the Bible told
me so. In the Morning Prayer of life I mixed faith and fairy tale, thinking God
a kindly giant, holding in his hands, as the song put it, the corners of the earth
and the strength of the hills. Thirty years have passed since I last saw St. Paul's,
and I have come down from the cool upland pastures and the safe fold of childhood to the hot lowlands. Instead of being neatly tucked away in a huge hand,
the world now seems to bound erratically, smooth and slippery, forever beyond
the grasp of even the most magical deity. Would that it were not so, and my
imagination could find a way through his gates, as the prayer says, with thanksgiving. Often I wonder what happened to the "faith of our fathers." Why if it
endured dungeon, fire, and sword in others, did it weaken so within me?

For me religion is a matter of story and community, a congregation rising   11
together to look at an Easter Bonnet, unconsciously seeing it an emblem of
hope and vitality, indeed of the Resurrection itself. For me religion ought to be
more concerned with people than ideas, creating soft feeling rather than sharp
thought. Often I associate religion with small, backwater towns in which tale
binds folk one to another. Here in a university in which people are separated
by idea rather than linked by story, religion doesn't have a natural place. In the
absence of community ceremony becomes important. Changeable and always
controversial, subject to dispassionate analysis, ceremony doesn't tie people together like accounts of pigeons and peonies and thus doesn't promote good
feeling and finally love for this world and hope for the next. Often when I am
discouraged, I turn for sustenance, not to formal faith with articled ceremony
but to memory, a chalice winey with story.

Not long ago I thought about Beagon Hackett, a Baptist minister in   12
Carthage, Tennessee. Born in Bagdad in Jackson County, Beagon answered the
call early in life. Before he was sixteen, he had preached in all the little towns
in Jackson County: Antioch, Nameless, McCoinsville, Liberty, and Gum
Springs. Although popular in country churches, Beagon's specialty was the all-
day revival, picnic, and baptizing, usually held back in the woods near places
like Seven Knobs, Booger Hill, Backbone Ridge, Chigger Hollow, and Twelve
Corners. Beagon made such a name that the big Baptist church in Carthage selected him as minister. Once in Carthage, Beagon tempered his faith to suit the

mood of the county seat. Only once a year did he hold a meeting out of doors. For his first four or five years in Carthage, he led a revival near Dripping Rock Bluff across Hell Bend on the Caney Fork River, the spot being selected for name not location.

The narrows of the river were swift and deep, and crossing Hell Bend was   13 dangerous, a danger Beagon celebrated, first reminding the faithful that Jesus was a fisher of men and then buoying their spirits up on a raft of watery Christian song: "Shall We Gather at the River," "The Rock That Is Higher Than I," and "Sweet By and By." Beagon's meetings across the Caney Fork were a success with people traveling from as far as Macon and Trousdale counties to be baptized. But then one spring Gummert Capron or Doodlebug Healy, depending on whose memory is accurate, became frightened in mid-river and tipping over a row-boat changed "Throw Out the Life-Line" from word to deed. If Homer Nye had not grabbed Clara Jakeways by the hair, the dark waters, as the hymn puts it, would have swept her to eternity's shore. As it turned out Clara's salvation turned into romance, and three months later she and Nye were married, much to the disappointment of Silas Jakeways who owned a sawmill and the Eagle Iron Works and who disapproved of Nye, until that time an itinerant bricklayer. Clara, Silas was reported to have said, would "have been better off if love hadn't lifted her from the deep to become the wife of a no-account." Whatever the case, however, Beagon never led another revival across Hell Bend; instead he stayed dry on the Carthage side of the Caney Fork, once a year holding a temperate affair, more Sunday outing than revival, on Myers Bottom.

After Beagon had been in Carthage for twenty years, he grew heavy and   14 dignified. No longer would he preside at river baptizings. In his church he erected, as Silas Jakeways said "a marble birdbath," a baptismal font, copied from one he saw in an Episcopal Church at Monteagle. In Carthage, though, pretension was always liable to be tipped over, if not by simple-minded folk like Gummert Capron or Doodlebug Healy, then by daily life. Addicted to drink, Horace Armitage, the disreputable brother of Benbow Armitage, occasionally cut hair at King's Barber Shop. One morning after a long night of carousing at Enos Mayfield's in South Carthage, Horace was a bit shaky, and while shaving Beagon cut him slightly on the chin. "That's what comes of taking too much to drink," said Beagon, holding a towel to his chin. "Yes, sir, Reverend" Horace replied, "Alcohol does make the skin tender."

Read More on the Web

Critique Magazine interview with Pickering: http://www.etext.org/Zines/
    Critique/writing/pickering.html

Review of Pickering's *The Blue Caterpillar and Other Essays:*
    http://www.upf.com/Spring1997/pickering.html

Questions for Discussion

1. Where in this essay does Pickering describe setting?
2. How does Pickering indicate the passage of time in paragraphs 6–9? In paragraphs 12–14?
3. To what end does the author include dialogue?
4. What do we learn about Miss Ida's character? What about Beagon Hackett's character? Why is it important for us to know about them?
5. Why does the author tell us that, on Christmas Eve at St. Paul's, "Bourbon was in the air" (paragraph 3)?
6. Explain the puns (plays on words) in paragraph 13.
7. What does Pickering mean by "pretension was always liable to be tipped over, if not by simple minded folk . . . then by daily life (paragraph 14)? How does the story of Horace Armitage's shaving Beagon Hackett illustrate this idea?
8. This essay seems to be in two parts: paragraphs 1–11 and paragraphs 12–14. In what way(s) are paragraphs 12–14 different from those that come before? In what way do these last three paragraphs shed light on what we read in paragraphs 1–11?

Thinking Critically

1. Pickering believes religion has more to do with people than with doctrine. What does he mean?
2. Why is the congregation happy about Miss Ida's return (paragraph 9)? How is her story related to the Easter theme?
3. The author doesn't think religion has a "natural place" in colleges and universities. Do you agree?

Suggestions for Journal Entries

1. Answer the journalists' questions to recall information about a humorous event that happened during a celebration—religious or not—that you attended.
2. In paragraph 10, Pickering tells us that his childhood vision of religion was a mixture of "faith and fairy tale." What was your childhood faith like? Recall an incident from those years that might help answer this question. Use listing or answer the journalists' questions to explain what happened.

Suggestions for Sustained Writing

1. If you responded to the first Suggestion for Journal Entries after Heaney's "Mid-Term Break," write an essay in which you explain your reaction or the reaction of someone you know to the death of a loved one. Now, add information to the notes you have already taken on this topic in your journal. If possible, interview or brainstorm with another person who has shared this loss—perhaps another family member or a close friend. Delve into your subject's character by explaining how he or she reacted to the shock, grieved over the loss, and dealt with the grief, if at all. Your narrative might span a few days, a few weeks, or even a few years.

   As you revise your first draft, add concrete details, figures of speech, and vivid verbs and adjectives. When you revise your second draft, try adding dialogue, and make sure you have described the setting and the people in your story well. Finally, check to see if you have included transitional devices and effective verbs to move the story along and to make it easy to follow. Next, edit your work for grammar; sentence structure, length, and variety; word choice; and punctuation and spelling. As always, proofread. This will probably be a powerful story—you don't want to spoil it with silly mistakes in writing or typing.

2. Use narration to explain what someone did to influence you either positively or negatively. Show how this person encouraged or discouraged you to develop a particular interest or talent; explain what he or she taught you about yourself; or discuss ways he or she strengthened or weakened your self-esteem.

   You need not express yourself in an essay. Consider writing a letter instead. Address it to the person who influenced you, and explain your appreciation or resentment of that influence. Either way, put your thesis—a statement of just how positively or negatively he or she affected you—in the introduction to your essay or letter.

   Before you begin, check the journal entries you made after reading the essay by Diaz-Talty. Then, write one or two stories from personal experience that show how the person in question affected you. After completing your first draft, try adding dialogue to your stories. Reveal your subject's attitude toward you by recalling words he or she used when answering your questions, giving you advice or instructions, or commenting on your efforts.

   As you revise your work further, make sure you have explained the results of this person's influence on you thoroughly. Add details as you move from draft to draft. Then, edit for grammar, punctuation, spelling, and other problems that can make your writing less effective.

3. The first of the Suggestions for Journal Entries after Diaz-Talty's "The Day I Was Fat" asks you to gather information about a painful experience that changed your life for the better. Use this information to begin drafting a full-length essay that explains what happened.

You might begin the first draft by stating in one sentence how this event changed you; this will be your working thesis. You can then tell your story, including only those materials that help explain or prove the thesis. For example, Diaz-Talty says that being called fat helped her regain her self-esteem and her figure; every detail in her story helps prove this statement.

As you write later drafts, add dialogue and descriptive detail about people in your story, just as Diaz-Talty did. If you are unhappy with your introductory and concluding paragraphs, rewrite them by using techniques explained in Chapter 4.

Before you get to your final draft, make certain your paper contains vivid verbs, adjectives, and adverbs, which will keep readers interested. If it doesn't, add them. Then, edit and proofread your work carefully.

4. Sandburg's "Child of the Romans" contrasts the shovelman's life with those of the railroad passengers. Show how difficult or easy your life seems when contrasted with the life of someone you know. If you made a journal entry after Sandburg's poem, you might have already gathered details for this paper.

Focus your essay on the other person; recall events that show the kind of life he or she has led. At the same time, remember that setting is important, so include details that reveal where or when these events took place.

A good way to introduce the essay is to explain how difficult or easy life seems to you. Then, write a thesis statement that contrasts your life with the life of the other person. Put the thesis at the end of your introduction. For example, say you start by complaining about the difficult courses you are taking, the many hours you work as a cashier, or the fact that you drive an old car. The thesis at the end of this introduction might be: "My life may be hard, but I count my blessings when I think about the sacrifices my cousin made to get through college."

However you begin, make the events you narrate in the body of your essay illustrate or prove your thesis. If they don't, revise the thesis or rewrite the body of the paper to include details that relate to the thesis more directly. Conclude your essay by explaining what this assignment has taught you about yourself or your society.

Finally, rewrite and edit the finished product. Make sure your information is well organized, your language is vivid and clear, and your grammar, sentence structure, punctuation, and spelling are correct.

5. Have you ever been treated unfairly, belittled, or held back because of your race, religion, nationality, physical handicap, personal belief, or any other reason? Tell your story vividly and completely. In the process, explain what the experience taught you about other people or society in general. Express this idea as your thesis statement somewhere in the essay.

Good examples of essays that use narration to develop a strong thesis statement are Schwartz's "The Colossus in the Kitchen" and Sagan's

"Frederick Douglass: The Path to Freedom." In her first paragraph, Schwartz defines apartheid as "a flaying of the innermost spirit," then uses the rest of her essay to support that idea. In his conclusion, Sagan tells us that "all his life, [Douglass] understood that literacy had been the way out" of bondage. This is the central idea he develops through the narrative.

Begin working by reviewing journal notes you made after reading the works of the authors mentioned above. Then outline and draft your paper. Like Schwartz and Sagan, you can focus on one event. On the other hand, you might narrate two or three events to support your thesis. Either way, include details about the people in your story as you draft or revise. Describe their personalities by revealing what they said or did. Then, as you edit for grammar, punctuation, and spelling, pay special attention to the vocabulary you have chosen. Include proper nouns as appropriate, and make sure your language is specific and vivid.

6. Did you respond to the first of the Suggestions for Journal Entries after "Faith of the Father"? If so, use the details you collected to get started on an essay that tells a humorous incident you witnessed or took part in during a religious, political, academic, or other kind of ritual, ceremony, or formal event.

Like Pickering, describe both the setting and the people of your story. Use dialogue whenever you can, and identify specific places and things—like the hymns in "Faith of the Father"—that will make your writing realistic and convincing.

A good way to introduce this essay is to describe a scene or to make a startling remark. You might conclude by using a quotation readers will remember, looking to the future, or offering advice.

When it comes time to rewrite your first draft, replace flat, uninteresting vocabulary with forceful verbs and vivid adjectives. Add transitions to make your story easy to follow. Use as much detail as needed to help your readers see the event as you did. If you write a truly entertaining paper, share it with your friends and family. First, however, remove any mechanical or stylistic errors that would reduce your essay's effect on them.

7. If you responded to the second journal suggestion after Pickering's essay, expand your entry into a full-length essay. Tell a story that will allow your readers to understand what religion meant for you when you were a child. Like Pickering, you need not have had an active role in the event or events you are narrating. Just make sure that what you write will be vivid and clear enough to explain the part religion played (and perhaps still plays) in your life.

If you run short on details, try interviewing others who witnessed or took part in what occurred. Otherwise, follow the advice offered in Suggestion 6 above.

8. Have you ever witnessed or experienced a car accident, robbery, mugging, house fire, serious injury, sudden illness, or other violence or misfortune? Tell what happened during this terrible experience and describe the people involved. However, spend most of your time discussing the reactions of people who looked on as the event took place. Were you one of them? What did they do or say? What didn't they do that they should have done?

  You might find inspiration and information for this project in the journal entries you made after reading the essay by Schwartz. Before you write your first draft, however, think about what the event itself and the onlookers' reactions taught you about human nature. Were you encouraged or disappointed by what you learned? Express your answer in a preliminary thesis statement. Write at least two drafts of your story, and make sure to include details that will support this thesis.

  Then revise at least one more time by turning what you have just written into a letter to the editor of your college or community newspaper. Use your letter to explain your approval or disappointment about the way the onlookers reacted, but don't mention their names. If appropriate, offer suggestions about the way your readers might respond if faced with an experience like the one you have narrated. Whether or not you send your letter to a newspaper, edit it carefully, just as if it were going to be published.

Writing to Learn: A Group Activity

Carl Sagan's "The Path to Freedom" explains how Frederick Douglass threw off the chains of slavery. However, there is more to know about Douglass's role in the freeing of other slaves and the abolition of slavery in general. Indeed, Douglass was part of an enormously important movement in American history, the particulars of which should never be forgotten. As such, your writing group might compile a list of people, events, and organizations important to the long struggle that resulted in the abolition of slavery.

THE FIRST MEETING

Assign each student to research four or five people, organizations, or developments that played a role in the struggle to abolish slavery. Limit your searches to topics that can be discussed in two or three paragraphs. Do not try to research complex topics such as the Civil War, for example. Below is a list of people, legal cases, laws, and organizations you might want to learn more about. Of course, you may want to add to this list:

John Brown	Nat Turner	Fugitive Slave Laws
Anthony Burns	*Amistad* Case	Kansas-Nebraska Act

Cassius Marcellus Clay	*Creole* Case	Missouri Compromise
Frederick Douglass	*Dred Scott* Decision	Underground Railroad
William Lloyd Garrison	Emancipation Proclamation	American Anti-Slavery Society
Abraham Lincoln	Fourteenth Amendment to the U.S. Constitution	Free-Soil Party
Lucretia Coffin Mott		Society of Friends
Harriet Tubman		*The Liberator*
Sojourner Truth		

RESEARCH

Print sources in your library's reference section should provide you with all the information you will need. However, many sites on the Internet also discuss topics in the list above. You might want to research each of these topics individually or search for terms such as *slavery* or *abolitionist movement*. In addition, your library should have a large variety of books that will help. Here are just five to look for:

Bontemps, Anna, *100 Years of Negro Freedom,* 1980

Blackett, R. J. M., *Beating against the Barriers,* 1986

Du Bois, W. E. B., *The Souls of Black Folk,* first published in 1903

Ebony editors, *Ebony Pictorial History of Black America,* 1971

Hughes, Langston, *A Pictorial History of Black America,* 1956, 1983

You are sure to find others in your library's catalog of books.

Take good notes on each topic you research. Try to focus on information that explains what made that person, organization, or development important to the struggle for freedom. Then put the notes you have taken on each topic into a well-developed paragraph or two. Each topic you discuss will become one entry in the glossary or listing your group is compiling.

Make enough copies of each entry you write to share with members of your group at your next meeting.

THE SECOND MEETING

Distribute and read each other's entries. Make suggestions for improvement in content. Make certain every entry explains the importance of the topic discussed to the eventual abolition of slavery. Assign each student the task of revising his or her work and of bringing copies to distribute at the next meeting.

THE THIRD MEETING

Distribute revised copies of the work you discussed during the second meeting. This time, make suggestions that will help the writer edit and proofread his or her work. Assign one person to collect the finished entries in a few days and to put them in alphabetical order before submitting them to the instructor.

Exposition

Many new writers begin to develop their skills by practicing the kinds of writing found in Section Three: Description and Narration. As you learned in previous chapters, description and narration usually involve writing about subjects that are concrete and, often, very specific—people, places, events, or objects that the reader can picture or understand easily. The primary purpose of description, of course, is to explain what someone or something looked like, sounded like, and so forth. The primary purpose of narration is simply to tell what happened, although many short stories and narrative essays do a great deal more.

At times, however, new writers face the challenge of discussing abstract ideas that can't be explained through narration and description alone. In such cases, they must rely on a variety of methods of development and techniques associated with exposition. *Exposition* is writing that explains.

Each essay selection in Chapters 10, 11, and 12 explains an abstract idea by using illustration, comparison and contrast, or process analysis as its *primary* method of development. However, these selections also rely on other methods explained earlier in this book (see Chapter 3). In fact, most writers of exposition combine methods to develop ideas clearly and convincingly. Comparison-and-contrast papers frequently contain definitions, anecdotes, and examples; process analyses include accurate, sometimes vivid descriptions; and illustration essays sometimes use comparisons, anecdotes, and descriptions.

Whatever your purpose and however you choose to develop ideas, you will have to know your subject well, include enough accurate information to make your writing convincing, and present that information in a way that is clear and easy to follow.

Explaining through Illustration

One of the most popular ways to explain an idea is illustration, a method of development you read about in Chapter 3. Illustration uses examples to turn an idea that is general, abstract, or hard to understand into something readers can recognize and, therefore, grasp more easily. As the word implies, an illustration is a concrete and specific picture of an idea that would otherwise have remained vague and undefined.

For instance, if you wanted a clearer and more definitive notion of what your friend meant when she claimed to have met several "interesting characters" since coming to school, you might ask her to describe a few of those characters specifically and to show you in what ways they were interesting. Each of the people she discussed would then serve as an illustration or picture of what she meant by the abstract word *interesting*.

Explaining through Comparison and Contrast

This method of development involves pointing out similarities or differences, or both, between two people, objects, places, experiences, ways of doing something, and the like. Writers compare (point out similarities between) and contrast (point out differences between) two things to make one or both more recognizable or understandable to their readers. Let's say you want to explain a computer monitor to someone who has never seen one. You might compare it with a television set. After all, both have glass screens on which electronic images appear. To make your explanation more complete and accurate, however, you might also need to contrast these two devices by pointing out that only on television can one watch a baseball game, a soap opera, or reruns of *I Love Lucy*. Contrast also comes in handy when you want to explain why you believe one thing is better than another. For example, "Watch the Cart!" an essay in the introduction to Chapter 11, points out differences to explain why the author thinks women are more adept at grocery shopping than men.

There are many reasons for comparing or contrasting the subjects you wish to write about. Whatever your purpose, you may find that comparing or contrasting will help you bring abstract ideas into sharper focus and make them more concrete than if you had discussed each of your subjects separately.

Explaining through Process Analysis

Process analysis is used in scientific writing to help readers understand both natural and technical processes such as the formation of rain clouds, the circulation of blood through the body, or the workings of a CD player, for example. However, it also has a place in nonscientific writing. For example, you might want to use process analysis to explain how U.S. presidents are elected, how money is transferred from one bank to another electronically, or even how your Aunt Millie manages to turn the most solemn occasion into a party.

Process analysis is useful when you need to provide the reader with directions or instructions to complete a specific task. Subjects for such essays might include "how to change the brakes on a Ford Mustang," "how to bake lasagna," or "how to get to school from the center of town."

In each of these examples, the writer is assigning him- or herself the task of explaining, as specifically and as clearly as possible, an idea that might be very new and unfamiliar to the reader. And, in each case, the essay will focus on how to do something or how something is done.

Though it may often seem deceptively simple, writing a process paper is often a painstaking task and must be approached carefully. Remember that your readers might be totally unfamiliar with what you're explaining and will need a great deal of information to follow the process easily and to understand it thoroughly.

As a matter of fact, the need to be clear and concrete often causes writers of process analysis to rely on other methods of development as well. Among them are narration, description, illustration, and comparison and contrast. Of these, writers of process analysis rely most heavily on narration. After all, a process is a story. Like narratives, process papers are often organized in chronological order and explain a series of events. Unlike narratives, however, process essays don't simply tell *what* happens; they also explain *how* something happens or *how* something should be done.

CHAPTER 10

Illustration

You have learned that the most interesting and effective writing uses specific and concrete details to *show* rather than to *tell* the reader something. This goes for all types of writing, including exposition. One of the best ways to show your readers what you mean is to fill your writing with clear, relevant examples. Examples are also referred to as *illustrations*. They act as pictures—concrete representations—of an abstract idea you are trying to explain, and they make your writing easier to understand and more convincing for your readers. Illustration can be used as the primary method to develop a thesis in your expository writing.

Effective illustrations make reference to specific people, places, and things—familiar realities that your readers will recognize or understand easily. Say that you want to convince them that your 2002 Wizbang is an economical car. Instead of being content to rely on their understanding of a vague word like *economical,* you decide to provide examples that show exactly what you think this term means. Therefore, you explain that the Wizbang gets about 65 miles per gallon around town, that its purchase price is $4,000 less than its least expensive competitor's, and that it needs only one $50 tune-up every 40,000 miles. Now that's economical!

Several types of examples are discussed below. The important thing to remember is that the examples you choose must relate to and be appropriate to the idea you're illustrating. For instance, you probably wouldn't cite statistics about the Wizbang's safety record if you wanted to impress your readers with how inexpensive the car is to own and operate.

Specific Facts, Instances, or Occurrences

A good way to get examples into your writing is to use specific facts, instances, or occurrences relating to the idea you are explaining. Let's say you want to prove that the Wizbang does not perform well in bad weather. You can say it stalled twice during a recent rainstorm or that it did not start when the temperature fell below freezing last week. If you want to show that people in your town are community-minded, you might mention that they recently opened a shelter for the homeless, that they have organized a meals-on-wheels program for the elderly, or that they have increased their contributions to the United Way campaign in each of the last five years. If you want to prove that the 1960s were years of turmoil, you can recall the assassinations of John and Robert Kennedy and Martin Luther King, Jr., the antiwar marches, and the urban riots.

The selections in this chapter use specific facts, instances, or occurrences to illustrate and develop ideas. Grace Lukawska's "Wolf" is full of revealing facts about this animal. Specific instances and occurrences can be found in Irina Groza's "Growing Up in Romania" and in Philip K. Howard's "The Death of Common Sense." In "Names," Jonathan Kozol recalls the wonderful names of children he has met to illustrate the aspirations, challenges, and values of inner-city families.

Statistics

Mathematical figures, or statistics, can also be included to strengthen your reader's understanding of an abstract idea. If you want to prove that the cost of living in your hometown has increased dramatically over the last five years, you might explain that the price of a three-bedroom home has increased by about 30 percent, from $100,000 to $130,000, that real estate taxes have doubled from an average of $1,500 per family to $3,000 per family, and that the cost of utilities has nearly tripled, with each household now spending about $120 per month on heat and electricity. Philip K. Howard's "The Death of Common Sense" makes good use of statistics.

Specific People, Places, or Things

Mentioning specific people, places, and things familiar to the readers can also help you make abstract ideas easier to understand and more convincing. If you want to explain that the American South is famous for the presidents and states-people it has produced, you might bring up George Washington, Thomas Jefferson, Henry Clay, Lyndon Johnson, Martin Luther King, and Jimmy Carter. If you need to convince readers that your city is a great place to have fun, you will probably mention its amusement park, professional football stadium, brand-new children's zoo and aquarium, community swimming pool, campgrounds, and public golf courses. Specific people, places, and things are mentioned throughout Howard's "The Death of Common Sense."

Anecdotes

As you probably know, anecdotes are brief, informative stories that develop an idea or drive home a point. They are similar to and serve the same purpose as specific instances and occurrences, and they are sometimes used with such il-lustrations to develop an idea more fully. However, anecdotes often appear in greater detail than other types of examples. Look for anecdotes especially in Groza's "Growing Up in Romania," Howard's "The Death of Common Sense," and Howe's "Covert Force," an essay about women who, disguised as men, fought in the Civil War.

Visualizing Examples

The following paragraphs are from Alleen Pace Nilsen's "Sexism in English: A 1990's Update." They explain interesting facts about etymology, the origins of words.

States her thesis.

. . . in American culture a woman is valued for the attractiveness and sexiness of her body, while a man is valued for his physical strength and accomplishments. A woman is sexy; a man is successful.

A persuasive piece of evidence supporting this view are the eponyms——words that have come from someone's name——found in English.

Creates an interesting contrast.

[After researching this subject] I had a two-and-a-half-inch stack of cards taken from men's names, but less than a half-inch stack from women's names, and most of those came from Greek mythology. In words that

Uses specific instances.

came into American English since we separated from Britain, there are many eponyms based on the names of famous American men: bartlett pear, boysenberry, diesel engine, franklin stove, ferris wheel, gatling gun, mason jar, sideburns, sousaphone, Schick test, and Winchester rifle. The only common eponyms taken from

Mentions specific people.

American women's names are *Alice blue* (after Alice Roosevelt Longworth), *bloomers* (after Amelia Jenks Bloomer) and *Mae West jacket* (after the buxom actress). Two out of the three feminine eponyms relate closely to a woman's physical anatomy, while the masculine eponyms (except for sideburns after General Burnsides) have nothing to do with the namesake's body, but instead honor the man for an accomplishment of some kind.

Although in Greek mythology women played a bigger role than they did in the biblical stories of the Judeo-Christian

Mentions specific mythological figures; mentions things readers will recognize.

cultures . . . the same tendency to think of women in relation to sexuality is seen in the eponyms *aphrodisiac* from Aphrodite, the Greek name for the goddess of love and beauty, and venereal disease, from Venus, the Roman name for Aphrodite.

Another interesting word from Greek mythology is *Amazon*. According to Greek folk etymology, the *a* means "without" as in *atypical* or *amoral* while *mazon* comes from *mazos,* meaning breast as still seen in *mastectomy.* In the Greek legend, Amazon women cut off their right breasts so that

Tells an anecdote.

they could better shoot their bows. Apparently, the story tellers had a feeling that for women to play the active, "masculine" role that the Amazons adopted for themselves, they had to trade in part of their femininity.

Revising Illustration Essays

Before writing "Wolf," student Grace Lukawska had completed a great deal of prewriting in her journal to get started. When she finished her first draft, however, she realized she would have to add more detail, restructure her essay, and improve some of her word choices to make her point effectively. By the time she finished, she had written several drafts, but the final product shows that careful revision is always worth the effort. Read these paragraphs from two versions of the complete paper, which appears in this chapter. Information in parentheses refers to Candace Savage's *Wolves*, a book in which Lukawska researched facts about her subject.

Lukawska—Rough Draft

Make introduction more interesting?

There are still popular misconceptions of the wolf as predator. Many people think that wolves kill for pleasure or just to show their dominance over other animals.

Include vivid details and examples to explain misconceptions?

However, the truth is that wolves are very fascinating and intelligent.

Their intelligence manifests itself in their behavior. Wolves belong to a group of animals who live in hierarchical groups. According to Candace Savage, a large, well-organized pack consists of an upper class——parents, a middle class——uncles and aunts, a lower class——children, and finally "helpers"

For what? Explain?

who are inexperienced hunters and who depend on the pack (55). Their role is to baby-sit youngsters while the other wolves are hunting (62).

Another example of wolves' aptitude is clear communication. The leader of the

Does this relate to communication?

group, usually the male, establishes regulations so that each animal knows whom it can boss and to whom it must <u>submit</u>. For instance, a middle-class wolf must obey the leader's orders; children and helpers must <u>submit</u> to their relatives. These rules help to prevent fights or disagreements in packs.

Say more about their language? Use examples?

Furthermore, wolves have their own language which is based on different sound levels in their voices. For example, according to Savage, a whimper indicates a friendly attitude; snarls convey warnings and admonitions (58).

Lukawska—Final Draft

For centuries, popular misconceptions have pictured the wolf as a terrifying predator

Creates vivid images that serve as examples.

that kills for pleasure. The name itself calls up nasty images: the glutton who "wolfs" down his food; the werewolf, who, during a full moon, grows hair all over his body, howls into the night, and claws

Mentions specific story, which readers might recognize

beautiful maidens to death. Even in fairy tales, such as "Little Red Riding Hood," the wolf is pictured as shrewd and bloodthirsty.

Makes thesis clearer, stronger.

But is the wolf really a cold-blooded killer? Not at all; the wolf is a magnificent animal which displays many of the characteristics we value in human beings.

The intelligence of the wolf manifests
itself in its behavior. The wolf's society
is well organized and hierarchical.

Mentions title of Savage's book.

According to Candace Savage, author of
Wolves,   a pack consists of an upper class——
parents, a middle class——uncles and aunts, a
lower class——children, and finally "helpers,"

Becomes more specific.

who are inexperienced hunters and <u>who depend</u>
<u>upon the pack for their food (55)</u>. Their
role is to baby-sit youngsters while the
other wolves are hunting (62). Like humans,
wolves practice adoption. If parents die,
their children are cared for by another
family.

New paragraph explains behavior, not communication.

The leader of the group, usually a male,
establishes regulations so that each animal
knows whom it can boss and to whom it must
submit. For instance, a middle-class wolf
must obey the leader's orders; children and
helpers must submit to their relatives.
This rule helps prevent disagreements and
fights.

Creates a new paragraph to discuss communication. Expands her discussion.

Another indication of the wolf's
intelligence is the ability to communicate.
Wolves have their own language, which is
based on the use of different intonations.
According to Savage, a whimper communicates
friendship, snarls convey warnings and
admonishments, and a "special chirplike tone

expresses sexual interest" (58). Like

dogs, wolves also use gestures and facial

Uses description to create examples. expressions to communicate. <u>By moving their</u>

<u>foreheads, mouths, ears, and eyes, they</u>

express their emotions and announce their

ranks. Frightened wolves keep their teeth

covered, "eyes slightly closed, ears flat to

the head" (Savage 55). They also bend their

legs and tuck in their tails. Wolves that

are self-confident, on the other hand, point

their ears forward and bare their teeth.

Includes concrete, specific vocabulary. Wolves of the highest rank reveal their

positions by <u>keeping their tails and ears up</u>

and by <u>looking directly</u> into the eyes of

other animals. Members of the pack show

respect for them; like dogs, they keep their

ears tucked in, their heads down, and their

legs slightly bent.

Practicing Illustration

Examples can be defined as concrete signs of abstract ideas. Below are several topic sentences expressing abstract ideas. Use the spaces below each to write a paragraph relating to each sentence. Develop your paragraph by using at least three examples of the kinds you have just read about. First, however, make a quick list of the examples you will use on a sheet of scratch paper. You can discuss them in detail when it comes time to write the paragraph.

Feel free to reword these sentences any way you like.

1. Wherever you go these days, people seem to be recycling.

   _____

   _____

_____

_____

_____

_____

_____

_____

_____

2. Some people I know are very materialistic.

_____

_____

_____

_____

_____

_____

_____

_____

3. A friend of mine often engages in self-destructive behavior.

_____

_____

_____

_____

_____

_____

_____

_____

4. _____(name a person) succeeds at whatever sport (or other type of activity) he (or she) pursues.

_____

_____

_____

_____

_____

_____

_____

_____

_____

5. Electronic devices play important roles in the modern home.

_____

_____

_____

_____

_____

_____

_____

6. People in my town seem to be getting richer and richer (or poorer and poorer).

_____

_____

_____

_____

_____

_____

_____

The illustrations found throughout this chapter make the abstract ideas they explain more interesting, more believable, and more easily understood. Keep this in mind as you read the essays that follow and especially as you begin to use illustration in your own writing.

Wolf

Grace Lukawska

Born in Boleslawiec, Poland, Grace Lukawska came to the United States in 1986. After studying English for speakers of other languages, she enrolled in a developmental writing course in which she wrote this paper. In Poland, Lukawska had seen many television specials on wild animals. When asked to write about a fascinating animal, she immediately thought of the wolf. Lukawska is now a medical assistant.

Preparing to Read

1. The author develops this essay with examples, but she also uses comparison and description.

2. Pay particular attention to the essay's good organization. Consider what Lukawska has done to keep her essay focused.

3. "Getting Started," the introductory chapter of this book, explains that summarizing written materials is a good way to gather information. Another is to quote directly from a source. Lukawska summarizes and quotes directly from Candace Savage's *Wolves.* She credits this book by indicating in parentheses the pages from which she took information. These entries are called parenthetical (internal) citations. She also provides full bibliographical information about the book at the end of her paper. You can learn more about crediting sources in the Appendix at the end of this textbook.

Vocabulary

admonishments (noun)	Condemnations, rebukes.
attribute (verb)	Associate with, blame for.
glutton (noun)	Someone who eats too much.
hierarchical (adjective)	Arranged by rank or importance.
intonations (noun)	Levels of sound, pitches.
manifests (verb)	Shows.
misconceptions (noun)	Incorrect opinions.
solidarity (noun)	Unity, mutual support, togetherness.

Wolf

Grace Lukawska

FOR CENTURIES, POPULAR misconceptions have pictured the wolf as a terrifying 1
predator that kills for pleasure. The name itself calls up nasty images: the
glutton who "wolfs" down his food; the werewolf, who, during a full moon,
grows hair all over his body, howls into the night, and claws beautiful maidens
to death. Even in fairy tales, such as "Little Red Riding Hood," the wolf is pictured as shrewd and bloodthirsty. But is the wolf really a cold-blooded killer?
Not at all; the wolf is a magnificent animal which displays many of the characteristics we value in human beings.

The intelligence of the wolf manifests itself in its behavior. The wolf's soci- 2
ety is well organized and hierarchical. According to Candace Savage, author of
Wolves, a pack consists of an upper class—parents, a middle class—uncles and
aunts, a lower class—children, and finally "helpers," who are inexperienced
hunters and who depend upon the pack for their food (55). Their role is to
baby-sit youngsters while the other wolves are hunting (62). Like humans,
wolves practice adoption. If parents die, their children are cared for by another
family.

The leader of the group, usually a male, establishes regulations so that each 3
animal knows whom it can boss and to whom it must submit. For instance, a
middle-class wolf must obey the leader's orders; children and helpers must submit to their relatives. This rule helps prevent disagreements and fights.

Another indication of the wolf's intelligence is the ability to communicate. 4
Wolves have their own language, which is based on the use of different intonations. According to Savage, a whimper communicates friendship, snarls convey
warnings and admonishments, and a "special chirplike tone expresses sexual interest" (58). Like dogs, wolves also use gestures and facial expressions to communicate. By moving their foreheads, mouths, ears, and eyes, they express their
emotions and announce their ranks. Frightened wolves keep their teeth covered,
"eyes slightly closed, ears flat to the head" (Savage 55). They also bend their legs
and tuck in their tails. Wolves that are self-confident, on the other hand, point
their ears forward and bare their teeth. Wolves of the highest rank reveal their
positions by keeping their tails and ears up and by looking directly into the eyes
of other animals. Members of the pack show respect for them; like dogs, they
keep their ears tucked in, their heads down, and their legs slightly bent.

Like people, wolves are sociable. In a group, they constantly check one an- 5
other by sniffing. To show affection, they nuzzle each other as if to kiss. To express hostility, they lick their cheeks, wag their tails, howl, and even stick out
their tongues. This kind of behavior serves not only to locate companions outside the pack but also to mark their territory and tell enemies of the family's sol-
idarity (Savage 59).

Regardless of rank or age, wolves enjoy playing games with other members   6
of their pack. Even the leader, who may appear to be aggressive and ruthless,
takes an active part in these activities, which include chasing one another and
rolling over. Another sign of intelligence, such exercises not only give them
pleasure, but also help them keep physically fit.

Wolves are natural-born strategists and planners. Hunting a large animal   7
like a deer or moose is very dangerous for a single wolf. Therefore, they hunt
in groups. After locating a herd, one might act as a decoy to draw males away
from the herd while the rest single out and attack the victim. Wolves kill only
weak or sick animals, and they never kill more than they need. In case there is
any excess, leftovers are buried near their dens.

The reputation from which wolves suffer is undeserved and unfair. Wolves   8
can be violent, and they are terrifying hunters. But they kill only to feed and
protect their families; they never commit distinctly "human" crimes such as
murder, theft, and rape. Wolves are not bloodthirsty monsters that should be
feared and eradicated. They are magnificent animals, and they deserve their
place on earth.

Works Cited: Savage, Candace. *Wolves.* San Francisco: Sierra Club, 1980.

Read More on the Web

NOVA site on wolves in the wild: http://www.pbs.org/wgbh/nova/wolves/
howl.html

International Wolf Center site: http://www.wolf.org/wolves/

Questions for Discussion

1. In Preparing to Read, you were asked what the author did to keep
   this essay focused and organized. What is the essay's thesis? What
   techniques does she use to maintain unity and coherence?
2. What kinds of examples does Lukawska rely on most in this essay?
   Does she ever refer to specific persons, places, or things?
3. Where in this essay does she use comparison?
4. Where does she create verbal images? Why are they so effective?
5. What techniques for writing introductions and conclusions has
   Lukawska used? (Check Chapter 4 if you need to review these
   techniques.)

Thinking Critically

1. Consider another animal that has a bad reputation: a rat, a snake, a bat, a pig, a spider, or some other unpopular beast. Then in a paragraph or two discuss the positive qualities of this creature. For example, many people hate and fear rats, but laboratory rats play an important role in medical research.

2. Reread Lukawska's introduction. Then list other examples that would illustrate the popular misconception of wolves as bloodthirsty monsters.

3. The author suggests that human beings can sometimes be more beastly than the beasts. What does she mean? Do you agree? Can you provide some examples?

Suggestions for Journal Entries

1. Think of an animal or species of animal you know well—your Siamese cat or all domestic cats, the neighbor's German shepherd or all shepherds, a bird that often visits your backyard or all common birds. List important things you know about this creature—anything that would provide clues about its behavior, lifestyle, or personality.

   Then ask yourself what this information tells you. Draw three or more general conclusions about the animal from the details you have listed. Write these conclusions in the form of topic sentences for paragraphs that you might later develop in an essay.

2. Are human families as well organized and as close as the wolf family? Think of your own family. Then write a paragraph in which you use illustrations to evaluate the kind of family to which you belong. Perhaps the best types of illustrations to use are anecdotes taken from your own experiences.

Growing Up in Romania

Irina Groza

When Irina Groza was a girl, Romania was a communist country, where personal freedom and economic opportunity were in short supply. Like other countries behind the iron curtain, Romania made it difficult for people to leave. But Groza was one of the lucky ones, and she was able to immigrate to the United States. Today, she is a registered nurse and is raising a family.

Preparing to Read

1. Groza shows that personal experience can be a rich source of illustrations to develop an abstract idea. She fills her essay with specific instances and anecdotes that explain how horrible life in Romania had become under a tyrannical and incompetent government.

2. Several types of writing can be used together to make a successful essay. Groza relies heavily on examples but also includes narrative and descriptive details.

3. In 1990, communist governments across eastern Europe fell from power. In Romania, dictator Nicolae Ceaușescu, his wife, and several members of his government were tried and executed for crimes against the people they had oppressed for over 30 years.

Vocabulary

brutalize (verb)	Treat cruelly or violently.
classics (noun)	Important and lasting works of literature.
compliance (noun)	Submission, agreement.
cult (noun)	Excessive or unnatural devotion to a person or idea.
egomania (noun)	Extreme pride and self-concern.
flawed (adjective)	Defective, faulty.
ideology (noun)	Ideas, beliefs, philosophy.
impoverishing (noun)	Making poor.
indoctrinate (verb)	Drill into, force to believe.
inflicted (verb)	Imposed.
jeopardy (noun)	Danger, risk.
magnitude (noun)	Size, extent.
prey on (verb)	Persecute, attack, victimize.
purge (verb)	Remove, eliminate.
regime (noun)	Government, rule.
stature (noun)	Standing, reputation.
suppress (verb)	Dominate, control.

Growing Up in Romania

Irina Groza

I GREW UP in a beautiful Transylvanian city called Arad, just a few miles from the Hungarian border. In the mid-fifties, when I was born, Romania was still recovering from the Second World War, and people were working hard to rebuild their country. I was in the third grade when our beloved president, Gheorghe Gheorghiu-Dej, died. He was succeeded by Nicolae Ceaușescu, a young and ambitious general who promised us a bright future. At his election, no one was able to foresee the magnitude of his egomania, ruthlessness, and incompetence. The tyranny that followed nearly destroyed Romania and inflicted widespread suffering on its people for many years.

At the beginning of Ceaușescu's presidency, life was still good. I remember going into town with my mother. The streets were busy places, filled with people who were smiling and laughing as they went about their business. The shops contained plenty of food; people stood in line only to buy fresh milk and bread. Slowly, however, certain foods began to disappear from store shelves and counters. It became much harder to get meat and fresh vegetables. Consumer goods such as clothing and small appliances became scarce. I heard my mother complain about the new president, but as a child I did not find these problems significant.

Then I started noticing a change in our school books. National heroes like Michael Eminescu and George Cosbuc, who had once been glorified, were deleted from our history texts. George Enescu and other great Romanian writers, artists, and musicians, who had been the symbols of our culture, were hardly mentioned. Classics were removed from our school library, and its shelves were overloaded with books about the new president and his regime. He was portrayed as a hero of the people who had fought for communism, but he was a hero we had never heard of before. School children had to take courses in politics designed to indoctrinate them with Ceaușescu's diseased ideology. We were forced to memorize his speeches, which were full of lies about the progress and prosperity his government had brought to Romania. Before long this sickening personality cult became obvious to everyone, and we knew that our country and our culture were being polluted by this madman.

Before long, new laws restricting people's personal freedom were put into effect. One of these prohibited travel outside the country, and Romanians found themselves prisoners in their own country. Another law required every family to have at least four children. Ceaușescu believed that increasing the population would make Romania powerful and increase his stature in the world. All contraceptives were removed from the shelves, and doctors who performed abortions were severely punished. But many people could not afford to support large families and were forced to turn their children over to state orphanages. As shown in recent news releases, these places were badly run and unsanitary. In fact, many of the children housed there contracted AIDS.

In another attempt to suppress the people and to destroy their spirit, the   5
government began a campaign to discourage church attendance. Celebrations
of religious holidays were prohibited, and people who openly expressed their
faith put themselves in jeopardy. One day a police officer stopped me and
ridiculed me in front of my friends because I was wearing a cross around my
neck. I felt embarrassed and angry, but there was nothing I could do. I had
heard that many people had been beaten by the police, and we lived in constant fear of them. Those who continued to oppose the system were thrown into
jail or put into mental institutions.

As soon as Ceauşescu took office, he began to purge those in the govern-   6
ment who might oppose him, and he surrounded himself with his supporters.
He also established the *Securitate,* a secret police force, which drew to its ranks
many misfits who were greedy for power and who had the stomach to swal-
low the government's lies. No special training was required of these people,
just blind compliance to the will of the regime and a desire to brutalize people. Members of the *Securitate* were privileged: they shopped in their own
well-supplied stores, and their salaries were about six times those of medical
doctors.

The *Securitate* was Ceauşescu's tool for holding down opposition to a   7
regime that the people knew was a miserable failure and that had succeeded
only in impoverishing the country and subjecting us to extreme economic
hardship. People worked hard, but the lines at food stores became longer and
longer. There were severe shortages of meat, milk, butter, flour, soap, deter-
gent, toothpaste, gasoline, and medical supplies. No one could understand
why a country that was so rich in natural resources and that possessed so many
acres of fertile farmland was unable to feed its people or supply them with simple necessities.

One reason was that Ceauşescu had broken the people's spirit. Another   8
had to do with his insane plan to crowd Romania's growing population into
large cities. On the outskirts of Arad were many private homes, each of which
sat on land of between half an acre and an acre. One year, the government decided to take this land from us and to build high-rise apartments on it. Neither
we nor our neighbors got paid for our property. On top of everything else, we
had to clear the land ourselves by cutting down our many fruit trees. Up to that
point, we had been able to supplement our food with the fruits and vegetables
we grew in our garden and with the animals we raised. But then the situation
became desperate, and we were barely able to feed ourselves. The president's
iron hand was felt by everyone, and hatred of him grew in everybody's heart.

Like everyone else, I missed the necessities that Ceauşescu's flawed eco-   9
nomic policy had taken from us. But I did not realize how badly the government
had mismanaged its finances and how corrupt it had become until my mother
became ill. Already retired by the time I left high school, she was suffering from
high blood pressure and had a heart condition. In an emergency, when I had to
call an ambulance, I was told to lie about my mother's age. Medical emergency

squads had been instructed not to pick up retired people. If they were left to die, the government would no longer have to pay their pensions.

As the economic crisis got worse and shortages of important supplies in- 10 creased, the crime rate began to soar. Alcohol abuse became a problem, as did theft, burglary, and assault. But the *Securitate* were busy searching for people who committed political crimes, and real criminals were given a free hand to prey on decent people. In fact, the police often paid common criminals to act as their informants.

I was seventeen and still in high school when I started working in a huge 11 textile factory. Once in the factory, no one was able to leave before quitting time unless he or she got a special pass from the boss. Every two weeks, we had to stay late to attend Communist Party indoctrination sessions. During these absurd meetings, the factory doors were locked, and no one was per-mitted to leave.

Our regular work week was six days long, but my boss often required us 12 to work on Sundays as well. In the beginning, I refused the overtime, remind-ing the boss that, according to our constitution, I had to work only six days a week. He in turn reminded me that if I refused overtime I could be assigned to the worst area in the factory. At this point, I had no choice but to accept the overtime, which paid the same wages as work on any other day.

Each day before we left the factory, we had to go through a room where 13 women guards body-searched us. One day, a guard thought that I was acting suspiciously and brought me to a special room where she asked me to remove all my clothes to see if I was hiding stolen material. I could not have concealed much under the thin summer dress I was wearing. She knew that because she had already body-searched me and had found nothing. I refused to obey. To clear myself, I called on another guard to search me again. At that moment, I felt embarrassment and outrage; I knew that the guard's purpose was only to exercise her power by humiliating whomever she wanted to.

My story is not unique. Ceauşescu's government tried to strip all Romani- 14 ans of their dignity, pride, and freedom. Everyone suffered in some way, and everyone has a personal tragedy to tell. As for me, I could not continue to live under the constant humiliation and the severe restrictions on personal freedom that I have described. I remember looking at the birds and envying them be-cause they were free to go anywhere in the world.

I promised myself I would never have children in Romania because I did 15 not want them to suffer as I had. In 1977, with the help of a brother who was living in the United States, I had the opportunity to leave. The day I emigrated, the course of my life changed for the better though my heart broke for those I left behind. Now, however, new hope blossoms for Romania. In December 1990, as part of the overthrow of corrupt communist governments across east-ern Europe, the people deposed the Ceauşescu regime and established a democracy.

Read More on the Web

History House site comparing Roman emperor Caligula and Ceauşescu:
  http://www.historyhouse.com/in_history/ceausescu/

History Guide lecture on fall of communism in Eastern Europe:
  http://www.historyguide.org/europe/lecture16.html#ceausescu

Comprehensive profile of life in Romania under Ceauşescu:
  http://www.enzia.com/Pages/Rev4.html

Questions for Discussion

1. Find Groza's thesis statement. What are the three main points she
    makes about Ceauşescu's government?
2. Which examples in this essay do you think best illustrate each of
    those three points?
3. How does Groza explain that Romania, a land rich in natural
    resources, was unable to feed its people?
4. What kind of people did the Ceauşescu government employ to
    carry out its policies? What examples of such people does Groza
    provide?
5. Why does she include details about life in Romania before Ceauşescu
    came to power?
6. How does Groza show that life in Romania was difficult for other
    people as well as for her?

Thinking Critically

1. In what way is this essay similar to Scamacca's "Oma," a selection that
    appears in Chapter 2? Does it discuss similar ideas? What might a
    conversation between Oma and Irina Groza be about?
2. Does this essay discuss ideas similar to those in Howard's "The Death
    of Common Sense," which appears in this chapter? On what points
    might Groza and Howard find agreement?

Suggestions for Journal Entries

1. The government Groza describes is monstrous. Have you ever lived
    under, read about, or heard about a government that suppresses
    personal freedom and keeps its people in fear and poverty as
    Romania's did? If so, use focused freewriting to record one or two
    well-developed examples of how that government treats or treated its
    people.

Another way to approach this assignment is to interview a person who has lived under a dictatorship. Find out what freedoms and opportunities your subject was denied, and explain his or her reaction to living in a country with such a government.

2. One major difference between a democracy and the communist society Groza describes is the freedom to criticize the government. Think of a law, policy, or practice of your government—federal, state, or local—with which you disagree. Brainstorm with others who share your opinion. Together, discuss the ways this law, policy, or practice affects people you know. Then, write down reasons it should be changed. If this topic doesn't interest you, focus on a school policy or regulation you want changed.

The Death of Common Sense

Philip K. Howard

This essay, which appeared in Reader's Digest, *was excerpted in 1995 from a book by the same title. The book's subtitle, which reveals much about its contents, is* How Law Is Suffocating America. *The author is an attorney who has done a great deal of research on the effect of the growing mass of government regulations on every segment of American society.*

Preparing to Read

1. This essay contains a variety of examples: specific instances and occurrences, statistics, and anecdotes. It also mentions familiar persons, places, and things. Look for such examples as you read it.
2. Find places where Howard uses dialogue. Ask yourself how this helps him make his point.
3. What clues about the essay's thesis and contents does the title provide?

Vocabulary

abode (noun)	Home, residence.
citing (adjective)	Criticizing, finding fault with, penalizing.
deplorable (adjective)	Terrible, distressing.
dictates (noun)	Rules, regulations.
edifice (noun)	Building.
explicitly (adverb)	Clearly, in an outspoken manner.
frailty (noun)	Weakness, fragility.
idiosyncrasy (noun)	Individuality, oddity, irregularity.
mammoth (adjective)	Huge.
pH (noun)	A measurement of acidity or alkalinity used in chemistry.
Providence (noun)	Heaven.
saris (noun)	A kind of dress worn by many women in India and Pakistan.
specific gravity (noun)	The mass of a volume of a substance as compared to the mass of an equal volume of water.

The Death of Common Sense

Philip K. Howard

IN THE WINTER of 1988, Mother Teresa's nuns of the Missionaries of Charity   1
walked through the snow in the South Bronx in their saris and sandals looking for abandoned buildings to convert into homeless shelters. They found two,
which New York City offered them at $1 each. The nuns set aside $500,000 for
the reconstruction. Then, for a year and a half, they went from hearing room to
hearing room seeking approval for the project.

Providence, however, was no match for law. New York's building code re-   2
quires an elevator in all new or renovated multiple-story buildings of this type.
Installing an elevator would add upward of $100,000 to the cost. Mother Teresa
didn't want to devote that much money to something that wouldn't really help
the poor. But the nuns were told the law could not be waived even if an elevator did not make sense.

The plan for the shelter was abandoned. In a polite letter to the city, the   3
nuns noted that the episode "served to educate us about the law and its many
complexities."

What the law required offends common sense. After all, there are proba-   4
bly over 100,000 walk-up apartment buildings in New York. But the law, as-
piring to the perfect abode, dictates a model home or no home.

Today, laws control much of our lives: fixing potholes, running schools,   5
regulating day-care centers and the workplace, cleaning up the environment—
and deciding whether Mother Teresa gets a building permit.

Our regulatory system has become an instruction manual, telling us ex-   6
actly what to do and how to do it. The laws have expanded like floodwaters
breaking through a dike—drowning the society we intended to protect.

In 1993, at Long Island's John Marshall Elementary School, the local fire   7
chief appeared around Halloween dressed as Officer McGruff, the police dog
that promotes safety. He noticed all the student art tacked to the walls. Within
days, McGruff had done his duty: the art was gone.

Why? The New York State fire code addresses this public hazard explicitly: 8
"[S]tudent-prepared artwork . . . [must be] at least two feet from the ceilings and
ten feet from exit doors and . . . [must] not exceed 20 percent of the wall area."

No one had ever heard of a fire caused by children's art. The school super-   9
intendent, accused of permitting a legal violation, suggested that he had used
a rule of thumb "on how much to decorate."

Liz Skinner, a first-grade teacher, was confused: "The *essence* of primary   10
education is that children show pride in their work." Now, said one observer,
the school looked "about as inviting as a bomb shelter."

Government has imposed fire codes for centuries. But only our age has   11
succeeded in barring children's art from school walls.

Safety also was the goal of Congress when in 1970 it created the Occupa-   12
tional Safety and Health Administration. For 25 years OSHA has been hard at

work, producing over 4,000 detailed rules that dictate everything from the ideal height of railings (42 inches) to how much a plank can stick out from a temporary scaffold (no more than 12 inches). American industry has spent several hundred billion dollars to comply with OSHA's rules. All this must have done some good.

It hasn't. The rate of workdays missed due to injury is about the same as 13 in 1973. A tour through the Glen-Gery brick factory near Reading, PA, indicates why.

People have been making bricks more or less the same way for thousands 14 of years. No hidden hazards have ever been identified. But OSHA inspectors periodically visit the Glen-Gery factory and walk around with measuring tapes. They are especially interested in railings, citing Glen-Gery for having railings of the wrong height.

Glen-Gery has never had a mishap related to railings. But inspectors won't 15 discuss if a violation actually has anything to do with safety. They are just traffic cops looking for violations. "We've done basically everything they asked for the last 20 years," says Bob Hrasok, Glen-Gery's full-time manager in charge of regulatory compliance.

As a result, warnings are posted everywhere. For example, a large "Haz- 16 ardous Material" sign was placed on one side of a storage shed—holding sand. OSHA categorizes sand as a hazardous material because sand—identical to the beach sand you and I sunbathe on—contains a mineral called silica, which some scientists believe under some conditions might cause cancer.

In 1994, Glen-Gery was required to include with shipments of brick a 17 form describing, for the benefit of workers, how to identify a brick (a "granular solid, essentially odorless," in a "wide range of colors") and giving its specific gravity (approximately 2.6). In fact, OSHA issued 19,233 citations in 1994 for not keeping its forms correctly. According to one expert, filling out these forms takes Americans 54 million hours per year.

Solid, objective rules, like the precise height of railings, satisfy lawmakers' 18 longing for certainty. Human activity, however, cannot be so neatly categorized. And the more precise the rule, the less sensible the law.

Until recently, Dutch Noteboom, 73, owned a small meat-packing plant in 19 Springfield, OR. The U.S. Department of Agriculture (USDA) had one full-time inspector on the premises and one supervisor who visited regularly. This level of attention is somewhat surprising, since Noteboom had only four employees. But the rules required it. Every day the inspector sat there, "often talking on the phone," says Noteboom. But they always found time to cite him for a violation: one was for "loose paint located 20 feet from any animal."

"I was swimming in paper work," says Noteboom. "You should have seen 20 all the USDA manuals. The regulations drove me out of business."

The Soviets tried to run their country like a puppeteer pulling millions of 21 strings. In our country, government's laws have become like millions of tripwires, preventing us from doing the sensible thing.

On the banks of the Mississippi River in Minneapolis, a mountain of 22 75,000 tons of lime sludge was built up over 60 years, the byproduct of a nearby plant. By the early 1980s, it sat in the path of a proposed highway.

Government rules designate any material with a pH of over 12.5 as "haz- 23 ardous waste." That may generally make sense, but not for lime, which is used to improve the environment by lowering the acidity of land and water.

The mountain of lime, whose alkalinity was also raised by dampness, had 24 a pH of 12.7. The highway was stopped dead in its tracks for many months because Minnesota had no licensed hazardous-waste-disposal site for the lime. Eventually, it was pushed onto adjoining land, where, with the help of the sun, it dried its way into lawfulness.

People tend to have their own way of doing things. But law, trying to make 25 sure nothing ever goes wrong, doesn't respect the idiosyncrasy of human accomplishment. It sets forth the approved methods, in black and white, and that's that. When law notices people doing it differently, it mashes them flat.

Gary Crissey and a partner have run a tiny coffee shop in New York's Lit- 26 tle Italy for years. Recently, some customers were dismayed when served with disposable plates and forks. Crissey explained that restaurant inspectors had stopped by and told him the law would not let him operate if he continued to wash dishes by hand. The code requires an automatic dishwasher or a chemical process. But the idea of using chemicals was unappealing, and Crissey's coffee shop is so small that it has no room for a dishwasher. The only solution was disposables. Now everything is plastic.

Today we have a world in which people argue not about right and 27 wrong, but about whether something was done the right way. With enough procedures, it's argued, no bureaucrat will ever again put his hand in the till. And so, by 1994, the Defense Department was spending almost half as much on procedures for travel reimbursement ($1.5 billion) as on travel itself ($3.5 billion).

Plato argued that good people do not need laws to tell them to act respon- 28 sibly, while bad people will find a way around law. By pretending procedure will get rid of corruption, we have succeeded only in humiliating honest people and have provided a cover of darkness and complexity for the bad.

By the mid-1980s, Brooklyn's Carroll Street Bridge, built in 1889, was in 29 disrepair. The city budgeted $3.5 million for an overhaul. Under procurement procedures, the renovation was estimated to take seven years.

But with the bridge's 100th anniversary approaching, Sam Schwartz, the 30 chief engineer responsible for bridges, thought the bridge should be fixed in time for a centennial party. Eleven months later, at a cost of $2.5 million, the bridge had been fixed. Practically the entire neighborhood participated in the centennial party, by all accounts a wonderful affair.

For his leadership in completing the job in one-seventh of the time and at 31 70 percent of budget, Schwartz received a reprimand.

Our modern legal system has achieved the worst of all worlds: a system of   32
regulation that goes too far—while it also does too little. A number of years ago,
two workers were asphyxiated in a Liberal, KS, meat-packing plant while
checking on a giant vat of animal blood. OSHA did virtually nothing. Stretched
thin giving out citations for improper railing height, OSHA reinspected only
once in eight years a plant that had admittedly "deplorable" conditions.

Then three more workers died—at the same plant. The government re-   33
sponse? A nationwide rule requiring atmospheric testing devices in confined
work spaces, though many of them have had no previous problems.

Most such legal dictates are stacked on top of the prior year's laws and   34
rules. The result is a mammoth legal edifice: federal statutes and rules now
total about 100 million words. The Federal Register, a daily report of new
and proposed regulations, increased from 15,000 pages in the final year of
John F. Kennedy's Presidency to over 68,000 pages in the second year of Bill
Clinton's.

Whenever the rules are eased, however, America's energy and good sense   35
pour in like sunlight through opened blinds. After the 1994 earthquake in Los
Angeles toppled freeways, Gov. Pete Wilson suspended the thick book of pro-
cedural guidelines and gave incentives for speedy work.

From law's perspective, the Los Angeles repair project was a nightmare of   36
potential abuse. The process wasn't completely objective; almost nothing was
spelled out to the last detail. When disagreements occurred, private contractors
and state bureaucrats had to work them out. Rather than specifying every iron
rod, state inspectors took responsibility for checking that the work complied
with general standards. The result? Instead of a $2\frac{1}{2}$-year trudge through government process, the Santa Monica Freeway was rebuilt in 64 days to a higher
standard than the old one.

"I'm proud," said Dwayne Barth, a construction supervisor. "It feels good   37
having a stake in rebuilding L.A."

When the rule book got tossed, all that was left was responsibility. No one   38
decided to spite Mother Teresa. It was the law. No one wants to take down children's art. It's the law.

"The idea of law," Yale professor Grant Gilmore cautioned in 1977, has   39
been "ridiculously oversold."

The rules, procedures and rights smothering us are aspects of a legal tech-   40
nique that promises a permanent fix for human frailty. This legal experiment,
we learn every time we encounter it, hasn't worked out. Modern law has not
protected us from stupidity and caprice, but has made stupidity and caprice
dominant features of society.

Energy and resourcefulness are what was great about America. Let judg-   41
ment and personal conviction be important again. Relying on ourselves—
rather than the law—to provide answers is not a new ideology. It's just common
sense.

Read More on the Web

Site of Common Good, a coalition chaired by Philip K. Howard and "dedicated to overhauling America's lawsuit culture": http://ourcommongood.com/

American Enterprise Institute-Brookings Joint Center site containing links to opinion papers on public policy, many of which are authored by Philip K. Howard: http://www.aei.brookings.org/publications/index.php?menuid=3&tab=date

Questions for Discussion

1. What is Howard's purpose? What is his thesis? Why did he use illustration to develop it? Would explaining how various laws came into being (process analysis) have been a good way to proceed?

2. Where does Howard cite statistics? Where does he use anecdotes?

3. How does his quoting people affected by overregulation help him achieve his purpose?

4. You know that it is not uncommon to find several methods of development in one essay. Where in this essay do you find comparison?

5. Where does Howard make use of figurative language? What does it say about his attitude toward his subject?

6. Howard's examples refer to a variety of regulations, occupations, people, and sections of the country. Explain how this variety contributes to the essay's success.

Thinking Critically

1. Read Glazer's "The Right to Be Let Alone" in Chapter 13. Explain the similarities between Glazer's ideas and Howard's in a short paragraph.

2. Is Howard against all government regulation? From what he has said, determine the kinds of regulations he might support to ensure workers' safety, to protect the environment, to maintain bridges, to keep schools safe, and so on. Reread the essay and make notes about such regulations in the margins. Then explain one of your examples in a well-developed paragraph.

3. Use the double-entry (summary/response) method you learned about at the beginning of this book in "Getting Started" to analyze and respond to three or four paragraphs in this essay. Don't be afraid to express your disagreement with anything Howard says. If you need to review how a double-entry notebook works, reread pages 36–38.

Suggestions for Journal Entries

1. List three laws or rules enforced by your college, community, or state that offend common sense. Then, brainstorm with a friend; gather details to show that these regulations should be changed to meet the needs for which they were intended. If you can't find a partner, do some freewriting or listing on your own.

2. Think of some rules enforced by your college, community, or state that make sense and that meet the needs for which they were intended. List them, and then explain briefly why you think they should not be changed.

3. Howard claims "people have their own way of doing things. But law, trying to make sure nothing ever goes wrong, doesn't respect the idiosyncrasy of human accomplishment." Freewrite for five minutes to explain what he means. Then list three examples to show that people who "break the rules"—who follow their own dreams instead of doing what they are told—sometimes accomplish a great deal. Take your examples from your own experiences, observations, or reading.

Names*

Jonathan Kozol

Born in 1936, Jonathan Kozol took his bachelor's degree at Harvard University and did graduate work at Oxford University in England. For more than thirty years, Kozol has written about the lives of the poor and homeless in America, the richest country in history. He is particularly concerned with the lives of poor and homeless children, arguing that we need to do more to provide them with an opportunity to share in the American dream. His best-known works are Rachel and Her Children: Homeless Families in America *(1988) and* Savage Inequalities: Children in America's Schools *(1992).* Amazing Grace *(1995), the book from which this selection is taken, discusses the problems of African-American and Latino children in New York City's Harlem, Washington Heights, and the South Bronx.*

Preparing to Read

1. Kozol took the title of his book *Amazing Grace* from a religious hymn of the same name. You can find the full text of this hymn at http://www.cyberhymnal.org/htm/a/m/amazgrac.htm
2. Delilah, the name of one of the children Kozol mentions, is a Biblical name. You can read the story of Samson and Delilah in the Old Testament, Book of Judges, Chapters 3-16.
3. Bernardo Rodriguez, whom Kozol mentions in paragraph 9, was killed when he fell down an elevator shaft in his apartment building. The elevator had been in need of repair for a long time, but the city, which maintained the building, had never taken precautions against its doors' opening accidentally.
4. Sojourner Truth, born Isabella in 1797, was a slave in northern New York until 1827, when slavery was outlawed in that state. After spending about 15 years as a housekeeper in New York City, she took the name Sojourner Truth and began traveling around Connecticut and Long Island, preaching about her faith in God and his justice and becoming an eloquent advocate for the human rights of blacks and of women.

Vocabulary

bondage (noun)   Slavery.
impulsively (adverb)   Without planning or forethought.

---

*Editor's title

inhibited (adjective)	Held back, restrained.
intensified (verb)	Became stronger.
pouty (adjective)	Given to sulking, complaining quietly.
smoldering (adjective)	Burning slowly.
sojourner (noun)	Person who stays in a place only temporarily, a boarder.

Names

Jonathan Kozol

WHENEVER I FEEL discouraged by the sheer accumulation of sad stories I've been told, I look for an excuse to go back to the elementary school on Cypress Avenue, because, although the things the children talk about are often sad, their unexpected ways of saying them seem to refresh the world. If possible, I spend time with them also in the playground during recess, since the energy released out in the schoolyard tends to make their comments more spontaneous and natural and less inhibited. 1

When I look through my notes after a day like this, I'm often fascinated by the names of many of the young black children I have met, especially the little girls. Some are African names, as well as poetically beautiful invented names that have an African sound. Increasingly, however, in the past few years, biblical names have come to be more popular again—or names that, while not literally biblical, evoke a biblical feeling and convey a powerful sense of gratitude to God. Some also symbolize a wish to mark a new departure from the bitterness or sorrows of the past. 2

"When I left the house of bondage," said Sojourner Truth, whose given name from her slave childhood was Isabella, "I left everything behind. I went to the Lord and asked Him to give me a new name." She did not want, she says, "to keep nothin' of Egypt on me"—"and the Lord gave me Sojourner . . . . Afterwards I told the Lord I wanted another name, 'cause everybody else had two names; and the Lord gave me Truth. . . . 'Thank you, God,' I said. 'Thou art my last master and Thy name is Truth.' " 3

I have never met a child named Sojourner in New York, but more than one who was named Charity, one in Roxbury named Prudence, one in New Orleans named Felicity (possibly for a street of that name close to where she lived), and a baby girl in the South Bronx named Easter. "She was born in the spring and I was hopeful, prayin' for a better life, for something better," said her mother, who had also, like Sojourner, done domestic work for many years. 4

One day, in a kindergarten class at P.S. 65, I met a truly angelic-looking child with a round face who was so affectionate and trusting that a mother who was helping in the classroom bent way down impulsively and gave her a big kiss when the child came right up with open arms and hugged her. 5

During a song-and-story period, the child sat on the floor with the other 6
children, sucking on one thumb and holding her other hand around one of her
ears. A boy sitting beside her, a thumb in his mouth too, was sound asleep. His
head was resting on her shoulder. When the teacher sang a song to the children
but forgot one line, all the children giggled, but this little girl laughed on and
on, as if it were the funniest thing that ever could be.

When I asked the mother what this little girl was named, she brought her 7
hands together as if to recite a prayer. "Her name is Destiny! God bless her!"

Destiny's name, I found, was neatly written on a card taped by the teacher 8
to her desk. I later asked if she would copy it for me on a piece of drawing paper. She gripped a pencil in her hand and wrote it once, then reached for a purple crayon and wrote it several times again. She did it slowly and seemed to take
tremendous satisfaction in the shaping of each letter.

Destiny's name, although unusual, is no more so than the names of many 9
other children at the school. In another kindergarten class, I met a child, with
her hair in beaded cornrows, named Delilah. Later, in a fifth grade class, I met
a tall and beautiful child named Mahogany, who turned out to be the older sister of Bernardo Rodriguez. Her eyes were filled with a smoldering anger that in-
tensified her beauty but also made it somewhat frightening.

Some months before, in one of the poorest homes I've ever visited, I met a 10
baby girl named Precious. The chubby infant sat on a sofa by my side, staring
at me with the greatest concentration while she held one of my fingers. I asked
her mother how she chose this name.

"When I was pregnant," she replied, "I said to God, 'I want a healthy child. 11
I want a pretty little girl who has long hair and I don't want no dummy.' He gave
me *exactly* what I ordered!

"For what you want," she said, "you got to be specific. One time I asked 12
Him for a handsome man and that's exactly what I got: a handsome man and
nothin' else. No brains, no money, no religion. I cannot deal with an ignorant
man who don't believe in nothin'. So I said, 'Next time I got to be specific. . . .'"

I asked her if she belonged to a church.   13

"I do," she said, "but I don't need to go to church to pray. If I want, I go in 14
the kitchen and I pray right there. I get on my knees and send it up!"

I asked her what she prays for.   15

"I pray to God to give my baby a better life, something more interesting. . . . 16
I'm lookin' at a doctor or a lawyer."

"Do you believe God hears your prayers?"   17

"God hears. He sit up high and look low, even here," she said with confi- 18
dence.

When I asked about her own job prospects, she said she was in a program 19
at a community college, where she was receiving training in "domestic services." I have since met other mothers in the South Bronx and in Harlem who
have told me that they studied "domestic sciences" in high school and also, in
one instance, in the Job Corps.

A 30-year-old woman whom I met once on the train, who was returning 20
with her daughter from a trip to Sing Sing, where she had been visiting her husband, a life prisoner, told me she'd attended Taft and felt it had prepared her
well for her employment. I asked her what she did, and she replied she was a
cook and household maid in Riverdale. Her daughter, a five-year-old, was
named Leticia, but, she said, "Her grandma calls her Blessing." She and Leticia
sang together in the choir at her church, she told me.

I asked the child, who wore patent-leather shoes and a frilly pink dress of 21
the kind a little girl might put on for a party, if she would sing a song for me.

"You don't need to slay the lamb no more . . .," the child sang, a gospel song 22
I'd never heard before.

Her mother pinched her cheeks after she sang the song. "She's smart—but 23
pouty! *Aren't* you?" she said, looking at the child. She told me that Leticia would
start school the next September.

"I have the highest hopes for her," she said.   24

Read More on the Web

Site linking to excerpts from two of Kozol's books: *Amazing Grace* and
    Savage Inequalities: http://www.thirdworldtraveler.com/
    Third_World_US/SI_Kozol_StLouis.html

Brandeis University site on Kozol and *Amazing Grace:* http://library.
    brandeis.edu/about/nsf/kozol/

Questions for Discussion

1. What is Kozol's thesis? What is his purpose in this essay?
2. Explain how each of the examples of names helps Kozol develop his
    thesis and achieve his purpose.
3. How does the conclusion of this selection relate to that purpose?
4. What do we learn about the parents of the children named in this
    selection? What light does that information shed on those names?
5. Re-read paragraphs 10–19. What does the story of Precious's mother
    tell us about the world in which these children are growing up?
6. Why does Kozol mention the story of Sojourner Truth?
7. What does Kozol tell us about Mahogany? Why is this information
    important?
8. What does the first line tell us about the nature and purpose of
    Kozol's *Amazing Grace,* the book from which this selection was taken?
9. This piece was given the title "Names" by the editor of this textbook.
    Can you think of a better title?

Thinking Critically

1. Why does Kozol include the story of Sojourner Truth? Is she mentioned simply to add another example of interesting names? Or does her presence in this selection signal hope?

2. What is Kozol saying about the educational opportunities available to the mothers of the children and, by extension, to the children themselves? In what way is this essay a criticism of public education?

Suggestions for Journal Entries

1. Make a list of the names you have been given by your parents, siblings, relatives, classmates, friends, co-workers, etc. In other words, include both your legal names and any shortened versions as well as any nick-names, affectionate or otherwise, that you might remember. Briefly, note the origin or significance of each name—why you were given it or what it said about you.

2. Do you know someone like Mahogany, the sister of Bernardo Rodriguez, whose eyes, facial expression, behavior, or other quality reflected a "smoldering anger" over a series of tragic or unfair events in her life? If so make a list of such events.

Covert Force

Robert F. Howe

This article first appeared in the October 2002 issue of Smithsonian *magazine. Robert F. Howe is a freelance writer based in California, who has published an article on Doolittle's Raiders in* Smithsonian.

Preparing to Read

1. Women are taking an increasingly active role in warfare. However, consider the position of women in America about 150 years ago. They didn't have the vote or, in most cases, the right to own property. They were discouraged from entering professions, and they certainly weren't admitted to the military. Keep this in mind as you determine the purpose of this essay.

2. Howe's essay uses information from *They Fought Like Demons: Woman Soldiers in the American Civil War,* a book by Lauren Cook and DeAnne Blanton, and he discusses these two contemporary women in addition to telling the stories of women Civil War soldiers. To fully appreciate his purpose, ask yourself how discussing Cook and Blanton fits into a discussion of women soldiers.

Vocabulary

a.k.a. (abbreviation)	"Also known as".
alluded (verb)	Suggested, implied.
avenge (verb)	Get revenge.
buffs (noun)	People with an avid interest in a particular subject.
compilation (noun)	Collection.
covert (adjective)	Hidden, secretive.
cursory (adjective)	Casual, superficial.
depraved (adjective)	Morally corrupt, evil.
deranged (adjective)	Mentally unbalanced, insane.
destitution (noun)	Poverty.
fending (adjective)	Fighting, defending against.
inebriated (adjective)	Drunk.
medic (noun)	Medical officer.
prevailing (adjective)	Accepted.
tilled (verb)	Worked the soil; cultivated.
unadulterated (adjective)	Pure.

Covert Force

Robert Howe

AUGUST 30, 1862, proved to be yet another bloody day. Henry Clark was in   1
the thick of things, fending off Federal troops in the Battle of Richmond,
Kentucky, when the Confederate private caught an enemy shell in the thigh.
Clark was swarmed by bluecoats and taken prisoner.

It was presumably when a Union medic treated Clark's wound that the sol-   2
dier's tightly held secret was unmasked. Henry's real name was Mary Ann. Indeed, she was a divorced mother of two.

When Federal troops realized that they had a woman on their hands, they   3
moved quickly to release her—as long as she swore to return to the life of a
proper lady. They even gave her a dress to wear. She agreed and was freed, then
quickly cast off the frock and made her way back to the rebel army, where she
was promptly promoted. Not long after, a young Confederate soldier—having
joined a crowd gathered around Clark, then apparently serving openly as a female officer—wrote home: "Pa among all the curiosities I have seen since I left
home one I must mention, a female Lieutenant."

A curiosity, yes, but to the surprise of many Civil War buffs even today,   4
Clark was by no means unique. She was one of an estimated 400 women who
took up arms in the war; they were not nurses, or laundresses or cooks, but actual female soldiers disguised as men, who marched, mastered their weapons,
entered into battle and even gave their lives.

Various histories have alluded to women's roles in combat during the War   5
Between the States, but none have made so detailed and convincing a case as
They Fought Like Demons: Women Soldiers in the American Civil War. Coauthors
Lauren Cook and DeAnne Blanton spent more than ten years combing through
letters, archives and news reports to document some 250 women warriors.

"No one has accumulated this much data," says Cook, 46, who first tilled   6
this turf in her 1994 *An Uncommon Soldier* (Oxford University Press), a compi-
lation of letters from a female Civil War soldier. The authors' mission was not
just to catalog the combatants. Their extensive research convinced them that
the prevailing notions about women's participation in the war—that they had
to be deranged or depraved—were way off the mark.

"We felt those women had not been given their due, that they were thor-   7
oughly misunderstood by military historians and the general public," says
Cook, a special assistant to the chancellor for communications at Fayetteville
State University-UNC in North Carolina. In fact, Cook contends, "they were
just as successful as their male comrades, and what enabled them to be so successful was that no one knew that they were women."

What would compel a woman to march into that terrible combat—and   8
how could she conceal her identity in what must have been uncomfortably
close quarters? Blanton and Cook offer a number of persuasive answers. In the
case of Clark, for example, a bad marriage and the death of a brother-in-law at

the hands of a pro-Union mob took such an emotional toll that she sought refuge in the military, according to a letter from her mother uncovered by the authors. But Martha Parks Lindley joined up just two days after her husband left for the 6th U.S. Cavalry. "I was frightened half to death," she told a newspaper. "But I was so anxious to be with my husband that I resolved to see the thing through if it killed me." It did not, and fellow troopers simply assumed that Lindley and the "young man" known as Jim Smith were just good friends. Then there was Charlotte Hope, who signed up in the 1st Virginia Cavalry to avenge the death of her fiancé, killed in a raid in 1861. Her goal: to slay 21 Yankees, one for each year of her beau's life.

Some joined to escape the misery of prostitution or destitution—a common problem with so few jobs open to women. Finance clearly figured into the decision of Sarah Rosetta Wakeman, alias Pvt. Lyons Wakeman, to sign up for the Union army. "I got 100 and 52$ in money," she wrote' proudly. "I can get all the money I want." 9

Loreta Velazquez, a.k.a. Lt. Harry T. Buford, was one of several women who fought simply for the unadulterated thrill of it: "I plunged into adventure for the love of the thing," she said after writing a postwar memoir called *The Woman in Battle*. Many women felt the keen tug of patriotism. Union soldier Sarah Edmonds, an immigrant from Canada, expressed thanks that she was "permitted in this hour of my adopted country's need to express a tithe of the gratitude which I feel toward the people of the Northern States." 10

"What surprised me most was the realization that women soldiers enlisted largely for the very same reasons as the men did," says Blanton, 38. "Some were rebelling against the strict roles that society confined them in, but then there were women who went because the pay was good, or because everybody else in the family was signing up, or because they wanted to defend their country. Some just signed up to run away from home, just like so many boys did." 11

To get to the front lines, each woman had to pass herself off as a man. Many were detected immediately and given the boot. But physical exams of the time tended to be cursory, and both armies were often so desperate for recruits that virtually anyone could pass. Occasions for discovery were limited; troops routinely slept in uniform, baths were a novelty and latrines were so foul that many soldiers sought refuge in nearby woods. A high-pitched voice or a lack of facial hair could be attributed to youth. Several women attempted to blend in by learning to cuss like sailors, taking up gambling, or even dating local young ladies. 12

Some female combatants were given away by ladylike mannerisms and others were undone by boastings while inebriated. But as with Clark, most were unveiled only when doctors stripped away their clothes to examine a war wound. 13

A native of Grand Rapids, Michigan, Cook had virtually no interest in the Civil War until 1987, when she toured the battle site at Gettysburg, Pennsylvania. She was so moved by the experience that she joined a fife and drum 14 corps and began participating in battle reenactments. Then, in 1989, during a re-creation of a military hospital at the Antietam National Battlefield in Sharpsburg, Maryland, she dressed as a male soldier "because I felt that was historically accurate." But when she visited the ladies' room, she caused a stir—not only among the women inside but with a ranger, who brusquely informed her that park rules did not allow women to participate in reenactments. "Their attitude was that the women of that era must have been oddballs, eccentrics and crazy, and didn't merit any kind of recognition or respect," says Cook. Her lawsuit against the Department of the Interior ultimately changed the rules.

A decade after teaming up to work on *Demons,* Cook and Blanton are still   15 fitting pieces of the puzzle. They cite the case, as it unfolded in letters written by soldiers, of a New Jersey woman who participated in the Union army's June 1862 siege of Richmond, Virginia, was wounded at the Battle of Antietam in September, and fought in the Union defeat at Fredericksburg in December. Just a few weeks later, on January 19, an astonished colonel in the Army of the Potomac wrote home: "A corporal was promoted to sergeant for gallant conduct at the battle of Fredericksburg—since which time the sergeant has become the mother of a child."

And there the story stops. "When she and her baby went home, was   16 she celebrated or shunned?" Blanton asks. "I hope that a descendant will read our book and call up and say, 'Hey, that lady was my great-great-great-grandmother.' "

Read More on the Web

Primary sources (letters, diaries, etc.) written by women during the Civil War: http://scriptorium.lib.duke.edu/women/cwdocs.html

Text of Loreta Velazqeuz's *The Woman in Battle:* http://docsouth.unc.edu/velazquez/menu.html

Questions for Discussion

1. What is the purpose of this essay? Was it simply to tell readers about the Civil War's women soldiers?
2. What is Howe's thesis? Can you tell if this thesis is similar to the thesis of Cook and Blanton's book?
3. In what ways were women's reasons for going to war the same as those of men?
4. In order to be effective, illustrations must be believable. Are the illustrations in this essay believable? What makes them so?
5. Why were so many women able to pass themselves off as men without being detected?

6. Why does the author mention *The Woman in Battle* by Loreta Velazquez, a.k.a Lt. Harry Buford?

7. Comment upon the fact that Howe quotes Cook and Blanton directly as well as including direct quotations from women Cook and Blanton quoted. What is the effect on the essay?

8. Why does the author introduce this essay with an illustration? Which other method for introducing essays, which you learned about in Chapter 4, does the Howe use? Which method for concluding essays, as explained in Chapter 4, does he use?

Thinking Critically

1. Re-read this essay carefully. As you do, make marginal notes that will point out similarities between the women who fought in the Civil War and today's American women.

2. What can you tell about Cook and Blanton that might explain why they might be so intent about telling the story of women combatants?

Suggestions for Journal Entries

1. It should not come as a surprise that today women can be found doing a variety of jobs once reserved for men. Women are fire fighters, police officers, doctors, mechanics, sanitation workers, etc. Make a list of women you know or have learned about who hold jobs that 30 years ago might have been reserved for men. Or, make a list of men you know who hold jobs that your parents or grandparents might have thought were suited only to women.

2. Use the Internet to find out more information about women combatants in the Civil War or on the role women played in other American wars. For example you might research the contributions women made on the home front and overseas during World War II. Or you might try to find out more about the American women who died in Vietnam. Print out any articles you find online and make notes in the margins using the techniques you read about in "Getting Started," which is at the beginning of this book.

Suggestions for Sustained Writing

1. If you responded to the first of the Suggestions for Journal Entries after Lukawska's "Wolf," you have already written three topic sentences that

express conclusions about the behavior or personality of a particular animal or species of animal.

Use these topic sentences in the body paragraphs of an essay that, like "Wolf," expresses your views on the character of this animal. Develop these paragraphs with illustrations. Perhaps some of the information in your journal will serve this purpose. Then, summarize in one statement the ideas expressed in your topic sentences; make this your essay's thesis.

After completing your first draft, return to your paper and insert additional details and examples that will make it more convincing and clear. In your third draft, work on creating an effective introduction; like Lukawska, try using a startling remark or challenging a widely held opinion. In your conclusion, rephrase your thesis or look to the future. Then, revise the entire paper once more to improve word usage and sentence structure. End this careful process by editing for grammar and by proofreading.

2. Have you ever lived in a land whose government was a dictatorship? Do you know someone who did? Write an essay that uses examples from personal experience—yours or someone else's—to explain what living in that country was like.

Collect information before starting your first draft. If you are writing about yourself, brainstorm with a family member who remembers as much about that time in your life as you do. If you are writing about someone else, try interviewing this person to gather examples about the kind of life he or she endured. In addition, read your response to the first journal suggestion after Irina Groza's "Growing Up in Romania."

Like Groza, use anecdotes and specific instances to explain what the government did to limit people's personal and economic freedom. Your essay doesn't have to be as long as hers, but it should be filled with examples that show how difficult living under a dictatorship can be.

Groza cared enough about her readers and her subject to complete the writing process step-by-step. She made several drafts, each of which developed her thesis in greater and more startling detail. Then she revised and edited her work to make sure it was well organized, coherent, and free of mechanical errors. Follow her example.

3. As an alternative to suggestion 2 write a letter to the editor of a local or college newspaper complaining about a law, regulation, policy, or practice in your community or on campus. Using examples from personal experience, explain why you are against it; show how negatively it affects you and others in your town or school.

Let's say your college library closes on Saturdays and Sundays. You decide to explain that this policy is hard on students who can't go to the library at other times. To develop your central idea, you might:

- Talk about the long trips to other libraries you and friends are forced to make on weekends.

- Discuss your many attempts to find a quiet place to study on Sunday afternoons.
- Explain that 10 of the 20 students in your history class didn't finish their midterm essays on time because they could not get information they needed.

You are trying to convince your readers of a particular opinion. So, pack your letter with examples, but remember that each example should relate directly to that opinion. As always, state your point clearly in a thesis.

Begin this assignment by looking to the journal responses you made after reading Groza's "Growing Up in Romania" and Howard's "The Death of Common Sense." That information might help you complete the first draft of your letter. Once again be thorough and careful when revising and editing your work.

4. Do some of the rules and regulations enforced by your college, community, or state offend common sense? Or do most laws that govern you seem reasonable? Take one or the other side of this issue or argue that some laws make sense while others are ridiculous. Either way, prove your point by discussing three or four laws, rules, or regulations as examples.

In any case, make your central idea clear from the very beginning. For example, argue that common sense, practicality, and the people's best interest should determine law—not some abstract theory or impractical principle. Then, in the body of the essay, show how the rules and regulations you are discussing meet or fail to meet this standard. If you are arguing both sides of the issue, make sure you discuss examples of both reasonable and unreasonable laws.

Before you begin, check the notes you made in your journal after reading "The Death of Common Sense." They should provide useful facts, insights, and examples with which to develop your paper. As always, apply common sense to your writing: revise, edit, and proofread.

5. If your responded to the first of the journal prompts after Kozol's "Names," turn your notes into a full-length essay that explains several of the different names you have been called to reveal things important to your personality or to your personal history. The examples you use can include legal names and nicknames given to you by friends, family, and classmates. As much as possible, comment upon the origin of each name—why you were given it—and what it says about you.

If this assignment does not interest you, try expanding the notes you made in response to the second journal suggestion after "Names." Use illustration to explain why someone you know harbors a "smoldering anger," as Kozol puts it in paragraph 9 of "Names." In other words, using events from this individual's life as examples, explain why this individual seems so angry with the world.

Whichever assignment you choose, be sure to include enough examples to make your essay convincing, concrete, and interesting. Add such information after writing your first draft if necessary. Then, make sure that your essay has a clearly stated thesis to which all your information relates.

6. If you responded to the first of the journal prompts after Howe's "Covert Force," turn your notes into an illustration essay explaining the fact that jobs once filled by members of only one of the sexes are now open to both. On the other hand, if you researched the role of women in wars, as suggested in item 2 of the Suggestions for Journal Entries after the essay by Howe, use this information to write an illustration essay that explains the role of women in a particular war. If you want, do some additional library or Internet research to gather more information. Make sure you cite any information taken from Internet or from print sources per the Modern Language Association style (or per any style sheet assigned by your instructor). MLA style is explained in the appendix to this textbook.

For both types of papers, remember that you need to develop illustrations that are credible and detailed. After you write your first draft, read it over carefully. Refine your thesis if necessary to make it clear and more focused. Then, add details and even whole events or instances that will better convince your reader of the validity of that thesis.

Writing to Learn: A Group Activity

In "Growing Up in Romania," Irina Groza writes about a government that denied people basic human liberties. In 1787, the Framers of the United States Constitution worried that the government they were creating might someday do the same. Therefore, they guaranteed the people certain fundamental rights, which they stated in the first ten amendments to the Constitution, now known as the Bill of Rights.

THE FIRST MEETING

Read and discuss the Bill of Rights (you can find it in any library or on the Internet). Then, choose the three or four amendments that your group believes are of greatest importance today. Ask each student to research one of these. The purpose of this assignment is to gather and present information that will help the group better understand the purpose and importance of each amendment.

RESEARCH

Search the Internet, the *New York Times Index, The Readers' Guide to Periodical Literature,* or an electronic database, such as ProQuest or InfoTrac, for information on the amendment you have chosen. Specifically, find information that will help you:

- Understand and explain what the amendment means. Be aware that experts on law and government disagree about the meaning and scope of certain amendments. This is especially true of the second amendment, the right to bear arms.
- Explain why the Framers of the Constitution thought it important to include the amendment. Briefly discuss one or two events, circumstances, or issues from history that might have influenced their decision.
- Explain why you think the amendment continues to be important. Discuss examples of the kinds of issues, circumstances, events, or problems to which the amendment applies today.

Take careful and complete notes. Then, write a well-developed paragraph responding to each of the three items above. Make copies of your work.

THE SECOND MEETING

Distribute copies of the paragraphs students have written and have them critique each other's work. Pay special attention to the clarity with which the writer explains what the amendment means. Then, evaluate the effectiveness of examples the writer uses in the second and third paragraphs. Offer concrete suggestions for additional research and/or revision. Arrange for one member of the group to collect and duplicate the final drafts of everyone's work before the next meeting.

THE THIRD MEETING

As a group, write one or two summary paragraphs that explain the importance of the Bill of Rights and that prepare readers for a discussion of the particular amendments your group has written about. Use this material as an introduction to a paper that contains each member's final draft. Use simple subheadings, such as **Amendment I,** to separate the three or four major sections of the body of the paper. Finally, assign someone to write a short concluding paragraph that comments on the good sense or perception of the people who wrote these amendments.

CHAPTER 11

Comparison
and Contrast

Comparison and contrast are methods of organizing and developing ideas by pointing out similarities and differences between subjects.

A comparison essay identifies similarities—even between subjects that seem different. For example, you might compare the government of the United States with that of ancient Rome; a newly patented drug with an age-old herbal treatment; the methods of building the Egyptian and Mayan pyramids with modern construction methods. A contrast essay identifies differences—even between subjects that seem alike; usually these subjects belong to the same general class or are of the same type. Such is the case in Cowley's "Temptations of Old Age," a selection in this chapter that discusses how two different types of people face the challenges of aging.

Comparison and contrast can also be used to argue for one or both sides of a question. For example, you might discuss the advantages and disadvantages of living in a particular city, the pros and cons of human cloning, or the strengths and weaknesses of a particular political ideology. In "High Anxiety: It Never Ends," student Nancy Terranova argues that, although the lifestyles of young adults differ from those of their parents and grandparents, they experience the same levels of fear and anxiety in their daily lives.

Organizing Comparison/Contrast Papers

One of the greatest advantages of using comparison or contrast is the simplicity with which it allows you to organize information. In fact, putting together a successful comparison or contrast essay doesn't have to be difficult if you follow either of the two standard methods of organization: point by point or subject by subject.

Which of the two methods for organizing a comparison or contrast paper is better for you? That depends on your topic and your purpose. The subject-by-subject method of organization is often used in short pieces. You can see it in Alan Paton's "The Road from Ixopo," a selection containing only a few paragraphs that contrast two places in the same mountains of South Africa. The point-by-point method, on the other hand, works well with essays that compare or contrast several aspects, qualities, or characteristics of two subjects. This arrangement allows readers to digest large quantities of information bit by bit. As such it helps eliminate the risk that they will forget what you said in the first half of your essay before they finish the second half. Stephen Moore's "New Blood for Cities" uses the point-by-point pattern.

Visualizing Methods of Comparison

THE POINT-BY-POINT METHOD

Using the point-by-point method, you compare or contrast one aspect or characteristic of both subjects, often in the same paragraph, before moving on to the next point in another paragraph. For example, if you were showing how economical your 2003 Wizbang automobile is by contrasting it to the 2003 Roadhog, your essay might be organized like this:

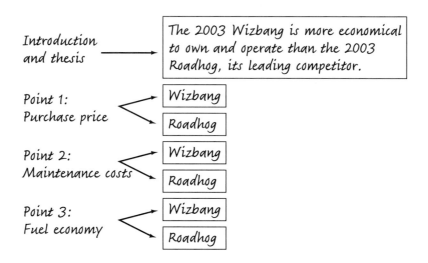

THE SUBJECT-BY-SUBJECT METHOD

Using the subject-by-subject method, you discuss *one* subject completely before going on to compare or contrast it with another subject in the second half of the essay. For example, you might outline the essay about the Wizbang and its competitor like this:

Introduction and thesis	The 2003 Wizbang is more economical to own and operate than the 2003 Roadhog, its leading competitor.
Subject 1: The Wizbang	• Purchase price • Maintenance costs • Fuel economy
Subject 2: The Roadhog	• Purchase price • Maintenance costs • Fuel economy

SEEING THE PATTERN IN A COMPARISON/CONTRAST PAPER

Student James Langley's "Watch the Cart!" which appears below, discusses differences between male and female shoppers. It follows the point-by-point pattern, which is often found in longer essays. Notes in the left margin explain how Langley organized his paper. Notes on the right explain how he developed it.

States thesis.

There is nothing similar to the way men and women shop for groceries. Believe me, I know because I work in a major supermarket. After watching scores of people shop for food day in and day out, I have become an expert on the habits of American consumers. I have noticed many things about them, but nothing stands out more clearly than the differences between men and women.

Establishes his expertise.

First of all, men never know where anything is. Nine times out of ten, it will be a man who asks an employee to find a product for him. I don't know how many guys come up to me in the course of a night to ask me where something is, but 50% of those who do invariably return to me in five minutes still unaware of the product's location. Men have no sense of direction in a supermarket. It's as if they're locked up in some life-sized maze. It has always been my contention that men who shop should be provided with specially trained dogs to sniff out the

Begins with topic sentence.

Point 1: How men search for a product

Includes a statistic.

Uses a simile.

products they desire. It would certainly
save me valuable time too often wasted as I
explain for the tenth time that soup is in
aisle 9.

**Point 1:
How women
search for
a product.**

<u>Women,</u> on the other hand, <u>rarely ask for
an item's location</u>. When they do, it is
usually for an obscure product only they
have heard of and whose name only they can
pronounce. Whenever a woman asks me where
some such item is, I always tell her to go
to aisle 11—the dog-food aisle. Send a man
there, and he'll forget what he was looking
for and just buy the dog food out of
desperation. Send a woman there, and she'll
be back in five minutes with the product in
hand, thanking me for locating it for her.

*Begins
with topic
sentence.*

*Uses an
example.*

**Point 2:
How quickly
men and
women shop.**

Another difference between men and women
is that women shop at speeds that would get
them tickets on freeways, while men shop
with the speed of a dead snail. A woman can
get her shopping done in the same amount of
time every time she goes. A man who shops
just as often gets worse and worse every
time.

*Begins
with topic
sentence.*

**Point 3:
How well
men and
women
manipulate
carts.**

The biggest difference between the sexes
in regard to shopping, however, involves the
manipulation of carts. A woman guides a
cart through the store so fluidly and
effortlessly that her movements are almost

*Begins
with topic
sentence.*

poetic. Men are an entirely different

story. A man with a shopping cart is a

menace to anyone within two aisles of him.

Men bounce their carts off display cases,   *Creates a*
vivid image.
sideswipe their fellow patrons and create

havoc wherever they go. They have no idea

of how to control the direction of carts.

To a man, a shopping cart is a crazed metal   *Uses a*
metaphor.
monster designed to embarrass and harass

him.

Conclusion
refers to
thesis and
restates
essay's main
points.

    Overall, then, women are far more

proficient shoppers than men. They are

efficient, speedy and graceful; men are slow

and clumsy. I know these things because I

work in a supermarket. I also know these

things because I am a man.

Revising Comparison/Contrast Papers

The following essay by Nancy Terranova was written after this student began to reflect upon the daily fears and anxieties faced by her generation, especially in light of the terrorist attacks of 9/11/01. Read the rough draft and an excerpt of the final draft of Terranova's paper. (You can read a full version of her final draft later in this chapter.) As you will see, the author did a thorough revision in which, among other things, she clarified her thesis, made the paper's organization more consistent and logical, and added information to develop her ideas more fully.

Terranova—Rough Draft—High Anxiety

In many ways the lives of young adults in 2002 are

different from those of their parents and far different

Make tone more formal? Use third-person "they" and "them."

from those of their grandparents. As members of Generation X, we seem to have all the answers and all the toys. Fax machines, email, voice mail, and call-waiting enable us to maintain unbroken strings of communication. Computer software makes us more productive students and business people. Take-home movies, television systems with hundreds of channels, electronic games, and downloads of popular music have allowed us transform ourselves into virtual coach potatoes. Speaking of food, consider the immediate gratification—if not the nutrition—that drive-up hamburger joints, sushi bars, and the makers of microwaveable pizzas provide.

Remove clichés?

Use quotation marks?

But are the important things in our lives really different? According to the French, the more things change the more they stay the same. We might be more technologically advanced than our parents and grandparents, but are our lives any happier and any less stressed-out than theirs?

State thesis explicitly?

Is subject-by-subject method best? Revise to use point-by-point method.

Over the last 100 years the longevity of Americans has increased. One reason for that is that, years ago, diseases such as polio, diphtheria, tuberculosis, pneumonia, tetanus, and even influenza took the lives of or crippled so many children and young adults. Back then, they worried about how to make a living as well. For example, many men and women of my parents' and grandparents' generations held factory or low-level office jobs. They

had to develop skills to get those jobs, which meant
finishing high school or learning a trade as an
apprentice. In those days, that wasn't so easy. My
grandparents remember the Depression, when 1 out
of 4 people was out of work. Many of them had to
leave high school in order to help support their
families, and sometimes finding someone to
apprentice with wasn't easy. Besides you could be
laid-off easily.

*How does
this relate
to thesis?
Strengthen
connection.*

*Finish
discussing
previous
point before
starting a
new one?*

Today, however, the Salk and Sabine vaccines
have virtually wiped out polio. Medicine has virtually
eliminated diphtheria and tuberculosis as well. And
pneumonia and tetanus are easily treated with
antibiotics. However, Generation X has other health
worries. For example the rates of teenage suicide are
much higher today. And young people seem to be
more susceptible to drug and alcohol. Sexually
transmitted disease including gonorrhea, syphilis
and AIDS are also much more prevalent today,
because members of my generation are far more
sexually active than before. Cases of anorexia and
bulimia, virtually unheard of 50 years ago, are
commonplace among women in their teens and
twenties, and men are getting them too.

*Support these
ideas with
research?*

*Develop
this point
more fully?*

Today, <u>they tell us</u>, our job opportunities are
greater too. But we need more education. Graduating
from high school will get you a job at Burger King.
The minimum to get started is a community college

*Who is
"they"?*

degree. And the best paying jobs require you to continue studying far beyond your bachelor's. However, even an advanced degree won't keep you from getting laid off, as so many employees of high-tech companies have found out in recent years. We may not be having a <u>depression like my grandparents</u>, but we have just come through a recession and that was bad enough. So anxiety about where your next meal is coming from is still around.

Correct illogical comparison.

Develop this point more fully?

And what about war, and national security? I remember my grandmother telling me about worrying so much about my grandfather who had had been shipped out to the Pacific during World War II. Today, we still have war fears, and many of my friends, who are in the reserves, might be called to fight in Iraq. And what about all the terrorism?

Add a formal conclusion?

Terranova—Final Draft—High Anxiety: It Never Ends

In 2002, the lives of people in their late teens and twenties are different in many ways from what they would have been if they had been born half a century earlier. Members of Generation X seem to have advantages their grandparents—and even their parents—never even hoped for. Fax machines, email,

Uses a more formal tone.

Has removed clichés.

voice mail, and call-waiting enable them to maintain unbroken strings of communication even with people across the globe. Computer software makes them more productive students and employees. Take-home movies, television systems offering hundreds of channels, electronic games, and downloads of popular music are, sadly, transforming them into a generation of overweight couch potatoes. And speaking of food, consider the immediate gratification—if not the nutrition—that drive-up hamburger joints, sushi bars, and the makers of microwaveable pizzas provide.

Adds quotation marks.

According to the French, however, "the more things change, the more they stay the same." Today's young adults might live in a technologically advanced environment, but are their lives any

States thesis explicitly.

happier and any less stressful than those of their parents and grandparents? As a matter of fact, they suffer the same kinds of anxieties that their elders experienced.

Switches to point-by-point method of organization.

Take concerns over staying healthy, for example. Through much of the 20th century, diseases such as diphtheria, tuberculosis, pneumonia, tetanus, and even influenza took the lives of many young adults or severely debilitated them. In the 1950's, the world went through a kind of polio hysteria, as bad as that caused by AIDS in the 1980s. According to Dr. Edmund Sass, the United States reported 52,000 new

Condenses what appeared in rough draft.

cases of polio in 1952 (3). Another 5000 new cases were reported in Canada (Rutty 1) for that year.

Makes connection with thesis stronger and adds researched material.

Today, medicine has virtually eliminated polio in the developed world. Diphtheria and tuberculosis, which plagued earlier generations, are in severe decline, and pneumonia and tetanus can be treated with antibiotics. However, Generation X has its own health worries. For example, according to the Centers for Disease Control:

Focus of paper now remains steady.

> Many more people die by suicide than by homicide in the United States. Suicide rates among youth have been increasing steadily for the past four decades; suicide is the third leading cause of death among children and youth between the ages of 10 and 24. (1)

Adds research to support thesis.

Moreover, young people seem to be more susceptible to drug and alcohol abuse. In a 1997 statement of the US Senate Judiciary Committee, Senator Orrin Hatch reported that the use of illicit drugs "among high school students [had] dramatically increased since 1991—from 11% to 24% in 1996 for 8th graders, from 21% to 38% for 10th graders, and from 29% to 40% for 12th graders" (1). Sexually transmitted disease including gonorrhea and syphilis are also much more prevalent today because members of Generation X are far more sexually active than their grandparents or even their parents were. AIDS, now at epidemic levels, was unknown fifty years ago.

Organization is uniform: point-by-point.

Adds research.

Rates of anorexia and bulimia have also increased in
the last two decades especially among women in
their teens and twenties. However, even young men
are suffering from these ailments.

People who came of age in the 40's, 50's, and 60's
worried about how to make a living. For example,
many men and women of our parents' and
grandparents' generations held factory or low-level
office jobs. They had to develop skills to get those
jobs, which meant finishing high school or learning a
trade as an apprentice. In those days, that wasn't so
easy. My grandparents remember the Depression,
when 1 out of 4 people was out of work. Many of
them had to leave high school in order to help
support their families, and sometimes finding
someone with whom to apprentice was difficult. In
addition, factory lay-offs were common.

Adds material to develop this point more fully. It now spans 2 paragraphs.

Today, college education is a necessity.
Graduating from high school qualifies one for an
entry-level job at Burger King. The minimum to
launch any worthwhile career is a community college
degree. And the best-paying jobs require continued
study far beyond the bachelor's.

However, even an advanced degree won't prevent
the possibility of being laid off, as so many employees
of high-tech companies have found out in recent
years. This generation may not be experiencing a
depression as our grandparents did, but we have just

come through a recession, and that was bad enough!
So anxiety about keeping a steady job and building a
rewarding career still abounds.

Practicing Comparison and Contrast

In the spaces provided, write paragraphs that respond to any four of the following items. Remember that comparison explains similarities while contrast explains differences.

Before you start writing a paragraph, gather details for it and make a rough draft. Before you begin your final draft, make sure the paragraph has a topic sentence.

1. Compare caring for a child and caring for an animal.

_____

_____

_____

_____

_____

_____

_____

2. Compare writing papers for English class and preparing for a mathematics test.

_____

_____

_____

_____

_____

_____

_____

3. Compare the cooking of two different cultures. For instance, compare Chinese with Italian, Indian with Mexican, Caribbean with Japanese, or Eastern European with American.

_____

_____

_____

_____

_____

_____

_____

4. Compare someone you know (perhaps yourself) to an animal. Start by writing "_____ is a snake" or "_____ is a workhorse."

_____

_____

_____

_____

_____

_____

5. Contrast your work or study habits with those of a friend.

_____

_____

_____

_____

_____

_____

6. Contrast the ways you and your parents (sister, brother, or other relative) view sex (marriage, education, religion, money, or your friends).

_____

_____

_____

_____

_____

_____

7. Contrast two hobbies you pursue, two sports you play or follow, or two jobs you have held.

_____

_____

_____

_____

_____

_____

_____

8. Contrast two pieces of music, films, paintings, books, or television shows that are about similar subjects or that have similar purposes.

_____

_____

_____

_____

_____

_____

_____

As you just learned, how you organize a comparison or contrast essay depends on your topic and on the reason you are writing about it. In general, there is no absolutely right or wrong method for arranging the details in such a paper. Sometimes you may simply want to use the pattern which you find easier. Just remember that comparing and contrasting are powerful tools for discovering ideas and expressing them effectively. In fact, the very act of pointing out similarities and differences may lead to important discoveries about your subjects that will make your writing richer in detail and more interesting.

The Road from Ixopo*

Alan Paton

An educator, writer, and vocal opponent of apartheid, Alan Paton (1903–1988) remains South Africa's best-known writer. His most widely read work is Cry, the Beloved Country, *of which this selection is the first chapter. This novel is an eloquent treatment of race and justice in a society tortured by an insane system of segregation. It is also the poignant story of parental love and the pain of loss experienced by two families, one black and one white. Among Paton's other works are* Ah, But Your Land Is Beautiful; Too Late the Phalarope; *and* Tales from a Troubled Land, *a book of short stories.*

Preparing to Read

1. Ixopo is not far from Paton's hometown of Pietermaritzburg, which is in the province of KwaZulu/Natal.
2. The Drakensberg Mountain range runs for about 600 miles in southeastern South Africa. Ingeli and East Griqualand are also place names in the area.

Vocabulary

bracken (noun)	Type of large fern.
forlorn (adjective)	Sad, despairing.
kloof (noun)	Ravine, gorge, cleft.
shod (adjective)	Wearing shoes.
unshod (adjective)	Not wearing shoes, barefoot.
veld (noun)	Open grassland of South Africa.

The Road from Ixopo

Alan Paton

THERE IS A lovely road that runs from Ixopo into the hills. These hills are   1
grass-covered and rolling, and they are lovely beyond any singing of it. The road climbs seven miles into them, to Carisbrooke; and from there, if there is no mist, you look down on one of the fairest valleys of Africa. About you there is grass and bracken and you may hear the forlorn crying of the titihoya, one of the birds of the veld. Below you is the valley of the Umzimkulu, on its

---

*Editor's title.

journey from the Drakensberg to the sea; and beyond and behind the river, great hill after great hill; and beyond and behind them, the mountains of Ingeli and East Griqualand.

The grass is rich and matted, you cannot see the soil. It holds the rain and the mist, and they seep into the ground, feeding the streams in every kloof. It is well-tended, and not too many cattle feed upon it; not too many fires burn it, laying bare the soil. Stand unshod upon it, for the ground is holy, being even as it came from the Creator. Keep it, guard it, care for it, for it keeps men, guards men, cares for men. Destroy it and man is destroyed. 2

Where you stand the grass is rich and matted, you cannot see the soil. But the rich green hills break down. They fall to the valley below, and falling, change their nature. For they grow red and bare; they cannot hold the rain and mist, and the streams are dry in the kloofs. Too many cattle feed upon the grass, and too many fires have burned it. Stand shod upon it, for it is coarse and sharp, and the stones cut under the feet. It is not kept, or guarded, or cared for; it no longer keeps men, guards men, cares for men. The titihoya does not cry here any more. 3

The great red hills stand desolate, and the earth has torn away like flesh. The lightning flashes over them, the clouds pour down upon them, the dead streams come to life, full of the red blood of the earth. Down in the valleys women scratch the soil that is left, and the maize hardly reaches the height of a man. They are valleys of old men and old women, of mothers and children. The men are away, the young men and the girls are away. The soil cannot keep them any more. 4

Read More on the Web

A short biography and a bibliography of Paton's work:
 http://www.kirjasto.sci.fi/apaton.htm
Teacher Resource File on Paton with several valuable links:
 http://falcon.jmu.edu/~ramseyil/paton.htm

Questions for Discussion

1. What pattern of comparison/contrast does Paton use to organize this selection? Why did he choose this one and not the other?
2. Identify three or four natural objects that the author uses as points of contrast.

3. Find examples of particularly vivid adjectives and verbs in paragraphs 1 through 3.
4. What vivid images does Paton create in paragraph 4? What is happening in each?
5. Besides contrast, what other method of development does Paton use?
6. In Chapter 7, you learned several ways to create emphasis. Find examples of such techniques in this selection, especially parallelism and repetition.

Thinking Critically

1. What important point or points is Paton making in this selection? Why did he use contrast to make it or them?
2. As you have learned, these four paragraphs make up the first chapter of *Cry, the Beloved Country.* This novel is, among many things, an indictment of apartheid (the forced segregation of nonwhites from whites) and of the brutal effects of that political system. Write a paragraph in which you speculate on how this first chapter might be preparing us for what is to come in the novel?

Suggestions for Journal Entries

1. Think of a natural environment you know well that has been damaged. Use listing to gather details that describe the effects of the damage and explain what caused it.
2. Gather details that might describe two different parts of your city, community, state, or campus.
3. In paragraph 2, Paton says "Destroy it and man is destroyed." Think about the information you put down in response to Suggestion 1 above. Now, use listing or clustering to gather details that might show how damaging this environment has affected the people who live in or frequent it.

New Blood for Cities

Stephen Moore

Stephen Moore is an economist at the Cato Institute, a think tank in Washington, DC. He has also worked on the U.S. Congress's Joint Economic Committee. His articles have appeared in The Wall Street Journal *and the* Los Angeles Times, *among other publications. He has appeared on television programs such as* The News Hour *with Jim Lehrer and* The McLaughlin Group, *and he is a contributing editor for* Human Events *and the* National Review. *His book,* Immigration for the Twenty-First Century, *was published in 1994. "New Blood for Cities" appeared in* The American Enterprise *magazine.*

Preparing to Read

1. "Balkanization" (paragraph 1) refers to the division, after World War I, of the area of the Balkan Mountains in southeastern Europe into several smaller nations, many of which were hostile to each other. These included Bulgaria, Greece, and Albania as well as several smaller states such as Serbia, Bosnia, and Croatia. Thus, *balkanization* means "to divide into opposing groups or factions."

2. Alexis de Tocqueville (1805–1859) (paragraph 2) was a French social philosopher. He wrote *Democracy in America* (1835), a book based on his travels in the United States. He believed American democracy would outlast European monarchy.

3. The heart of this contrast essay is paragraphs 5 through 10. But read paragraphs 1 through 4 and 11 carefully. They reveal Moore's purpose and thesis.

Vocabulary

assesses (verb)	Evaluates, measures, appraises.
compelling (adjective)	Impressive, convincing.
demographic (adjective)	Relating to population.
fiscal (adjective)	Financial; in this case, relating to public finances and budgets.
infusion (noun)	A flowing into.
per capita (adjective)	Per person, per head.
refute (verb)	Disprove, rebut.
virtually (adverb)	Essentially, practically.

New Blood for Cities

Stephen Moore

IMMIGRATION, WARNS A recent *New York Times Magazine* story, is leading to the 1
"balkanization" of America's once-mighty industrial cities. "In the last half of
the 1980s, for every ten immigrants who arrived in New York, Chicago, Los Angeles, and Houston, nine residents left for elsewhere," the article informs us.
Meanwhile, city officials and antiimmigration groups charge that immigrants
impose large economic burdens on America's inner cities.

Not so fast, argues a new study from the Alexis de Tocqueville Institution 2
(ADTI) in Alexandria, VA. Certainly immigrants have a profound demographic,
economic, and fiscal impact on America's largest central cities. More than half
of all immigrants reside in just seven cities: Los Angeles, New York, Chicago,
Miami, San Diego, Houston, and San Francisco. And true, immigrants impose
special strains on these cities—heavier demands for social services, schools,
and housing; language problems; and tighter labor markets. But the benefits of
an infusion of fresh blood may offset these costs, the ADTI study suggests.

It assesses the local impact of immigration by contrasting the economic 3
condition of cities with the highest immigration and those with the lowest immigration from 1980–90 (and through 1994 where more recent data is available). The 85 most populous U.S. cities, population 200,000 or more, are
examined using Census Bureau data on nine different economic and fiscal
measures.

The study's findings challenge much conventional wisdom: 4

- In the 1980s cities with the highest immigration had a job-creation 5
  rate twice as high as cities with the lowest immigration.

- Residents of high-immigrant cities are, on average, 15 percent richer 6
  than residents of low-immigrant cities. And incomes grew faster in
  high-immigrant areas as well. Residents of the cities with the most
  immigrants in 1980 experienced a 95 percent growth in per capita
  income that decade, versus an 88 percent growth in income for
  residents in the cities with the fewest immigrants in 1980.

- Poverty rates were 20 percent higher in 1990 in the cities with the 7
  fewest immigrants than in the cities with the most immigrants. The
  poverty rate from 1980–90 grew almost twice as fast in the cities with
  fewest immigrants in 1990 as in the cities with the most immigrants.

What about social conditions? No single factor has contributed to the de- 8
clining livability of America's inner cities more than crime. Since at least the
turn of the century, when the great wave of Germans, Italians, and Irishmen arrived through Ellis Island, Americans have often seen immigrants as a source of
criminality.

Immigrants and Crime Don't Really Mix

High-Immigrant Cities	Foreign-Born, 1990	Crime Rate, 1991
Hialeah	69%	8 per 1,000
Miami	59	18
Santa Ana	51	8
Glendale	45	5
Los Angeles	38	10
San Francisco	34	9
Anaheim	28	7
New York	28	9
San Jose	27	5
Jersey City	26	9
Average, high-immigrant cities		9

Low-Immigrant Cities	Foreign-Born, 1990	Crime Rate, 1991
Jackson	1%	14 per 1,000
Shreveport	1	10
Birmingham	1	13
Memphis	1	10
Louisville	2	6
Richmond	2	12
Indianapolis	2	7
Mobile	2	13
Nashville	2	9
St. Louis	2	16
Average, low-immigrant cities		11

True or not in the past, crime and immigration do *not* go together today. The table shows that high-immigrant cities in 1990 had a crime rate of 9 per 1,000 residents. Low-immigrant cities had a crime rate of 11—or about 22 percent higher. Only Miami, which has a very heavy concentration of immigrants and also the second highest crime rate of all major cities, is a major exception to the rule.   9

The ADTI study does not answer the critical question of whether the immigrants cause urban conditions to improve, or whether improved urban conditions cause the immigrants to come. But it does provide compelling evidence to refute the belief that the economic decline of cities is *caused* by immigration. The assertion cannot be true, because, with few exceptions, the U.S. cities in greatest despair—Detroit, St. Louis, Buffalo, Rochester, and Shreveport, for example—have virtually no immigrants.   10

Some 200 years ago James Madison wrote: "That part of America that has   11
encouraged [foreign immigration] has advanced most rapidly in population,
agriculture, and in the arts." That observation may be as true today as it was at
the birth of the nation.

Read More on the Web

American Family Immigration History site, Ellis Island: http://www.
    ellisisland.org/default.asp

Alexis de Tocqueville Institute Immigration Page: http://www.adti.net/
    gw-immigration.html

Site of the National Immigration Forum: http://www.immigrationforum.
    org/

Homepage of the Federation for American Immigration Reform (FAIR):
    http://www.fairus.org/

Questions for Discussion

1. Which of the two patterns for organizing comparison/contrast essays
    does this essay use?
2. Moore's introduction is four paragraphs long. What is the function of
    each of these paragraphs?
3. Why does the author mention the *New York Times Magazine* story in
    paragraph 1? How does doing so help him make his point?
4. What kinds of details does Moore use most frequently to support the
    central ideas of paragraphs 5 through 10?
5. Does Moore believe the presence of large numbers of immigrants
    makes living in a place better? If not, what is his thesis?
6. What method for concluding essays explained in Chapter 4 does
    Moore use?

Thinking Critically

1. Explain the effect of Moore's including the table entitled "Immigrants
    and Crime Don't Really Mix." Couldn't he have just summarized this
    information in another paragraph or two?
2. You might agree with everything Moore has to say. Nonetheless, there
    are two sides to every story, even if one is more convincing than the
    other. Reread this essay. Offer an objection or counterargument to
    each of the author's arguments in paragraphs 5 through 10.

Suggestions for Journal Entries

1. Are you an immigrant, the child of an immigrant, or even the grandchild of an immigrant? If so, make a list of all of the good things people of your family or your ethnic group have contributed to the community, the state, or the country in general.

2. Think of other advantages that the presence of immigrants brings to a community. For example, you might mention that many new Americans start small businesses that provide new products and employment opportunities. You might talk about various types of music, art, or sports that immigrants have brought to America. Or, you could mention how the variety of ethnic restaurants, started by immigrants, has made your city a more interesting place to live.

3. For Moore, the notion that immigration is a burden on the cities is clearly a misconception. Think of three or four popular misconceptions about immigrants in general or about members of a particular immigrant group. List these in a sentence or two. Then list an argument or fact that would refute each of these misconceptions.

Temptations of Old Age*

Malcolm Cowley

Malcolm Cowley (1898–1989) was a writer, editor, literary critic, and historian noted for his energy and productivity up until his death at 90. In the last decade of his life, Cowley wrote The View from 80, *a book that explains his very positive attitude toward aging and that offers excellent advice about the latter stages of life.*

Preparing to Read

1. This selection is from a chapter of Cowley's book that discusses several temptations of old age and explains ways to avoid them. Among these temptations are greed, vanity, and a desire to escape life's problems through alcohol. But the greatest temptation, as shown in the following paragraphs, is "simply giving up."

2. Renoir, mentioned in paragraph 4, was a French painter of the nineteenth and twentieth centuries. Goya was a Spanish painter of the eighteenth and nineteenth centuries.

3. What hint about the selection's contents does the word "temptations" provide?

Vocabulary

ailments (noun)	Illnesses, disorders, diseases.
compelling (adjective)	Convincing, strong, valid.
distinguished (adjective)	Well-respected.
distraction (noun)	Amusement, diversion.
infirmities (noun)	Illnesses, weaknesses, ailments.
lithographs (noun)	Prints.
outwitted (verb)	Outsmarted, outmaneuvered.
Rolls-Royce (noun)	Expensive British automobile.
senility (noun)	Forgetfulness and decrease in mental powers affecting some elderly people.
stoical (adjective)	Brave, uncomplaining.
unvanquished (adjective)	Undefeated.

---

*Editor's title.

Temptations of Old Age

Malcolm Cowley

NOT WHISKEY OR cooking sherry but simply giving up is the greatest tempta-   1
tion of age. It is something different from a stoical acceptance of infirmi-
ties, which is something to be admired.

The givers-up see no reason for working. Sometimes they lie in bed all day   2
when moving about would still be possible, if difficult. I had a friend, a distinguished poet, who surrendered in that fashion. The doctors tried to stir him to
action, but he refused to leave his room. Another friend, once a successful
artist, stopped painting when his eyes began to fail. His doctor made the mistake of telling him that he suffered from a fatal disease. He then lost interest in
everything except the splendid Rolls-Royce, acquired in his prosperous days,
that stood in the garage. Daily he wiped the dust from its hood. He couldn't
drive it on the road any longer, but he used to sit in the driver's seat, start the
motor, then back the Rolls out of the garage and drive it in again, back twenty
feet and forward twenty feet; that was his only distraction.

I haven't the right to blame those who surrender, not being able to put my-   3
self inside their minds or bodies. Often they must have compelling reasons, physical or moral. Not only do they suffer from a variety of ailments, but also they are
made to feel that they no longer have a function in the community. Their families and neighbors don't ask them for advice, don't really listen when they speak,
don't call on them for efforts. One notes that there are not a few recoveries from
apparent senility when that situation changes. If it doesn't change, old persons
may decide that efforts are useless. I sympathize with their problems, but the men
and women I envy are those who accept old age as a series of challenges.

For such persons, every new infirmity is an enemy to be outwitted, an ob-   4
stacle to be overcome by force of will. They enjoy each little victory over themselves, and sometimes they win a major success. Renoir was one of them. He
continued painting, and magnificently, for years after he was crippled by arthritis; the brush had to be strapped to his arm. "You don't need your hand to
paint," he said. Goya was another of the unvanquished. At 72 he retired as an
official painter of the Spanish court and decided to work only for himself. His
later years were those of the famous "black paintings" in which he let his imagination run (and also of the lithographs, then a new technique). At 78 he escaped a reign of terror in Spain by fleeing to Bordeaux. He was deaf and his eyes
were failing; in order to work he had to wear several pairs of spectacles, one
over another, and then use a magnifying glass; but he was producing splendid
work in a totally new style. At 80 he drew an ancient man propped on two
sticks, with a mass of white hair and beard hiding his face and with the in-
scription "I am still learning."

"Eighty years old!" the great Catholic poet Paul Claudel wrote in his jour-   5
nal. "No eyes left, no ears, no teeth, no legs, no wind! And when all is said and
done, how astonishingly well one does without them!"

Read More on the Web

Washington Post obituary and an interview with Cowley's son: http://
www.geocities.com/Heartland/Hollow/5913/interests/cowley.html

Short biography of Cowley with excerpts from his major works:
http://www.spartacus.schoolnet.co.uk/USAcowleyM.htm

Questions for Discussion

1. Pick out particularly vivid verbs and adjectives in this selection.
2. Where does Cowley signal a transition from one subject to another?
3. Various methods can be combined to develop one idea. Where in this piece does Cowley use examples?
4. Do you think the conclusion of this selection is effective? Why or why not? If necessary, review ways to write conclusions in Chapter 4.
5. Why, according to the author, do some elderly people simply give up?
6. What does he mean when he says that others see "every new infirmity" as "an obstacle to be overcome by force of will" (paragraph 4)?

Thinking Critically

1. Cowley quotes directly from the "unvanquished." Why doesn't he also quote from "those who surrender"?
2. This selection uses the subject-by-subject pattern. Why does the author begin with the "givers-up" and not end with them? Should he have discussed Renoir, Goya, and Claudel first?
3. Would "Temptations of Old Age" have been better organized point by point? Why or why not?

Suggestions for Journal Entries

1. What Cowley says might apply to folks of all ages. Do you know someone who seems to face all the challenges life has to offer? Spend five minutes freewriting about the way this person reacts to such challenges. Then do the same for someone you might call a "giver-up." Try to include facts about their lives that will describe their personalities.
2. In what way are you like the people in your family who have come before you? Think about a parent, grandparent, great-aunt, or other older relative. Use listing or focused freewriting to explain what is similar about your personalities, interests, lifestyles, or your opinions about music, politics, other people, or anything else you can think of.

High Anxiety: It Never Ends

Nancy Terranova

The student who wrote this essay majored in English and is now working part-time as an editor for a large publishing house. When asked to write a comparison/contrast essay, she reflected on the kinds of anxieties young American adults were experiencing, especially in the aftermath of the terrorist attacks of 9/11/01. "Nancy Terranova" is a pen name.

Preparing to Read

1. "Generation X" is a term that defines the current generation of young adults, roughly from their mid-teens to about thirty.

2. Note that Terranova uses a two-paragraph introduction and that she follows the point-by-point pattern to organize her essay. However, in the rough draft of this essay, which appears in the chapter's introduction, Terranova began with the subject-by-subject method, then switched to point-by point. Her final draft is far more consistent and logical.

3. Several bits of researched information appear in this essay, along with a Works Cited page, arranged in Modern Language Association style. If you want to learn more about MLA style, turn to the Appendix of this textbook. For now, pay particular attention to how researched information is introduced into this essay and how it helps support the thesis.

Vocabulary

abounds (verb)	Is plentiful.
anxiety (noun)	Worry, uneasiness.
debilitated (adjective)	Weakened.
despots (noun)	Tyrants.
gratification (noun)	Satisfaction.
hysteria (noun)	Extreme agitation, mass fear.
illicit (adjective)	Illegal.
prevalent (adjective)	Common.
susceptible (adjective)	Vulnerable, exposed to.
virtually (adverb)	Nearly, almost totally.

High Anxiety: It Never Ends

Nancy Terranova

IN 2002, THE lives of people in their late teens and twenties are different in   1
many ways from what they would have been if they had been born half a
century earlier. Members of Generation X seem to have advantages their
grandparents—and even their parents—never even hoped for. Fax machines,
email, voice mail, and call-waiting enable them to maintain unbroken strings
of communication even with people across the globe. Computer software
makes them more productive students and employees. Take-home movies, television systems offering hundreds of channels, electronic games, and downloads of popular music are, sadly, transforming them into a generation of
overweight couch potatoes. And speaking of food, consider the immediate
gratification—if not the nutrition—that drive-up hamburger joints, sushi bars,
and the makers of microwaveable pizzas provide.

According to the French, however, "the more things change, the more they   2
stay the same." Today's young adults might live in a technologically advanced
environment, but are their lives any happier and any less stressful than those of
their parents and grandparents? As a matter of fact, they suffer the same kinds
of anxieties that their elders experienced.

Take concerns over staying healthy, for example. Through much of the   3
20th century, diseases such as diphtheria, tuberculosis, pneumonia, tetanus,
and even influenza took the lives of many young adults or severely debilitated
them. In the 1950's, the world went through a kind of polio hysteria, as bad as
that caused by AIDS in the 1980s. According to Dr. Edmund Sass, the United
States reported 52,000 new cases of polio in 1952 (3). Another 5000 new cases
were reported in Canada (Rutty 1) for that year.

Today, medicine has virtually eliminated polio in the developed world.   4
Diphtheria and tuberculosis, which plagued earlier generations, are in severe
decline, and pneumonia and tetanus can be treated with antibiotics. However,
Generation X has its own health worries. For example, according to the Centers for Disease Control:

> Many more people die by suicide than by homicide in the United
> States. Suicide rates among youth have been increasing steadily for
> the past four decades; suicide is the third leading cause of death
> among children and youth between the ages of 10 and 24. (1)

Moreover, young people seem to be more susceptible to drug and alcohol abuse.
In a 1997 statement of the US Senate Judiciary Committee, Senator Orrin Hatch
reported that the use of illicit drugs among adolescents had "dramatically
increased since 1991—from 11% to 24% in 1996 for 8th graders, from 21% to
38% for 10th graders, and from 29% to 40% for 12th graders" (1). Sexually
transmitted diseases including gonorrhea and syphilis are also much more

prevalent today because members of Generation X are far more sexually active than their grandparents or even their parents were. AIDS, now at epidemic levels, was unknown fifty years ago. Rates of anorexia and bulimia have also increased in the last two decades especially among women in their teens and twenties. However, even young men are suffering from these ailments.

People who came of age in the 40's, 50's, and 60's worried about how to make a living. For example, many men and women of our parents' and grandparents' generations held factory or low-level office jobs. They had to develop skills to get those jobs, which meant finishing high school or learning a trade as an apprentice. In those days, that wasn't so easy. My grandparents remember the Great Depression, when 1 out of 4 people was out of work. Many of them had to leave high school in order to help support their families, and sometimes finding someone with whom to apprentice was difficult. In addition, factory lay-offs were common. 5

Today, a college education is a necessity. Graduating from high school qualifies one for an entry-level job at Burger King. The minimum to launch any worthwhile career is a community college degree. And the best-paying jobs require continued study far beyond the bachelor's. However, even an advanced degree won't prevent the possibility of being laid off, as so many employees of high-tech companies have found out in recent years. This generation may not be experiencing a depression as our grandparents did, but we have just come through a recession, and that was bad enough! So anxiety about keeping a steady job and building a rewarding career still abounds. 6

Then there are the questions of war and national security. The previous two generations lived through the horrors of World War II and the Korean War, not to mention the Cold War, which is now, we are told, far behind us. But this generation has to deal with its fear of terrorism, which became all too real on 9/11/01. We are leery about boarding airplanes, and we have accustomed ourselves to listening for warnings from the newly created Department of Homeland Security. Some of us might soon be called to fight in the Middle East as did our older brothers and sisters in the 1990 Persian Gulf War or in Kosovo. 7

No one knows what tomorrow will bring. Perhaps being human means living with anxiety and even fear. If the past is any indication of what the future holds, this generation will follow the example of its predecessors and come through. The American people have distinguished themselves during the past fifty years. After all, they have conquered major diseases, ended the Cold War, invented the computer, helped establish democracies in countries once ruled by despots, strengthened the rights of women and minorities in their own land, and, through it all, managed to maintain the highest standard of living the world has ever known. If the current generation can do half that much, it will be just fine. 8

Works Cited

Centers for Disease Control and Prevention. *Suicide Among Youth.*
12 July 2002. 15 July 2002. http://www.cdc:gov/
communication/tips/suicide.htm.

Rutty, Christopher J. *Do Something . . . Do Anything! Poliomyelitis
in Canada, 1927–1962.* Apr. 1995. Health Heritage Research
Services. 12 July 2002 <http://www.healthheritageresearch.
com/PolioPHD.html>.

Sass, Edmund. "A Polio History Quest." *Polio History Pages.* 22
Apr. 2002. 12 July 2002 <http://www.cloudnet.com/
~edrbsass/poliohistoryquest.htm>.

United States Senate Judiciary Committee. *Drug Abuse Among
Our Children: A Growing National Crisis.* By Senator Orin
Hatch, Chairman. June 1998. 15 July 2002 <http://www.
senate.gov/~judiciary/oldsite/ogh61798.htm>.

Read More on the Web

Essay written by a Case Western Reserve University professor who claims
that young adults are living in an age of anxiety: http://www.cwru.
edu/pubaff/univcomm/anxiety.htm

Ohio State University site on dealing with anxiety in young adults:
http://anxiety.psy.ohio-state.edu/Adolescents.htm

Questions for Discussion

1. The author discusses three major areas of similarity. What are they?
2. Explain why the subject-by-subject method of organization would
    not have been as appropriate to Terranova's purpose as the point-by-
    point method?
3. This essay makes many comparisons; it points out similarities. What
    differences between the sources of anxiety for one generation and
    those for another does Terranova point out? In other words, where
    and why does she use contrast?
4. What does the author's subtitle add to the essay? How does it help
    the reader?
5. Where in this essay do you find illustration used? How about the
    cause-and-effect method?
6. Much of this essay's success is due to its use of concrete detail.
    Analyze one paragraph you think is particularly illustrative of
    Terranova's ability to use such detail.

Thinking Critically

1. Terranova spends a great deal of time explaining the anxieties young people feel over their health. Do you agree with her assessment? Are you worried about the kinds of problems she mentions? Are you worried about other problems? Are you not worried at all about health problems?

2. Terranova argues that today's young adults have as much to worry about as their parents and grandparents did. If this is so, in what ways are their lives better than those of their predecessors? In what ways are they worse?

Suggestions for Journal Entries

1. Terranova spends less time on questions of health and employment than on national security. Perhaps, for her, the first two are simply more relevant and more immediate. Which one of the concerns that she mentions has the most relevance for you? Use focused freewriting to add details of your own to Terranova's discussion, but focus on only one of the three areas she discusses. If you have no interest in any of the areas that Terranova covers, write about another source of anxiety that is especially important for you.

2. Interview at least two parents, grandparents, or any members of an earlier generation. Begin by talking about the prevailing views of your generation on a certain subject such as sex, war, getting married, religion, or any other issue or concern that affects the lives of people your age. Then, ask the people you are interviewing to identify both similarities and differences in the ways their generation viewed such questions. Like Terranova, you might want to discuss various types of anxieties suffered by your generation and theirs. Or you might ask them about their generations' views on race relations, education, war, the government, patriotism, religion, dating, or drinking.

Suggestions for Sustained Writing

1. Did you respond to the second of the Suggestions for Journal Entries after Paton's "The Road from Ixopo"? If so, turn your notes into an essay that details major differences between two parts of your community, city, state, or campus. In the process, explain what accounts for or has created these differences.

   As Paton did in "The Road from Ixopo," try using the subject-by-subject method. In fact, you might use the selection by Paton as a model. Begin by writing an outline containing two major headings under each of which you will discuss one of the areas you are contrasting. Then, under the first heading list several points, topics, ideas, or facts about the area that you will discuss. Under the second heading, list points, topics, ideas, or facts that parallel, mirror, or complement those found under the first.

Now, using this blueprint, write your rough draft. When you revise this draft, take another tip from Paton. Add the kind of concrete, specific, and vivid language that he uses and that you learned about in Chapters 5 and 6 of this textbook. In addition, draw verbal images that will make your contrast starker and more convincing to your reader. Then, edit your final draft carefully.

2. If you have not responded to all three of the items for journal writing after Moore's "New Blood for Cities," do so now. Then, read over all of your notes and use them to start an essay that contrasts at least three common misconceptions or false ideas about immigrants with the truth about them. You might devote your entire paper to one particular group of immigrants. Then, again you might attack misconceptions about three or more different groups.

The point-by-point method, which Moore uses, is probably the best way to organize this paper. Begin by making an outline much like the one you see in the diagram that helps explain the point-by-point method on page 438. Like Moore, make sure to write an interesting introduction and a memorable conclusion. State your thesis clearly in the beginning or at the end of your essay.

You need not rely heavily on statistics, as Moore does. If possible, however, you can include some simple statistics, even those you have gathered through personal observation. Of course, description, anecdotes, and examples might provide all the details you will need to develop your ideas successfully. In any event, use language that is specific and concrete. When revising your work, add vivid verbs and adjectives and create verbal images that will keep the reader's interest. Finally, edit your best draft and proofread your final product.

3. In talking about people who are 80, Malcolm Cowley describes two different types: those who fight on and those who give up. But we see these types in every generation, even our own. In fact, you may have begun discussing such people in your journal. Use these notes in an essay about people you know who fit Cowley's personality types: those who face life bravely and those who just give up.

On the other hand, if you don't like this topic, you can start from scratch and choose your own basis for contrast. For example, discuss two very different types of students: those who are serious about getting an education and those who are not. Here's an example of a thesis for such a paper:

> While serious students study hard, do extra reading, and compare notes with classmates, those who just want to get by spend much of their time playing cards or watching television.

Cowley uses the subject-by-subject method; you might want to do the same. However you decide to organize your essay, discuss two or three people you know as examples of *each* personality type. Begin with a rough draft, adding details with each revision to make your paper clearer and more convincing. In the process, include an effective introduction and conclusion.

Then, rewrite your paper once more. Make sure it has a clear thesis, is easy to follow, and is free of mistakes in grammar, punctuation, spelling, and the like.

4. If you responded to the second journal entry after "High Anxiety: It Never Ends," you interviewed two members of an earlier generation to get their views on how people in their day viewed a particular problem, question, or concern that is also affecting people of your generation. Write an essay that both compares and contrasts the ways that members of your generation and of their generation view this problem. Like Terranova, you might want to do some research—on the Internet or in the library—that will support your thesis. If so, remember to follow principles for including and citing such information as explained in the Appendix to this textbook, which discusses writing a research paper using the Modern Language Association style.

5. What was your hometown, neighborhood, or street like when you were a child, and what is it like now? Has it changed for the better or for the worse?

Describe important changes in a well-developed essay that uses the subject-by-subject method. If you wish, begin by describing what the place was like before, then discuss what it has become. Rely on your senses, and use language that is specific, vivid, and concrete. Examples of such language are found throughout this chapter but especially in the work of Paton and Cowley. Other selections that describe places and things well appear in Chapter 8.

As you write your first draft, focus on a thesis that expresses your approval or disapproval of the changes you have seen. Put that thesis in your introduction or conclusion. Here are two examples:

> What's happened to the downtown area in the last ten years has convinced me that even the most rundown city can be saved.
> What's happened to Elm Street in recent years has made me an opponent of urban renewal.

If you responded to the journal suggestions after Paton's "The Road from Ixopo," you might already have the information and inspiration to begin this project.

Writing to Learn: A Group Activity

In "New Blood for Cities," Stephen Moore draws our attention to the question of immigration. Should we leave our current immigration policy as is, or should we limit the number of immigrants? What effect—negative or positive—does the current system have on this country's economy, health care, schools, welfare system, and tax rates? Here's your chance to present both sides of the issue.

THE FIRST MEETING

Brainstorm to identify research questions concerning the impact that immigration is having on the country. For example, one of you might research immigration's effects on health care. Another might find information on immigration and the welfare system. Still others might research its impact on education, the economy, or employment. Someone could even learn about the changes immigration is bringing to American culture, especially in cuisine, entertainment, and fashion. Before you adjourn, make sure someone agrees to report on major aspects or regulations of the current U.S. immigration policy.

RESEARCH

Stick to current sources. Check the Internet, but also use your library's online and print databases to find relevant articles in periodicals. For example, try InfoTrac or ProQuest as well as the most recent installments of the *New York Times Index,* the *Readers' Guide to Periodical Literature,* and the *Social Sciences Citation Index.* Find information and opinions on both sides of the question you are researching. Bring your notes and photocopies of pages from your sources to the next meeting.

THE SECOND MEETING

The purpose of this assignment is to present both sides of the issue. Therefore, make sure everyone has gathered enough information to compose a paper that fully explains both the pros and cons of each question researched. Write an outline for a paper that will address each of these questions in a separate section. Then, ask each student to write at least two paragraphs addressing his or her assigned question. Ask the person who researched the current U.S. immigration policy to write an introduction that summarizes that policy and introduces points to be discussed in the rest of the paper.

THE THIRD MEETING

Critique each other's work and offer suggestions for improvement. Make sure everyone has fully discussed both the pros and cons of the question he or she researched. Pick one student to collect the final versions of everyone's writing and put together a draft of a complete paper that will be distributed and reviewed next time.

THE FOURTH MEETING

Distribute and read the draft of the paper. Make revisions as needed. Ask one student to edit the paper and another to type and proofread it.

CHAPTER 12

Process Analysis

Like illustration and comparison and contrast, process analysis is a way to explain complex ideas and abstract concepts. It can be used to show how something works or how something happens. It also comes in handy when you want to give readers instructions.

Organization, Purpose, and Thesis

Process explanations are organized in chronological order, much like narrative essays and short stories. In narration, however, the writer's purpose is to tell *what* happens. In process analysis, it is to explain *how* something happens (or happened) or *how* it is done.

You would be explaining a process if you wrote an essay discussing how the body uses oxygen, how electric light bulbs work, how a CD player produces sound, or how the Grand Canyon was formed. An example of such an essay in this chapter is Carl Sagan's "The Measure of Eratosthenes."

As you can see, process analysis is an important tool in scientific writing. But it can also be applied to topics in history, sociology, economics, the arts, and other subjects. For example, a process paper might be a good way to explain how the U.S. Constitution was ratified, how the stock market works, how people celebrate a holiday or tradition, or how a particular type of music developed. As Kenneth Kohler shows in "How I Came Out to My Parents," this type of writing can even explain how people deal with important personal issues. In fact, Dave Barry's "Florida's Fire Ants Headed for Trouble" proves that process analysis can be used to create humor.

Process analysis is also used in writing instructions. Scientists, doctors, engineers, and computer experts, for example, must often write careful directions to show their readers how to use a tool or machine, how to complete a procedure safely, how to conduct a test to achieve accurate results, or how to run complicated computer software. As a beginning writer, you might want to discuss a more limited subject by showing your readers how to change a tire, hang wallpaper, stop smoking, lose weight, study for a math exam, or accomplish another important task or goal. In this chapter, selections that instruct readers are Adam Goodheart's "How to Fight a Duel," and Triena Milden's "So You Want to Flunk Out of College," which appears in the introduction.

The thesis in a process analysis essay is usually a statement of purpose; it explains why a process is important, why it occurs or occurred, or why it should be completed. For example, if you want to explain how to change the oil in a car, you might begin by saying that changing oil regularly can extend the engine's life. In addition to a statement of purpose, writers often begin with a broad summary or overview of the process so that readers can understand how each step relates to the whole procedure and to its purpose.

Clarity and Directness

As with all types of writing, clarity and directness are important in process writing. You must explain the various steps in your process specifically and carefully enough that even readers who are unfamiliar with the subject will be able to follow each step easily. To be clear and to maintain your reader's interest, keep the following in mind:

1. *Use clear, simple language:* Use words that your readers will have no trouble understanding. If you *must* use terms your readers are not familiar with, provide a brief definition or description. Depending on how much your readers know about how to change a tire, for example, you might have to describe what a lug wrench looks like before you explain how to use it.

2. *Use the clearest, simplest organization:* Whenever possible, arrange the steps of your process in chronological order. In addition, use plenty of connective words and phrases between paragraphs (especially to show the passage of time); this will keep your writing coherent and easy to follow.

3. *Mention equipment and supplies:* Let readers know what equipment, tools, supplies, and other materials are involved in the process. Define or describe items that might be unfamiliar to them. If you are giving instructions, list these materials *before* you start explaining the steps in your process. Otherwise, the reader will have to stop in mid-process to find a needed item. This can be frustrating and time consuming.

4. *Discuss each step separately:* Reserve an entire paragraph for each step in the process; this is especially important when giving instructions. Explaining more than one step at a time can confuse readers and cause you to leave out important information.

5. *Discuss simultaneous steps separately:* If you need to explain two or more steps that occur at the same time, write about these steps in separate paragraphs. To maintain coherence between paragraphs, use connective elements such as "At the same time," "Meanwhile," and "During this stage of the process."

6. *Give all the necessary information:* Always provide enough information to develop each step in the process adequately, and don't forget the small, important details. For instance, if you're explaining how to change the oil in a car, remember to tell your readers to wait for the engine to cool off before loosening the oil-pan bolt; otherwise, the oil could severely burn

their hands. On the other hand, the oil should be warm enough so that it all drains off.

7. *Use the right verb tense:* If you're explaining a recurring process (one that happens over and over again), use the present tense. In writing about how your student government works, for instance, say that "the representatives *are elected* by fellow students and *meet* together every Friday afternoon." But if you're writing about a process that is over and done with, such as how one individual ran for election, use the past tense.

8. *Use direct commands:* When giving instructions, make each step clear and brief by simply telling the reader to do it (that is, by using the imperative mood). For example, don't say, "The first thing to do is to apply the handbrake." Instead, be more direct: "First, apply the handbrake."

Visualizing Process Analysis

The following diagram illustrates how you might organize the instructions on removing a flat tire. Transitions are underlined.

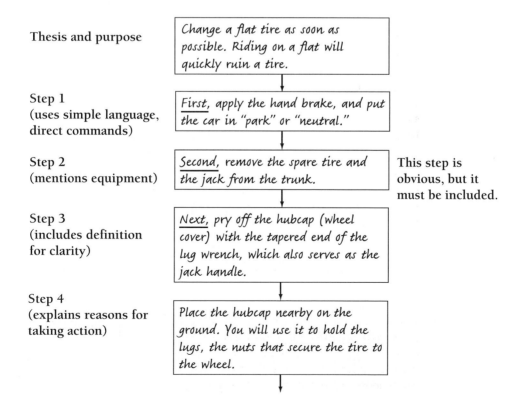

Thesis and purpose	*Change a flat tire as soon as possible. Riding on a flat will quickly ruin a tire.*
Step 1 (uses simple language, direct commands)	*First, apply the hand brake, and put the car in "park" or "neutral."*
Step 2 (mentions equipment)	*Second, remove the spare tire and the jack from the trunk.* **This step is obvious, but it must be included.**
Step 3 (includes definition for clarity)	*Next, pry off the hubcap (wheel cover) with the tapered end of the lug wrench, which also serves as the jack handle.*
Step 4 (explains reasons for taking action)	*Place the hubcap nearby on the ground. You will use it to hold the lugs, the nuts that secure the tire to the wheel.*

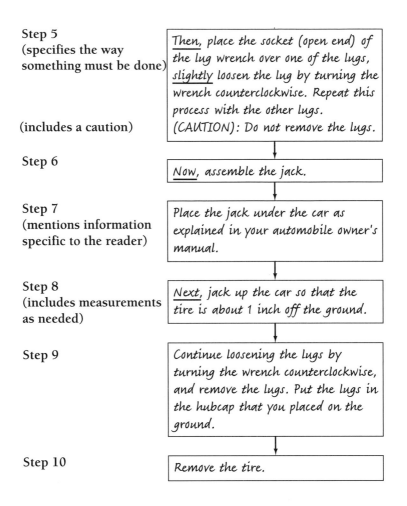

Step 5
(specifies the way
something must be done)

Then, place the socket (open end) of the lug wrench over one of the lugs, slightly loosen the lug by turning the wrench counterclockwise. Repeat this process with the other lugs.

(includes a caution)

(CAUTION): Do not remove the lugs.

Step 6

Now, assemble the jack.

Step 7
(mentions information specific to the reader)

Place the jack under the car as explained in your automobile owner's manual.

Step 8
(includes measurements as needed)

Next, jack up the car so that the tire is about 1 inch off the ground.

Step 9

Continue loosening the lugs by turning the wrench counterclockwise, and remove the lugs. Put the lugs in the hubcap that you placed on the ground.

Step 10

Remove the tire.

SEEING THE PATTERN IN A PROCESS ANALYSIS PAPER

The following essay, "So You Want to Flunk Out of College," takes a humorous approach to a serious issue. Student author Triena Milden uses irony by arguing the opposite of what she believes. Nonetheless, her tongue-in-cheek essay illustrates several techniques important to process analysis.

Flunking out of college is a relatively easy task. It requires little effort and might even be considered fun. Though it is hard to imagine why anyone would purposefully try to flunk out of college, many people accomplish

States thesis.

this task easily. In fact, whatever the reason one might want to flunk out of college, the process is quite simple.

Uses present tense.

First, *do not show up* for classes very often. It is important, however, to show up occasionally to find out when tests will be scheduled; the importance of this will become apparent later in this essay.

Uses transitions for clear, simple organization.

Uses direct commands.

When in class, *never raise your hand* to ask questions and never volunteer any answers to the teacher's questions. If the teacher calls on you, either answer incorrectly or say "I don't know." Be sure your tone of voice conveys your lack of interest.

Discusses each step separately.

Another thing to avoid is homework. There are two reasons for this. First and most important, completing homework assignments only reinforces information learned earlier, thereby contributing to higher test scores. Second, although teachers credit homework as only part of the total grade, every little bit of credit hurts. Therefore, make sure that the teacher is aware that you are not doing your homework. You can do so by making certain that the teacher sees you writing down the answers as the homework is discussed in class.

Provides all necessary information.

Uses simple language.

The next area, tests, can be handled in two ways. <u>They can either not be taken or be failed.</u> If you do not take them, you run the risk of receiving an "incomplete" rather than a failing grade. In order to flunk out of college, failing grades are preferable.

Continues to use direct commands.

Therefore, <u>make sure to take and fail all exams.</u> Incidentally, this is where attendance and homework can really affect performance. Attending class and doing homework regularly can be detrimental to obtaining poor test scores.

Since you won't know the correct answers to test questions, make sure to choose those that are as absurd as possible without being obvious. Even if you guess a few correctly, your overall grade will be an *F* as long as the majority of your answers are wrong. By

Keeps to the present tense.

the way, one sure way to receive that cherished zero is t<u>o </u>be caught cheating: all teachers <u>promise</u> a zero for this.

The same ideas <u>pertain</u> to any reports or term papers that you are assigned. If you

Provides all necessary information.

fail to turn them in, you might get an "incomplete." Therefore, hand in all papers, especially if they're poorly written. Make sure to use poor organization, to present information in a confused manner, and to

write on the wrong topic whenever you can.
The paper should be handwritten, not typed,
and barely legible. Misspellings should be
plentiful and as noticeable as possible.
Smudged ink or dirty pages add a nice touch
to the finished product. Finally, try to get
caught plagiarizing.

By following these few simple
suggestions, you will be assured of a
failing grade. Try not to make it too
obvious that your purpose is to fail.

Ends with a memorable conclusion.

However, if a teacher shows concern and
offers help, be sure to exhibit a poor
attitude as you refuse. Should you decide to
put extra effort into failing, you may even
finish at the bottom of the class. Someone
has to finish last. Why not you?

Revising Process Analysis Papers

When Kenneth Kohler wrote the first draft of "How I Came Out to My Parents,"
he used narration. Later, he decided that telling what happened was less important than explaining how it happened. Paragraphs from the draft and revision of his paper show how he changed his narrative into process analysis. They
also show that he added information, removed unnecessary words and details,
and combined sentences to make his writing more efficient. The entire essay
appears later in the chapter.

Kohler—Early Draft

My struggle to "come out of the closet" grew
out of several needs. First, I had a need
to be closer to my parents and to share my
life with them. Second, I had a need to be

Combine these two reasons?

honest with them about who I really was.

And third, I needed to let them know that — *Is "And" needed?*

there was someone special in my life. By

Remove? Isn't this clear already? [coming out to my parents, I would risk

alienation and rejection for the hope that — *Save for later paragraph?*

they would gain a little more understanding

of the man whom they called their son.

. . .

I had no idea how my parents might react

when I came out to them. I knew that if my

parents reacted violently or negatively it

Repeats ideas from above. Remove? [could take years to heal the damage that — *Wordy? Remove unnecessary words?*

would be done by their reaction. It was a

chance I had to take. I had to risk telling

them my deepest secret in an attempt to get

closer to them. It was a risk my brother — *Do readers need to know this?*

never had to take.

Kohler—Final Draft

My struggle to "come out of the closet" grew

out of several needs. First, I wanted to be — *Combines ideas.*

closer with my parents and to be honest

about who I was. Second, I needed to let — *Has removed ideas that belong in a later paragraph.*

Adds information to strengthen and clarify purpose. [them know that there was someone special in

my life. Finally, I had agreed to speak at

my church about being gay, and I felt it

important to tell my parents about my

lifestyle before informing my congregation.

. . .

Adds information important to purpose.

I had no idea how they might react when I came out to them. I knew that if they responded violently or negatively it could take years to heal the damage. I also knew that I might never see them again. It was

Has removed unnecessary words, details.

for this reason that I had avoided coming out to them before. However, because of my pending public announcement, the time had come to let them know.

Adds a paragraph to trace steps in the process.

I planned what I had to say carefully. Something so important could not simply be announced and forgotten. I had actually begun to prepare for this moment years

Step 1

before by reading as much as I could about homosexuality and by talking to gay friends. It was necessary for me to accept myself as a gay man before expecting others to do so. I had to develop a positive self-image, and this took several years. Then, in the week

Step 2; Note transition.

prior to my announcement, I began to rehearse my lines. I made notes for various approaches I could take. I wanted to feel secure in my delivery and didn't want to appear ashamed of my lifestyle. "Why should I be?" I thought. I had never felt differently. I imagined my parents' every reaction and tried to predict my responses. I even prepared myself for the worst, afraid they would tell me to "Get out and never come back!"

Step 3

Practicing Process Analysis

Reread Visualizing Process Analysis and the diagram of it on pages 473–477. Use the method you see there to list instructions on doing a simple task. Write these steps in the boxes below, one step per box. Be complete; if you need more boxes, draw them on a piece of paper. As always, make a rough draft first. Here are examples of the task you might write about.

How to brush your teeth.
How to make a pot of coffee.
How to address an envelope.
How to make out a check.
How to start a car.
How to take a two-minute shower.
How to do laundry in a washing machine.
How to heat leftovers in a microwave.

**State task's
purpose**

Step 1

Step 2

Step 3

Step 4

Step 5

Step 6

Step 7

Step 8

Enjoy the four selections that follow. They are well written and should provide you with effective examples of the techniques found in writing that makes good use of process analysis.

How to Fight a Duel

Adam Goodheart

Adam Goodheart was an associate editor with Civilization *magazine, published by the Library of Congress in Washington, DC. Goodheart wrote a column called "Lost Arts" in which he explained how to master arts, skills, or activities from the past. Among these intriguing articles are "How to Host a Roman Orgy" and "How to Fly a Zeppelin." "How to Fight a Duel" appeared in 1996.*

Preparing to Read

1. Tort reform (paragraph 1) is a movement to change laws governing suits brought to gain compensation for injury to one's person, property, or reputation.

2. In paragraph 4, Goodheart mentions a "second." This is a person who accompanied and assisted the duelist and even took his or her place if necessary.

3. As with the other articles in his column, Goodheart explains a serious subject humorously. One way he does this is to mix formal, even exotic, language with everyday vocabulary, including slang.

Vocabulary

à la terre (adverb)	To the ground (French).
blunderbuss (noun)	A gun with a wide muzzle used at close range.
calumniating (adjective)	Slandering, making malicious and untrue statements about.
frock coat (noun)	Close-fitting, knee-length coat.
impertinent (adjective)	Arrogant, rude, presumptuous.
languid (adjective)	Listless, lacking in energy or spirit.
lanky (adjective)	Tall and thin.
latitude (noun)	Degree of freedom.
litigious (adjective)	Given to lawsuits, argumentative.
prescribed (verb)	Directed, specified.
prevaricating (adjective)	Speaking falsely or in a misleading way.
provoke (verb)	Incite, anger.
sangfroid (noun)	Cold-bloodedness, cool-headedness (French).
trifle (noun)	Something of no importance.

How to Fight a Duel

Adam Goodheart

TORT REFORM IS for wimps. If we really want to fix our litigious society, how   1
about reviving the old-fashioned pistol duel? As the author of *The Art of Du-*
elling wrote in 1836, "It is certainly both awful and distressing, to see a young
person cut off suddenly in a duel . . . but the loss of a few lives is a mere trifle,
when compared with the benefits resulting to Society at large"—such as enforcing good manners. Though you may protest that you don't know a flintlock
from a fife cleaner, the rules for duels are really quite simple.

Equipment

Two (2) smoothbore flintlock pistols.

Gunpowder.

Some round lead bullets and linen patches.

A surgeon's kit.

A frock coat.

A handkerchief.

A mortal enemy.

1. The Challenge. In the 18th and 19th centuries, elaborate manuals pre-   2
scribed the exact circumstances under which duels were fought. A slur against
one's wife or mistress was a common motive, though the Irish dueling code of
1777 ruled such insults justified if they had "the support of ladies' reputations."
(But ladies dueled too; in 1721 the Countess de Polignac plugged Lady de Nes-
tle over the handsome Duc de Richelieu.)

Still, if the offense has not been obvious, you'll often find it necessary to   3
provoke a challenge by insulting your would-be enemy. Here, more creative lat-
itude is permitted. Some insults for you to choose from: "impertinent puppy"
(Major Oneby to a Mr. Gower, 1720); "prevaricating, base, calumniating
scoundrel, poltroon and coward" (Gen. James Wilkinson to Rep. John Ran-
dolph, 1807); "Baron—of Intellect" (Harry Maury to Baron Henri Arnous de
Riviere, 1858). Or you can bypass such formalities like Lord Cobham who, in
1750, simply seized Lord Hervey's hat and spat into it.

2. Preliminaries and Precautions. Once a duel has been agreed upon, it   4
is customary simply to exchange cards and then leave all further arrangement
to your seconds. The challenger's second then calls upon the challenged party
to arrange the confrontation. Such a visit should be cordial if not exactly
friendly; sangfroid, at least, is essential. In an 1870 duel, Prince Pierre Bona-
parte grew flustered and fired a bit prematurely—killing, that is to say, the unfortunate second who had come to deliver a challenge.

Traditionally, the duel must take place within the next 48 hours—to re- 5 duce practice time—and preferably at dawn. Pick a secluded spot; if there's a state or national boundary handy, fight near enough to it so you can escape across if you prove victorious. And be discreet, even with friends and family. In 1898, a Berlin duel was cut short when the opponents' fathers burst out of the shrubbery and began thrashing the young men with canes.

3. Taking the Field. Arrive properly attired in a dark frock coat—one 6 without gilt buttons and with lapels to hide your white collar, since these make easy targets. (In 1806, Andrew Jackson scandalized Kentucky—a tough feat in those days—by fighting Charles Dickinson wearing a loose dressing gown draped over his lanky frame.) Greet your antagonist and take your place. The more serious the dispute, generally, the closer you will stand. Anywhere from 10 to 50 paces is customary, although in 1819 Armistead Mason and John Mc-Carty—they were rival politicians—blasted holes in each other with shotguns at four paces. Before shots are exchanged, the seconds can try to effect a reconciliation. If your thirst for vengeance is implacable, proceed to Step 4.

4. Ready, Aim, Fire. You and your antagonist will fire simultaneously on 7 cue, usually the dropping of a handkerchief. You should be standing sideways to offer as narrow a target as possible—though not if you're built like British politician Charles James Fox, who exclaimed at a 1779 duel, "Why, man, I'm as thick one way as the other!" If you're considering firing into the air, inform yourself as to local custom. While the languid Brits thought it unsporting under any circumstances to take careful aim, the Germans were deeply offended if you didn't shoot to kill.

If both bullets miss, you can either declare the affair settled or go for an- 8 other round. If you hit your foe, advises *The Art of Duelling,* "An expression of regret should always precede [your] quitting the field." If you're hit, the handbook continues, "treat the matter coolly"; if you happen to die, "go off with as good a grace as possible."

Warning Don't try any fancy stuff. In 1808, two Frenchmen fought a duel with 9 blunderbusses in balloons; M. Grandprée sent M. le Pique plummeting *á la terre.* Late in the century, the "dynamite duel" came into vogue—participants would hurl sticks of TNT at each other. But gentlemen prefer pistols at 10 paces.

Read More on the Web

Original essay by Adam Goodheart on one of Thomas Edison's worst inventions: http://flyingmoose.org/truthfic/edison.htm

Original essay by Goodheart on how to mummify a pharoah: http://lancefuhrer.com/mummify_a_pharoah.htm

Questions for Discussion

1. Earlier in this chapter you read about techniques writers of process analysis use to keep their work interesting and clear. Find examples of such techniques. For example, where does Goodheart use direct commands? What verb tense does he use?

2. As you would expect, Goodheart lists steps involved in a duel in chronological order. Why does he arrange these steps into four separate categories?

3. What does the author propose as the purpose for dueling?

4. What method or methods of development that you learned about in Chapter 3, other than process analysis, does this essay use?

5. Why does the author include a separate list of equipment? Why didn't he just include these items in the text as he went along?

6. You learned in Preparing to Read that Goodheart creates humor by mixing informal and formal language. You can find one such example in paragraph 1. Look for at least one other and explain why it is funny.

Thinking Critically

1. Considering what you have learned about dueling, what can you add to the warning given at the end of the essay?

2. Paragraph 3 reports that Harry Maury called Henri Arnous de Riviere the "Baron—of Intellect." How do you interpret his insult?

3. What does paragraph 5 say about the image of dueling even in the past?

Suggestions for Journal Entries

1. What is worth fighting for? Make a list of people, beliefs, or ideas for which you might risk your well-being or even your life.

2. Defined broadly, a duel could be any confrontation, contest, or encounter between two people. Consider the following:

> Bargaining when buying a car.
> Convincing a child to do something he or she does not want to do.
> Asking for a raise or time off at your job.
> Talking your way out of a traffic ticket.
> Convincing someone you dislike to stop calling or annoying you.

These are only a few examples. You can probably think of many more. Focus on one such "duel"; use clustering, freewriting, or brainstorming with a friend to gather information that might explain how to prepare for and fight your particular duel successfully.

The Measure of Eratosthenes

Carl Sagan

Carl Sagan was a professor of astronomy at Cornell University and the author of many books on science. He published "The Measure of Eratosthenes" (er-uh-TAHS-thuh-neez) to honor the Greek thinker who, 17 centuries before Columbus, measured the Earth and proved it was round. Another essay by Sagan can be found in Chapter 9.

Preparing to Read

1. In paragraph 4, Sagan claims that "in almost everything, Eratosthenes was 'alpha.' " Alpha is the first letter of the Greek alphabet.
2. Papyrus, mentioned in paragraph 5, is a plant from which paper was made in ancient times.
3. What might Sagan mean by "measure" in the title?

Vocabulary

cataract (noun)	Large waterfall.
circumference (noun)	Distance around a circle or globe.
compelling (adjective)	Difficult to ignore.
deduced (verb)	Concluded, discovered.
inclined (adjective)	Slanted.
intergalactic (adjective)	Between galaxies.
intersect (verb)	Cross.
musings (noun)	Thoughts.
pronounced (adjective)	Significant.
randomly (adverb)	By chance.

The Measure of Eratosthenes

Carl Sagan

THE EARTH IS a place. It is by no means the only place. It is not even a typical   1
place. No planet or star or galaxy can be typical, because the cosmos is mostly empty. The only typical place is within the vast, cold, universal vacuum, the everlasting night of intergalactic space, a place so strange and desolate that, by comparison, planets and stars and galaxies seem achingly rare and lovely.

If we were randomly inserted into the cosmos, the chance that we would   2
find ourselves on or near a planet would be less than one in a billion trillion

trillion (10^{33}, a one followed by 33 zeros). In everyday life, such odds are called compelling. Worlds are precious.

The discovery that the earth is a *little* world was made, as so many impor-   3
tant human discoveries were, in the ancient Near East, in a time some humans call the third century BC, in the greatest metropolis of the age, the Egyptian city of Alexandria.

Here there lived a man named Eratosthenes. One of his envious contem-   4
poraries called him "beta," the second letter of the Greek alphabet, because, he said, Eratosthenes was the world's second best in everything. But it seems clear that, in almost everything, Eratosthenes was "alpha."

He was an astronomer, historian, geographer, philosopher, poet, theater   5
critic, and mathematician. His writings ranged from "Astronomy" to "On Free-dom from Pain." He was also the director of the great library of Alexandria, where one day he read, in a papyrus book, that in the southern frontier outpost of Syene (now Aswan), near the first cataract of the Nile, at noon on June 21 vertical sticks cast no shadows. On the summer solstice, the longest day of the year, as the hours crept toward midday, the shadows of the temple columns grew shorter. At noon, they were gone. A reflection of the sun could then be seen in the water at the bottom of a deep well. The sun was directly overhead.

It was an observation that someone else might easily have ignored. Sticks,   6
shadows, reflections in wells, the position of the sun—of what possible impor-tance could such simple, everyday matters be? But Eratosthenes was a scientist, and his musings on these commonplaces changed the world: in a way, they made the world.

Eratosthenes had the presence of mind to do an experiment—actually to   7
observe whether *in Alexandria* vertical sticks cast shadows near noon on June 21. And, he discovered, sticks do.

Eratosthenes asked himself how, at the same moment, a stick in Syene   8
could cast no shadow and a stick in Alexandria, far to the north, could cast a pronounced shadow.

Consider a map of ancient Egypt with two vertical sticks of equal length,   9
one stuck in Alexandria, the other in Syene. Suppose that, at a certain moment, neither stick casts any shadow at all. This is perfectly easy to understand—pro-vided the earth is flat. The sun would then be directly overhead. If the two sticks cast shadows of equal length, that also would make sense on a flat earth: the sun's rays would then be inclined at the same angle to the two sticks. But how could it be that at the same instant there was no shadow at Syene and a substantial shadow at Alexandria?

The only possible answer, he saw, was that the surface of the earth is   10
curved. Not only that: the greater the curvature, the greater the difference in the shadow lengths. The sun is so far away that its rays are parallel when they reach the earth. Sticks placed at different angles to the sun's rays cast shadows of different lengths. For the observed difference in the shadow lengths, the dis-tance between Alexandria and Syene had to be about seven degrees along the

surface of the earth; that is, if you imagine the sticks extending down to the center of the earth, they would intersect there at an angle of seven degrees.

Seven degrees is something like one-fiftieth of 360 degrees, the full circumference of the earth. Eratosthenes knew that the distance between Alexandria and Syene was approximately 800 kilometers, because he had hired a man to pace it out. 11

Eight hundred kilometers times 50 is 40,000 kilometers; so that must be the circumference of the earth. (Or, if you like to measure things in miles, the distance between Alexandria and Syene is about 500 miles, and 500 miles times 50 is 25,000 miles.) 12

This is the right answer. 13

Eratosthenes' only tools were sticks, eyes, feet, and brains, plus a taste for experiment. With them he deduced the circumference of the earth with an error of only a few percent, a remarkable achievement for 2,200 years ago. He was the first person accurately to measure the size of a planet. 14

Read More on the Web

Sagan's obituary: http://www.news.cornell.edu/general/Dec96/
   saganobit.ltb.html

Planetary Society's Tribute to Sagan: http://www.planetary.org/society/
   tributes/

Questions for Discussion

1. What does paragraph 6 tell us about the purpose for which Sagan wrote this essay?

2. Where does Sagan refer to the scientific process of making observations and of drawing conclusions from those observations?

3. Where does Sagan define important terms?

4. You have read that each step in a process should be discussed thoroughly. In what paragraph or paragraphs does Sagan's essay illustrate this principle?

5. Does this essay list separate steps in a process one by one? Explain your answer.

6. What methods of development, other than process analysis, does Sagan use?

Thinking Critically

1. Why does the author tell us so much about the life of Eratosthenes? Explain your answer in a short paragraph.
2. Make notes in the margins that explain each step in the process by which Eratosthenes measured the earth's circumference. Then put your notes into a well-organized paragraph.

Suggestions for Journal Entries

1. Make a brief, informal list of steps you might use to explain how a simple machine or natural process works. Pick something you have had experience with or know a lot about. Here are examples:

Machine	Process
Sling shot	Circulation of the blood
Bow and arrow	Formation of rain clouds
Bottle opener	Photosynthesis
Cork screw	Osmosis
Food blender	Pollination of flowers by bees
Pliers	Transmission of a particular disease
Water wheel	Movement of the tides
Fishing reel	Formation of a fossil

2. Follow the advice in Suggestion 1 for a process that human beings have learned or invented to survive or to improve the quality of their lives. Examples include the process by which a broken bone is set, artificial respiration is given, an incandescent bulb turns electricity into light, solar energy is used to heat a house, a serious disease is treated, or a food crop is grown or harvested.

Florida's Fire Ants Headed for Trouble

Dave Barry

Dave Barry is humor columnist for the Miami Herald, but his work appears regularly in hundreds of newspapers around the world. Among the twenty-four books that Barry has published are Dave Barry Hits Below the Beltway (political satire), Dave Barry Is Not Taking This Sitting Down (collected columns), Dave Barry Is from Mars and Venus, and Dave Barry's Book of Bad Songs. Two of his books have been used as the basis for the television sitcom Dave's World. "Florida's Fire Ants Headed for Trouble," published in 2003, is one of his syndicated columns.

Preparing to Read

1. This essay explains a natural process. Because it is so humorous, it is not typical of scientific writing. Yet, it does contain ingredients important to pieces of process analysis found in the world of science. For example, Barry explains the purpose of the process when, early in the essay, he says the "phorid fly" has been introduced to control fire ants.

2. One characteristic common to many of Barry's columns is that they poke as much fun at their author as at the subjects they discuss. Make sure to mark places in this essay where the author turns the comedy on himself.

3. To create humor, writers often manipulate language in several ways. Here are only a few tools that Barry uses:

    *   **Hyperbole** (exaggeration). For example, Barry claims that fire ants have 5684 eyes.

    *   **Irony**, saying the very opposite of what is meant. According to Barry, being attacked by a fire ant "was my own stupid fault: I sat on my lawn."

    *   **Sarcasm**, a type of irony with an edge. The author pokes fun at a late-night television personality when he compares the thickness of a snake to a "thigh of Anna Nicole Smith."

    *   **Figurative language.** Barry compares being bit by a fire ant to sticking his hand into "a Toaster-oven set on 'pizza' " (simile). He also personifies the fire ant "Arnie."

    *   **Unusual or unconventional wording.** Notice the phrase "Special Recipe fire-ant venom."

Vocabulary

carnivorous (adjective)	Meat-eating.
crabgrass (noun)	An unsightly weed that often appears in lawns.
ecosystems (noun)	Natural groupings of organisms living together.
maggot (noun)	Insect larva or offspring
pheromones (noun)	Hormones secreted by animals to get a response from others of their species.
predatory (adjective)	Associated with animals that hunt.
seething (adjective)	Fuming, boiling, overflowing

Florida's Fire Ants Headed for Trouble

Dave Barry

ALMOST THE first thing that happened to me when I moved to South Florida   1
was that I got attacked by a fire ant. This was my own stupid fault: I sat on
my lawn.

I thought this was safe because I had come from Pennsylvania, where   2
lawns are harmless ecosystems consisting of 93 percent crabgrass (my lawn
was, anyway); 6 percent real grass; and 1 percent cute little critters such as
worms, ladybugs and industrious worker ants who scurry around carrying objects that are 800 times their own weight. (They don't USE these objects; they
just carry them around. That's how industrious they are.)

Your South Florida lawn, on the other hand, is a *seething* mass of predatory   3
carnivorous organisms, including land crabs, alligators, snakes ranging in
thickness from "knitting needle" to "thigh of Anna Nicole Smith," lizards the
size of small dogs, and giant hairy spiders that appear to have recently *eaten*
small dogs, and are now wearing their pelts as trophies.

But the scariest South Florida lawn-dweller is the fire ant, a quarter-inch-   4
long insect that can easily defeat a full-grown human in hand-to-hand combat.
That's what happened to me. I sat on my lawn, put my hands down and YOW
a fire ant—let's call him Arnie—injected me with his Special Recipe fire-ant
venom, and then watched, with a merry twinkle in each of his 5,684 eyes, as I
leaped up and danced wildly around, brushing uselessly at my hand, which felt
as though I had stuck it into a toaster-oven set on "pizza." I'm sure the other
ants had a hearty laugh when Arnie got back to the colony and communicated
this story by releasing humor pheromones ("Then this MORON puts his HAND
down! Yes! On the LAWN! Ha ha! Must be from Pennsylvania.")

That happened 17 years ago, and my hand just recently finished healing.   5
So I am not a fan of fire ants. This is why I was excited when I read a story by
Jennifer Maloney in the *Miami Herald* about a U.S. Department of Agriculture
program, right in my neighborhood, to control fire ants by releasing a wondrous little creature called the decapitating phorid fly. This is an amazing fly
that kills fire ants via a method that, if insects wrote horror novels, would have
been dreamed up by the fire-ant Stephen King.

What happens is, the female phorid fly swoops in on a fire ant and, in less   6
than a tenth of a second, injects an egg into the ant's midsection. When the egg
hatches, the *maggot* crawls up inside the ant, and—here is the good part—*eats
the entire contents of the ant's head.* This poses a serious medical problem for the
ant, which, after walking around for a couple of weeks with its insides being
eaten, has its head actually fall off. At that point it becomes a contestant on *The
Bachelorette.*

No, seriously, at that point the ant is deceased. Meanwhile, inside the de-   7
tached head, the maggot turns into a fly, and, when it's ready crawls out and
goes looking for more ants.

You can see an amazing video of phorid flies in action at www.cmave.saa.   8
ars.usda.gov/fireant/news1.htm. The video, which has a soundtrack of wild,
jungle-style drum music, shows female flies zipping around fire ants like tiny
fighter planes, giving the ants FITS. The video also shows how, when a fly isn't
fast enough, it gets turned into Purina Ant Chow.

On a recent Friday I went to watch University of Florida Extension Agent   9
Adrian Hunsberger, and Miami-Dade County biologist Ruben Regalado, release
phorid flies on the grounds of Baptist Hospital in Kendall. To start the procedure, Ruben stuck a shovel into a fire-ant mound and turned over a bunch of
dirt. Immediately, fire ants charged out and began scurrying angrily around.

"They're looking for whoever disturbed their mound," said Adrian.   10

"I HAD NOTHING TO DO WITH DISTURBING YOUR MOUND," I   11
shouted at the ants. "RUBEN DISTURBED YOUR MOUND. I AM HERE AS A
JOURNALIST."

It's important to maintain your objectivity.   12

While the mound was swarming, Adrian opened a vial and released a   13
bunch of phorid flies. The flies, which are almost invisible—little swooping
specks—immediately went after the ants. At least the female flies did. Presumably the males, observing the Universal Guy Top Priority, tried to mate with the
females.

Anyway, I think it's a terrific idea, using natural enemies to attack fire ants.
To the Department of Agriculture, I say: Good work! To the female phorid flies,
I say: You go, girls! And to any fire ants that happen to be crawling on this col-
umn, I say: REMEMBER, I DID NOT DISTURB YOUR MOUND.

Read More on the Web

Links to some of Barry's other columns: http://www.miami.com/mld/
 miamiherald/living/columnists/dave_barry/
Dave Barry's Official Website: http://www.davebarry.com/

Questions for Discussion

1. As you learned in Preparing to Read, process essays often include statements of purpose. What, besides creating humor, is the purpose of this essay? In other words, what problem does it address?
2. Where does Barry explain the process itself? Express each of the steps of that process in your own words.
3. Process analysis pieces often contain statements cautioning or warning readers about dangers to life and property. Can you find anything resembling a caution or warning in Barry's essay?
4. Where in Barry's essay do you find examples of hyperbole, irony, or any of the other methods for creating humor mentioned in Preparing to Read?
5. Find examples of transitions in and between paragraphs.
6. What does "decapitating" mean? Where does Barry define this term? What methods of development—other than process analysis and definition—which you learned about in Chapter 3 does this essay use?
7. What is the purpose of Barry's including a reference to a website in paragraph 8?

Thinking Critically

1. Find examples of Barry's making fun of himself. Why does he do this? What can you tell about the speaker of this essay?
2. Read Adam Goodheart's "How to Fight a Duel," which also appears in this chapter. What does it have in common with "Florida's Fire Ants Headed for Trouble"?

Suggestions for Journal Entries

1. Access the website that Barry mentions in paragraph 8 or look up information on using phorid flies to control fire ants on any other

website or in any printed source. In your own words, summarize the process by which these flies kill fire ants.

2. Use freewriting or clustering to make notes on how you might get rid of a pest—any pest. You might include information on höw to control ants or cockroaches, to keep birds and squirrels out of your attic or moths out of your closet, to check the spread of mold or mildew in a bathroom, or to limit the number of weeds in a flower or vegetable garden. Then again, you might explain how you to get rid of another type of pest, such of a "friend" who has become annoying or a former sweetheart who just won't let go. Another possibility is to offer advice on how to deal with tele-marketers or how to get rid of SPAM that plagues you while you are retrieving email.

How I Came Out to My Parents

Kenneth Kohler

When his freshman English instructor encouraged the class to "write from the heart," Ken Kohler decided to explain how he accomplished one of the most difficult and meaningful tasks in his life—telling his parents he was gay. Kohler's recollection of the process by which he came to the decision and finally confronted his parents shows how deeply concerned he was about their feelings and about the kind of relationship he would have with them once they knew of his sexual preference.

This essay represents the best of what process writers can achieve, for it combines the author's emotional commitment to his subject with clear, logical analysis. Ken Kohler is now a computer programmer.

Preparing to Read

1. Like other process essays, "How I Came Out to My Parents" is organized as a narrative. But this is not just another story. What is really important here is not *what* happened, but *how* it happened— the agony Kohler endured to tell his family about his homosexuality.

2. This selection is divided into two sections. The first explains how Kohler made the decision and found the courage to tell his parents he was gay. The second discusses the results of that decision.

Vocabulary

acknowledged (verb)	Admitted.
acutely (adverb)	Greatly, sharply.
alienation (noun)	State of loneliness, exclusion.
congregation (noun)	Church members.
disclosure (noun)	Announcement, revelation.
irreparably (adverb)	Beyond repair.
pending (adjective)	Upcoming, expected.
predict (verb)	Know ahead of time.
rejection (noun)	Disapproval.

How I Came Out to My Parents

Kenneth Kohler

BEING A MINORITY within your own family can be a source of conflict. I had   1
always known that I was different from my brother and my sister. My parents, too, may have sensed the difference, but they never acknowledged it to

me. For many years, I had struggled with the idea of letting them know how different I was from my older brother. I was gay and didn't know how they would react if they ever found out.

My struggle to "come out of the closet" grew out of several needs. First, I wanted to be closer with my parents and to be honest about who I was. Second, I needed to let them know that there was someone special in my life. Finally, I had agreed to speak at my church about being gay, and I felt it important to tell my parents about my lifestyle before informing my congregation. 2

Rejection was my greatest fear. At the time, I had friends who had not spoken to their families for years after revealing they were gay. Their parents could not understand how their children could be "fags" or "dykes." These were terms their families had previously applied only to strangers. Some friends even told me about the violent reactions their families had had to the news. One of them said his father chased him around the house with a butcher knife. I had also known people who had used their homosexuality as a weapon against their families. Never did I want to hurt my parents; I merely wanted to break down the barriers between us. 3

I had no idea how they might react when I came out to them. I knew that if they responded violently or negatively it could take years to heal the damage. I also knew that I might never see them again. It was for this reason that I had avoided coming out to them before. However, because of my pending public announcement, the time had come to let them know. 4

I planned what I had to say carefully. Something so important could not simply be announced and forgotten. I had actually begun to prepare for this moment years before by reading as much as I could about homosexuality and by talking to gay friends. It was necessary for me to accept myself as a gay man before expecting others to do so. I had to develop a positive self-image, and this took several years. Then, in the week prior to my announcement, I began to rehearse my lines. I made notes for various approaches I could take. I wanted to feel secure in my delivery and didn't want to appear ashamed of my lifestyle. "Why should I be?" I thought. I had never felt differently. I imagined my parents' every reaction and tried to predict my responses. I even prepared myself for the worst, afraid they would tell me to "Get out and never come back!" 5

I also knew it was possible that none of the negative things that had happened to my friends would happen to me. In fact, I thought my parents might have already suspected I was gay. After all, I had been living with a man for three years. My partner at the time said, "They probably already know about you, the way you swish around!" I knew he could be right, but I was still afraid. Would my disclosure actually draw me closer to them as I had hoped, or would it push me away? Would they accept my partner as they had in the past? How would I cope with the loss of their love? These were just a few of the many questions that swept through my mind as I called my mother to ask if I could visit and talk about something important. 6

My heart was racing and my palms were sweating as I stopped the car in   7
front of their house. I turned off the ignition, took a deep breath, and stepped
out. "This is it," I thought. "This is what I've been thinking about doing for
years." The walk to the front door had never seemed so long. I was acutely
aware of my heartbeat pounding in my ears. My breath seemed suspended in
the frigid February night air. Time seemed to stop as I nervously straightened
my jacket, threw my shoulders back, swallowed hard, and opened the front
door.

My father was sitting in the recliner watching the television. My mother   8
was folding laundry. "Hi, how are you doing?" I said, trying to hide my nerv-
ousness. They both looked up and smiled. As I walked over to give each of
them a hug, I wondered if they would ever smile at me again.

I took off my coat, sat down next to my mother, and began to help her fold   9
the laundry. We talked about how fast my niece was growing up. While we
spoke, I tried to form the words that I feared would hurt them irreparably, but
I realized there was only one way to say it. "Mom. Dad. I've been thinking about
telling you this for some time now." I swallowed hard and took a good look at
them. "I'm not telling you this because I want to hurt you. I love you. Please try
to understand." I paused and took a deep breath. "I'm gay."

There was silence. Finally, with much hesitation, my mother asked, "Are   10
you sure?"

There was still no response from my father. I wondered what was racing   11
through his head. His silence was deeper than I could remember. Again my
mother spoke. "Are you happy?"

"Yes," I replied with hesitation. I was not sure what would happen next. I   12
could almost hear the silent screams that I imagined howling in each of them.

"Well," she paused, "you've always been good to us, and you've never given   13
us any problems."

"Here it comes," I thought, "the guilt trip."   14

"I guess if you're happy," she continued slowly as if weighing every word,   15
"then I'll try to understand."

A smile spread over my face as I leaned over and gave her a long, warm   16
hug. Never had I felt so close to her. It was only then that my father piped up,
"I hope you aren't sleeping with someone new every night." I assured him that
I wasn't as I gave him a hug.

"You know, it's funny," my mother said. "We always thought your friend   17
was gay, but we didn't know you were." I tried hard to keep from laughing as I
thought of my partner's remarks. Deep down, I suspected that they had always
known but had denied it.

When I explained that I was going to speak at my church about what it was   18
like to be gay, my mother's brow became dark and furrowed. "Do you think you
should? What if you lose your job? What if someone tries to hurt you?" she
responded.

I tried to assure her that everything would be all right, but I really had no   19
idea what might happen. Of course, I knew my parents would struggle with my
gayness just as I had, but I was overjoyed that they were asking such questions.
A great burden had been lifted from my shoulders; I felt like laughing and dancing around the room. I realized I no longer had to hide my private life, to
change pronouns, or to avoid questions about whom I was dating. More important, I had discovered how deeply my parents loved me.

Read More on the Web

Site of Parents, Families, and Friends of Lesbians and Gays:
  http://www.pflag.org/
Site for parents of gay children: http://www.outproud.org/
  brochure_for_parents.html

Questions for Discussion

1. Why did Kohler feel the need to "come out of the closet"?
2. Discuss the fears he dealt with before deciding to tell his parents he
    was gay.
3. What steps did he take to prepare *himself* for the moment when he
    would tell his parents he was gay?
4. What steps did he take to prepare his *parents* for this moment?
    Should he have done more to get them ready?
5. Why does the author tell us how the parents of his friends reacted
    when they announced they were gay? Does including this
    information help him explain a process?

Thinking Critically

1. This essay and Sagan's "The Measure of Eratosthenes" tell us how
    something was done. What other similarities do you find between
    these selections? Make notes in the margins of Kohler's essay to
    identify them.
2. Had Kohler asked you for advice about approaching his parents, what
    would you have told him? Put your comments in the form of a letter.

Suggestions for Journal Entries

1. Recall a time when you told someone something he or she did not
    want to hear. Perhaps you had to tell your parents that you had
    wrecked the family car, or had to persuade a sweetheart that your
    relationship was over, or had to inform a friend or relative that a

loved one had died. Freewrite for about five minutes to explain how hard this was.

2. Kohler's decision to tell his parents he was gay came from a strong desire to be honest with them. Write about a time when you needed to reveal something about yourself to a loved one who might find it difficult to accept. List a few steps that explain how you did this.

Suggestions for Sustained Writing

1. Triena Milden takes an ironic or tongue-in-cheek approach to academic studies in "So You Want to Flunk Out of College," which appears in the chapter's introduction (pages 474–477). You too may be able to provide advice to help someone fail at something important. Write an ironic but complete set of instructions for this purpose. Put them in a letter to someone you know well.

   If you follow Milden's lead, begin your letter by explaining how hard or easy it is to fail at the task you are discussing. Somewhere in your letter, perhaps in the introduction or conclusion, you might also explain why anyone would want to fail at it in the first place. In any case, revise and edit your letter to make sure it's clear, easy-to-follow, and fun to read.

2. If Suggestion 1 doesn't appeal to you, write an essay that explains how *not* to do something. Here are some topics you might choose:

   > How not to study for an important exam.
   > How not to do laundry.
   > How not to light a barbecue grill.
   > How not to start exercising.
   > How not to lie to your parents, children, spouse, or sweetheart.
   > How not to drive a car if you want it to last.
   > How not to become depressed when life gets difficult.
   > How not to become addicted to tobacco, drugs, alcohol, or other substances.
   > How not to get hooked on watching TV or any other activity.

3. The word *duel* can have many meanings. If you responded to the second journal suggestion after Adam Goodheart's essay, you have probably gathered some pointers on how to prepare for and fight a modern duel (contest, confrontation, or encounter) such as the kind people face every day. Read your notes, and use them as the basis of a paper that provides complete instructions.

Begin with an outline that, as in Goodheart's essay, divides the process chronologically into major components. Let's say you want to teach your reader how to bargain over the price of a car. You might list headings such as Adopting the Right Attitude, Researching Dealer Costs, Visiting Several Dealerships, Making an Offer, and Closing the Deal. As you write your first draft, list and explain particular steps under each of these headings in detail.

When you revise your first draft, make sure you have explained each step separately and clearly, used direct commands, and provided all needed information. If necessary, include a list of supplies/equipment in your introduction and a warning in your conclusion. Now, ask a fellow student to read and comment on your work. Revise it once more. Then edit and proofread.

4. Item 2 in the Suggestions for Journal Entries after "The Measure of Eratosthenes" asks you to list steps in a process that human beings have learned or invented to survive or to improve the quality of their lives. If you did not respond to that suggestion, do so now.

    Use your list as the outline to an essay that fully explains the process. Write your first draft by following this outline. As you revise, develop each step in greater detail until you are sure the process is clear and complete. When you are ready to write an introduction, discuss the reason or reasons this process is important, thereby giving your essay an identifiable purpose and focus. In other words, let your readers know from the very start that the essay is worth their time.

    As you edit your final draft, check for coherence—adding connectives and linking pronouns as necessary. Then proofread.

5. If you responded to the second of the journal prompts after Barry's "Florida's Fire Ants Headed for Trouble," turn the notes you made into a fully developed essay that explains how you got rid of a pest or that provides instructions on how to get rid of one. Remember that the pest you choose to discuss can be an insect or other animal, a plant, a mold or fungus, a human being, or even an electronic pest such as computer SPAM.

    Your essay can be straightforward and serious. However, you will have more fun if, like Barry, you take a humorous approach. In fact, you might use some of the devices for making readers laugh that Barry used: hyperbole, irony, sarcasm, figurative language, and interesting phrasing. However, this is a process paper; you must explain things clearly. As always, remember that writing itself is a process, so revise, edit, and proofread your work carefully.

6. Ken Kohler's "How I Came Out to My Parents" explains the painful process of telling people a truth they might not want to hear. Have you ever been in a similar situation? Did you ever have to confess that you smashed up the family car, misplaced an important document or tool at work, or lost

your younger brother in a shopping mall? Have you ever said good-bye to a loved one or told somebody a close relative or friend died?

Write an essay explaining how you did what had to be done. As you draft and rewrite, include details to show how painful the process was. Remember that this is not simply a narrative. Don't just say that you got the courage to face the situation or that you overcame emotional hurdles. Show *how* you did these things step by step.

You can begin by explaining how you got yourself ready. Next, recall the things you did to prepare your listener(s) for the news. Then, tell how you made the announcement, and describe the way your listener(s) reacted. Finally, like Kohler, explain how you felt when the experience was over.

Check your journal for notes that will help you get started. As you write your paper, remember that Kohler's essay is so powerful because he revised and edited it carefully. Do the same with yours.

Writing to Learn: A Group Activity

In his column in *Civilization*, Adam Goodheart gave instructions on "lost arts." Have some fun by writing instructions on how to perform an art, skill, or other activity that today is rarely or no longer practiced.

THE FIRST MEETING

Choose a lost art to research. Here are some suggestions. How to:

> Plan and prepare a Christmas dinner for George and Martha Washington.
>
> Make a stained glass window for a church or cathedral.
>
> Build an ancient pyramid (Egyptian, Aztec, or Mayan).
>
> Plan and build a Buddhist pagoda.
>
> Lead a camel caravan across desert trade routes.
>
> Construct an Iroquois long house.
>
> Make and bury a mummy.
>
> Use leeches to treat a patient suffering from a fever or other illness.

After you have decided on a subject, brainstorm to identify questions to research. Let's say your group decides to explain how to construct and use a Roman catapult. One of you might investigate the purpose for which this war machine was developed. Another could find information classifying various types of Roman catapults. Still another could learn about their construction and operation. Someone else might research the dangers of operating a catapult.

RESEARCH

Research the Internet, specialized encyclopedias and other works in your library's reference section, or books listed in the card or online catalog. Bring the notes you take and photocopies of pages from your sources to the next meeting.

THE SECOND MEETING

Make sure the group has gathered enough information to compose a paper that (1) explains the purpose of the process, (2) lists and explains all necessary materials, and (3) provides step-by-step instructions for carrying out the process. Then, write an outline of a paper that addresses each of these items in a separate section. Have each student write two or three paragraphs for one of these sections. You might also ask someone to write an attention-grabbing introduction and a warning paragraph that identifies hazards or dangers involved in the process. Bring photocopies of your work to the next meeting.

THE THIRD MEETING

Critique each other's contributions; offer suggestions for revision. Make sure your work is clear and easy to follow. Assign one student to collect the final versions of everyone's work and to create a draft of a complete paper to be distributed at the next meeting.

THE FOURTH MEETING

Distribute and read the draft of the paper. Make last-minute suggestions for revision. Ask one student to edit the paper and another to type and proofread it.

Argumentation and Persuasion

Argumentation and persuasion are similar, and they often work together. In fact it is rare to find an essay that is pure argumentation without the slightest hint that the author is trying to persuade the readers. It is even rarer to find an effective persuasive essay that is not based on a logical argument. However, argument and persuasion are not identical.

Establishing Purpose: Choosing to Argue or Persuade

To begin with, a formal "argument" is not a fight, altercation, or heated discussion with tempers flaring and threats being exchanged. *Argument* is the defense of an opinion or of a position on an issue that is supported by concrete evidence and that is presented logically. The purpose of a written argument is limited: to prove a point, a thesis—sometimes referred to as a proposition. Scientists use argument to prove a theory or hypothesis. Historians engage in argumentation when they dispute theories about the causes of a war or of an economic depression. A psychologist might argue that genetic factors caused someone to become a serial killer, and an economist could use argumentation to present theories about the business cycle or the effects of taxation.

Persuasion begins with logical argument. It too uses logic and concrete evidence to make a point, to prove a thesis. However, *persuasion* goes beyond argument and also appeals to the reader's emotions, values, and self-interest. The Declaration of Independence, a classic piece of persuasion, even attempts to inflame our passions. Finally, the purpose of persuasion is not simply to prove a point; it is to get readers to act. Lawyers use persuasion to get judges and juries to rule in favor of their clients. Politicians use persuasion to get voters to support them.

So first of all, you need to decide if your purpose is to argue or to persuade. Your decision will affect the word choices you make, the tone of your paper, and even its content. You would be writing an argument if you tried to convince your readers that the Internet and other electronic means of publishing information will someday replace the printed books and paper journals now on college library shelves. You would also be arguing if you proved that devoting too much time to a job while attending college full-time reduces the chances for academic success. On the other hand, you would be writing persuasively if you tried to convince your college president to reduce the library's book budget and allocate the money to the purchase of CD ROMs or subscriptions to periodical databases. You would also be trying to persuade if you wrote a letter to your college newspaper so as to convince students to reduce their work hours and spend more time on their studies.

Appealing to Your Audience

The kind of audience you are writing to will often have as much influence on whether to argue or to persuade as your purpose does. For example, let's say you have been assigned to write a paper on the effects of regular aerobic exercise on the emotional health of people over 65. Your paper will be duplicated and read by all of the members of your class, none of whom happens to be over 65. So you decide to stick to pure argument and simply lay out the facts in support of an opinion. You cite statistics from journal articles published by senior-citizen groups and insurance associations, draw on studies in the *New England Journal of Medicine,* and quote a cardiologist you have interviewed to support the idea that aerobics promote emotional health in seniors. In short you write an essay that argues.

Now, take another scenario. You have been asked to write a similar article for a magazine read primarily by senior citizens. Your purpose this time is not simply to prove a point. You also want to get your readers to follow your advice—to get them on that tread mill or into that jazzercize class. So, in addition to doing research on your subject, you spend time evaluating your readers' goals, interests, and values and even their preconceived notions about aerobic exercise so that you can address these "motivational" factors when you write your essay. For example, your paper might appeal to your readers' desire to maintain their emotional health in order to enjoy their children and grandchildren better. It might even suggest that regular aerobic exercise improves sex, regardless of age. Now that's motivation!.

NOTE: As you consider your audience, keep the following in mind:

- If you are trying to persuade your readers, make sure you are familiar with their needs, their interests, and their opinions.
- Assess the readers' familiarity with the issue. Include background information as necesaary to help readers new to the issue understand it fully. However, include only enough explanatory information and data to make your claims clear and convincing. Don't include three illustrations and six sets of statistics when only one will do.
- Express yourself clearly and simply. Don't use highly sophisticated or technical vocabulary unless you are sure your readers will understand it. Otherwise, they might suspect you are trying to confuse them or to cloud the issue.

Choosing a Thesis (Claim) That Is Debatable, Supportable, and Focused

The thesis for an argumentative paper is often referred to as the claim—the opinion the writer wishes to prove, defend, or support. Start with a preliminary thesis, but remember that writing is a process of discovery. So, as you become more knowledgeable about your thesis by gathering information for, outlining, and drafting your paper, you might see the need to rewrite the thesis by revising your stand on the issue or even changing it completely.

Unless your instructor assigns a specific topic, write on a question you already know something about or are concerned about, such as health care, animal rights, the homeless, affirmative action, school choice, the criminal justice system, or the environment, for example. Those ideas can lead to the framing of a thesis—at least a preliminary thesis. Writing about something you believe is important provides the intellectual energy and commitment to complete an effective argumentative or persuasive essay.

At the same time, keep the following three criteria in mind as you frame your preliminary claim or thesis:

1. **An effective claim is debatable.** It is more than a simple statement of fact or of personal opinion, which will not lead to a sustained discussion.

    STATEMENT OF FACT: My college major requires that I complete 28 hours of laboratory science.

    DEBATABLE THESIS: My college needs to install more up-to-date equipment in the chemistry labs.

    The first item cannot be debated. Either your major requires 28 hours of laboratory science or it doesn't. The second item, on the other hand, can yield sustained discussion through evidence that the current lab equipment does not enable students to keep up with advances in the chemical industry.

    Personal Opinion or Preference: A vegetarian diet is as satisfying as one that includes meat and fish.

    Debatable Thesis: Following a vegetarian diet can help lower cholesterol and prevent heart disease.

    The first item is based on personal taste, an invalid criterion for argument. The second can be discussed in light of objective medical research.

NOTE: You don't have to take one side of an issue exclusively. For example, you can argue against illegal immigration while expressing your understanding for the reasons that people from poor countries try to enter the United States illegally.

2. **An effective claim is defensible.** Before taking a position, think it through and decide if you can collect enough evidence to argue it effectively.

> **Indefensible:** People who wear leather and fur are cruel to animals.
>
> **Defensible:** People who wear leather and fur support industries whose harvesting methods are cruel to animals.

The first claim requires the writer to prove an impossibility: that the wearing of fur or leather itself is cruel. The second can be argued by calling upon evidence from government or industry sources, eye-witness testimony, or scientific research.

3. **An effective claim is focused.** For most college assignments, your thesis must be focused enough to be argued effectively in a short essay.

> **Too General:** Policies at two public colleges in my state violate students' rights.
>
> **Focused:** Policies governing speech at two public colleges in my state violate rights guaranteed to students by the First Amendment to the Constitution.

The first item would result in an essay whose length might exceed what was assigned. It covers too wide a range of policies. Moreover it does not focus on particular "student rights," as does the second item. Writing an essay on the second item would be much easier.

Read More on the Web

Here are three websites on writing thesis statements for argument/persuasion papers:

Humboldt University Argumentation and Critical Thinking Tutorial: http://www.humboldt.edu/~act/about.html

University of Nebraska Communications 109 Home Page: http://www.unl.edu/speech/comm109

Purdue University Online Writing Center: http://owl.english.purdue.edu/handouts/general/gl_argpers.html

Gathering Evidence to Support Your Thesis

Many ways to develop any essay, as explained in Chapter 3, can be also be used to approach an argument. For example, to argue that your college's policies restrict students' freedom of speech, you might first define the right of free speech and reveal the source of that right. If you argue that the college's lab equipment needs to be replaced, you might use cause-and-effect to explain the difficulties new chemistry graduates are having when they get jobs in industry. Whatever your approach, communicate your position through sufficient concrete evidence to be convincing.

The most effective types of supportive evidence are documented facts, and statistics; expert testimony; and illustrations.

DOCUMENTED FACTS AND STATISTICS

To argue that being overweight contributes to heart disease and stroke, you can quote data published in scientific journals. You might also use statistics taken from medical studies or insurance sources to show that obese people suffer higher mortality rates from coronary disease and stroke than others do.

NOTE: Too many statistics can overwhelm or bore some readers, especially those who are not used to analyses of issues based on mathematical evidence.

EXPERT TESTIMONY

Including what experts in a particular field say or have written strengthens your argument. When you introduce such material, however, state your source's credentials. In other words, explain why your expert is in fact an expert. Mention academic degrees, professional experience, publications, awards, and other information that will convince readers of your source's value.

You might use expert testimony in the form of statements from college faculty, staff, and students to prove that the college's laboratories are outdated. You might quote constitutional lawyers, judges, or government experts to support your claim that the college's policies restrict free speech.

Read More on the Web

Cite sources of facts, statistics, and expert testimony by using MLA, APA, or other acceptable formats:

http://www.wisc.edu/writing/Handbook/DocMLA.html
http://owl.english.purdue.edu/handouts/research/r_mla.html
http://webster.commnet.edu/mla/mla_original.htm
http://www.apastyle.org/elecref.html

ILLUSTRATIONS

As you learned earlier in this book, illustrations are factual examples or instances of the idea you are trying to support. You would be using illustrations if you wrote about specific cases in which college policy was invoked to punish or silence students who had expressed unpopular opinions on controversial campus issues. Always make sure these examples are concrete and well-developed. Mention names of the people involved, include statements of the charges and punishments, explain the "offense," summarize arguments, quote testimony from hearings, and reference specific parts of the college policy. Finally choose examples that are directly relevant to your claim and that appeal to your audience. For example, in discussing an alleged violation of the college policy, you would do more than claim that Oscar Outspoken criticized the History Department. You might add that he did so in a polite, well-reasoned letter to the college newspaper, which calls itself "the student's voice." You might even quote directly from that letter.

Of course, most argumentative essays use a combination of these kinds of evidence. For example, to strengthen your claim that college policy violates students' rights of free speech, you might include the testimony of legal experts when you cite examples. Again, the important thing is that you use enough concrete evidence to be convincing.

Determining Tone and Content

The tone and language of an argument are usually objective, neutral, specific, and rational. The argument might draw on the testimony of experts, on statistics, or on historical or scientific studies. Experts and authorities in a particular field who have a reputation for evaluating issues fairly are often cited by writers of argument. Argument depends on logic. In persuasive essays, writers also use language that is more personal and emotionally charged. They sometimes involve themselves in the essay by viewing things subjectively; they focus on particular people and incidents more than on abstract studies and statistics; and they usually defend their positions vigorously and even passionately.

Let's say you are writing an argument that victims of violent crime ought to be compensated by the government. You might include Department of Justice statistics on the annual medical bills for victims of crime nationwide. You might remind readers that the government often helps victims of natural disasters and cite specific instances or programs in which such aid has been distributed. You might even describe a program used in another country that forces convicted criminals to work so as to fund a compensation program for crime victims. The tone of your argument would be dispassionate, and your presentation logical.

On the other hand, if you are writing an article to gather support for a rally to get Congress to pass a crime-victims bill, you might describe the long-term emotional and physical effects that specific crime victims are suffering. You might create vivid images of people no longer able to walk, to work, or to live pain-free lives. You might also appeal to the readers' self-interest by asking them to predict the horrors they might endure if ever victimized by some thug. Your language will probably be emotionally charged, and the images you paint will be startling. This is what we see in Angela Brandli's research essay, which appears in the Appendix at the end of this book. So persuasive was the author that she convinced state legislators to pass a bill that increased compensation for victims of violent crime.

Expressing a Voice

Although argument relies on logic and although persuasion can appeal to the reader's emotions as well, the line between pure argument and pure persuasion sometimes gets blurred. In fact, writers of argument frequently reveal their feelings about a topic, if ever so subtly. In "The Right to Be Let Alone" (Chapter 13), Barry Glazer uses emotionally charged language when he asserts that if he were "in the throes of terminal cancer or facing the horror of Alzheimer's disease" he should be allowed to commit suicide. Thus, while his purpose is not to move his readers to action, Glazer does touch our emotions, and we are the more convinced. An effective argument needs to be logical and well supported, but no writer should ever refrain from expressing his or her personal voice in a piece of formal writing, as long as it remains reasonable and restrained.

Being Fair, Accurate, and Logical

You will learn more about specific techniques you can use when writing either argumentation or persuasion essays in the next two chapters. However, whether you are writing argument or persuasion, remember to be accurate and fair. Being persuasive is not a license to mislead your readers. Unfortunately, sometimes both argument and persuasion suffer from logical fallacies. In many cases, writers commit such fallacies unknowingly. Dishonest writers do so intentionally.

Ten Logical Fallacies

Errors in logic, though sometimes subtle and hard to detect, appear in political speeches and advertisements, in television commercials, in newspaper editorials, and even in well-written and sincere arguments of bright college students. Here is a list of ten logical fallacies that you should look for when reading or listening to argumentation or persuasion and that you should avoid in your own writing.

Generalizations Supported by Insufficient Evidence   Writers sometimes draw conclusions not justified by the amount or kind of information they have gathered. Failing to consider enough or the right kind of evidence can lead to faulty generalizations. Here are a few examples of insufficient evidence:

1. My neighbors never finished high school, but they have built a very lucrative plumbing company. Therefore, the claim that education improves one's chances for success is false.

2. The president will veto a bill lowering tax rates for married couples. Obviously, he doesn't want to help families.

3. The directory assistance operator could not find the name or number of a company that I know is listed. The telephone company should train their employees better.

4. The Supreme Court refused to review a lower court's judgment against the tobacco industry. Obviously, the Supreme Court is antibusiness.

The Straw Man   As the name implies, the straw man is an argument that is weak and easy to knock down. The straw man comes into play when a writer falsely claims that the opposing side supports an idea that is indefensible. The writer then refutes this obviously bad idea and, in the process, casts the opposition in a bad light. The straw man is a pretense; it has little to do with the point being debated, nor does it represent the opponent's views fairly and accurately. In fact, it is often used only to distract readers from valid arguments of the opposition.

> **Your position:** You argue that we should create a plan to force those convicted of violent crime to compensate their victims and their victims' families. You propose that prisons establish small factories in which prisoners must work so as to earn the money to compensate their victims.
> **Your opponent's position:** Using the "straw man," your opponent argues that you are suggesting a return to the chain-gang system of punishment and that you are in favor of slave labor.

> **Your position:** You argue that people who have no children in the public school system should pay less school tax than those who do.
> **Your opponent's position:** You are an elitist who cares little for public education and is concerned only with educating the children of the rich, most of whom attend private schools.

> **Your position:** You argue that the government should preserve thousands of acres of untouched wilderness that happens to be located upon huge oil reserves.
> **Your opponent's position:** You care more about trees and wildlife than you do about the consumers who would benefit from cheaper heating oil and gasoline prices.

The Ad Hominem Argument   *Ad hominem* is Latin for "to the person." When writers indulge in this unethical tactic, they attack the person's character rather than his or her position, logic, opinions, or history.

For example, when John F. Kennedy ran for president in 1962, some unscrupulous people attacked him because he was a Roman Catholic. They ignored the fact that Kennedy had on numerous occasions affirmed his commitment to the separation of church and state. When Ronald Reagan ran for governor in California in the 1970s and, again, when he ran for president, some opponents attacked him because he had been an actor, not because of the issues he supported.

You would be arguing *ad hominem* if you claimed that Senator Alvarez cannot represent the interests of families because she is single, or that Representative Kelly will not fight to increase community-college funding because he attended a private university. On the other hand, you would be arguing fairly if you mentioned that Senator Alvarez has consistently opposed pro-family legislation or that Representative Kelly has made several speeches arguing for an increase in community-college tuition so as to decrease state funding for such schools.

Begging the Question   This fallacy occurs when a writer draws an invalid conclusion from a false assumption or an assumption that cannot be proven. Thus, the writer avoids addressing the real issue or question.

For example, you would be begging the question if you argued that, because Angela is a member of Alcoholics Anonymous, she could not have been the one you saw having a beer at Calhoun's Saloon last night. The false assumption here is that members of Alcoholics Anonymous never fall back into their old habits. The argument begs the question: *Did Angela drink a beer at Calhoun's Saloon last night?*

The Red Herring   The red herring distracts the audience from the real issue at hand. It gets its name from a practice used by farmers to protect their newly planted fields from fox hunters and their dogs. Farmers often dragged a red herring along the edge of their fields where it would leave a strong scent. This scent distracted the dogs and kept them and the hunters from trampling the crops.

Most visibly, red herrings can be found in commercials and advertisements. Automobile commercials picture cars and their drivers winding through beautiful mountain passes as they head toward stunning sunsets; exercise machines are pictured against exotic, tropical landscapes populated by people with perfect bodies; soft drinks are promoted through television spots that picture athletic young people engaged in exciting sports such as rock climbing, hang gliding, or surfing. None of these tells us much about the product. They are selling an image that, like the farmer's red herring, is supposed to draw our attention away from what is really being sold.

One commercial goes so far as to portray a four-wheel-drive vehicle as an adult toy. It suppresses the fact that most people really buy cars for one practical reason—safe and reliable transportation. It encourages the notion of "fun" and, red-herring fashion, distracts us from the reality that, in order to pay for this "toy," we will have to work extra hard and, in most cases, tie ourselves to an all-too-real auto loan that takes three, four, or five years to pay off!

Non-Sequitor   A Latin term, *non-sequitor* translates roughly to "does not follow." It occurs when a statement does not proceed logically from the previous statement. Here are two examples.

> My 90 year-old grandfather smokes a pack of
>
> cigarettes a day. Therefore, smoking can't be bad for
>
> one's health.

> Gina finds accounting a challenging course. She will
>
> never succeed in business.

Neither of these statements follows directly from the other. The fact that one man who smokes heavily has reached the age of ninety in no way contradicts the massive research proving that, for the vast majority of people, smoking is a health hazard. Similarly, although Gina finds accounting challenging, the time and effort she puts into studying this subject may enable her to master it eventually. On the other hand, a mastery of sophisticated accounting principles may not be necessary to success in the kind of business she plans to pursue.

False Analogy   An argument based on a false analogy incorrectly assumes that because situations may be alike in some respects, the same rules, principles, or approaches apply to both or the same conclusions can be drawn about both. You would be guilty of false analogy if you wrote:

> Jason's father had a heart attack at fifty; Jason will
>
> suffer from heart disease too.

The analogy presumes that the only cause for heart disease is heredity. But what if Jason has a healthy lifestyle, while his father smokes heavily, fails to exercise, and eats a high-fat diet?

Before the United States invaded Afghanistan in the fall of 2001, many political pundits predicted a long, drawn-out conflict with thousands of casualties. Their prediction was based on a false analogy between the US's involvement and the Soviet Union's disastrous military occupation of Afghanistan in the 1980s. But there were significant differences in the goals and preparedness of the two armies. Moreover, the Afghani political situation in 2001 had changed from what it was in the 1980s.

Either. . .Or Fallacy   Failing to see all the aspects or all the choices associated with a problem or situation can result in an "either. . .or" fallacy. You would create such a fallacy if you wrote:

> The only way students get through Prof. Wilson's
>
> history class is to cheat on her exams or resign
>
> themselves to a D.

Of course, no matter how demanding the instructors, there is a third alternative: to study hard.

Erroneous Cause   In Latin, this is called the *Post Hoc, Ergo Propter Hoc (After this; therefore, because of this)* fallacy. It occurs when the writer assumes that because one thing follows another it must necessarily have resulted from (been caused by) the other. Here's an example:

> The College restricted student parking to Lots A and
>
> B last semester, so Rachel got more parking tickets
>
> than ever.

The reason Rachel got more parking tickets was not directly caused by the college's decision to restrict student parking. After all, Lots A and B might be sufficient to hold all student cars. Rachel's getting more tickets is a direct result of her choosing to park where she shouldn't.

Going-Along or Bandwagon Fallacy   This fallacy assumes that an idea, action, or proposal must be valid if a great many people support or believe in it. Recall that in some primitive cultures the vast majority of people believed in the practice of human sacrifice to appease their gods. You would be falling into this logical error if you wrote:

> Overwhelming popular support for the new mayor
>
> shows she can achieve greatness.

Read More on the Web

Web Site on Justice Louis Brandeis: http://faculty.purduenc.edu/bbk/brandeis.htm

Purdue University site on right to privacy: http://faculty.purduenc.edu/bbk/privacy.html

CHAPTER 13

Argumentation

As you have learned in the introduction to Section Five, a formal, written argument is very different from a loud or excited discussion about a point of controversy! In fact, when it comes to writing, *argumentation* is an attempt to prove a point—also known as a thesis or proposition—or to support an opinion through calm if vigorous logic and the presentation of evidence.

Mastering Deduction and Induction

Traditionally, two types of thinking have been used in argumentation: induction and deduction. Both support an opinion or belief the writer expresses in a conclusion. Of course, since all persuasive essays begin with logical arguments, as you will see in Chapter 14, induction and deduction are also important components of persuasion. Deduction moves from general premises to a limited conclusion; induction moves from specific evidence to a general conclusion.

DEDUCTION: FROM GENERAL TO SPECIFIC

Deduction draws a limited conclusion from premises, ideas upon which that conclusion is based. Using deduction, writers start with a general statement or idea they believe their readers agree with. Next, they apply a specific case or example to that statement. Finally, they draw a limited conclusion from the two. The logical structure through which this is done is called a syllogism. You would be using deduction if you argued:

> **General statement:** All full-time students can use the college exercise room free of charge.
> **Specific case:** I am a full-time student.
> **Conclusion:** Therefore, I can use the college exercise room free of charge.

Alice Callaghan uses deductive reasoning in "Desperate to Learn English," an essay that appears later in this chapter. Her argument goes something like this:

> **General statement:** Mastering English is essential to success in school.
> **Specific case:** Bilingual education makes it harder for non-native speakers to learn English.
> **Conclusion:** Bilingual education should be abolished.

INDUCTION: FROM SPECIFIC TO GENERAL

Inductive thinking involves collecting separate facts, reasons, or other pieces of evidence and then drawing a conclusion from that information. Say you come down with a case of food poisoning—cramps, vomiting, a headache, the works. When you call the other five people with whom you shared a pot of stew the night before, each tells the same horrible story about cramps, vomiting, and so on. It's safe to say the stew made you sick. That's your conclusion. Support for that conclusion comes in the form of six separate tales of woe.

As a matter of fact, induction is the kind of thinking behind conclusion and support, one of the methods of developing paragraphs and essays explained in Chapter 3. Papers developed through this method express a conclusion or opinion in a formal thesis statement. A good example is Philip K. Howard's "The Death of Common Sense" in Chapter 10. Howard claims that America is being overregulated. This is his *conclusion,* which he expresses in his thesis. He then goes on to discuss *supportive evidence* from which he drew that conclusion.

Here's an example of a paragraph developed using the conclusion-and-support method. It is based upon information from an essay by Lester Brown:

> In the next century, increases in the levels of air pollution caused by the burning of fossil fuels will force us to seek alternative sources of energy. *Thankfully, such alternatives are plentiful.* Around the equator and in deserts, homeowners and industries will install solar panels on rooftops and on the summits of hills to collect energy that will generate electricity or heat water directly. People living on wind-swept prairies will create their own power by using windmills. Geothermal energy may be tapped by those living in countries around the Mediterranean Sea. Finally, governments might once again fund large-scale hydroelectric projects, such as those created by the Tennessee Valley Authority during the Great Depression.

The second sentence (in italics) in this paragraph is the *conclusion,* which is expressed as the paragraph's topic sentence: "Thankfully, such alternatives are plentiful." This is the point the writer wishes to make, the proposition he wishes to prove. The rest of the paragraph provides evidence to *support that conclusion.*

Induction and deduction are two different ways of reasoning, but they almost always complement each other. In fact, logical and well-supported arguments often reflect both types of thinking.

Reasoning Through the Use of Claims and Warrants

British rhetorician Steven Toulmin designed a technique for argumentation and persuasion, which he believed is close to the way people actually debate. Resembling the inductive method in some ways, Toulmin's "Layout of Argumentation" is applicable to any discipline, issue, or question. As you read about his method, you may decide to incorporate parts of it into your own brand of argumentation or persuasion. It contains six major components:

1. **Data:** Information that leads the writer/speaker to take a position on a question or issue.
2. **Claim:** A statement of the position being defended; the thesis.
3. **Warrants:** Major ideas used to support a claim. There are three types of warrants: authoritative, substantive, motivational. Warrants must relate directly and logically to the claim.
4. **Backing:** Evidence used to support or prove a warrant. It comes in three forms: expert testimony, data and statistics, and concrete illustrations.
5. **Reservation:** Statement anticipating an opposing argument before it decreases your argument's credibility.
6. **Qualifier:** Statement or phrase that restricts the scope of the claim.

As you read above and in the introduction to Section Five, Toulmin's "claim" is another word for the thesis, the point you are trying to prove. However, he also uses "warrants" in his "Layout of Argumentation." These are major ideas that relate directly to and support the claim. In some ways, they resemble topic sentences, ideas that support a thesis. They, in turn, are developed via concrete evidence, which Toulmin calls "backing." There are three types of warrants:

> **The authoritative warrant** relies on theories, opinions, and studies put forth by experts. Such information may be paraphrased, summarized, or quoted directly. For example, if you claimed that listening regularly to classical music increases IQ in children, you might quote experts in child development, psychologists, and testing specialists. You might also make reference to scientific studies conducted by universities, professional organizations, or government agencies.

> **The substantive warrant** uses a variety of rhetorical modes—especially the conclusion-and-support, comparison/contrast, cause-and-effect, and process analysis methods—to present concrete facts, data, and illustrations that support the claim. For example, you might explain how (process analysis) listening to classical music affects the human brain in the formative stages. You might compare (comparison/contrast) those effects to the effects of listening to other kinds of music or of being exposed to no musical stimulation. In addition, you can cite hard statistics found in professional studies (conclusion and support) to help

develop this warrant. Or you can describe the effects of classical music documented in case studies (illustration) of children who were exposed to the works of Mozart and Beethoven on a regular basis.

The motivational warrant can be used if the writer feels knowledgeable about the nature of the audience, their needs, and their opinions. In such cases, he or she might appeal to their personal and professional beliefs, their values, their pride, or even their self-interest. As you might assume, the motivational warrant is particularly **useful when writing persuasion,** which is discussed in the next chapter. For example, if you know that you are writing to the parents of school age children, you will want to link exposure to classical music to the child's performance on standardized mathematics tests in grammar and high school. You might also point out that, later on, such scores will surely help the student's chances of being admitted to a prestigious college and even of being awarded an academic scholarship.

Read More on the Web

For more on the Toulmin method, refer to these websites:

http://www.unl.edu.speech/comm109/Toulmin/
http://writing.colostate.edu/references/reading/roulmin/

Developing Ideas in an Argument

In Chapter 3, you learned that there are several ways to develop a paragraph or essay whether your purpose is to explain or to argue or persuade. One of the most popular is conclusion and support, the method you just learned about. As the selections in this chapter show, however, writers of argument often use a combination of methods to provide evidence that proves a point or supports a proposition (thesis). For example, in "Free Speech on Campus," Nat Hentoff uses comparison, mentions the opinions of others via direct quotations, and includes examples to make his point. Student Barry Glazer appeals to authority in "The Right to Be Let Alone" when he makes specific reference to the U.S. Constitution and quotes Supreme Court Justice Louis Brandeis. Alice Callaghan uses narration and statistics effectively in "Desperate to Learn English."

The most important thing to remember about an effective argument is that it is both *logical* and *well supported.* You can use inductive reasoning, deductive reasoning, or both, but your arguments must be reasonable and easy to follow. You can support ideas with examples, facts, statistics, the knowledge or opinions of experts, analogies, comparisons, definitions, first-hand observations, and the like. But your writing must contain enough supportive information to be clear, convincing, and easily understood.

Establishing Your Authority

Of course, the best way to establish your authority—to show that you are knowledgeable about a subject and that you should be believed—is to amass relevant facts and opinions that show you know what you are talking about. In some cases, there is no need for the author to establish his or her credentials. Nat Hentoff, whose essay "Free Speech on Campus" appears in this chapter, doesn't need to tell us he is an expert on this topic because his reputation as a defender of the First Amendment is widespread. On the other hand, it sometimes helps to remind readers of your credentials and experience. That's what Dudley Barlow does in the beginning of his essay on bilingual education, which appears in this chapter, when he alludes to the fact that he is an experienced teacher.

Anticipating and Addressing Opposing Opinions

It is always a good idea to think about points of view in opposition to your own. Doing so shows that you are open-minded, that you have considered more than one side, that you have thought out your position and others' well, and that you are knowledgeable about your subject. In short, it lends authority to your writing. This is very important when writing persuasion, but it also plays a part in argument. One way to address an opposing opinion is simply to show that it lacks validity, when this is the case. Another effective way is to recognize the validity of your opponent's argument while offering your own as the more realistic or logical alternative. To succeed, each of these tactics requires you to demonstrate to your reader your fair and accurate understanding of the opposing view. Barry Glazer's "The Right to Be Let Alone" and the two essays discussing bilingual education in this chapter illustrate ways in which to deal with opposing arguments.

Visualizing Strategies for Argument

Read the following editorial, published in *USA Today*. Then, read the two discussions that follow it, which show how it uses both deduction and induction.

Drug Tests Fail Schools

IMAGINE YOU wanted to go out for your company's softball team and your boss told you: "Pee in this cup—in front of me."   1

Most adults would consider such a demand outrageous. Yet, that's what some public schools were demanding from student athletes in the war against drugs when 12-year-old James Acton came along in 1991.   2

The would-be seventh-grade football player put a damper on such demands. First, he told Vernonia, OR, public school officials that he wouldn't go along. Then he went to court. His claim: The district's drug tests—required of all those trying out for sports—violate Fourth Amendment rights to privacy.   3

Last year, a federal appeals court in San Francisco agreed. In doing so, it made such testing illegal in nine Western states under its jurisdiction. And it discouraged schools elsewhere from starting testing programs until the Supreme Court rules on the case.   4

Today, the high court hears arguments. And if students, schools and taxpayers are lucky, it will kill all such required drug tests for student athletes by next fall.   5

Drug testing can be smart, when it's conducted to protect public safety and security, as with transportation workers and drug enforcement agents. And it may even be sensible when it's done to ensure role models, such as professional and college athletes, don't abuse narcotics.   6

But it wastes money and violates rights when forced upon thousands of youngsters.   7

Vernonia began its program mostly because of increased disciplinary problems.   8

But school officials chose not to focus on the problem kids. They lassoed mostly innocent ones. Of 500 students tested in 41/2 years, a mere 12 tested positive, not many for a district claiming huge problems.   9

And who paid for the willy-nilly testing? Not local folks, but deficit-riddled Uncle Sam through the federal drug-free schools program. Vernonia's cut: $7,500 a year.   10

History shows there's a fairer way. Teen drug use was cut substantially during the 1980s, not because a few schools tested students for drugs but because most taught students the dangers of abuse and involved parents in their programs.   11

Schools should do the same today. They should call parents of kids suspected of drug use and get permission for any testing.   12

That would save money, focus the drug fight on those causing problems and not invade the privacy of innocent kids whose only crime is trying out for a sport.   13

Deduction in "Drug Tests Fail Schools"   As you have learned, deduction moves from general to specific. The process starts with a general statement, to which a specific case or example is applied. Then, a conclusion is drawn from these two. Here's how deduction works in "Drug Tests Fail Schools":

> **General statement:** Drug testing should be permitted only to protect public safety or to ensure that role models don't abuse drugs (paragraph 6).
>
> **Specific case or example:** Forcing students to test for drugs only wastes money and violates rights; it does not protect public safety (paragraph 7).
>
> **Conclusion:** Therefore, forcing students to take drug tests should be stopped.

Induction in "Drug Tests Fail Schools"   Earlier you read that induction is the basis of the conclusion-and-support method for developing a paper. Support for a conclusion comes in the form of evidence or reasons behind it. Here's how induction works in "Drug Tests Fail Schools":

> *Support*
> A federal appeals court ruled that forcing students to take drug tests violates the Fourth Amendment (paragraph 4).

> *Support*
> Of 500 students tested for drugs in Vernonia, Oregon, only 12 tested positive (paragraph 9).

> *Support*
> Testing for drugs in Vernonia cost taxpayers $7,500 (paragraph 10).

> *Support*
> Studies show teen drug use can be cut through education and parental involvement (paragraph 11).

> *Conclusion*
> Forcing students to take drug tests should be stopped.

Revising Argument Papers

An argument requires logical and clear writing, and such writing takes hard work. Barry Glazer, a student whose essay appears in this chapter, wrote several drafts of a paper on individual rights before he arrived at a version with which he was satisfied. His rough draft contained the germ of an idea and several good examples but by the time Glazer wrote his final draft, the paper had been transformed into a first-rate argument paper. Even the title had changed.

Glazer—Rough Draft

It Ain't Nobody's Business but My Own

Help? In what way? ⌐ Government is <u>supposed to help people</u>, not

hurt them. Those we elect to public office

are there to make things better for

everyone. However, many of them are doing

What kinds of things? things that <u>annoy</u> and <u>frighten</u> me. If I am

not hurting anybody, the government should

Expand? Clarify? stay out of my private affairs. What I do,

if it isn't causing anyone else harm, is no

one's business but my own.

Support this claim.   If I have a terminal disease, I should be

allowed to kill myself or get a doctor to

help me do so.

They don't? Support this claim.   If I am driving home late at night <u>the</u>

<u>police have no right</u> to stop me just because

I am young and look suspicious. Recently, I

was walking around the block at three in the

morning and the police stopped and

questioned me. Yet, all I was doing was

taking a late-night stroll.

. . .

What kinds of things?

Yes, we need government to take <u>care of</u> <u>important things</u>. But the government and the police should stay out of people's lives when it is none of their business. They should just leave us alone.

Glazer—Final Draft

The Right to Be Let Alone. *Revises title.*

Government is the instrument of the people,

Appeals to authority.

says the <u>United States Constitution</u>. Those to whom the people entrust power are charged

with <u>maintaining justice</u>, <u>promoting the</u> <u>general welfare</u>, and <u>securing the blessings</u> <u>of liberty for us all</u>. Recent newspaper

Explains how government "is supposed to help people".

Explains what he meant by "things that annoy and frighten me."

opinion polls, however, suggest that many Americans are dissatisfied with the men and women running our communities, our states, and our nation. More and more of us have come to believe that our leaders are isolated from the realities ordinary people face. We fear we are losing control.

Instead of helping to alleviate this feeling of impotence, however, politicians and bureaucrats continue to make and enforce regulations that constrain our lives and constrict our freedoms. To help people regain a rightful measure of control, government—whether national, state, or local—should stay out of our private lives

Appeals to authority.

whenever possible. As Supreme Court Justice Louis Brandeis noted, Americans treasure their "right to be let alone."

Supports claim with convincing details.

There is no reason for the government to interfere in our lives if our behavior does not adversely affect others or if there is no immediate necessity for such interference. Were I in the throes of terminal cancer or facing the horror of Alzheimer's disease, I should be allowed to kill myself. Faced with the agonizing degeneration of my memory and personality, I

Appeals to emotions.

would probably want to end my life in my own way. But the government says this is illegal. Indeed, were I to call upon a doctor to assist me on this final quest, she would stand a good chance of being charged with murder.

Supports claim by appealing to authority.

The government should also stay out of an individual's life if there is no reason to believe he is doing wrong. The Bill of Rights protects us from unlawful searches and seizures. Yet, if I drive home from work in the early morning, I stand a reasonable chance of being stopped without cause at a police roadblock. While armed, uniformed officers shine flashlights in my face, I can be subjected to questions about my destination and point of origin. I can

Appeals to reader's self-interest and personal values.

be told to produce my papers and to step out of my car. I can be made to endure the embarrassment of performing tricks to prove my sobriety. Allowing the police such powers is hardly in keeping with our government's mission to promote justice, security, and liberty.

Appeals to emotions.

. . .

Supports preceding statement.

Clearly, government is a necessity. Without it, we would face anarchy. Yet, those who roam the halls of power should remember from where their power originates and should find ways to reduce the burden of unnecessary regulations heaped on the backs of the American people.

Appeals to emotions.

Practicing Strategies for Argument

Practice Deduction   Read the following general statements. Think of a specific case or example that applies to each. Then draw a conclusion. Write your responses in the spaces provided.

1. **General statement:** Students who have had three years of high school mathematics can enroll in Math 101.

    Specific case: _____

    _____

    _____

    _____

    Conclusion: _____

    _____

    _____

2. **General statement:** Students who commute to the college by car must buy parking decals.

   Specific case: _____

   _____

   _____

   _____

   Conclusion: _____

   _____

3. **General statement:** Cars more than five years old must be inspected once per year.

   Specific case: _____

   _____

   _____

   _____

   Conclusion: _____

   _____

4. **General statement:** People whose families have a history of heart disease should have annual coronary examinations.

   Specific case: _____

   _____

   _____

   _____

   Conclusion: _____

   _____

5. **General statement:** People who don't vote should not complain about the way government is run.

   Specific case: _____

   _____

   _____

   _____

   Conclusion: _____

   _____

Practice Induction   Read each group of supportive statements below. Then, using induction, draw a general conclusion from it. Write the conclusion in the space provided.

1.   **Support:** None of the restaurants on the east side of town offers meals for under $30.

       Support: The east side is full of luxury high-rise apartment buildings.

       Support: The east side has no discount clothing, drug, or grocery stores.

       Conclusion: _____

       _____

2.   **Support:** Students who attend Professor Villa's class regularly have a good chance of passing her tests.

       Support: Professor Villa encourages students to come to her office for extra help.

       Support: Professor Villa's assignments are clear and practical.

       Conclusion: _____

       _____

3.   **Support:** The lock on the door had been broken.

       Support: I couldn't find my jewelry.

       Support: Furniture, pictures, and pillows had been moved.

       Conclusion: _____

       _____

4.   **Support:** Serena dragged herself into the apartment and turned on the light.

       Support: There were circles under her eyes.

       Support: In about five minutes, the apartment was dark again.

       Conclusion: _____

       _____

5.   **Support:** Miguel Hernandez plans to attend medical school after getting his bachelor's degree in biology.

       Support: His sister wants to become a dentist.

       Support: His brother is enrolled in a five-year program in architecture.

       Conclusion: _____

       _____

The Right to Be Let Alone

Barry Glazer

Barry Glazer became interested in writing when he enrolled in a basic-skills composition class during his first semester in college. He went on to major in history and English, to become editor of his college newspaper, and to take a bachelor's and a master's degree.

Preparing to Read

1. This essay is logical, clear, and well developed, but it goes beyond pure argument and often appeals to the emotions.

2. Glazer organizes his work around three principles by which he would restrict the government's ability to interfere with our lives. Identify these principles as you read "The Right to Be Let Alone."

3. Louis Brandeis, mentioned in paragraph 2, was associate justice of the United States Supreme Court (1916–1939). He was a champion of individual rights.

Vocabulary

adversely (adverb)	Negatively.
alleviate (verb)	Reduce, lessen, relieve.
anarchy (noun)	Chaos, disorder, lawlessness.
bureaucrats (noun)	Government officials.
constrain (verb)	Restrain, hold in check, bind.
constrict (verb)	Bind, choke, squeeze.
endure (verb)	Suffer, bear, submit to.
entrust (verb)	Give to for safekeeping.
impotence (noun)	Lack of power.
reflect (verb)	Think.
refrain from (verb)	Stop, cease, avoid.
throes (noun)	Agony, pain.

The Right to Be Let Alone

Barry Glazer

GOVERNMENT IS THE instrument of the people, says the United States Consti-   1
tution. Those to whom the people entrust power are charged with maintaining justice, promoting the general welfare, and securing the blessings of
liberty for us all. Recent newspaper opinion polls, however, suggest that many
Americans are dissatisfied with the men and women running our communities,
our states, and our nation. More and more of us have come to believe that our
leaders are isolated from the realities ordinary people face. We fear we are losing control.

Instead of helping to alleviate this feeling of impotence, however, politi-   2
cians and bureaucrats continue to make and enforce regulations that constrain
our lives and constrict our freedoms. To help people regain a rightful measure
of control, government—whether national, state, or local—should stay out of
our private lives whenever possible. As Supreme Court Justice Louis Brandeis
noted, Americans treasure their "right to be let alone."

There is no reason for the government to interfere in our lives if our be-   3
havior does not adversely affect others or if there is no immediate necessity for
such interference. Were I in the throes of terminal cancer or facing the horror
of Alzheimer's disease, I should be allowed to kill myself. Faced with the agonizing degeneration of my memory and personality, I would probably want to
end my life in my own way. But the government says this is illegal. Indeed, were
I to call upon a doctor to assist me on this final quest, she would stand a good
chance of being charged with murder.

The government should also stay out of an individual's life if there is no   4
reason to believe he is doing wrong. The Bill of Rights protects us from unlawful searches and seizures. Yet if I drive home from work in the early morning,
I stand a reasonable chance of being stopped without cause at a police roadblock. While armed, uniformed officers shine flashlights in my face, I can be
subjected to questions about my destination and point of origin. I can be told
to produce my papers and to step out of my car. I can be made to endure the
embarrassment of performing tricks to prove my sobriety. Allowing the police
such powers is hardly in keeping with our government's mission to promote
justice, security, and liberty.

Finally, the government should refrain from creating unnecessary burdens   5
for the American people. It should stay out of a person's private business if such
involvement burdens the individual unnecessarily or unfairly. Recently, my
faithful dog Linda was dying. Because of years of abuse at the hands of her previous owner, she was no longer able to walk and had to be carried in my arms.
At that time, the dog warden knocked on my door and threatened me with fines
for my continued refusal to license the animal. When I told him that Linda was
unable to walk, let alone leave my property, he threatened to return with the
police.

Similarly, when I wanted to convert my garage into a den, I was over-　6
whelmed by official red tape. The cost of construction permits and of measures
to meet complex building codes cost more than the lumber, wall board, and
other supplies for the project. Another example of governmental red tape became evident when I attempted to enroll in a Japanese language course at a
community college. I was told the state required that I take a mathematics
placement test or pass a course in elementary algebra first!

Clearly, government is a necessity. Without it, we would face anarchy. Yet　7
those who roam the halls of power should remember from where their power
originates and should find ways to reduce the burden of unnecessary regulations heaped on the backs of the American people.

Read More on the Web

Website on Justice Louis Brandeis: http://faculty.purduenc.edu/bbk/
　　brandeis.htm

Purdue University site on right to privacy: http://faculty.purduenc.edu/
　　bbk/privacy.html

Privacy Rights Clearinghouse site with links to other sources: http://
　　www.privacyrights.org/

Article by George Mason University professor Walter Williams, a noted
　　social critic: http://www.gmu.edu/departments/economics/wew/
　　articles/99/Left-Alone.htm

Questions for Discussion

1. What one sentence in this essay best expresses Glazer's purpose and
   central idea?
2. In Preparing to Read, you learned that the author defends three
   principles by which he would limit government interference. What
   are these principles?
3. What method of development does Glazer rely on most?
4. Pick out vocabulary that appeals to the reader's emotions.
5. Why does Glazer bother to tell us that Justice Brandeis is the source
   of the quotation in paragraph 2 (and of the essay's title)?
6. Find examples of deductive and inductive reasoning in this essay.
7. Where does the author address an argument that an opponent might
   use to dispute his?

Thinking Critically

1. What side would Barry Glazer take in the debate over mandatory testing of school-age athletes as expressed in the selection earlier in the chapter "Drug Tests Fail Schools"? Support your answer with reference to both reading selections.

2. If you haven't done so already, read Howard's "The Death of Common Sense," an essay in Chapter 10. On what points might Glazer agree and disagree with Howard?

Suggestions for Journal Entries

1. Glazer calls up several examples from experiences similar to those you or people like you might have had. Use focused freewriting to narrate an incident that explains how a government rule or regulation interferes with the right of privacy. Interpret the word *government* broadly; write about the federal, state, local, or college regulation you most disagree with. You might even address a rule followed by your family, your athletic team, or other group to which you belong.

2. Play the role of Glazer's opponent by responding to at least one of the examples he uses to support his thesis. Explain why requiring licenses for all dogs is reasonable; why strict building codes are important; why the police should have the right to stop and question drivers; why doctors should not be allowed to help terminally ill patients commit suicide; or why states should set academic standards in public colleges.

3. Even if you agree with Glazer, you may know of instances in which people welcome government "interference." List as many examples of such beneficial interference as you can.

A Cool and Logical Analysis of the Bicycle Menace

P. J. O'Rourke

A satirist whose targets are politics and social mores, P. J. O'Rourke graduated from Miami University of Ohio. In 1978, he was appointed editor-in-chief of The National Lampoon. *His articles have appeared in* American Spectator, Esquire, Vanity Fair, Harper's, *and many other well-known magazines. O'Rourke is now on staff with* Rolling Stone *and frequently contributors to* The Atlantic Monthly. *He is the author of ten books including* Parliament of Whores *(1991)* All the Trouble in the World *(1994),* Age and Guile Beat Youth, Innocence, and a Bad Haircut *(1996), and* The Bachelor Home Companion *(1997). His latest book is* The CEO of the Sofa *(2002). "A Cool and Logical Analysis of the Bicycle Menace," which appears in* Republican Party Reptile *(1987) reveals O'Rourke as the master of the ironic.*

Preparing to Read

1. As you learned above, this essay is an example of irony, a technique used by writers to create humor by saying something that is different from—often the very opposite of—what they really mean. Often referred to as the tongue-in-cheek method, verbal irony can be used to produce biting satire or simply to create humor. In this essay, O'Rourke is obviously using the latter.

2. Among the products of O'Rourke's irony are several examples of the kinds of logical fallacies explained in the introduction to Section Five: Argumentation and Persuasion. After you read this essay for the first time, re-read it and try to find examples of some of those fallacies.

3. Paragraph 16 mentions UNICEF, the United Nations Children's Fund. Paragraph 18 mentions the DOT, the Department of Transportation; CAFE, Corporate Average Fuel Economy standards; and NHTSA, the National Highway Traffic Safety Administration.

Vocabulary

eons (noun)	Ages.
faddist (noun)	Someone who follows a fashion or trend.
ferrules (noun)	Metal sleeves.
haplessly (adverb)	Unluckily, unfortunately.
impuissant (adjective)	Powerless, ineffective.
phalanx (noun)	A body of troops in close formation.
Pleistocene (noun)	An early geological period.
savanna (noun)	Flat grassland.

A Cool and Logical Analysis of the Bicycle Menace

P. J. O'Rourke

OUR NATION IS afflicted with a plague of bicycles. Everywhere the public   1
right-of-way is glutted with whirring, unbalanced contraptions of rubber, wire, and cheap steel pipe. Riders of these flimsy appliances pay no heed to stop signs or red lights. They dart from between parked cars, dash along double yellow lines, and whiz through crosswalks right over the toes of law-abiding citizens like me.

In the cities, every lamppost, tree, and street sign is disfigured by a bicycle   2
slathered in chains and locks. And elevators must be shared with the cycling faddist so attached to his "moron's bathchair" that he has to take it with him everywhere he goes.

In the country, one cannot drive around a curve or over the crest of a hill   3
without encountering a gaggle of huffing bicyclers spread across the road in suicidal phalanx.

Even the wilderness is not safe from infestation, as there is now such a   4
thing as an off-road bicycle and a horrible sport called "bicycle-cross."

The ungainly geometry and primitive mechanicals of the bicycle are an of-   5
fense to the eye. The grimy and perspiring riders of the bicycle are an offense to the nose. And the very existence of the bicycle is an offense to reason and wisdom.

Principal Arguments Which May Be Marshaled Against Bicycles

1. BICYCLES ARE CHILDISH.

Bicycles have their proper place, and that place is under small boys delivering   6
evening papers. Insofar as children are too short to see over the dashboards of cars and too small to keep motorcycles upright at intersections, bicycles are suitable vehicles for them. But what are we to make of an adult in a suit and tie pedaling his way to work? Are we to assume he still delivers newspapers for a living? If not, do we want a doctor, lawyer, or business executive who plays with toys? St. Paul, in his First Epistle to the Corinthians, 13:11, said, "When I became a man, I put away childish things." He did *not* say, "When I became a man, I put away childish things and got more elaborate and expensive childish things from France and Japan."

Considering the image projected, bicycling commuters might as well pro-   7
pel themselves to the office with one knee in a red Radio Flyer wagon.

2. BICYCLES ARE UNDIGNIFIED.

A certain childishness is, no doubt, excusable. But going about in public with   8
one's head between one's knees and one's rump protruding in the air is nobody's idea of acceptable behavior.

It is impossible for an adult to sit on a bicycle without looking the fool.   9
There is a type of woman, in particular, who should never assume the bicycling
posture. This is the woman of ample proportions. Standing on her own feet she
is a figure to admire—classical in her beauty and a symbol, throughout history,
of sensuality, maternal virtue, and plenty. Mounted on a bicycle, she is a laugh-
ingstock.

In a world where loss of human dignity is such a grave and all-pervading   10
issue, what can we say about people who voluntarily relinquish all of theirs and
go around looking at best like Quixote on Rosinante and more often like something in the Macy's Thanksgiving Day parade? Can such people be trusted? Is a
person with so little self-respect likely to have any respect for you?

3. BICYCLES ARE UNSAFE.

Bicycles are topheavy, have poor brakes, and provide no protection to their rid-   11
ers. Bicycles are also made up of many hard and sharp components which, in
collision, can do grave damage to people and the paint finish on automobiles.
Bicycles are dangerous things.

Of course, there's nothing wrong, *per se,* with dangerous things. Speed-   12
boats, racecars, fine shotguns, whiskey, and love are all very dangerous. Bicycles, however, are dangerous without being any fun. You can't shoot pheasants
with a bicycle or water-ski behind it or go 150 miles an hour or even mix it with
soda and ice. And the idea of getting romantic on top of a bicycle is alarming.
All you can do with one of these ten-speed sink traps is grow tired and sore and
fall off it.

Being dangerous without being fun puts bicycles in a category with open-   13
heart surgery, the war in Vietnam, the South Bronx, and divorce. Sensible people do all that they can to avoid such things as these.

4. BICYCLES ARE UN-AMERICAN.

We are a nation that worships speed and power. And for good reason. Without   14
power we would still be part of England and everybody would be out of work.
And if it weren't for speed, it would take us all months to fly to L.A., get involved in the movie business, and become rich and famous.

Bicycles are too slow and impuissant for a country like ours. They belong   15
in Czechoslovakia.

5. I DON'T LIKE THE KIND OF PEOPLE WHO RIDE BICYCLES.

At least I think I don't. I don't actually know anyone who rides a bicycle. But   16
the people I see on bicycles look like organic-gardening zealots who advocate
federal regulation of bedtime and want American foreign policy to be dictated
by UNICEF. These people should be confined.

I apologize if I have the wrong impression. It may be that bicycle riders are   17
all members of the New York Stock Exchange, Methodist bishops, retired Marine Corps drill instructors, and other solid citizens. However, the fact that they

cycle around in broad daylight making themselves look like idiots indicates that they're crazy anyway and should be confined just the same.

6. BICYCLES ARE UNFAIR.

Bicycles use the same roads as cars and trucks yet they pay no gasoline tax, 18 carry no license plates, are not required to have insurance, and are not subject to DOT, CAFE, or NHTSA regulations. Furthermore, bicyclists do not have to take driver's examinations, have eye tests when they're over sixty-five, carry registration papers with them, or submit to breathalyzer tests under the threat of law. And they never get caught in radar traps.

The fact (see No. 5, above) that bicycles are ridden by the very people who 19 most favor government interference in life makes the bicycle's special status not only unfair but an outright incitement to riot.

Equality before the law is the cornerstone of democracy. Bicycles should be 20 made to carry twenty-gallon tanks of gasoline. They should be equipped with twelve-volt batteries and a full complement of taillights, headlamps, and turn signals. They should have seat belts, air bags, and safety-glass windows too. And every bicycle rider should be inspected once a year for hazardous defects and be made to wear a number plate hanging around his neck and another on the seat of his pants.

7. BICYCLES ARE GOOD EXERCISE.

And so is swinging through trees on your tail. Mankind has invested more than 21 four million years of evolution in the attempt to avoid physical exertion. Now a group of backward-thinking atavists mounted on foot-powered pairs of Hula-Hoops would have us pumping our legs, gritting our teeth, and searing our lungs as though we were being chased across the Pleistocene savanna by saber-toothed tigers. Think of the hopes, the dreams, the effort, the brilliance, the pure force of will that, over the eons, have gone into the creation of the Cadillac Coupe de Ville. Bicycle riders would have us throw all this on the ash heap of history.

What Must Be Done About the Bicycle Threat?

Fortunately, nothing. Frustrated truck drivers and irate cabbies make a point of 22 running bicycles off the road. Terrified old ladies jam umbrella ferrules into wheel spokes as bicycles rush by them on sidewalks. And all of us have occasion to back over bicycles that are haplessly parked.

Bicycles are quiet and slight, difficult for normal motorized humans to see 23 and hear. People pull out in front of bicycles, open car doors in their path, and drive through intersections filled with the things. The insubstantial bicycle and its unshielded rider are defenseless against these actions. It's a simple matter of natural selection. The bicycle will be extinct within the decade. And what a relief that will be.

Read More on the Web

O'Rourke's "Liberty Manifesto": www.libertarian.org/cato/manifesto.html

"All People Are Crazy": An *Atlantic* online interview with O'Rourke:
http://www.theatlantic.com/unbound/interviews/int2002-08-08.htm

Questions for Discussion

1. What is O'Rourke's thesis? Where does he state it? What does this thesis tell you—ironically at least—about the way he will defend it?

2. In which paragraphs does O'Rourke use induction?

3. Paragraphs 6, 18, and 20, among others, use deduction. Create syllogisms that trace O'Rourke's logic in at least two such paragraphs.

4. Where does O'Rourke anticipate opposing arguments? How does he respond to such arguments? Does he ever acknowledge the validity of such arguments?

5. How does the author defend his not knowing anyone who rides a bicycle (paragraph 16)?

6. Find an example in this essay of what Toulmin would call "data," information that leads the writer to take a position on an issue.

7. Find an example of what Toulmin would call a "substantive warrant." Why doesn't O'Rourke include authoritative warrants?

8. Find examples of at least five of the logical fallacies discussed in the introduction to Section Five: Argumentation and Persuasion.

Thinking Critically

1. The nation of Czechoslovakia, which O'Rourke mentions in paragraph 15, no longer exists. (In the early 1990s, it divided into two separate countries: Slovakia and the Czech Republic). Explain O'Rourke's reference to Czechoslovakia. You might have to read more about this country on the Internet or in your library.

2. In item 8 under Questions for Discussion, you were asked to find examples of five logical fallacies in this essay. Now, explain how each of those examples illustrates the fallacy you think it represents.

Suggestions for Journal Entries

1. Using clustering or any other prewriting technique you read about in "Getting Started," gather information to include in your own humorous "analysis" of a particular activity. Remember, your purpose here is to collect reasons that might be used in an ironic, tongue-in-cheek, essay. Like O'Rourke, you will want to show—ironically, of course—why the activity is "a menace" or why it should be stopped. Here are a few suggestions to choose from, but you can probably think of a better one yourself:

   - Exercising on a regular basis.
   - Shopping in a supermarket or other kind of store.
   - Going shopping with a spouse or member of the opposite sex.
   - Going camping, hiking, boating, skiing, etc.
   - Reading the daily newspapers.
   - Driving an SUV, a pickup truck, or any other kind of car or truck.
   - Majoring in (you pick it).
   - Following a low-fat or any other type of diet.
   - Beginning work on a research paper more than one day before it's due.

2. Use clustering or any other prewriting technique you read about in "Getting Started" to gather information that you might use in a serious essay endorsing or criticizing a particular activity. In other words, your purpose here is to gather reasons that might get people to adopt or reject this activity.

Free Speech on Campus

Nat Hentoff

Nat Hentoff (1925–) is one of the most important defenders of free speech in America. He writes a regular column for The Village Voice, *a New York weekly, and he contributes regularly to prestigious newspapers, magazines, and journals across the country. A native of Boston, Hentoff attended Northeastern and Harvard Universities as well as the Sorbonne in Paris, where he studied on a Fulbright fellowship. Although he writes on many subjects, his reputation rests chiefly on his defense of the First Amendment of the U.S. Constitution and his consistent opposition to censorship. Among his books is* The First Freedom: The Tumultuous History of Free Speech in America *(1989).*

Hentoff is generally considered a liberal in politics, but when it comes to free speech he is nonpartisan. In recent years, he has found fault with the Left for its attempts to silence those whose opinions it finds offensive or distasteful. This essay is excerpted from a longer piece, which first appeared in The Progressive *(1989).*

Preparing to Read

1. The First Amendment to the U.S. Constitution states that "Congress shall make no law respecting the establishment of religion, or prohibiting the free exercise thereof; or abridging the freedom of speech, or of the press; or the right of the people peaceably to assemble, and to petition the Government for a redress of grievances."

2. The Fourteenth Amendment (paragraph 21) guarantees due process and equal protection under the law. Due process (paragraph 13) allows citizens to defend themselves in both criminal and civil actions against accusations that can have legal, financial, or other serious consequences.

3. Lenny Bruce, Richard Pryor, and Sam Kinison, who are mentioned in paragraph 13, have used language that some might find offensive or even obscene in their comedy acts.

4. Affirmative action (paragraph 16) is the name given to government regulations that set goals for the admission of minorities to educational institutions and for the hiring of minorities in both the private and public sectors.

5. "Politically correct" is a term used by critics of the Left. They accuse liberals of insisting that only certain beliefs and behaviors are legitimate despite Constitutional and other legal guarantees.

6. Oliver Wendell Holmes was a U.S. Supreme Court Justice famous for his writings on the First Amendment.

Vocabulary

aggravated (adjective)	Heightened, made worse.
condemnation (noun)	Blame, censure.
constitute (verb)	Make up or equate to.
derogatory (adjective)	Degrading, disdainful.
dissented (verb)	Refused to conform or obey.
inquiry (noun)	Questioning, exploration, debate.
knownothingism (noun)	A term that has come to mean intolerance and bigotry. The Knownothing Party of the nineteenth century wished to close U.S. borders to further immigration.
malignancies (noun)	Cancers.
orthodoxy (noun)	Strict adherence to a doctrine or set of beliefs.
pall (noun)	Gloom, sadness.
pariah (noun)	Social outcast, renegade.
perpetuate (verb)	Continue, keep alive.
pietistic (adjective)	Solemn, but in an affected or false way.
resurgence (noun)	Rebirth.
sanctions (noun)	Punishments.
scant (adjective)	Little.
secular (adjective)	Worldly.
short shrift (noun)	Little attention.
stifling (adjective)	Suffocating.
tempered (adjective)	Balanced, controlled.
ukase (noun)	Proclamation, decree, order.

Free Speech on Campus

Nat Hentoff

A FLIER DISTRIBUTED at the University of Michigan some months ago pro- 1
claimed that blacks "don't belong in classrooms, they belong hanging
from trees."

At other campuses around the country, manifestations of racism are be- 2
coming commonplace. At Yale, a swastika and the words WHITE POWER!
were painted on the building housing the University's Afro-American Cultural
Center. At Temple University, a White Students Union has been formed with
some 130 members.

Swastikas are not directed only at black students. The Nazi symbol has 3
been spray-painted on the Jewish Student Union at Memphis State University.
And on a number of campuses, women have been singled out as targets of
wounding and sometimes frightening speech. At the law school of the State

University of New York at Buffalo, several women students have received anonymous letters characterized by one professor as venomously sexist.

These and many more such signs of the resurgence of bigotry and   4
knownothingism throughout the society—as well as on campus—have to do solely with speech, including symbolic speech. There have also been physical assaults on black students and on black, white, and Asian women students, but the way to deal with physical attacks is clear: call the police and file a criminal complaint. What is to be done, however, about speech alone—however disgusting, inflammatory, and rawly divisive that speech may be?

At more and more colleges, administrators—with the enthusiastic support   5
of black students, women students, and liberal students—have been answering that question by preventing or punishing speech. In public universities, this is a clear violation of the First Amendment. In private colleges and universities, suppression of speech mocks the secular religion of academic freedom and free inquiry.

The Student Press Law Center in Washington, D.C.—a vital source of le-   6
gal support for student editors around the country—reports, for example, that at the University of Kansas, the student host and producer of a radio news program was forbidden by school officials from interviewing a leader of the Ku Klux Klan. So much for free inquiry on that campus.

In Madison, Wisconsin, the *Capital Times* ran a story in January about   7
Chancellor Sheila Kaplan of the University of Wisconsin branch at Parkside, who ordered her campus to be scoured of "some anonymously placed white supremacist hate literature." Sounding like the legendary Mayor Frank ("I am the law") Hague of Jersey City, who booted "bad speech" out of town, Chancellor Kaplan said, "This institution is not a lamppost standing on the street corner. It doesn't belong to everyone."

Who decides what speech can be heard or read by everyone? Why, the   8
Chancellor, of course. That's what George III used to say, too.

University of Wisconsin political science professor Carol Tebben thinks   9
otherwise. She believes university administrators "are getting confused when they are acting as censors and trying to protect students from bad ideas. I don't think students need to be protected from bad ideas. I think they can determine for themselves what ideas are bad."

After all, if students are to be "protected" from bad ideas, how are they go-   10
ing to learn to identify and cope with them? Sending such ideas underground simply makes them stronger and more dangerous.

Professor Tebben's conviction that free speech means just that has become   11
a decidedly minority view on many campuses. At the University of Buffalo Law School, the faculty unanimously adopted a "Statement Regarding Intellectual Freedom, Tolerance, and Political Harassment." Its title implies support of intellectual freedom, but the statement warned students that once they enter "this legal community," their right to free speech must become tempered "by the responsibility to promote equality and justice."

Accordingly, swift condemnation will befall anyone who engages in "re-   12
marks directed at another's race, sex, religion, national origin, age, or sex preference." Also forbidden are "other remarks based on prejudice and group
stereotype."

This ukase is so broad that enforcement has to be alarmingly subjective.   13
Yet the University of Buffalo Law School provides no due-process procedures
for a student booked for making any of these prohibited remarks. Conceivably,
a student caught playing a Lenny Bruce, Richard Pryor, or Sam Kinison album
in his room could be tried for aggravated insensitivity by association.

When I looked into this wholesale cleansing of bad speech at Buffalo, I   14
found it had encountered scant opposition. One protester was David Gerald
Jay, a graduate of the law school and a cooperating attorney for the New York
Civil Liberties Union. Said the appalled graduate: "Content-based prohibitions
constitute prior restraint and should not be tolerated."

You would think that the law professors and administration at this public   15
university might have known that. But hardly any professors dissented, and
among the students only members of the conservative Federalist Society spoke
up for free speech. The fifty-strong chapter of the National Lawyers Guild was
on the other side. After all, it was more important to go on record as vigorously
opposing racism and sexism than to expose oneself to charges of insensitivity
to these malignancies.

The pressures to have the "right" attitude—as proved by having the "right"   16
language in and out of class—can be stifling. A student who opposes affirmative action, for instance, can be branded a racist.

At the University of California at Los Angeles, the student newspaper ran   17
an editorial cartoon satirizing affirmative action. (A student stops a rooster on
campus and asks how the rooster got into UCLA. "Affirmative action," is the answer.) After outraged complaints from various minority groups, the editor was
suspended for violating a publication policy against running "articles that per-
petuate derogatory or cultural stereotypes." The art director was also suspended.

When the opinion editor of the student newspaper at California State Uni-   18
versity at Northridge wrote an article asserting that the sanctions against the editor and art director at UCLA amounted to censorship, he was suspended too.

At New York University Law School, a student was so disturbed by the pall   19
of orthodoxy at that prestigious institution that he wrote to the school newspaper even though, as he said, he expected his letter to make him a pariah
among his fellow students.

Barry Endick described the atmosphere at NYU created by "a host of   20
watchdog committees and a generally hostile classroom reception regarding
any student comment right of center." This "can be arguably viewed as symp-
tomatic of a prevailing spirit of academic and social intolerance of . . . any idea
which is not 'politically correct.' "

He went on to say something that might well be posted on campus bul-   21
letin boards around the country, though it would probably be torn down at

many of them: "We ought to examine why students, so anxious to wield the Fourteenth Amendment, give short shrift to the First. Yes, Virginia, there are racist assholes. And you know what, the Constitution protects them, too."

Not when they engage in violence or vandalism. But when they speak or 22 write, racist assholes fall right into this Oliver Wendell Holmes definition— highly unpopular among bigots, liberals, radicals, feminists, sexists, and college administrators: "If there is any principle of the Constitution that more imperatively calls for attachment than any other, it is the principle of free thought—not free only for those who agree with us, but freedom for the thought we hate."

The language sounds like a pietistic Sunday sermon, but if it ever falls 23 wholly into disuse, neither this publication nor any other journal of opinion— right or left—will survive.

Read More on the Web

Site explores university responses to censoring the Internet. Includes useful bibliography: http://hsb.baylor.edu/ramsower/ais.ac.97/papers/peace.htm

Nat Hentoff Archives: Three years of Hentoff columns on the Web: http://www.jewishworldreview.com/cols/hentoff.archives.asp

American Civil Liberties Union online essay: "Racist Speech on College Campuses": http://archive.aclu.org/library/aahate.html

Questions for Discussion

1. What use of expert testimony and opinion does Hentoff make?
2. What use of anecdotes does he make? Of contrast?
3. Analyze the essay's introduction. What techniques are used here to draw our attention?
4. What is the question Hentoff asks in paragraph 4? How does this question help him introduce his essay?
5. In what way is symbolic speech similar to speech? Why does Hentoff bother to mention symbolic speech?
6. What distinction does the author draw between speech and action? Why is this distinction important to his thesis? What is his thesis?
7. Why does Hentoff quote Professor Carol Tebben (paragraph 9) and David Gerald Jay (paragraph 14)? What do their words add to the author's argument?

8. You learned earlier that, at times, writers of argument reveal their feelings about an issue, if only subtly. Where does Hentoff do this?

9. Where does the author address opposing opinions?

10. Describe the intended audience for this piece.

Thinking Critically

1. Reread Barry Glazer's essay, which appears earlier in this chapter. How might Hentoff respond to Glazer's arguments?

2. Reread Hentoff's essay. Then, using deduction, summarize it into a syllogism. In your own words, state its major premise, its minor premise, and its conclusion.

Suggestions for Journal Entries

1. Can you think of any circumstances when you might agree that speech should be censored? Make a list of such circumstances; then, explain why each might warrant limitations on free speech.

2. Are you in favor of unlimited free speech under all circumstances? If so, explain your reasons. As a way to anticipate arguments opposed to your own, explain how and why you would defend the rights of people to speak—verbally or symbolically—in ways that you might find distasteful, immoral, abhorrent, or even dangerous.

3. Consider an issue on your campus that you feel strongly about. It doesn't have to have earth-shaking consequences. The benefits of keeping the library open all night, the need for more parking spaces, or the advantages of majoring in a particular subject area might make fine topics for argumentation. Use freewriting or clustering to gather information you might later use to argue your position and to anticipate opposing arguments in a formal, full-length essay.

Bilingual Education: Opposing Views

"Desperate to Learn English" by Alice Callaghan
"Melting Pot or Tossed Salad" by Dudley Barlow

A priest in the Episcopal Church, Alice Callaghan directs Los Familias del Pueblo Community Center in Los Angeles, California. "Desperate to Learn English" first appeared on August 15, 1997, on the New York Times *op-ed page.*

Dudley Barlow is a high-school teacher in Canton, Michigan. He writes "The Teachers Lounge" and "Education Resources" for Education Digest, *a research journal in education. "Melting Pot or Tossed Salad" appeared in the March 1996 issue of that journal.*

Preparing to Read

1. In November 1997, *U.S. News & World Report* magazine claimed that a "measure that would virtually eliminate bilingual education in California" would most certainly appear on the ballot in 1998. A referendum limiting state funding for bilingual education was passed by the voters in that year.

2. Analyze each of the titles of the essays presented here. What do the titles tell us about the contents of the essays to which they belong?

Vocabulary

acknowledge (verb)	Admit, recognize.
adios, amigo (verb/noun)	Spanish for "goodbye, friend." Used sarcastically.
advocates (noun)	Supporters.
assimilation (noun)	Absorption.
ballot initiative (noun)	Referendum putting a question to a public vote.
compatriots (noun)	Colleagues, co-workers.
confines (noun)	Borders.
critical mass (noun)	Extremely large number, breaking point.
denounced (verb)	Severely criticized, condemned.
entrenched (adjective)	Dug in, securely established.
ethnic (adjective)	Relating to a race or nationality.
havens (noun)	Safe places.
languish (verb)	Lose strength or energy, fade.
lectern (noun)	A podium or platform from which a speaker addresses listeners.
linguistic (adjective)	Relating to language and the study of language.

monoglots (noun)	Speakers of only one language.
proficiency (noun)	Skill, ability.
relinquished (verb)	Gave up, surrendered.

Desperate to Learn English

Alice Callaghan

JUANA AND FLORENCIO left the poverty of their rural Mexican village in 1985   1
and came to Los Angeles to work in the garment district's sweatshops. In
1996, they pulled their three children—all born in Los Angeles—out of school
for nearly two weeks until the school agreed to let them take classes in English
rather than Spanish.

Seventy other poor immigrant families joined this school boycott in Feb-   2
ruary 1996, insisting that their children be allowed out of the city's bilingual
program, which would not teach English to children from Spanish-speaking
homes until they learned how to read and write in Spanish. In the end, the parents prevailed.

Yet, throughout California and elsewhere in the country, many Hispanic   3
parents are worried that bilingual education programs are keeping their children from learning English.

These children live in Spanish-speaking homes, play in Spanish-speaking   4
neighborhoods and study in Spanish-speaking classrooms. With little exposure
to English in the primary grades, few successfully learn it later.

This is why many Latino parents are backing a California ballot initiative   5
that would end bilingual education for most children in the state. The measure will be put to a vote in June if enough signatures are gathered to put it on
the ballot.

School administrators, Latino politicians and other advocates of bilingual   6
education have denounced the measure. Though they acknowledge the failings
of the system, they insist they can fix it with time.

Yet after 25 years, bilingual education has few defenders among Latino par-   7
ents. In a *Los Angeles Times* poll this year, 83 percent of Latino parents in Orange County said they wanted their children to be taught in English as soon as
they started school. Only 17 percent of those surveyed said they favored having their children taught in their native language.

One reason bilingual education is so entrenched is money. Bilingual teach-   8
ers in Los Angeles are paid extra, up to $5,000 a year; schools and school dis-
tricts receive hundreds of dollars for each child who is designated as having
limited proficiency in English. About $400 million in state and Federal money
supports bilingual educational programs in California. Because such money is
not readily relinquished, students languish in Spanish-language classes.

Moreover, there are not enough bilingual teachers. In Los Angeles, the   9
shortfall has been so severe that the city has granted emergency credentials

to people whose only claim to a classroom lectern is their ability to speak Spanish.

Latino parents know that placing their children in English-language classes 10 will not cure the many problems plaguing California schools, where the Latino dropout rate is 40 percent and Latino students have consistently low achievement test scores. Unless these students can learn in English, future school reform efforts will not help them.

Most parents who participated in the school boycott last year labor in garment 11 district sweatshops. Others wait on tables, clean downtown offices or sell fruit or tamales on street corners. All struggle on average monthly incomes of $800.

Education is their only hope for a better future for their children. The first 12 step is learning English.

Melting Pot or Tossed Salad

Dudley Barlow

It was a student named Brian, during my first year of teaching, who intro- 1 duced me to Hyman Kaplan, the main character in Leonard Q. Ross's wonderful little book, *The Education of H*y*m*a*n K*a*p*l*a*n*. The character is a German Jewish immigrant in his forties, and he is in Mr. Parkhill's class entitled "American Night Preparatory School for Adults." Kaplan first came to Parkhill's attention when the class turned in an assignment on common nouns and their plural forms. Kaplan's paper read: "house . . . makes . . . houses, dog . . . makes . . . doggies, library . . . makes Public library, cat . . . makes . . . Katz."

Throughout the book, we watch as Kaplan plunges enthusiastically into 2 this puzzle of a new and difficult language. On the final exam, he writes Parkhill a note because, "In the recass was som students asking if is right to say Its Me or Its I . . . a planty hard question, no? Yes."

Kaplan has the whole puzzle neatly solved. "If I am in hall and knok, knok, 3 knok; and I hear insite (insite the room) somebody hollers 'Whose there'—I anser strong 'Its Kaplan'!!

"Now is fine! Plain, clear like gold, no chance mixing up Me, I, Ect.   4

"By *Thinking* is Humans making big edvences on Enimals. This we call 5 Progriss."

Kaplan came to my mind as I started writing this column. He was fortu- 6 nate to be able to struggle with this new language in the company of the long-suffering Parkhill. A few weeks ago, I saw a news story on television about two non-English speakers who were not so fortunate.

The story concerned a bar owner somewhere in the state of Washington 7 who refused to serve two Mexican patrons because they did not speak English. I believe she even went so far as to have the two men thrown out of the establishment. On the wall of the bar was a sign that said something like, "If you don't speak English, adios, amigo." When the TV reporter covering the story asked the woman about the incident, she said, "I thought this was America. In America, we speak English."

This woman reminded me of something my wife's uncle, Joe Zadzora, once 8 told me. Joe was born in a coal town in Pennsylvania in the early 1920s, and he worked in the mines before joining the army during World War II. He told me about the ethnic groups—including Poles, Slavs, Russians, Irish, and Hungarians—who mined the coal and lived in the company town above the shafts. They had come to this country for the same reasons that immigrants have always come here: There was work to be had in America, and if they worked hard at difficult and sometimes dangerous jobs, maybe they could make it possible for their children to have better jobs and better lives.

Many, perhaps most, of them did not speak English. They did not need it. 9 They could cut, blast, and shovel coal below ground with their compatriots, and above ground they lived in ethnic neighborhoods where the languages of their homelands worked just fine. But for their children, it was a different story. They went to school to learn, among other things, how to speak English to fit into this new land. English was the first key to assimilation into the broader culture beyond the company town.

The first generation born here would speak two languages with ease: the 10 old world language used at home and English in the larger world. The next generation would have a new mother tongue, but would still be able to understand their grandparents. By the third generation, though, they would be monoglots again, and their ancestral languages would be lost.

This has been pretty much the normal course of events for immigrant families here. Big cities with their ethnic neighborhoods sometimes provided linguistic havens where the old languages could hang on for generations. Foreign-born folks less adventuresome than Hyman Kaplan could find everything they needed within the confines of a few blocks and within the familiar tongues of their former homes.

Ultimately, though, assimilation was what everyone wanted. Immigrants 12 wanted to acquire our language to be able to partake of the American Dream, and we knew that they were right in wanting to be like us.

Now, though, things are changing. In some parts of our country, in the 13 Southwest in particular, non-native English speakers are reaching a critical mass which has weakened the arguments for learning English.

The melting pot is becoming a tossed salad in which the various elements are 14 mixed together but retain their individual identities. So, how do we respond to this new situation? What do government printing offices do? Does the Internal Revenue Service print forms in Spanish as well as English? What about road signs: Do cities in California, Arizona, and Texas print directions in both languages?

And how do those of us in the education business respond to this new 15 situation? What are schools where Spanish-speaking students outnumber English-speaking students to do?

Some policymakers would respond the way the owner of that Washington 16
pub did, and insist that "In America, we speak English." This "English only" approach would have all lessons taught only in English to force non-English speakers to learn our language.

Others would have us offer bilingual instruction designed to communicate 17
with students in the language with which they are most familiar while trying to equip them with the language that would carry them beyond the confines of their own ethnic group.

There must also be a third group that would argue that, if a class is made 18
up entirely or even predominantly of Spanish speakers, the lessons should be taught entirely in Spanish. To force these students to abandon Spanish for English, this group would argue, is a form of linguistic racism.

My sympathies are with the second group. If a school has a student popu- 19
lation made up primarily of Spanish speakers, I think it would be foolhardy not to communicate with them in the language they understand best. At the same time, we need to recognize (and these students need to understand) that the language of commerce—the language of the widest range of opportunities in our country—is English. For this reason, these students also need to acquire English language skills.

And what about the road signs and IRS forms? We need to take a cue from 20
business here. The instructions telling me how to set up my computer came in English and Spanish, and the instructions in a box of film or cough syrup come in several languages. As Kaplan would say, "This we call Progriss."

As a footnote, one final comment about the Washington bar owner who re- 21
fused to serve the patrons who did not speak English. I believe her name was Orlander. Something tells me that her first ancestors to reach American soil didn't speak English, either. Someone must have served them.

Read More on the Web

Links to sites for and against bilingual education: http://www.wellesley.edu/Spanish/NEWEduc308/bilingual1.html

Site which explains California's Proposition 227 with links to full text: http://primary98.ss.ca.gov/VoterGuide/Propositions/227.htm

Questions for Discussion

1. Where in her essay does Callaghan use statistics?
2. Does Callaghan rely on authority to support her opinions? Where?
3. How does she anticipate arguments of the opposition?
4. Comment on Callaghan's introduction. What purpose does it serve?
5. Find examples of deductive reasoning in Callaghan's essay.
6. Explain how Callaghan tries to appeal to our emotions.

7. What methods of development does Barlow use in "Melting Pot or Tossed Salad"?

8. Where does Barlow address opposing arguments?

9. Why is Barlow's introduction so long?

10. Why does he quote Hyman Kaplan so extensively?

11. What is the thesis of "Melting Pot or Tossed Salad"?

12. How does the author's contrasting the metaphors of the "melting pot" and the "tossed salad" describe the current U.S. population?

13. Why does Barlow mention three different positions on bilingual education (paragraphs 16, 17, and 18)? Why doesn't he limit himself to the two opinions in paragraphs 16 and 17?

Thinking Critically

1. Is Callaghan being fair in her criticisms of the bilingual-education establishment (paragraph 8 and 9)? Why or why not?

2. Early in "Desperate to Learn English," we learn that 71 families joined in the school boycott. Is this statistic convincing? Why or why not?

3. What does Barlow mean when he claims that "non-native speakers are reaching a critical mass, which has weakened the arguments for learning English"? Do you agree with this statement?

4. If these two authors met in a debate, on what points would they definitely disagree? Are there any points on which they might agree?

Suggestions for Journal Entries

1. What's your opinion? Should we abolish bilingual education, keep it as it is, or change it in some way? Interview educators (including those who teach in bilingual programs, if possible) to gather insights.

2. Think of a particular change we should make in public education and list arguments that would support that change. Here are some examples of changes one might advocate:

> Increase services for learning-disabled students.
>
> Increase or decrease the number of electives high school students can take.
>
> Grant tax credits to parents whose children attend private or parochial schools.
>
> Require foreign-language study from first through twelfth grade.
>
> Fund all public schools in America by allocating the same amount of tax money for every student regardless of the community or state in which he or she lives.

Exporting Democracy: Opposing Views

"Freedom: Our Best Export" by Lou Dobbs
"Republic or Empire?" by Joseph Wilson

The last U.S. diplomat to meet with Saddam Hussein before the Persian Gulf War, Joseph Wilson was the Deputy Chief of Mission at the U.S. Embassy in Baghdad, Iraq, from 1988–1991. He also served as deputy ambassador, and he is responsible for the release of hundreds of American hostages held in Iraq. He is now a member of the Middle East Institute in Washington, D.C.

Lou Dobbs is the host and producer of CNN's "Moneyline." One of the most respected financial and international affairs reporters, Dobbs also writes "The Dobbs Report," a weekly column for US News & World Report, *in which his essay first appeared on March 10, 2003.*

Preparing to Read

1. In paragraph 1 of "Republic or Empire," Wilson mentions Desert Shield, an action in which US troops guarded Saudi Arabia from Iraqi invasion in 1990. Desert Storm was an allied operation that in 1991 ousted Iraq from Kuwait.

2. In criticizing American foreign policy, Wilson makes reference to Rome, both as a republic and an empire. You can recognize this allusion in his title. In paragraph 2, he mentions "Pax Americana," Latin for "American Peace," and a play on "Pax Romana." In paragraph 3, he compares American diplomats to "pro-consuls," the men Rome sent out to rule conquered lands.

3. Colin Powell, mentioned in Wilson's fifth paragraph, became Secretary of State under Pres. George W. Bush in 2001. He was also head of the Joint Chiefs of Staff during Desert Storm.

4. The Baath Party, mentioned in paragraph 3 of Dobbs's essay, is a secular political party that ruled Iraq and that was led by Saddam Hussein.

Vocabulary

cajoling (adjective)	Coaxing.
ceded (adjective)	Yielded, surrendered.
constrain (verb)	Limit, hold back.
disconsolate (adjective)	Dejected, dispirited.
dissent (noun)	Expression of opposition.
eschewed (verb)	Turned away from, avoided.
hegemony (noun)	Authority over, dominance.
hubris (noun)	Arrogance.

impending (adjective)	Upcoming, imminent.
intransigence (noun)	Refusal to cooperate, stubbornness.
jettison (verb)	Throw away, discard.
linchpin (noun)	Component or event on which entire process depends.
myopia (noun)	Shortsightedness.
obliqueness (noun)	Not being straightforward or direct.
partisan (adjective)	Favoring one side.
precipitously (adverb)	Suddenly, quickly.
restive (adjective)	Uneasy, unstable.
sanctioned (adjective)	Approved.
vassal (adjective)	Subservient, controlled.

Freedom: Our Best Export

Lou Dobbs

PRESIDENT BUSH last week laid out in broad terms his vision of a Middle East free of Saddam Hussein and the fear of weapons of mass destruction. The president said, "A liberated Iraq can show the power of freedom to transform that vital region by bringing hope and progress into the lives of millions." Some critics of the president's decision to disarm Saddam Hussein absolutely, and by force if necessary, either suggest or claim outright that U.S. policy is being motivated by oil. Along with a number of journalists who were invited to the White House last week, I heard this president say without reservation and with absolute conviction that the U.S. policy is peace and freedom in the region, which he sincerely believes are essential to the safety of the American people. 1

The critics of the war against terror and the absolute disarmament of Saddam Hussein must overcome their partisan myopia and do their best to understand that there's nothing at stake here less than the very survival of our nation and democratic civilization. 2

In my opinion, the president has set us upon exactly the right course on the Middle East. Yes, it is in the interest of this energy-hungry nation to have stability in the region. But far more important is the elimination of dictators and despots who oppress their people and deny them even basic freedoms whether in the name of the secular Baath Party or radical Islamist ideology. 3

Trade in values. We have imported their oil and exported our dollars far too long without exporting as well democratic and capitalist market values. Democracy and markets offer the people of the Middle East their best hope for prosperity and freedom. The widespread impoverishment and unchecked extremism among radical Islamist factions will breed only further dangers to our way of life and democratic civilization everywhere. 4

The threat of terrorism and the uncertainty and impending prospect of war with Saddam Hussein continue to depress our markets and stifle business, 5 investment and economic growth. Consumer confidence is now at the weakest level in nine years, and investor confidence is at a historical low. "Our company's surveys have shown that business spending decisions have clearly been delayed because of uncertainty about the war," says Jason Trennert, senior managing director of ISI Group. Even Federal Reserve Chairman Alan Greenspan has warned about Iraq's drag on the economy and the markets. As he told Congress last month, "Worries about the situation in Iraq contributed to an appreciable increase in oil prices. These uncertainties, coupled with ongoing concerns surrounding macroeconomic prospects, heightened investors' perception of risk." Stunningly clear talk from a man better known for obliqueness.

Israel's current problems are troubling proof of the cost of allowing uncertainty over terror to continue. Since Israeli-Palestinian peace negotiations broke down in September of 2000, the main index of the Israeli stock market (the TA 100) has plunged 44 percent. Israel's economy has slowed from 6 percent annual growth to recession. And as you would expect, Israel's unemployment rate has increased dramatically to 10 percent. 6

Soundly defeating Saddam will also be an important disincentive to other states and radical Islamist terrorist groups who would harm Americans. As President Bush also said last week, "The passing of Saddam Hussein's regime will deprive terrorist networks of a wealthy patron that pays for terrorist training and offers rewards to families of suicide bombers." And, as Mr. Bush added, "Other regimes will be given a clear warning that support for terror will not be tolerated." 7

Of course, even after Saddam is long gone, the cost of the threat of terrorism won't go away. We'll still face the danger from further attacks from al Qaeda and other radical Islamist groups. As a report from the Joint Economic Committee last year found, there are significant long-term costs of terrorism, such as the expense of additional security measures, or a "terrorist tax." That's in addition to the economic resources diverted toward security and away from private-sector activity. 8

But the best way to create a disincentive to terrorists in the future is to fight the war against Saddam with all of the resources and resolve we possess today. Saddam's threat to our security needs to be eliminated once and for all, and the message needs to be sent that terror against the United States from any radical group or state won't be tolerated. Otherwise, the cost of terror will only rise precipitously—both in economic terms and human life. 9

Republic or Empire

Joseph Wilson

A S THE SENIOR American diplomat in Baghdad during Desert Shield, I advocated a muscular US response to Saddam's brutal annexation of Kuwait in flagrant violation of the United Nations charter. Only the credible threat of 1 force could hope to reverse his invasion. Our in-your-face strategy secured the release of the 150 American "human shields"—hostages—but ultimately it took war to drive Iraq from Kuwait. I was disconsolate at the failure of diplomacy, but Desert Storm was necessitated by Saddam's intransigence, it was sanctioned by the UN and it was conducted with a broad international military coalition. The goal was explicit and focused; war was the last resort.

The upcoming military operation also has one objective, though different   2
from the several offered by the Bush Administration. This war is not about weapons of mass destruction. The intrusive inspections are disrupting Saddam's programs, as even the Administration has acknowledged. Nor is it about terrorism. Virtually all agree war will spawn more terrorism, not less. It is not even about liberation of an oppressed people. Killing innocent Iraqi civilians in a full frontal assault is hardly the only or best way to liberate a people. The underlying objective of this war is the imposition of a Pax Americana on the region and installation of vassal regimes that will control restive populations.

Without the firing of a single cruise missile, the Administration has already   3
established a massive footprint in the Gulf and Southwest Asia from which to project power. US generals, admirals and diplomats have crisscrossed the region like modern-day proconsuls, cajoling fragile governments to permit American access and operations from their territories.

Bases have been established as stepping stones to Afghanistan and Iraq, but   4
also as tripwires in countries that fear their neighbors. Northern Kuwait has been ceded to American forces and a significant military presence established in Bahrain, Saudi Arabia, Qatar, the United Arab Emirates and Oman. The over-the-horizon posture of a decade ago has given way to boots on the ground and forward command headquarters. Nations in the region, having contracted with the United States for their security umbrella, will now listen when Washington tells them to tailor policies and curb anti-Western dissent. Hegemony in the Arab nations of the Gulf has been achieved.

Meanwhile, Saddam might well squirm, but even without an invasion, he's   5
finished. He is surrounded, foreigners are swarming through his palaces, and as Colin Powell so compellingly showed at the UN, we are watching and we are listening. International will to disarm Iraq will not wane as it did in the 1990s, for the simple reason that George W. Bush keeps challenging the organization to remain relevant by keeping pressure on Saddam. Nations that worry that, as John le Carré puts it, "America has entered one of its periods of historical madness" will not want to jettison the one institution that, absent a competing military power, might constrain US ambition.

Then what's the point of this new American imperialism? The neoconser-   6
vatives with a stranglehold on the foreign policy of the Republican Party, a party that traditionally eschewed foreign military adventures, want to go beyond expanding US global influence to force revolutionary change on the region. American pre-eminence in the Gulf is necessary but not sufficient for the hawks. Nothing short of conquest, occupation and imposition of handpicked leaders

on a vanquished population will suffice. Iraq is the linchpin for this broader assault on the region. The new imperialists will not rest until governments that ape our worldview are implanted throughout the region, a breathtakingly ambitious undertaking, smacking of hubris in the extreme. Arabs who complain about American-supported antidemocratic regimes today will find us in even more direct control tomorrow. The leader of the future in the Arab world will look a lot more like Pakistan's Pervez Musharraf than Thomas Jefferson.

There is a huge risk of overreach in this tack. The projection of influence   7
and power through the use of force will breed resistance in the Arab world that will sorely test our political will and stamina. Passion for independence is as great in the Arab world as it is elsewhere. The hawks compare this mission to Japan and Germany after World War II. It could easily look like Lebanon, Somalia and Northern Ireland instead.

Our global leadership will be undermined as fear gives way to resentment   8
and strategies to weaken our stranglehold. American businessmen already complain about hostility when overseas, and Arabs speak openly of boycotting American products. Foreign capital is fleeing American stocks and bonds; the United States is no longer a friendly destination for international investors. For a borrow-and-spend Administration, as this one is, the effects on our economic growth will be felt for a long time to come. Essential trust has been seriously damaged and will be difficult to repair.

Even in the unlikely event that war does not come to pass, the would-be   9
imperialists have achieved much of what they sought, some of it good. It is encouraging that the international community is looking hard at terrorism and the proliferation of weapons of mass destruction. But the upcoming battle for Baghdad and the lengthy occupation of Iraq will utterly undermine any steps forward. And with the costs to our military, our treasury and our international standing, we will be forced to learn whether our republican roots and traditions can accommodate the Administration's imperial ambitions. It may be a bitter lesson.

Read More on the Web

Review of *Exporting Democracy: Fulfilling America's Destiny* by Joshua
    Muravchik: http://www.danielpipes.org/article/877
CNN.com site on possible war with Iraq, with numerous resources for
    further study: http://www.cnn.com/2002/fyi/lesson.plans/09/27/
    cnnpce.showdown.iraq.da/
Brookings Institution site on Middle East policy: http://www.brook.edu/
    fp/saban/sabancenter_hp.htm/

Questions for Discussion

1. Wilson's purpose goes beyond criticizing U.S. plans to invade Iraq. What else is he criticizing?

2. Put Wilson's thesis, which appears in paragraph 2, into your own words.

3. In paragraph 8, Wilson uses deduction to argue that invading Iraq would weaken our economy. Explain the process by which he comes to this conclusion.

4. Wilson argues that America's purpose is to "force revolutionary change in the region." From this, he concludes that "Nothing short of conquest, occupation and imposition of handpicked leaders on a vanquished population will suffice" (paragraph 6). What evidence does he offer to support this argument?

5. In paragraph 9, Wilson acknowledges that some of what the United States achieves might be "good." Does doing this weaken his argument?

6. Where does Wilson establish his authority?

7. In paragraph 2, Wilson claims that "virtually all agree war will spawn more terrorism." How might Dobbs respond?

8. Dobbs believes that the primary reason behind invading Iraq is to export democracy and capitalism so as to stabilize the Middle East. How might Wilson respond to that idea?

9. How does Dobbs respond to those who claim the United States would invade Iraq for oil? Does he totally disagree?

10. Explain Dobbs's use of deduction in paragraph 4.

11. Explain Dobbs's use of induction (the conclusion-and-support method) in paragraphs 5, 6, and 7.

12. What appeals to expert authorities does Dobbs make? Do you find them effective in supporting his argument?

Thinking Critically

1. Interestingly, Wilson and Dobbs share the same views on some points having to do with American Middle-East policy. Explain these similarities. Then explain the differences in their opinions. Make specific reference to the texts.

2. Explain the connection between Rome and America that Wilson makes. Does drawing this comparison strengthen his argument?

Suggestions for Journal Entries

1. Dobbs tells us that fostering stability in the Middle East is in our best interest. Defeating Saddam Hussein, he adds, would be a "disincentive to other states and radical Islamist terrorist groups who would harm Americans" (paragraph 7). Wilson says that "war will spawn more terrorism" (paragraph 2). Research ways that security experts recommend we fight terrorism. Read several sources, online or in print, and pick one that makes particular sense to you. Make marginal and textual notes on your copy of this document, as recommended in "Getting Started: Becoming an Active College Reader" (pages 31–41). Then, summarize the document's contents in your journal.

2. These two essays raise several important questions besides those having to do with invading Iraq:

    • Is America too dependent on foreign oil? Should we do more to tap domestic sources of oil? Should we promote research into alternate fuel sources more aggressively?

    • What should our stand be in regard to countries that harbor terrorists?

    • Do the problems between the Israelis and the Palestinians increase hatred for America in Islamic countries and serve to encourage terrorism?

    • Should America try to export democracy and capitalism to parts of the world that have not yet experienced these systems?

    • Does the US really want to control the Middle East as Wilson claims?

    Choose one of these questions or any question you can draw from your reading of Wilson's and Dobbs's essays. (Make sure that your instructor approves the question you have selected.) Then, through Internet or library research, find at least two sources, one on each side of the issue. Make marginal and textual notes on your copies of these articles. Then summarize them in your journal.

Suggestions for Sustained Writing

1. Like Barry Glazer, many of us have strong opinions about the right of privacy. Perhaps you discussed some of your own in your journal after reading "The Right to Be Let Alone."

    Write an essay arguing that some government regulations interfere unnecessarily with the way we live. Use examples of federal, state, or local laws you think limit our freedom. If you interpret the word *government* broadly, you can even focus on rules enforced by your college, your family, or another group to which you belong.

One way to introduce this essay is to show readers that you are reasonable. Begin by admitting that some rules are necessary and should be fully enforced. For example, voice your support for tough laws against child abuse, rape, and drunk driving. At the end of your introduction, however, state your thesis forcefully: explain that some rules enforced by the government, by your family, or by another group are inappropriate and should be abolished. Then, like Glazer, develop your essay with examples from your experiences or from those of people you know or have read about.

Read your first draft carefully, adding details as you go along to make your opinions clear and convincing. Then, edit your work thoroughly.

2. Read "The Right to Be Let Alone" again. Then, write an essay in which you play Glazer's opponent. Argue that, although some government regulations are inappropriate, the ones he criticizes should be strictly enforced.

One way to organize your paper is to defend the regulations Glazer attacks in the same order he presented them. As such, you might outline the body of your essay like this:

Terminally ill patients should not have the right to commit suicide.

Police have the right to stop and question motorists at random.

Pets should be licensed.

Strict building codes are necessary.

Colleges should enforce academic requirements.

Develop each of these points in concrete and convincing detail using any of the methods mentioned earlier in this chapter. After completing several drafts, write a conclusion that restates your thesis or that uses one of the methods for closing explained in Chapter 4. As always, be sure your final draft is organized and edited well.

3. If you responded to either of the Suggestions for Journal Entries after O'Rourke's "A Cool and Logical Analysis of the Bicycle Menace," use these notes as the basis for an essay in which you present reasons to adopt or to reject a particular activity. If you responded to the first journal suggestion, you have probably gathered information that will help you write a humorous essay. If you responded to the second journal prompt, you will most likely write a serious argument.

In either case, state a thesis clearly and defend that thesis by explaining numerous reasons for it. In fact, you might want to develop your essay by including what Toulmin calls "substantive warrants," as well as "authoritative warrants," if appropriate. If you include "authoritative warrants"— researched information and ideas—make sure to cite your sources. (The Appendix to this textbook explains how to do so using Modern Language

Association style.) When it comes time to edit and proofread your paper, make sure to double check quotations and correct any mistakes with in-text citations or with the items in your list of sources.

4. Reread the notes that you made in response to the first two Suggestions for Journal Entries after Nat Hentoff's "Free Speech on Campus." Turn these notes into a full-length essay in which you argue one of the following:

> Some circumstances allow for limiting free speech.
>
> Free speech should be limited under no circumstances.

If this assignment doesn't interest you, write an essay based on the notes you made in response to Suggestion 3 after Hentoff's essay.

Whichever option you choose, be as complete and convincing as you can by gathering sufficient information to support your proposition. You might want to gather additional details, ideas, and opinions by brainstorming with fellow students or interviewing professors who can offer expert testimony. Also, try looking for more information on the Internet. If possible, use direct quotations.

Whether you organize your essay primarily around deduction or induction, check to be sure that you have not committed any of the logical fallacies discussed in the introduction to Section Five. You can do this when you revise your first draft. Also, make sure that your thesis is clearly stated and that your paper is well organized and easy to follow. As with other papers, edit and proofread carefully. Grammar, mechanical, spelling, and other such errors weaken an argument's effectiveness and lose your reader's trust.

5. Read the notes you made in response to the second of the Suggestions for Journal Entries after the essays by Callaghan and Barlow. (If you have not responded; do so now.)

Add to your notes, and write a preliminary thesis statement for an essay that would argue for a particular change in public education. Make sure you limit yourself to a specific question. For example, don't argue that all students should learn more about the fine arts. Instead, argue that a year of art appreciation and a year of music appreciation be required of all high school graduates.

As you draft your paper, make sure to anticipate and address opposing arguments. You can do this by exposing those arguments as unsupported, illogical, or untrue; or you can admit that they have value while arguing that yours make even better sense. If you wish, use your introduction to accomplish this. Then, devote the body of your paper to supporting your own point of view.

Revise your paper several times, adding information as needed, and make sure your opinion is clear, logical, and well supported. Conclude your work on this project with meticulous editing and proofreading.

6. If you responded to the first of the journal suggestions that followed the essays by Wilson and Dobbs (under "Exporting Democracy: Opposing Views"), use what you have put into your journal as a starting point for a research paper that argues for a particular strategy to fight terrorism.

If you responded to the second journal suggestion after these essays, you have already researched materials on both sides of a particular question—either one mentioned in Suggestions for Journal Entries (item 2) or one of your own choosing. Continue your research until you feel comfortable writing a thesis that expresses your own opinion on this question. Then, write a research paper that defends this opinion. As you draft your paper, make sure to anticipate and address opposing arguments. (You probably found at least one argument opposing yours when you researched this question for your journal.)

Whichever assignment you choose, make sure to document your research. Use the Modern Language Association style sheet in the Appendix to this book, or check with your instructor as to the format he or she wishes you to follow.

Writing to Learn: A Group Activity

Should institutions of higher learning regulate speech? If so, to what extent should they regulate it? What kinds of speech should be prohibited, if any, and for what reasons? And who should do the regulating? As a group, review and critique at least two college or university speech policies. (Note: a *critique* is not necessarily a criticism of a document; it is an evaluation.) Begin by finding and photocopying your own school's speech code if it has one. If it doesn't, find the policies of two other schools that are similar to yours or that are located in your county or state. You can do this by searching for these institutions' websites on the Internet. Make copies of both policies for everyone.

THE FIRST MEETING

Distribute copies of the policies. Read and discuss them as a group. Most speech policies are not long, so you might be able to do this during your meeting. Then, come to a consensus about the contents of each policy, item by item or point by point. Does the group agree or disagree with each of the points? (If you can't reach a consensus, rely on a majority vote.) Then, decide if you agree or disagree with the overall philosophy and purpose of the documents under discussion.

RESEARCH

Ask each group member to search the Internet and/or the library's periodical indexes for articles (online or on paper) that discuss free speech on college campuses. One source you might find effective is the American Civil Liberties Union's website (http://www.aclu.org). Take notes on and bring copies of informative articles to the next meeting.

THE SECOND MEETING

Invite each group member to share his or her research by distributing copies of the materials found and by summarizing important points and ideas orally. After discussing these points and reading from relevant portions of useful articles, start discussing the speech policies you began to consider at your last meeting. Have your views on these policies changed in light of the research?

Whatever your answer, use both the group's reactions to the policies and the insights gained through research to list major points you might develop in a critique of the policies. Ask one student to write a draft of an essay that critiques the first policy and another to write a draft of an essay that critiques the second. Remind them to:

• Address the points the group has agreed to develop.

• Make frequent reference to their primary sources (the policies themselves).

• Include information and insights gathered through research.

Finally, ask them to bring photocopies of the completed drafts to the next meeting, enough for each group member.

THE THIRD MEETING

Distribute copies of the drafts. Then, revise the critiques by adding or deleting information, clarifying ideas, and making the structure of the essays easier to follow. When you are finished, assign a third student to combine all of this into a single essay and to write an appropriate introduction and conclusion. Also, ask this person to write a thesis statement that expresses the group's opinion of the speech codes or of speech codes in general. As before, remind the writer to photocopy this draft.

THE FOURTH MEETING

Distribute copies of the draft mentioned above and, together, revise it for logic, clarity, and development. Next, edit it for grammar, sentence structure, punctuation, and other language considerations. After the group has agreed to all changes, assign a fourth student to type, proofread, and photocopy a final draft. Submit the original to the instructor and distribute copies to the group members. (You might even want to send a copy to the editor of your college paper for publication.)

CHAPTER 14

Persuasion

As you learned in the introduction to Section Six, effective persuasion always begins with a solid argument based on evidence that is presented logically. However, persuasion goes beyond pure argument. Writers engage in persuasion not only to prove a point but also to convince readers to adopt their point of view and to act on it.

So, if you want to convince readers that your stand on a controversial issue has merit or that a conclusion you have drawn about a complex issue is correct, a strong argument is probably enough. If you need to change people's attitudes or urge them to action, on the other hand, logic and evidence might not be enough to get the job done. You will need to be persuasive. Thus, while remaining clear-headed and fair, you might also want to appeal to the reader's values, pride, emotions, and even self-interest. Before doing so, you will have to consider the attitudes and opinions of your audience.

Appealing to the Reader's Values and Pride

Let's say your college is having a problem with litter, which makes the campus unsightly and even causes minor sanitation problems. As a member of the Student Senate, you are asked to write an open letter to the student body. Your letter will appear on the front page of the college newspaper accompanied by pictures of a parking lot where people have emptied ashtrays or left empty bottles, of a lunchroom table covered with trash, and of classrooms in which papers, used pens, a stray sneaker, and other refuse have been left behind.

Your job is to persuade students to clean up after themselves and to stop trashing the campus. You begin by explaining that common courtesy and concerns over health and sanitation demand that people deposit their garbage properly. The campus is a public place, you argue, and as such it demands that those who use it respect it and keep it clean for others. You also explain that keeping the grounds clean is easy if only everyone participates.

After reading your letter, you decide that your opinions are reasonable and fair. No one would disagree with them. In fact, your letter might be the very model of an effective written argument. However, you realize that it will not convince people to act on your recommendations—it simply does not go far enough.

The next step is to appeal to your readers' values and pride. You start by addressing their sense of fellowship, their pride in being members of an academic community. Remind them that they are college students, not adolescents who need to be taught table manners. You can also appeal to their self-image by explaining that the way students behave reflects their respect—or lack of respect—for the college, for professors, for classmates, and for themselves.

Appealing to the Reader's Emotions

If you are dealing with an especially hard-to-convince group, ask them to put themselves into the shoes of other students, of faculty, and of visitors—not to mention the janitorial staff—who enter the cafeteria to find tables and floors covered with soiled plates and napkins, half-eaten sandwiches, and dirty coffee cups. Express your disgust over the cigarette butts, empty bottles, and paper bags dumped in the parking lots. Complain about yogurt containers, aluminum cans, and other debris left in student lounges. In the process, use colorful images, concrete nouns, and strong verbs, adjectives, and adverbs to get your point across and shake up your audience. Use figures of speech: ask your readers not to turn the place into an academic "pigsty"; or compare the cafeteria at day's end to a "small village that has been looted and trashed by invading barbarians." You will see several excellent examples of speech that appeals to the emotions in Wilfred Owen's "Dulce et Decorum Est," a poem that appears in this introduction.

Appealing to the Reader's Self-Interest

Often this is the only way to move an especially obstinate audience. Try arguing that the dirtier the campus, the more unpleasant it is to be there, and remind your fellow students of the amount of time each of them spends on campus. You might even suggest that it is easier to study and to learn in a clean, attractive setting than in a dump! More important, explain that a dirty campus must be cleaned up and that this increases the cost of janitorial services. Of course, higher operating costs translate into higher tuition levels, so students might have to work longer hours to pay for college, or their parents might have to sacrifice a bit more to send them there.

Anticipating and Addressing Opposing Opinions

You learned in Chapter 13 that anticipating and responding to an opposing argument is important to making your point. Doing this is even more important when engaging in persuasive writing. When you argue, you need show only that, while other opinions have merit, your case is the strongest. When it comes to persuasion, on the other hand, you are asking readers to make a choice and to act on that choice. If they have any doubt that your opinion stands out as the strongest and wisest, they will not follow your lead, and they may, in fact, decide to do nothing. As you read the selections that follow, try to find places where writers address and respond to opposing arguments. More important, make use of this practice whenever you write to persuade.

Establishing Your Authority

Again, you read in Chapter 13 that, when writing argument papers, it is important to gain the confidence of your readers by convincing them you know what you are talking about. This is even more important when writing persuasively. If readers are going to follow your lead and act as you suggest, they will have to trust in your knowledge. As with all writing, the best way to show you are knowledgeable is to use concrete facts—hard evidence—to support your opinions. In addition, however, you might want to explain the source of your knowledge of a particular topic or problem. In "Education Is the Priority," student Nicholle Palmieri persuades her readers that working too many hours can often interfere with one's studies. She establishes her authority by explaining that, while working in the dean's office, she encountered too many students who had failed to make academics their priority and, as a result, were about to flunk out!

Using Conciliation—The Rogerian Approach

As you learned earlier, it is always appropriate to anticipate opposing arguments and to recognize their validity when possible. Sometimes, however, you will have to go even further. In some cases, you will be writing or speaking to an audience whose positions on a particular issue are so solidified that nothing you say will change minds. Think about writing to or addressing an audience whose views on subjects such as abortion, gun control, the 9/11 attacks, the Iraq War, or homosexuality are diametrically opposed to yours. In such cases, an approach developed by psychologist Carl Rogers might be helpful. Rogers believed that before people who hold entrenched positions can begin to discuss issues productively, some conciliation must be made. His method involves the following:

Establish Common Ground   You will first need to prove to your audience not simply that that you understand and appreciate their position but that you accept it as viable. One way to do this is to establish common ground by identifying points on which you can agree. For example, say you were to write a letter to your college newspaper arguing for the creation of a foreign-language graduation requirement for students in all majors. It's a good bet that most of your readers oppose adding new graduation requirements. So, you might first explain that:

- Like your readers, you are enrolled in a curriculum already packed with requirements and that adding more requirements will make it even more demanding.
- Adding requirements might prevent both you and your readers from taking a few electives particularly relevant to your individual career plans.

- Adding requirements might delay graduation and add tuition costs for you and your readers.
- Taking a foreign language will yield no immediately measurable benefit for either you or them.

You can then start to present arguments in favor of requiring foreign languages by explaining the importance of learning about other cultures, the emergence of a global economy, the advantages of using a foreign language when traveling, and the need to communicate with people of other cultures both in English and in their languages in order to promote international understanding.

Use Non-threatening Language   It's one thing to tell an audience of gun-control opponents that their right to own guns is the thing that is causing so much crime. It's another to explain that limiting the right to own guns will decrease violent crime and make their lives safer. The first statement is negative, the second far more positive. The same is true of this pair:

Threatening:	If we do not improve homeland security and impose stricter security regulations at airports, in bus and train terminals, and in public buildings, the events of 9/11 will be repeated.
Non-threatening:	Strengthening homeland security and instituting careful screening procedures at airports, in bus and train terminals, and in public buildings will make the country safer.

Express Opposing Views Accurately and Fairly   Let's say that you are opposed to the enactment of an on-campus speech policy that the college administration is introducing in order to enforce professional decorum in academic discussions, to protect the institution from the legal repercussions of slanderous and libelous statements made by employees or students, and to make the library a quieter place to study. You could certainly argue that any speech policy, albeit benign in purpose and design, would limit the students' Constitutional right to free speech. However, it would probably be unfair and inaccurate to characterize this policy as an attempt to limit student participation in class, to prevent people from speaking out against college policies and regulations, or to treat the students as if they were high school adolescents.

Visualizing Strategies for Persuasion

The following antiwar poem was written by Wilfred Owen (1893–1918), a British soldier who witnessed the horror of trench warfare in World War 1. The title is Latin for "It is sweet and fitting." The last lines, taken from the Latin poet Horace, translate to "It is sweet and fitting to die for one's country."

Dulce et Decorum Est — *Uses an ironic title.*

Bent double, like old beggars under sacks,

Knock-kneed, coughing like hags, we cursed through sludge,

Till on the haunting flares we turned our backs

And towards our distant rest began to trudge.

Opens with a startling image; uses figures of speech.

Men marched asleep. Many had lost their boots

But limped on, blood-shod [shoed in blood]. All went lame; all blind;

Drunk with fatigue; deaf even to the hoots

Of tired, outstripped Five-Nines that dropped behind.

Includes vivid verbs and adjectives.

Gas! Gas! Quick, boys!—An ecstasy of fumbling,

Fitting the clumsy helmets just in time;

Startles readers with the soldiers' cries.

Narrates action vividly.

But someone still was yelling out and stumbling,

And flound'ring like a man in fire or lime.

Dim, through the misty panes and thick green light,

As under a green sea, I saw him drowning.

Creates an extended metaphor to describe the horror of a gas attack.

In all my dreams, before my helpless sight,

He plunges at me, guttering, choking, drowning.

Uses adjectives to evoke an emotional response.

Addresses readers directly to get them to change their minds.

If in some smothering dreams you too could pace

Behind the wagon that we flung him in,

And watch the white eyes writhing in his face,

His hanging face, like a devil's sick of sin;

If you could hear, at every jolt, the blood

Come gargling from the froth-corrupted lungs

Obscene as cancer, bitter as the cud

Of vile, incurable sores on innocent tongues,—

My friend, you would not tell with such high zest

To children ardent [eager] for some desperate glory,

The old Lie: Dulce et decorum est

Pro patria mori.

Continues direct address; persuades readers to stop glorifying war.

Obviously, this is a message to stir our passions. Startling words, images, and figures of speech appeal to the emotions and create in us the sense of the horror that Owen experienced. The poem's central idea is, of course, that war is *not* sweet and fitting and that we must stop lying about it to children. In the last stanza (verse paragraph), the poet addresses his readers directly. He does this first in order to make his argument strike home more directly, to make it more compelling. He appeals to the readers' self-interest; after all they too might be asked to send their sons to war. He also does this so as to answer an opposing argument offered by people who have not seen war close up. We lie to children—"ardent for some desperate glory"—when we romanticize war. In no way is it sweet and fitting to die for one's country, and the poet demands that we stop telling them it is.

Considering Visuals That Persuade

Commercial advertisements and editorial cartoons often combine words and pictures that persuade. Consider the following examples. As you do, identify the intended audiences and determine which tools ordinarily found in written persuasion each item uses. Then, write a paragraph or two that responds to the exercise prompt following each visual.

1. SOME PRESENTATIONS YOU DON'T WANT MESSED WITH

This advertisement for Adobe Acrobat 5.0 pictures Moses holding three tablets with fifteen commandments. It appeals to the readers' need for electronic document security and maintenance.

 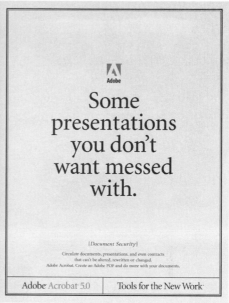

©2002 Adobe Systems, Inc., Courtesy of Goodby, Silverstein & Partners.

Exercise: Make sure you know the Biblical story of Moses. You can find it in the Bible, in an encyclopedia, or on the Internet (a helpful site is http://www. newadvent.org/cathen/10596a.htm). Write a paragraph or two that identifies the message the ad conveys, and explain how Moses' holding three tablets helps the manufacturers of Adobe Acrobat 5.0 make their point.

2. HELP EDITORIAL CARTOON

This cartoon, originally appearing in the *Chicago Tribune,* was reprinted in the July 29, 2002 issue of *National Review,* a magazine whose editorial policy is politically conservative. It addresses a lawsuit to prohibit the reciting of the Pledge of Allegiance in public schools. The suit was brought by people who believe that the presence of the word "God" in the pledge violates the First Amendment to the Constitution: "Congress shall make no law respecting an establishment of religion." It also references a Supreme Court decision that, several years ago, struck down a state law prohibiting the burning of the American flag.

Exercise: Write a paragraph that explains the sources of this cartoon's appeal to readers. How would you describe those readers? How does the cartoon appeal to their pride, emotions, and values?

HELP!!!!

Dick Locher, *The Chicago Tribune,* 2002. Reprinted with permission from Tribune Media Services.

3. PREVENT CHILD ABUSE AMERICA PUBLIC SERVICE ANNOUNCEMENT (PRINT AD)

This advertisement dramatizes the horrors and pain of child abuse. At the same time, it urges the reader to take specific action to help prevent the abuse of children, including finding out more about this problem.

Exercise: Analyze this ad. Discuss the images created by the reference to macaroni and cheese. What images are suggested by the stove top? Why are the words "sorry for what he did" so much larger than those in the rest of the sentence? How would you characterize the advice offered under the picture? Is it effective? Why or why not?

©Reprinted courtesy of Prevent Child Abuse America, the Advertising Council and Lowe.

4. WHICH ONE REALLY NEEDS A HEART?

A Steve Benson creation, this cartoon, published on February 25, 2003, addresses a controversy over an illegal alien's receiving an organ transplant at the expense of US taxpayers.

Steve Benson reprinted by permission of United Feature Cyndicate, Inc.

Exercise: Analyze the two characters in this cartoon. What kinds of emotions do these two portraits tap in you?

5. WE ALWAYS WANTED TO HAVE A NEIGHBOR JUST LIKE YOU

This Randy Bish cartoon honors Fred Rogers, the host of *Mr. Rogers' Neighborhood,* a children's television program. It shows that editorial comment need not be negative, sarcastic, or caustic.

Exercise: Write a paragraph explaining what Bish is advocating? How does he get his point across? What can you tell about Fred Rogers and about *Mr. Rogers' Neighborhood* from this cartoon?

We always wanted to have a neighbor just like you

FRED ROGERS 1928-2003

Randy Bish reprinted by permission of United Feature Syndicate, Inc.

Revising Persuasion Papers

Revising any kind of paper takes hard work, but persuasion papers often ask the reader to accomplish tasks or goals or to change deeply held views, so it is important that they be as clear, logical, well supported, and strong as possible. Student Nicholle Palmieri rewrote "Education Is the Priority," which appears in this chapter, to make it the kind of paper she thought would get her fellow students to decrease the emphasis they placed on work in favor of their real goal— to get a college education.

Palmieri—Early Draft

Education Is the <u>First</u> Priority ⎤ *Redundant.*

About a year ago, I quit my full-time job to

return to college. Despite all of the

Wordy. ⎡ obstacles <u>that stood</u> in my way, I was lucky

enough to find <u>a job in the office of Dean</u> ⎤ *More*

<u>Russell</u>. I say "lucky" for many reasons. ⎦ *information needed.*

The dean and her administrative assistant,

Karen Gormish, are two of the <u>nicest people</u> *Cliché.*
<u>on the face of the earth</u>, not to mention the

fact that I don't have to worry about my job

interfering with my studies. I am able to

fit my work hours around my class schedule,

and I still manage to get in enough hours to

sufficiently cover my bills.

Vague. Working there, though, <u>has been quite a</u>
<u>learning experience</u>. Almost every day, at

least one student comes into the <u>office</u>, *Language seems flat, unappealing.*
<u>their eyes scared, pleading</u> to be taken off *Wrong pronoun*
academic probation. I am often the first *agreement.*

Wordy. person that greets them and, therefore, <u>I</u>
<u>have the privilege of seeing their appeals</u>
<u>firsthand</u>. Most of these students have

failed to make their educations their <u>top</u> *Redundant.*

priority, and they are paying for it dearly,

and there is one claim that almost all have

in commo<u>n their</u> hours at work have taken *Fused sentence.*

precious time away from their college

studies. Mind you, most of these kids (I

Develop the notion of their being "kids"? say "kids" because that is what the majority
of them are) are living at home and taking
about 15 credits per semester. Most of them

occupy menial positions at fast-food

Use language that appeals to emotions. restaurants or retail stores. They take
orders from <u>tough supervisors and work long</u>
<u>hours</u> toward their future in hopes of

Add details about their situations? Appeal to the emotions?

someday having a real job. From what I understand, most of these students work such hours under threat by their managers of being fired if they refuse.

I find fault with this whole scenario.

Smooth out syntax.

Fifty years ago, it was <u>unheard of that</u>

<u>full-time college students should even work</u>

<u>two hours a week let alone</u> forty, and that

was for a good reason.

Support this with research?

Palmieri—Final Draft

Education is the Priority   *Removes redundancy.*

About a year ago, I quit my full-time job to

Eliminates wordiness.

return to college. <u>Despite all of the</u>

<u>obstacles in my way,</u> I was lucky enough to

find a job as a work-study assistant in the

office of Dean Bernadette Russell. I say

"lucky" for many reasons. The Dean and her

Adds information about her job.

administrative assistant, Karen Gormish, are

supportive of students and are willing to

accommodate their needs. Because of their

Replaces cliché with fresher language.

support and flexibility, I don't have to

worry about my job interfering with my

studies. I am able to fit my work hours

around my class schedule—<u>not the other way</u>

<u>around</u>—and still manage to work enough hours

Adds emphasis.

to pay my bills.

Uses language that is more evocative.

Adds important information.

Eliminates wordiness.

Uses language that is clearer, more specific.

Removes redundancy.

Inserts colon to correct fused sentence.

Defines notion of "kids" by contrasting them to "seasoned adults."

Working in the Dean's office has taught me a great deal about college students and their priorities. Almost every day, at least one of them comes into the office, eyes fraught with desperation. They plead to be taken off academic probation, restriction, or suspension. Some beg to have their dismissals lifted and to be allowed to re-enroll.

I am often the first person who greets them and, therefore, I see their appeals first. Most of these students have failed to make education their priority, and they are paying for it dearly. In fact, there is one claim that almost all have in common: their hours at work have taken precious time away from their college studies. Mind you, most of these kids (I say "kids" because that is what the majority of them are) are living at home and taking about 15 credits per semester. It is not as if they are seasoned adults who have worked at full-time jobs for fifteen years, have learned to manage their time, and are able to squeeze in a course or two in the evenings and weekends. On the contrary, most of them work at menial positions in fast-food restaurants or retail stores. They take orders from <u>demanding,</u> <u>unreasonable</u> supervisors, and they work <u>asinine,</u> <u>exhausting</u> hours that no human being should have to work—certainly not someone who is attending college classes full-time and <u>devoting hours of endless study</u> toward earning an education and <u>entering a rewarding</u> <u>career.</u> From what I understand, most of these students work such hours under threat of being fired by their managers if they refuse.

Adds words and information that appeal to emotions.

Smooths out syntax.

I find the whole scenario appalling. Fifty years ago, it was unheard of that full-time college students should even work two hours a week, let alone forty, and that was for a good reason. According to the website of the Division of Student Affairs at Virginia Polytechnic Institute and State University, being a successful college student requires "about two hours of preparation for each hour in the classroom. This means that [a student carrying fifteen credits] has at least a forty-five hour work week, and is consequently involved in a full-time occupation"(1). At Newbury College, incoming freshmen are advised to attend classes regularly ("This is a

Finds supportive information through research.

Adds direct quotations from

must!"), seek help at the Academic Resources
Center, visit their professors regularly
during office hours, enroll in "the Academic
Enrichment Program," and join a student
study group (1). These activities take
time—the bulk of your time—but in order to
be successful in college you must commit to
them. That also means that you will have
little time for work outside your studies.
For a full-time student, most college
counselors recommend no more than 15 hours
of work per week. Consider this: If you
fail to nurture your education, you will
find yourself on academic probation,
restriction, or suspension. Even worse, you
might get yourself dismissed, a blow from
which it is hard to recover even if you
manage to transfer to another college.

*authorities
on
succeeding
in college.*

Practicing Strategies for Persuasion

Reread Wilfred Owen's poem, "Dulce et Decorum Est," on pages 565–566. Pay
close attention to the language Owen uses to stir our emotions and appeal to
our self-interest. Now use vivid, moving language in a *persuasive* paragraph or
two responding to each of the following:

1. Describe the effects of cigarette smoking to persuade someone to kick the
    habit.

    _____

    _____

    _____

    _____

2. Explain the dangers of drinking and driving to a group of teenagers so as to get them to choose a designated driver whenever they attend parties where alcohol is served.

_____

_____

_____

_____

3. Discuss the serious, even dangerous effects of promiscuous and/or unprotected sex to a group of 18-year-old males. Your ultimate purpose is to persuade them to abstain from sex until marriage.

_____

_____

_____

_____

4. Explain the effects of a high-fat diet and a lack of physical exercise to convince a friend to change his or her lifestyle.

_____

_____

_____

_____

5. Allow readers to visualize the long-term consequences of marrying a particular person, entering a particular career, or making another important life decision. You can either defend or attack this decision.

_____

_____

_____

_____

Review your responses to the five items above. Then, in each case, write a paragraph that addresses an appropriate opposing argument.

In addition to the selections that follow, you can find another piece of persuasive writing in the Appendix at the end of this textbook. This persuasive essay is entitled "Victims of Violent Crime: Equal Treatment under the Law." Written by student Angela Brandli, "Victims of Violent Crime" was first drafted as a letter to legislative leaders in New Jersey. It was so persuasive that Brandli was asked to draft a version of a bill to increase compensation for crime victims in that state. The bill was passed by the state legislature and signed by Governor Christine Todd Whitman in 1999, and it has come to be known as the "Brandli Bill."

In the last few pages, you have read a lot about how to write persuasively. As with all kinds of writing, the most important ingredient in persuasion is your knowledge of the subject. Think of yourself as a lawyer. To argue a case or defend a client effectively, you will need to know the evidence well. Otherwise, you will have a hard time convincing judge or jury. Wise readers approach new opinions cautiously. Some will be open to persuasion. Others may even be eager to accept your point of view. But all will expect you to present evidence logically, clearly, and convincingly before they make your opinions their own.

Education Is the Priority

Nicholle Palmieri

Nicholle Palmieri wrote this essay as a letter to the editor of her college newspaper. As a work-study assistant in the office of the Dean of Liberal Arts, Palmieri came into contact with many full-time students who were doing poorly in their studies because they had not made education a priority. The vast majority of these had underestimated the amount of time a successful college career demands, and they were spending too many hours at their jobs. Some of them even held full-time jobs while attending college full-time.

Much of what Palmieri discusses here was inspired by her own experiences. As a junior in high school, she held a job as a sales clerk at a store in a large shopping mall. When she told her boss that she could not work overtime because she had to study for an exam the next day, he threatened to fire her. But this student knew her priorities, and she quit before he could do so. Palmieri graduated from Douglass College with a major in English. She is now pursuing a career in publishing.

Preparing to Read

1. Palmieri's title is, essentially, her thesis. As you learned above, she wrote this selection as a letter to her college newspaper. What does this tell you about her purpose and her audience?

2. The biographical note on this student author reveals something about her personality. What might that be? How will this character trait be reflected in the selection that follows?

3. Palmieri appeals to the reader's emotions, values, and self-interest. Underline places where she does this as you read her essay.

4. The author uses the terms academic "probation," "restriction," and "suspension" to designate the statuses of students whose grades need immediate improvement. "Dismissal" occurs when a student's grades are so low that he or she is asked to leave the college.

Vocabulary

accommodate (verb)	Meet or serve.
appalling (adjective)	Shocking.
asinine (adjective)	Foolish, idiotic.
fraught with (adjective)	Accompanied by, filled with.
menial (adjective)	Low level.
nurture (verb)	Care for, provide for, nourish.

priority (noun)	Item of greatest importance.
scenario (noun)	Situation.
seasoned (adjective)	Experienced.
serf (noun)	Slave, someone bound to the land or to a master.

Education Is the Priority

Nicholle Palmieri

ABOUT A YEAR ago, I quit my full-time job to return to college. Despite all of   1
the obstacles in my way, I was lucky enough to find a job as a work-study
assistant in the office of Dr. Bernadette Russell, Dean of Liberal Arts at my college. I say "lucky" for many reasons. The Dean and her administrative assistant,
Karen Gormish, are supportive of students and are willing to accommodate
their needs. Because of their support and flexibility, I don't have to worry about
my job interfering with my studies. I am able to fit my work hours around my
class schedule—not the other way around—and still manage to work enough
hours to pay my bills.

Working in the Dean's office has taught me a great deal about college stu-   2
dents and their priorities. Almost every day, at least one of them comes into the
office, eyes fraught with desperation. They plead to be taken off academic probation, restriction, or suspension. Some beg to have their dismissals lifted and
to be allowed to re-enroll.

I am often the first person who greets them and, therefore, I see their ap-   3
peals first. Most of these students have failed to make education their priority,
and they are paying for it dearly. In fact, there is one claim that almost all have
in common: their hours at work have taken precious time away from their college studies. Mind you, most of these kids (I say "kids" because that is what the
majority of them are) are living at home and taking about 15 credits per semester. It is not as if they are seasoned adults who have worked at full-time jobs
for fifteen years, have learned to manage their time, and are able to squeeze in
a course or two in the evenings and weekends. On the contrary, most of them
work at menial positions in fast-food restaurants or retail stores. They take orders from demanding, unreasonable supervisors, and they work asinine, exhausting hours that no human being should have to work—certainly not
someone who is attending college classes full-time and devoting hours of endless study toward earning an education and entering a rewarding career. From
what I understand, most of these students work such hours under threat of being fired by their managers if they refuse.

I find the whole scenario appalling. Fifty years ago, it was unheard of that   4
full-time college students should even work two hours a week, let alone forty,

and that was for a good reason. According to the website of the Division of Student Affairs at Virginia Polytechnic Institute and State University, being a successful college student requires "about two hours of preparation for each hour in the classroom. This means that [a student carrying fifteen credits] has at least a forty-five hour work week, and is consequently involved in a full-time occupation"(1). At Newbury College, incoming freshmen are advised to attend classes regularly ("This is a must!"), seek help at the Academic Resources Center, visit their professors regularly during office hours, enroll in "the Academic Enrichment Program," and join a student study group (1). These activities take time—the bulk of your time—but in order to be successful in college you must commit to them. That also means that you will have little time for work outside your studies. For a full-time student, most college counselors recommend no more than 15 hours of work per week. Consider this: If you fail to nurture your education, you will find yourself on academic probation, restriction, or suspension. Even worse, you might get yourself dismissed, a blow from which it is hard to recover even if you manage to transfer to another college.

Why would anyone want to do that to herself for the sake of some no-   5
brainer, dead-end job that pays $5.05 per hour? I understand that many students need money because they have bills to pay, not the least of which might be tuition. However, there comes a point when enough is enough. I too have bills to pay, and I manage to pay them by working 15 hours a week or less. I could not possibly devote sufficient time to my studies if I worked a minute more, and my supervisor understands this. Managers who don't understand this aren't worth working for, and they would do students in their employ a favor by firing them.

No words can overemphasize the importance of education. Without one,   6
the "kids" I mentioned earlier might be condemned to work as under-paid, under-appreciated, under-respected cashiers and stock clerks for the rest of their lives. It is time college students put their educations first and told their supervisors at McDonald's or Burger King to find another serf if they don't like it. This is a free country. There is nothing—least of all a dead-end job or a cranky fast-food manager—that can deprive you of your right to a quality education and to a successful future.

Works Cited

Division of Student Affairs Home Page. Division of Student Affairs, Virginia
     Polytechnic Institute and State University. 4 Mar. 2000
     <http://www.ucc.vt.edu/stdysk/htimesch.html>.

How to Be a More Active Learner at Newbury College. Newbury College.
     4 Mar. 2000 <http://www.newbury.edu/support/active.htm>.

Read More on the Web

SUNY Brockport site on working while in college: http://www.brockport.
edu/career01/upromise.htm

University of Michigan college survival tips: http://www.flint.umich.edu/
departments/advising/SurvTips.htm

Wisconsin Student Public Interest Research Group report on working
while in college: http://www.wispirg.org/student/wicampus.
asp?id2=6478

Questions for Discussion

1. What is Palmieri's thesis? Where does she state it most clearly?
2. Does this selection illustrate the uses of deduction, which you learned
   about in Chapter 13? Explain Palmieri's thinking by creating a
   syllogism in your own words: start with a general statement, apply a
   specific case to that statement, and then draw a conclusion.
3. Where in this essay does the author rely on induction, which you
   also learned about in Chapter 13?
4. Where does the author appeal to her audience's values? To their self-
   interest?
5. What use does she make of testimony of experts on her subject? Why
   did she choose these sources to quote directly? Why not include
   direct quotations from students "fraught with desperation," whom
   she met in the dean's office?
6. Palmieri chooses her persuasive vocabulary well. Identify and analyze
   a paragraph or two in which her language appeals to our emotions.
7. Does the author anticipate and answer opposing arguments? Where?
8. Why does Palmieri tell us so much about herself in this essay,
   especially in her introduction?

Thinking Critically

1. Reread "Study Calculus" by William J. Bennett in Chapter 2 and
   "Burger Queen" by Erin Sharp in Chapter 3. How might each of them
   react to Palmieri's essay?
2. Palmieri criticizes employers who do not accommodate students who
   work for them. How might an employer respond to her comments?

Suggestions for Journal Entries

1. Think about the opposing argument Palmieri addressed in paragraph 5. Can you make a case for this argument? Are there other reasons for working more than 15 hours per week while carrying a full academic load? Brainstorm with two or three classmates to gather relevant information you might use later on to write a rebuttal to Palmieri's essay.

2. Think about an issue that is crucial to student success in college and that you might write about in a letter to the editor of your student newspaper. Palmieri's essay focuses on making education, not work, the priority. Yours might discuss study habits, time management, stress management, participation in community service projects, the dangers of alcohol or drug abuse among students, or any other issue you believe is important to your fellow students. If you need inspiration picking a topic, visit either of the two Internet sites Palmieri mentions in her works-cited list, or go to the websites of other colleges and universities.

I Have a Dream

Dr. Martin Luther King, Jr.

After graduating from Morehouse College at nineteen, Martin Luther King, Jr. (1929–1968), entered the seminary and later became a minister in Atlanta's Ebenezer Baptist Church, where his father was pastor. In 1957, he founded the Southern Christian Leadership Conference, a civil-rights organization. Influenced by the philosophy of human-rights activist and pacifist Mahatma Gandhi, King led several important demonstrations against racial segregation in the South and in the North. Among the most famous was the march in Birmingham, Alabama, in 1963, for which King was arrested. It was during this imprisonment that he wrote "Letter from Birmingham Jail," a landmark in the literature of American human rights. In that same year, King made a stirring speech during the great March on Washington. Delivered before 200,000 people assembled at the Lincoln Memorial, the text of this speech has come to be known as "I Have a Dream." King won several awards for his work in support of human rights, including the Nobel Prize for Peace in 1964. On April 4, 1968, Dr. King was assassinated while he spoke with other civil-rights leaders on a motel balcony in Memphis, Tennessee.

Preparing to Read

1. King refers to the Declaration of Independence and the U.S. Constitution as a "promissory note to which every American was to fall heir." If you haven't done so already, read these documents. You can find them in any college or public library or on the Internet.

2. Look up Martin Luther King, Jr., and/or the American Civil Rights Movement in a library reference book or on the Internet to familiarize yourself with some of the issues and events that King refers to in this speech.

3. Given the fact that King was a Christian minister, what allusions and references might he use in this speech to support his advocacy of civil rights and to move his audience?

Vocabulary

defaulted (verb)	Failed to pay a debt.
devotees (noun)	Disciples, those who believe in.
hallowed (adjective)	Holy, sacred.
inextricably (adverb)	Permanently, unable to be removed.
interposition (noun)	Attempts to stop the enforcement of laws, in this case those guaranteeing civil rights.

jangling (adjective)	Clanking, clattering.
languishing (adjective)	Lying weak and ill.
manacles (noun)	Handcuffs.
militancy (noun)	Aggressiveness, willingness to do battle.
momentous (adjective)	Extremely important, weighty.
nullification (noun)	Refusal to enforce or recognize laws, in this case those guaranteeing civil rights.
redemptive (adjective)	Redeeming, saving.
unalienable (adjective)	Natural, undeniable.
withering (adjective)	Decaying, dying.

I Have a Dream

Dr. Martin Luther King, Jr.

FIVE SCORE YEARS ago, a great American, in whose symbolic shadow we stand, signed the Emancipation Proclamation. This momentous decree came as a great beacon light of hope to millions of Negro slaves who had been seared in the flames of withering injustice. It came as a joyous daybreak to end the long night of captivity. 1

But one hundred years later, we must face the tragic fact that the Negro is still not free. One hundred years later, the life of the Negro is still sadly crippled by the manacles of segregation and the chains of discrimination. One hundred years later, the Negro lives on a lonely island of poverty in the midst of a vast ocean of material prosperity. One hundred years later, the Negro is still languishing in the corners of American society and finds himself an exile in his own land. So we have come here today to dramatize an appalling condition. 2

In a sense we have come to our nation's capital to cash a check. When the architects of our republic wrote the magnificent words of the Constitution and the Declaration of Independence, they were signing a promissory note to which every American was to fall heir. This note was a promise that all men would be guaranteed the unalienable rights of life, liberty, and the pursuit of happiness. 3

It is obvious today that America has defaulted on this promissory note insofar as her citizens of color are concerned. Instead of honoring this sacred obligation, America has given the Negro people a bad check; a check which has come back marked "insufficient funds." But we refuse to believe that the bank of justice is bankrupt. We refuse to believe that there are insufficient funds in the great vaults of opportunity of this nation. So we have come to cash this check— a check that will give us upon demand the riches of freedom and the security of justice. We have also come to this hallowed spot to remind America of the fierce urgency of *now*. This is no time to engage in the luxury of cooling off or to take the tranquilizing drugs of gradualism. *Now* is the time to make real the promises of Democracy. *Now* is the time to rise from the dark and desolate valley of 4 segregation to the sunlit path of racial justice. *Now* is the time to open the doors of opportunity to all of God's children. *Now* is the time to lift our nation from the quicksands of racial injustice to the solid rock of brotherhood.

It would be fatal for the nation to overlook the urgency of the moment and   5
to underestimate the determination of the Negro. This sweltering summer of the Negro's legitimate discontent will not pass until there is an invigorating autumn of freedom and equality. Nineteen sixty-three is not an end, but a beginning. Those who hope that the Negro needed to blow off steam and will now be content will have a rude awakening if the nation returns to business as usual. There will be neither rest nor tranquility in America until the Negro is granted his citizenship rights. The whirlwinds of revolt will continue to shake the foundations of our nation until the bright day of justice emerges.

But there is something that I must say to my people who stand on the warm   6
threshold which leads into the palace of justice. In the process of gaining our rightful place we must not be guilty of wrongful deeds. Let us not seek to satisfy our thirst for freedom by drinking from the cup of bitterness and hatred. We must forever conduct our struggle on the high plane of dignity and discipline. We must not allow our creative protest to degenerate into physical violence. Again and again we must rise to the majestic heights of meeting physical force with soul force. The marvelous new militancy which has engulfed the Negro community must not lead us to a distrust of all white people, for many of our white brothers, as evidenced by their presence here today, have come to realize that their destiny is tied up with our destiny and their freedom is inextricably bound to our freedom. We cannot walk alone.

And as we walk, we must make the pledge that we shall march ahead. We   7
cannot turn back. There are those who are asking the devotees of civil rights, "When will you be satisfied?" We can never be satisfied as long as the Negro is the victim of the unspeakable horrors of police brutality. We can never be satisfied as long as our bodies, heavy with the fatigue of travel, cannot gain lodging in the motels of the highways and the hotels of the cities. We cannot be satisfied as long as the Negro's basic mobility is from a smaller ghetto to a larger one. We can never be satisfied as long as a Negro in Mississippi cannot vote and a Negro in New York believes he has nothing for which to vote. No, no, we are not satisfied, and we will not be satisfied until justice rolls down like waters and righteousness like a mighty stream.

I am not unmindful that some of you have come here out of great trials and   8
tribulations. Some of you have come fresh from narrow jail cells. Some of you have come from areas where your quest for freedom left you battered by the storms of persecution and staggered by the winds of police brutality. You have been the veterans of creative suffering. Continue to work with the faith that unearned suffering is redemptive.

Go back to Mississippi, go back to Alabama, go back to South Carolina, go   9
back to Georgia, go back to Louisiana, go back to the slums and ghettos of our

northern cities, knowing that somehow this situation can and will be changed. Let us not wallow in the valley of despair.

I say to you today, my friends, that in spite of the difficulties and frustra- 10 tions of the moment I still have a dream. It is a dream deeply rooted in the American dream.

I have a dream that one day this nation will rise up and live out the true 11 meaning of its creed: "We hold these truths to be self-evident; that all men are created equal."

I have a dream that one day on the red hills of Georgia the sons of former 12 slaves and the sons of former slaveowners will be able to sit down together at the table of brotherhood.

I have a dream that one day even the state of Mississippi, a desert state 13 sweltering with the heat of injustice and oppression, will be transformed into an oasis of freedom and justice.

I have a dream that my four little children will one day live in a nation 14 where they will not be judged by the color of their skin but by the content of their character.

I have a dream today. 15

I have a dream that one day the state of Alabama, whose governor's lips are 16 presently dripping with the words of interposition and nullification, will be transformed into a situation where little black boys and black girls will be able to join hands with little white boys and white girls and walk together as sisters and brothers.

I have a dream today. 17

I have a dream that one day every valley shall be exalted, every hill and 18 mountain shall be made low, the rough places will be made plain, and the crooked places will be made straight, and the glory of the Lord shall be revealed, and all flesh shall see it together.

This is our hope. This is the faith with which I return to the South. With 19 this faith we will be able to hew out of the mountain of despair a stone of hope. With this faith we will be able to transform the jangling discords of our nation into a beautiful symphony of brotherhood. With this faith we will be able to work together, to pray together, to struggle together, to go to jail together, to stand up for freedom together, knowing that we will be free one day.

This will be the day when all of God's children will be able to sing with new 20 meaning

My country, 'tis of thee,
Sweet land of liberty,
　Of thee I sing:
Land where my fathers died,
Land of the pilgrims' pride,
From every mountain-side
　Let freedom ring.

And if America is to be a great nation this must become true. So let free- 21
dom ring from the prodigious hilltops of New Hampshire. Let freedom ring
from the mighty mountains of New York. Let freedom ring from the heighten-
ing Alleghenies of Pennsylvania!

Let freedom ring from the snowcapped Rockies of Colorado! 22

Let freedom ring from the curvaceous peaks of California! 23

But not only that; let freedom ring from Stone Mountain of Georgia! 24

Let freedom ring from Lookout Mountain of Tennessee! 25

Let freedom ring from every hill and molehill of Mississippi. From every 26
mountainside, let freedom ring.

When we let freedom ring, when we let it ring from every village and every 27
hamlet, from every state and every city, we will be able to speed up that day
when all of God's children, black men and white men, Jews and Gentiles,
Protestants and Catholics, will be able to join hands and sing in the words of
the old Negro spiritual, "Free at last! free at last! thank God almighty, we are
free at last!"

Read More on the Web

The Martin Luther King, Jr. Papers Project at Stanford University: http://
www.stanford.edu/group/King/

National Civil Rights Museum site: http://www.mecca.org/~crights/
mlk.html

Questions for Discussion

1. King's central idea is expressed most forcefully in the sentences that
    begin "I have a dream . . ." Of these, which has the greatest effect on
    you?
2. Where in this speech does King appeal to written authority?
3. Where does he use facts to support his point of view?
4. Why does King mention so many Southern states by name?
5. In what parts of this address does the speaker appeal to his audience's
    values?
6. Where does he appeal to the self-interest of the African-Americans in
    his audience?
7. Where does he appeal to the self-interest of whites?
8. The speaker uses parallelism to evoke our emotions. Find examples
    of this rhetorical technique. If necessary, review what you learned
    about parallelism in Chapter 7.

9. Another way King rouses our emotions is by using figures of speech. Find several examples of figurative language.

10. King addresses two sets of opposing arguments in this speech. Explain how he does this.

Thinking Critically

1. Reread paragraphs 2 and 3. Explain the extended metaphors used in them.

2. Turn back to Chapter 7 in this book, and read Lincoln's Gettysburg Address. Pay particular attention to the word "hallowed," used in paragraph 2 of that document. This is the same word King uses in paragraph 4 here. What other similarities can you identify in these two addresses?

3. Who is King's audience? Is it only the 200,000 people assembled at the Lincoln Memorial?

Suggestions for Journal Entries

1. Have we made progress in guaranteeing the civil rights of minorities since Dr. King spoke these words? Make a list of the most important advances. Start by reviewing "I Have a Dream" and deciding if the wrongs mentioned there have been dealt with. You might want to do some Internet research on the history of the American Civil Rights Movement—as already suggested in Preparing to Read—to gather facts. You might also want to interview a professor of history, literature, or government at your college to find out more about this question.

2. Do you have your own dream for the world? What major problem affecting the United States or another country would you like to see solved in the next few decades? Perhaps you might address poverty, illiteracy, drug abuse, or teenage pregnancy in America, the AIDS epidemic in Africa, or famine in any of several parts of the world.

   Again you might have to do some library or Internet research or interview a professor who is knowledgeable about the issue you are addressing.

Government Reparations for Slavery: Opposing Views

"US Needs to Pay Reparations for Slavery" by David A. Love

"Reparations for Slavery?" by Thomas Sowell

David A. Love received a B.A. in East Asian Studies from Harvard College in 1989, and a J.D. from the University of Pennsylvania Law School in 2003. Prior to attending law school, Love was a producer for Pacifica Radio's "Democracy Now!" news program, a newspaper op-ed columnist for the Progressive Media Project and Knight-Ridder Tribune News Service, and a staff member with the Center for Constitutional Rights. In addition, he was a contributor to the book States of Confinement: Policing, Detention and Prisons *(Joy James ed., St. Martin's Press 2000). Love completed the Joint Programme in International Human Rights Law at New College, University of Oxford, and participated in the Amnesty International UK National Speakers Tour.*

Thomas Sowell is a senior fellow at the Hoover Institution at Stanford University and a frequent contributor to the public affairs journal the Jewish World Review. *Among his latest books are* The Quest for Cosmic Justice *(1999) and* Conquests and Cultures *(1998).*

Preparing to Read

1. Both Love and Sowell use relatively short paragraphs. One of the reasons for this is that their essays were written for magazines read by the general public. Another is that both knew that their work would eventually appear on the Internet; on a computer screen, short paragraphs are easier to read than long ones.

2. In paragraph 8, Love mentions bill H. R. 40, introduced by Rep. John Conyers. H. R. stands for the House of Representatives (Congress) in Washington, D. C. In paragraph 12, Sowell explains that the word "slave" is derived from Slavs. The Slavs are an ethnic group comprising Poles, Czechs, Slovaks, Russians, Ukrainians, and other peoples of Eastern Europe.

3. Love's thesis is implied. It is the answer to the rhetorical question (question to which the answer is obvious), which he asks at the end of paragraph 2. Sowell's thesis is stated. Look for it at the end of his first paragraph.

Vocabulary

compensation (noun)	Payment.
advocates (noun)	Supporters.
allocation (noun)	Grant.
coerced (verb)	Compelled, forced.
demagogues (noun)	Agitators, rabble-rousers.
legacy (noun)	Inheritance.
manifestation (noun)	Demonstration, show.
potent (adjective)	Powerful
reparations (noun)	Payments to make up for a wrong.
unctuous (adjective)	Insincere.
unwittingly (adverb)	Unknowingly.

US Needs to Pay Reparations for Slavery

David A. Love

IN DECEMBER, officials from Germany, Eastern Europe and the United States   1
signed a historic agreement to pay $5 billion in reparations to Nazi slave la-
borers and their families. U.S. Secretary of State Madeleine Albright called the
deal the first serious attempt to compensate "those whose labor was stolen or
coerced during a time of outrage and shame. It is critical to completing the unfinished business of the old century before entering the new."

Unwittingly, Albright was making the perfect case for reparations to the de-   2
scendants of African slaves in America. Since the United States has pressured
the German and Swiss governments to own up to the sins of their past, should-
n't our country own up to the sins of its past?

Randall Robinson, executive director of TransAfrica and author of the new   3
book, "The Debt: What America Owes to Blacks" (Dutton, 2000), believes that
the nation's racial problems cannot be solved unless the United States com-
pensates blacks for the massive crime of slavery, the "grievous wrong that has
been committed against African Americans, and takes steps to redress that
wrong."

Robinson notes that the U.S. government requested 100 slaves to construct   4
the Capitol in Washington, a potent symbol of freedom and democracy. Mas-
ters who agreed to lend their slaves to the government received $5 per month
per slave. Subsequently, forced labor helped clear the land for the rest of the
District of Columbia.

Advocates for reparations point not only to the past injustices of slavery,   5
but to the present racial inequalities that are a manifestation of slavery's legacy.

In 1996, 39.5 percent of black children lived in poverty, as compared to 15.5 percent of white children, according to "The Social Health of the Nation" (Oxford University Press, 1999). The infant-mortality rate for African Americans in 1996 was more than twice as high as for whites, a proportional gap larger than in 1970.

Social injustice is accompanied by inequalities in the criminal-justice system. According to Human Rights Watch and the Sentencing Project, African Americans make up 13 percent to 15 percent of all drug users, yet account for 36 percent of all arrests for drug possession. In 1996, the incarceration rate for black men was eight times that of white men.   6

In 1865, following the end of the Civil War, Congress passed a bill that called for the seizure of Confederate property and the allocation of 40 acres of land and a mule to each of the former enslaved blacks. President Andrew Johnson vetoed the bill.   7

In every legislative session since 1989, Rep. John Conyers, D-Mich., has introduced bill H.R. 40—for "40 acres and a mule"—legislation that would establish a commission to examine slavery and its lingering effects on African Americans and the country as a whole. The commission would then make recommendations to the Congress on appropriate remedies.   8

"What we're trying to do is start a discussion," says Conyers. "This is the most averted subject matter in the congressional agenda."   9

Others suggest that the road to reparations is possible through legal action. The National Coalition of Blacks for Reparations in America, based in Washington, D.C., plans to sue the U.S. government on this issue.   10

"Our team is convinced that a solidly crafted lawsuit will help us achieve our reparations," says the group's attorney, Adjoa Aiyetoro. "Much like our ancestors who fought for 250 years to end chattel slavery, we cannot refuse to demand reparations in every forum because it appears that the government is unlikely to give it to us or that we do not have agreement as to what form it will take."   11

America, your silence on reparations smacks of hypocrisy.   12

Reparations for Slavery?

Thomas Sowell

THE FIRST THING to understand about the issue of reparations for slavery is that no money is going to be paid. The very people who are demanding reparations know it is not going to happen.   1

Why then are they demanding something that they know they are not going to get? Because the demagogues themselves will benefit, even if nobody else does. Stirring up historic grievances pays off in publicity and votes.   2

Some are saying that Congress should at least issue an official apology for   3
slavery. But slavery is not something you apologize for, any more than you apologize for murder. You apologize for accidentally stepping on someone's toes or
for playing your TV too loud at night. But, if you have ever enslaved anybody,
an apology is not going to cut it. And if you never enslaved anybody, then what
are you apologizing for?

The very idea of apologizing for what somebody else did is meaningless,   4
however fashionable it has become. A scholar once said that the great economist David Ricardo "was above the unctuous phrases that cost so little and yield
such ample returns." Apparently many others are not.

The only thing that would give the idea of reparations for slavery even the   5
appearance of rationality is an assumption of collective guilt, passed down from
generation to generation. But, if we start operating on the principle that people
alive today are responsible for what their ancestors did in centuries past, we will
be adopting a principle that can tear any society apart, especially a multi-ethnic
society like the United States.

Even if we were willing to go down that dangerous road, the facts of his-   6
tory do not square with the demand for reparations. Millions of immigrants arrived in this country from Europe, Asia and Latin America after slavery was
over. Are their descendants guilty too and expected to pay out hard cash to re-
deem themselves?

Even during the era of slavery, most white people owned no slaves. Are
their descendants supposed to pay for the descendants of those who did?

What about the effect of all this on today's black population? Is anyone   7
made better off by being supplied with resentments and distractions from the
task of developing the capabilities that pay off in a booming economy and a
high-tech world? Whites may experience a passing annoyance over the reparations issue, but blacks—especially young blacks—can sustain more lasting
damage from misallocating their time, attention and efforts. Does anyone seriously suggest that blacks in America today would be better off if they were in
Africa? If not, then what is the compensation for?

Sometimes it is claimed that slavery made a great contribution to the de-   8
velopment of the American economy, from which other Americans benefitted,
so that reparations would be like back pay. Although slaveowners benefitted
from slavery, it is by no means obvious that there were net benefits to the economy as a whole, especially when you subtract the staggering costs of the Civil
War.

Should the immoral gains of dead people be repaid by living people who   9
are no better off than if slavery had never existed? The poorest region of the
United States has long been the region in which slavery was concentrated.

The same is true of Brazil—and was true of 18th century Europe. The   10
worldwide track record of slavery as an economic system is bad. Slaveowners
benefitted, but that is not saying that the economy as a whole benefitted. The

last desperate argument for reparations is that blacks have lower incomes and occupations than whites today because of the legacy of slavery. Do the people who say this seriously believe that black and white incomes and occupations would be the same if Africans had immigrated voluntarily to this country?

Scholars who have spent years studying racial and ethnic groups in countries around the world have yet to come up with a single country where all the different groups have the same incomes and occupations. Why would people from Africa be the lone exception on this planet? Groups everywhere differ too much in too many ways to have the same outcomes. 11

Slavery itself was not unique to Africans. The very word "slave" derives from the name of a European people—the Slavs, who were enslaved for centuries before the first African was brought to the Western Hemisphere. The tragic fact is that slavery existed all over the world, for thousands of years. 12

Unfortunately, irresponsible demagogues have also existed for thousands of years. 13

Read More on the Web

"The Case for Slavery Reparations" by Brandt Williams on Minnesota Public Radio website: http://news.mpr.org/features/200011/13_williamsb_reparations/

University of Dayton site on reparations for slavery: http://academic.udayton.edu/race/02rights/repara00.htm

"Does American Owe Reparations?" by Dr. Walter Williams of George Mason University: http://www.gmu.edu/departments/economics/wew/articles/01/reparations.html

"The Controversial Anti-Reparations Ad" by David Horowitz: http://www.adversity.net/reparations/anti_reparations_ad.htm

Questions for Discussion

1. In paragraphs 1 and 2, Love connects the agreement to pay reparations to "Nazi slave laborers" to doing the same for "African slaves." Explain how this appeals to the reader's values.
2. Does Love anticipate opposing arguments? How does he do this?
3. Where does Love appeal to authority? How does he establish his own authority on this issue?
4. Does Love appeal to the reader's emotions?
5. What are the reasons Love believes reparations should be paid for slavery?
6. What is Sowell's thesis? Does this thesis undercut Love's argument? Why or why not?

7. How would you describe Sowell's intended audience? Explain how Sowell appeals to the interests of people of various races, including African-Americans.

8. Explain how he appeals to their values.

9. Where does Sowell anticipate opposing arguments? Does he do so effectively?

10. How does Sowell establish his authority to speak on this issue?

11. Find examples of both authors' referencing historical events to support their arguments. To what end do they include such information?

Thinking Critically

1. In paragraphs 5 and 6, Love adds "present racial inequalities" to the past horrors of slavery to support his thesis. Is doing so logical? Is it effective? Explain what his doing this reveals about his intended audience.

2. In paragraph 4, Sowell includes a quotation about David Ricardo. Find out more about David Ricardo on the Internet (Try http://cepa.newschool.edu/het/profiles/ricardo.htm) Then, explain what the quotation from Ricardo means and how it helps support Sowell's thesis.

Suggestions for Journal Entries

1. Make notes in the margins of the text of both essays in order to mark ideas or arguments with which you disagree or which you find illogical. (Re-read information on logical fallacies that appears in the introduction to Section Four, pages 510–513, before you do this.) Then, use focused freewriting or listing to record your responses to these ideas and arguments in your journal.

2. On which side of this question do you stand? Or do you adopt a third position? Summarize your position and the reasons behind it in a paragraph or two. Make reference to the essays by Love and Sowell in the process. However, also make sure your position is clearly stated in one statement, which you will be able to use as the thesis for a paper responding to one of the Suggestions for Sustained Writing.

Farming and Wearing Fur: Opposing Views

"Fur Is Dead" by People for the Ethical Treatment of Animals (PETA)

"Fur Is Natural and Environmentally Sound" by Mark Schumacher

According to its website, People for the Ethical Treatment of Animals (PETA) "is dedicated to establishing and protecting the rights of all animals. PETA operates under the simple principle that animals are not ours to eat, wear, experiment on, or use for entertainment."

Mark Schumacher is the Vice President of the Schumacher Fur Company. His letter first appeared in the newsletter of the National Animal Interest Alliance (NAIA) and later on its website. The NAIA describes itself as "an association of business, agricultural, scientific, and recreational interests formed to protect and promote humane practices and relationships between people and animals."

Preparing to Read

1. The PETA article appeared on its website. This is an excerpt of a longer piece, which you can read by going to http://www.furisdead.com/animals-expose.html.

2. Schumacher's letter is a response to a letter from a sixth grade student who is against fur farming and the selling of furs. Schumacher is a member of the NAIA.

3. As you read each piece, notice that PETA's approach to persuasion appeals chiefly to our emotions and values while Schumacher's approach appeals chiefly to our values and our self-interest.

Vocabulary

biodegradable (adjective)	Able to decompose, rot.
cervical (adjective)	Having to do with the neck.
dehydration (noun)	Loss of body fluids.
labia (noun)	Lipped-shaped parts of the vagina.
offal (noun)	Leftovers from a butchered animal that are not edible by humans.
self-mutilating (adjective)	Having to do with the process of injuring oneself.

sustainable (adjective)	Able to be maintained, kept in existence.
toxic (adjective)	Harmful, poisonous.
vertebra (noun)	Bone that is found in the spine.

Fur Is Dead

People for the Ethical Treatment of Animals

A LIFETIME IN A CAGE

Animals raised to become someone's fur coat spend their days exposed to the   1
elements in row after row of barren, tiny, urine- and feces-encrusted cages. Investigations have found animals with gruesome injuries going without medical
care and foxes and minks pacing in endless circles, crazy from the confinement.

Minks, foxes, chinchillas, raccoons, and other animals on fur farms spend   2
their entire lives confined to tiny, filthy cages, constantly circling and pacing
back and forth from stress and boredom, some animals even self-mutilating or
cannibalizing cagemates. Foxes are kept in cages measuring only 2.5 feet
square, with one to four animals per cage. Minks and other species are generally kept in cages only 1 foot by 3 feet, again with up to four animals per cage.
The cramped and overcrowded conditions are especially distressing to solitary
animals, like minks.

During the summer, hundreds of thousands of animals endure searing heat   3
and suffer from dizziness and vomiting before dying of heat exhaustion. Baby
animals are the most common victims, as they succumb faster to dehydration.
In the winter, caged animals have nowhere to seek refuge from freezing tem-
peratures, rain, sleet, and snow.

No federal law protects animals on fur farms. Farmers often kill animals by   4
anal or genital electrocution, which causes them to experience the intense pain
of a heart attack while fully conscious. Other killing methods include neck-
breaking and suffocation. Sometimes animals are only stunned and are then
skinned alive.

PETA has gone undercover numerous times to document the cruelty on fur   5
farms firsthand.

GENITAL ELECTROCUTION: A REAL-LIFE SHOCK-HORROR STORY

Row after row of tiny wire-mesh cages, stacked four high and about 25 in a row,   6
chinchillas peering watchfully through the wires, a rack of pelts hanging on a
far wall, and except for a radio playing softly in one corner of the room, a
morgue-like hush. That's the scene that two PETA investigators found at a fur
"factory" farm secluded in a quiet, snow-covered town in Michigan. PETA's Research & Investigations Department sent two undercover teams into fur "farms"
in five states. Our investigators witnessed not only how animals live, but also

how they die in the seedy world of fur farming. One method they documented had never been made public before: genital electrocution.

LITTLE ANIMALS, BIG SUFFERING

During genital electrocution, the killer attaches an alligator clamp to the ani-   7
mal's ear and another to her labia and flips a switch, or plugs the wire into the wall socket, sending a jolt of electricity through her skin down the length of her body. She jerks and stiffens. But, according to biologist Leslie Gerstenfeld-Press, although the electrical current stops the heart, it does not kill her: In many cases, the animal remains conscious. The electrical current causes unbearable muscle pain, at the same time working as a paralyzing agent, preventing the victim from screaming or fighting. A chinchilla farmer who uses genital electrocution told our investigators that he leaves the clips on "for one or two minutes" to make sure the heart doesn't start up again but that some-times animals revive and those who do remember the pain. In front of our in-vestigators, one rancher unplugged the animal, listened to the heart and said, "Nope, still beating," and plugged the cables back in for another 30 seconds.

NOT KILLING THEM SOFTLY

As one farmer observed, "Sometimes you'll get one that'll argue with you." The   8
chinchillas, like all animals, do not go willingly; although they make no noise as they wait—held upside down as the rancher attaches the clips—their whiskers and mouths tremble constantly until the electrical charge freezes all movement. For the benefit of our investigators, the farmer laid the animal's body on a table, although normally, he said, he would just hang the animal by the tail from a clip.

For small animals, neck "snapping" or "popping" is easy and cheap. The   9
owner of one farm that PETA visited wraps the fingers of one hand around the neck of the chinchilla, grasps the lower body with the other hand and jerks the animal's vertebra out of the socket, breaking the neck. Neck-snapping takes just a second, but for "about five minutes" afterward, according to one rancher, the animal jerks and twitches. It might take two minutes for an animal to be-come brain-dead from cervical dislocation; in the meantime, as shown in our investigator's video, she or he kicks and struggles.

No federal law regulates the killing of animals raised for fur. The methods   10
vary from one company to another, but all emphasize concern for the pelt, not for the animal. It takes at least 100 chinchilla pelts to make just one full-length coat.

Some people believe that animals raised in captivity on fur "ranches" do   11
not suffer. This is not the case. Trapping and "ranching" have both similar and disparate cruelties involved, and neither is humane. "Ranched" animals, mostly minks and foxes, spend their entire lives in appalling conditions, only to be killed by painful and primitive methods.

Filth and Frenzy

Approximately one half of the fur coats made in the United States and Canada   12
come from captive animals bred, born, and raised on fur farms. These operations range from family-owned businesses with 50 animals to large operations
with thousands of animals. But regardless of their size or location, "the manner
in which minks (and other furbearers) are bred is remarkably uniform over the
whole world," according to one study. As with other intensive-confinement animal farms, the methods used on fur farms are designed to maximize profits,
always at the expense of the animals' welfare and comfort, and always at the expense of their lives.

In the United States there are approximately 500 fur farms, down from   13
1,615 in 1970.(1) About 90% of all ranched fur bearers are minks. Foxes, rab-
bits, and chinchillas account for most of the remainder, though fur farmers
have recently diversified into lynx, bobcats, wolves, wolverines, coyotes, and
beavers. All of these animals live only a fraction of their natural lifespans; minks
are killed at about five months of age, and foxes are killed when they are about
nine months old. Breeding females live somewhat longer. The animals' short
lives are filled with fear, stress, disease, parasites, and other physical and psychological hardships, all for the sake of an industry that makes huge profits
from its $648 million-a-year sales.(2)

Minks, foxes, and chinchillas are fed meat and fish by-products so vile that   14
they are unfit even for the pet food industry. These animals are also fed minced
offal, which endangers their health because of bacterial contamination. Newly
weaned kits and pups are especially vulnerable to the food poisoning this diet
can cause.

Water on fur farms is provided by a nipple system from which the animals   15
can drink at will—except, of course, when the system freezes in the winter.

The Choices

Every fur coat represents the intense suffering of up to several dozen animals,   16
whether they were trapped or ranched. These cruelties will end only when the
public refuses to buy or wear fur products and rejects the propaganda of trap-
pers, ranchers, and furriers whose monetary motives cause unjustifiable misery
and death. Those who learn the facts about furs must help educate others, for
the sake of the animals and for the sake of decency.

References:

McCann, Dennis, "Tough Times in the Fur Trade," *The Milwaukee Journal
Sentinel Magazine,* April 9, 1995.

Fur Statistics, The Humane Society of the United States, Sept. 1993.

Fur Is Natural and Environmentally Sound

Mark Schumacher

THIS LETTER was written to a sixth grade student by Mark Schumacher, an NAIA board member and furrier.

Dear Ms. Norte:

1 Your Animal Rights club is an interesting idea, as I support freedom of thoughts and association. However, freedom of thoughts and the expression of those thoughts should be founded on solid facts, not emotion.

2 The concept of Animal Rights states that we should not use animals for any human purposes, including food, clothing, entertainment, or medical research. If you want to be consistent in your thoughts, you may not eat or drink anything which is made from an animal life form: meat, poultry, eggs, fish, milk, cheese, honey, bakery products using butter and eggs, marshmallows, and on and on. You may not have leather shoes, belts, purses, furs, wool, circuses, rodeos, or keep pets. Furthermore, you should not use any medicines or cosmetics which have been tested for safety using animals.

3 Now then, if you are concerned about animal welfare, that is a different issue. Some people abuse animals, pets, livestock, etc., and they should not. However, most farmers take excellent care of their animals because it is in their best economic interest to do so. Sick or abused animals do not produce a salable product.

4 If the planet Earth is going to be saved from destruction, we cannot rely on synthetic clothing for our future existence. The extraction of oil is killing the environment by the spilling of oil and the taking of the animals' habitat or home. The processing plants used to make artificial fibers pollute the air (acid rain and the depletion of ozone), streams and rivers and create toxic waste. The clothing (fake furs, nylons, rayons, and polyester) made from these synthetic products fill up our landfills and are not biodegradable.

5 As to the extinction of animals, the fur industry does not use any endangered or threatened species and will not in the future. Ninety-five percent of the mink used by the fur industry are farm-raised. They eat fresh byproducts from the agricultural industry which are not desired by humans but are loved by the mink. If it were not for the mink, these byproducts would fill up our landfills, rivers, or be burned, none of which is environmentally sound.

6 The animals are not tortured or otherwise abused during their lives, as this would not produce a desirable pelt. The mink are killed by cool carbon monoxide. It is painless.

7 The manure produced by the mink is spread on the mink rancher's farm and is a natural fertilizer, not oil-based and not polluting. The tanning of the mink uses salt and alum, which are put into the sewer system and welcomed

by sewage treatment plants because they help to break down the sewage. There are no harmful or polluting chemicals used by our industry.

To make a fur coat requires only cotton thread, electricity for our sewing 8 machines and silk for the lining—no large polluting factories or large amounts of energy.

The fur coat will last 40 years or more, thus requiring only one purchase in 9 a lifetime. Thus fur can be restyled and reused from generation to generation. Finally, when it has finished its useful life, it biodegrades (rots) in six months, back to the earth from where it originally came. In Genesis 1:28 and Genesis 3:21, God gave man use of animals for his benefit and put skins of animals on Adam and Eve. I think that using natural fibers is the way God intended us to live. They are renewable, sustainable, reusable, biodegradable, and environmentally compatible. The use of animals has been Mother Nature's choice for one million years. I think it's the natural choice for one million more years.

You are correct: there is only one world. I ask that you think about whether 10 or not synthetics are the way of the future for this world rather than the agricultural products managed and used by man in a well thought-out, scientific manner.

I took the time to answer your letter because I feel you are smart enough 11 to think through these long-term environmental questions. One day maybe you will be part of a Natural Fibers Club. It will definitely be the only way of the future for the Planet Earth. I invite the Animal Rights Club to come to Schumacher Fur Company so I may show you our natural product and talk about our planet and what we can do for its future.

Thank you for your concern,
Mark Schumacher, vice president
Schumacher Fur Company

Read More on the Web

Website of People for the Ethical Treatment of Animals: http://www. peta.org/

Website of the National Animal Interest Alliance: http://www. naiaonline.org/

Website of association of furriers: http://www.furcommission.com/

List of websites relating to anti-fur movement: http://www.furfreefriday. com/links.htm

Questions for Discussion

1. How would you describe the language used in "Fur is Dead"? How does it compare with what we read in Schumacher's letter?

2. One of the qualities that makes "Fur Is Dead" compelling is its use of specific details to create images. Are these images effective, or do they overwhelm and repel you?

3. Where do the authors of "Fur Is Dead" appeal to our values?

4. Where in that selection do the authors use direct quotations to support their argument? Does doing so make their arguments more credible? Explain how.

5. Where do the authors of "Fur Is Dead" anticipate the opposition?

6. What information about raising and harvesting fur in Schumacher's letter contradicts what you read in "Fur Is Dead"?

7. What fundamental principle of PETA and the animal rights movement does Schumacher try to undercut (see paragraph 2).

8. Schumacher claims that fur farmers "take excellent care of their animals." Should he have expanded his discussion of this statement? What types of information might he have added? Look to the contents of the PETA essay for clues.

9. In Preparing to Read, you learned that PETA's approach to persuasion appeals chiefly to our emotions and values while Schumacher's approach appeals chiefly to our values and our self-interest. Defend this statement by making specific reference to the both texts.

10. Does Schumacher's addressing the environmental aspects of fur farming strengthen his position? How might PETA respond to his environmental arguments?

Thinking Critically

1. Schumacher's authority is established when we learn that he is a furrier, thereby making his opinions more credible. In what way does the fact that he is a furrier make his argument less credible?

2. Schumacher says that minks are killed in a painless manner. This is a direct contradiction of what we read in the PETA article. Conduct Internet research (begin with the sites listed under Read More on the Web) to decide whose claim is closer to the truth.

Suggestions for Journal Entries

1. Using the Internet or print sources, research some other concerns about animal rights that PETA has identified over the years. For example, you might research PETA's views on the leather industry or the use of circus animals. Print out one or two relevant documents and read them critically, using methods explained in "Getting Started under Becoming an Active College Reader" (pages 31–47). In other

words, make marginal comments and mark the text to record your evaluation and response to PETA's argument. Finally, summarize your responses in your journal.

2. Follow the directions for item 1, but find views opposing PETA's on the subject you researched above. For example, if you researched PETA's stand on leather, find information that supports the use of animal skins to manufacture, shoes, clothing, wallets and briefcases, or furniture.

Suggestions for Sustained Writing

1. Write an essay that tries to persuade your readers that working more than 15 hours a week while pursuing a full-time academic career is reasonable. You might explain that working longer hours is necessary if you are to pay your expenses. You might also explain that some full-time students are so organized or talented that they can handle more than 15 hours of work. If this idea does not interest you, write an open letter to your fellow students trying to persuade them to adopt a particular behavior or attitude concerning an issue important to them. For example, offer advice on time or stress management, persuade them to change their study habits, encourage their participation in community service, or warn them about the dangers of alcohol abuse. If you responded to either of the journal suggestions after Palmieri's essay, look over the notes you made before you begin this assignment.

   Another alternative is to write an essay in which you try to persuade your fellow students to devote 100 percent of their time to school and to quit even the least demanding part-time job. Of course, you will have to suggest alternative sources of income—such as scholarships, loans, and other types of financial aid—that students might tap to pay tuition and living expenses.

   Like Palmieri, try to support your arguments with the testimony of experts and present your arguments logically. However, remember that this is a persuasive assignment. Use language that will appeal to your fellow students' pride, self-interest, and emotions. Try to rouse them if you can! In addition, however, make sure to raise and to address opposing arguments. If you are using researched materials, credit your sources with internal citations, as Palmieri did, and include a list of works cited. More information on how to do this can be found in the Appendix of this book. It discusses documentation principles used by the Modern Language Association.

2. Look back to the journal notes you made after reading Dr. King's "I Have a Dream." Whether you responded to item 1 or 2 in the Suggestions for Journal Entries, expand your notes into a persuasive address that you might deliver to a large group of people if you had the opportunity.

    If you responded to item 1, you might be satisfied by relating the progress the United States has made in the decades since Dr. King spoke at the Lincoln Memorial. In the process, you could take the position that we have done enough in this area, and that further measures will simply be redundant and even counterproductive. Then again, you might argue that not enough has been done, and you could persuade your listeners that we need to take additional steps to assure everyone's civil rights. However you approach this question, try to be as specific and detailed as you can, relying on library or Internet research and/or using information you have acquired through interviews with faculty members on your campus.

    If you responded to item 2, write a speech in which you try to persuade your listeners to support measures to solve a serious problem that threatens our people, society, culture, or environment or that affects the people, environment, or society of another part of the world. Again, be as specific and detailed as you can and rely on research.

3. Research the question of providing reparations for slavery by reading the sources listed under Read More on the Web, which appears immediately after Love's and Sowell's essays. Then read the notes you made for both of the journal prompts after these essays. If you have not responded to both of those prompts, do so now.

    Next, use the thesis you put into your journal notes as a working thesis for an essay that expresses your views on reparations for slavery. You may side with either Love or Sowell, or you may adopt a third view. As you draft your essay, include information you have gathered through research. Remember to cite sources of such information appropriately. Your instructor can tell you the documentation style you should use. (Modern Language Association style is explained in the Appendix of this book.)

4. Look over the information you gathered and the notes you compiled in response to the two journal entry prompts following the selections under "Farming and Wearing Fur: Opposing Views." (If you haven't responded to both those prompts yet, do so now.) Perhaps you researched materials on the treatment of circus animals or on the harvesting of leather. Now write down a preliminary (working) thesis that states your opinion on this issue. Do you agree or disagree with PETA? Or do you take a third or middle position? Now do some more library and/or Internet research to gather additional information and insights that you can use in a persuasive essay defending your thesis.

Remember that, as you do additional research, you have the right to amend or even completely change your thesis. Also remember that this is a research paper, so you will have to cite sources appropriately. Check with your instructor as to the documentation style he or she wishes you to use. (Modern Language Association style is explained in the Appendix of this book.)

Writing to Learn: A Group Activity

In the introduction to this chapter (page 568), you saw a cartoon relating to the controversy over reciting the Pledge of Allegiance in public schools. According to people who have filed suit against reciting the Pledge, the words "under God" added to it in the 1950s, violate part of the First Amendment to the US Constitution: "Congress shall make no law respecting an establishment of religion. . ." However, the First Amendment is even better known for its protection of free speech. "Congress shall make no law . . . abridging the freedom of speech or of the press. . . ."

Although seemingly simple the First Amendment has been the subject of various interpretations and much debate. What's your opinion? Should we protect freedom of expression no matter what the circumstances, who is involved, or what the consequences?

THE FIRST MEETING

Brainstorm a list of circumstances or situations that might cause you to argue for limiting free speech. The classic example was put forth by Supreme Court Justice Oliver Wendell Holmes. The First Amendment, he argued, does not protect one from falsely shouting "Fire!" in a crowded theater, for doing so would cause panic and endanger lives. More recently, the courts ruled child pornography illegal. However, other restrictions of the freedom of expression are still being debated. Here are some you might use to start brainstorming a list of your own:

Regulating the content of the Internet.

Censoring or rating radio and television shows.

Regulating or rating films, CDs, or other entertainment products.

Enforcing criteria for what is shown, displayed, or performed in public places such as city museums, train stations, public squares, municipal buildings, or public schools.

Setting criteria for what public libraries put on their shelves.

Writing policies or codes governing speech on college campuses.

After you have brainstormed a list of your own issues (include those above if you like), assign each student the task of researching one particular topic. Ask him or her to find information and opinions on both sides of the issue.

RESEARCH

Search the Internet as well as print and online periodical indexes for articles on your topic published in the last five or six years. Bring your notes and photocopies of pages from sources to the next meeting. For general information on the First Amendment, try the American Civil Liberties Union website on the Internet (http://www.aclu.org).

THE SECOND MEETING

Distribute copies of articles students have read and notes they have taken. Make sure each has gathered information on both sides of his or her topic. After the group has read these materials, debate the pros and cons of each question and, if possible, take a group stand or position on it. (Ask each student to take notes on the group's discussion of the question he or she researched.)

Before closing the meeting, ask everyone to write one or two paragraphs explaining both sides of his or her issue and stating the group's position on it. Encourage him or her to incorporate both researched information and the opinions of fellow group members. Finally, remind everyone to bring copies of this work to the next meeting.

THE THIRD MEETING

Distribute, read, and critique each other's writing; offer suggestions for revision. Ask one student to collect the final versions of everyone's work and use them in a draft of a complete paper that takes positions on the free-speech questions members of your group researched. If possible, have a second student write the introduction and the conclusion to this paper.

THE FOURTH MEETING

Distribute and read the draft of the paper. Make last-minute suggestions for revision. Ask a third student to edit the paper and a fourth to type and proofread it.

Writing a Research Paper Using Modern Language Association (MLA) Style

The Modern Language Association (MLA) is a professional organization of teachers and scholars of language and literature. Like many other professional associations, the MLA has created a style sheet for authors who write about subjects in the disciplines it covers. The following pages explain ways to include and cite (identify the sources of) researched material using MLA style in research papers such as the ones you might be assigned in first-year composition classes and in other college courses. You can find out more about MLA style in Joseph Gibaldi's *MLA Handbook for Writers of Research Papers,* 6th ed., 2003.

Identify the Source of All Researched Information

Most college research papers contain some of the student's own ideas and first-hand knowledge. However, research papers also rely on information, ideas, and direct quotations taken from other sources including books, professional journals, newspapers, pamphlets, and online resources, to name only a few examples. All materials taken from a source other than yourself must be identified as such in the body of the paper. This is known as citing, a process by which you (1) identify the source of the words and/or materials you have researched and (2) provide readers with information they can use to locate this source on their own.

Here are three ways to take information from a source other than yourself to:

- **Use a direct quotation:** A direct quotation uses the source's exact words and is indicated by quotation marks ("/") except when quotations of more than four lines are used. In such cases, the quotation is double spaced and indented 10 spaces from the left margin.
- **Paraphrase:** When paraphrasing, the writer uses the source's ideas but expresses them in his or her own words.
- **Summarize:** A summary is like a paraphrase, but when summarizing, the writer condenses a large amount of information from the source into a sentence or two. Again, the writer expresses that material in his or her own words.

A common mistake among beginning writers is to think that only direct quotations need citations. This is NOT TRUE. In fact, whether you quote from, paraphrase, or summarize someone else's work, you must include a citation. In other words, you must identify and give credit to the source. Otherwise, you might be committing plagiarism.

AVOID PLAGIARISM

Plagiarism is a form of academic dishonesty, and it is as serious a matter as copying answers from someone else's test paper or having a friend write an essay and submitting it as your own work. Remember that words and ideas taken from a source other than yourself need to be cited and that direct quotations must be indicated by quotation marks.

Of course, plagiarism when writing a research paper can sometimes be done unintentionally. When paraphrasing, for example, you might accidentally incorporate some of your source's original vocabulary or sentence structure into your notes without using quotation marks. When writing your paper, you might just forget to include an internal citation for ideas you have summarized, or you might simply neglect to type quotation marks around the quoted words or sentences. This is no excuse. Whether intentional or unintentional, plagiarism is a serious misuse of someone else's words or ideas because it presents those words and ideas as if they were your own.

It is especially important to remember that when paraphrasing or summarizing, you need to guard against letting a few of the author's exact words or phrases slip into your own writing without quotation marks. You must also try to avoid following the source's exact sentence structure, plugging your own words into a pattern he or she has already established.

In a paraphrase or summary, the words you use and the order that you present them in should be yours alone. The following sample paragraphs illustrate this idea.

ORIGINAL PARAGRAPH FROM H. L. MENCKEN'S ESSAY "THE PENALTY OF DEATH"

Of the arguments against capital punishment that issue from uplifters, two are commonly heard most often. . . .

1. That hanging a man (or frying him or gassing him) is a dreadful business, degrading to those who have to do it and revolting to those who have to witness it.
2. That it is useless, for it does not deter others from the same crime.

PARAPHRASE OF MENCKEN CONTAINING SOME PLAGIARISM

According to Mencken, there are two arguments most commonly made against capital punishment. One is that it degrades the executioners and revolts those who witness it; the second is that it does not deter others from the identical crime.

The problem here is that the paraphrase uses some of Mencken's own words and even his sentence/paragraph structure.

ACCEPTABLE PARAPHRASE

According to Mencken, opponents of the death penalty claim that it debases those who must administer it. They also claim that it is ineffective in lowering the murder rate.

Note that this *acceptable* paraphrase must now be *cited*.

For another example, compare an original paragraph from an essay on date rape by Camille Paglia and the two paraphrases of that paragraph, which follow it:

ORIGINAL PARAGRAPH FROM PAGLIA'S "IT'S A JUNGLE OUT THERE"

The only solution to date rape is female self-awareness and self-control. A woman's number one line of defense is herself. When a real rape occurs, she should report it to the police. Complaining to college committees because the courts "take too long" is ridiculous. College administrations are not a branch of the judiciary. They are not equipped or trained for legal inquiry. Colleges must alert incoming students to the problems and dangers of adulthood. Then colleges must stand back and get out of the sex game.

PARAPHRASE OF PAGLIA CONTAINING PLAGIARISM

For Camille Paglia, college women have to defend themselves against the possibility of date rape. They need to be aware and take control. When an actual rape occurs, for example, they should report it to legal authorities, not to college administrators, who are not part of the judiciary and are not equipped to pursue legal inquiry. The only thing colleges should do is warn incoming students of the dangers of adulthood, but they should stay away from refereeing the college sex game.

ACCEPTABLE PARAPHRASE OF PAGLIA

College women need to take responsibility for protecting them-selves against sexual assault. Legal, not campus authorities, should be notified when rape occurs. Colleges are not courts of law, and college administrators are not prosecutors or judges. Acade-mia's responsibility goes no further than to warn new students of the potential dangers of dating in a college setting. It does not ex-tend to defining rape and determining when it has occurred.

Note: Like direct quotations, all acceptable paraphrases and summaries must still be cited.

Identify Sources through Parenthetical Citations

Using MLA style, you identify the source of quoted, paraphrased, or summa-rized material by using parenthetical (internal) citations. They are called "par-enthetical" because they identify the source within parentheses ( ). Ordinarily, the information within parentheses is brief and includes the author's name and the page number of the book, article, or other sources from which the re-searched material was taken. However, the form of parenthetical citations can vary depending upon the kind of document being cited and the way the mate-rial is introduced. The information in an internal citation must be accurate, for it will lead readers to your Works Cited list (this is usually the last page of your paper), which lists each source you have used in alphabetical order according to the author's last name. Each entry in this list contains all the publication in-formation your readers will need to locate the source on their own. Instructions on completing a Works Cited list appear later in this Appendix.

Cite Researched Information in the Body of Your Paper: Using Parenthetical Citations

The way that you cite a source in the body of your paper depends on whether you are paraphrasing/summarizing or quoting directly. It also de-pends upon the source from which you are taking information. Study the following examples:

Citing Paraphrased or Summarized Material

The most direct way to cite materials you have paraphrased or summarized is to write the author's last name followed by the page number in parentheses directly after the paraphrase or summary. In the following example, a student paraphrases information from a book by the columnist George F. Will:

> Imposing term limits on members of the U.S. Congress
>
> would increase the public's respect for our legislators
>
> and encourage more ordinary citizens to run for office
>
> (Will 7).

The citation above includes the author's last name and the number of the page from which the student took this information.

Introducing a Direct Quotation with the Author's Last Name

A good practice when quoting directly is to introduce the quotation with the author's last name in a phrase such as "Dr. Lee says . . ."; "According to Professor Gonzalez, . . ."; or "Robinson believes that. . . ." The following example uses a direct quotation from an article by Terry Eastland:

> Commenting on the U.S. Constitution, Eastland argues:
>
> "The framers designed and empowered the presidency so
>
> that it would provide the energy that the government
>
> under the Articles of Confederation lacked" (72).

Introducing a Direct Quotation without the Author's Last Name

If you have mentioned a name only a few lines before and want to avoid repetition, you might introduce another direct quotation from that author without mentioning his or her name. In such cases, simply place the author's name in parentheses followed by the page number. For example, take this direct quotation from Marc Breslow's article, which appeared in *Dollars and Sense:*

> The debate on how to overcome poverty in America
>
> continues. One economist believes that government
>
> spending is the answer: "To the degree that the War on
>
> Poverty failed, it was because we spent too little on it, not
>
> too much" (Breslow 121).

Combining a Direct Quotation with Your Own Sentence

You can combine a direct quotation with your own sentence by placing quotation marks ("/") in the appropriate places. Make sure that the quotation fits with your words naturally and correctly. Then, indicate the author's last name and the page number in parentheses.

> Anti-gun-control advocates believe that "guns don't increase
>
> . . . crime and violence—but the continued proliferation of gun-
>
> control laws does" (Polsby 54).

Note: The ellipses (. . .) that come between "increase" and "crime" indicate that the writer of the paper has removed words from the quotation. This practice is appropriate as long as it does not change the meaning or intent of the quotation.

Using a Direct Quotation Longer than Four Lines

MLA format requires that quotations longer than four lines be double spaced and indented 10 spaces from the left margin. Don't place quotation marks around this material (the indentation takes their place) except where the material already contains quotation marks of its own.

> In On the Make: The Rise of Bill Clinton, Meredith L. Oakley
>
> explains one of the reasons for Clinton's victory in the 1992
>
> presidential election:
>
>> A fighter, a survivor, a crusader: It was this image, not
>>
>> that of a draft-dodger, womanizer, prevaricator, and
>>
>> opportunist, that was supposed to emerge in the 1992
>>
>> presidential campaign, and for the most part, it did.
>
> (16-17)

Note: With a long, *indented* quotation, the page numbers in parentheses come *after* the period; for a short quote that is not set off, the citation goes *before* the period.

Including Material for Which No Author Is Named

If no author is named, place the title of the source within parentheses followed by the page number. If the title is long, you can use only the first two or three words, but make sure to provide enough information so that your readers can easily find this source in your Works Cited page. The following quotation was taken from "Finding Deals, Small Businesses Buy More Online," which appeared on page C4 of *The New York Times* on May 15, 2000:

> According to a survey report in <u>The New York Times,</u>
>
> "small-business owners are going online in droves
>
> looking for deals, particularly on computer equipment,
>
> office supplies, and travel reservations . . ." ("Finding
>
> Deals" C4).

Including a Quotation Found in Another Source

If you are using information that contains a direct quotation from yet another source, use the phrase "qtd. in" for "quoted in" in the parenthetical citation:

> According to Charles de Gaulle, "the graveyards are full
>
> of indispensable men" (qtd. in Byrne 35).

Including Information from a Selection in an Anthology

An anthology is a collection of individual works (essays, poems, short stories, etc.) selected and arranged by an editor. Cite information from individual works by using the name of the selection's author, not the name of the anthology's editor.

> In "Unfair Game," Susan Jacoby defines the "code of
>
> feminine politeness," which she says "is no help in
>
> dealing with the unwanted approaches of strange men"
>
> (303).

Taking Information from Two or More Works by the Same Author

If you are using two or more works by the same author, introduce the material by including the author's name in the text of your paper. Then, write the name of the work (in an abbreviated form, if necessary) in the internal citation along with the page number:

> Jonathan Kozol claims that the cause of homelessness in
>
> the United States is not the "deinstitutionalization" of

mental patients but the lack of affordable housing for the poor ("Distancing the Homeless" 1). Kozol also claims that "early death or stunted cognitive development" as well as "severe emotional damage" are common in homeless children in the United States (<u>Rachel and Her Children</u> 83).

Using Material from the Bible

Indicate the edition of the Bible, the book, chapter, and verse(s) when referencing the Bible. You can do this in the body of the text or in a parenthetical citation. In the following example, the book, Proverbs, is mentioned in the text; edition, chapter (18) and verse (24) are mentioned in the parenthetical citation.

Proverbs shows us two sides of friendship: "Some friends bring ruin upon us, but a true friend is more loyal than a brother" (<u>King James Bible,</u> 18: 24).

Using Material from a Corporate Author

If authorship is claimed by an organization, use the name of the organization to introduce the information or include the name in parenthetical citation:

President Herbert Hoover personally supervised the removal of important government documents from the Oval Office during a fire on Christmas Eve 1929 (White House Historical Association 147).

Including Ideas from an Entire Work

To include ideas from an entire work, just indicate the author's name in the text or parenthetical citation. Obviously, no page number can be given. Take this example that references Pete Hamill's autobiography, *A Drinking Life*.

Although the book depicts the life of a popular American journalist, <u>A Drinking Life</u> also chronicles many of the events, trends, and philosophies that helped shape New York City in the 1930s, 40s, 50s, and 60s (Hamill).

Including Information from a Work That Is Not Paginated

You need not worry about including page numbers if the work you are citing is not paginated. Instead, simply use paragraph numbers:

> Tortorice's explanation of the formation of the aquifer
>
> accounts for several properties attributed to the region's
>
> groundwater (paras. 4–7).

Using Material from Two Different Authors with the Same Last Name

Make sure to indicate each author's first name when you include information from his or her work:

> "The endless struggle between the flesh and the spirit
>
> found an end in Greek art" (Edith Hamilton 65).

Including Information from Two Works in the Same Sentence

Use a semicolon to separate that author and page number(s) of each work in the parenthetical citation.

> A few important differences marked the religious
>
> practices of the Greeks and the Romans even though the
>
> gods they worshipped were essentially the same (Romero
>
> 52; Christiansen 184).

Including Material from a Source Whose Author Is Unknown

If the author's name is not available, use the title of the work to introduce the information or include it in the internal citation. If you choose the latter, you may abbreviate the title.

> The National Woman's Conference held in Houston,
>
> Texas, in 1977, produced a "25-point, revised national
>
> Plan of Action," which was to set the agenda from the
>
> Woman's Rights Movement for the next decade (70 Years
>
> in Review 66).

Incorporating Material from a Work in More than One Volume

If you take information from one volume in a multivolume work, indicate the volume number in the parenthetical citation. Separate the volume and page numbers with a colon.

> In The Encyclopedia of Philosophy, Arthur Wooldruff
>
> explains that the British chemist and physicist Michael
>
> Faraday (1791–1867) became interested in science while
>
> he was apprenticed to a bookbinder (3: 18).

Prepare a Works-Cited List

As you learned above, a works-cited list includes sources from which you took information and which are cited (identified) in your paper. Arranged alphabetically (by author's last name, in most cases), each item in this list contains all of the publication data readers of your paper will need to locate the source mentioned.

Typically, a works-cited list is the last thing a research-paper writer completes, and it appears at the very end of the paper. However, before you begin even to take notes from a particular book, article, or other source, be certain to record all pertinent publication information about that source. You can do this on a index card (3″ × 5″ should be large enough), one source per card, or in a computer file. (There are programs designed specifically for this, though you could just as well use a table in MS. Word or another word processing program.) This information will come in handy when it comes time to compile your list of works cited. For a book, the information would contain the author's or authors' full names, the full title of the book, the place and date of publication, and the name of the publisher. For a magazine article, it would include the author's name, the title of the article, the title of the magazine, the date of publication, and the number(s) of the page(s) upon which the article appeared. Here is an example of a bibliography card for a magazine article:

Zinmeister, Karl.	**Name of author**
"Divorce's Toll on Children."	**Title of article**
Current	**Title of magazine in which article appears**
February 1997	**Date of publication**
Pages 29–33	**Pages on which article appears**

The Modern Language Association uses various formats for items in a works-cited list depending upon the type of source being referenced. Below is a comprehensive list of such formats for the kinds of sources you might use. However, the overall organization of a works-cited list follows three principles:

1. Items appear in alphabetical order according to the author's last name or according to the first major word in the title if no author is indicated (short newspaper articles often do not carry the author's name). Items by more than one author are alphabetized according to the author whose name appears first.
2. Items are double spaced, and are separated from each other by two lines.
3. Each item begins at the left margin. If more than one line is needed to complete the entry, subsequent lines are indented five spaces.

Sample Entries for a Works-Cited Page—Print Sources

A Book by a Single Author

MacLean, Harry. *In Broad Daylight.* New York: Harper & Row, 1988.

MacLean, Harry.	Name of author, last name first, followed by a period
In Broad Daylight.	Title of book, underlined or in italics, followed by a period
New York:	Place of publication, followed by a colon
Harper & Row,	Publisher, followed by a comma
1988.	Date of publication, followed by a period

A Book with a Subtitle

A subtitle follows the main title and a colon (:).

> Westervelt, Saundra D. Shifting the Blame: How
>
> Victimization Became a Criminal Defense. New
>
> Brunswick, NJ: Rutgers UP, 1998.

Note: Except when the source has been published in a major U.S. or world city such as Atlanta, Berlin, Boston, Chicago, Dallas, London, Los Angeles, Miami, Montreal, New York, Toronto, Washington, DC, and so on, you should indicate the state, province, or country in which the city is located. In the item above, "NJ" indicates that New Brunswick is in New Jersey. The "UP" stands for "University Press."

A Book by Two Authors

Type the first author's name, last name first, followed by a comma and the word "and." Then type the second author's name, first name first. In the next example, the authors are Gilbert Geis and Leigh B. Bienen.

> Geis, Gilbert, and Leigh B. Bienen. Crimes of the Century:
>
> From Leopold and Loeb to O. J. Simpson. Boston:
>
> Northeastern UP, 1998.

A Book by Three Authors

Type the first author's name, last name first, followed by a comma. Then type the second author's name, first name first, followed by a comma and the word "and." Then type the third author's name, first name first, followed by a period. In the next example, the authors are Mark Umbreit, Robert B. Coates, and Boris Kalanj.

> Umbreit, Mark, Robert B. Coates, and Boris Kalanj. <u>Victim</u>
>
> <u>Meets Offender: The Impact of Restorative Justice</u>
>
> <u>and Mediation.</u> Monsey, NY: Criminal Justice P, 1994.

A Book by More than Three Authors

Type the name of the first author, last name first, followed by "et al." This is the abbreviation for "et alia," a Latin phrase meaning "and others."

> Malikin, David, et al. <u>Social Disability: Alcoholism, Drug</u>
>
> <u>Addiction, Crime, and Social Disadvantage.</u> New York:
>
> New York UP, 1973.

Two or More Works by the Same Author

List works in alphabetical order according to the first major word in their titles. Type the author's name, last name first, in the first entry. Type three hyphens (---) in place of the author's name in subsequent entries.

> Kelleher, Michael. <u>Murder Most Rare: The Female Serial</u>
>
> <u>Killer.</u> Westport, CT: Praeger, 1998.
>
> ———. <u>New Arenas for Violence: Homicide in the</u>
>
> <u>American Workplace.</u> Westport, CT: Praeger, 1996.

A Book in a Series

Type the series name and the series number, if any, between the editor's name, which follows the title, and the publication information. Do not underline or italicize the name of the series.

> Dickens, Charles. <u>Great Expectations.</u> Ed. Janise Carlisle.
>
> Case Studies in Contemporary Criticism. Ser. 4.
>
> Boston: Bedford/St. Martin's, 1996.

A Book in More than One Volume

Treat such a work as you would any other book, but indicate the number of volumes the book contains immediately after the title.

> Norwich, John Julius. <u>The Normans in Sicily.</u> 2 vols.
>
> London: Penguin, 1970.

Note: If you are taking information from only one of the volumes, type the number of that volume. Then, type the total number of volumes at the end of the entry.

> Norwich, John Julius. <u>The Normans in Sicily.</u> Vol 1.
>
> London: Penguin, 1970. 2 vols.

The Bible

Ordinarily, the Bible does not appear in a works-cited list, but you might want to indicate a specific version of the Bible in the internal citation.

An Editor of a Book

If you are using information from a book's editor (anthologies and collections are normally put together by editors, who introduce and comment on the selections), use the abbreviations "ed." or "eds." as in the following example:

> Curtis, Lynn A., ed. <u>Policies to Prevent Crime:</u>
>
> <u>Neighborhood, Family, and Employment Strategies.</u>
>
> Newbury Park, CA: Sage, 1987.

An Edited Book

If you are using information from the author of a book that has been edited, indicate the author's name first, followed by the title, followed by the name of the editor or editors preceded by the abbreviation "Ed." or "Eds."

> Twain, Mark. <u>A Connecticut Yankee in King Arthur's</u>
>
> <u>Court.</u> Ed. Allison E. Ensor. New York: Norton, 1982.

A Later Edition

If you are referencing a work that has been republished in a later edition or editions, indicate the number of the edition you are using.

> Gibaldi, Joseph. <u>MLA Handbook for Writers of Research</u>
>
> <u>Papers.</u> 6th ed. New York: Modern Language
>
> Association, 2003.

A Foreword, Introduction, or Afterword of a Book

Forewords, introductions, and afterwords to a book are often written by someone other than the book's author. If you are using information from such a section in a book, start with the name of the author of the foreword, introduction, or afterword. Then type the word "Foreword," "Introduction," or "Afterword" followed by the title of the book. Continue by typing the name of the book's author (first name first). Finally, indicate place of publication, publisher, and date of publication.

> Smith, Elmer W. Foreword. <u>Social Disability: Alcoholism,</u>
>
> <u>Drug Addiction, Crime, and Social Disadvantage.</u> By
>
> David Malkin, et. al. New York: New York UP, 1973.

A Translation

> Dostoyevsky, Fyodor. <u>Crime and Punishment.</u> Trans.
>
> Sidney Monas. New York: New American Library,
>
> 1980.

A Work by an Association, Organization, or Corporation

Type the name of the organization or corporation first, followed by a period. Then type the title of the work. Then, type the name of the publisher, even if the publisher and the author are the same.

> White House Historical Association. <u>The White House: An</u>
>
> <u>Historic Guide.</u> Washington, DC: White House
>
> Historical Association, 1982.

A Work by an Unknown Author

Begin the entry with the title of the work.

> <u>A History of Crime in Bucks County.</u> Philadelphia:
>
> Cyclops, 1957.

A Signed Article in a Magazine

> Mackenzie, Dana. "The Shape of Madness." <u>Discover</u> Jan.
>
> 2000: 79-83.

Mackenzie, Dana.	Name of author, last name first, followed by a period
"The Shape of Madness."	Title of article in quotation marks, followed by a period
<u>Discover.</u>	Title of magazine, underlined or in italics, followed by a period
Jan. 2000:	Date of publication (*Discover* is a monthly magazine), followed by a colon
79-83.	Pages in magazine on which article appears, followed by a period

An Unsigned Article in a Magazine

Begin with the title of the article in quotation marks.

"United States: Defining Hate." Economist 10 April

1999: 27.

A Signed Article in a Scholarly Journal with Continuous Pagination within a Volume

Libraries often bind monthly, bimonthly, or quarterly issues of journals together in yearly or half-yearly volumes. Some scholarly journals, such as the one in the following example, use continuous pagination through a volume. The number 42 in the example below is the volume number. The article appears on pages 215–227 of that volume.

Umbreit, Mark S. "Victim-Offender Mediation in Canada:

The Impact of an Emerging Work Intervention."

International Social Work 42 (1999): 215–227.

A Signed Article in a Scholarly Journal with Separate Pagination for Each Issue within a Volume

Some scholarly journals paginate each issue of a volume separately. For example, if issue 1 of volume 23 runs from page 1 through page 129, issue 2 of volume 23 starts with page 1, not with page 130. Therefore, it is important to include the issue number as well as the volume number when listing such journals.

Eden, Kathy. "Great Books in the Undergraduate

Curriculum." Academic Questions 13: 2 (2000):

63–69.

Note: This article appears in issue number 2 of volume 13 of the journal *Academic Questions.*

An Article in a Weekly or Biweekly Magazine

Use the same format that you use for a monthly magazine, but indicate the day as well as the month and year of publication.

Gladreeper, Robert. "Siren Song." New Republic 19 April

1999: 8–10.

A Signed Article by Multiple Authors in a Scholarly Journal

Type the name of the first author last name first, followed by a comma. Type the names of subsequent authors first name first.

> Belknop, Joanne, Bonnie S. Fisher, and Francis T. Cullen.
>
> "The Development of a Comprehensive Measure of
>
> the Sexual Victimization of College Women." <u>Violence</u>
>
> <u>Against Women</u> 5 (1999): 185–214.

An Unsigned Article in a Scholarly Journal

> "Victims." <u>Columbia Journalism Review</u> 37 (1999): 12–13.

An Article in an Edited Collection

> Hattemar, Barbara. "Cause and Violent Effect: Media and
>
> Our Youth." <u>Our Times: Readings from Recent</u>
>
> <u>Periodicals.</u> Ed. Robert Atwan. Boston: Bedford, 1995:
>
> 241–249.

A Signed Newspaper Article

> Purdy, Matthew. "Extending a Hand, Not Cuffs." <u>New York</u>
>
> <u>Times</u> 2 Feb. 2000: A5.

An Unsigned Newspaper Article

> "Mexican Drug Cartel May Be Linked to 3 US Dead." <u>The</u>
>
> <u>Los Angeles Times</u> 12 May 2000: 5.

An Editorial in a Newspaper

Since editorials are normally unsigned, you can use the same format as you would for an unsigned article except that you must type the word "Editorial" immediately after the title.

> "The Gun Windmills." Editorial. <u>The Wall Street Journal</u>
>
> 13 Dec. 1999: A34.

A Letter to the Editor

> Miller, Thomas V. Letter. <u>The Washington Post</u> 20 Oct.
>
> 1999: M04.

A Book Review

> Preston, William J. "The Politics of Hysteria." Rev. of <u>Many Are the Crimes: McCarthyism in America,</u> by Ellen Schrecker. <u>The Los Angeles Times</u> 31 May 1998: Book Reviews 6.

An Entry from a Reference Book

> "Crime." <u>The Encyclopedia Britannica: Micropedia.</u> 15th ed. 1991.

Motion Picture or Video Cassette

> <u>Victory at Sea: Full Fathom Five.</u> Videocassette. Video Treasures, Inc., 1986. 20 min.

A Personal or Telephone Interview

> Cornell, Matthew. Personal Interview. 9 June 1998.

An Article from an Online Magazine

> Cullen, David. "Overruled." <u>Salon</u> 28 Oct. 1999. 3pp. 3 May 2000 <http://www.salon.com/news/feature/1999/10/28/laramie/index.html>.

Cullen, David.	Name of author, last name first, followed by a period
"Overruled."	Title of article in quotation marks, followed by a period
Salon 28 Oct. 1999. 3pp.	Title of magazine, underlined or in italics Date of publication, followed by a period Number of pages, paragraphs, or other numbered sections if indicated
3 May 2000 <http://www.salon.com/news/feature/1999/10/28/laramie/index.html>.	Date you accessed the article URL in angle brackets with period at the end

Note: If some of the needed information is not available, follow the advice of the Modern Language Association: include what is readily accessible. Just make sure that your readers will be able to find the article you are citing.

Article from an Online Professional Journal

> Iribarren, Carlos MD, et al. "Association of Hostility with Coronary Artery Calcification in Young Adults." Journal of the American Medical Association 283.19 (2000). 25 May 2000 <http://jama.ama-assn.org/ issues/v283n19/full//joc91868.html>.

Article from an Online Newspaper or News Service

> Babinek, Mark. "Railroad Killer Gets Death Penalty." San Francisco Examiner 22 May 2000. 27 May 2000 <http://examiner.com/ap_a/AP_Railroad_Killer.html>.

Full-Text from a Library Database or Other Subscription Service

> Valentine, Barbara. "The Legitimate Effort in Research Papers: Student Commitment Versus Faculty Expectations." The Journal of Academic Librarianship 27 (2001): 107–115. Academic Search Premier. EBSCOhost. Middlesex County College Library, Edison, NJ. 31 Aug. 2002 <http://search.epnet.com>

Valentine, Barbara.	Name of author, last name first, followed by a period
"The Legitimate Effort in Research Papers: Student Commitment Versus Faculty Expectations."	Title of article in quotation marks, followed by a period
The Journal of Academic Librarianship	Title of journal, underlined or in italics
27 (2001):	Volume number and date (include issue number if given)
107-115.	Paging or indication of length in paragraphs, followed by a period
Academic Search Premier	Name of database, underlined, or in italics, followed by a period
EBSCOhost.	Name of database publisher, followed by a period
Middlesex County College Library, Edison, NJ.	Name of library and location, followed by a period
31 Aug. 2002	Date you accessed article
<http://search.epnet.com>	Full web address

Article from a Portable Database

Halloway, Marguerite. "On the Trail of Wild Elephants."

Scientific American. December 1994: 48–50.

Expanded Academic ASAP. CD-ROM. New York:

Information Access Company. April 2, 1995.

Article in a Reference Database

"Gadsden Purchase." Encyclopædia Britannica online.

2003. Encyclopædia Britannica. 11 Mar. 2003

<http://search.eb.com/>.

Book on the WWW

Hardy, Thomas. Jude the Obscure. London 1895. Project

Gutenberg. Ed. John Hamm. Aug 1997. 28 May 2000

<http://promo.net/pg/history.htm>.

Note: This book was originally published in 1895. The date of its electronic publication is August 1997. The electronic producer of the text is Project Gutenberg, a public database of books on the WWW.

E-Books from NetLibrary

Crane, Steven. The Red Badge of Courage. Columbus, OH:

Charles E. Merrill, 1969. Netlibrary. 2001. 13 Mar.

2002 <http://emedia.netlibrary.com/reader/reader.

asp?product_id=2010654>.

CD-ROM in a Single Edition

"Criminology." Encyclopedia Britannica. CD-ROM. London:

Encyclopedia Britannica, 1998.

CD-ROM Issued Periodically

CD-ROM databases are updated periodically. Treat articles in such databases the same way you would printed versions. However, add the name of the database ("SIRS Government Reporter," for example), the medium (CD-ROM), and the company that maintains the database ("SIRS"). End with the date that the article was published electronically, followed by a period.

Gilreath, James. "History of a Book: Madison Council Told

of First Book Printed in America." <u>Library of</u>

<u>Congress Information Bulletin</u> 1 May 1995: 200-202.

SIRS Government Reporter. CD-ROM, SIRS. Fall 1998.

Personal Site

Mallin, Robert J. Home page. 15 Nov. 2001 <http://www.

bobmallin.com>.

Poem on the WWW

Frost, Robert. "Birches." <u>Mountain Interval.</u> New York,

1921. <u>Representative Poetry Online.</u> Ed. Ian

Lancashire. 1997. U of Toronto. 26 June 1998

<http//www.library.utoronto.ca/utel/rp/poems/

frost6.html>.

Posting on a Forum

Harrington, J. K. "Publishing." Online posting. 19 May

2000. The Writing Life: Inkspot Writers' Community

Forums. 25 May 2000 <http://writers-bbs.com/

inkspot/threads.cgi?action=almsgs&forum=writing

life>.

Note: Forums are open to people who may or may not be experts in their fields. As with all researched information, make sure of the appropriateness and validity of the source.

Professional Site on the WWW

<u>ERIC Clearinghouse on Urban Education</u>. Columbia U.

12 Dec. 1998 <http//.eric-web.tc.columbia.edu/

home_files/eric_cue_desc.html>.

Scholarly Project

> Smith, Charlotte Turner. <u>The Emigrants, A Poem in Two</u>
>
> <u>Books.</u> London, 1793. <u>British Women Romantic Poets,</u>
>
> <u>1789–1832.</u> Ed. Nancy Kushigian. 1999. U. California,
>
> Davis. 5 Mar. 2003 <http://www.lib.ucdavis.edu/
>
> BWRP/Works/SmitCEmigr.htm>.

Read More on the Web

<http://owl.english.purdue.edu/handouts/research/r_mla.html#Print>
<http://owl.english.purdue.edu/handouts/research/r_mla.html#Electronic>
<http://owl.english.purdue.edu/handouts/research/r_mla.html#other>
<http://www.westwords.com/guffey/mla.html>
<http://webster.commnet.edu/mla/index.shtml>
<http://www.wisc.edu/writing/Handbook/DocMLAWorksCited.html>
<http://www.aresearchguide.com/10works.html#sampleworks>

EVALUATE THE USEFULNESS OF INTERNET SOURCES

Like all other materials you use, those found on the Internet need to be evaluated for accuracy and timeliness. The Internet is a wonderful tool, which allows everyone to publish his or her ideas and opinions on a system that reaches hundreds of millions of people. Be aware, however, that not everyone who publishes on the Internet is an expert on the topic he or she discusses. For example, in searching for information on Sir Thomas More, you might come upon a piece by Richard Marius, the noted Harvard biographer of this sixteenth-century lawyer. Then again, you might find a research paper on More written by a high-school senior. Which one would be more authoritative?

Also be aware that many people who publish electronically, like those who publish on paper, may not have an unbiased view on an issue, may have done faulty research, or may simply be inaccurate. Here are some questions you might ask to help you evaluate Internet sources:

1. Who is the author and what are his or her credentials? Can you tell if this person has worked in the field about which he or she

is writing? Is he or she connected with a university, prominent think tank, government agency, professional journal?

2. Who is the website sponsor? Is it an educational institution, arm of government, business, or professional organization? Or is this just a personal website?

3. Are the website author and sponsor unbiased? For example, you could have confidence in the impartiality of an article on the effects of chewing tobacco appearing in the website of the *New England Journal of Medicine.* Could you put as much confidence in an article on the same subject appearing on a website sponsored by the Down Home Tobacco Growers' Association?

4. Is there any overt bias in the material you have read? Does the author make claims that are unsubstantiated or unconvincing? Does the author contradict him- or herself?

5. Has the author provided a list of sources from which he or she has taken information? Are these sources reputable and unbiased? Are there hyperlinks to other sites? Do you find that materials in those sites seem reasonable, unbiased, and accurate? Who are the authors and sponsors of those sites?

6. Can you tell if the site is updated regularly? Is the data the author relies on current? Are links to other pages and sites current?

7. Is the material well written, or are there grammatical and spelling errors. Does the author rely heavily on flashy graphics rather than on hard data and convincing prose?

8. Was the document published in a print version as well as on the Web? If not, could it have been?

Other Sources

Government Publication

Ordinarily, the government (whether federal, state, or municipal) is considered the author of such works. After typing the name of the government, type the name of the specific agency that published the work.

> United States. Bureau of the Census. <u>Historical Statistics</u>
>
> > <u>of the United States: Colonial Times to 1970.</u>
> >
> > Bicentennial ed. Washington: GPO, 1975.
>
> New Jersey. Division of Youth and Family Services.
>
> > <u>Children at Risk 1995–96.</u> Trenton: NJ Division of
> >
> > Youth and Family Services, 1998.

Pamphlet

As with a book, begin the entry with the author's name if known. If the author is unknown, treat the pamphlet as a book whose author is unknown.

> Webrogan, Signe I. <u>Projections of the Population of States</u>
>
> > <u>by Age, Sex, and Race: 1989–2010.</u> Washington: GPO,
> >
> > 1990.

Published Dissertation

Treat a published doctoral dissertation as a book. However, add the abbreviation "Diss." after the title as well as the name of the university that granted the doctorate and the year the dissertation was completed. End with the publication information as usual.

> Edwards, Flora Mancuso. <u>The Theater of the Black</u>
>
> > <u>Diaspora: A Comparative Study of Black Drama in</u>
> >
> > <u>Brazil, Cuba, and the United States.</u> Diss. New York
> >
> > University, 1975. Ann Arbor: Xerox University
> >
> > Microfilms, 1987.

Unpublished Dissertation

Begin with the author's name, followed by the title of the dissertation in quotation marks. Then type the abbreviation "Diss." as well as the name of the university that granted the doctorate and the year that the dissertation was completed.

> Dann, Emily. "An Experimental Pre-Statistics Curriculum
>
> > for Two-Year College Students." Diss. Rutgers
> >
> > University, 1976.

Abstract of a Dissertation

Begin with the author's name, followed by the title of the dissertation in quotation marks. Then, type the abbreviation "Diss." and the name of the university at which the dissertation was written, followed by the date of its completion. End with the abbreviation *DA* or *DAI* (*Dissertation Abstracts* or *Dissertation Abstracts International*), followed by the volume, year of publication, and page number.

> Szabo, Lydia. "America in the Making: History and the
>
> > Hybrid Poetics of Emily Dickinson, Gertrude Stein,
> >
> > and William Carlos Williams." Diss. Duquesne
> >
> > University, 1997. <u>DAI</u> 5912A (1998): 4430.

Published Interview

Begin with the name of the person interviewed. Follow with the title of the interview, if any, in quotation marks. If the title of the interview does not include the word "interview" or if the interview has no title, simply type "Interview" after the subject's name.

> Johnson, Paul. "Live with TAE: Interview with Paul
>
> Johnson." The American Enterprise Sept./Oct. 1998:
>
> 20–23.

Musical Composition

Begin with the composer's name, followed by the title of the work. Underline or italicize the titles of operas, ballets, and works that have a name, as in the first of the following; note that there are no italics for the second:

> van Beethoven, Ludwig. Eroica.
>
> Mendelssohn, Felix. Piano Concerto no. 1 in G. op. 25.

Personal Letter

Begin with the writer's name, followed by "Letter to the author" and the date.

> Cornell, Matthew Robert. Letter to the author. 9 June
>
> 1998.

Lecture or Address

Begin with the speaker's name, followed by the title of the presentation in quotation marks and the name of the sponsoring organization. End with the place and date of the presentation.

> Partopillo, Alessandro. "Giotto and the Dawn of the Italian
>
> Renaissance." Art League of Madison. Eagle Hotel,
>
> Madison, OR. 8 May 1999.

Live Performance of a Play

Begin with the title of the play, underlined or in italics, followed by the name of its author. Next, indicate the names of the director and the principal actors. End with the name of the theater, its location, and the date of the performance you saw.

> The Iceman Cometh. By Eugene O'Neill. Dir. Howard
>
> Davies. Perf. Kevin Spacey and Tony Danza. Brooks
>
> Atkinson Theater, New York. 22 June 1999.

Map or Chart

Treat such a document as you would a book by an unknown author. Begin with the title underlined or italicized, followed by the word "Map" or "Chart." Then include publication data.

> Rocky Mountain National Park, Colorado. Map.
>
> Washington DC: GPO, 1996.

Radio or Television Interview

Begin with the name of the person interviewed followed by the word "Interview." Then include the title of the program underlined or italicized. End with the name of the network and city, and the date the program was aired.

> Bush, George W. Interview. Hardball. CNBC: New York. 29
>
> June 1999.

Radio or Television Program

If you are drawing information from a titled episode of a program, begin with the title of that episode in quotation marks. If not, begin with the name of the program underlined or italicized. Then, indicate the name of the host, narrator, or director, if available. Next, type the name of the network, the city, and the date of the broadcast.

> "The Great Chain." The American Revolution. Host
>
> William Curtis. The History Channel. New York. 3
>
> July 1999.

Sound Recording

Begin with the name of the composer or speaker, followed by the title of the work. Then, include the name of the conductor, orchestra, chorus, and leading performers. Conclude by naming the manufacturer of the recording and the date of its publication.

> Puccini, Giacomo. La Boheme. Perf. Luciano Pavarotti,
>
> Mirella Freni, Elizabeth Hardwood, and Gianni
>
> Maffeo. Opera of Berlin Chor. and Berlin Phil. Orch.
>
> Cond. Herbert von Karajan. London, 1972.

Work of Art

Begin with the artist's name, if known, followed by the title of the work, underlined or italicized. Next, type the name of the institution and the city in which the work is housed.

> Hopper, Edward. Nighthawks. Art Institute. Chicago.

A Student Research Paper

Victims of Violent Crime: Equal Treatment under the Law
by Angela Brandli

A former community college student, Angela Brandli is majoring in public health at Rutgers University. When asked to choose a topic for a freshman composition research paper, Brandli picked something with which she was intimately familiar. Having been a victim of a violent crime that left her severely injured. Brandli decided to research and argue for victims' rights.

This project eventually led Brandli to petition the New Jersey State Legislature to establish a Catastrophic Injury Fund granting $25,000 to victims severely injured as a result of violent crime in order to help with the cost of rehabilitation. In fact, she even drafted a version of a bill that was passed by the New Jersey Senate and the Assembly and signed into law by Governor Christine Whitman on July 15, 1999.

Her research paper illustrates the best of what academic research papers should be: a natural blending of the author's own knowledge and insights with those taken from authorities on the subject through careful and accurate research. Brandli's works-cited list shows that she conducted research both in the library and online. She also gained a great deal of information through a personal interview with an expert in the field.

Angela Brandli

Professor Buscemi

English Composition II

10 April 2001

VICTIMS OF VIOLENT CRIME:

EQUAL TREATMENT UNDER THE LAW

ll. 2–5: Brandli
prepares us for her
thesis statement,
which appears at the
end of the second
paragraph, lines
24–29.

Victims of violent crime are a growing minority in the

United States. However, despite significant progress

made by the Victims' Rights Movement, little assistance

is available for the rehabilitation of violent-crime

victims. In fact, while more and more rights seem to be   5

extended to violent criminals, the rights of law-abiding

citizens victimized by these individuals have received

little real attention from the government.

ll. 9–29: Brandli
quotes from and
references various
Amendments to the
United States
Constitution. No
internal citations are
needed here.
Moreover, the
Constitution and its
Amendments need
not be mentioned in
the works-cited
page, for only one
official version of
these documents
exists.

The Bill of Rights was added to the U.S. Constitution

to secure certain individual rights and to protect the   10

citizenry from injustices committed by government.

Relying on the ideas of Beccaria and other philosophers

of the Enlightenment, the framers of the Constitution

desired to protect the rights of the accused prior to

conviction. For example, the Fourth Amendment   15

guarantees that no citizen shall be liable to search,

seizure of goods, or arrest without probable cause. The Fifth Amendment ensures that "no person . . . shall be deprived of life, liberty, or property without due process of law . . .," and the Sixth Amendment guarantees the accused "speedy and public trial by an impartial jury. . . ." Moreover, should the accused be found guilty, the Eighth Amendment demands that the punishment administered be fair and humane. At the same time, however, the Fourteenth Amendment certifies that no state can deny any person equal protection under the law, thereby supporting the notion that the government owes victims of violent crime as much as, if not more than, it provides the perpetrators of such crime.

Nonetheless, over the last decades, extending equal protection under the law seems to have done more to provide loopholes for the guilty than to protect the innocent. We have allowed rights once designed to protect us from a tyrannical justice system to become sources by which law-abiding citizens can be victimized. Although perpetrators of violent crimes violate and even kill members of the community, it is that same community that must bear the expense of providing for their personal needs and must often assume many of their familial responsibilities after incarceration. Our prisons are full of criminals demanding that they be

ll. 24–29: The writer states her thesis.

20

25

30

35

40

l. 47: Brandli uses an internal citation to reveal the source (Long) of summarized material found in this paragraph. This information comes from page 29 of Long's book, whose title and publication information appear on Brandli's works-cited list.

l. 48: Brandli introduces a paraphrase of information from an article (found on her works-cited list) by constitutional scholar Gary McDowell by using his name. On line 52, she indicates the page number (262) of the article from which the information was taken. She does not need to repeat the source's name; for it was mentioned only five lines above.

ll. 53–59: Brandli adds her own ideas to those she has researched.

treated in accordance with the rights afforded free citizens, and too many politicians and bureaucrats oblige them. Yes, they are entitled to humane treatment, but by virtue of their crimes they have forfeited their claim to civil rights afforded those who obey the law (Long 29). 45

According to constitutional scholar Gary McDowell, confusion over the origins of the rights of the accused have, ironically, caused the courts—the protectors of everyone's rights—to weaken the Constitution's role in protecting the civil liberties of the law-abiding (262). Indeed, prisoners are often provided with unnecessary services and comforts that taxpayers, working long and hard, can sometimes ill-afford to provide themselves. But the greatest irony is that victims and/or their families actually help fund these expenses involuntarily through taxes, while little is done to compensate these people for their suffering. 50 55

Family advocates argue that the family of a criminal should not have to suffer for his or her wrongdoing, that spouses and children of criminals are victims too. This argument has merit, but it has been taken to an 60

ll. 60–72: The writer drew these insights from her reading of several different written sources and from studying several state laws. Thus, this information may be considered common knowledge and does not require a citation.

extreme. Some states provide assistance to a criminal's family if the offender's incarceration results in financial hardship—this is in addition to funding programs to assist indigent families with dependent children. In essence, then, they give preferential treatment to the families of the incarcerated. Yet this assistance is not available to the family of the criminal's victim—even in murder cases. If a criminal's children should not be made to suffer for his or her crime, should this suffering be then visited upon the victim's children? In many cases, the victim's family is even more affected than the criminal's family, yet only the latter is entitled to government assistance. Clearly, granting aid to some victims while ignoring others is discriminatory and violates the right to fair and equal treatment under the law.

ll. 80–87: The information in these lines comes from "Crime Victims' Rights," a journal article for which no author is indicated. Therefore the source is cited by title.

The U.S. crime victims' movement began in the 1960s. California was the first state to set up a victims' compensation program in 1965, but it wasn't until the early 1970s that victims' rights groups, led by feminists and rape victims, made their appearance. It took an additional ten years for victims' rights reform to reach the federal level. Finally, Congress passed the 1984 Victims of Crime Act ("Crime Victims' Rights" 634). This

65

70

75

80

85

law established the Crime Victims' Fund to provide

grants to the states for their victims' compensation

funds. Financed through fines paid by federal criminals,   90

the fund can be accessed only at the state level. Monies

from the fund can be applied to a wide range of

expenses incurred as a direct result of crime but only if

insurance and other recovery sources are unavailable

(United States Office for Victims of Crime). What's more,   95

the amount of compensation a victim of violent crime

can receive varies from state to state. Nine states offer

more than $25,000; twenty-one states offer a maximum

of $25,000; and twenty states provide up to $10,000.

The only thing that all the funds clearly have in   100

common is that they limit the amount of assistance a

victim can access ("Crime Victims' Rights" 637).

The establishment of a federal Crime Victims' Fund

has been viewed by many politicians as well as the

general public as a victory for crime victims. But the   105

program emerged ostensibly to satisfy the needs of

victims before the scope of their needs was even

l. 95: The information in the previous two lines is taken from a pamphlet called the *Office for Victims of Crime Fact Sheet.* The author is a government agency, the U.S. Office for Victims of Crime, and the publisher is the Department of Justice.

l. 102: The source for this information is "Crime Victims' Rights," the same article cited earlier in this paragraph. Since additional information from another source has intervened, however, a second citation for "Crime Victims' Rights" with the appropriate page number is necessary.

ll. 103–109: Brandli paraphrases from page 349 of an essay by Robert Elias, which is listed in the works-cited page.

determined (Elias 349). This might be a victory for politicians but not for victims!

Some states are making progress in aiding crime victims. In Wisconsin, for example, a Victim's Crime Amendment was added to the state constitution, providing several services to crime victims. The website of the Wisconsin Victim Resource Center lists the following:

110

115

ll. 116–132: This information comes from page 1 of the website of the Wisconsin Office of Crime Victim Services. Notice that the list of services, which is a direct quotation and which is longer than four lines, is indented 10 spaces from the left margin and is double spaced. The source has been named in the text of Brandli's paragraph and the page number of the website follows the quoted list. Brandli includes this infor-mation to show that some progress on victims' rights is being made. In this way, she attempts to give opponents to her argument a fair hearing. At the same time, she uses this information both to argue that what is being done is still

· Telephone counseling.

· Information and referrals for crime victims who are experiencing problems.

· Problem-solving assistance relative to victimization.

· Victim/witness assistance services in matters the Attorney General's Office is prosecuting and when no other services are available.

· Resource person to district attorneys in counties with no victim/witness program.

· Informational materials on topics such as sexual assault, child sexual abuse and victims' rights in Wisconsin.

120

125

not enough and to show that she has researched the question thoroughly, thereby making her argument even more convincing.

l. 133: Brandli introduces information she took from a personal interview by indicating her source. Since interviews obviously have no pages, no internal citation of a page number is needed here.

· An advocate for victims in exercising their

state constitutional rights.   130

· Crime victim compensation assistance.

· Victim Appellate Notification Services. (1)

Nonetheless, as reported by Renee Lane of the New

Jersey Violent Crime Compensation Board, financial

compensation to victims and their families remains   135

limited. The NJ Criminal Injuries Act (1971) addresses

the rights and services of victims and witnesses, and it

provides protection and reimbursement to witnesses

incurring expenses while testifying at trials or

otherwise cooperating with the courts. There are no   140

stated limits to reimbursement pertaining to witnesses,

but violent crime compensations are limited to $25,000.

Surviving victims and members of murder victims'

families are eligible to apply to the Violent Crimes

Compensation (VCC) Board, which handles claims. On   145

the other hand, family members of surviving victims

are not eligible to apply even if the crime results in

financial hardship to the victim's spouse and/or

children.

Awards are made with the understanding that if the   150

claimant is successful in recovering money from any

other source, he or she must notify the Board to

arrange for reimbursement. On the other hand, none of the money granted for the assailant's defense, care, and rehabilitation has to be repaid, even if his or her circumstances later change. Tax dollars that support criminals are spent and forgotten (Lane).

155

l. 157: The internal citation indicates that the information has been taken from an interview with Renee Lane. An internal citation is necessary in this paragraph because the information being cited in this paragraph was not introduced by the source's name.

Furthermore, no programs exist to pay for the rehabilitation of victims, and, as stated above, victims may be required to repay any limited compensation awards they receive. Such awards are funded by fines imposed upon criminals, but they are subject to availability. Currently, over $15 million owed New Jersey's fund remains uncollected (Lane). No wonder compensation awards must be limited!

160

165

l. 164: This internal citation again indicates that Lane is the source of the information.

ll. 167–206: All of the information in these lines is taken from personal experience and common knowledge. No citation is necessary.

In short, then, the compensation some victims of violent crime receive through the VCC Program is grossly inadequate and does not satisfy the state's responsibility of providing fair and equal treatment under the law. The fact that the program was designed to be funded by fines against offenders—hardly reliable sources of income—displays a lack of concern for crime victims. It is a bone thrown to appease victims' rights advocates. Indeed, if tax dollars can fund programs that assist flood, fire, hurricane and other victims, why can't

170

175

they be used to assist victims of violent crime? Excluding crime victims and their families from tax-funded assistance violates the Fourteenth Amendment. It is clearly another act of discrimination against a minority group.   180

The needs of violent crime victims vary depending upon the nature of the crime and the seriousness of the injury. However, I have learned from personal experience that the injury is often only the beginning of the nightmare. In 1990, I sustained a spinal cord   185 injury in a nearly fatal stabbing. The pain I suffered and my ongoing recovery cannot be comprehended fully by anyone who has not had a similar experience. But my government's failure to assist me adequately in confronting the challenges I face while fighting to   190 rebuild my life has been the cruelest blow. No government agency funds my rehabilitation. I spend hours developing strategies to combat one insurance cut after another, and I live with conditions that restrict my independence because I lack the funds to provide an   195 adapted environment that meets the needs of my disability. Consequently, my family has had to take on the burden of my care. The one-time compensation grant of $25,000 that the New Jersey Violent Crime Compensation Board granted me was a good beginning,   200 but it fell short of providing the resources to rebuild my

life. I have learned first hand that fair and equal treatment is a concept that America only claims to provide its people. The reality is that fair and equal treatment has a dollar limit imposed at the discretion of   205
our government.

Admitting that more must be done to help finance the needs of crime victims, the U.S. House of Representatives voted 431 to 0 on February 8, 1995, for a bill requiring federal convicts to pay restitution to   210
their victims. Unfortunately, the Victim Restitution Act applies only to federal violations and not to most assaults, rapes, and violent street crimes, which are state offenses (Seelye). As reported by Laurie Asseo in SF Gate News, an online news service, this concept was   215
underscored by a recent U.S. Supreme Court decision declaring unconstitutional "a key provision of the 1994 Violence Against Women Act," which "let rape victims sue their assailants in federal court" (1). However, even if the Victim Restitution Act covered assaults, rapes, and   220
violent street crimes, it is unlikely that victims would see a single dollar of compensation. In fact, as Bruce Shapiro, himself a violent-crime victim, argues, federal

l. 214: The information in the first part of this paragraph comes from Katherine Seelye, whose *New York Times* article appears on the works-cited page.

l. 214: Brandli introduces a direct quotation by using the name of the author: Laurie Asseo. The page number of the Web source follows the quote on line 219.

ll. 222–227: Brandli both paraphrases and quotes directly from an article by Bruce Shapiro. Since she introduces this information with the name of the author, only the page number appears in the internal citation. Note that the words "debtors' prisons" are in quotation marks. At times, you might want to quote only a word or short phrase and include it along with a paraphrase. In such cases, quotation marks are still required.

ll. 232–240: Brandli quotes directly from Shapiro. Since the quotation is more than three lines long, she indents 10 spaces from the left margin and double spaces the quotation. No quotation marks are necessary in such cases. However, the page number(s) from which this material is taken must appear in parentheses at the end of the quotation and after the final period. Note that Brandli adds the words "crime victims" in brackets [/] for clarity. These are her own words. Adding them to the quotation is permissible for clarity as long as the intent of the quoted material is not affected.

courts might be jammed up with new waves of damage claims with jailed criminals claiming that the government had acted unconstitutionally by creating "debtors' prisons" (451). In August 1994, Shapiro and seven other people were stabbed while they sipped coffee in a Connecticut café near his home. He remains skeptical as to the effectiveness of victims' compensation laws:

> On the surface it is hard to argue with the principle of reasonable restitution—particularly since it implies community recognition of the victim's suffering.
>
> But I wonder if these laws really will end up benefiting [crime victims]—or if they are just empty, vote-getting devices that exploit victims and could actually hurt our chances of getting speedy, substantive justice. (451–452)

Victims of violent crime are being denied their rights, and their inability to obtain adequate assistance endangers the health and welfare of them and their families. The public's indifference to their severe needs and the denial of public funds to help them address monumental obstacles resulting from their

225

230

235

240

245

victimization amount to unconstitutional discrimination. Unless we recognize our responsibility to provide victims of violent crime with viable avenues for both compensation and rehabilitation, we will have done many innocent people a great disservice while, ironically, succoring the very criminals who victimized them.

250

Works Cited

Asseo, Laurie, "Court Rejects Law Allowing Rape Victims to Sue Attackers in Federal Court." <u>SFGate</u> 15 May 2000. 4 pp. 26 May 2000 <http://www.sfgate.com/ cgi-bin/article.cgi?file-/news/archive/2000 . . . / national1017EDT0545.DT>.

"Crime Victims' Rights." <u>The CQ Researcher</u> 4: 27 (1994): 625–648.

Elias, Robert. "The Politics of Victimization." <u>Taking Sides: Clashing Views on Controversial Issues in Crime and Criminology.</u> Ed. Richard C. Monk. 2d ed. Guilford, CT: Dushkin, 1991: 344–350.

Lane, Renee. Personal Interview. 9 Jan. 1996.

Long, Hamilton A. <u>The American Ideal of 1776: The Twelve Basic American Principles.</u> Philadelphia: Heritage, 1976.

McDowell, Gary L. "The Supreme Court Has Distorted
the Meaning of the Bill of Rights." The Bill of Rights:
Opposing Viewpoints. Ed. William Dudley. San Diego:
Greenhaven, 1994. 257–267.

Seelye, Katherine O. "House Backs Bill to Require
Restitution from Criminals." New York Times 8 Feb.
1995: A16.

Shapiro, Bruce. "One Violent Crime." Nation 3 April
1995: 437, 446–452.

United States. Department of Justice. National Victims
Resource Center. Washington, DC: Department of
Justice, 1991.

United States. Office for Victims of Crime. Office for
Victims of Crime Fact Sheet. Washington:
Department of Justice, 1993.

Wisconsin Victim Resource Center. 6 May 2000 State of
Wisconsin Office of Crime Victim Services.
<http://www.doj.state.wi.us/cvs/vrc.htm>.

abstract language   Words that represent ideas rather than things we can see, hear, smell, feel, or taste. The word *love* is abstract, but the word *kiss* is concrete because we can perceive it with one or more of our five senses. (See Chapters 5 and 6.)

allusion   A passing reference to a person, place, event, thing, or idea with which the reader may be familiar. Allusions can be used to add detail, clarify important points, or set the tone of an essay, a poem, or a short story.

analogy   A method by which a writer points out similarities between two things that, on the surface, seem quite different. Analogies are most often used to make abstract or unfamiliar ideas clearer and more concrete. Chapters 3 and 4 contain examples of analogy.

anecdote   A brief, sometimes humorous story used to illustrate or develop a specific point. (See Chapter 10.)

argument   A type of writing that relies on logic and concrete evidence to prove a point or support an opinion. (See Chapter 13.)

central idea   The idea that conveys a writer's main point about a subject. It may be stated explicitly or implied. Also known as the *main idea* or *controlling idea,* it determines the kinds and amount of detail needed to develop a piece of writing adequately. (See Chapter 1.)

chronological order   The arrangement of material in order of time. (See Chapter 9.)

coherence   The principle that writers observe in making certain that there are logical connections between the ideas and details in one sentence or paragraph and those in the next. (See Chapter 2.)

conclusion   A paragraph or series of paragraphs that ends an essay. Conclusions often restate the writer's central idea or summarize important points used to develop that idea. (See Chapter 4.) A conclusion can also be defined as a principle, opinion, or belief a writer supports or defends by using convincing information. (See Chapters 3 and 13.)

concrete language   Words that represent material things—things we can perceive with our five senses. (See *abstract language* above, and see Chapters 5 and 6.)

coordination   A technique used to express ideas of equal importance in the same sentence. To this end, writers often use compound sentences, which are composed of two independent (main) clauses connected with a coordinating conjunction. "Four students earned scholarships, but only three accepted them" is a compound sentence. (See Chapter 7.)

deduction   A kind of reasoning used to build an argument. Deductive thinking draws conclusions by applying specific cases or examples to general principles, rules, or ideas. You would be thinking deductively if you wrote: All students must pay tuition. I am a student. Therefore, I must pay tuition. (See Chapter 13.)

details Specific facts or pieces of information that a writer uses to develop ideas.

emphasis The placing of stress on important ideas by controlling sentence structure through coordination, subordination, and parallelism. (See Chapter 7.)

figurative language (figures of speech) Words or phrases that explain abstract ideas by comparing them to concrete realities the reader will recognize easily. Analogy, metaphor, simile, and personification are types of figurative language. (See Chapter 6.)

image A verbal picture made up of sensory details. It expresses a general idea's meaning clearly and concretely. (See Chapter 5.)

induction A kind of reasoning used to build an argument. Inductive thinking draws general conclusions from specific facts or pieces of evidence. If you heard the wind howling, saw the sky turning black, and spotted several ominous clouds on the horizon, you might rightly conclude by induction that a storm was on its way. (See Chapter 13.)

introduction A paragraph or series of paragraphs that begins an essay. It often contains a writer's central idea in the form of a thesis statement. (See Chapter 4.)

irony A technique used by writers to communicate the very opposite of what their words mean. Irony is often used to create humor. An effective example of irony can be found in Milden's "So You Want to Flunk Out of College," which appears in the introduction to Chapter 12.

linking pronouns Pronouns that make reference to nouns that have come before (antecedents). They are one of the ways to maintain coherence in and between paragraphs. (See Chapter 2.)

main point The point that a writer focuses on in a thesis or topic sentence. (See Chapter 1.)

metaphor A figure of speech that, like a simile, creates a comparison between two things to make the explanation of one of them clearer. Unlike a simile, a metaphor does not use *like* or *as*. "The man is a pig" is a metaphor. (See Chapter 6.)

parallelism A method to express facts and ideas of equal importance in the same sentence and thereby to give them added emphasis. Sentences that are parallel express items of equal importance in the same grammatical form. (See Chapter 7.)

personification A figure of speech that writers use to discuss animals, plants, and inanimate objects in terms normally associated with human beings: for example, "Our neighborhoods are the *soul* of the city." (See Chapter 6.)

persuasion A type of writing that supports an opinion, proves a point, or convinces the reader to act. (See Chapters 3 and 14.)

point of view   The perspective from which a narrative is told. Stories that use the first-person point of view are told by a narrator who is involved in the action and who uses words such as *I, me,* and *we* to explain what happened. Stories that use the third-person point of view are told by a narrator who may or may not be involved in the action and who uses words such as *he, she,* and *they* to explain what happened. (See Chapter 9.)

simile   A figure of speech that, like a metaphor, compares two things for the sake of clarity and emphasis. Unlike a metaphor, however, a simile uses *like* or *as.* "Samantha runs like a deer" is a simile. (See Chapter 6.)

subordination   A technique used to emphasize one idea over another by expressing the more important idea in the sentence's main clause and the other in its subordinate clause. (See Chapter 7.)

syllogism   The logical structure through which a writer uses deduction. To create a syllogism, a writer makes a general statement, then applies a specific case or example to that statement, and then draws a limited conclusion from the two. You would be using deduction in a syllogism if you wrote:

> **general statement:**   All lifeguards must know how to swim.
> **specific case:**   Marvin does not know how to swim.
> **conclusion:**   Marvin cannot be a lifeguard.

thesis statement   A clear and explicit statement of an essay's central idea. It often appears in an introductory paragraph but is sometimes found later in the essay. (See Chapter 1.)

topic sentence   A clear and explicit statement of a paragraph's central idea. (See Chapter 1.)

transitions (connectives)   Words or phrases used to make clear and direct connections between sentences and paragraphs, thereby maintaining coherence. (See Chapter 2.)

unity   The principle that writers observe in making certain that all the information in an essay or paragraph relates directly to the central idea, which is often expressed in a thesis statement or topic sentence. (See Chapter 2.)

ACKNOWLEDGMENTS

Albrecht, Ernest. From "Sawdust" by Ernest Albrecht. Reprinted by permission of the author.

Annan, Kofi. "In Africa, AIDS Has a Woman's Face." *The New York Times,* December 29, 2002. Copyright © 2002 The New York Times. Reprinted by permission.

Aronowitz, Paul. "A Brother's Dreams" by Paul Aronowitz. Copyright © 1988 by The New York Times Company. Reprinted by permission.

Barlow, Dudley. "Melting Pot or Tossed Salad?" Reprinted from *The Education Digest,* March 1996, Ann Arbor, MI. Reprinted with permission.

Barry, Dave. "Florida's Fire Ants Headed for Trouble" Copyright © 2003 by Tribune Media Services. Reprinted with permission.

Bennett, William. Reprinted with the permission of Simon & Schuster Adult Publishing Group, from *The De-Valuing of America: The Fight for Our Culture and Our Children* by William J. Bennett. Copyright © 1992 by William J. Bennett. All rights reserved.

Brownback, Sam. "All Human Cloning Is Wrong." *USA Today,* January 3, 2003.

Callaghan, Alice. "Desperate to Learn English." *The New York Times,* August 15, 1997. Copyright © 1997 The New York Times. Reprinted by permission.

Cannon, Angie. "Jeffrey Dahmer, Cannibal." *U.S. News and World Report,* December 6, 1999. Copyright © 1999 by U.S. News and World Report, L.P. Reprinted with permission.

Chelminsky, Rudolph. "The Curse of Count Dracula" by Rudolph Chelminsky. Copyright © 2003 by Rudolph Chelminsky. Originally appeared in *Smithsonian,* April 2003. Reprinted by permission of the author.

Cowley, Malcolm. "The View from 80" by Malcolm Cowley as appeared in *Life,* December 1978. Reprinted by permission of The Estate of Malcolm Cowley.

Dobbs, Lou. "Freedom: Our Best Export," *U.S. News and World Report,* March 10, 2003. Copyright © 2003 U.S. News and World Report, L.P. Reprinted with permission.

Ericson, Jr. Edward E. From "Gen X is OK" by Edward E. Ericson, Jr. Reprinted with permission of The American Enterprise, a magazine of Politics, Business and Culture. On the web at *www.TAEmag.com.*

Fang, Bay. "I Don't Know What God Wants," *U.S. News and World Report,* April 8, 2002. Copyright © 2002, U.S. *News and World Report,* L.P. Reprinted with permission.

Fields, Suzanne. "Macho Girls and Vanishing Males" by Suzanne Fields. Copyright © 2002 by Suzanne Fields. Reprinted with permission of the author from *The Washington Times.*

Fox, Stephen. From "The Education of Branch Rickey" by Stephen Fox. First appeared in *Civilization* magazine, September/October 1995. Copyright © 1995 by Stephen Fox. Reprinted by permission of the Robins Straus Agency, Inc. as agent for the author.

Fu, Shen C. Y. From "A Closer Look at Chinese Calligraphy" by Shen C. Y. Fu. Courtesy of Freer Gallery of Art, Smithsonian Institution, Washington, D.C.

Fulghum, Robert. "I Was Just Wondering" from *All I Really Need to Know I Learned in Kindergarten* by Robert L. Fulghum. Copyright © 1986 by Robert L. Fulghum. Used by permission of Villard Books, a division of Random House, Inc.

Glanz, James. "The Haunting Final Worlds: 'It Doesn't Look Good, Babe.'" *The New York Times,* June 6, 2002. Copyright © 2002 by The New York Times Co. Reprinted with permission.

Goodheart, Adam. "How to Fight a Duel" by Adam Goodheart. Reprinted by permission, from the May/June 1996 issue of *Civilization.*

Hayden, Robert. "Those Winter Sundays." Copyright © 1966 by Robert Hayden, from *Collected Poems of Robert Hayden* by Robert Hayden, edited by Frederick Glaysher. Used by permission of Liveright Publishing Company.

Heaney, Seamus. "Mid-Term Break" from *Opened Ground: Selected Poems 1966-1996* by Seamus Heaney. Copyright © 1998 by Seamus Heaney. Reprinted by permission of Farrar, Straus and Giroux, LLC and Faber and Faber, Ltd.

Hentoff, Nat. "Free Speech on Campus." Copyright © 1989 by Nat Hentoff. Reprinted by permission of the author. Nat Hentoff is a columnist/author for *The Village Voice* and United Media Newspaper Syndicate.

Howard, Philip K. Excerpt from *The Death of Common Sense* by Philip K. Howard. Copyright © 1994 by Philip K. Howard. Used by permission of Random House, Inc.

Howe, Robert F. "Covert Force," *Smithsonian,* October 2002. Copyright © 2002 by Robert F. Howe. Reprinted by permission of the author.

Hughes, Langston. "Harlem" from *The Panther and the Lash* by Langston Hughes. Copyright © 1951 by Langston Hughes. Reprinted by permission of Alfred A. Knopf, Inc.

Kazin, Alfred. Excerpt from *A Walker in the City.* Copyright © 1951 and renewed 1979 by Alfred Kazin. Reprinted by permission of Harcourt, Inc.

King, Jr., Martin Luther. From "I Have a Dream" by Martin Luther King, Jr. Reprinted by arrangement with The Heirs to the Estate of Martin Luther King, Jr., c/o Writer's House, Inc., as agent for the proprietor. Copyright © 1963 by Martin Luther King, Jr. Copyright renewed 1991 by Coretta Scott King.

Kozol, Jonathan. Excerpt from *Amazing Grace* by Jonathan Kozol, copyright © 1995 by Jonathan Kozol. Used by permission of Crown Publishers, a division of Random House, Inc.

Kozol, Jonathan. "The Human Cost of an Illiterate Society" from *Illiterate America* by Jonathan Kozol. Copyright © 1985 by Jonathan Kozol. Used by permission of Doubleday, a division of Random House, Inc.

Levine, Samantha. "Josephine Baker: The Daring Diva," *U.S. News and World Report,* January 27, 2003. Copyright © 2003 U.S. News and World Report, L.P. Reprinted with permission.

Lord, Lewis. "The Way We Were," *U.S. News and World Report.* Copyright © 1999 by U.S. News and World Report, L.P. Reprinted with permission.

Love, David A. "U.S. Needs to Pay Reparations for Slavery." Copyright © 2000 by David A. Love. Reprinted by permission of the author.

Marius, Robert. "Writng and Its Rewards" by Robert Marius. Copyright © Robert Marius. Reprinted by permission of the author.

McPhee, John. "The Woods from Hog Wallow" from The Pine Barrens by John McPhee. Copyright © 1967, 1968 by John McPhee. Reprinted by permission of Farrar, Straus and Giroux, LLC. Published in Canada by Macfarlane, Walter & Ross, Toronto. Used by permission.

Moore, Stephen. "New Blood for Cities" by Stephen Moore. Reprinted from *The American Enterprise,* by Washington-based magazine of politics, business and culture, September/October 1997 with permission.

Moyer, Tena. "Code of Denial." Copyright © 1999 by Tena Moyer. Reprinted with permission from the October 1999 issue of *Discover* magazine.

Nilsen, Alleen Pace. From "Sexism in English: A 1990's Update" by Alleen Pace Nilsen. Reprinted by permission of the author.

O'Rourke, P. J. "A Cool and Logical Analysis of the Bicycle Menace" from *Republican Party Reptile* by P. J. O'Rourke. Copyright © 1987 by P. J. O'Rourke. Used by permission of Grove/Atlantic, Inc.

O'Rourke, P. J. Two short excerpts from *A Parliament of Whores* by P. J. O'Rourke. Copyright © by P. J. O'Rourke. Used by permission of Grove/Atlantic, Inc.

Owen, Wilfred. "Dulce et Decorum Est" from *The Collected Poems of Wilfred Owen,* copyright © 1963 by Chatto & Windus, Ltd. Reprinted by permission of New Directions Publishing Corp.

Parks, Gordon. From *Voices in the Mirror* by Gordon Parks, copyright © 1990 by Gordon Parks. Used by permission of Doubleday, a division of Random-House, Inc.

Paton, Alan. Reprinted with the permission of Scribner, an imprint of Simon & Schuster Adult Publishing Group, from *Cry the Beloved Country* by Alan Paton. Copyright © 1948 by Alan Paton; copyright renewed © 1976 by Alan Paton.

People for the Ethical Treatment of Animals (PETA) "Fur is Dead." *http://www.furisdead.com* Reprinted with permission.

Po Chu-i. "Watching the Reapers" from *Chinese Poetry* translated by Arthur Waley, 1962. Reprinted by permission of the Arthur Waley Estate.

Pickering, Samuel. "Faith of the Father" from *Still Life.* Copyright © 1990 by University Press of New England. Reprinted by permission.

Rainie, Harrison. "The Buried Sounds of Children Crying." *U.S. News and World Report,* May 1, 1995. Copyright © 1995 by U.S. News and World Report, L.P. Reprinted with permission.

Ringle, Ken. "Uncommon Valor." *Smithsonian,* September 2002. Copyright © 2002 by Ken Ringle. Reprinted by permission of the author.

Romero, Leo. "What the Gossips Saw" from *Agua Negra* by Leo Romero. Copyright © 1981 by Leo Romero. Reprinted by permission of Ahsahta Press at Boise State University.

Russell, Bertrand. Excerpt from *Autobiography* by Bertrand Russell. Reprinted by permission of Routledge.

Ryan, Michael. From "They Track the Deadliest Viruses" by Michael Ryan, *Parade,* April 23, 1995. Copyright © 1995 by Michael Ryan. Reprinted by permission of the author and *Parade.*

Sagan, Carl. From *The Demon-Haunted World* by Carl Sagan. Copyright © 1996 by Carl Sagan and Ann Druyan. Reprinted with permission from Ann Druyan and the Estate of Carl Sagan.

Sagan, Carl. "The Measure of Eratosthenes" by Carl Sagan, *Harvard Magazine,* September/October 1980. Copyright © 1980 by Harvard Magazine. Reprinted by permission of Harvard Magazine and the author.

Sandburg, Carl. "Child of the Romans" from *Chicago Poems* by Carl Sandburg. Copyright © 1916 by Holt, Rinehart and Winston and renewed 1944 by Carl Sandburg. Reprinted by permission of Harcourt, Inc.

Schrof, Joannie M. "The Last Safe Haven" by Joannie M. Schrof from *U.S. News and World Report,* December 26, 1994. Reprinted by permission.

Schumacher, Mark. "Fur is Natural and Environmentally Sound." Reprinted by permission of National Animal Interest Alliance (NAIA) *http://www.naiaonline.org.*

Selzer, Richard. From "A Mask on the Face of Death" by Richard Selzer. Copyright © 1987 by Richard Selzer. Reprinted by permission of Georges Borchardt, Inc. for the author. First appeared in *Life* magazine.

Sharp, Erin. "Burger Queen" by Erin Sharp. From *The American Enterprise* magazine. Reprinted with permission.

Shlachter, Barry. "Charisma Fortified by "Chutzpah.' " By Barry Shlachter, KRT News Service, September 7, 1997. Reprinted with permission of Tribune Media Services, Inc.

Simon, Paul. "The Silent Superstar." *The New York Times,* March 9, 1999. Copyright © 1999 The New York Times. Reprinted by permission.

Sowell, Thomas. "Reparations for Slavery?" Reprinted by permission of Thomas Sowell and Creators Syndicate, Inc.

Steinbeck, John. From "The Chrysanthemums" by John Steinbeck. Copyright 1937, renewed © 1965 by John Steinbeck; from *The Long Valley* by John Steinbeck. Used by permission of Viking Penguin, a division of Penguin Putnam, Inc.

USA Today. "Drug Tests Fail Schools." *USA Today,* March 28, 1995. Copyright © 1995, USA Today. Reprinted with permission.

USA Today. "Overreaction to Cloning Poses Other Risks," *USA Today,* January 3, 2002. Copyright © 2003 USA Today. Reprinted with permission.

Wallis, Claudia. "How to Live to be 120" by Claudia Wallis, *Time,* March 6, 1995. © 1995 Time, Inc. Reprinted by permission.

Wellstone, Paul. Excerpt from "If Poverty is the Question" by Paul Wellstone. Reprinted by permission, from the April 14, 1997 issue of *The Nation* magazine.

Whitehead, Barbara DaFoe. "All is Not Well with the Women of Generation X." Copyright © 1998 by *The American Enterprise* magazine. Reprinted with permission.

Wiesel, Elie. A Prayer for the Days of Awe." *The New York Times,* October 2, 1997. Copyright © The New York Times. Reprinted by permission.

Wilson, Joseph. "Republic or Empire? Reprinted with permission, from the March 3, 2003 issue of *The Nation.* For subscription information, call 1-800-333-8536. Portions of each week's Nation magazine can be accessed at http://www.thenation.com.

Wong, Jade Snow. from *Fifth Chinese Daughter* by Jade Snow Wong. Copyright © 1950/1989 by Jade Snow Wong. Used by permission of the University of Washington Press.

Zanoza, Daniel. "Back from the Brink" by Daniel Zanoza. Reprinted from *The American Enteprise,* a Washington-based magazine of politics, business and culture, September/October 1997, with permission.